SPECIAL EDITION

USING

Microsoft®

Office
2003

Student-Teacher Edition

Ed Bott

Woody Leonhard

800 East 96th Street
Indianapolis, Indiana 46240 USA

SPECIAL EDITION USING MICROSOFT® OFFICE 2003, STUDENT-TEACHER EDITION

International Standard Book Number: 0-7897-3466-4

Library of Congress Catalog Card Number: 2005933310

Printed in the United States of America

First Printing: February 2006

09 08 07 06   4 3 2 1

Trademarks

Warning and Disclaimer

Bulk Sales

Que Publishing offers excellent discounts on this book when ordered in quantity for bulk purchases or special sales. For more information, please contact

U.S. Corporate and Government Sales
1-800-382-3419
corpsales@pearsontechgroup.com

For sales outside the United States, please contact

International Sales
international@pearsoned.com

Associate Publisher
Greg Wiegand

Executive Editor
Rick Kughen

Development Editor
Rick Kughen

Managing Editor
Charlotte Clapp

Project Editor
Tonya Simpson

Indexer
Aaron Black

Proofreader
Suzanne Thomas

Publishing Coordinator
Sharry Lee Gregory

Interior Designer
Anne Jones

Cover Designer
Anne Jones

Page Layout
Nonie Ratcliff

CONTENTS

III Using Word

ABOUT THE AUTHORS

Ed Bott is a best-selling author of more than two dozen computer books and an award-winning technology journalist with two decades of experience in the personal computer industry. For nearly 10 years he was responsible for *PC Computing* magazine's extensive coverage of every conceivable flavor of Microsoft Windows and Microsoft Office. For a recent book on computer security, Ed won an international award of merit from the Society for Technical Communication. He is a three-time winner of the Computer Press Award, and he and Woody Leonhard won the prestigious Jesse H. Neal Award, sometimes referred to as "the Pulitzer Prize of the business press," in back-to-back years for their work on *PC Computing*'s "Windows SuperGuide." He lives in an extremely civilized corner of the Southwest with his wife, Judy, and two amazingly smart and affectionate cats, Katy and Bianca.

Woody Leonhard describes himself as a "Certified Office Victim." With more than 25 computer books under his belt, he's seen parts of Office that would curl your hair. Woody's best known for his website, AskWoody.com, which combines the latest no-bull news with one of the Web's best-known all-volunteer "Help" sites. Woody has won eight Computer Press Awards and, with Ed, two American Business Press Association awards. He now basks in the glorious sun on Phuket Island, Thailand.

DEDICATION

To my brother Don, an award-winning teacher who has inspired countless kids to become great journalists.—Ed

To Add, for filling my life with happiness. And to Justin, for keeping me on my toes.—Woody

ACKNOWLEDGMENTS

Thanks to all the folks at Que, who made sure that all the pieces of this book came together on time and in the right order. And we owe a big, big shout-out to the corps of fellow beta testers and Microsoft techies who helped us decode, decipher, unravel, and ultimately explain the mysteries of Office 2003 Student-Teacher Edition.

WE WANT TO HEAR FROM YOU!

As the reader of this book, *you* are our most important critic and commentator. We value your opinion and want to know what we're doing right, what we could do better, what areas you'd like to see us publish in, and any other words of wisdom you're willing to pass our way.

As an associate publisher for Que, I welcome your comments. You can email or write me directly to let me know what you did or didn't like about this book—as well as what we can do to make our books better.

Please note that I cannot help you with technical problems related to the topic of this book. We do have a User Services group, however, where I will forward specific technical questions related to the book.

When you write, please be sure to include this book's title and author as well as your name, email address, and phone number. I will carefully review your comments and share them with the author and editors who worked on the book.

Email: feedback@quepublishing.com

Mail: Greg Wiegand
            Associate Publisher
            Que Publishing
            800 East 96th Street
            Indianapolis, IN 46240 USA

For more information about this book or another Que Publishing title, visit our website at www.quepublishing.com. Type the ISBN (excluding hyphens) or the title of a book in the Search field to find the page you're looking for.

INTRODUCTION

In this introduction

Microsoft Office has been around, in one version or another, for more than a decade. We—that is, Woody and Ed—have been writing about Office since the very beginning. In books, on the Web, and in magazine articles and e-mail newsletters, we've guided lost souls through the Office labyrinth, held Microsoft's feet to the fire over bugs and security breaches, and passed out praise for the many innovations that the Office development team has delivered through the years.

In previous editions, we focused on the needs of people using Microsoft Office in the office. For those books, we focused on budgets, annual reports, e-mails from the boss, and other staples of dull corporate life.

This edition is different. Microsoft Office Student and Teacher Edition is packaged and sold for people who plan to use it at home. Although its individual parts are identical to those found in the Office version used in corporate settings, the day-to-day tasks you're likely to tackle are a little different. That's why, in this book, we've shifted the focus to explain how you can use Word, Excel, PowerPoint, and Outlook to produce school reports, family newsletters, and projects for civic and social organizations. Of course, if you want to use the same technique to sneak in a little work on the weekend, we won't tell.

The audience may be different, but the depth of our coverage hasn't changed. We still assume you're smart, curious, and able to figure out the truly basic stuff on your own. We show you how to use and customize the common parts of Office 2003—toolbars, task panes, and other interface elements—so that when you learn how to customize one Office program you can transfer the same skills to others.

Office 2003 still has odd inconsistencies, as well as bugs, features that don't work as advertised, and basic interface elements guaranteed to drive expert users crazy. But as we researched the third edition of this book, we were pleasantly surprised to see how many longtime Office annoyances have finally been fixed. Office 2003 isn't perfect—not by a long shot—but it is indisputably the most stable, usable, and productive version we've ever worked with.

Some of what you see in *Special Edition Using Microsoft Office 2003* will be familiar to you if you've worked with an earlier edition of this book. We've gone through every chapter, sentence by sentence, testing, verifying, updating, revising, and adding a wealth of new information to ensure that this book is accurate and absolutely up to date.

WHO SHOULD BUY THIS BOOK

If you need an Office 2003 reference book you can rely on—one that won't bore you with the obvious, pull punches when Office comes up short, or turn mealy-mouthed when you hit the really hard parts—you have the right book in your hands.

As with other titles in Que's best-selling *Special Edition Using* series, this book focuses on the unique needs of students, teachers, and anyone using Office 2003 at home. We assume you're experienced with Windows, the Web, and, for the most part, previous versions of

Microsoft Office. If you're like most people, you've probably only scratched the surface of the capabilities in Office and you'd like to learn a lot more without taking a graduate course on the software. We're also certain you've experienced your fair share of Office bugs and annoyances firsthand. Because we're confident you've already figured out the basics, we've spent our time figuring out how these programs *really* work. Trust us—Office still has bugs and poorly designed features, and Microsoft doesn't always make it easy to see how you can combine features or customize applications to increase productivity.

We figure you're smart enough to experiment with basic features and to read the online help when you want to know how an Office program is *supposed* to work. That's why you won't find beginner-level instructions in this book. Instead, you'll find what isn't in the official documentation—key details, insight, and real-world advice you can't find anywhere else. And it's all arranged so that you can get in, find the answer you need, apply it to your work at hand, and get out. This book may weigh a ton, but if you need the straight scoop on anything related to Office, this is where you should look first.

How This Book Is Organized

Special Edition Using Microsoft Office 2003 is organized into six parts. Naturally, each of the major applications in the Office suite gets its own section. Before diving into specific features of Outlook, Word, Excel, and the rest, however, we recommend you read through the sections that cover the techniques common to all applications.

Part I, "Common Tasks and Features," covers the essentials of Office, including techniques you can use to transform the Office interface into your own personal productivity center. For instance, we show you how to customize the Office Open and Save As dialog boxes so that you can find your working files with the fewest possible clicks. This section also covers Office 2003's stellar graphics and document-scanning tools. Clippit, the annoying Office Assistant, has been downgraded to bit-player status in this version; if the pesky paper clip somehow survived the upgrade process on your computer, we show you how to make it disappear, permanently, in Chapter 1.

With each succeeding version, Outlook 2003 gets a sweeping makeover, and this one is no exception. Its roster of new features includes a revamped (but still sometimes overwhelming) interface you can use to tie together contacts, calendars, tasks, and e-mail. In Part II, "Using Outlook," we help you tame the flood of e-mail, banish spam forever with Outlook's new and surprisingly effective junk-mail filter, keep your address book up to date, and set up reminders so that you never miss another appointment.

Part III, "Using Word," covers the oldest and most polished productivity application in Office. We walk you through every customization option (including a few you probably never even knew you needed). We also show you how to supercharge your text-editing and formatting skills, how to manage long documents, and how to automate everyday documents so that they practically write themselves.

Part IV, "Using Excel," shows you tricks you never realized you could perform with this incredibly versatile tool. Check out the examples in our formatting chapters to see how you can turn drab rows and columns into eye-catching data graphics. We explain how to master any of Excel's 300+ functions, as well as which ones are worth memorizing. We'll show you how to use PivotTables (and their graphic cousins, PivotCharts) to give you a completely different view of data. Do you have a list of names, addresses, or other information? We also show you how to use the effective new list editing tools to sort, filter, and organize lists like an expert.

Of all the Office applications, PowerPoint is probably the least appreciated. In Part V, "Using PowerPoint," we explain how this program really works, and we help you create compelling presentations that you can deliver in front of a large audience or a small one— or completely unattended over the Web.

In Part VI, "Advanced Tasks and Features," we focus on ways to extend the capabilities of Office. We explain how to automate Office with macros written in Visual Basic for Applications (VBA). We also explain how you can create, edit, and publish sophisticated web pages without having to tangle with HTML tags. And in the final chapter, we intro-duce a few features that you'll need to know if you use Office on a portable computer, espe-cially a Tablet PC.

CONVENTIONS USED IN THIS BOOK

Special conventions are used to help you get the most from this book and from Office 2003.

TEXT CONVENTIONS

Various typefaces in this book identify terms and other special objects. These special type-faces include the following:

Type	Meaning
Italic	New terms or phrases when initially defined. An italic term followed by a page number indicates the page where that term is first defined.
Monospace	Information that you type, Web addresses, or onscreen messages.
UPPERCASE	Typically used to indicate Excel objects, such as functions and cell references.
Initial Caps	Menus, dialog box names, dialog box elements, and commands are capitalized.

Key combinations are represented with a plus sign. For example, if the text calls for you to enter Ctrl+S, you would press the Ctrl key and the S key at the same time.

SECRETS OF THE OFFICE MASTERS

While using Office, you'll find many features that work well together or others that simply don't work well at all without some poking and prodding. We've used this chapter-ending element to point out some key areas in which you can combine features or find startlingly productive new uses for everyday features.

SPECIAL ELEMENTS

Throughout this book, you'll find Tips, Notes, Cautions, Sidebars, Cross References, and Troubleshooting Tips. These elements provide a variety of information, ranging from warnings you shouldn't miss to ancillary information that will enrich your Office experience, but isn't required reading.

ED AND WOODY'S "SIGNATURE" TIPS

TIP FROM

Ed & Woody

> Tips are designed to point out features, annoyances, and tricks of the trade that you might otherwise miss. These aren't wimpy, run-of-the-mill tips that you learned the first week you used Office and don't need us to tell you. Watch for our signatures on the tips to indicate some industrial-strength—and in many cases never-before-documented—information.

NOTES

NOTE

> Notes point out items that you should be aware of, although you can skip these if you're in a hurry. Generally, we've added notes as a way to give you some extra information on a topic without weighing you down.

CAUTIONS

CAUTION

> Pay attention to Cautions! These could save you precious hours in lost work. Don't say we didn't warn you.

TROUBLESHOOTING NOTES

 We designed these elements to call attention to common pitfalls that you're likely to encounter. When you see a Troubleshooting note, you can flip to the "Troubleshooting" section at the end of the chapter to learn how to solve or avoid a problem.

CROSS REFERENCES

Cross references are designed to point you to other locations in this book (or other books in the Que family) that will provide supplemental or supporting information. Cross references appear as follows:

→ For a full discussion of the wonders of PivotTables, **see** "How PivotTable and PivotChart Reports Work," **p. 652**.

SIDEBARS

Want to Know More?
Sidebars are designed to provide information that is ancillary to the topic being discussed. Read these if you want to learn more about an application or task.

PART

I

COMMON TASKS AND FEATURES

CHAPTER 1

GETTING STARTED WITH OFFICE 2003

In this chapter

WHAT IS OFFICE STUDENT AND TEACHER EDITION 2003?

Microsoft's most popular software package is aimed at businesses. With a name like Office, that's only natural. And sure enough, most of the new features Microsoft has introduced to Office in recent years are aimed at helping people in corporations work more closely.

So, what's the deal with Microsoft Office Student and Teacher Edition 2003? Students and teachers work in classrooms, not offices, after all. As it turns out, both groups use computers, and people who spend their days in classrooms do many of the same things their office-bound counterparts do: They write reports, perform mathematical calculations, give presentations, and communicate via e-mail, among other things. Those are exactly the tasks that the individual programs in Microsoft Office are designed to accomplish.

So, despite the slightly misleading name, Microsoft decided to make an Office 2003 Standard Edition available in a special package for people who don't normally work in offices.

In fact, the only thing different about the Student and Teacher Edition of Microsoft Office is the license agreement. To legally install and use the software, you must be a "qualified educational user" (or the parent or legal guardian of a qualified educational user who is a minor). You qualify if you're a full- or part-time student, a home-schooled student, a full- or part-time faculty or staff member of an accredited educational institution, or a member of a household with at least one person who fits in these categories.

As a qualified educational user, you get a significant price break on the cost of the Office software. You also get the right to install Office on up to three computers in your household. (Other editions of Office allow installation on only one primary computer and one portable computer that is not used at the same time as the primary copy.)

So what's the catch? There are a few:

The license you get with Office Student and Teacher Edition 2003 is a "personal learning license." You're not allowed to use the software for any commercial purpose or in any way related to the operation of a business. But that's a legal requirement, not a technical one. You don't have to prove that you're actually a student or a teacher to buy the software or to install it, and the software police won't kick down your door if you use your copy of Office to produce a business plan or catch up on some paperwork that you've brought home from the office.

In this book, we assume that you're primarily using the software for educational purposes, which is why most of our examples relate to activities you'll encounter in a classroom or a home. But if you notice that we occasionally mention a feature that just might help you be more productive at work…well, we won't tell if you won't tell.

OFFICE 2003 STUDENT AND TEACHER EDITION, PIECE BY PIECE

Four programs form the core of Office 2003 Student and Teacher Edition—Outlook, Word, Excel, and PowerPoint. In addition, the package includes a handful of smaller programs, such as the Picture Manager utility.

NOTE

This book covers the four programs found in Office 2003 Student and Teacher Edition. If you've purchased a different Office edition, the program code for these programs is exactly the same and our advice applies just as well. In particular, if you use the Standard edition of Office, you'll find everything you need in here. We do not include coverage of programs that are included with other Office editions, such as Publisher and Access, nor do we include the more distant members of the Office family, such as FrontPage, Project, and Visio.

OUTLOOK 2003

Outlook 2003 is an e-mail program and a whole lot more. As even a cursory examination of the Outlook interface makes clear, you can keep track of contacts, appointments, tasks, and e-mail messages. To switch between Outlook modules, you can use the customizable Navigation pane (see Figure 1.1) or an Explorer-style folder list. You can create shortcuts to your favorite folders and define *search folders* that automatically find messages based on criteria you define.

Figure 1.1
In Outlook 2003, a customizable Navigation pane replaces the old Outlook Bar and Folder List.

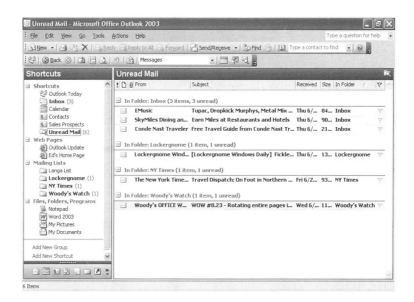

➔ For details on how to work with the Navigation pane, **see** "Using and Customizing the Outlook Interface," **p. 166**.

Using the Reading pane, you can skim e-mail messages quickly. With e-mail rules, desktop alerts, and custom view options, you can quickly sort and group e-mail messages. You can use as many e-mail accounts as you like, and even create a custom e-mail signature for each one.

Outlook 2003 includes a wealth of privacy and security tools as well. Junk-mail filters effectively block most spam; you can customize the lists of blocked and safe senders to prevent wanted messages from being incorrectly identified as junk. The program also protects your privacy by blocking images in e-mail messages from unknown senders; these so-called Web bugs can signal to a spammer that your e-mail address is active. Outlook 2003 also blocks attachments that can contain viruses and other hostile programs. We explain how these features work (and how to work around them) in Chapter 9, "Stopping Viruses, Spam, and Other Security Threats."

WORD 2003

The oldest and most mature of the Office programs, Word is also the most widely used. It's an extremely versatile tool—ideal for creating short documents, such as letters and reports, with enough layout and graphics-handling capabilities to also make it suitable for sophisticated publishing chores. Thanks to its HTML-editing capabilities, it's also an excellent starting point when you want to create a web page.

At its core, Word 2003 is easy enough to use. The basic tools for formatting text, viewing documents, and putting pages on paper have been part of Word for years. If you dig a little deeper, you'll find some useful features in the task panes. The Research pane, in particular, is tailor-made for use with Word documents, giving you access to an encyclopedia, a dictionary, and other reference books that can simplify the process of writing a paper. More than any other Office program, Word takes full advantage of Smart Tags, such as those used for AutoCorrect options. The most noteworthy innovation to the Word 2003 interface is the addition of a new Reading Layout view, which is optimized to make documents easier to read onscreen (see Figure 1.2).

➔ For full details on Word's new Reading view, **see** "Choosing the Right Document View," **p. 326**.

EXCEL 2003

Excel is an incredibly useful all-purpose number-crunching tool, suitable for tasks as simple as balancing a checkbook or as complex as creating a doctoral dissertation in macroeconomic analysis. Excel is also a fabulous tool for keeping track of lists. When you designate a range as a list, you can automatically add totals to it, easily insert new columns and rows, import and export lists, and share those lists on an intranet. A new List and XML toolbar helps turn many of these tasks into single-click exercises. (For an extensive discussion of these tools, read Chapter 20, "Working with Lists and PivotTables.")

Figure 1.2
Word's Reading Layout view hides most editing tools and reformats your document to make it easy to browse onscreen.

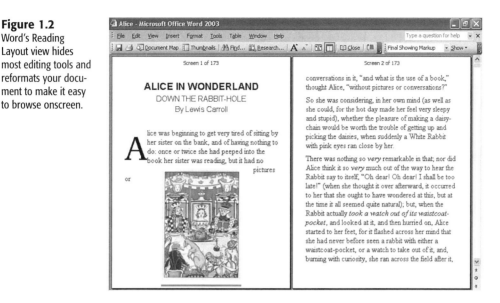

POWERPOINT 2003

PowerPoint has always been an effective way to create PC-based slide shows for presentations in front of a large audience. Recent versions add the capability to create effective web-based presentations as well. You can't truly appreciate the effectiveness of web-based presentations until you create one. PowerPoint can turn slide titles into a table of contents in the left pane of a frame, and then display each slide on the right, with the viewer pointing and clicking to drive the show.

An increasing number of schools are using PowerPoint presentations in the classroom as well. They've discovered that it's an excellent way for kids to learn how to organize their thoughts, and it adds a whole new dimension to the classic "show and tell" day.

→ For step-by-step instructions that will help you get a PowerPoint presentation into web format in record time, **see** "Creating Presentations for the Web," **p. 788**.

For novices and experts alike, PowerPoint has earned a reputation as the most user friendly program in the Office family. That's good news, because many PowerPoint users dust off the program only every few months, unlike Word and Excel. If you can't remember how to create a specific type of slide, look at the Slide Design task pane, which lets you see and preview design templates, color schemes, and animation effects while the slide is visible.

You can add annotations to the slides in your presentations and save those comments for later. You can also embed multimedia clips into your presentation and show them using the full screen. Using the Package for CD utility, it's simple to put your slides on a CD and play them back on any PC, even one that doesn't have Office installed.

Unlike the documentation—or other Office books—we also show you exactly how to use each of PowerPoint's many file formats.

OTHER OFFICE PROGRAMS

In addition to the major programs, Office 2003 includes an assortment of utilities and add-ins. Some are positively ancient and of limited value; a good example is the Organization Chart tool, which is accessible from the Insert, Diagram menu on any Office program. A handful of Office utilities, though, are brand-new or greatly improved, and one in particular deserves special mention.

Microsoft Office Picture Manager (found in the Microsoft Office Tools group on the All Programs menu) lets you organize collections of image files that you've taken with a digital camera, scanned from original photos, or saved from websites. You can compress and resize images and perform basic image-editing tasks, such as removing "red eye" from portraits (see Figure 1.3). You can also convert images to alternative formats (from the space-hogging Bitmap format to the more efficient JPEG or GIF format, for instance, a trick that comes in especially handy when creating web pages.

Figure 1.3
Use Picture Manager to perform basic image-editing chores.

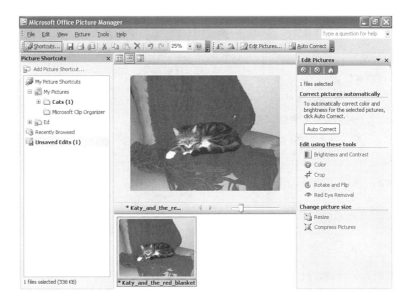

SETUP ESSENTIALS

For most people, installing Office 2003 is ridiculously simple. Pop the CD in the drive, enter the 25-character product key from the yellow sticker inside the software case, choose the default installation options, and let the Setup program go about its business. No rebooting is required.

The Office program files themselves are included in a large collection of compressed files stored in the Cabinet File format (using the extension .cab). During the installation process, the Setup program automatically copies these files, along with the Installer package files and a handful of additional files, to the Local Install Source. This is a hidden folder named Msocache, which is stored in the root folder of your system drive.

The purpose of the Local Install Source is to eliminate the need to insert the Office CD whenever you install an optional feature, add a patch or service pack, or modify the existing installation in any way.

Having these files handy can save the aggravation of having to insert the Office CD when you make a change to your existing Office setup. However, the Local Install Source does occupy several hundred megabytes of disk space, and on some computers that can cause problems. As a result, you can eliminate this folder in either of two ways:

- In the final phase of Setup, select the check box that offers to automatically remove the installation files.
- After Setup is complete, run the Disk Cleanup Wizard (cleanmgr.exe), select the Office Setup Files check box from the Files to Delete list, and click OK.

CAUTION

> Don't just delete the Msocache folder. Although that action appears to solve the problem, the fix is only temporary. As soon as you take any action that changes your Office installation, the Setup program re-creates the Local Install Source.

Two aspects of setup deserve special mention here. One is Office Product Activation, a controversial anti-piracy technology designed to prevent casual copying; the other is the need to check for updates after installation is complete.

ACTIVATING YOUR COPY OF OFFICE

After you complete the Office 2003 Setup process, you can begin using Office programs immediately. However, you will be required to complete one final step before you can continue using Office past an initial trial period: You must *activate* the product by contacting Microsoft over the Internet or by phone. This measure is intended to stop piracy; as we noted earlier, you can install and activate Office 2003 on up to three computers. However, if you try to activate Office 2003 a fourth time using the same product key, you'll be refused.

For most users with an Internet connection, product activation happens automatically and takes only a few seconds. The activation process generates a "fingerprint" based on the hardware in your system and then associates that ID code with your 25-character Product ID. If you reinstall the software on the same computer (after reformatting the hard drive, for instance), reactivation should be automatic. In fact, you can reinstall Office 2003 an unlimited number of times on the same computer. The activation server is intelligent enough to recognize from the hardware fingerprint that your computer hasn't changed.

If you've used all three of your permitted activations and you try to install the software on a new computer, or on an old computer that you have upgraded with substantially different hardware, you might have to call Microsoft to get a new activation code. Simply changing a video card or adding a new hard drive won't trigger a request to reactivate Office, but a

1

major upgrade, such as swapping the motherboard *and* switching hard drives *and* replacing the network card, might.

NOTE

> Retail versions of Windows XP also require activation. However, the rules and regulations for the two products are slightly different. Windows XP allows you to continue using the operating system for up to 30 days before shutting down, whereas Office allows 50 uses before forcing you to activate. Windows Product Activation is also more generous about hardware changes than Office. For more details about Office Product Activation, visit `http://www.microsoft.com/office/editions/prodinfo/activation.mspx`.

A product activation reminder pops up each time you start a new Office program. If you don't have ready access to the Internet, you can delay activation, but don't wait too long. Without activating the product, you can use individual Office programs a maximum of 50 times (each time you launch a different program counts as a single use, even if you are forced to restart after a crash); after you use your 50 free starts, a process that can take less than a week, Office switches into a "reduced functionality" mode, in which you are allowed to open and print files but not edit or save them.

INSTALLING UPDATES AND SERVICE PACKS

At irregular intervals, Microsoft releases software *updates*. Available for download from Microsoft's website, these updates are executable programs, usually small in size, intended to fix specific bugs or to plug security holes in Office programs. Less frequently, Microsoft releases comprehensive updates to Office called *service packs*. Because they're typically quite large, service packs are usually made available both via download and on CD.

NOTE

> Service Packs and updates can be installed on any version of Microsoft Office, including Student-Teacher Edition. The update program installs all files that are required for your version.

Because updates often fix issues that affect the reliability and security of your computer, it's crucial that you install all available updates. You can take your pick of two tools to help you tackle this task:

- **Microsoft Update**—This service, introduced in 2005 as an upgrade to the Windows Update service, automatically checks for updates to Windows, Office, and other Microsoft products; to install it, visit `http://update.microsoft.com/microsoftupdate`. (Note that you must be logged on as a member of the Administrators group to enable this service.)

- **Office Update**—This web-based service scans your system and identifies any updates you need, based on the Office version you have installed. Unlike Windows Update and

Microsoft Update, this service is not automatic. You have to visit the site, install an ActiveX control, and manually scan for updates. The easiest way to reach Office Update is to open any Office program and choose Help, Check for Updates.

CAUTION

> Don't assume that you should immediately install every update you find on the Office Update site. We strongly recommend installing anything identified as a critical update, but for optional updates, read the documentation carefully and decide whether the update applies to you before installing it.

CUSTOMIZING YOUR OFFICE INSTALLATION

When you select the Typical Install or Upgrade options to install Office 2003, Setup uses the following default options:

- Program files go in the Microsoft Office Subfolder in the folder that the %program-files% variable points to. (On most systems, this is C:\Program Files.) In Office 2003, you can specify a different location, although we strongly recommend using the default location.

- Setup removes your previous Office installation (if any) and replaces all installed programs. In the process, it migrates your personal settings and preferences to Office 2003.

- Setup installs a standard set of programs and features. In the case of an upgrade, it automatically replaces all previously installed components with new versions, even if they're not normally part of the Typical Install.

TIP FROM

> If you're not sure whether to use the Custom Install option, choose it anyway. When you do, Setup lets you review all options, and if you accept the default settings at every opportunity, the effect is the same as if you had chosen a Typical Install.

To change any of these options, you need to select one of the other available installation types:

- Complete Install selects every Office program and feature. For most Office users, this option is overkill. If you need additional features, you can add them at any time by rerunning Setup from the Add or Remove Programs option in Control Panel.

- Minimal Install selects a stripped-down group of programs and features. If you're upgrading from a previous version, you'll be prompted to specify which programs you want to replace; all old versions are removed.

- Custom Install offers the widest assortment of options, allowing you to specify precisely which programs and features you want to install and how you want them configured.

When you choose the Custom Install option, you'll use two dialog boxes that allow you to change which pieces of Office are installed. The Windows Installer distinguishes between *applications*, which are major pieces of the package, and *installation options*, which comprise the files, programs, *dynamic link libraries (DLLs)*, and Registry entries that make up each feature.

The wizard screen shown in Figure 1.4 lets you choose not to install specific programs. By default, on a system that does not currently have any version of Office installed, all check boxes are selected; clear the check mark to the left of a program to specify that you want to skip that application.

Figure 1.4
For maximum control over how Office programs are installed, choose the Advanced Customization option at the bottom of this dialog box.

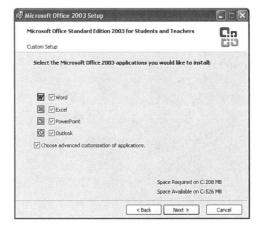

If you select Choose Advanced Customization of Applications, clicking Next displays the Advanced Customization dialog box shown in Figure 1.5. The icon to the left of each feature shows how it will be installed. A white box with a drive icon means all options will be installed using the method you've specified; a gray box with a drive icon means that some of the options available in that feature will not be installed. Click the plus sign to the left of each feature to see a list of options and adjust each one as needed.

Figure 1.5
By using a custom installation, you can select installation options for each Office application.

NOTE

As you select each item in the list, text at the bottom of the dialog box offers a capsule description of the feature or program.

In Office 2003, as in earlier versions, you can configure each Office feature separately, saving considerable disk space. For example, if you use Outlook, Word, and Excel regularly but you're sure you'll never use PowerPoint, you can set up the first three programs to run from your local computer but skip the installation of PowerPoint.

Up to four settings are available for each feature and options. Click the drop-down arrow to the left of any feature to see of the available options, as shown in Figure 1.6.

Figure 1.6
When setting up Office, you can choose whether and how to run each feature.

- When you choose Run from My Computer, Setup copies all associated program files to the specified location on the user's hard disk, and the application runs the feature locally. This option results in the best performance. Choose Run All from My Computer to apply this setting to all options under the selected feature.

- When you specify Installed on First Use for a feature, Setup creates a menu item or shortcut for the specified feature, but does not install the files associated with the feature. In the Typical Install, a number of little-used features are installed using this option. When you first use that menu choice or shortcut, the Windows Installer copies the necessary files to the local hard disk just as if you had chosen the Run from My Computer option. You might be prompted to insert the Office CD to complete the installation.

TIP FROM

ED & Woody

Be extremely careful when using this option on portable computers. If you configure a system option to Installed on First Use, the Windows Installer must be able to access the CD-ROM or the Local Install Source to complete the installation. If you're away and the CD is on your desk back home and you've cleaned away the local installation files, you will be unable to use this feature until you return home.

- Choose Not Available when you do not want to install a feature or create shortcuts that refer to it. In some cases, built-in menus include options that refer to features you've chosen not to install; if you select one of these menus, you'll see an error message that instructs you to rerun Setup.

FIXING SETUP PROBLEMS

Thanks to the Windows Installer, Office 2003 Setup is extremely robust. As the Setup program does its work, it keeps track of each action it takes. If you click the Cancel button in the middle of the process, Setup uses this feature to "roll back" all the changes—undoing any Registry changes and deleting any files you've copied so far. If Setup is interrupted for any other reason—by a system crash or power failure, for example—you should be able to restart Setup and resume at the place where it stopped previously.

TIP FROM

Ed & Woody

> The Windows Installer creates a hidden folder called Config.msi to store files it removes during the Setup process so that you can roll back to the previous installation if necessary. If you find this folder on your computer after successfully installing Office 2003, you can safely eliminate it and recover the disk space without any dire consequences.

Unless you specify otherwise, Setup also creates and saves log files that contain information on all Setup actions—changes to the Registry, files copied, and so on. You can locate these files in your system's Temp directory; each one begins with the name of the Office version, followed by the word Setup and a number. You can open each file by using any text editor.

USING SETUP IN MAINTENANCE MODE

When you run Setup on a computer that has Office installed already, you'll see the Maintenance Mode Options dialog box shown in Figure 1.7. Use this dialog box when you want to add or remove features, when you need to repair an Office installation that is not functioning properly, or when you want to completely uninstall Office 2003.

You can start Setup in Maintenance mode by running Setup from the CD, or by using the Add or Remove Programs option in Control Panel.

Figure 1.7
After you install Office 2003, running Setup displays the Maintenance Mode Options dialog box.

1

ADDING AND REMOVING OFFICE FEATURES

To change the list of installed Office features after running Setup for the first time, run Setup in Maintenance mode and click the Add or Remove Features button. The resulting dialog box is nearly identical to the list of features available when you perform a custom installation, as described previously. You can also use this dialog box to change the configuration of a feature—for example, to change a feature that is not currently installed so that it's installed on first use—using one of these techniques:

- To add a feature so that it is available at all times, select the Run from My Computer or Run All from Computer check box.
- To configure a feature so that it is available for installation when needed, select the Installed on First Use option.
- To remove a feature, select Not Available.

REPAIRING AN OFFICE INSTALLATION

The Windows Installer maintains a complete record of all Office components you've installed. If you accidentally delete a file or a Registry entry becomes corrupted after installation, the Windows Installer can automatically reinstall the component the next time you try to use it. In most cases, these repairs are automatic: If one of the essential system files for PowerPoint is missing when you attempt to launch the program, for example, the Installer starts automatically and reinstalls the missing file from the original installation source. You might need to supply the Office CD to continue.

If you suspect that some features of an application might be damaged, you can force Setup to inspect all essential files for that application and reinstall any files that are missing or corrupted. To use this option, choose Help, Detect and Repair. You'll see the dialog box shown in Figure 1.8; click Start to continue.

Figure 1.8
If you've inadvertently deleted one or more shortcuts for an application, use the Detect and Repair option to restore the shortcuts and any missing program files.

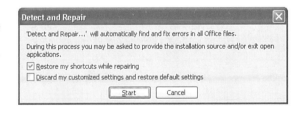

The Detect and Repair option works only on the program from which you run it. If you're unable to start that program, or if you suspect that several programs are damaged, rerun Setup in Maintenance mode and choose Repair Office. This option lets you choose whether to completely reinstall Office using all the settings you originally specified, or whether the Windows Installer should look for missing or corrupted files and Registry settings and repair them as needed.

UNINSTALLING OFFICE 2003

The final option in the Maintenance Mode dialog box, Uninstall Office, lets you completely uninstall Office 2003 and all associated features and components. When you choose this option, you see one and only one dialog box asking you to confirm that you want to remove Office completely. If you click OK, the Windows Installer begins the uninstall process immediately.

TIP FROM

Thanks to the Windows Installer's rollback capability, you can abort the uninstall process at any time before completion, and Setup restores your system to its previous state. A progress bar moves from left to right as the Windows Installer removes components; if you click the Cancel button, watch the progress bar move from right to left as the Windows Installer undoes its actions and restores the original configuration.

You should be aware of two caveats when uninstalling Office:

■ Using the Uninstall Office option effectively deletes virtually all program files and associated Registry entries. However, it leaves behind a considerable number of Registry entries associated with user settings and preferences, as well as some files that contain user settings. If you attempt to reinstall Office later, the new installation will use these settings. For instance, if you've defined alternate locations for documents, these will appear in your new installation, as will Excel macros in a leftover Personal Macro Workbook.

■ If you upgraded over an earlier version of Office, removing Office 2003 will not bring back the previous version. The only way to preserve older Office versions is to specifically choose that option by performing a custom install of Office 2003 in the first place.

TIP FROM

If you want to make a completely clean start by first removing previous Office versions, use the Microsoft Office Removal Wizard (`offcln.exe`). This utility can be found on the Office CD, in the `Files\Pfiles\Msoffice\Office11` folder.

GETTING HELP

Each Office program includes detailed help content for Office users at any level, regardless of technical sophistication or experience. If your computer is connected to the Internet, Office 2003 automatically updates the local Help files and supplements their content with articles, training courses, templates, downloads, and links to Office newsgroups.

The jumping-off point for all these disparate types of content is the Help task pane, which replaces the old-style Help window. To open this pane, click the Help button on the standard toolbar, press F1, or click the arrow to the right of the task pane title bar and choose

Help from the drop-down list. As Figure 1.9 illustrates, the Help task pane is divided into three sections.

Figure 1.9
Looking for answers?
Start with the Office
2003 Help task pane.

- **Assistance**—This section consists of local help content (with online updates), plus a search box. Click the Table of Contents link to see an outline-style list of all available Help topics.
- **Office Online**—Here, you'll find links to online resources. Clicking any of these links opens your browser to the linked page.
- **See Also**—The links in this section point to a grab bag of locations, including Web pages and a dialog box that you can use to configure Help options.

The contents of the Help task pane change dynamically. For instance, if you click the Table of Contents link, the search box and other links disappear, leaving only an expandable list like the one shown in Figure 1.10. Click any closed-book icon to expand that section. Individual help topics are denoted with a question-mark icon that matches the one on the Help button.

TIP FROM

E℘ & Woody

> Remember that the task pane is expandable. When working with the Help pane, the default width cuts off most topics. Drag the inside edge to the left to make the pane large enough to comfortably view all topics.

Figure 1.10
Browse through the table of contents to find how-to information by category.

Using the Table of Contents is the right strategy when you want to start with a general subject and dig deeper. To search for answers to more specific questions, enter a word or phrase in the Search box and click the green arrow to its right (or press Enter). By default, Office searches all available information sources, online and offline, returning the results in the task pane, as shown in Figure 1.11.

Look carefully at the results that the search in Figure 1.11 returned. Unlike previous Office versions, this search returns not only help topics but articles, templates, training courses, and links to commercial services. If you don't find what you're looking for, revise the keywords in the Search box at the bottom of the results pane and try again. The list above the Search box lets you narrow the list of sources to be searched. To search for only help topics—no articles, templates, or other content—choose Assistance from the list of sources to be searched. To look only in the local help file, choose Offline Help.

TIP FROM

E℘ & Woody

> Of course, sometimes the best interface is no interface. If all you want is answers, without having to deal with dialog boxes or a cartoon character, type a keyword or phrase into the tiny box at the top right corner of any Office program window. (You can't miss it; look for the light gray "Type a question for help" prompt.)

To return to the main Help task pane, click the small green Back arrow at the top of the task pane, just below the title bar.

Figure 1.11
The default search returns help topics, articles, templates, and more.

VIEWING A HELP TOPIC

Normally, when you click a link that points to a Help topic, Office resizes the currently active program window and displays the topic in its own window just to the right of the program window. When you close the Help topic, the program window returns to its previous size. Even on a high-resolution system, this arrangement doesn't work particularly well; because the Help task pane remains visible, your program window shrinks to a skinny, nearly useless sliver. A much better arrangement is to allow the Help window to float. In this configuration, in fact, you can keep a topic open but minimized while you work, so that you can return to it as needed. Click the Untile button at the top left of the Help window to allow the Help pane to float; click it again to restore the Auto Tile configuration.

As the example in Figure 1.12 shows, all the individual Help topics look and behave like web pages (with single-click "hot" links, Back and Forward buttons for navigation, and so on). That shouldn't be surprising, because they are written in HTML. In fact, links to Help topics come directly from Microsoft's website unless you disable the option to search online.

TIP FROM

EQ & Woody

Try as we might, we can't find any easy way to save a Help topic for future reference. The Office Help engine doesn't allow you to create bookmarks or customize the Help pane by designating Favorites. If you find an especially helpful topic, you can use any of these three strategies: Click the Print button to produce a hard copy; use the Clipboard to select some or all of the topic and then right-click and use the Clipboard to copy the text to a Word document or e-mail message; or right-click, choose Properties, copy the URL of the Help topic, and create a shortcut to that topic.

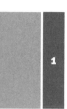

Figure 1.12
Every Help topic is actually a mini-web page, available either from a local file or from Microsoft's website.

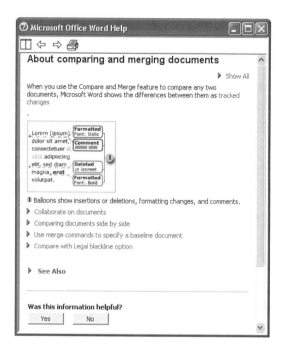

Office 2003 offers only a limited menu of options for configuring how Help works. At the bottom of the main Help task pane, click Online Content Settings to display the dialog box shown in Figure 1.13. Clear Show Content and Links from Microsoft Office Online to disable all online access. Clear the Search Online Content When Connected check box if you want Office to use only the local Help files but still search for articles and templates. You'll see a warning at the top of the Help task pane whenever online searches are disabled.

Figure 1.13
Use these check boxes to customize Office Help searches.

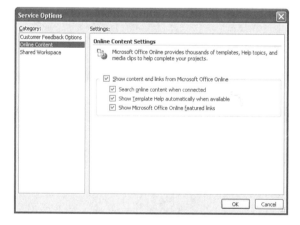

USING THE OFFICE ASSISTANT

The Office Assistant Character is the single most provocative Office feature, past or present. In previous versions of Office, that %$#@! paper clip was in your face from the moment you started each program. Apparently, Microsoft's research has determined that most people prefer to do without Clippit, because the Office Assistant is not included with a default installation. Even if you go out of your way to keep this "social interface" around (by choosing Help, Show the Office Assistant), the character's role is greatly reduced. If the Assistant is visible, it displays some warning messages, but results from searches you start with the Office Assistant appear in the Help task pane.

To get rid of a too-persistent Assistant, right-click and choose the Hide button. After a few tries, the Assistant will get the hint and offer to disappear permanently. To eliminate all traces of the Office Assistant, re-run Setup using the Add or Remove Features option, find the Office Assistant option under Office Shared Features, and set it to Not Available.

CHAPTER 2

MAKING OFFICE 2003 WORK YOUR WAY

In this chapter

POINT, CLICK, CUSTOMIZE

Microsoft Office is filled with features you'll never use. Every Office program contains an assortment of menus and toolbars that were designed for someone who has almost nothing in common with you. You *could* spend weeks or months learning how to ignore all those irrelevant features and find the secret paths to the ones you actually use day in and day out. But we have a better suggestion: Make a few small adjustments.

You might be tempted to skip over this chapter and go straight to one that's directly related to the program you're trying to use right now. That's fine. But be sure to come back and read this one after you've used a program for a while. When you've used a program for a while, you learn which features are most important to you. In this chapter, we explain how to clear away the clutter and put the menus and toolbars you use most often where they belong—a click or two away. We also show you how task panes work, how to set up spell-checking options, and how you can get a dictionary definition or a quick translation of a foreign phrase without leaving the friendly confines of your Office program. All in all, learning the techniques in this chapter can save you time and make Office easier to use. Good news: Most Office programs work in identical fashion, so once you learn how to tweak a toolbar and modify a menu in Word, you can use the exact same techniques in Excel, PowerPoint, and Outlook.

MAKING MENUS AND TOOLBARS CONSISTENT

Every Office program plays a confusing game of "now you see 'em, now you don't"—at least until you get around to disabling the *personalized menus and toolbars* feature. In most Windows programs, toolbars and pull-down menus are fixed. When you click a menu item, a list drops down showing you all the choices available on that menu. Toolbars show buttons that you can click to perform common tasks.

But that's not the way Office programs work. In Office, menus and toolbars change dynamically as you use the program. When you click a menu, you see a short list of available choices instead of the full menu. To make matters even more confusing, the short list changes over time, as each Office program monitors your usage patterns and "personalizes" menus and toolbars. The idea is to reduce clutter and simplify your work by showing you only the menu choices you use regularly, rather than overwhelming you with a long menu that contains many choices. In the case of toolbars, where there's not always enough room on the screen to see every button, Office programs take note of the buttons you use and move them onto the visible part of the toolbar, hiding those you haven't used lately.

When we talk to people who actually use Office 2003, they tell us that personalized menus and toolbars actually make the Office interface *more* confusing. Menu choices and toolbar buttons disappear and reappear, seemingly at random. The problem is especially acute if you use a particular program extensively and depend on knowing exactly which choices are on a program's menus.

You can configure the precise way in which personalized menus and toolbars behave, and if you don't like this feature, you can disable it completely. In his section, we explain how the process works and how you can take charge of it.

NOTE

> With Windows XP, you can and should create a separate user account for each member of your family. Having a separate account enables you to keep your personal data files in their own private folder; it also gives you a place to store your own Office 2003 settings. You can adjust toolbars, menus, and templates without having to worry that someone else will come along and change your carefully customized settings without your permission. You'll find the User Accounts option in Control Panel; if you are an administrator on your computer, you can set up a new user account for yourself or for any other member of your family with just a few clicks.

HOW PERSONALIZED TOOLBARS AND MENUS WORK

In Office 2003, the personalized menus option is turned on for every program when you first use it, and this option remains enabled until you turn it off. When you click any item on the menu bar, you see only a subset of the choices available under that menu. (You might see truncated versions of cascading menus as well.) Figure 2.1 shows a typical personalized menu in Word. The double-headed arrows at the bottom of the main menu and the cascading menu to its right indicate that some of the choices on both menus are currently hidden.

Figure 2.1
The double-headed arrow, or chevron, at the bottom of each menu shown indicates that some menu choices are hidden.

If the choice you want isn't on the short menu, force the full set of menu options to appear by using any of the following three techniques:

- Click the chevron character at the bottom of the short menu.
- Leave the short menu open for more than three seconds without moving the mouse off the top-level menu (File, Edit, and so on).
- Click a top-level menu item twice in a row; the first click displays the short menu, and the second expands it to the full menu.

TIP FROM

Ed & Woody

> If you don't like personalized menus, but you find yourself working on another computer or in another user account where this option is enabled, here's how to keep your sanity: Get in the habit of double-clicking top-level choices on the main menu bar. By double-clicking, you'll blast right past the short menus and see all the choices right away.

Don't confuse the grayed-out choices on a menu with hidden choices. As in all Windows programs, grayed-out menu choices mean that an option is unavailable in the current context; in Word, for example, several options on the Table menu are unavailable until you create a table and click to position the insertion point in that table.

How does Office decide which menu options and toolbar buttons should be hidden? It examines the way you use each program over time and then makes decisions based on the following rules:

- When you first install Office 2003, you see a default short menu when you click the top-level menus (File, Edit, and so on) in each program. If you leave the Standard and Formatting toolbars on a single row, you'll see a default short selection for each of these toolbars as well, with some buttons hidden.

- These default menu items remain visible for at least six different program sessions on six different days in which you use other items on the same menu. If you use Excel every day but you use the Data menu only once a month, for example, it might be six months or more before the default choices on that menu change.

- Each time you use a menu item or toolbar button that is hidden in the initial default settings, that menu item or button is promoted to the list of visible entries. If your toolbar is already using the full width of the program window, Office might hide another button to make room for the newly promoted button.

- Menu items remain visible for at least three different sessions on three different days after you use them.

- The more you use a menu item, the longer it stays around. If you work on a PowerPoint presentation for several weeks and regularly use the Action Buttons choice on the Slide Show menu, that option will remain visible for much longer than if you just clicked it one day to see what the option was for and then never clicked it again.

- Office never changes the *order* of items on toolbars and menus (although you can use customization options to do so). When an Office program promotes a menu choice or makes a toolbar button visible, it appears in the exact same position (relative to other menu choices) as when you display full menus.

DISABLING ON-THE-FLY INTERFACE CHANGES

In our experience, most people find this constant shifting of menus and toolbars more confusing than helpful. If you agree, you can disable personalized menus and toolbars. Select Tools, Customize, click the Options tab, and click to put a check mark in both boxes in the Personalized Menus and Toolbars section, as shown in Figure 2.2.

Figure 2.2
To force Office to display full menus and toolbars at all times, put a check mark in both boxes in the top section of this dialog box.

RESTORING DEFAULT MENUS AND TOOLBARS

You might be one of the rare people who actually prefers personalized menus. Or maybe you're allowing one of your kids who is just getting started with Office to practice with an existing user account and you feel this option will make her work easier. To restore personalized menus and toolbars to their default settings, select Tools, Customize, click the Options tab, and click the Reset Menu and Toolbar Usage Data button. Then clear both check boxes in the Personalized Menus and Toolbars section.

You also might want to select this option if you give someone a hand-me-down computer without setting up a new user account or after a training session in which the student explores a number of features they probably won't use regularly.

NOTE

> The Reset Menu and Toolbar Usage Data option has no effect on buttons or menu choices you add or remove using the customization techniques described in the next few sections. It also has no effect if you've chosen the Always Show Full Menus option.

CUSTOMIZING TOOLBARS

Each program in the Office family includes an assortment of toolbars in addition to the Standard and Formatting toolbars. Some, such as Word's Outlining toolbar and Excel's PivotTable toolbar, appear automatically when you begin performing specific tasks. You can show specific toolbars and arrange them onscreen when they're needed and then hide them when you're finished working with them. You can also customize most toolbars by adding and removing buttons, and you can create new custom toolbars that contain exactly the buttons and menu choices you specify.

TIP FROM

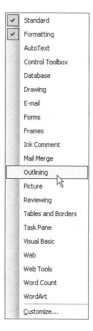

If your monitor is set to a limited resolution, such as 800×600 pixels, you might prefer to keep the Standard and Formatting toolbars on one row most of the time and switch to the two-row configuration only when you need to do a lot of formatting. In Office 2003, this option is always available, without requiring that you dive into dialog boxes. Click the drop-down arrow at the right of either toolbar and choosing the appropriate menu option—Show Buttons on One Row or Show Buttons on Two Rows.

SHOWING, HIDING, AND ARRANGING TOOLBARS

To display or hide toolbars, right-click any visible toolbar or right-click the menu bar to see a list of commonly available toolbars, similar to the one in Figure 2.3. Click any item in the list to display that toolbar; if one of the toolbars listed has a check mark next to its name, click to clear the check mark and hide the toolbar.

Figure 2.3
This list of toolbars shows only a subset of those that are actually available; use the Customize dialog box to see a more complete listing.

✓	Standard
✓	Formatting
	AutoText
	Control Toolbox
	Database
	Drawing
	E-mail
	Forms
	Frames
	Ink Comment
	Mail Merge
	Outlining
	Picture
	Reviewing
	Tables and Borders
	Task Pane
	Visual Basic
	Web
	Web Tools
	Word Count
	WordArt
	Customize...

To reduce confusion and clutter, this pop-up list shows only some of the available toolbars. If you work with a Word document in Normal view, for example, you'll see a selection of 20 or so toolbars on this list, although more than 30 are actually available. To make any of these additional toolbars available, select Tools, Customize, and click the Toolbars tab (see Figure 2.4). Select the check box to the left of any item on the list to make that toolbar visible.

Figure 2.4
This list of available toolbars offers more choices than the simple pop-up menu you see when you right-click a toolbar.

TIP FROM

If you use the Customize dialog box to display a toolbar that isn't on the shortcut menu, you don't need to go through all those clicks to hide it again. Right-click on any menu or toolbar to display the list of available toolbars and you'll see that the toolbar you added now appears on that menu. Click its name to hide the toolbar.

When you're working with toolbars, you have three options for positioning each toolbar on the screen:

- You can dock any toolbar to any side of the screen. By default, for example, the Standard and Formatting toolbars are docked just below the menu bar in every Office program, and the Drawing toolbar attaches itself to the bottom of the screen. To move the toolbar, aim the mouse pointer at the sizing handle (the thin horizontal bar at the left or top edge of a docked toolbar) until it turns into a pointer with four arrows. Then click and drag the toolbar to any other edge of the screen and release the mouse button to snap it into its new position.

TIP FROM

Not all toolbars actually work properly when docked to the side of the screen. Some drop-down lists that normally appear on a toolbar, such as the Style, Font, and Font Size choices on the Formatting toolbar or the Line Style selector on the Borders toolbar, aren't visible on a toolbar that's docked to the side of the screen. Pull-down menus can be harder to read when displayed sideways. Toolbars that contain only buttons, such as the Picture toolbar in Word, Excel, and PowerPoint, work well when docked on either side of the screen.

- You can dock two or more toolbars on the same edge, side by side, or one above the other. Drag the sizing handle to move a toolbar on its row.

- You can also drag any docked toolbar into the program window to let it "float" above the document you're working on. This option is best suited for controls you use when designing forms and charts, creating macros, working with pictures or drawings, and editing PivotTables. In fact, Excel's PivotTable Field List toolbar does not allow you to dock it to the bottom of the screen because doing so would render it practically useless.

When you add more buttons to a toolbar than will fit in the current screen width, or when you dock two or more toolbars on the same row, there might not be enough room to display all buttons. In that case, the program shows only those buttons you have used most recently; click the down arrow at the right of the toolbar to see additional choices, as we've done in Figure 2.5.

Figure 2.5
Click the arrow to the right of a toolbar to see buttons that are hidden because they don't fit in the available space.

ADDING AND REMOVING BUTTONS

Instead of relying on personalized menus and toolbars, which try to guess what you really want, why not customize the built-in toolbars so they contain the buttons you use and aren't cluttered with those you don't need? If you never use the Align Right or Justify buttons on the Formatting toolbar, for example, it's easy to get rid of them. Click the Toolbar Options arrow (the slim, downward-pointing arrow at the right side of every toolbar), select Add or Remove Buttons, and choose the name of the toolbar to display the list of available buttons, as in Figure 2.6 (if you add a button, it appears on this list as well). A check mark next to any item on the list means that the button is currently visible; click to toggle this check mark and display or hide the button.

When customizing the selection of buttons on a toolbar, you're not limited to choices on the Add or Remove Buttons menu. In any Office program, you can add any command, macro, or existing menu to a toolbar. In Word, you can add fonts, styles, and AutoText entries as well. If you're editing a long report and you want certain paragraphs to be formatted in a specific font, you can make the task easier by adding that font to a toolbar.

To add a command to a visible menu or toolbar, follow these steps:

Figure 2.6
Click the arrow at the right of any toolbar to add or remove buttons easily.

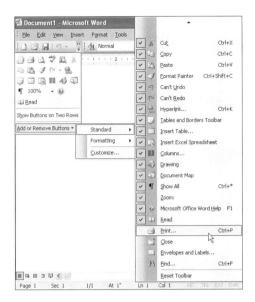

1. Select Tools, Customize (or right-click any toolbar or menu and choose Customize from the bottom of the shortcut menu). The Customize dialog box opens.

2. If the toolbar you want to customize is not visible, click the Toolbars tab and click the check box for that toolbar.

3. Click the Commands tab, select an entry from the Categories list on the left, and then select the command you want to add from the Commands list on the right, as in Figure 2.7.

Figure 2.7
Drag items from the list on the right side of this dialog box to create new toolbar buttons.

NOTE

The items in the Categories list typically correspond to top-level menu choices, built-in toolbars, and some collections of tools. Only Word includes an All Commands category that consists of an alphabetized list of every available command. If you're not sure what a particular command does, select it from the Commands list and click the Description button.

4. Drag the command from the Customize dialog box to the toolbar where you want to add the button. When you see a thick black I-beam in the correct position, drop the button to add it.

5. Repeat steps 3 and 4 to add more buttons to any toolbar.

6. When you've finished working with the toolbar, click Close to put away the Customize dialog box.

If you never use certain toolbar buttons, clear them away to make room for the buttons you do use. It's ridiculously easy to remove a button from a toolbar: Point to the button you want to remove, and then hold down the Alt key as you drag it off the toolbar—when the pointer displays a tool icon with an X, release the mouse button to delete the item. If the Customize dialog box is open, you can remove any button or menu item by dragging it off the menu bar, without having to hold down the Alt key.

TIP FROM

Ed & Woody

Use these same drag-and-drop techniques to move buttons and menu items, either on the same toolbar or between toolbars. From any editing window, hold down the Alt key and drag a button to move it to a different place on the same toolbar or to a different toolbar altogether. With the Customize dialog box visible, hold down the Ctrl key and drag any button to create a copy. And here's an undocumented shortcut we guarantee you haven't read anywhere else: Hold down the Alt key as you drag a button onto the same toolbar or on another toolbar. Then (while continuing to hold down the Alt key) press the Ctrl key and release the button. This shortcut creates a copy of the button, without opening the Customize dialog box. This technique is especially effective if you want to create slightly different versions of the same toolbar for different tasks: Create a new toolbar based on an existing toolbar, and then drag buttons from the old toolbar to the new copy. Switch between the two toolbars for different tasks.

Office 2003 offers an alternative way to customize toolbars and menus, even when those interface elements are currently hidden. From any Office program, choose Tools, Customize, click the Commands tab, and click the Rearrange Commands button. In the Rearrange Commands dialog box (see Figure 2.8), choose any menu, submenu, or toolbar. The Controls list shows all items currently available on the menu or toolbar you selected. The five buttons to the right allow you to add, delete, move, or edit a toolbar button, using the techniques described in the next section.

Figure 2.8
Using the Rearrange
Commands dialog box
is less convenient
than drag-and-drop
techniques, but is
valuable for editing
menus and toolbars
that are not currently
visible.

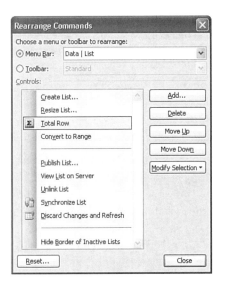

2

CREATING A NEW TOOLBAR

You're not limited to the selection of built-in toolbars—you can also create custom toolbars in any Office program, adding your own selection of buttons and menus to each new toolbar. Let's say you use Word to create a monthly newsletter for your school's swim team. With a custom toolbar, you can give yourself one-click access to the styles and fonts you use in the newsletter, as well as adding buttons for commands you use frequently, such as the Columns and Drop Cap commands. To create a new toolbar, select Tools, Customize, click the Toolbars tab, and click the New button. Give the new toolbar a name and click OK to create an empty toolbar and begin adding commands (buttons and menu items) to it.

How do you make a new toolbar available for all new documents and worksheets? The procedure is slightly different for each Office program. Use Word's Organizer to copy a toolbar from one document or template to another. Unless you choose a different location, Word stores a new toolbar in the Normal document template, `Normal.dot`, to make it available for all documents.

→ To learn more about copying elements between templates, **see** "Managing Styles and Templates,"
p. 465.

When you create a new toolbar in PowerPoint, it's automatically available for all presentations you open or create using that user account. If you open an Excel workbook that contains a custom toolbar created by someone else, you can copy it to your Personal Macro Workbook (`Personal.xls`). Open both workbooks, and then switch to `Personal.xls` and select Tools, Customize. Click the Toolbars tab and click the Attach button. Select the toolbar you want to copy from the Custom toolbars list on the left, and then click the Copy button to transfer it to the Personal Macro Workbook.

N O T E

> Outlook enables you to create custom toolbars. Because the program stores all customizations as part of the program options rather than associating them with data files, there's no need to copy these toolbars to a different location.

CUSTOMIZING THE APPEARANCE OF TOOLBAR BUTTONS

You'll encounter unique design challenges when you create custom toolbars that mix built-in commands with macros, styles, and AutoText items. If the toolbar includes standard button and menu options, you can decide whether you want to see only an image, only text, or both.

For buttons you use infrequently, the default icon might not give you a very good clue as to what that button actually does. By showing both the icon and the text, you don't have to constantly hover the mouse pointer over the button so you can use the ScreenTip to remind you what it does. (Outlook, for example, uses this option effectively to show the Reply, Reply to All, and Forward buttons on the Standard toolbar in the Inbox.) Select Tools, Customize to display the Customize dialog box, and then right-click any button to display the shortcut menu shown in Figure 2.9.

Figure 2.9
Use this shortcut menu to change the text and icon that describe a toolbar button or menu choice.

The four choices on this menu let you decide whether to show icons only, text only, or a combination of both. (The Default Style choice uses the setting that Microsoft's interface designers have determined is most appropriate for most users. That may or may not match what *you* want.)

Most built-in commands include their own images that Office programs can use as the icon on a toolbar button. You can change the image on any button, and if you're a decent icon designer, you can use the built-in Button Editor to create your own custom button images.

TIP FROM

Ed & Woody

> Although you can create an icon from scratch, it's usually best to start with an existing button image. If you see an image that you like on a built-in toolbar button, copy it to your custom icon using the Copy Button Image and Paste Button Image choices on the shortcut menu for each icon; then edit the pasted image. If you make a mistake, click Reset Button Image and start over.

When you have a group of buttons that work together, use a separator line to define the group. On the Standard toolbar in every Office program, for example, the Cut, Copy, Paste, and Format Painter buttons are all in a group with a separator line at either side. If the Customize dialog box is open, right-click the icon that begins the group and select Begin a Group from the shortcut menu. To quickly add a separator line without leaving the normal editing window, hold down the Alt key, click the button to the right of the place where you want the line to appear, and drag slightly to the right. To remove a separator line without having to go through a dialog box, hold down the Alt key, click the button to the right of the line, and drag the button to its left, over the line.

EDITING A TOOLBAR BUTTON'S ICON AND LABEL

To edit the text and icon associated with any button, first make sure the toolbar is visible. Then open the Customize dialog box and click to select the button you want to change. Click in the Name box to enter the text that will appear on the button when you select any display option other than Icon Only. The text you enter here will also appear as a ScreenTip for that button.

To edit the existing icon, simply right-click again and select Edit Button Image. This opens the Office Button Editor (see Figure 2.10). Click any color in the color box, and use the pointer to paint that color over any pixel.

Figure 2.10
Use the Office Button Editor to create images for use on toolbar buttons. Each image is limited to this palette of colors and a total size of 16 pixels square.

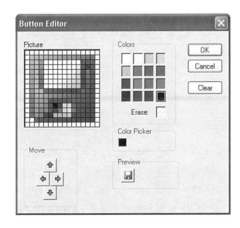

To create a custom icon, right-click the button and select Change Button Image. You can start with any of the icons shown in Figure 2.11 or build a new icon from scratch.

Figure 2.11
Office lets you choose from this assortment of somewhat hokey custom icons, or you can cut, paste, and edit an icon from an existing button.

ASSIGNING A HYPERLINK TO A TOOLBAR BUTTON

All Office programs allow you to attach a hyperlink to a toolbar button, although the procedure for doing so is cumbersome. You can create a hyperlink to a web page or to any file on your computer or to a shared file on another computer that you access over a network. You can assign a graphic file to a toolbar button, so that clicking that button inserts a logo or other graphic you use regularly. You can even create a hyperlink to an e-mail address, with a ready-made subject line and body text—this option is especially useful if you send out a weekly e-mail report to a school group or club using a standard template, and you want to automate the process of starting each one.

To attach a hyperlink to a toolbar button, you first must create a toolbar button and then customize it. Only Excel enables you to create a blank button or menu item; in other programs, you first must add a button—any button—using an existing command, and then customize it.

With the Customize dialog box open, right-click the button to which you want to assign the hyperlink. Select the text in the Name box and replace it with a short description of the link you want to create. Then select Assign Hyperlink. Click Open if you want the button to open a file or web page, or click Insert Picture if you want to create a link to a graphic file.

In the Assign Hyperlink dialog box (see Figure 2.12), click the Existing File or Web Page button and select the item you want to link to the button. Click OK to create the link.

→ To learn more about using the Office hyperlinking features, **see** "Working with Hyperlinks," **p. 847**.

→ Use AutoText to enter large blocks of text and graphics with a few simple keystrokes; **see** "Entering Text and Graphics Automatically with AutoText and AutoCorrect," **p. 341**.

To remove a hyperlink from a toolbar button, open the Customize dialog box, right-click the button, and select Edit Hyperlink, Remove Link.

Figure 2.12
Select a file or web page and assign it to a toolbar button as a hyperlink, and then open the file or insert a picture with a single click.

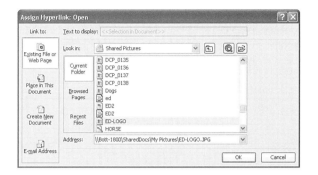

CUSTOMIZING BUILT-IN MENUS

If you've mastered the art of customizing toolbars, you already know how to modify menus. That's because menus in Office programs are simply toolbars without icons. You can mix and match menus and buttons on any toolbar; in fact, the default menu bar in each Office application is actually just another toolbar, and you can rearrange top-level items as well as menu items and even submenus.

In this section, we show you how to rearrange the built-in menus in any Office program; how to add new menus to any Office toolbar (whether it's the built-in variety or a custom toolbar you create); and how to modify right-click shortcut menus in Word and PowerPoint.

REARRANGING PULL-DOWN MENUS

Customizing the default menus for any Office application is a tricky proposition. Yes, you can remove menu items to simplify the range of available choices, but when you take items off the menu, you make it extremely difficult to gain access to those functions if you discover you need them at a later date. Likewise, if you drastically change the order of menu items or add new items, you might create confusion for yourself or for someone who borrows your computer and expects to see each menu choice in a standard location.

 For tips on how to recover if you customize a menu or toolbar a little too much, see "Back to Square One" in the "Troubleshooting" section at the end of this chapter.

To add, remove, or rearrange menus, use the same procedures described earlier in this chapter, in the "Customizing Toolbars" section. Select Tools, Customize, and then (with the Customize dialog box open) click and drag to add commands, macros, and other items to a menu, or to move an item to a different location within the pull-down menus. Drag items off the menus to remove them. Right-click any item and change the text in the Name box to rename it. If you're more comfortable working within the confines of a dialog box, click the Commands tab on the Customize dialog box; then click the Rearrange Commands button and choose the menu you want to work with from the drop-down Menu Bar list.

TIP FROM

Ed & Woody

> All Office programs give you quick access to top-level menus through the Customize dialog box. Click the Commands tab, scroll to the bottom of the Categories list, and select Built-in Menus to select from a full list of top-level menus and add them to any toolbar; the Excel version of this list includes not only all top-level menus but cascading menus under them as well.

CREATING NEW MENUS

Adding a new cascading menu item to an existing menu or toolbar is an excellent way to organize fonts, styles, commands, macros, and other shortcuts for quick access. For example, you might create a new cascading menu called Favorites on Word's Format menu and use it to hold a collection of shortcuts to the handful of fonts and styles you use most often. Or, you could add a similar menu to the Drawing toolbar containing hyperlinks to pictures you can insert in any Word document or PowerPoint presentation.

To add a new menu to any toolbar (including the default menu bar), be sure the toolbar you want to customize is visible, and then select Tools, Customize. Click the Commands tab and select New Menu from the bottom of the Categories list. Drag the New Menu item from the Commands list and drop it in your correct position on the toolbar.

Right-click to rename the new menu. Then add buttons and menu items by dragging and dropping commands, macros, and other objects from the Customize dialog box or from other toolbars. When you drag an item over a pull-down menu, the menu drops down so you can drop it in the correct location.

TIP FROM

Ed & Woody

> For Word users, one of the most powerful menus you can add is buried at the bottom of the Built-in Menus list and is completely undocumented. The Work menu lets you build a list of files you work with regularly so you can get to them anytime. Drag the Work menu onto the menu bar or any toolbar; when you open a file that you know you'll want to work with again, select Work, Add to Work Menu. To quickly remove a file from this list, press Ctrl+Alt+- (hyphen) and point to the file on the list. Note that you must use the hyphen key on the top row of the keyboard; the hyphen on the numeric keypad won't work.

MODIFYING SHORTCUT MENUS

The context-sensitive shortcut menus found throughout Office—the ones that appear when you right-click within a document or on a bit of selected text, for example—are powerful timesavers, but they're not perfect; for example, Microsoft's interface designers chose not to add the Paste Special command to the shortcut menus that pop up when you edit a Word document or a PowerPoint presentation. Customizing these shortcut menus can make you more productive by placing the commands you use most frequently within easy reach and removing those you don't use.

Word and PowerPoint allow you to customize shortcut menus; unfortunately, there's no easy way to customize shortcut menus in Excel or Outlook.

To add the Paste Special command to Word's shortcut menus, follow these steps (the technique is virtually identical for PowerPoint):

1. Select Tools, Customize, click the Toolbars tab, and select the Shortcut Menu check box. The Shortcut Menu toolbar appears (see Figure 2.13). Note that these menus are organized by category; Word, for example, uses separate shortcut menus for editing text, working with drawings, and managing tables.

Figure 2.13
Use the special-purpose Shortcut Menu toolbar to customize right-click menus in Word and PowerPoint (but not Excel or Outlook).

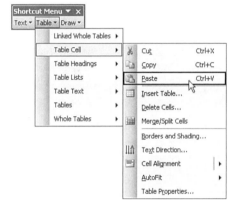

> **NOTE**
>
> Even if you leave the Shortcut Menus check box selected, this toolbar disappears when you close the Customize dialog box. This special toolbar is available only for customization, not for regular use.

2. Click the Commands tab, select Edit from the Categories list and Paste Special from the Commands list, and then drag the command over the Text choice on the Shortcut Menus toolbar. The full list of shortcut menus appears; drag the new menu item down to the Text menu, which will cascade to the right. Drop the Paste Special item on the menu, beneath Paste.

3. Repeat this process with other menus you want to customize from the drop-down lists on the Shortcut Menus toolbar. At a minimum, add the Paste Special choice to the List and Headings menu under the Text group. If you want the Paste Special command to be available when you edit tables as well, add this choice to every shortcut menu under the Table group.

4. Click Close to close the Customize dialog box and return to Word.

If shortcut menus don't work as you expect, see "Broken Shortcut Menus?" in the "Troubleshooting" section at the end of this chapter.

BYPASSING MENUS WITH KEYBOARD SHORTCUTS

Office includes a literally overwhelming number of keyboard shortcuts for nearly every task. Some shortcuts use mnemonic devices to make it easier for you to remember what they do—Ctrl+B (Bold), Ctrl+U (Underline), and Ctrl+I (Italic) are common to every Office application. Others follow Windows standards, such as the universal Ctrl+X (Cut), Ctrl+C (Copy), and Ctrl+V (Paste) shortcuts. Still others give you access to commands that are nearly impossible to access any other way. For example, there's no menu choice in Word to convert field codes to their results; you have to know the shortcuts: Ctrl+6 (from the numeric keypad, not the row of numbers above the QWERTY keys) or Ctrl+Shift+F9.

Office applications are remarkably consistent in their use of keyboard shortcuts, with one notable exception: Outlook is the black sheep, with many, many nonstandard keyboard shortcuts. Throughout every other Office application, for example, you use Ctrl+F to display the Find and Replace dialog boxes; in Outlook, however, that key combination forwards an item via e-mail. To find text in Outlook, press F4, which works as the Repeat key everywhere else in Office.

No one expects you to memorize every Office keyboard shortcut, but learning a select few can dramatically increase your productivity, especially for commands and functions you use regularly.

TIP FROM

Ed & Woody

To make discovering keyboard shortcuts for a particular Office program easier, turn on the option that displays keyboard shortcuts along with ScreenTips. Select Tools, Customize, click the Options tab, and select the Show Shortcut Keys in ScreenTips check box. We do not highlight every keyboard shortcut in the text of this book because there are so many of them that the text would be practically unreadable. If we think a keyboard shortcut is important enough for you to consider memorizing, we'll call it out in the text.

Of all the Office-wide keyboard shortcuts, one stands out as by far the most useful. F4 is the Repeat key, which repeats the previous action; it comes in handy in a wide variety of situations. For example, you can use F4 to apply a new style to a series of paragraphs scattered throughout a Word document. Click in the first paragraph and select the style from the drop-down list. Click in the next paragraph and press F4 instead of going back to the Style menu; F4 will continue to apply that style until you perform another action, such as typing or formatting. Add or delete a row in an Excel worksheet, and then move the insertion point and press F4 to add or delete another row, again without using menus.

Printing out an exhaustive list of shortcut keys for each Office application would take hundreds of pages. To see a generally complete list organized by category, search in each application's online help for a topic called "Keyboard Shortcuts."

Of all Office programs, only Word enables you to easily customize keyboard shortcuts. Select Tools, Customize, and then click the Keyboard button to select a command, a macro, an AutoText entry, a font, a style, or a common symbol. The Customize Keyboard dialog box displays the current key combination assigned to each item you select (see Figure 2.14).

Figure 2.14
Only Word enables you to easily customize keyboard shortcuts.

To add or change a key combination, first select the item you want to assign; then click in the Press New Shortcut Key box and press the key combination. Look at the text just below this box to see whether the key combination you've selected is already assigned to another function; if the option is available, click Assign. Look in the Current Keys box to see whether a key combination is already assigned to that function; to remove that definition, select the item and click Remove.

 For details on how to restore default keyboard shortcuts if you inadvertently reassign the wrong key, see "Restoring Default Shortcut Keys" in the "Troubleshooting" section at the end of this chapter.

CONFIGURING COMMON OFFICE FEATURES

In every Office program, you'll find most customization settings on the Options dialog box. Select Tools, Options to adjust these settings. Although the available settings vary widely, you can typically customize the following:

- Control the number of files on the recently used file list. The default is four, and the maximum is nine for most Office applications.

- Set spelling preferences, as explained in the following section.

- Enter user information, including your name and initials, for use with comments.

- Control whether you see and hear animation and sound effects when you use menus and other interface elements. If sound effects annoy you, turn them off here.

- Set AutoRecover options (Word, Excel, and PowerPoint) to automatically save snapshots of files in memory at regular intervals so that the program can recover them in the event of a system crash. (This is not a substitute for saving your work regularly!)

- Hide or show status bars at the bottom of each program window. These typically display information about the current document, worksheet, presentation, or other data file.

- Hide or show rulers, scrollbars, and other interface elements.

→ For a discussion of text entry, editing, and formatting options used throughout Office, **see** Chapter 4, "Entering, Editing, and Formatting Text," **p. 87**.

CUSTOMIZING TASK PANES

Task panes are small windows that dock within an Office program window (typically along the right side) to provide easy access to commands and program functions. Task panes give you access to search functions, the Office Clipboard, clip art, online help, research tools, and file management tasks throughout Office.

Despite their widespread use, task panes are mostly fixed and barely customizable (unless you are a skilled programmer developing an Office add-in). The one and only task pane option lets you make the Getting Started task pane visible each time you start an Office program without opening a saved document. In Word, Excel, and PowerPoint, choose Tools, Options, click the View tab, and select the Startup Task Pane check box to enable this option.

TIP FROM

Most task panes can be docked to the left or right side of the program window. You can also dock a task pane on the top or bottom of the window, although this arrangement rarely makes the contents of the task pane easier to work with. You can even allow the task pane to float over the current document, undocked. To move the pane, point to the sizing handle at the left of the pane's title bar; when the mouse pointer changes to a four-headed arrow, click and drag the pane to its new position. You can also change the width of the pane by dragging the edge that's next to your document; this option is especially useful with the Clip Art task pane.

When the task pane is visible, you can switch to a different task pane by using the drop-down list at the top of the pane. Use the back and forward buttons just below the task pane title bar to move between task panes you've used in the current session. Click the Home button to return to the Getting Started task pane. To quickly hide or show the task pane in any Office program, use the keyboard shortcut Ctrl+F1.

CUSTOMIZING SMART TAGS

Smart Tags are tiny button/menu combinations that appear automatically after certain types of actions. For example, a Smart Tag appears whenever you paste something (text, a picture, whatever) into any Office document. If the results of the paste operation aren't what you expect, you can use options on the Smart Tag menu to change the way the data appears. Smart Tags assist in error checking in Excel worksheets and are used for layout functions in PowerPoint. They can also automatically identify words or phrases that meet certain criteria. For instance, you can configure Word to automatically recognize the names of persons (as in Figure 2.15), or ask Excel to recognize stock ticker symbols.

Figure 2.15
Word automatically adds a Smart Tag to names in a document. Click the button to add the name to your Outlook Contacts folder, paste in the contact's address, or perform other tasks.

Subtle indicators mark the positions of each Smart Tag in an Office document. In a Word document, a faint purple line under a name means a Smart Tag is buried there. In Excel, a triangular indicator in the corner of a cell marks the presence of a Smart Tag. Hover the mouse pointer over the Smart Tag to display an Action button; click the button to see a list of actions you can take in response to the tag.

A wide array of options is available for customizing Smart Tags. To adjust these options for any Office program, select Tools, AutoCorrect Options, and click the Smart Tags tab. Figure 2.16, for instance, shows the full range of options available in Word. Using this dialog box, you can specify which types of data will be recognized or turn off Smart Tags completely.

Figure 2.16
If you find Smart Tags more annoying than helpful, clear this check box to turn them off for good.

TIP FROM

EQ & Woody

> Because Smart Tags use a standard format called XML, software developers can create Office-compatible add-ins that work as Smart Tags. The Office Update website lists a selection of available Smart Tags that you can purchase or download for free. Most of these add-ins are intended for businesses, but it's still worth checking to see if you might find one useful. For quick access to this site, choose Tools, AutoCorrect Options. In the AutoCorrect dialog box, click the Smart Tags tab, and click the More Smart Tags button.

If an Office program insists on incorrectly recognizing a word, phrase, or name and assigning a Smart Tag to it, use the actions menu to clean up the clutter. You can remove a single Smart Tag, stop recognizing a certain word or phrase in a particular type of Smart Tag, or tell Office to completely ignore a particular word or phrase when checking for Smart Tags.

SETTING UP SPELL-CHECKING OPTIONS

Unless you're the National Spelling Bee champion, chances are you need occasional help with a tricky word. That goes double if your fingers insist on hitting the wrong keys every so often. All Office programs have access to a powerful spell-checking module. No matter what program you're working in, you can check the spelling of a word or a paragraph or a whole document with a few clicks. And if you use technical terms or proper nouns that aren't in the built-in dictionaries, you can add those words to your custom dictionary. Your changes are stored in a single text file, which you can easily open and edit, and when you add a word using one Office program, the term is available to the spell-checking feature in every other Office program.

To adjust spelling options in Office, use the following techniques.

For Word, select Tools, Options, and click the Spelling & Grammar tab. Use the dialog box shown in Figure 2.17 to adjust options.

Word has the most extensive set of spelling options, including the capability to add supplemental dictionaries for specialized vocabularies, such as those used in a medical or legal practice.

 To tame some of Word's aggressive spell-checking tendencies, see "Word Changes Text Mysteriously" in the "Troubleshooting" section at the end of this chapter.

→ For more details on how Word automatically uses suggestions from the spelling-checker, **see** "Checking Spelling and Grammar," **p. 351**.

With Excel's Spelling options (see Figure 2.18), you can specify the language you want to use, as well as which dictionary file you want to use when adding words.

PowerPoint's spelling options are far less comprehensive. Select Tools, Options, and click the Spelling and Style tab to display the dialog box shown in Figure 2.19.

Figure 2.17
Word's spelling options are by far the richest of any Office program.

Figure 2.18
Excel users might want to create separate custom dictionaries to recognize specialized financial terms in worksheets.

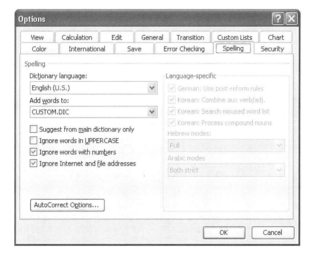

To hide the red squiggly line under spelling errors for a given presentation, check the Hide All Spelling Errors box. To turn off automatic spell-checking completely, clear the check box next to the Check Spelling As You Type box.

If you use Word to compose new e-mail messages in Outlook, all of Word's spell-checking features are available. If you use the Outlook message editor, you can set its spell-checking options separately: select Tools, Options, and click the Spelling tab. The Outlook editor lets you check spelling on any message you compose, including replies. It doesn't automatically mark possible typos with a red squiggly underline, however, unless you use Word as your e-mail editor.

Figure 2.19
PowerPoint's spelling options are far less extensive than those in other Office programs.

All Office spelling tools share the following dictionary files:

- A main dictionary, as determined by your language settings; on a system configured for U.S. English, for example, this file is `Mssp3en.lex`.

- A custom dictionary, which stores words you add while spell-checking; the default name for this file is `Custom.dic`.

Where will you find these dictionary files? The exact location depends on how you installed Office and how you've configured Windows. In most cases, the main dictionary file will be in `%programfiles%\Common Files\Microsoft Shared\Proof`.

TIP FROM

E Q & Woody

> Why are some words enclosed between percent signs in these locations? Those are called *environment variables*. If you click Start, Run and type `%userprofile%` (including the percent signs), Windows opens an Explorer window and displays the contents of your user profile. You don't have to know the drive letter or any other details.

The custom dictionary file, on the other hand, should appear in a personal data folder, such as `%userprofile%\Application Data\Microsoft\Proof`. Because the custom dictionary file is a simple text file, shared by all applications, you can use any text editor to edit it. The easiest way to do this is with the help of Word. Open the Spelling & Grammar dialog box (Tools, Options, Spelling & Grammar) and click the Custom Dictionaries button. Select the correct file from the list, if necessary—normally you'll have only the one Custom.dic file—and click Modify. This opens up a neat dialog box where you can add a word at a time, as in Figure 2.20.

Figure 2.20
To edit the Office-wide Custom dictionary, click the Modify button in Word's Spelling & Grammar dialog box.

CONFIGURING THE RESEARCH TASK PANE

Office 2003 gives you access to an extensive collection of reference books and online research services. All of them are available whenever you're working in any Office program. To quickly find the definition of a word or phrase, select the text, right-click, and choose Look Up from the shortcut menu. The Research task pane opens, with the Encarta dictionary definition of the word you selected in place, as shown in Figure 2.21. Scroll down through the list to see other information, such as synonyms, or to translate the word or phrase into another language. Click the drop-down list below the search term to look in additional reference books, such as the Encarta Encyclopedia.

To go beyond the basic look-up tools, open the Research task pane and enter a name or phrase to look up using any of several online references. The MSN Search option enables you to look up any word or phrase on the Internet without having to leave the document you're working on. It's free, but other services are typically available only with a paid subscription. The MSN Encarta encylopedia, for example, provides a small amount of basic information free of charge, but you'll need to pay extra to get full details about the topic you selected. In most cases, clicking a link in the Office Research pane opens Internet Explorer, where a Research sidebar mirrors the results found in the Office task pane. The results of the online search appear in the browser window.

The list of books and services shown in the Research task pane is customizable. This is especially useful for anyone studying a foreign language; if you're writing papers in French, add the French-language Encarta dictionary and thesaurus to your Research pane. You can remove any existing service or add new services by visiting the Microsoft Office website. To access these options, open the Research task pane and click the Research Options link at the bottom. Figure 2.22 shows the complete list.

Figure 2.21
Definitions, drawn from a built-in dictionary and thesaurus and from online services, appear in the Reference task pane.

Figure 2.22
Select or clear these check boxes to add services to the Research task pane.

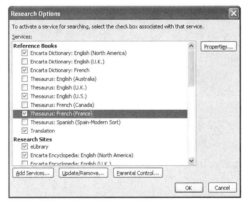

TIP FROM

Parents who are setting up Office for use by young people should strongly consider enabling the Parental Control features in the Research task pane. Click the Parental Control button on the Research Options dialog box and click the Turn On Content Filtering to Make Services Block Offensive Results option. You'll need to enter a password before clicking OK; this prevents your kids from changing these settings without your permission.

SETTING SECURITY OPTIONS

Security isn't just for Windows. Office 2003 has an assortment of security settings as well, all designed to protect your computer from being compromised by viruses and hackers. The default security settings are designed to protect you, and we don't recommend that you change them unless you are sure you know what the consequences will be. To see the security options for any Office program, select Tools, Options, and click the Security tab. Figure 2.23 shows this dialog box for Word, which offers the most extensive set of options of any Office program.

Figure 2.23
Every Office program includes a Security dialog box similar to this one. Word's privacy options are more extensive than other programs.

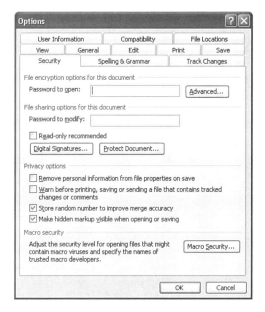

In general, you'll find three categories of options in this dialog box:

- **Password Protection**—These options apply to the current document, worksheet, or presentation only. You can assign a password, set encryption levels, and add a digital signature here.

- **Privacy Options**—Office documents typically include information about a document's creator and company, as well as other details that might be added during editing. For documents you intend to publish outside your organization, you might want to delete this information. Excel and PowerPoint allow you to check a box to remove this information when saving a file; Word goes a step further, letting you remove this information before printing or e-mailing a file. New in Office 2003 is an option to show hidden markup (comments, revision, and so on) when you open or save a file, giving you a chance to remove potentially embarrassing content before sending a document to someone else.

2

TIP FROM

Word embeds a random number in every document. This feature, originally intended to improve mail merge accuracy, can inadvertently affect your privacy by adding a unique identifier to a document. In theory, someone could use this random number as a "finger-print" to identify you as the author of a document. Clear the Store Random Number check box under Privacy Options to remove this possibility.

- **Protection from Macro Viruses**—Click the Macro Security button to select one of four levels for determining which macros will run in each Office program. By default, macro security is set to high, meaning only macros from trusted sources will run properly. In a home or school setting, most users will never encounter a macro created by someone else. But if you do receive such a document, even from a trusted source, any macros contained in that document will not run. If you're certain the macro is safe, dropping the security level to medium might be required. With a medium security setting, Office gives you the option to run or disable macros each time you open a document containing macros.

→ For more details on macro security issues, including a discussion of when it's safe to lower security levels, **see** "Macro Security," **p. 816**.

TIP FROM

If you don't use antivirus software, you're simply begging to lose data or suffer catastrophic loss. The best antivirus programs integrate tightly with Office to protect you from infection when you open a document from the Internet or receive one as an e-mail attachment. Check with the maker of your antivirus software to determine whether you need an update for compatibility with Office 2003. If you're not sure which antivirus program to use, start by visiting ICSA Labs at `http://www.icsalabs.com`. Browse their list of ICSA-certified programs and find the one that represents the best match for your needs and budget.

SAVING AND RESTORING PERSONAL SETTINGS

So, you've followed our advice and painstakingly customized each Office program so that the toolbars and menus match the way you work. What happens if you get a new PC? You can use a backup program to move your data files from the old PC to the new one, but you need to take an extra step to transfer all of your Office options and preferences to the new computer. Typically, Microsoft offers multiple ways to perform this task. Here are the two that we recommend:

- **Save My Settings Wizard**—This simple utility saves your settings in a file; you can copy this file to another computer and rerun the wizard to restore your settings. To use it, click the Microsoft Office 2003 Save My Settings shortcut (in the Microsoft Office Tools group on the All Programs menu).

- **Windows XP Files and Settings Transfer Wizard**—This tool comes with every copy of Windows XP (it's available on the All Programs menu, in the Accessories\System Tools group, or you can run it from the Windows XP CD). You run the wizard on your old system, saving your settings in a file that you can copy to a CD or a USB flash memory key. Then you run the wizard again on the new computer and point it to the file you saved. The wizard copies all your settings, including e-mail and addresses from Outlook.

TROUBLESHOOTING

BACK TO SQUARE ONE

You've customized menus and toolbars a bit too much, and now you can't find several options and buttons you need.

You can restore any toolbar, including the main menu bar, to its default settings. Select Tools, Customize, and click the Toolbars tab. Choose the toolbar whose customized settings you want to remove (select Menu Bar for the main menus) and click Reset. If you're doing this in Word, you can specify whether the change applies to the current document only or to all documents based on the current template.

BROKEN SHORTCUT MENUS?

You've customized shortcut menus in Word or PowerPoint, but they don't behave as you expect.

Be sure you customized the correct menu. When you edit tables, for example, Word uses different shortcut menus depending on whether you're working with a table heading, text within a table cell, an entire cell, or the whole table. If you want the Paste Special command to be available whenever you work on a table, you must customize each of these shortcut menus.

RESTORING DEFAULT SHORTCUT KEYS

After assigning a shortcut key to one function, you discover that the keyboard combination you used applies to a useful system shortcut, and you want to reset it.

When you assign a keyboard shortcut to a specific function, Office removes that shortcut for any other function that uses the same combination. To restore the shortcut, select the original function and reassign the key combination that's normally associated with it. To restore every default Word key combination (and wipe out any custom shortcuts you've created), select Tools, Customize, click the Keyboard button, and click the Reset All button in the Customize Keyboard dialog box.

WORD CHANGES TEXT MYSTERIOUSLY

As you create a document, you discover that Word is consistently changing some words or abbreviations you type. You've checked thoroughly, and you know the text being changed is not in the AutoCorrect list. What's up?

Word thinks you're mistyping the text in question, and it is convinced that it knows exactly what you meant to type. This behavior is controlled by a well-hidden spell-checking option. To stop it, select Tools, AutoCorrect Options, click the AutoCorrect tab, and clear the check mark from the Automatically Use Suggestions from the Spelling Checker box.

EXTRA CREDIT: CUSTOM TOOLBARS FOR QUICK HIGHLIGHTING

While working on this book, we regularly used Word's yellow and green highlighters to mark text for specific tasks and then cleared the highlighting when the task was complete. Using the highlighter is an ideal way to remind yourself of a paragraph that needs to be rewritten, or to call out a sentence that needs a little more research. Because Word's Highlighter icon remembers the last color you select, this routine often takes two clicks—one click to display the drop-down list of available colors and a second click to select a color (or None, to erase highlighting).

To make highlighting a one-click process, we first created three nearly identical macros, using the following code:

```
Public Sub NoHighlight()
Selection.Range.HighlightColorIndex = wdNoHighlight
End Sub
Public Sub YellowHighlight()
Selection.Range.HighlightColorIndex = wdYellow
End Sub
Public Sub GreenHighlight()
Selection.Range.HighlightColorIndex = wdGreen
End Sub
```

(For more details on how to create a macro and save it as part of the Normal document template, see Chapter 26, "Using Macros to Automate Office Tasks.")

We then created a new toolbar and assigned each macro to a button on the new toolbar. To assign a macro to a toolbar button in Word, follow the same steps as you would to add a command button; on the Commands tab of the Customize dialog box, select Macros from the Categories list and the name of the macro from the Commands list. If you have macros stored in different Word templates or in the document itself, you must select the correct location from the Save In drop-down list.

Finally, we used a brightly colored icon and text label to clearly identify each highlighting option, as in Figure 2.24. (Note that this toolbar also includes buttons to add strikethrough formatting, show field codes, update field codes, and unlink field codes—all tasks that are difficult or impossible to do using Word's menus.)

Figure 2.24

Although you can't tell it from this page, the button next to each toolbar label is the same color as the highlighting choice. Creating the icons was simple—we started with the "happy face" icon and used the Button Editor to cover the inside of the face with the highlight color associated with each macro.

KEEPING TRACK OF YOUR FILES AND SETTINGS

GETTING ORGANIZED (AND STAYING THAT WAY)

You're about to start working on a new report or presentation. What's the best way to get started? Where should you save your file? How do you find that file tomorrow, or next week, or next month? How do you protect yourself from the inconvenience (to put it mildly) of losing a document you've worked on for hours?

Those are the questions we tackle in this chapter. Relax—we're not going to force you to change the way you handle your homework or your projects. It helps if you can stick to a sensible file-naming strategy, and you'll have best results if you have a clear understanding of where and how Office stores files. Whether you file every scrap of paper that goes across your desk or just throw everything into a shoebox, Office has a set of tools for you to use. At the end of this chapter, we introduce you to an amazing search tool that can help you pick out any Office document, even if all you can remember is a word or phrase it contained.

WHERE SHOULD YOU KEEP YOUR FILES?

In Windows XP, the files you create belong in one place: the My Documents folder. This folder is a part of your personal profile, which is created when you set up your user account in Windows XP. Using this folder as the default location for your personal data files makes it easier for you to find and back up files you create.

In Windows XP, the My Documents icon is never more than two clicks away—it's located at the top of the right column in the Start menu, and in Windows Explorer it's just below the Desktop. When you click the File menu and choose Open or Save As from within any Office program, the resulting dialog box takes you straight to the My Documents folder. As we'll discuss a bit later in this chapter, you can also get to the My Documents folder by clicking its icon in the Places Bar along the left side of those dialog boxes.

TIP FROM

Ed & Woody

> Although most of your files will be stored in the My Documents folder, you might need to store files elsewhere under certain conditions. For example, if you've created a PowerPoint presentation and you want someone else to be able to work with it, you might choose to save it in the Shared Documents folder (you'll find the icon for this folder in the My Computer window). Files in this folder can be opened by anyone who logs on to the same computer, even if they do so with a different user account. Those files can also be accessed over a local network.

The My Documents icon on the desktop, in Windows Explorer windows, and on the Windows XP Start menu is actually a *shell extension*—a virtual folder like the My Computer and My Network Places icons, not an actual physical location. Opening this shortcut opens the folder that's registered as the Documents location for the user who's currently logged on. The exact physical location of the My Documents folder varies, depending on which Windows version you have installed and whether it was a clean installation or an upgrade.

On most computers running Windows XP, the My Documents folder appears in your *user profile*, normally C:\Documents and Settings*<username>*\My Documents.

If you currently store data files in other locations and you're willing to reorganize your storage system, you can substantially increase the odds that you'll find files you're looking for when you need them. Doing so also makes it easier to back up data files.

You can change the default location that individual Office programs use for data files; it's also possible to point the My Documents shortcut to another location. (Oh, and if the name bugs you, just change it.)

TIP FROM

Ed & Woody

> To move the My Documents folder to a new location, right-click the My Documents icon, choose Properties, and click Move. Pick the folder where you want your personal documents to be stored, and then click OK or Apply. If you want to leave all your documents in their current location and point the My Documents folder to a new location, enter the full path to that folder in the Target box and click OK. To rename the My Documents folder, open Windows Explorer, right-click the My Documents icon, and choose Rename from the shortcut menu. Renaming the shortcut doesn't change the actual name of the folder to which it points.

3

Finally, you can change the default working folder for any individual Office program, although the exact procedure is slightly different, depending on the program you're working with. Why would you want to reset the default working folder? Maybe you're working on an extended class project that requires constant access to files on a shared network folder. In that case, you might want to define that location as the default working folder; whenever you choose File, Open or File, Save As, the dialog box will display the contents of this folder. Follow these steps, for example, to adjust the default document folder in Word:

1. Choose Tools, Options, and click the File Locations tab. The dialog box shown in Figure 3.1 lets you specify a wide range of system folders.
2. In the File Types list, select the Documents entry.
3. Click the Modify button; then use the Modify Location dialog box to browse through drives and folders. Select the correct folder and click OK.
4. Click OK to close the Options dialog box and save your change.

Follow the same basic procedure for Excel and PowerPoint, with the following exceptions: In Excel, click the General tab; in PowerPoint, click the Save tab. In the box labeled Default File Location, enter the full name and path of the folder that you want to specify as the new default. Only Word allows you to browse through drives and folders to find the one you want; with other Office programs, you must enter the full directory path (complete with drive letter and backslashes to separate folder names) manually.

Figure 3.1
Use the Options
dialog box to adjust
the default working
folder for any Office
program.

3

The default file location setting for each application is independent. If you set Word's
default Documents folder to a location on your network, for example, Excel and PowerPoint
continue to open to the default location—typically the local My Documents folder.

TIP FROM

Ed & Woody

> Curiously, several other settings in Word's File Locations dialog box apply across the
> board to all Office applications. If you change the location of the Templates or
> Workgroup Templates folder in Word, that change applies to Excel and PowerPoint as
> well. Specifying the Workgroup Templates folder here is an ideal way to make sure that
> individual users on a network always have access to the most current templates in the
> three main Office programs. Users can continue to save and open personal templates in
> their own folders, but any Word, Excel, or PowerPoint template in the Workgroup
> Templates folder will "automagically" appear in the New dialog box of all three applica-
> tions. This setting is most useful on a business or school network.

Behind the scenes, Office creates and uses an additional group of subfolders in the
Application Data folder within the user's personal profile. These subfolders represent standard locations where Office stores customization data, such as your Excel Personal macro
workbook, any custom templates that you create in any program (stored in the Templates
folder), custom dictionaries (in the Proof folder), and Word startup templates (in the
\Word\STARTUP folder). On a default Office installation, these subfolders are typically located
within the %appdata%\Microsoft folder. Office maintains separate subfolders for each application, special-purpose folders for use by all Office programs, and a folder for Office itself.

TIP FROM

In the previous paragraph, `%appdata%` refers to an *environment variable* that uniquely identifies a system folder on a computer running Windows XP. Typing this variable, complete with the surrounding percent signs, opens the target folder. Using this variable saves you keystrokes and enables you to create shortcuts that work for different users without modification and without having to worry about the exact drive or folder location. You can use environment variables in the Run dialog box, in an Open or Save dialog box, or in the Target box of a file or program shortcut, for example. Other useful Windows environment variables that we use in this book include `%programfiles%` (which opens the Program Files folder) and `%userprofile%` (which goes directly to the personal profile of the currently logged-on user). To see a full list of environment variables, open Control Panel's System option and click the Advanced tab.

Finally, Office stores a small number of data files in a second Application Data folder. This subfolder is stored in the hidden Local Settings folder within each user's profile. Most notably, this is the default storage location for Outlook Personal Store (PST) files, which contain, among other things, each user's Outlook e-mail and Contacts.

→ To learn more about how to manage PST files, **see** "How Outlook Stores Data," **p. 186**.

OPENING AND SAVING FILES OVER A NETWORK

Office 2003 lets you work with files over a network or on the Web in much the same way that you access files and folders on a standalone PC. If you are connected to a network at your office or school, contact your network administrator to find locations on the network where you're permitted to read or write files. You should get a network share address for the location, using *UNC syntax* (`\\Servername\Sharename\`). Unless the network administrator has restricted your rights, you can create and manage your own subfolders in this location.

Although you can type UNC-style network addresses directly from within Open or Save As dialog boxes, doing so is usually more trouble than it's worth. For easier access, browse to the My Network Places folder and click your way to the correct server, share, and folder.

Aside from the additional navigation steps, there is no difference between using network shares and using local drives, assuming that you have proper authorization from your network administrator.

STORING FILES ON THE WEB OR AN INTRANET

If you're using Office to create documents that will be used on the Web, you can save your files directly to a web server or to an FTP server—the process is almost as simple as working with files on a local network. You can usually open a Web-based file by copying the URL from your web browser's Address box and pasting it into the File Name box on the Office program's Open dialog box. On servers that support the Web-based Distributed Authoring and Versioning (WebDAV) standard, you need only the URL for the location (for example, `http://www.example.com/someplace` or `ftp://example.com/incoming`) and logon credentials (a username and password) to save files to that location. In Windows Explorer, collections of documents on a WebDAV-compatible server appear as folder icons in the My Network Places folder. (In previous Windows and Office versions, this feature was known as *Web folders*.)

NOTE

> For more information about the WebDAV standard, including technical information and lists of compatible servers and applications, visit Greg Stein's superb WebDAV Resources site at `http://www.webdav.org`.

To save a file to a web server or an FTP site on the Internet or an intranet, choose File, Save As and click the My Network Places icon in the Places Bar. If the list of available network places includes the location you want to use, double-click it and then enter a filename. If the location does not have an icon in the My Network Places folder, enter the full URL for the location and then fill in your logon credentials when prompted.

By default, Windows automatically populates the My Network Places folder with the names of all available WebDAV-enabled servers and shared network folders on the local network. You can manually add, remove, or rename a network place—on a local network, on a remote server, or on the Internet—by opening the My Network Places folder in Windows Explorer and clicking the Add Network Place shortcut.

NOTE

> Intranets are most commonly found in larger businesses. They're still rare in small businesses and school networks. From a technical standpoint, there are almost no differences between publishing to an intranet web server and publishing to one on the Internet. The format of the URL that you use likely will be different—intranet servers are typically identified with a one-word name (such as `http://marketing`) rather than a fully qualified domain name (such as `http://www.example.com`). You'll likely encounter different security issues, including password-protected logons and possibly disk quotas (which limit the amount of disk space that a user can fill with web content) on both types of server.

CREATING NEW FILES

When you choose File, New in an Office 2003 program, the New Document, New Workbook, or New Presentation task pane opens (the exact name varies depending on the Office program in use). As Figure 3.2 illustrates, these task panes are well organized and fairly self-explanatory. Choose an option from the New block at the top of the task pane to create a blank document or to create a new workbook, database, or presentation from an existing file. Select from the Templates list if you want to see a complete list of available templates.

Figure 3.2
Every Office program offers a variation of this task pane, which gives you options for creating a new blank file or one based on existing content.

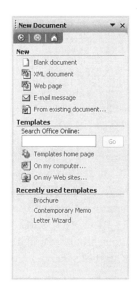

The top of the Templates section includes a search box and link that go directly to Microsoft's Office Online site. Click here to open your web browser and look for custom templates that match the needs of your current project. Click On My Computer to select from templates available in the current Office program; the resulting tabbed dialog box is built on the fly from two (and, in some cases, three) sources:

- The default collection of Office templates is stored in a subfolder that corresponds to the system's current language settings; on a default U.S. English installation, this is `%programfiles%\Microsoft Office\Templates\1033`. All users of the current system see these templates.

- Each user's custom templates are stored in the location specified for User Templates. By default, this is `%appdata%\Microsoft\Templates`. The actual location can be changed in Word's File Locations dialog box. Choose Tools, Options, and, on the File Locations tab, click User Templates and then Modify.

- If you've used Word's File Locations dialog box to specify a Workgroup Templates folder, Office displays templates from this location in the New dialog box as well. If a template in the Workgroup Templates location and one in the User Templates location have the same name, the Office program displays and uses only the one from the User Templates location.

NOTE

The default Office installation does not install all available templates; instead, you'll find shortcuts to some templates in the task pane and New dialog box. The first time you use one of these templates, Office attempts to install the supporting files. Word, Excel, and PowerPoint templates are covered in Chapter 15, "Mastering Styles and Templates"; Chapter 17, "Getting Started with Excel"; and Chapter 22, "Getting Started with PowerPoint," respectively.

If you're having trouble finding templates that you've saved, see "Putting Templates in Their Place" in the "Troubleshooting" section at the end of this chapter.

Although you can manage the contents of template folders in an Explorer window, the easiest and safest way to make new templates available to an Office program is to save the file in Template format. After creating the Word document, Excel workbook, or PowerPoint presentation that you want to use as a template, follow these steps:

1. Choose File, Save As.

2. From the Save As Type drop-down list, choose Document Template (Word), Template (Excel), or Design Template (PowerPoint). The dialog box displays the contents of your User Templates folder.

3. To add the new template to one of the existing tabs, click the Create New Folder button and add a folder with the same name as the existing tab. If you want to create a custom tab for the Templates dialog box, specify a new folder name. If you don't select a subfolder here, your new template will appear on the General tab of the Templates dialog box.

4. Type a name for the template and click Save.

NAMING DOCUMENTS

After you create a new file, the first thing you should do is save it, and as you work on it you should get in the habit of saving it regularly. What's the best name to use? If the file is for your own personal use, you can make up your own file-naming system. If you're working as part of a team in a small office or classroom, you'll want to devise a standard that everyone can agree on, and then follow that standard.

Whether the file-naming system is just for you or for an entire team, the most important guideline is to be consistent. As we explain in this chapter, you can use a variety of search tools to find just about any file. But a file with a descriptive name is much easier to pick out of a list. Some people begin each filename with a keyword (*report*, *homework*, *budget*) that helps define the type of content. You might want to add the creation date (using a format *YYYYMMDD*) to help you see at a glance which version of a file is the most recent one: "Homework - English 101 – 20051031" is pretty descriptive, wouldn't you say?

Regardless of how you choose to name files, be sure you know the file-naming rules that apply to all Office documents:

- A filename can contain any *alphanumeric* character, including the letters A to Z and numbers from 0 to 9.

- A filename can be as short as 1 character and as long as a total of 255 characters, including the full path—drive letter, colon, backslashes, and folder names included.

CAUTION

> The rules governing maximum length of a filename include the full path. For this reason, moving a file with a long name can cause problems, especially when the destination folder is deeply nested. In practice, you can avoid this problem and still have descriptive names if you keep filenames to a maximum length of about 40 characters.

- The following special characters are allowed in a filename: $ % - _ @ ~ ` ! ( ) ^ # & + , ; =.
- You may use spaces, brackets ([ ]), curly braces ({ }), single quotation marks, apostrophes, and parentheses within a filename.
- You may not use a slash (/), a backslash (\), a colon (:), an asterisk (*), a question mark (?), a quotation mark ("), or angle brackets (< >) as part of a filename. These characters are reserved for use with the file system, and you'll see an error message if the name you enter includes any of these characters.
- Office files typically include a three-letter *extension*, which is added automatically by the application that created the file (such as .doc for files created by Word). File extensions define the association between a document type and the program that is used to create it. However, a file extension is not required, nor are file extensions restricted to three characters. We don't recommend changing extensions unless you understand the full consequences of doing so. To force an Office program to use the exact name and extension that you specify, enter the full name, including the extension, between quotation marks. (Filename extensions are normally hidden; to make them visible, open Control Panel, Folder Options, click the View tab, and clear the Hide Extensions for Known File Types check box.)

CAUTION

> If you use a nonstandard file extension, you might be unable to open the file from an Explorer window. Also, files that include unregistered file extensions do not appear in the Open dialog box unless you choose All Files from the drop-down list of file types.

- A filename may contain one or more periods. Windows treats the last period in the name as the dividing line between the filename and its extension.

NOTE

> Windows filenames are not case sensitive. Office ignores all distinctions between upper- and lowercase letters when you enter a filename in an Open or Save As dialog box.

USING AND CUSTOMIZING COMMON DIALOG BOXES

The Open and Save As dialog boxes used throughout Office have a series of shortcut icons on the left side, called the *Places Bar* (see Figure 3.3), and are designed to speed navigation through common file locations. With a small amount of effort, you can easily customize these icons in dialog boxes used in all Office programs. The default icons are as follows:

Figure 3.3
Customize the Places Bar by adding short-cuts to commonly used data folders; to see more choices, right-click the Places Bar and choose Small Icons from the shortcut menu.

NOTE

Although these dialog boxes look exactly like the ones you find in other Windows pro-grams that aren't part of the Office family, they aren't the same. If you customize the Places Bar in Windows (using Microsoft's very cool but unsupported Tweak UI Power Toy), your changes do not extend to the Places Bar in Office programs. Likewise, if you customize the common dialog boxes in Office, the changes don't appear when you use other Windows programs.

■ **My Recent Documents**—Opens the Recent folder, which contains shortcuts to files and folders that you've worked with. When you click this icon from within an Office program, Office displays only shortcuts appropriate to the program you're using.

NOTE

Don't confuse the Office Recent folder with the Windows system folder of the same name. Office manages a separate Recent folder for each user profile on a system. To manage the Office shortcuts from an Explorer window, enter `%appdata%\Microsoft\Office\Recent` in the Run dialog box or in the Address bar of an Explorer window.

TIP FROM

Ed & Woody

> The Recent folder is just one of many Most Recently Used (MRU) lists in Windows. Some people prefer not to keep this list, either for privacy reasons or out of a desire to reduce clutter. You can empty the Recent folder at any time by opening it in Windows Explorer, pressing Ctrl+A to select all files, and then pressing Shift+Delete (use the Shift key to bypass the Recycle Bin and permanently delete the selected shortcuts). To turn off tracking of recently used files in Office, you need to use the Registry Editor (Regedit.exe). This tool is for experts only, so don't attempt this unless you're comfortable poking around in the Registry. Navigate to `HKEY_CURRENT_USER\Software\Microsoft\Office\11.0\Common\Open Find`. Delete the entire Open Find subkey to remove all MRU lists for all Office programs. This change isn't permanent—Office will begin building a new set of MRU lists the next time you use an Office program.

- **Desktop**—Opens or saves files on the Windows desktop. Use the desktop as a holding area when you want to create a file and move it elsewhere using Windows Explorer. Using the desktop as a permanent storage area is generally a bad idea because most Office applications have a tendency to create temporary files in the same location as the file you're working with.

- **My Documents**—Opens the personal data folder for the user currently logged on. As noted earlier in this chapter, Windows enables you to change the target folder that Office opens when you click this icon.

- **My Computer**—Displays icons for local drives and document folders.

- **My Network Places**—Lets you manage files stored in shared folders on your network or on WebDAV-compatible servers.

In Open and Save dialog boxes, Office includes two features that make it easier to find a file by name:

- As you type in the File Name box, the *AutoComplete* feature suggests the first name that matches the characters that you've typed so far. Keep typing, or press Enter to accept the suggestion. Note that the list of files does not scroll as you type.

- If you click in the list of files and then type a character, Office selects the first file that begins with the letter or number that you typed. If you quickly type several characters in rapid succession, the selection moves to the first file that begins with those characters. If you pause for more than a second between characters, this type-ahead feature resets. Note that as you select files in this fashion, Office does not fill in the File Name box.

To adjust the display of files in the Open and Save As dialog boxes, use the Views button. The drop-down arrow lets you choose from a list of views, or you can click the button to cycle through the following icon arrangements:

- Thumbnails, Tiles, Icons, and List views mirror their counterparts in Windows Explorer.

■ Details view displays size, file type, and other information, as shown in Figure 3.4; click any heading to sort the list by that category. (If you think that the information in the Type column is useless, we agree.)

Figure 3.4
Click the Views button to change the arrangement of icons in the Open and Save As dialog boxes.

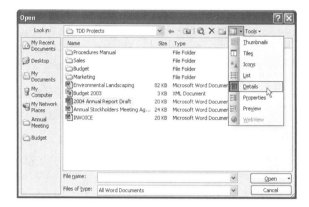

3

■ Properties displays summary information about the selected document in the right half of the dialog box.

■ Preview displays a thumbnail version of the document in the right half of the dialog box as you move from file to file in the list. In general, you should avoid this option because of the performance penalty you pay: As you scroll through a dialog box, the program that you're working with has to open each file; find an import filter, if necessary; and generate the preview. Switch to this view when you want to quickly verify that the file you're about to open is the correct one, and then switch back to List or Details view after peeking at the file.

■ WebView uses an HTML template to display files stored in a SharePoint document library. If you don't have a SharePoint server on your network (most people don't) this option is grayed out and unavailable.

 Some files, especially certain Excel worksheets, can't be seen in the Preview pane. For suggestions on the possible reasons, see "No Preview in Common Dialog Boxes," in the "Troubleshooting" section at the end of this chapter.

TIP FROM

Ed & Woody

To manage files in Open and Save As dialog boxes, select the filename and right-click. Shortcut menus here work just as they do in an Explorer window. You can move, copy, delete, or rename a file, for example, as long as the file you select is not currently open.

CUSTOMIZING COMMON DIALOG BOXES

The Places Bar can be customized to make it easier and faster to get to frequently used folders. To add your own folders to the Places Bar, select the icon for the folder that you want to add, and then choose Tools, Add to "My Places." To remove a custom location from the Places Bar, right-click its icon and choose Remove from the shortcut menu. (You can't rename or delete the five default locations on the Places Bar.)

TIP FROM

Ed & Woody

> If you add more icons than can be displayed in the Places Bar, small scroll arrows appear at the top and bottom of the list. You can see more icons in the Places Bar if you right-click it and choose Small Icons. Put no more than 15 locations in the Places Bar; with any more, you'll spend too much time scrolling.

To rearrange folders in the Places Bar, right-click an icon that you want to move, and choose Move Up or Move Down.

TIP FROM

Ed & Woody

> Both the Open and Save As dialog boxes can be resized by clicking and dragging on any of the edges or corners.

3

Changes you make to the Places Bar apply to all Office programs.

USING ALTERNATIVE FILE FORMATS

By default, Office applications save data files in their own *binary* formats. When you double-click on the saved file, it opens using the program you created the file with. That's the correct choice in most circumstances, but when you share files with friends, neighbors, and co-workers who don't use Office 2003, you might need to open or save a file in a different format.

TIP FROM

Ed & Woody

> In previous Office versions, *Rich Text Format (RTF)* was often your best choice for saving a file and using it with other programs, especially from software companies other than Microsoft. No more. Nowadays you'll probably find that the easiest way to share data is HTML, which is virtually guaranteed to be readable by any other person on any computer, because they can open it directly in their web browser. (Of course, they won't be able to edit the file, but if your goal is to share information, that shouldn't matter.)

Office includes a wide range of file converters to help translate files into other popular formats, including those for earlier versions of Office. Normally, Office programs open any file created in a compatible format without requiring any extra work on your part. The file that you want to convert might not be visible in the Open dialog box if it ends with an extension that the Office program doesn't recognize. To see all files with extensions normally associated with a given file type, such as WK1 and WKS files for Lotus 1-2-3 spreadsheet files, select the appropriate entry from the Files of Type drop-down list. (If you can't see any extensions in Explorer windows or dialog boxes, open Windows Explorer and click Tools, Folder Options; in the Folder Options dialog box, click the View tab and clear the Hide File Extensions for Known File Types check box.)

TIP FROM

Ed & Woody

> To see all files in the Open dialog box, regardless of their extension, choose All Files from the Files of Type drop-down list. Some other distinctions in this drop-down list are less obvious but still useful. For example, selecting Word Documents filters the list to show only files with that file type and the *.doc extension, whereas All Word Documents includes web pages (*.htm) and Word templates (*.dot), as well as ordinary Word documents. Likewise, the All PowerPoint Presentations choice includes any HTML file in addition to PowerPoint presentations and shows.

3

To save a file in an alternative format, choose File, Save As. In the Save As dialog box, choose an entry from the Save as Type drop-down list.

Office displays the full range of compatible file types in both the Open and Save As dialog boxes. In some cases, you might need to supply the Office CD to install a particular converter before opening or saving a file in that format.

STORING EXTRA DETAILS ABOUT YOUR DOCUMENTS

Windows XP keeps track of a few essential details about each file: its size, when it was created, and when you last modified it, for example. You can see all these standard details when you open Windows Explorer. So what happens when you save a document using an Office program? You get the option to store extra details called *properties*; these include the author's name, a title and a subject for the file, and comments or keywords that you can use to search for documents later. If you're an obsessive organizer, you can open a Custom properties sheet for any document and keep track of more than two dozen built-in categories or add your own.

Some properties are filled in automatically by Office, but to really take advantage of this feature you need to go a little bit out of your way and fill in extra details for every document you work with. Why should you bother?

- **It helps you find stuff later**—When you use the Advanced File Search task pane in Office or a third-party search tool, you can search for any property of any Office file. If you've trained an entire department to enter details about a client, project, or product line in the Properties dialog box (or if you've automated this process with macros), it's trivially easy to locate all the files associated with that activity.

- **It helps you keep projects organized**—In Windows Explorer's Details view, you can add columns for many Office file properties. For example, in a folder filled with Word documents, right-click any column heading to display a list of available columns, and then click Title and Author to add those fields to the display. That way, you can scan through a list and see more than just the file name.

■ **It lets you reuse data**—You can look up file properties in any document and then use those values in fields and in macros that you create by using Visual Basic for Applications. Using fields, you can automatically fill in data within a document based on the values you enter in the properties dialog box. You can also create AutoNew macros that prompt you for key information every time you create a new document based on a particular Word template. You can then use that information to file the document when you save it.

➔ For more ideas and techniques using VBA, **see** Chapter 26, "Using Macros to Automate Office Tasks," **p. 801**.

To view and edit the properties of a file currently open in an Office program, choose File, Properties. The dialog box that appears resembles the one in Figure 3.5.

Figure 3.5
The Properties dialog box displays summary information about Office file types.

3

The Properties dialog box for an Office file includes the five tabs described in Table 3.1.

TABLE 3.1   OFFICE FILE PROPERTIES

Properties	Description
General	Basic information from the Windows file system: name, location, size, and so on.
Summary	Information about the current file and its author, including fields for company name, category, and keywords. The Comments field is particularly useful because the comment text appears in the status bar at the bottom of any Windows Explorer window when you select the saved file. It also appears in the ScreenTips that appear when you hover the mouse pointer over a file name in Windows Explorer.

continues

TABLE 3.1   CONTINUED

Properties	Description
Statistics	Details about the size and structure of the file, such as the number of words in a document or the number of slides in a presentation; also displays revision statistics and total editing time. This tab is not visible when inspecting file properties from within Windows Explorer; instead, the information is displayed on the Advanced view of the Summary tab. This information is frequently incorrect, especially when you inspect it from within an Explorer window. If you rely on these statistics to stay within a specific word count when working on a homework assignment, always nspect them from within the document itself to guarantee that the information is up to date.
Contents	The parts of the file, such as the outline of a Word document, based on heading styles; worksheet titles in an Excel workbook; or slide titles in a PowerPoint presentation. This tab is not visible when inspecting file properties from within Windows Explorer.
Custom	Twenty-seven built-in fields that are useful when creating business documents, including Client, Document Number, and Date Completed. In addition, you can enter a field of your own creation, such as the name of a class or a teacher. Custom fields can contain text, dates, numbers, or Yes/No information; they can also be linked to Word bookmarks, named Excel ranges, or PowerPoint text selections.

N O T E

> You can inspect most Office file properties by right-clicking a filename in Windows Explorer and choosing Properties from the shortcut menu. Information in this dialog box is arranged differently from what you see within an Office program, and many properties are not available when the file is open for editing.

For simple projects, you might choose to ignore file properties and just give each document a descriptive filename that tells you everything you need to know about the file. For more complicated documents, however, adding file details—including keywords and categories—can help you quickly find a group of related data files, even months or years after you last worked with them. Use the Comments box to add freeform notes about a given file.

To enter additional details about an Office file, you must open the Properties dialog box, fill in the appropriate fields, and then save the file. If you use this feature regularly, you can configure Word, Excel, and PowerPoint to display the File Properties dialog box every time you save a file.

→ To learn more about the common features found within the Office applications, **see** "Configuring Common Office Features," **p. 47**.

DEFAULT DOCUMENT PROPERTIES

If you just click the Save button without entering any additional data, Office programs save only a few document properties along with the saved file. Windows stores the standard file details, of course, including the name and size of the file as well as the date and time the file was modified. All Office programs add your name and your organization's name (using whatever name the program finds on the User Information tab of the Options dialog box) in the Author and Company fields, respectively. Word and PowerPoint fill in the Title field as well, using the first few words of a Word document or the title of a PowerPoint presentation.

CAUTION

In Word documents in particular, this capability can lead to embarrassing consequences if you're not careful. By default, if you don't take any special steps to enter document properties, Word picks up the opening line of your document and plops it in the Title field—up to the first paragraph mark or 126 characters, whichever comes first. If you begin composing an angry letter and save the file as a draft, Word fills in your initial angry words in the Title field. Those angry words might remain in the Title field even if you calm down and delete them from the final version of the document. That fact alone is an excellent reason to configure Word to pop up the Properties dialog box whenever you save a new document.

3

If you want to add categories, keywords, or comments to any Office file, do so on the Summary tab.

USING CUSTOM PROPERTIES TO ORGANIZE FILES

Custom properties make it easier to keep track of files in an office environment where many people create and share files. In a legal office, for example, you might use the Client, Status, and Recorded Date fields to track the progress of Word documents. Members of a team producing budget worksheets might use the Checked By and Forward To fields as part of a document management system. Use the Office applications' Search task panes to find files whose properties match a particular set of criteria. Figure 3.6 shows a Word document that includes several custom properties.

To enter custom criteria for any Office file, follow these steps:

1. Open the file and choose File, Properties.
2. Click the Custom tab to display the dialog box shown previously in Figure 3.6.
3. Choose a field from the Name list. To create a new field, type its name here.
4. Choose one of the available data types from the Type drop-down list.
5. Type the data for the selected field in the Value text box.

Figure 3.6
Record additional file properties on the Custom tab; later, use the Find tool in Office common dialog boxes to search for files that match these criteria.

3

CAUTION

If you specify Number or Date as the data type for a custom field, you must enter the value in a matching format. If you enter dates in a nonstandard format or you include text in a field that should contain only numbers, Office enters the value as text.

6. Click Add. The new entry appears in the Properties list at the bottom of the dialog box.

7. Repeat steps 3–6 for any additional custom fields. To remove an item from the Properties list, select its entry and click Delete. Click OK to close the dialog box and return to the program window.

The Link to Content check box is grayed out and unavailable unless you're working with a Word document that contains bookmarks, an Excel workbook that contains named ranges, or a PowerPoint presentation containing linked text. In any of those cases, you can enter a custom field name, select the Link to Content check box, and then choose the bookmark or named range. In a PowerPoint presentation, you must select the text you want to link to a custom field before opening the Properties dialog box.

USING WINDOWS EXPLORER TO VIEW FILE PROPERTIES

To view any Office file's properties without opening the file itself, open a Windows Explorer window, right-click the file's icon, and then choose Properties. In most Windows versions, you can edit most file properties for Word documents, Excel workbooks, Publisher publications, and PowerPoint presentations directly from an Explorer window. Regardless of which Windows version you use, only the most basic summary information is available when you view the properties of an Access database from an Explorer window.

In Windows XP, you can see some Office file properties, such as the author's name, in the info pane along the left side of a Windows Explorer window, as shown in Figure 3.7. You can also see a thumbnail of the file itself in this region, but only if you selected the Save Preview Picture check box on the Summary tab of the Properties dialog box. By default, this check box is cleared for Word documents and Excel workbooks and is selected for PowerPoint presentations.

Figure 3.7
In Windows XP, you can view some information drawn from an Office file's properties from within Windows Explorer. The thumbnail preview is available only if you check an option when saving the file.

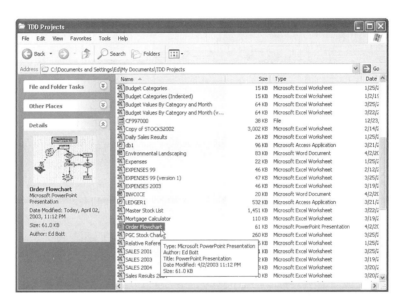

 To save a preview of an Excel workbook, you must check this box when you first save the file; see "No Preview in Common Dialog Boxes" in the "Troubleshooting" section at the end of this chapter for more details.

SEARCHING FOR OFFICE FILES

The Open dialog box displays a list of all files and subfolders in a single folder. Searching for a specific file can be tedious if the folder is full of files with similar names, or if it's organized into many subfolders. So how do you find the exact file you're looking for? From any Office program, you can open the Search task pane, which enables you to search for files, Outlook items, or web pages by using almost any criteria. If you can remember a few scraps of information about the file—part of the name, a date, or even a word or phrase that you remember using in the document—you can probably find it.

NOTE

The Office search tools are capable, but if you have lots of documents on your computer, you'll get better results from a desktop search tool that integrates directly with Windows XP. For details, see "Extra Credit: Find Files Faster with Desktop Search Tools" at the end of this chapter.

For example, you might look in your homework folder for all files that you created or updated in the past week. You might search for files that include the word *report* and that are not marked as completed. If you're trying to clean out clutter in your My Documents folder, you can search for all Office files that were last modified more than six months ago, and then burn them to a CD or move them to an archive folder.

In Office 2003, the file search tools are tightly integrated into Office programs. To display the Basic File Search task pane (see Figure 3.8), choose File, File Search.

Figure 3.8
Search for a file or Outlook message by using simple search criteria in the Basic File Search task pane.

CAUTION

> Office 2003 does *not* allow you to save and reuse search criteria. You can bring back the most recently used Search by clicking the Restore button, but there is no capability to store searches within Office programs. For that task, you'll have better results using a desktop search utility that allows you to save shortcuts.

Basic searches are quick and simple. Enter your search text, select the locations you want to search, choose what file types you want the search to return, and then click Go to begin the search. Basic searches follow these rules:

- The search looks for any files that contain the search text, whether that text appears in the body of the file, in keywords, or in file properties.

- Search results also include files that contain forms of the words you entered as search text, such as plurals or alternate verb forms (*paying* or *paid* instead of *pay*, for example).

- You can use wildcards in basic searches. An asterisk (*) substitutes for a group of characters, whereas a question mark (?) fills in for a single character.

- You'll have better results when searching the My Network Places option if you specify only the network locations you want to search. Many network locations do not support searches, and others allow searches only in document libraries.

- When searching Outlook messages, you can use natural language rather than keywords, entering a phrase such as *show me all messages received this week.*

Advanced searches, on the other hand, can be complex, with sophisticated logic and multiple criteria. To make the switch, click the Advanced File Search link at the bottom of the Basic File Search task pane. Figure 3.9 shows a typical advanced search.

Figure 3.9
Be careful when using AND/OR logic in the Advanced File Search task pane. The correct order affects your search results.

You construct a search by adding criteria to a list. Each entry in the criteria list consists of three pieces:

- **Property**—Includes file system properties (name, date created, and file size, for example), statistics (such as the number of slides in a PowerPoint presentation or the number of paragraphs in a Word document), and Office custom properties.

- **Condition**—Defines the comparison that you want Office to make. The list of available conditions depends on the property you selected previously.

- **Value**—Defines the specific text, number, or other data type for which you want Office to search.

A pair of buttons (And, Or) at the left of the criteria definition boxes enable you to combine criteria, and you can specify that Office search multiple folders and subfolders.

Criteria can be extremely simple—for example, all files last modified this week. For more sophisticated searches, combine criteria to quickly filter a huge group of files into a manageable list. After you enter the first set of conditions, click the Add button. After you've entered all your search criteria, click the Search button. Options at the bottom of the pane let you restrict file types and locations using check boxes.

To improve the performance of searches on your local computer, especially those that have to chug through folders filled with large numbers of documents, you'll need to enable the Windows Indexing Service, which is referred to in the Basic and Advanced File Search panes. Don't confuse this feature with the old, much-despised FindFast feature from past Office versions. The Indexing Service is a Windows feature that also benefits other programs and runs only when the system is idle. Although you might see some performance degradation on computers with low system resources (in particular, those with 128MB or less of RAM), in practice the effect should be unnoticeable.

To turn on the Indexing Service, open the Basic File Search task pane, click the Search Options link, and select the option to enable the Indexing Service.

FINDING FILES OR MESSAGES BY CONTENT

To conduct a simple search by content—whether you're looking for a file, a message, a contact, an appointment, a task, a note, or a web page—bring up the Basic Search task pane and follow these steps:

1. Type the text (content) that you're looking for in the Search Text box. You can use wildcards: ? stands for any single character (m?t searches for *met* or *mat*, but not *meet*); * stands for one or more characters (b*nk searches for *bank* and *blank* but not *band*).

2. In the Search In list, specify where you want Office to look. You can narrow the search to specific drives or folders in My Computer or Outlook; you can also limit the search to specific locations in My Network Places.

3. In the Results Should Be box, specify which types of Office files and Outlook items to look for; you can also search in web pages.

4. Click the Go button. The matching items appear in a list. If you click once on a filename, the appropriate Office application opens the file. You can also choose from a drop-down list to the right of the filename if you want to create a new file based on the selected one.

USING DOCUMENT PROPERTIES TO LOCATE FILES

Use the Advanced File Search task pane in conjunction with file properties to construct a powerful document-management system. It takes training and discipline for a group of workers to routinely enter the correct information in file properties. You can automatically add some of these details by customizing templates or using Visual Basic for Applications. For example, you might use simple AutoNew, AutoOpen, and AutoClose macros, which run automatically when you open or close a document, to prompt the user to enter specific details about a document.

All built-in file properties are available from the Property drop-down list in the Advanced File Search task pane. To search for properties that you've added to the Custom tab, you need to manually enter the name of the property.

WORKING WITH MULTIPLE FILES

In Word, Excel, and PowerPoint, you can open and view or edit more than one file at a time. To open multiple files using the common dialog boxes, follow these steps:

1. Choose File, Open (or press Ctrl+O) to display the Open dialog box.
2. Hold down the Ctrl key and click to select multiple filenames.
3. Click the Open button or press Enter to open all selected files.

To open multiple files from an Explorer window, hold down the Ctrl key and click each icon; then right-click and choose Open.

You can also open any file by dragging its icon from an Explorer window into an Office program window. When you drag an Excel or PowerPoint icon from an Explorer window into an open program window, Office opens the new file in its own window. On the other hand, if you drop a Word icon into an open document window, Word assumes that you want to insert the file at the point where you dropped it. To open the document in a new window instead, drop the icon onto the title bar of the Word program window.

Each data file gets its own button on the Windows taskbar, and you can switch between document windows the same way you switch between programs.

Unfortunately, the techniques for handling multiple document windows are inconsistent among Office programs, which can cause you no end of confusion. Unless you change its default behavior (see the following tip), each Word document exists in its own window; there's no way to display two or more Word documents in the same window, and closing one Word document has no effect on other windows. Using Excel and PowerPoint, on the other hand, you can rearrange two or more document windows within a single program window, and if you click the Close (X) button on an Excel or PowerPoint window, you close all open workbooks or presentations.

TIP FROM

Ed & Woody

> You can have Word put multiple documents inside its window like the other Office applications do (the so-called *multiple document interface*, or MDI). With Word in this condition, you can, for example, choose Window, Arrange All to have multiple documents appear inside Word without multiple copies of the menus and toolbars hanging around cluttering up the screen. To do so, choose Tools, Options; on the View tab, clear the Windows in Taskbar check box. Unfortunately, when you do this, individual documents no longer appear in the Windows taskbar.

3

SETTING UP AUTOMATIC BACKUP AND RECOVERY OPTIONS

No roller coaster can compete with the sinking feeling you get when an Office program hangs, crashes, or simply disappears. With most programs, you can kiss your unsaved work goodbye. But Office 2003 comes with "air bags" designed to make crashes less frequent, to make them less devastating when they do occur, and to increase your chances of recovering a document when Office does crash. These are the important points to keep in mind:

- If an Office application "hangs"—goes out to lunch and doesn't come back—you should shut it down using the Office Application Recovery program. Click Start and open the All Programs menu; then click Microsoft Office, Microsoft Office Tools, and choose Microsoft Office Application Recovery. (Figure 3.10 shows this utility in action.) Avoid using Task Manager or the other Windows tools—Office is one of the few Windows programs that ships with tools specifically designed to dislodge a "hang."

Figure 3.10
If an Office program quits responding, try to use the Application Recovery utility to recover your work.

- When you restart an Office program that has crashed, chances are good that you'll be presented with the Office Document Recovery task pane (see Figure 3.11). Documents that are listed as [Original] probably aren't as up-to-date as those marked [Recovered]. Choose the version that you want to keep, click it, and then Close the Document Recovery task pane.

- It might be worthwhile to save several [Recovered] documents and compare the versions to see which (if any) have worthwhile changes. To do so, click the down arrow to the right of the [Recovered] filename and choose Save As.

TIP FROM

Ed & Woody

Automatic Backup and Recovery—the "air bags for Office"—isn't foolproof. Sometimes it works; sometimes it doesn't. It's definitely not a substitute for saving your work regularly and keeping backup copies in a safe place. For projects that are especially important, burn your backups to a CD or copy them to a USB flash drive for extra protection.

Figure 3.11
Office's Document
Recovery task pane
appears on the left
side of the screen.

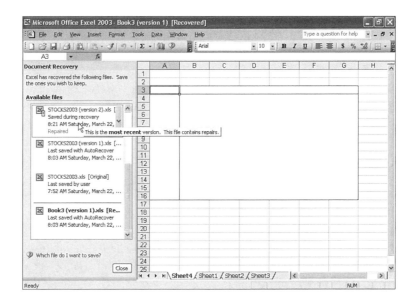

In some cases, the recovery procedure will actually repair damage to a file when reopening it. In this case, you can use the drop-down menu to open a dialog box that shows you which repairs were made.

TROUBLESHOOTING

PUTTING TEMPLATES IN THEIR PLACE

I created a group of templates and saved them along with the standard Office templates in the %programfiles%\Microsoft Office\Templates\1033 *folder. But when I choose File, New, none of my custom templates are visible.*

Microsoft designed the folder that stores system templates so that users cannot add templates to it. Instead, you should save your templates to the default User Templates location. The safest way to save templates to this location is one at a time. If you choose Template from the Files of Type list in the Save As dialog box, all Office programs will save your work to the correct location. If you want to add a large number of files to this location, open Word and choose Tools, Options; then click the File Locations tab and verify the User Templates location.

NO PREVIEW IN COMMON DIALOG BOXES

I selected Preview from the drop-down menu of views in an Office common dialog box, but when I click a file in the pane on the left, Windows displays the words Preview not available *instead of showing my file.*

The preview pane shows a static snapshot of the document as it existed the last time you saved it. By default, this option is not selected because it tends to add roughly 60KB to every file that you create. To make this preview picture available, you must choose File, Properties and check the Save Preview Picture box on the Summary tab. You can do this at any time with a Word document or PowerPoint presentation. However, this option is effective with Excel workbooks only if you use it when you first create the file. Checking this box on an Excel workbook after you've saved it with this option off has no effect at all. To enable the preview, select the Save Preview Picture check box and save the file under a new name. Then close the file and use Windows Explorer to delete the old version and rename the new one with the old name.

EXTRA CREDIT: FIND FILES FASTER WITH DESKTOP SEARCH TOOLS

You don't need to open an Office program to find a missing document. Desktop search utilities index the entire contents of your hard drive, including e-mail messages, Office documents, music files, digital photos, and just about anything else. By entering a search term or two, you can display all matching documents and quickly zero in on the one you need.

All the leading desktop search utilities have the capability to index, find, and preview files saved in Office formats. Typically, you install a small program, allow it to create an index of your hard disk, and then begin searching. (The index process can take several hours, so don't install one of these programs if you need to find a file right away.)

Our two favorite programs in this category are Copernic Desktop Search (http://www.copernic.com) and Windows Desktop Search, which is included with the MSN Search Toolbar (http://desktop.msn.com/). Both programs are free, easy to use, and amazingly fast and accurate.

CHAPTER 4

Entering, Editing, and Formatting Text

In this chapter

ENTERING TEXT: MORE THAN JUST TYPING

How hard can it be to enter text in an Office document? You click, you type. As long as your fingers hit the right keys, everything just happens, right? Well, not exactly. What happens when you need to enter a character that isn't on the keyboard: a currency symbol such as ¥, perhaps, or a Greek character such as π?

In fact, Office 2003 contains full support for the *Unicode standard*, a universally recognized character set containing tens of thousands of letters, ideographs, and other symbols, which spans the majority of all written languages. If the operating system you are using supports the characters used in a specific language, those characters are available in Office. You won't find all those characters on your 102-key keyboard, of course, but they're only a few taps and clicks away, once you learn the secrets.

INSERTING SYMBOLS AND SPECIAL CHARACTERS

If you're writing a paper about world currencies, how do you enter the symbols associated with currencies other than your own? When you're citing sources written in a foreign language, how do you enter accented characters? Office supports three relatively easy methods to place a single symbol or other special character in an Office document:

- Your first stop should be the Symbol dialog box. Choose Insert, Symbol and then click the Symbols tab to scroll through a comprehensive and easy-to-use list of every character available in normal or decorative fonts (see Figure 4.1). The magnified preview makes it easy to select the correct symbol.

Figure 4.1
The frequently overlooked Subset list for Insert Symbol's normal text option offers quick access to different groups of characters.

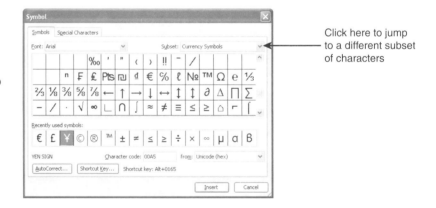

Click here to jump to a different subset of characters

TIP FROM

E.Q & Woody

When you click a symbol, a short description of the character, as well as its character code, appears at the bottom of the Symbol dialog box. Most characters include a keyboard shortcut, typically triggered by holding down the Alt key while entering a four-digit numeric ANSI code from the numeric keypad (the numbers on the top row of the keyboard do not work for these shortcuts). Although these shortcuts are usable in any Windows program, the shortcut hint is only visible when you open the Symbol dialog box in Word.

NOTE

> After you insert a character, the Symbol dialog box remains open so that you can insert additional characters, if necessary. To dismiss this dialog box, press Esc or click Close (X) or Cancel.

- The Special Characters tab in the Symbol dialog box (see Figure 4.2) gives you quick access to the most common punctuation characters (also known as *special characters*). The tab is only available in Word and Excel (and in Outlook when you use Word as your e-mail editor). If you are tired of scrolling through the Symbol dialog box's detailed lists, this is the place to turn. The shortcut-key reminders are visible in Word only.

Figure 4.2
The Special Characters tab includes only a small subset of the characters listed on the Symbols tab, but the ones that are there are easier to find.

- If you know that you're going to be using a specific symbol or special character repeatedly, set up an AutoCorrect entry for it by clicking the AutoCorrect button on the Symbol dialog in Word (or in Outlook when using the Word editor), or by choosing Tools, AutoCorrect Options in Excel, Access, Publisher, or PowerPoint. For example, if you use the ¥ (Japanese Yen) symbol frequently, tell Office to AutoCorrect the two characters Y= to ¥. The entry will work in Outlook, Word, Excel, Publisher, or PowerPoint.

→ To learn more about saving and reusing text, **see** "Using AutoCorrect to Type Faster," **p. 98**.

NOTE

> To find various dashes, "curly" quotes, daggers, ellipses, and many more common marks quickly, open the Symbol dialog box and choose General Punctuation from the Subset list on the Symbols tab.

When it comes to inserting symbols into your documents, you have many more choices. For example, you can use the Windows Character Map applet (Charmap.exe), or you can click the buttons on the Word version of the Symbol dialog to create AutoCorrect entries or shortcut keys. You can write a macro in any Office application that inserts a specific character and assigns it to a toolbar button or key combination. You can also choose from an endless assortment of keyboard macro and Clipboard management utilities designed for general-purpose use with Windows.

ENTERING ACCENTED AND INTERNATIONAL CHARACTERS

If you use the U.S. English version of Office 2003 and you have only occasional need for an accented, inflected, or otherwise altered character common in European languages, Word and Outlook recognize the shortcuts in Table 4.1.

TABLE 4.1 WORD AND OUTLOOK'S ACCENTED CHARACTER SHORTCUTS		
To Type Any of These Accented Characters	First, Press This Key Command	Then Type the Desired Letter
ÀàÈèÌìÒòÙù	Ctrl+`	AaEeIiOoUu
ÁáD´dÉéÍíÓóÚúÝý	Ctrl+'	AaDdEeIiOoUuYy
ÂâÊêÎîÔôÛû	Ctrl+Shift+^	AaEeIiOoUu
ÄäËëÏïÖöÜüŸÿ	Ctrl+Shift+:	AaEeIiOoUuYy
ÃãÑñÕõ	Ctrl+Shift+~	AaNnOo
ÆæŒœß	Ctrl+Shift+&	AaOos
Çç	Ctrl+,	Cc
Åå	Ctrl+Shift+@	Aa
Øø	Ctrl+/	Oo

To enter an inverted question mark or exclamation point (¿, ¡) for use with Spanish text, press Alt+Ctrl+Shift+? or Alt+Ctrl+Shift+!.

ENTERING TEXT IN ANOTHER LANGUAGE

Office interprets the keys on your keyboard according to the conventions established inside Windows. To change the mapping of keys to characters, use the Control Panel's Keyboard applet: Click Start, Settings, Control Panel, double-click Keyboard, and then click the Input Locales tab.

TIP FROM

EQ & Woody

It's easy to set up a keyboard shortcut that changes languages. On the Keyboard applet's Language or Input Locales tab, use the Switch Languages (or locales) option. In Windows 2000 and XP, you'll need to click the Change Key Sequence button in the Hot Keys for the Input Locales section.

When you switch keyboards, Word automatically switches fonts to those that are designed for the language and sets the proofing language for spell checking and grammar checking.

Before you can edit text in those other languages, you need to have Office install the features demanded by that particular language. To do so, click Start, All Programs, Microsoft Office, Microsoft Office Tools, Microsoft Office 2003 Language Settings. On the Enabled Languages tab (see Figure 4.3), select the languages you want Office to recognize.

Figure 4.3
Office 2003 supports a wide variety of languages, even if you have only the U.S. English version.

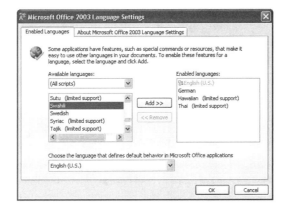

The actual tools involved vary from language to language. For example, if you install Thai language support, the Font dialog box (choose Format, Font) will, from that point on, include a selection for complex scripts (that is, text that includes Thai characters; see Figure 4.4).

Figure 4.4
Choose to enable Thai language support, and the Font dialog box enables you to specify a font for Complex scripts. Note the "Sample" in Thai at the lower right.

4

NOTE

Some languages require additional tools. Arabic, Hebrew, and Farsi, for example, need *bidirectional support*, because they are input and read from right to left. Ideographic languages need the Microsoft Input Method Editor to make it possible to type "text" (ideograms) at all. (*Ideograms*, the cornerstone of several written Asian languages, are symbols more related to ideas or things rather than a spoken sound. Ideographic languages are notoriously difficult to input into a computer because they typically contain thousands of "characters.") For more details, consult the online Help topic "About Multilingual Features in Office."

SELECTING TEXT

Text selection is one of the most fundamental of Office activities, but the specific techniques used in each program vary widely. In fact, mastering the different shortcuts each Office application uses to handle text selection is a key step on the road to becoming an Office master.

When you select text with a mouse, the following shortcuts apply:

- Double-clicking a word selects the word in all Office applications. In the text-centered Office programs—Outlook, Word, and PowerPoint—double-clicking also selects the word's trailing space(s), if any; in Excel, it does not. That can be somewhat confusing when switching between applications.

- Triple-clicking selects an entire paragraph in Outlook, Word, and PowerPoint. Triple-clicking in Excel does not select an entire cell.

- In Word, moving the mouse pointer to the left margin changes it from an I-beam insertion point to an arrow that points up and to the right. When you see this pointer, you can click once to select the current line; twice to select the paragraph; or three times to select the entire document. The Outlook e-mail editor does not have a similar capability.

- In Word, Outlook, and PowerPoint, the selection automatically extends to include entire words when you click and drag over more than one word. All four applications allow you to turn this feature off using the Edit tab on the Options dialog box (choose Tools, Options to get there); clear the box marked When Selecting, Automatically Select Entire Word.

→ To learn more ways you can customize Word, **see** "Customizing the Word Interface," **p. 359**.

- When working with text boxes in the drawing layer, Office takes on the clicking conventions of the underlying application: Triple-clicking in a paragraph in an Excel text box does nothing; the same action in Word or PowerPoint selects the entire paragraph.

→ For an explanation of how the drawing layer works, **see** "Working with the Drawing Layer," **p. 114**.

Many advanced Word users—especially proficient typists—prefer to use the keyboard to select characters and words. If you work with lots of documents that use special characters, memorizing a few simple commands can help you avoid the mouse and get text on the screen much more quickly. Keyboard-selection techniques stay fairly uniform throughout Office (see Table 4.2).

TABLE 4.2   KEYBOARD SELECTIONS VALID IN ALL OFFICE PROGRAMS

To Select	Press
Next character to right	Shift+Right Arrow
Next character to left	Shift+Left Arrow
To end of word	Ctrl+Shift+Right Arrow
To beginning of word	Ctrl+Shift+Left Arrow
To end of line	Shift+End
To beginning of line	Shift+Home
Entire document	Ctrl+A

In addition, Outlook and Word have two important shortcuts that you will want to memorize (see Table 4.3). These shortcuts come in handy when you're trying to select blocks of text in large documents, "from this point to the beginning" or "from this point to the end." No menu or toolbar button equivalents exist for either.

TABLE 4.3   KEYBOARD SELECTIONS VALID ONLY IN OUTLOOK AND WORD

To Select	Press
To end of document	Ctrl+Shift+End
To beginning of document	Ctrl+Shift+Home

In Word (and in Outlook when using Word as the e-mail editor), you can select noncontiguous characters—that is, characters that are not next to each other—by holding down the Ctrl and Shift keys simultaneously as you make your selections. (If you hold down Ctrl when you click, your initial selection extends to a complete sentence.) In Excel you can select noncontiguous cells the same way. In PowerPoint, you're allowed to select noncontiguous slides. But you can't select noncontiguous text in Excel or PowerPoint, or when using the built-in Outlook e-mail editor.

FINDING AND REPLACING TEXT

When you want to find or replace a piece of text in an Office document, the method varies depending on which application you use. To find a particular text string, do the following:

1. Choose Edit, Find. Type the text you want to locate in the Find What box. Word's Find and Replace dialog box is shown in Figure 4.5.

2. Set up the parameters, known as *criteria*, for your search. Depending on which Office application you are using, the process of setting up your search criteria will vary:

   • In Outlook and Word, you can choose whether you want to search Up (toward the beginning of the document) or Down (toward the end). (To reach this option in Word, click the More button.) In Excel (see Figure 4.6) or PowerPoint, you have no choice as to direction—the first Find uncovers the first occurrence of the string; subsequent Find Next selections move to later occurrences. In Word, you can choose the Search All option, which finds the first occurrence of your search text in the current document or database object, the same as an Excel or PowerPoint Find.

Figure 4.5
Word has the most comprehensive Find and Replace options, all of which are available in Outlook as well if you use Word as the e-mail editor.

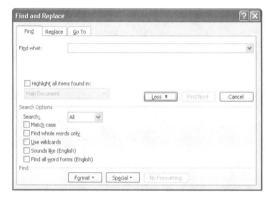

Figure 4.6
Excel's Find and Replace is remarkably different from Word's.

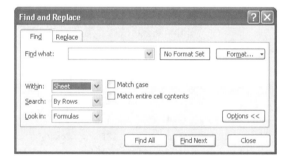

- Excel enables you to choose whether you want to search *row-major* ("Search By Rows" going across the current row before dropping down to the next one) or *column-major* ("Search By Columns" going down the current column before looking at the next one to the right). Make your choice in the Search box. Excel also enables you to look at formulas or values (that is, formula results). If you have a cell that contains the formula =SUM(A1:B3), for example, searching the formulas for B3 results in a hit, whereas searching the values doesn't.

NOTE

Excel allows you to easily search for text in comments. This feature can come in handy if you're scanning for comments from a specific individual or those that apply to a given topic. To do so, select Comments in the Look In box.

- All the Office applications allow you to specify that you want to Match Case (as in the PowerPoint dialog box shown in Figure 4.7). With this check box selected, the capitalization shown in the Find What text box must match the capitalization of the text in the document precisely to get a "hit."

Figure 4.7
PowerPoint's Spartan Find dialog box is limited.

- Using the Find dialog box in Outlook, Word, and PowerPoint, you can select a check box that restricts the search to Find Whole Words Only. When this option is enabled, the text in the Find What field must appear in the document preceded and followed by a space or punctuation mark: beast, for example, will match beast but not beasts. Excel has a comparable check box that limits hits to cells where the entire cell contents matches the text in the Find What box.

3. With the find criteria established the way you want, click Find Next and the application selects the next occurrence of the text.

Outlook, Word, Excel, and Access accept wildcards:

- * matches one or more letters. For example, s*ap will turn up hits on snap or strap, but not on sap.

- ? matches one single letter. For example, b?t will match bit or bat, but not boot.

- In Excel only, the tilde character (~) followed by a ~, ?, or * matches ~, ?, or *. So hop~* matches hop*, but not hop? or hope, and tr~?p matches tr?p but not tr*p or tr~p or trip.

Word has an enormous number of additional search features; the other Office applications pale in comparison.

→ To learn more about Word's powerful search features, **see** "Finding and Replacing Text and Other Parts of a Document," **p. 345**.

CONVERTING SCANNED DOCUMENTS TO TEXT

Office 2003 includes a surprisingly good optical character recognition (OCR) system that can convert a paper document into a Word file with relative ease. You can scan the document and dump its text directly into Word in a single operation; or start with a scanned document, perform OCR, and then select some or all of the recognized text to use in any Office program.

If you have a scanner connected to your PC, use the Microsoft Office Document Scanning utility to scan the document. It creates a file in the Tagged Image File Format (TIFF) and then performs OCR on that file in one operation. You'll find the Document Scanning program in the Microsoft Office Tools group on the All Programs menu. The Scan New Document dialog box (see Figure 4.8) is fairly easy to use: Click the Scanner button to check and, if necessary, adjust the settings of your scanner, and then click the Scan button.

Figure 4.8
When scanning a multi-page paper document, be sure to select the option to prompt for additional pages.

The resulting document includes two components: a graphic representation of the scanned page, in TIFF format, and a version that includes OCR information. The results appear in the Microsoft Office Document Imaging utility. If you have a saved TIFF file, you can open it directly in this program (you'll find its shortcut in the Microsoft Office Tools group as well).

TIP FROM

Options available for the Document Scanning utility depend on your hardware. Some drivers support automatic page feeders; others include the option to "re-stitch" documents that are printed on both sides of the paper. You scan one side and then the other, and the software puts the two halves together, in sequence. It's a very handy feature.

The Document Imaging utility (see Figure 4.9) includes an enormous number of options—too many to describe here. Pages in a multi-page document appear in the thumbnail pane on the left; right-click here to add, delete, or rearrange pages. Clicking the Selection arrow can select a portion of the page.

The speed at which the Document Imaging Utility converts your scanned document to text depends on how much horsepower your computer has, but the results can be exceptional. After performing OCR, you can select a portion of the recognized text, right-click, and copy the selection to the Clipboard as an image or as text. Click the Send Text to Word icon to export just that portion to a new Word document. As Figure 4.10 shows, the Document Imaging program lets you decide what to export.

Selection arrow

Figure 4.9
When scanning a multi-page paper document, be sure to select the option to prompt for additional pages.

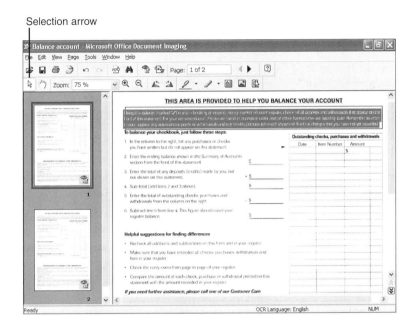

Figure 4.10
After making a selection, you can export all or part of the recognized text to Word.

How successful will you be turning scanned documents into text? That depends on the original document. In our experiments scanning a perfectly clean printout using typical business text in 12-point Times New Roman font, recognition was nearly perfect. When we started with a faxed report containing multiple tables, originally printed on an impact printer, complete with authentic coffee cup stains, Office still managed to recognize more than 80% of the characters.

Whether that's good enough for you is largely a matter of how the scanned documents will be used. If you're trying to avoid retyping a 20-page report, recognition that gets 98% of the text right might be good enough. But you might find it easier to re-key a short document than to go through the hassle of scanning, converting, and proofreading.

USING AUTOCORRECT TO TYPE FASTER

You see the result of AutoCorrect when you type a word like *teh* and Word instantly transforms in into *the*. Don't take AutoCorrect's name too literally. Yes, it's true that AutoCorrect watches over you, correcting typos in Outlook or Word—for example, type *isn;t* and AutoCorrect converts it to *isn't*. But it does much more:

- AutoCorrect works in all of the big four Office programs: Word, Outlook, Excel, and PowerPoint. When using Outlook's built-in e-mail editor, AutoCorrect works only on plain text and RTF messages and is disabled when composing HTML messages. Customized AutoCorrect entries you create in one program work in all the others (with one exception discussed later in this section); if you tell Word to change `mouses` into `mice`, the correction applies in all other Office applications.

- You can create your own AutoCorrect entries to supercharge your typing—say, changing your shorthand `tpfp` into the `Party of the First Part` or `otoh` into `on the other hand`.

- If you commonly work with boilerplate text, AutoCorrect can handle it for you. Do you have a description of the history and goals of your local civic organization that you put at the end of letters and e-mail messages to potential new members? Set up a code you can remember—such as `history1`—so it automatically expands on demand. An AutoCorrect entry can consist of paragraphs, even pages, of text, footnotes, and the like.

- In Word (and in Outlook when using Word as your e-mail editor), AutoCorrect entries can include graphics. This is handy if you frequently reuse the same graphic image. For example, you might want to scan your signature and turn it into an AutoCorrect entry called `mysig`. Then, wherever you type `mysig`, your scanned signature appears.

- AutoCorrect can even help you with odd capitalization. For example, if you're preparing a presentation about a company called `ZapItInc`, you might have trouble getting the caps right when you type the company name. Set up an AutoCorrect entry for `zapitinc` (all lowercase) and have it corrected to `ZapItInc`. Then every time you type `zapitinc`— or `Zapitinc`, `ZapItinc`, `ZapitInc`, or even `zApitiNc`—AutoCorrect automatically changes the word to `ZapItInc`.

Word has a similar feature, called AutoText, which can be more appropriate than AutoCorrect in certain situations.

→ To learn when you should use AutoText instead of AutoCorrect, **see** "Entering Text and Graphics Automatically with AutoText and AutoCorrect," **p. 341**.

TIP FROM

EQ & Woody

In all Office applications except Excel, a Smart Tag appears whenever AutoCorrect changes something you've typed. Hover your mouse over the changed text and click the Smart Tag (look for the lightning bolt icon) for easy access to all AutoCorrect options—including the capability to undo, or even permanently turn off, whatever correction was made.

HOW AUTOCORRECT WORKS

The AutoCorrect engine watches as you type. Whenever you press the spacebar, type a punctuation mark, or press Enter, this Office component looks to see whether the preceding characters match an entry in your AutoCorrect list. If it finds a match, it replaces the old text with the contents of the AutoCorrect entry.

In a default installation, the AutoCorrect list includes a large collection of commonly misspelled words and phrases. Figure 4.11 shows an AutoCorrect entry that changes accomodate to accommodate. Because of this entry, if you ever type accomodate followed by a space, punctuation mark, or paragraph mark, the misspelling will be automatically changed to accommodate.

Figure 4.11
The AutoCorrect dialog box includes a ready-made list of commonly mistyped words and phrases.

The entry must match precisely. Using the default AutoCorrect entry shown in Figure 4.11, Word would not change accomodated to its correct spelling—unless, of course, you add a custom AutoCorrect entry to handle that word.

If AutoCorrect changes a word and you want the original back, click to position the insertion point within the changed word. Then let the mouse pointer hover over the underline beneath the changed word, click the lightning bolt icon to reveal the action menu, and choose Undo Automatic Corrections. Alternatively—and much more quickly—you can immediately press Ctrl+Z, or you can choose Edit, Undo AutoCorrect, or click the Undo button. Any of these actions will reverse the change made by AutoCorrect and restore what you typed to its original state. The same action menu lets you quickly remove an entry from the AutoCorrect Options list or stop AutoCorrect from performing a certain type of correction.

SETTING AUTOCORRECT OPTIONS

In addition to replacing one string of text with another, Office has four additional AutoCorrect settings:

- When you select the Correct TWo INitial CApitals check box, AutoCorrect examines each word you type in an Office program; if it detects a word that starts with two consecutive capitals and that word appears in the dictionary, Word changes the second letter to lowercase. For example, if you miscapitalize AHead, Word changes it to Ahead; but if you type JScript or IDs, Word leaves it alone. You might want to override AutoCorrect on certain two-capital combinations. To do so, click the Exceptions button and add the entry manually.

  You can bypass this dialog box and automatically add words that begin with two capital letters to the Exceptions list by immediately undoing the change. If you're writing a paper about a new club whose name is the GOphers, for example, and Word, Publisher, or PowerPoint "corrects" the entry to Gophers, click the AutoCorrect Smart Tag for the changed text and choose Stop Automatically Correcting GOphers from the action menu. (You can also press Ctrl+Z in any application to undo the change.) Office restores the second capital letter and adds the word to the Exceptions list in one operation. To disable this feature, click the Exceptions button on the AutoCorrect dialog box and clear the Automatically Add Words to List check box.

- The Capitalize First Letter of Sentence box is built around the belief that Office can recognize when you're starting a new sentence. That's not an easy task. If this setting causes Office to make capitalization mistakes more frequently than you like, turn it off. Office generally assumes that you're about to start a new sentence when it detects the presence of a period followed by a space, but tempers that judgment by a lengthy list of exceptions, including approx. and corp., which rarely signal the end of a sentence (see Figure 4.12).

- The Capitalize Names of Days check box works as you would expect.

- The Correct Accidental Usage of cAPS LOCK Key check box, however, comes into play only when you type one lowercase letter, followed by

Figure 4.12

pushing the Caps Lock key, and then continue typing. With this box checked, Office turns the first character into a capital, makes the other characters lowercase, and turns off the Caps Lock function.

Word offers two more AutoCorrect check boxes, which are also available in Outlook when you use Word as the default e-mail editor. The first, Capitalize First Letter of Table Cells, works much like the Capitalize First Letter of Sentences setting. The second option, Automatically Use Suggestions from the Spelling Checker, configures Word to consult the spelling checker if the usual AutoCorrect lookup doesn't find the word in question in the AutoCorrect list. If the spelling checker comes back with one—and only one—suggested correct spelling, the word you typed is replaced with the one offered by the spell checker.

CAUTION

You could have an embarrassing mistake if Word substitutes the absolute wrong word for a misspelled one. However, Word's automatic substitution routines don't seem to generate vulgar expressions. In addition, AutoCorrect will not change proper nouns and other capitalized words (so, for example, if you type `Mr. Turkye`, it will remain `Turkye`, and not be AutoCorrected to `Turkey`).

→ To learn more about Word's spelling checker, **see** "Checking Spelling and Grammar," **p. 351**.

If you type *tiime*, and there's no entry for *tiime* in the AutoCorrect list, Word consults the spelling checker. The spelling checker offers only one correct spelling—*time*—so, with this box checked, *tiime* is replaced by *time*.

CUSTOMIZING THE AUTOCORRECT LISTS

Office maintains two AutoCorrect lists. The first one includes all unformatted Word AutoCorrect entries, plus all entries for the other Office applications. The second AutoCorrect list exclusively handles formatted entries available in Word (and in Outlook when you use Word as its editor).

Use a formatted AutoCorrect entry whenever it's important that formatting be applied in the replaced text. For example, if you're writing a paper for your civics class and you always want the term *Congressional Record* to appear in italic text, you might set up a formatted AutoCorrect entry called cr that always produces `Congressional Record` (see Figure 4.13).

Adding your own formatted entries to the AutoCorrect list is easy:

1. Select the text you want AutoCorrect to produce. Apply whatever formatting you want.

2. Choose Tools, AutoCorrect Options. The text you've selected appears in the With box. Click the Formatted text button.

3. Type the text you want to trigger an AutoCorrect replacement in the Replace box. In Figure 4.13, we instructed Office to replace cr with `Congressional Record`.

4. Click Add.

Figure 4.13
Formatted
AutoCorrect entries
are available only
in Word.

Formatted AutoCorrect entries apply only to Word (and Outlook when using Word as your e-mail editor). If you add the formatted *cr* entry shown earlier in Figure 4.11 and then type *cr* in Excel or PowerPoint, nothing happens. The text *cr* is AutoCorrected only in Word and Outlook.

To add an unformatted AutoCorrect entry, choose Tools, AutoCorrect Options, and type the entry name in the Replace box and the replacement text in the With box. Click Add.

CAUTION

> When Word searches for AutoCorrect entries, it looks for formatted entries first. Building on the previous example, if you create a formatted entry for *cr* in Word and then create an unformatted (plain text) entry for *cr* in another program, typing *cr* in Word will bring up the formatted entry, but typing *cr* in Excel or PowerPoint will bring up the unformatted (plain text) entry. To make things even more confusing, only the unformatted entry will show in the Word AutoCorrect list, although the formatted entry will still be used. If you can't make sense of a specific AutoCorrect entry, your best bet is to first remove the unformatted entry from Excel or PowerPoint, then remove the entry from Word, and start over.

You can also add AutoCorrect entries while performing a spell check. Right-click a word with a red squiggly underline, choose AutoCorrect, and select the correct spelling. Office corrects the misspelling and adds a matching AutoCorrect entry automatically.

Deleting AutoCorrect entries is as easy as adding them. Open the AutoCorrect dialog box, select the entry you want to remove, and click Delete.

If you type the name of the entry you want to delete in the Replace box, Office jumps immediately to that part of the list.

Word fields can appear in AutoCorrect entries, but only as Formatted Text. If you switch to Plain Text when creating an AutoCorrect entry that contains a field, Word converts the field to its field result before storing the entry.

Unformatted AutoCorrect entries are stored in a file that includes the extension .acl in the `%appdata%\Microsoft\Office` folder. In a default U.S. English installation, this file is called MSO1033.acl. The file can be moved from one computer to another along with other Office personal information. Formatted AutoCorrect entries are stored in Word's global template, Normal.dot.

→ To move AutoCorrect entries and other saved settings to a new computer, **see** "Saving and Restoring Personal Settings," **p. 56**.

Also consider adding words you commonly type that have odd punctuation—Yahoo! comes to mind—so the capitalizing routine will operate properly. You might have other abbreviations that appear frequently in your writing: tb. perhaps, or exec.. To add these exceptions, choose Tools, AutoCorrect Options, and then click the Exceptions button. Type `Yahoo!` and click Add. Type `tb.` and click Add again; type `exec.`, and click Add one last time.

The AutoCorrect list is filled with hundreds of entries—not all of which might be to your liking. Consider removing the ones you find obtrusive (choose Tools, AutoCorrect Options, select the entry, and click the Delete button). For example:

- Several combinations of colons, semicolons, dashes, lines, and parentheses are automatically turned into smiley faces. If you don't want smiley faces to appear in your documents and e-mail messages, delete those entries from the AutoCorrect list. They're all near the beginning of the list.

TIP FROM

EQ & Woody

When using Word as your Outlook e-mail editor, AutoCorrect will not replace emoticons such as :-) with smiley faces if you work in Plain Text mode (select Plain Text from the Format menu). Working in Plain Text also short-circuits AutoCorrect entries that would generate odd characters, such as the copyright symbol. Outlook's built-in e-mail editor supports AutoCorrect.

- If you commonly create numbered lists by hand, and use (a), (b), (c), and so on within the numbers, you'll quickly discover that (c) is automatically turned into a copyright symbol. To override that behavior, use the lightning bolt icon that appears when you hover over the copyright symbol and choose Stop Automatically Correcting "(c)".

- Another AutoCorrect entry turns a standalone lowercase i into an uppercase I. That, too, can be problematic if you create numbered lists by hand. To get around it, click the AutoCorrect Smart Tag (the lightning-bolt icon) and use the action menu.

■ One AutoCorrect entry changes three consecutive periods (...) into an ellipsis. The ellipsis is a single character that looks like three periods, squished close together (…). As long as your documents are destined to be used only by other Office programs, the ellipses pose no problem. But when you copy the text into an e-mail message, for example, or post the document on the Web, the ellipsis character can turn into something totally inscrutable. To keep Office from changing three periods to an ellipsis, use the AutoCorrect action menu.

ADVANCED AUTOCORRECT TECHNIQUES

Any situation that involves boilerplate text is a likely candidate for AutoCorrect. If you commonly construct letters that contain five or six paragraphs selected from a pool of many dozens—or hundreds—you can set up AutoCorrect entries for each of the possible paragraphs and, based on a printed list that's memorized or easily accessible, construct the letter rapidly.

In fact, by using {fillin} fields, you can prompt for specific pieces of text to further customize the boilerplate text.

→ To learn more about creating user input forms using Word fields, **see** "Prompting for Input," **p. 506**.

This feature is handy if you're starting several classes in which you're required to produce weekly papers that use standard elements, such as a title page, an abstract, and a bibliography.

You can set up each of these elements as an AutoCorrect entry with custom text that includes the class and teacher name—*title101*, *abstract101*, and *biblio101*, for example; then you can "type" that entire letter with three simple lines:

```
title101

abstract101

biblio101
```

In addition, if you set up the {fillin} field at the indicated location in the first paragraph, when you type *title101*, Word prompts you for the date of the letter. You type in the date and it appears in place of the {fillin} field.

By customizing these elements for different classes and changing the AutoCorrect entry names to match, you can make the process of getting started with a paper that much easier. These techniques are also useful in business, for writing form letters and other documents that use mix-and-match blocks of text.

AUTOCORRECT DO'S AND DON'TS

The most common problem with AutoCorrect entries arises when you create an entry that has unexpected side effects. For example, while working on a paper for a civics class you might create an entry called *econ* that AutoCorrects to *Council of Economic Advisors*. Then, a few days or weeks later, you might be writing an e-mail message to a friend and include this line:

```
I'm thinking of signing up for Econ 101…
```

and the AutoCorrect entry kicks in:

```
I'm thinking of signing up for Council of Economic Advisors 101…
```

 If you find it difficult to locate some AutoCorrect entries, see "Finding Obscure AutoCorrect Entries" in the "Troubleshooting" section at the end of this chapter.

To minimize the chances for side effects like these, many Office experts use punctuation marks in their AutoCorrect entries. You might be tempted to set up an AutoCorrect entry called usr, for example, to "correct" into `United Steel & Resources, Inc.` Unfortunately, every time your finger slips on the keyboard and you misspell use as usr, AutoCorrect kicks in and you get gibberish. If you define the entry as `usr.`, on the other hand—note the trailing period—you can type the entry almost as quickly as usr, and the chance for accidental side effects are greatly reduced.

USING AND MANAGING FONTS

The first law of *typography*: Don't use more than three different fonts (typefaces) in any single document—one for the body text, one for headings, and at most one more for the masthead or main titles. Using these guidelines, you might settle on Garamond for body text, Arial for headings, and Verdana for the title page.

The second law of typography: Nobody follows the first law.

Unless you have a compelling reason to flout convention, most business letters and memos use at most two fonts: one font for the logo, return address, or any other fixed text at the top and bottom of the first sheet; and a second font for all the rest. Most teachers insist on having papers printed out in a standard format designed for readability, not good looks. In the United States, it's customary to use a *serif* font as the main font (for body text), and *sans serif* fonts are commonly used for heading text; in Europe, sans serif is almost as common as a body font, with serif fonts frequently used in headings.

TIP FROM

Ed & Woody

> A serif font, such as Times New Roman, has curlicues on the ends of the letters, sometimes referred to as feet; a sans serif font, such as Arial, has straight ends.
>
> For example
>
> This is Serif.
>
> This is Sans Serif.
>
> You can mix and match as you like, of course, but be aware that each font you add to a document increases the likelihood that typography will obscure, not enhance, your message. The sure sign of an amateur document designer is a wild mixture of fonts, of varying sizes, with *lots* of italic and ***even more*** bold italic.

4

When you include the fonts that come with Windows and the fonts included with different Office programs, you have more than 150 fonts at your disposal. Third-party programs add still more fonts, sometimes by the hundreds. That's enough to overwhelm anyone who isn't a design expert.

If you find your collection grows unmanageable (and it surely will by the time you hit 300–400 fonts), invest in a third-party font management program. These programs enable you to load and store groups of fonts, bringing them up when they're needed. One of our favorite programs in this category is Printer's Apprentice, from Lose Your Mind Development (`http://www.loseyourmind.com`).

COMMON FORMATTING OPTIONS

Although each Office program enables you to modify font formatting, and those with paragraphs (Outlook, Word, and PowerPoint) enable you to change paragraph formats, only Word and Outlook use the same dialog boxes to do so, and each application has its own quirks.

CHANGING CHARACTER ATTRIBUTES

To change character formatting, follow these steps:

1. In all Office programs, select the characters you want to change. In Word, Publisher, or PowerPoint, if you don't make a selection, your changes apply to the entire word in which the insertion point is located.

2. In Word (see Figure 4.14), Outlook, or PowerPoint, choose Format, Font. In Excel (see Figure 4.15), choose Format, Cells, and click the Font tab.

Figure 4.14
Word offers the greatest variety of font-formatting options of any Office application.

Figure 4.15
Excel font formatting applies to the entire cell unless you make a selection.

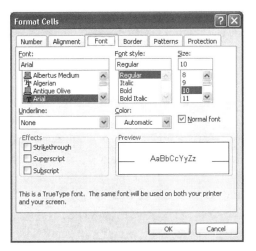

3. Set the characteristics. All Office programs enable you to change the font (that is, the typeface), size (in fractional increments), style (regular/roman, bold, italic, or bold italic), color, and single-line underline. Excel has several different kinds of underlines, strikethrough, superscript, and subscript. PowerPoint enables you to specify the super/subscript distance, shadow, and emboss.

TIP FROM

In theory, the Automatic color (available in every application except Outlook) tells Office to choose a color that contrasts with the color of the background. If you choose Automatic for the text color, for example, and then change the background to black, the text color changes to white and you can still read it. Unfortunately, thanks to a wide-ranging bug in Office, this feature works only in Word documents and tables. If you specify the Automatic color in a PowerPoint text placeholder, an Excel worksheet cell, or a text box in any application, Office ignores your request and formats the text as black. If you then change the background to black, your text disappears from sight.

4. Click OK to change the selected text.

→ To learn more about adding different formatting to your text in Word, **see** "Changing Text Formatting," **p. 384**.

Three Office programs—Word, Excel, and PowerPoint—include check boxes that refer to the Default or Normal font. Each of these boxes works in completely different ways; only Word's actually changes the default font for new documents:

- In Word, the Default button sets the properties you want to use for the default font in all documents created in the future, from the current template. When you click the Default button, Word asks whether you want to use the font settings for all new documents based on the current template. Click Yes. That sets the character formatting for the Normal style in the current template.

- In Excel, by contrast, whenever you check the Normal Font box, Excel sets the font, style, and size of the current selection to match the characteristics of the current workbook's Normal style. To change the standard font used in Excel—in other words, to set the font for the Normal style in new workbooks you create—choose Tools, Options, and modify the Standard font entry on the General tab.

- In PowerPoint, you can set the font, style, size, and so on, and then click the box marked Default for New Objects. That merely sets the default font for newly created items in the drawing layer—basically the size of the font in new Text Boxes and Auto Shapes in the current presentation.

USING BULLETS AND NUMBERS TO SET OFF LISTS

Bulleted and numbered lists come in handy both to emphasize and to organize. In general, you'll use bulleted lists to draw attention to important members of collections, and you'll want to save numbered lists when there's some sort of internal hierarchy (for example, a top-ten list), or when the sequence of points is important (for example, when describing each step in a complex procedure).

Word, Publisher, and PowerPoint all offer a Bullets and Numbering option on the Format menu. In each case, you choose the paragraphs you want to bullet or number, and then choose Format, Bullets and Numbering. If you don't make a selection, the formatting applies to the current paragraph and any succeeding paragraphs until you either turn off the formatting or press Enter twice.

NOTE

> When using Outlook's e-mail editor to create HTML messages, bullets and number formatting are applied as HTML list tags. You can apply formatting using toolbar buttons, right-click shortcut menus (choose Format, then click Bullets or Numbers), or from the Style list on the Format menu.

Using the Bullets and Numbering menu allows you to choose a picture or any character as a bullet. You can control whether the numbering continues from the previous number or starts fresh. You can also start AutoNumbering by typing a number followed by a period and space or tab. The primary differences:

- Word allows outline numbering, where you construct numbering schemes such as 1.A.3, 1.A.4, and so on. Word also applies bullet formatting automatically if you type a *, >, -, or a similar character, followed by a space or tab.

→ To learn more about constructing customized numbering schemes in Word, **see** "Formatting Simple Lists with Bullets and Numbers," **p. 396**.

- PowerPoint enables you to easily scale the size of the bullet so you can select the best size for your presentation.

→ To learn how to create effective bulleted and numbered lists in PowerPoint, **see** "Working with Bulleted and Numbered Lists," **p. 730**.

UNDOING AND REDOING CHANGES

All Office applications include Undo features. If you make a mistake, click the Undo icon, or choose Edit, Undo, or press Ctrl+Z. Every Office program supports at least one level of Undo, and some enable you to undo a number of successive changes. If you discover you made a mistake five minutes ago, you might be able to recover by clicking the Undo button repeatedly. If you close your file, however, all bets are off—all Office programs clear the Undo history when you close the document.

Word includes a virtually unlimited number of Undo levels, a feature you can exploit in Outlook when using Word as the default e-mail editor. As long as you don't close the document, you can undo anything you've done. (There are some physical limitations to the size of the Undo file, but in practice they aren't significant.)

Word's tremendously powerful Undo capability enables you to bring back material that you might have thought was lost. For example, if you're working on a paper and you decide the opening paragraph you started with is better than the one you ended with, you can easily restore it. First, save your current document! If anything goes wrong while using Undo in this way, you can exit without saving and reopen your document to start over.

4

TIP FROM

Click the drop-down Undo list and scroll all the way to the bottom, selecting every action on the list. When you release the mouse button, Word undoes everything you've done in the current session, restoring your document to the state it was in when you first opened it. Next, select the text you want to restore and copy it to the Clipboard (do not, under any circumstances, use the Cut command). Now scroll to the bottom of the drop-down Redo list and click to redo every action you just undid. Your document is now back to the state it was in before you performed the multiple-level undo, and you're free to paste in the paragraph from the Clipboard.

If you've lost the ability to Redo changes in Word, see the tip "Cutting Text Clears the Redo List" in the "Troubleshooting" section near the end of this chapter.

Excel, on the other hand, limits you to 16 levels of Undo. This relatively severe limitation has been part of Excel for years, since the Undo feature was first introduced. We know of no way to work around this limitation.

→ For more details about this limitation, **see** "Extra Credit: Beware of Undo," **p. 558**.

PowerPoint enables you to select the number of levels of Undo you want to support. (Choose Tools, Options, click the Edit tab, and spin the Maximum Number of Undos box.) The default value is 20, but you can increase this to a maximum of 150.

CAN YOU REALLY ENTER TEXT BY SPEAKING?

With each passing year, speech recognition technology improves. This exciting capability is still in its infancy, however, and Office's implementation only underscores that fact. Speech recognition can be a godsend to those who are physically challenged; however, text input using dictation rates as little more than a novelty to serious Office users. Voice Command mode doesn't fare much better.

Before you even attempt speech recognition, make sure you have the following:

- A PC running at 400MHz or faster (Microsoft's recommendation). Our experience suggests that you shouldn't even try dictation with a CPU running at less than 2GHz.
- At least 128MB of memory.
- Windows 2000 with Service Pack 3 or later, or any version of Windows XP.
- A high-quality headset microphone that comfortably sits within an inch of your mouth. USB microphones perform best.

Start using speech recognition by choosing Tools, Speech. You will go through a 15-minute "training" exercise, where the speech recognition software learns to recognize the words you say. Training is required even if you're only going to use speech recognition for commands. When you finish the training, Office connects to the Web and runs a video.

When Speech Recognition is activated (choose Tools, Speech), a free-floating bar called the Language bar appears in the upper-right area of the screen.

TIP FROM

EQ & Woody

> The Language bar might look like a plain-vanilla Office toolbar, but it isn't. You can't hide it or make it appear by choosing Tools, Customize, Toolbars. It won't dock. It's available to all of Windows, so the toolbar doesn't travel with an application's window when it's minimized. To get rid of the bar, right-click the left or right ends, and choose Close the Language bar.

Clicking Voice Command on the Language bar sets up voice recognition so you can choose menu items: File <pause, pause, pause> Open <pause, pause, pause> will reliably bring up the Open dialog box, for example. After the dialog box appears, you can navigate to a greater or lesser extent by using the names of tabs on tabbed dialog boxes, or drop-down lists. For example, if you want to open the fifth document in your My Documents folder, you would say: File <pause, pause, pause>, Open <pause, pause, pause>, Down <pause, and so on>, Down, Down, Down, Open. (Assuming all your commands were understood, and you didn't end up opening the Views list, for example.)

Choosing Dictation on the Language bar enables you to dictate into the document. Microsoft claims an initial recognition rate of 85%–90%, providing you use a high-quality microphone, you're working in a dead-silent room, and you consistently keep the microphone in the same location close to your mouth. Our tests didn't measure up to that claim, but your results might vary.

> Do the math. If you commonly put 2,000 characters in a typical single-page business letter, and your error rate is a mere 10%, you'll have to change 200 characters on that page before it's usable. Spell checking and grammar correction help speed up the process of correcting individual documents, but using the built-in Word tools doesn't help "train" the voice recognition system.

Microsoft claims a recognition rate of 95% if you devote a sufficient amount of time to "training"—and you can go back to training at any time. Every time you use the Correction tool on the Language bar, you're helping train the speech recognition system, as well.

> The most important fact a typical Office user needs to know about speech recognition is how to remove it. Go into Control Panel (Start, Settings, Control Panel) and double-click Add/Remove Programs. Choose Microsoft Office, click Change. Choose Add or Remove Features. Pull down the list under Office Shared Features and under Alternative User Input, turn the icon in front of Speech to a big red X (Unavailable). Click Update, and speech recognition goes away.

TROUBLESHOOTING

FINDING OBSCURE AUTOCORRECT ENTRIES

A rogue AutoCorrect entry is causing unwanted text to appear in my documents, but I can't find the offending entry in the AutoCorrect list.

Most of the time, it's fairly easy to figure out which entry is causing the problem. Unfortunately, AutoCorrect isn't always so simple. In particular, note that AutoCorrect entries can have embedded spaces so, for example, an entry for *any where* might correct to *anywhere*. That behavior can be puzzling until you realize that you might be the victim of an AutoCorrect entry that begins with *any*.

CUTTING TEXT CLEARS THE REDO LIST

I used Word's multiple-level Undo capability to roll back a large number of changes, and then cut a block of text. But when I wanted to restore my document to its previous state, the Redo button was grayed out.

Did you save your changes before you performed the Undo operation? If so, exit the document without saving, and restore your saved copy. If not, you're out of luck. When you use Word's multilevel Undo, you can *copy* anything you want to the Clipboard; if you use the Cut command, however, you wipe out the Redo list, and nothing will bring it back.

EXTRA CREDIT: USING AUTOCORRECT TO ADD A SCANNED SIGNATURE TO WORD DOCUMENTS

If you have a scanner, it takes only a few minutes to set up an AutoCorrect entry that will replace the text you type in Word with a scanned image of your signature. For example, you can have Word replace the text mysig with a scanned image of your signature. A signature slug can be useful for "signing" daily correspondence, and it's indispensable if you want to sign a fax that is sent out electronically.

Start by scanning the signature into a Word document by choosing Insert, Picture, From Scanner or Camera. Use your scanner's software to crop the image and insert it into the document. Select the scanned image and choose Tools, AutoCorrect. Make sure the Formatted Text button is selected, and type the text entry in the Replace box.

Make sure you don't allow others to use the scanned signature without your permission.

Figure 4.16

CHAPTER 5

USING PICTURES AND DRAWINGS

In this chapter

GOING BEYOND PLAIN TEXT

Documents that consist of only words are, frankly, boring. Photographs add visual interest to reports. Charts and diagrams can help you instantly tell a story with numbers that would otherwise be lost in a table. Even whimsical illustrations do wonders to make printed documents more readable, web pages more accessible, workbooks more lively, and presentations more engaging. Office 2003 includes a full set of drawing tools you can use, even if you aren't a trained graphic designer, plus a few features expressly aimed at making digital photos easier to use.

In this chapter, you'll find a thorough explanation of the often-confusing drawing tools used throughout Office. If you're not sure of the difference between an AutoShape and a Clip Art object, or if you can't tell the difference between a drawing canvas and a drawing object, you should read this chapter closely.

In addition, Office 2003 includes one brand-new program that's undeservedly buried under several layers of subfolders on the Start menu. Microsoft Picture Manager enables you to pull together even enormous collections of digital photos. Using its healthy assortment of editing tools, you can crop, resize, compress, and generally tweak those images so they fit perfectly in Office documents.

Office 2003 also includes an assortment of tools and techniques for working with clip art, and it offers you the capability to download additional clip art from the Office Online website. In this chapter, we explain how to use these cool (and often underrated) tools.

USING OFFICE DRAWING TOOLS

5

When you installed Office 2003, it added an assortment of applications designed to help you create, insert, edit, and manage graphics. We'll get to those programs a little later in this chapter. First, we want to tell you about the graphics tools that are built directly into Office. With a few clicks you can insert a prebuilt diagram directly into Word, Outlook, Excel, or PowerPoint; you can take your pick of diagrams chosen from six basic categories, each with many options. With the help of the Drawing toolbar, you can add geometric shapes, lines, arrows, and text boxes to a document, worksheet, or presentation, and then add colors, shadows, and backgrounds to create images with impact. These aren't simple one-dimensional shapes, either—you can stretch, layer, and combine Office *AutoShapes* to create complex flowcharts and diagrams.

WORKING WITH THE DRAWING LAYER

Before you can even hope to harness the power of Office's Drawing tools, you need to come to terms with a fundamental concept: Word, Excel, and PowerPoint documents, as well as formatted (HTML) Outlook e-mail messages, are *layered*.

NOTE

When we use the term *document* in this chapter, we're referring to any Office data file that includes a drawing layer, including formatted (HTML) Outlook e-mail messages, Word documents, Excel worksheets, and PowerPoint presentations.

It's tempting but misleading to think of an Office document as two-dimensional and directly analogous to a piece of paper or a computer screen. Actually, that finished product is only a snapshot of the real document, which consists of multiple layered drawings in addition to the main layer of the document itself; by changing the order, grouping, and arrangement of these drawings and the main layer you can dramatically change a document's appearance.

The main layer is called the *text layer*. The graphic material is in a *drawing layer*, which exists independently of—but can interact with—material in the text layer. Technically, just one drawing layer is present; however, because you can position each object within the drawing layer independently, from front to back—and the text layer can be set at any depth—it's more useful to think of each object as a layer unto itself.

Think of the layered transparencies that have been used for several generations in high school biology classes. As you peel back each layer, a dissected frog appears, with each layer revealing some additional aspect of the frog's anatomy. The drawing layer works like that: Objects in the drawing layer are arranged from top to bottom (called the *Z order*), as if each drawing were on its own sheet, and each drawing can be moved independently toward the top or sent toward the back.

When you begin working with the drawing layer, it helps to visualize a complex document as consisting of many transparencies, each with its own data and properties:

- Because each layer, including the text layer, is transparent, you can see the contents of any one layer through all other layers.
- Although the text layer is normally at the bottom of the stack, with individual drawing objects in front of it, you can also position a drawing object behind the text layer.
- The contents of the text layer can be wrapped around a drawing layer.
- You can reorder and reposition virtually every object in the drawing layer; you can also group drawing items together and treat them as a single object, and then ungroup them to work on each individually.

Virtually all of the text-formatting and data-management capabilities we discuss elsewhere in this book—everything from search-and-replace to master formatting functions—apply only to the text layer. If you enter text in the drawing layer of a long report, it will not appear in the table of contents, nor will the appearance of the drawing layers change if you alter the formatting of your document.

You generally work with the drawing layer through the Drawing toolbar. To display this toolbar, right-click any toolbar or the main menu bar and choose Drawing from the list of available toolbars (see Figure 5.1). (You'll also find a button on the Standard toolbars in Word and Excel that toggles the Drawing toolbar.)

By default, the Drawing toolbar docks itself to the bottom of the document window. As with any toolbar, you can move it to the top or side, or let it float over the window.

Figure 5.1
The starting point for Office Drawing objects is the Drawing toolbar and AutoShapes.

WORKING WITH A DRAWING CANVAS

Frequently you want to treat several drawings as a group so they can be moved or resized together, or so you can be sure that they will always appear on the same page together. That's the reason for the *drawing canvas*, which acts as a frame that forms a boundary between drawing objects and helps hold them together. The drawing canvas appears explicitly only in Word (and in Outlook when using Word as your e-mail editor), although you'll see vestiges of its design when you use drawing objects throughout the other Office applications.

Unless you change the default settings, Word places a drawing canvas in your document whenever you insert a drawing object. Continuing the analogy we used in the preceding section, you can think of the drawing canvas as a transparent sheet that can be cut to almost any size (as long as it is rectangular). You can then position any number of drawing objects on this canvas. You can move and resize individual objects, but when you select the drawing canvas, it handles all of the objects together as a single unit.

If you open a blank Word document (or position the insertion point within text in an existing document) and then select any drawing object from the Drawing toolbar in Word, Word creates a new drawing canvas in your document window and displays the Drawing Canvas toolbar. (You can have more than one drawing canvas in a Word document.)

TIP FROM

You can disable this behavior by choosing Tools, Options and then on the General tab, clear the box marked Automatically Create Drawing Canvas When Inserting AutoShapes.

The corners and edges of a drawing canvas are characterized by a distinctive bold outline (see Figure 5.2). When you click and drag any edge or corner of a drawing canvas, you change the size of the canvas, but the size and position of each drawing on that canvas remains unchanged. When the document is printed, all of the drawings in the canvas will appear on one page.

Figure 5.2
The short, bold corner and edge lines distinguish a drawing canvas.

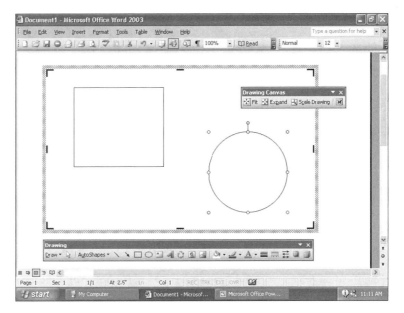

After a drawing canvas is selected, if you insert a drawing object (a picture or AutoShape, for example) into your document, the drawing is placed inside the canvas, where you can move and resize it along with the other objects on that canvas. To remove the drawing from the canvas, click it and drag it to any spot outside the borders of the canvas.

The Drawing Canvas toolbar, which appears whenever a drawing canvas is selected, has the following options:

- **Fit**—Make the canvas as small as possible, without moving any of the drawing objects on the canvas, by moving the borders in until they reach the outside edge of any existing objects on the canvas.

- **Expand**—Increase the size of the canvas in small increments, by adding space around all four edges of the existing canvas.

- **Scale Drawing**—When this option is selected, any resizing of the drawing canvas increases or decreases the size of the drawings on the canvas proportionally.

- **Text Wrapping**—Displays a menu that allows you to control whether (and how tightly) text flows around the canvas. By default, a new drawing canvas is configured to wrap in line with text.

To apply formatting to the drawing canvas (outline, background color, and so on) right-click the border and choose Format Drawing Canvas.

DRAWING SIMPLE SHAPES

Use the Line, Arrow, Rectangle, and Oval buttons on the Drawing toolbar to draw simple geometric shapes.

TIP FROM

EQ & Woody

For many shapes, holding down the Shift key while you drag makes the shape symmetrical. For example, Shift+drag with the rectangle shape to produce a square; use the same technique with the oval shape to draw a perfect circle.

If you routinely create complex shapes that aren't represented on the Drawing toolbar, you can easily customize the Drawing toolbar to include your preferred shapes. For example, to add an octagonal stop sign shape to the Drawing toolbar, do the following:

1. Click the AutoShapes button and choose Basic Shapes.

2. Click and drag the horizontal sizing handle at the top of the Basic Shapes list to tear the list away and create a free-floating Basic Shapes toolbar.

3. Hold down the Ctrl and Alt keys simultaneously, and drag the octagonal "stop sign" icon onto the main part of the Drawing toolbar.

When you no longer want the stop sign on the main Drawing toolbar, hold down the Alt key, and then click and drag the button off the Drawing toolbar.

WORKING WITH AUTOSHAPES

One of the easiest ways to add high-quality graphics to a document is through the use of *AutoShapes*, geometric shapes that form the basis for graphics and charts.

In addition to rectangles, ovals, and other basic shapes, the library of AutoShapes covers most of the important bases in diagramming: flowchart symbols, generic geometric shapes, and display arrows. You can also add *callouts*, balloon-shaped drawing objects that contain text and are typically used to provide information on specific items in a document; for example, you might add a callout to a table or chart within a report to explain the reason for a sudden change in the chart. PowerPoint goes even further, providing Action Buttons—not unlike controls on a form—that can be set to execute commands or macros when clicked.

TIP FROM

EQ & Woody

Put related AutoShapes into a single drawing canvas so you can move or resize all of them simultaneously.

If you're creating a diagram that includes several instances of the same AutoShape, a useful approach is to create one example of the graphic item you need, and then copy that AutoShape to the Clipboard and paste it in position as needed.

TIP FROM

EQ & Woody

When you click the AutoShapes button on the Drawing Toolbar, don't overlook the More AutoShapes entry. That choice takes you to a good-sized collection of shapes in the Insert Clip Art task pane.

Instead of having to eyeball a shape, you can set specific dimensions for it. The best approach is to start by drawing in the rough dimensions of your shape with the mouse, right-click the shape, choose Format AutoShape, and click the Size tab. Options in this dialog box enable you to specify a precise size for the shape.

USING LINES AND ARROWS

After you have your basic shapes down, you'll frequently want lines, dashed lines, and arrows to connect them all, and illustrate the relationships in your charts.

Excel and PowerPoint provide true charting *connectors*—lines that stay connected to preset positions on shapes—for every shape in a document. As you move the shapes, the connectors move with them without requiring you to manually redraw them. Word and Outlook have connectors, too, as long as all the connected shapes sit in the same drawing canvas.

To create a connector, do the following:

1. Draw the shapes you want to connect. In Word (or in Outlook when using Word as your e-mail editor), make sure all of the shapes are in the same drawing canvas.

2. On the Drawing toolbar, choose AutoShapes, Connectors. Pick the type of connector you want to use—straight, elbow, or curved, with or without arrows.

3. Move the mouse pointer over one of the shapes you want to connect. The pointer turns into a square with four radiating lines and the predefined connection points for the shape appear as colored dots on the perimeter of the shape. Click the starting point for your connector.

4. Repeat the previous step at the desired connector point on the shape where you want the connector to end.

To change a connection point, click the connector, and then click and drag one of the red connection boxes at the beginning or end of the connector. Move it over the shape until you see the colored dots that indicate automatic connection points, and then pick one of those points to snap the connector into position.

If you've moved an AutoShape so that its connectors are on the incorrect side of the shape, let Office make a more logical connection for you; right-click the connector and choose Reroute Connector. (This option is only available when Office determines that your connections are incorrect.)

In addition to the connector capability, Excel and PowerPoint also include *snap* and *grid* settings—crucial tools for placing lines and other shapes. Word offers similar capabilities, although they are implemented differently.

5

When you use the drawing layer, you can take advantage of a hidden layout grid. By default, drawing objects align to this grid. Although it's usually a helpful shortcut, this *Snap To Grid* feature can be a problem when you're drawing a line manually. Because the edges of shapes are tied to grid positions, they might not line up visually with other shapes that are arranged in slightly different positions on the grid. The fix is to *snap objects to other objects* (in Excel it's called *Snap To Shape*) so, for example, the end point of a line connecting two shapes ends up at a reasonable point on each shape.

NOTE

> The ability to snap objects to other objects is off by default in Word and PowerPoint, but Snap to Shape is enabled in Excel.

To set the Snap to Grid and Snap to Shape values in Excel, choose Draw from the Drawing toolbar, and then Snap, and toggle the To Grid or To Shape settings.

To set the Snap to Grid and Snap to Shape values in Word (and to perform other tasks, such as making the grid visible or resetting the grid), choose Draw from the Drawing toolbar, and then choose Grid. In Word, you'll see the Drawing Grid dialog box shown in Figure 5.3.

Figure 5.3
Normally, the grid is hidden in Office applications; make it visible in Word, and then "snap" drawing objects to the grid for precise alignment.

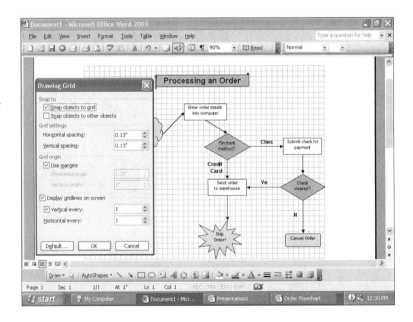

To set these options in PowerPoint, click Grid And Guides from the Draw menu on the Drawing toolbar. The options in PowerPoint are more limited than those in Word, but the basic functions are similar. Select the Snap Objects to Grid and Snap Objects to Other Objects check boxes.

NOTE

> Don't be confused by the terminology. In this case, a "shape" in Excel is identical to an "object" in Word and PowerPoint.

It's possible to move one or more objects in very fine increments without completely disabling the grid. Hold down the Alt key as you drag the object, and it moves freely rather than following the grid. You can also use the keyboard to move objects. Normally, when you select one or more objects and press any arrow key, the selection moves to the next point on the grid. If you make a selection and then hold down the Ctrl key while pressing any arrow, the selection moves in much finer increments.

CHANGING BACKGROUND COLORS AND LINE FORMATS

Using the Office drawing tools, you can draw shapes and lines galore, but they won't look right unless you can make them blend in with your document.

AutoShape backgrounds can have their own colors. (A background color is called a "fill" color.) By default, the fill color is white—rarely a good choice because it obscures everything underneath the AutoShape.

Color backgrounds can come in handy if you're working with a color medium—color printer, onscreen documents, or web pages. But the same technology that makes background color inviting can also jump up and bite you: Unless you choose high-contrast color combinations to differentiate text from background, your message can be lost completely. Remember that PC monitors in particular are notorious for not reproducing colors accurately. A color scheme that you carefully craft to look good on one monitor can morph into an illegible splotch on another.

In addition to the fill color, all AutoShapes have borders around the outer edge. You can adjust the border width, style (dashed lines, for example), color, and size. In many cases, the border is superfluous and detracts from the appearance of your document; don't hesitate to get rid of it.

To edit an AutoShape or line, follow these steps:

1. Select one or more of the shapes or lines in the drawing layer.
2. Right-click and choose Format AutoShape. In the Format AutoShape dialog box, click the Colors and Lines tab (see Figure 5.4).
3. Adjust the fill color, lines, and arrows per the dialog box. If you want to be able to see through the shape, make sure you change the Color setting to No Fill, or adjust the Transparency slider to a value greater than 0%. The higher the value set here, the clearer the object underneath it will appear. At 70% Transparency, for example, black text beneath a drawing will appear as fuzzy gray but quite readable.

Figure 5.4
Use the Format
AutoShape dialog box
to add colors and
change the appear-
ance of lines and
borders.

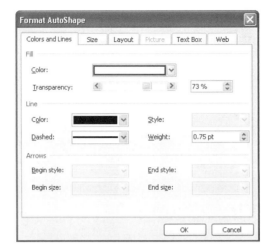

> After you adjust formatting settings—fill color, line size, arrow types, and so on—you can
> configure Office to use those settings for all new shapes in the current document. Right-
> click the object and choose Set AutoShape Defaults.

ADDING SHADOWS AND 3D EFFECTS

3D effects rarely add to, and frequently detract from, the effectiveness of a document.
Before you consider using a 3D effect, ask yourself—repeatedly—whether the inherently 2D
medium you're working with will be able to properly convey that third dimension. The
answer is usually no.

Shadows, on the other hand, if applied consistently and with attention to detail, can add
depth to a document without detracting from the main story.

To apply Shadow or 3D effects, follow these steps:

1. Click once on the shape you want to modify, or Ctrl+click to select several.
2. Click the Shadow Style or 3D Style button on the Drawing toolbar.
3. A tear-off menu of effects opens up. Click the effect you want, and Office transforms
   the selected shapes.

In addition to the choice of effects, each menu also includes a Settings button for fine-
tuning the effects. For example, you can change the depth and "lighting" of a 3D object, or
the extent and placement of the shadow.

> A few effects go a long way. A chart is not abstract art; if you use a red 3D rectangle for
> one particular item, then similar items also should be red 3D rectangles.

Adding Text to a Drawing

In some drawings, you will want to put text inside your AutoShapes—to identify the steps in a flowchart, for example, or the decision points in a decision matrix. All the AutoShapes (except lines) can be converted to text boxes, if you know the trick.

One particularly effective way to draw your attention to specific locations in a picture is to use callouts. (In this book, for example, we sometimes use callouts to identify screen elements in figures.) In Office parlance, a callout is a text box with a line attached to it. You can move, resize, and format the text box, line, and connector independently. Several of the built-in Office callouts look like dialog balloons, similar to those you see in a comic strip. Here's how to use them:

1. On the Drawing toolbar, open the AutoShapes menu and click Callouts. From the tear-off Callouts menu, choose the callout type you want—in this case, the Cloud Callout choice in the upper-right corner.

2. Click in the drawing layer where you want the callout to originate from, and then drag to form the rest of the callout.

3. Immediately begin typing; the text you type appears in the callout.

4. Right-click the callout and set its formatting. In the example in Figure 5.5, we set the balloon to have a light yellow fill, retained the border line, and then adjusted the size of the balloon to match the text.

Figure 5.5
AutoShape callouts come in many different forms. This one looks like a thought balloon from a comic strip.

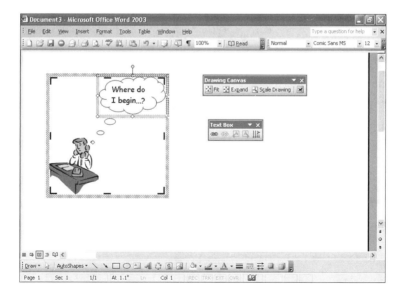

TIP FROM

Don't worry about getting the text or formatting in a callout perfect the first time. To change text in a callout, click once in the callout text, and then add, delete, or edit the text. To change formatting in a callout, select the text, right-click, and choose an option from the shortcut menu.

ALIGNING AND GROUPING GRAPHIC ELEMENTS

Depending on the naked eye to center shapes in a drawing isn't always reliable. Office has built-in drawing tools with the capability to bring symmetry out of chaos. When *aligning* objects, the key is to do it one step at a time, carefully planning out what you need to do to redistribute or align them, and in which order.

If you have four objects on the drawing layer above an Excel worksheet and you want to organize them as shown in Figure 5.6, follow these steps:

Figure 5.6
Use the Drawing toolbar's alignment tools to make your graphics line up.

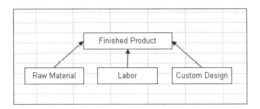

1. Select the bottom three rectangles by holding down the Shift key as you click each one.
2. To evenly space the three shapes, click the Drawing toolbar's Draw menu, and then choose Align or Distribute, Distribute Horizontally.
3. To line up the three shapes, click Draw, Align or Distribute, Align Top.
4. Now align the top rectangle with the middle one. Select both shapes, and then choose Draw, Align or Distribute, Align Center.

After you have properly formatted, connected, aligned, and distributed all your AutoShapes, you can take one more step to *group* them all into a single graphic object. This step is crucial; it enables you to preserve the relationships between objects and it helps prevent the chance that you'll accidentally move or resize a shape.

Select all the elements you want to group, and then choose Draw, Group.

TIP FROM

E&Woody

> When you're creating complex drawings that consist of several AutoShapes, it's easy to leave one out accidentally. After selecting multiple items for grouping, it's always a good practice to drag the collection left and right just a little; you can see whether any odd pieces are hiding behind other shapes. If you missed one, press Ctrl+Z to undo the move, and regroup.

The individual elements in a group can't be edited independently. For example, if you have a text box in a group, you won't be able to change the text in the box as long as it remains grouped.

If you find you need to make a revision, you can ungroup, make your edits, and then regroup. To ungroup a composite graphic, select the graphic, and then choose Draw, Ungroup.

WRAPPING, LAYOUT, AND STACKING

Graphics don't always appear where you want them—at least not without a bit of persuading. When you insert a complex graphic into a Word document, for instance, the graphic shoves the text in your report out of the way. In this case, you may prefer to *wrap* the text around a drawing object.

The solution? Use layout options (which are available only in Word) to adjust the placement of graphics relative to the text layer. Right-click the graphic object (or the drawing canvas, if all your drawing objects are enclosed in a drawing canvas) and choose the Format option (Format AutoShape or Format Drawing Canvas, for instance). In the Format dialog box, choose the Layout tab.

- To lay out your graphic so that it appears as a background to the document, choose Behind Text or In Front of Text. When using this option, use only very light-colored graphic objects; otherwise, the graphic will overwhelm the text on the page and make it unreadable.

- Use the standard Square method to wrap text around the rectangular borders of the graphic. This option is most appropriate when the graphic has a defined border.

- Use Tight wrapping if the graphic object or drawing layer does not have a border. With this option selected, Word ignores the empty spaces of the graphic and wraps the text snugly up to the drawing elements themselves.

In Word, Excel, and PowerPoint, you can also change the order of objects so that one is in front of another. By default, when you create or position a graphic object so that it overlaps another graphic object (including a drawing canvas), the new element appears on top of the old one. To change the front-to-back ordering, right-click the graphic element or drawing canvas you want to move, and choose Order. At that point, you can

- Float the graphic all the way to the top (Word calls it Bring to Front) or sink it all the way to the bottom (Send to Back).

- Bring the graphic up one level (Bring Forward) or push it down one level (Send Backward).

- Move the graphic so it's on top of the text layer (Bring in Front of Text), or place it behind the text layer (Send Behind Text). These options are not available in Excel or PowerPoint.

When should you use each wrapping option? The simplest rule of thumb is this: If you want to turn a single graphic into a background or an overlay for a Word document, use the Layout tab. If you have multiple graphic elements or drawing canvases you want to arrange in the document, go with the Order tools.

TIP FROM

> Adjusting the order also enables you to create sophisticated effects interweaving the text and graphics. For example, you can use Word's Bring in Front of Text layout option to place a group graphic on top of the text, and then ungroup and move some elements of it under the text.

ADDING PICTURES TO OFFICE DOCUMENTS

Clip art has its place, especially in presentations and informal documents, where you want to make your audience laugh or just provide some visual relief. But certain types of reports require realistic graphics such as photographs or image files produced by professional graphic artists. A report for an art history class might benefit from photographs of paintings or sculptures, with enlarged detail sections for sections that discuss specific details. For a geography or history paper, you might include maps or photographs that help the reader visualize the locations under discussion.

Pictures can be useful outside the classroom as well. When you submit a claim to your insurance company, for example, your letter will have a lot more impact if you embed digital pictures of the damage. And your annual holiday letter will be much more interesting if you can show, not just tell, what's been going on with your family throughout the year.

Office can read any graphics file format for which it has "filters," the software that converts the graphic format into data usable inside the Office application. Windows XP includes support for the Windows Bitmap (*.bmp), Windows Metafile (*.wmf), and Tagged Image File Format (*.tif, *.tiff) formats. A default installation of Office 2003 adds filters for the following widely used formats:

- Encapsulated PostScript (*.eps)
- WordPerfect Graphics (*.wpg)
- Portable Network Graphics (*.png)
- Macintosh Graphics (*.pict)
- Graphics Interchange Format (*.gif)
- Joint Photographics Expert Group (*.jpg, *.jpeg)
- Computer Graphics Metafile (*.cgm)
- CorelDRAW (*.cdr)
- Kodak PhotoCD (*.pcd)

Filters for the last three formats in the preceding list are available for use by Office programs but are not actually installed until first use.

To add graphic files to Office documents, choose Insert, Picture, From File. Browse to the folder that contains the picture, select the filename, and click Insert. By default, Office programs insert a copy of the selected picture directly in the document as an inline object. You can change this default setting so that pictures are automatically inserted as floating objects; to do so, choose Tools, Options, click the View tab, and use the drop-down Insert/Paste Pictures As list to select a different layout setting than the default In Line with Text.

CHOOSING EMBEDDING OR LINKING

When you place a picture file into an Office document, it automatically goes in the text layer, not the drawing layer. As Figure 5.7 shows, Word gives you three choices; PowerPoint offers only the Insert and Link to File options; Excel includes only the Insert option.

Figure 5.7
Word lets you Insert, Link to File, or Insert and Link a picture in a file.

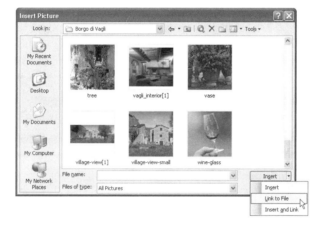

- **Insert**—This choice *embeds* the picture, physically placing it in the document. This is the default option in all Office programs. If you aren't overly worried about file sizes, don't need any history telling you where the picture came from, and don't care whether the picture gets updated, this is your best choice.

- **Link to File**—This choice puts a pointer to the picture at the place in the document where you want the picture to appear. The picture itself is not stored in the document. Instead, it's brought in as needed to display on the screen, or print on the printer. If there's a chance the picture will be changed, and your document *must* reflect those changes, this is your only option.

- **Insert and Link**—This hybrid option is available only in Word (and in Outlook messages created using Word as an e-mail editor). It puts a copy of the picture in the document, but maintains a link as well. When the picture is needed, Office first looks for the linked file. If the picture file is unavailable, it reverts to the copy stored in the document. This option is especially useful for business documents stored on portable computers, because it ensures that graphics will be available when you are away from the office and your network, while still allowing the option to update the image when you reconnect to the network.

5

Office frequently uses fully qualified filenames as the links, which can cause problems if you move either the picture file or the document. If you link the picture %userprofile%\My Documents\My Pictures\Corplogo.jpg in a document and then send the document as an e-mail attachment, the picture must be located in the exact same folder hierarchy or Office won't be able to find it, and will substitute a meaningless placeholder (see Figure 5.8).

Figure 5.8
The dreaded "missing link" placeholder graphic. If you see this placeholder, it means Office couldn't find the picture.

When should you embed graphics and when should you link? Follow these guidelines:

- If you repeatedly use the same graphic in printed documents—for example, a letterhead logo—link to it and make sure it doesn't move. This helps reduce the size of all your saved documents.

- If you're connected to a network or using Office on a computer that is shared by several members of your family, linking works if the graphic is in the Shared Documents folder or in a *shared network folder* that's accessible to everyone who wants to use the document. If you don't have ready access to the shared folder, insert the graphic.

- If you plan to distribute documents externally, either as e-mail attachments or on a CD or other media, you must insert the graphics. (Documents you save on a CD will show linked graphics if you save all the files in the same folder as the document, but the links will be broken as soon as the document is copied to another location.)

 If you discover broken image links in your document, see "Fixing Broken Image Links" in the "Troubleshooting" section at the end of this chapter.

WORKING WITH SCANNED IMAGES

Word, Excel, and PowerPoint directly support scanners and digital cameras that include Windows Driver Model (WDM) drivers. This option does not require any separate image-editing software.

To scan a picture directly into an Office document, choose Insert, Picture, From Scanner or Camera. The dialog box you see next varies, depending on the capabilities of your input source. Typically, you can choose the image type and resolution; some software also lets you choose the image size.

TIP FROM

Ed & Woody

> The scanning capability, in combination with Office's graphics layer, provides a solution to a relatively new problem: How do you type up a printed form when you don't have a typewriter anymore? The answer: Scan the form into a Word document, and then insert it as a picture in the document header. Crop and resize the image as needed, and format the picture layout as Behind Text. Exit from the header, and you can type over the form.
>
> Alternatively, scan the form and place the image in the main text layer. Crop and resize as needed, and then format the graphic object by using the Behind Text option. Add a text box on top of each field in the form; use the ordering options to place this layer in front of the form and make the box semitransparent.

➔ For instructions on how to translate scanned documents into editable Word documents, **see** "Converting Scanned Documents to Text," **p. 95**.

VIEWING, EDITING, AND MANAGING PICTURES

Digital pictures usually need a bit of manipulation—and sometimes major surgery—before they fit properly into a document. For most tasks, you can use the internal image-editing tools that are installed along with Office 2003. Using buttons on the Picture toolbar, you can crop, compress, lighten, darken, rotate, and colorize digital images. When you do this sort of manipulation, the original image file remains untouched; your changes affect only the image included in the Office file.

If you have a full-featured image editing program, you can use it to manipulate pictures, save the results, and then insert the edited image files into your documents. If you don't have a favorite image editing program (or if you're unhappy with the one you're using), take a look at Microsoft Picture Manager. This standalone program, which is included with Office, lets you organize collections of image files from local hard disks and shared network folders, including pictures you take with a digital camera as well as those you save from websites. You can perform most of the same image editing and compression tasks as you can with the built-in Office tools, and then some. On images afflicted with red eye, for instance, you can get the red out with one click. You can also convert images to alternative formats (from the space-hogging Bitmap format to the more efficient JPEG or GIF format, for instance), a trick that is impossible with the built-in Office tools.

To open Picture Manager, click Start, All Programs; then click Microsoft Office, Microsoft Office Tools, and finally click the Microsoft Office Picture Manager shortcut. The Picture Manager main window is divided into three parts, as shown in Figure 5.9:

- **Picture Shortcuts pane**—Gather shortcuts to folders that contain pictures in this pane. Your pictures remain in their original location. By default, the list includes the My Pictures folder and any folders you browse for pictures. Click the Add Picture Shortcut link to manually add a shortcut to the list; choose File, Locate Pictures to search for picture files in other folders on your computer or on shared network folders.

5

- **Preview pane**—View pictures in this center pane. Use the Preview toolbar at the top of the pane to switch between thumbnails, filmstrip, and individual picture views. Use the Zoom slider to make the image appear larger or smaller.

- **Edit pane**—Editing tools appear in this pane, including compression options, red-eye reduction, and cropping tools.

Figure 5.9
Image shortcuts appear in the left pane, with image editing tools in the task pane on the right.

CAUTION

Watch out for one interface "gotcha" in Picture Manager's Picture Shortcuts pane. Yes, it's true that every folder listed here is a shortcut to an external location. However, if you right-click the shortcut and choose Delete Folder, the program really does delete the underlying folder and all of the files in it, not just the shortcut! To get rid of a shortcut in this pane, right-click and choose Remove Shortcut.

When you use Picture Manager to make any changes to image files, the resulting changed files appear in the Unsaved Edits folder at the bottom of the Picture Shortcuts pane. For instructions on how to save those changed files, see "Editing Image Files," later in this chapter.

TIP FROM

The first time you run Picture Manager, it displays a dialog box that allows you to specify which image formats it should open automatically. If you want to change these settings later, choose Tools, File Types, and select or clear the check boxes for the formats you want to use.

RESIZING AND CROPPING PICTURES

When you insert a picture into a document, it appears full size. If the picture file is six inches wide, that's what you'll see in your document. More often than not, you'll need to make some adjustments to fit the picture to the document. You can *crop* the picture—that is, cut away portions of the image to show only the parts you want to see in your document. Or you can *resize* the picture, leaving the image intact but changing its height and width (and thus the number of pixels it occupies). You can also combine the two operations, cropping to the correct proportions and resizing to fit the page. (Although you can expand a small image to fit a larger space, the more typical task in Office documents is to shrink large digital images to a manageable file size.)

You have two choices:

- Make a copy of your original picture and then crop or resize it using Picture Manager or another photo editor. If you use the photo editor to adjust the image to the exact size and shape you need, you can import it into your document without requiring any additional work.

- If you want your original picture to remain the same, or if you're still designing your document and you think you may want to do additional cropping or resizing, use the built-in Office tools.

To crop an image within an Office document, first select the image, and then click the Crop button on the Picture toolbar. The mouse pointer changes to match the icon on the Crop button. To begin cutting away portions of the picture, point to any of the eight cropping points, one on each corner of the image and one in the center of each side; then click and drag toward the center of the image. Hold down the Ctrl key and drag the handles in the center of any side to crop identical amounts from the top and bottom or left and right; to maintain the exact same *aspect ratio* and crop equal amounts from all sizes, hold down the Ctrl key and drag any of the corner handles in.

TIP FROM

Ed & Woody

> In Word, you can avoid some sizing hassles by drawing a text box where you want to place the graphic and then inserting the graphic into the text box. The graphic is resized automatically. If the picture is already in the document, click it once, and then click the Text Box button on the Drawing toolbar to surround the image with a box.

If you make a mistake while cropping, click the Reset Picture button on the Picture toolbar and start over.

Buttons on the Picture toolbar also allow you to make a few adjustments in picture quality: contrast, brightness, color, and the like. Again, any changes you make here affect only the picture in the document, not the original source file.

5

EDITING IMAGE FILES

If you want to start a raging debate, gather a bunch of graphics professionals in one place and ask them to name their favorite image-editing program. Then duck. Web designers and desktop publishers are typically passionate about their editing tools, and you'll probably get an earful.

The Picture Manager utility can't compete with professional-strength editing packages. However, its collection of features matches those found in many freeware and shareware image-management programs. If you're already experienced with one of these tools, you should at least look at Picture Manager and decide whether you want to make the switch.

To use Picture Manager's editing tools, first select one or more images, and then click the Edit Pictures button to open the task pane shown in Figure 5.10.

Figure 5.10
Click any of the editing options shown here to open a new task pane with specialized tools for that task.

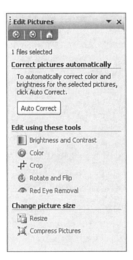

The Auto Correct button adjusts brightness, contrast, and color automatically. For images that appear washed out or dull, you should always try this option first (if the results are unsatisfactory, press Ctrl+Z to undo the changes and start over). Use any of the following editing tools to alter specific parts of an image:

- **Brightness and Contrast**—Use this feature to correct pictures that appear too light or too dark. Try the Auto Brightness button first; then adjust manually.

- **Color**—Click to adjust the hue and saturation of the image. This option is useful for "punching up" dull pictures or fixing images where poor lighting caused unnatural tints.

- **Crop**—Remove extraneous portions of an image. You can crop out unnecessary elements or choose from the drop-down Aspect Ratio list to select a specific size—3×5, for instance. This option is not available when multiple images are selected.

- **Rotate and Flip**—Change an image from landscape to portrait orientation, and vice versa, or use the By Degree control to fix a scanned image that's slightly crooked or a digital photo that's askew.

- **Red Eye Removal**—This feature allows you to remove those ghostly red dots caused by your camera's flash. This option is available only when a single image is selected.

- **Resize**—Change the dimensions of a picture without cropping out any information, by choosing a predefined or custom height and width or selecting a percentage of the original size. This feature is most useful for reducing file size for images you plan to use in e-mail messages or on web pages.

As you edit images, Picture Manager keeps track of the changes you make. Click the Unsaved Edits icon in the Picture Shortcuts page to see any changes you have not yet saved. If you close Picture Manager, you'll be given the chance to save your changes, discard the changes, or cancel. Be careful! Choosing Save Changes will overwrite the original images; if you don't have backup copies, those originals will be gone for good.

When in doubt, open the Unsaved Edits folder and review your changes. Then click the File menu and choose any of the following options:

- **Save**—Accept the changes for a selected image or images and overwrite the original file.

- **Save As**—Specify a new name or location for the changed file. This option is available only when a single image is selected.

- **Save All**—Accept changes for all images and overwrite the original files. This operation cannot be undone.

- **Export**—Offers a wide range of options using the Export task pane (see Figure 5.11). You can change the name, location, file format, and size of one or more files.

Figure 5.11
The Export option offers the most options for saving images you edit with Picture Manager.

Picture Manager offers one especially elegant way to add a consistent naming strategy to a disorganized folder made up of image files gathered from many different sources. Add the folder to the Picture Shortcuts pane and press Ctrl+A to select all images in the folder. Then click the Rename Pictures link in the Getting Started task pane. Choose from the impressive array of options for using names and numbers to bring order out of chaos. This option is also available when you click Rename Pictures in the Export task pane.

COMPRESSING GRAPHICS FOR WEB PAGES AND PRESENTATIONS

Unless you're going to print a graphic on a high-resolution printer—in which case you can probably use all the detail you can get—chances are good that you will want to squeeze down the size of external graphic files for use in Office documents. This is especially true with images that were originally captured with high-resolution digital cameras in uncompressed format, where file sizes can be 3MB or more.

To cut image files down to size outside of Office, use the Compress Pictures button in Picture Manager. To shrink a photo or graphic image that is already inserted in an Office document, use Office's built-in Compress feature. Although this option does remove data from the selected image, the practical effect is rarely noticeable and the reduction in document size can be profound. To compress a graphic in Word, Excel, or PowerPoint, follow these steps:

1. Click to select the graphic object.

2. Right-click and choose Format Picture.

3. On the Picture tab, click the Compress... button. The Compress Pictures dialog box appears (see Figure 5.12).

Figure 5.12
Office includes built-in tools to shrink the size of embedded graphics, thus reducing the size of a document or presentation.

4. Choose from Web/Screen resolution (at a nominal 96 dots per inch, which is fine for most monitors); Print (nominal 200 dots per inch, which will produce a fuzzy but legible picture). Select No Change if you have used the built-in Office tools to crop

portions of a picture and you want to delete the cropped data without affecting the resolution of what remains visible. Be sure to select the Delete Cropped Areas of Pictures check box.

5. Click OK.

USING ADVANCED PICTURE EFFECTS

Inserted graphics can be grouped, ordered, wrapped, layered, and given colored backgrounds, borders, and 3D or shadow effects, just like other Office graphics. They can also be placed inside a drawing canvas. Note that in Word, assigning layout formatting to a linked graphic breaks the link.

AutoShape 3D effects are not available for pictures (both clip art and imported files) when they are in the text layer, but a limited number of shadow effects are. The full complement of effects is available if you put a text box around the picture. This enables you to frame your art in a way that can spell the difference between a document that looks routine and one that looks like it was created by a professional graphic artist.

One popular professional graphics effect in Excel involves replacing colored or textured bars, wedges, and other chart components with pictures. Open the workbook that contains the chart you want to work with, and follow these steps:

1. Right-click the chart object where you want to use a picture (a data series in a column chart, for example) and choose the appropriate Format option—Format Data Series, in this example.

2. Click the Patterns tab, and then click the Fill Effects button. On the Fill Effects dialog box, choose the Pictures tab.

3. Click the button marked Select Picture, and choose the picture you want to use.

4. If you want the picture to be distorted so a single image fits on the chart object, click Stretch. If you want pictures to be placed one on top of the other, choose the Stack option. Click OK twice to place the picture on the chart object.

5

This technique works best with graphic images that have been carefully sized for the chart in question. Use Picture Manager or another image-editing program to crop and resize the image to the exact proportions you'll need. If you use a photo of a person or place in an Excel chart, the results will typically be unsatisfactory and often ludicrous.

CREATING GRAPHICS FROM TEXT

In addition to pure graphics, Office programs also include features you can use to turn text into graphics. The result can add personality and visual interest to documents without requiring more than a modicum of artistic talent on your part.

USING TEXT BOXES TO CREATE PULL QUOTES

One well-known technique for livening up text is to throw in a *pull quote*—a usually provocative excerpt from the text that is enclosed in a box and formatted with large type. Newspaper editors and magazine designers use pull quotes as visual cues to "draw in" readers who are casually flipping through the pages looking at headlines and pictures without reading the body text. Word has an exceptionally cool technique to create pull quotes:

1. Select the text excerpt you want to use. Press Ctrl+C to copy it, and then paste a copy in the general location where you want to create the pull quote.

2. Select the copied text and click the Text Box button on the Drawing toolbar. Word immediately creates a text box containing the selected text (see Figure 5.13).

Figure 5.13
Word can create an instant "pull quote" by using a text box in the drawing layer.

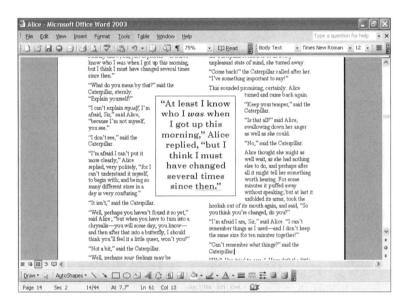

3. Select the text within the text box and adjust its font, alignment, and other formatting.

4. Format the text box, resize, and move it to your desired location.

Text boxes can be used to put free-standing text of any kind in your document. The device works for a short sidebar; for example, to highlight a point, you can use the method described in the preceding section to combine a text box with an AutoShape.

The term *text box* is a bit misleading, at least in Word. More accurately, this drawing object is a subdocument that appears in the drawing layer over (or under) the text layer of the document. In Word, you can insert a picture into a document, select the picture, and then insert a text box, which has the practical effect of enclosing the picture completely within the text box. You can then add text or other graphics to the "text box." In Excel and PowerPoint, however, a text box can contain only text (although you can group text boxes with other shapes).

TIP FROM

> If you want to make it easy to move and position a picture on a Word document or PowerPoint slide, insert the picture into a text box. Move the text box, and the picture goes along for the ride.

USING WORDART FOR LOGOS

WordArt is an Office program you can use to manipulate TrueType fonts and save the result as a graphic image. The resulting picture can be dropped into the drawing layer of documents, charts, or slides. Don't let the name fool you into thinking this utility is just for Word—the WordArt program is available in Excel and PowerPoint, too.

For the small business without a graphic arts department, WordArt can form the basis of a simple logo. You can take advantage of WordArt's capabilities to lay text out vertically, curve it, and add 3D effects.

To create a WordArt picture in an open document, worksheet, or presentation, follow these steps:

1. Click the Insert WordArt icon on the Drawing toolbar, or click Insert, Picture, WordArt. Office responds with the WordArt Gallery shown in Figure 5.14.

Figure 5.14
WordArt makes for attention-getting text effects or easy logos.

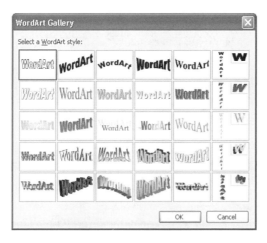

2. Choose the basic style of WordArt you want to construct, and then click OK.
3. In the Edit WordArt Text dialog box, type the text you want to use as WordArt; select the font, font size, and treatment (bold or italic), and click OK.

TIP FROM

> WordArt uses only TrueType fonts, meaning that your PostScript fonts can't be used as WordArt. Start with a simple font, such as a basic serif font. Decorative fonts generally produce horrible WordArt.

4. After the WordArt object appears in the drawing layer, click and drag any of the sizing handles to change its appearance, or use the Free Rotate icon on the Drawing toolbar to slant the WordArt object up or down.

The WordArt toolbar includes a large collection of shapes under the WordArt Shapes button that you can use to further bend, stretch, and modify existing pieces of WordArt. Additional buttons enable you to move and size text and adjust character spacing. A shortcut also exists for wrapping text around the WordArt. If the WordArt toolbar isn't visible, right-click any toolbar or the main menu bar and choose WordArt from the list of available toolbars.

USING CLIP ART

Clip art—reusable drawings, photos, and the like—derives its name from the not-so-distant past, when designers actually clipped images from books and pasted them onto layout boards to produce master images for printed documents. The electronic versions of these tools are easier to use, but the effect is the same: to enliven an informal document. Much depends on the audience you want to reach and the effect you want to achieve.

A dynamite piece of clip art can tell a story worth a thousand words. A really poor piece of clip art hinders communication, leaving people scratching their heads and wondering "What's *that* all about?"

Gratuitous clip art—that is, clip art that doesn't relate to the topic at hand or otherwise impedes the flow of your documents—distracts your audience and often detracts from the point you're trying to make.

In Office 2003, the clip art collection is accessible through its own task pane. The built-in clip art collection includes more than 1,600 graphic images, bullets, lines, and a few media files. The Clip Art task pane is tightly connected to the Office Online Clip Art and Media page, where you can download thousands of additional images, sounds, video clips, animated graphics, and the like. The result is organized in a fully indexed and searchable graphics database, sorted into collections, categorized by keywords, and eminently customizable.

At its simplest, you can search for relevant images by category or keyword. From any Office program, choose Insert, Picture, Clip Art to open the Insert Clip Art task pane. Then proceed in this order:

1. Click the drop-down arrow to the right of the Search In box to display the list of available collections.

2. Select or clear check boxes to choose the collections you want to search. This list includes three main groups:
   - **My Collections**—This group consists of clips you've added to your personal collection. In a default Office installation, it is empty.

5

- **Office Collections**—These are the files installed on your hard disk with the initial Office setup, plus any files you've added from the Office Online site.

- **Web Collections**—This group consists of content available from the Microsoft Office Online website.

Click a top-level collection to clear all existing check marks and then select only the specific categories you want.

3. In the Results Should Be box, choose the media type you're looking for (see Figure 5.15). Click the plus sign to the left of each category heading to display the full list of options and narrow your search to very specific types of media (for example, photographs in JPEG format and clip art in Windows Metafile format).

4. Type keywords in the Search For box, and click Go.

Figure 5.15
To keep from being overwhelmed with results, select the specific types of clip art files you're looking for.

The results of your search appear in the scrolling pane at the bottom of the Clip Art task pane. If one of the images meets your needs, click to insert it in the current document, worksheet, or presentation. To see additional choices, click the drop-down arrow at the right side of every clip. You can copy an item to the Clipboard for use in another program, for example, or make it available offline in one of your personal collections. You can also preview the clip in a larger window that shows additional properties, as shown in Figure 5.16.

The keywords and other saved details for clips that are part of Office clip art collections, whether they're stored locally or pulled from the Web, are not available for editing. In clips that are stored in your personal collections, however, you're free to customize the built-in keywords and captions. To set your own keywords for a particular clip, follow these steps:

1. Right-click the clip and choose Edit Keywords. The Keywords dialog box opens (see Figure 5.17).

2. In the Caption box, type a descriptive name for the clip. The caption can be virtually any length, and may include punctuation marks and other special symbols. The caption text will appear as a ScreenTip when you hover the mouse pointer over the clip in the task pane.

3. In the Keywords for Current Clip box, add or remove keywords for the particular clip.

Figure 5.16
To see a larger view of search results, open this dialog box. Scroll through all search results by using the left and right arrows beneath the large preview.

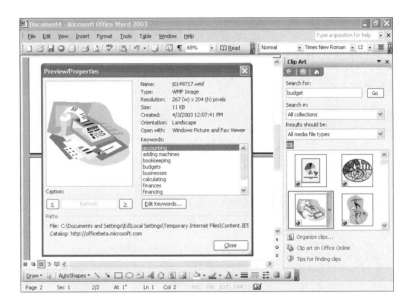

Figure 5.17
Add your own keywords and descriptive captions for clips in your collections.

CAUTION

Office helps you maintain consistency in your keywords by use of the drop-down list. If you're careful to use uniform keywords, your efforts will pay off later with more effective searches.

You can also add photographs and graphic images from files on an individual computer or on the company network to your personal collection, with the option to move or copy a graphic onto your computer or link the item in the collection to the original file location. If you regularly produce graphics-intensive documents using a library of images you've drawn from many sources, you may find it useful to make those images available in the Clip Art pane.

To open the Clip Organizer, click Organize Clips… at the bottom of the Insert Clip Art task pane. You can also open the Clip Organizer on its own, without having to go through the Clip Art task pane—its shortcut is in the Microsoft Office Tools group on the All Programs menu. Then choose File, Add Clips to Organizer. You can have the Clip Organizer automatically scan your disk for compatible files, or click the On My Own option to specify a location from which you want to import graphics files.

The Clip Organizer is also the ideal way to add files from the Office Online collections. Click the Clips Online button to visit the website and select clips you want to download. The Office Online site installs an ActiveX control that makes it easy to import new clips, which show up in the Downloaded Clips category (see Figure 5.18).

Figure 5.18
Clips you download from Office Online show up in your Personal Collection.

Images you download from Office Online go into the Microsoft Clip Organizer subfolder in your My Pictures folder. The index to your personal collection is stored in a Media Catalog file (with the extension *.mcg) in the `%appdata%\Microsoft\Clip Organizer` folder.

CREATING AND EDITING CHARTS AND DIAGRAMS

In addition to the picture-editing and drawing tools we've discussed so far in this chapter, Office includes a handful of generic charting and diagramming tools. They're useful when you need to knock out a quick chart in a standard format, but don't expect highly polished results.

SIMPLE CHARTS

The least impressive member of Office's portfolio of graphics tools is Microsoft Chart. You can access this venerable utility in Word and PowerPoint by choosing Insert, Picture, Chart. It also appears automatically when you create PowerPoint slides with chart placeholders.

The number one bit of guidance to give you on Chart is: If you have more than just a few numbers, don't use it. Chart is a leftover from the days before Microsoft Office, when customers typically purchased a standalone copy of Word or PowerPoint. It was available so you could pretend you were incorporating Excel material in your documents.

Because you use Office, of course, you *do* have Excel, and there is nothing Chart can do that can't be done much more easily and with vastly more impressive results in Excel. If you do give Chart a try, you'll see that it starts out with a prefab chart and datasheet. Add your own data, select the chart type, and choose File, Update to insert the chart into your document.

It is just as easy to click Insert, Object, select Microsoft Excel Chart from the pull-down list, and insert a real chart into Word or PowerPoint. You'll get the same model chart to adapt to your needs as with the limited charting module, but you'll have the full power of Excel at your command.

ORGANIZATION CHARTS

It's physically possible to put together organizational charts with AutoShapes. Drawing charts this way is exhaustingly tedious, but if you're persistent and patient, the results can be aesthetically pleasing.

TIP FROM

Ed & Woody

> Although the objects and terminology in the Organization Chart program assume you're creating a chart for a business, you can use this program for other tasks, including family trees, assignment sheets for volunteer organizations, and any sort of chart that suggests the evolution of something—including ideas, schools of philosophy, and even musical genres. Use your imagination!

A much easier alternative is to use the Organization Chart program included with Office. To use it, choose Insert, Picture, Organization Chart.

The Organization Chart object appears in its own drawing canvas (even in Excel, which doesn't normally use drawing canvases). Click once on each placeholder to add names and titles. To add ready-made boxes for Assistants, Coworkers, and Subordinates, click the appropriate block in the organization chart and then select an item from the Insert Shape list. Limited formatting tools let you change fonts, box styles, shadowing, and lines.

TIP FROM

> To make it easier and faster to add new people to the chart, "tear off" the Insert Shape toolbar and let it float on the screen.

Click the Layout button on the Organization Chart toolbar to choose from a menu of useful formatting options for the chart itself, including options to fit the chart to the drawing canvas. Click the AutoFormat button to select from a sophisticated collection of interesting designs.

DIAGRAMS

Office comes with five additional prebuilt diagramming tools, similar to the organization chart tool mentioned in the previous section. These tools can be used for constructing any of the following:

- **Cycle diagrams**—Bits of text arranged in a circle, with lines or arrows between the blurbs

- **Radial diagrams**—Bits of text with one blurb in the middle, and the rest arranged around it, with lines emanating from the center to the outside blurbs

- **Pyramid diagrams**—A triangle in the background is adorned with evenly spaced blurbs down the middle

- **Venn diagrams**—Overlapping circles with blurbs arranged outside the circles (note that the amount of overlap cannot be adjusted)

- **Target diagrams**—A bull's-eye has superimposed callout lines and spaces for blurbs in a single heap at the side

The tools here are rudimentary, but they can be useful, particularly if your intent is to convey a general idea, as opposed to a mathematical exactitude. Other tools, notably Visio, give you much more control over the appearance of your diagrams.

TROUBLESHOOTING

FIXING BROKEN IMAGE LINKS

I created a link to an image stored on a networked computer and everything worked fine. When I opened the document later, however, the image link was broken.

If links get messed up, you have one tool at your disposal, short of directly editing Word field codes to fix the broken links. Choose Edit, Links, and use the tools provided by the application to change or correct the links. You also can use this approach to change linked files to embedded files.

EXTRA CREDIT: A PROFESSIONAL FLOWCHART

Office AutoShapes give you the opportunity to create almost any kind of basic process-related diagram. Note how this flowchart emphasizes clean, simple phrases, and places them in color and shape-coded boxes. A simple, clean flowchart can do wonders for explaining an otherwise difficult procedure. And with the use of standard Office Drawing tools, this flowchart is equally at home in a PowerPoint presentation, a Word document, or an Excel workbook.

Figure 5.19

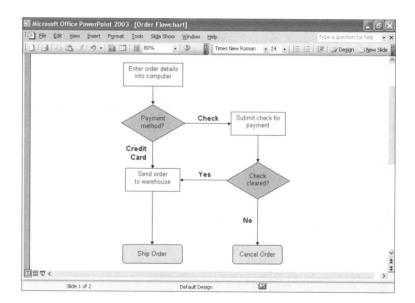

CHAPTER 6

USING OFFICE PROGRAMS TOGETHER

SHARING DATA BETWEEN OFFICE PROGRAMS

Every Office program produces its own type of data files. Each has its strengths and weaknesses, and sometimes creating the best document means snipping a piece from a data file produced by one program and dropping it into a document from a completely different source. Done poorly, this process can result in Frankenstein's monster. But when you know how to use each program properly, the final document can be much greater than the sum of its parts.

The possibilities are limited mostly by your imagination. The most common scenario is to use Excel's superb analytical tools to create eye-catching charts and tables and insert them into a Word document or a PowerPoint slide. You can even save the resulting file as a web page so that anyone can view it, with or without their own copy of Office.

The fundamental tool for shifting data from one program to another, the Windows Clipboard, is as old as Windows itself. In Office 2003, Microsoft has enhanced the capabilities of the venerable Clipboard. The result—a Clipboard task pane that holds up to 24 items—is a mixed success at best. In this chapter, we'll show you how to use the Office 2003 Clipboard.

The second most popular technique for moving and copying data is dragging it from place to place with the mouse. Office 2003 makes the process of arranging program windows on the screen relatively easy; a choice on the Window menu, Compare Side By Side, automatically arranges two open documents next to one another so that you can compare their contents and drag data between them easily.

USING THE OFFICE CLIPBOARD

The Windows Clipboard holds one item at a time. Period. When you cut or copy something, it immediately and irrevocably displaces the current contents of the Windows Clipboard. That makes some cut-and-paste jobs almost unbearable. To borrow bits and pieces of one document to use in another, you have to copy the first bit, switch to the second document, paste, and then return to the first document to do it again, repeating the process until your mouse finger finally screams in protest.

Using the Office Clipboard, you can gather as many as 24 Office objects and then paste them—one at a time or all at once—into an Office document. The enhanced Clipboard can hold any data type that will fit in the Windows Clipboard, including text from a Word document; graphics (even the animated variety) for use in PowerPoint presentations; and Excel charts or ranges.

Using the Office Clipboard, you can tackle any of the following tasks:

- Pull together excerpts from a large report to create a summary or digest.
- Gather background information from scattered files and assemble the appropriate parts into the first draft of a report or presentation.

- Take a collection of notes, one from each member of a group, and stitch them together into a single report.
- Quickly collect a list of names or figures you expect to use repeatedly in a document.

The enhanced Clipboard is available in any Office program. It appears automatically (see Figure 6.1) if you copy some data, paste it, and then copy another piece of data, all within the same Office program. The Clipboard task pane also appears if you copy or cut two Office items in sequence without an intervening paste or if you press Ctrl+C twice in a row. To display the Office Clipboard task pane manually, choose Edit, Office Clipboard. (You can also click the task pane title bar, if it is visible, and select Clipboard from the drop-down list.)

Figure 6.1
Use the Office Clipboard to copy up to 24 items, and then paste them, one at a time or all at once, into any Office document.

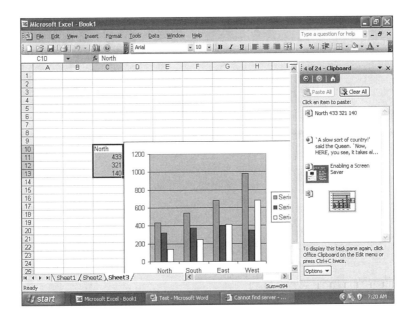

→ To learn more about working with task panes, **see** "Configuring Common Office Features," **p. 47**.

Each item on the Office Clipboard is represented by an icon that depicts the program from which the item was copied. The Clipboard task pane also displays a thumbnail view of the copied item, whether it consists of text, numbers, or a graphic.

When you start an Office program, the first entry on the Clipboard task pane consists of the current contents of the Windows Clipboard. Whenever an Office program is running, any item you cut or copy using the standard Windows Clipboard techniques (even from a non-Office program) creates a new entry on the Office Clipboard. The Windows Clipboard keeps discarding its contents every time you cut or copy something new, but the contents of the Office Clipboard remain available as long as any Office program is running.

6

Each new item appears at the top of the Office Clipboard pane. When the Office Clipboard is visible and reaches its maximum of 24 items, cutting or copying another item drops the oldest item from the Office Clipboard.

To paste the contents of one specific copied item, click in your document to position the insertion point where you want the item to appear, and then click the button for that item. To paste all the copied items into a document in the same order they were added to the Clipboard task pane (beginning with the oldest at the bottom of the list and working up), click Paste All.

 If you're frustrated because the Paste All button is grayed out, see "Paste All and the Office Clipboard" in the "Troubleshooting" section at the end of this chapter.

To remove an individual item from the Office Clipboard, click the arrow to the right of the item and choose Delete. To clear all the Clipboard contents at once, click the Clear All button.

NOTE

> The Windows Clipboard continues to operate just as it always does, without regard to the contents of the Office Clipboard. Every time you cut or copy a new item, it replaces the current contents of the Windows Clipboard. Whenever you use the Paste command in a non-Office program, the Windows Clipboard uses the last item you cut or copied.

Don't expect miracles from the Office Clipboard. Among its many limitations worth noting are the following:

- You're limited to 24 items, period.
- It works only with Office programs. Although you can copy text and graphics from programs outside the Office family onto the Office Clipboard, you can't paste clips to those programs.
- Your saved clips stay in memory only as long as you have an Office program open. The Office Clipboard contents vanish when you close the last Office program in memory, and you can't save the list.
- You can't edit clips, nor can you see any more than the tiny preview in the Clipboard task pane.

TIP FROM

Ed & Woody

> The Office Clipboard is useful, but for power users its limitations are all too apparent. If you really want to put some power in the Windows Clipboard, we recommend replacing it with a third-party utility. Mike Lin's Clipomatic (`http://mlin.net/Clipomatic.shtml`) is free and useful. For shareware utilities with a full set of features, try ClipCache Plus, from XRayz Software (`http://www.xrayz.co.uk`), or ClipMate, from Thornsoft Development (`http://www.thornsoft.com`). Unlike the Office Clipboard, these add-ons work with any Windows program. You can save hundreds or even thousands of clips for reuse later—when filling in forms, for example—and assign keyboard shortcuts to those you use regularly. You can even clean up clips—removing the >>> used as e-mail forwarding indicators, for instance, or converting the case of text in a clip.

CUSTOMIZING THE OFFICE CLIPBOARD

Click the Options button at the bottom of the Clipboard task pane to display a shortcut menu that lets you customize its operation in any of the following ways:

- If you find the Clipboard pane annoying, clear the Show Office Clipboard Automatically check box. In this configuration, the Clipboard pane will appear only when you specifically choose to display it.

- With the preceding option disabled, you may want a keyboard shortcut to display the Clipboard task pane. Select the Show Office Clipboard When Ctrl+C Pressed Twice option, and you can reveal the task pane by pressing Ctrl+C without changing the current selection. (This shortcut will not work if you change the selection between the first and second press of this key combination.)

- If you want to collect a number of items but don't want the Clipboard pane to clutter up your workspace, select the Collect Without Showing Office Clipboard option.

- When the Office Clipboard is active, a small icon appears in the notification area (also known as the system tray) at the right of the taskbar, and a brief message appears each time you copy an item. The two items at the bottom of the Options menu let you hide either or both of these indicators.

- To stop the Office Clipboard from collecting any additional items, right-click the icon in the system tray and choose Stop Collecting from the shortcut menu. This immediately closes the Clipboard pane and removes the tray icon. It does not, however, clear the contents of the Office Clipboard.

CONVERTING CLIPBOARD DATA INTO ALTERNATIVE FORMATS

When you paste an item from the Clipboard into an Office document, the Office program examines the item to determine its data format—simple text, HTML, formatted text (so-called Rich Text Format), worksheet data, or one of many picture formats, for example. Before the Office program pastes the Clipboard contents, a negotiating procedure takes place in which the program attempts to discover the format that's most appropriate for the current contents.

Most of the time, Office makes the correct guess about what to do with the Clipboard's contents. In some cases, however, you might want to convert the Clipboard contents to a different format when pasting into another program (or even within the same program). For instance, when copying formatted text from one Office program to another—for example, the contents of an HTML-based Outlook e-mail message into Word—you typically don't want the original formatting to appear in the document where you're pasting the data. Instead, you want to transfer just the text, letting it take on the paragraph formatting defined in the Word document.

6

In Office 2003, you have two opportunities to override the Office defaults and switch formats when using the Clipboard:

- Instead of using the default format, choose Edit, Paste Special, and select any available format from the As box (see Figure 6.2). In this case, Unformatted Text is the best choice.

Figure 6.2
Use Paste Special when you want to choose the format of copied data before pasting it into a new document.

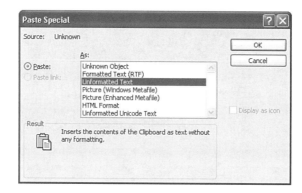

- After pasting the data, you can change its format by choosing from the Paste Options action menu, available by clicking the Smart Tag (see Figure 6.3). In this example, we copied a range of cells from an Excel worksheet and pasted them into a PowerPoint slide. The Smart Tag shows additional formats available for the pasted data.

Figure 6.3
After pasting data into an Office program, click the Paste Options Smart Tag to change the format of the data.

TIP FROM

The Paste Options Smart Tag may seem like a little thing, but it's one of the most useful improvements in Office in years. Whenever you use the Clipboard to copy data from one place to another within Office, it pays to click the Smart Tag to see which options are available on the action menu.

With an Excel worksheet range on the Clipboard, for instance, you can choose any of the following formats when using Paste Special to paste the data into a Word document:

- **Microsoft Excel Worksheet Object**—Used with the Paste Link option, this is a good choice if you plan to update the data in the worksheet and you want to ensure that the latest numbers appear in the Word document whenever it's opened.

- **Formatted Text (RTF)**—This option converts the Excel range to a Word table, retaining text formatting such as fonts and colors from the original data.

- **Unformatted Text, Unformatted Unicode Text**—These options force the text to take on the surrounding formatting in Word. Use the Unicode option if your original text includes any characters outside of the normal alphanumeric character set.

- **Picture, Bitmap, Enhanced Metafile**—Choose one of these formats to enable scaling and cropping, and to allow other kinds of picture formatting. You won't be able to edit text after pasting it in this format.

- **HTML Format**—Select this option if you intend to use the resulting Word document on a web page.

You can generalize from these formats to other options in other situations. Various Object types enable you to link or embed data from one program into another (an option discussed in more detail later in this chapter). Unformatted text options strip all the original formatting away, so the pasted data picks up whatever formatting is applied to the destination. Pasting in a picture format can cause formatting to become distorted, and you'll make the distortion worse if you try to resize the pasted-in picture after the fact. The good news with all these options is that you're free to experiment. Try a Paste Special format—if you don't like the results, click the Undo button and try another until you get the results you want.

NOTE

> The Paste as Hyperlink choice on Word's Edit menu has the same effect as choosing the Paste Link option in the Paste Special dialog box, and then choosing Word Hyperlink.

DRAGGING AND DROPPING DATA

All Office programs support standard Windows drag-and-drop actions. Dragging with the left mouse button within a document, worksheet, or presentation moves the item from one place to the other. All Office programs also enable you to drag with the right mouse button; when you do, you see a shortcut menu from which you can choose the correct action. For example, in Word, right-dragging a selected item enables you to choose whether to copy or move it to the new location, or to insert it as a shortcut or hyperlink (see Figure 6.4).

6

Figure 6.4
All Office programs allow you to drag text or objects with the right mouse button; in Word, use this technique to move text.

Excel allows right drags and provides even more choices than Word: Move Here, Copy Here, Copy Here as Values Only, Copy Here as Formats Only, Link Here, Create Hyperlink Here, Shift Down and Copy, Shift Right and Copy, Shift Down and Move, Shift Right and Move, Cancel.

If you hold down the Ctrl key while dragging, the default action changes. In Excel, for example, use this technique on a worksheet tab to create a copy of the sheet. In PowerPoint's Slide Sorter view (page x), Ctrl+drag copies the slide.

→ To learn more about moving and copying Excel data, **see** "Moving, Copying, Inserting, and Deleting Worksheets," **p. 516**.

Drag and drop is not limited to single documents or even single programs. By arranging document windows on your screen, you can easily drag and drop data from one window to the other. (For our advice on the best ways to work with multiple documents, see "Extra Credit: Side by Side with Office," at the end of this chapter.)

Dragging text between Word documents is a powerful and quick way to reuse material from one document in another. For example, if you select a phrase in one document, right-drag it to another document, release, and choose Create Hyperlink Here, you'll create a fully functional hot link between the two documents.

If you're trying to work with two or more Word documents at the same time and find that you can't see enough of each document to perform any meaningful copying or pasting, see "Giving Word Documents More Editing Room" in the "Troubleshooting" section at the end of this chapter.

PowerPoint has terrific drag-and-drop capability in Slide Sorter view (see Figure 6.5). Drag or Ctrl+drag a slide from one presentation to another and you not only copy the slide, it automatically takes on the master style of the target presentation.

Figure 6.5
When you drag and drop in PowerPoint's Slide Sorter view, slides you copy between presentations are transformed to the target presentation's style.

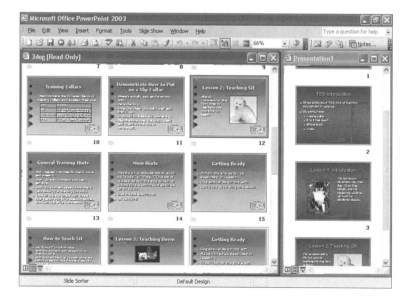

To drag and drop between Office programs, arrange the windows on your screen so you can see both, and then drag some Word text into an Excel cell or a PowerPoint slide into Word.

TIP FROM

Ed & Woody

If you have a Word outline that's properly formatted, you can import it directly into PowerPoint and turn it into a presentation. But if your Word document doesn't conform to the official formatting rules, you can still assemble a presentation quickly: Set up a Word window next to a PowerPoint window, and click and drag text from Word to the PowerPoint outline.

When you want to drag between Office programs, but you want to work with each program at full size, use the Windows-standard *drag-and-hover* technique. Select the data from the original program, click, and then drag your mouse pointer over the target document's button on the Windows taskbar. Don't release the mouse button. Instead, allow the pointer to hover over the button for a moment, until the target window appears. Move the pointer to the correct location and release the mouse button to complete the drop.

CONVERTING AND IMPORTING FILES BETWEEN OFFICE PROGRAMS

One very common intra-Office data sharing task involves retrieving contact names and addresses from Outlook to put in a Word letter, a process more commonly known as *mail merge*. Unfortunately, both Word and Outlook conspire to make that common activity uncommonly difficult. In this book, we explain the secrets for simplifying the connection.

→ To learn how to retrieve Outlook addresses for use in a Word document, **see** "Addressing Letters with the Outlook Contacts List," **p. 477**.

→ For more information on working with Outlook Contacts, **see** Chapter 10, "Organizing Your Contacts List," **p. 275**.

→ To see how Word can help you create mass mailings, reports, envelope labels, and more using any list (including one created in Excel), **see** "Using Mail Merge to Personalize Form Letters," **p. 481**.

In most cases, Office programs cannot open files created and saved in the native file format of another program. One exception is when you open a Word file in PowerPoint. In that case, PowerPoint attempts to construct a presentation based on the file structure. This operation is most effective when the Word file is a simple outline.

6

NOTE

If you try to use an Office program to open an HTML file generated by any of the Office programs, the file opens—but Office reads the XML tag in the file and launches the originating program to load the file.

To export all or part of a Word file to PowerPoint, choose File, Send To, Microsoft PowerPoint. You can also send slides and notes from PowerPoint to Word by choosing File, Send To, Microsoft Word.

COMBINING TWO OR MORE DATA TYPES IN ONE DOCUMENT

After you get beyond simple letter writing and number crunching, you get to the really interesting—and perhaps overly technical—aspects of Office as a unified system. Using a few esoteric techniques, you can build *compound documents* by combining data created in a variety of sources—starting with a Word document and integrating an Excel worksheet into it, for instance, or incorporating an Excel chart into a PowerPoint presentation.

The most common use of compound documents is in business, where you can incorporate data from a "live" database into a Word document. Every time you open the document, the document goes out to the database and updates itself, so it's always up to date.

If you're using Office at home or in the classroom, of course, you're not going to be connecting to a corporate database, so these fancy techniques don't apply. But you can still benefit from creating compound documents. For example, if you're managing a list in Excel, you can link the range containing your list to a Word document so that the document is automatically updated when you make changes to the worksheet. Using this strategy, you don't have to remember to copy the Excel data into your report when it changes; the link between the two Office documents handles this chore automatically.

This all works because Office has an *object design*: Each Office document is essentially a container into which several kinds of information can be poured.

You'll see references to *OLE objects*, *COM objects*, and *ActiveX objects* in the online documentation and elsewhere. For everyday use, these terms all refer to the same thing. For simplicity's sake, we call them "objects" in this book.

NOTE

> You'll also see *OLE container*, *ActiveX container*, and *COM container* in the Help files and online articles. Don't be confused. These terms refer to Office files—documents, workbooks, and presentations.

EMBEDDING VERSUS LINKING

Office offers two very different methods for putting objects (such as text, charts, pictures, or a worksheet range) into a Word document, Excel worksheet, Access database, Outlook item, or PowerPoint presentation. The two methods are called *embedding* and *linking*:

- Embedding stores the data as an object inside the document, including an indication of which program made the object. So, if you embed an Excel chart in a Word document, all the data for the chart resides inside the Word document and Word "knows" it can be edited with Excel. The data for the chart is not available as an external file; thus, you can't start Excel and edit the chart directly. Instead, you must start with your Word document to edit the chart.

■ Linking, on the other hand, inserts a pointer to data stored in an external file. When you create a link, the container document (the one that contains the link) might include a snapshot of the data, but it also attempts to update the link whenever necessary. Thus, if you insert a named range from an Excel worksheet stored in the file `C:\Documents And Settings\Ed\My Documents\Members.xls` into a Word document, the document stores a code that instructs Word to retrieve that range from the file in that exact location whenever you open or print the document. Because the data exists in an external file, you can use Excel to update `Members.xls` at any time, and your changes will be reflected the next time you open or print the Word document that contains the link.

NOTE

Pictures frequently appear in documents as, simply, pictures—they're neither embedded nor linked.

Embedded objects are edited in-place: If you double-click an Excel worksheet embedded in your Word document, for example, Excel's menus and toolbars replace the Word equivalents—even though you're still working in the Word window (see Figure 6.6).

Figure 6.6
When editing an embedded Excel worksheet in Word, note that the window title says Word, but Excel takes over the menus and toolbars.

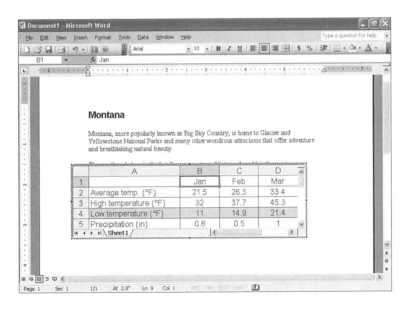

On the other hand, if you double-click a linked object, the originating program opens and loads the data from the linked external file. If you double-click an Excel chart linked in a PowerPoint presentation, Excel opens, loads the file containing the linked chart, and lets you begin working with it.

When you consider whether to link, embed, or place objects in documents, you must juggle three competing considerations:

- **File Size**—Will the objects make the document file too large? An embedded Office object (an Excel chart, say) can take up twice as much room as a picture of that same object. This isn't as much of an issue as it used to be, thanks to CD burners and USB flash memory keys.

- **Update Capability**—Will the object change? If so, you need to keep your options open. Yes, you can paste an Excel range into a Word document as a table, and then convert it back to an Excel range for updates. But if you plan to update the data frequently, it's easier to embed or link the data.

- **Portability**—Will the document and objects stay on a single computer? If you think you'll distribute the file to one or more people over e-mail, or if you plan to take the file to work on at your school's computer lab, you'll need to include all linked files. If one or more of the linked files are missing, anyone who opens the original document won't be able to see the updates and will have to deal with annoying error messages.

With those three goals in mind, here's how to select the best method for putting an object into a document:

- If you're not particularly worried about file size, and you won't need to update the object or change its formatting, forget about linking or embedding. Insert the data—picture, table, chart, whatever—into the document.

- If file size is the overriding concern and you don't expect to move documents from their original locations, use links to external data such as pictures and charts. If you need to move documents from one computer to another, just be sure to duplicate the folder structure for documents and linked objects.

- If portability is the main concern, and it's possible you'll need to update the object or move the file that contains the source data, use embedding. That way, you'll always have the object at hand—the object and its data travel with the document.

TIP FROM

Ed & Woody

> You can quickly tell whether an object in Word is embedded or linked. Choose Tools, Options, and select the Field Codes check box on the View tab. An embedded object appears with an {Embed} field code; a linked object appears as a {Link} field code. Pictures that are part of the file won't have any field code, and you can see the picture.

CREATING AND EDITING EMBEDDED OBJECTS

The easiest way to embed an object from one Office program into a document from another Office program is to use the Clipboard. For example, if you've created a table in Excel and you want to embed that table in Word, follow these steps:

1. Select the range that you want to use in your Excel worksheet.

2. Press Ctrl+C, or choose Edit, Copy.

3. Switch to the Word document and choose Edit, Paste Special.

4. Choose the Paste (not Paste Link!) option and select Microsoft Office Excel Worksheet Object from the As list.

5. Click OK.

Under some circumstances, you might want to create a brand-new embedded object. If you're adding a simple chart to a Word document, for instance, you might want to take advantage of Excel's powerful charting capabilities without creating a new worksheet. By creating a new object, you can enter your data and create the chart object directly. The general method for creating any kind of new embedded object in Word or Excel is as follows:

1. Click to place the insertion point where you want to add the object.

2. Choose Insert, Object, and click the Create New tab. You'll see the Object dialog box shown in Figure 6.7.

Figure 6.7

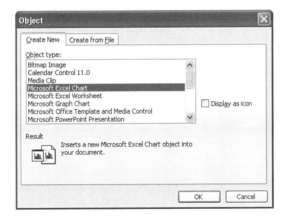

3. Scroll through the Object Type box until you find the type of object you want to insert. Select it, and then click OK. The new object appears, ready for editing, using the menus and toolbars for the program associated with that object.

4. Edit the object as needed. When you're done, click outside the object area to return to the main document.

When you're back in the container document, right-click the object and select Format Object to set text wrapping, colors, size, layout, cropping, and the like.

PowerPoint works similarly, although the dialog boxes are labeled a little differently.

 If you become frustrated trying to format or resize an embedded object, see "Formatting or Resizing Embedded Objects" in the "Troubleshooting" section at the end of this chapter.

6

In some cases, you can right-click and drag to create an embedded object. For example, if you right-drag a picture file from Windows Explorer and drop it onto a Word document, Word displays a shortcut menu. Choose Copy Here to embed the picture.

CREATING AND EDITING LINKED OBJECTS

You can create a link to an existing object in many ways. The easiest way to reliably create a link to an entire file is to follow these steps:

1. Click to position the insertion point at the location in the document (worksheet, presentation, and so on) where you want to add the link.

2. Choose Insert, Object, and click the Create from File tab. You'll see the Object dialog box shown in Figure 6.8.

Figure 6.8
If the object already exists, you can embed or link to it from this dialog box.

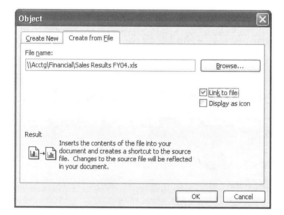

3. Use the Browse button to find the object, make sure the Link to File box is selected, and click OK.

Other ways to link to objects include the following:

- Use Ctrl+C or Edit, Copy to place the object on the Clipboard. Then click in the document where you want the link to appear and choose Edit, Paste Special. Select a format, choose the Paste Link option, and click OK.

- Choose Insert, Picture, From File and select a picture. Instead of clicking the Insert button, click the down-arrow to its right and choose Link to File.

- In Word, choose Insert, File. Then, instead of choosing the Insert option, click the down-arrow to the right of the button and choose Insert as Link.

In Word, if you choose Insert and Link from the Insert Picture dialog box, you'll get an embedded picture that's linked to the source file. A copy of the picture travels with the document, but each time the link is updated, Word goes out to the linked file and refreshes the picture.

It's all done with something called an {includepicture} field, which implements this strange hybrid of embedding and linking you won't find anywhere else in Office.

TIP FROM

> If you're trying to link to a picture using the Clip Art task pane, you're out of luck. Office doesn't offer any direct way to link to clips stored in a Clip Art collection. If you insist on doing so, you need to track down the location where the underlying file is stored and then create a link directly to that file.

MANAGING LINKS BETWEEN DOCUMENTS AND OBJECTS

Try as you might, links break easily. Because a link is just a pointer—a fully qualified file-name, possibly with some ancillary information such as a range name—any time the path to the file changes, the link goes kaput. If you change the name or folder location of the object, the link breaks. If the link extends over a network and you lose the connection to the server or the shared folder on which the object is stored—for whatever reason—the link breaks as well. This is a particular concern on portable computers.

If you have placeholder links instead of the pictures that should be in your document, see "Broken Links to Image Files" in the "Troubleshooting" section at the end of this chapter.

When you work with a Word document, Excel workbook, or PowerPoint presentation that includes one or more linked items, the Edit menu changes to include several new choices. Choose Edit, Links to see a dialog box that lists all linked items in the current document, as shown in Figure 6.9.

Figure 6.9
When a link breaks, use this dialog box to fix it.

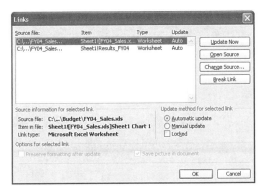

From the Links dialog box, you can change the object (using the Change Source button), update the linked object manually, or break the link altogether. If you're planning to send a document to someone via e-mail and they don't need to edit it, you should consider break-ing the links first so they don't get any confusing error messages.

When you break the link, a format conversion takes place, changing the linked object into a picture, which is then placed in the document.

TROUBLESHOOTING

PASTE ALL AND THE OFFICE CLIPBOARD

Why is the Paste All button on the Office Clipboard grayed out?

When you click the Paste All button, the effect is the same as if you were to paste each item individually, pressing Enter (if necessary) between items. In some cases, the data types are incompatible with the current location of the insertion point. For example, if you've clicked in a cell within an Excel worksheet, you won't be able to paste a collection that contains a mix of text and graphics items. In that case, Office disables the Paste All button. Delete the incompatible data types from the Clipboard task pane, or paste the items one at a time.

GIVING WORD DOCUMENTS MORE EDITING ROOM

I want to view two or three Word documents at once, so I can cut and paste data between them, but the document area is nearly impossible to see.

Try disabling any toolbars that aren't absolutely necessary (right-click any toolbar and clear the check mark to the left of any toolbar you don't need). Turn off the horizontal scrollbar and status bar by choosing Tools, Options, and clearing the appropriate check boxes on the View tab of the Options dialog box. Repeat for each document.

FORMATTING OR RESIZING EMBEDDED OBJECTS

An embedded object is the wrong size, but there are no obvious options for reformatting or resizing it.

Formatting, resizing, and cropping an embedded object is difficult because embedded objects use formatting from their native program and generally ignore formatting from the host program. To complicate matters, the inserted object is frequently sized arbitrarily. In Word, try selecting the object and then enclosing it within a text box (Insert, Text Box). If you can't get the formatting correct from outside the object, double-click it and see whether you can change settings in the program that created it.

BROKEN LINKS TO IMAGE FILES

There are placeholder icons in my document instead of the pictures that should be visible there.

Those placeholder icons represent broken links to image files. If the links point to files on shared drives, check the permission on the shared drive or folder. If it's necessary to move the linked files, you might need to re-create the links.

EXTRA CREDIT: SIDE BY SIDE WITH OFFICE

You have two copies of a document—an early draft and one that includes comments and annotations from a teacher or reviewer. You want to arrange both documents on the screen so you can compare their contents and move or copy data from one to the other. Here's how.

In Word or Excel, choose Window, Compare Side By Side; this is absolutely, positively your preferred option when you need to see two documents alongside one another.

The Compare Side By Side option is grayed out and unavailable until you have at least two documents or workbooks open. When you have exactly two documents open, the Compare Side By Side menu option changes to include the name of the other open document. If you have more than two documents or workbooks open, the menu changes to Compare Side By Side With. Click this menu in one of the files you want to use, and then choose the name of the other document from the Compare Side By Side dialog box.

The side-by-side view arranges both windows neatly on the screen and adds a Compare Side by Side toolbar. The button at the left of this toolbar allows you to synchronize scrolling of the two documents, so you can compare them without constantly switching back and forth. If you maximize one of the documents to make some changes or take a closer look, click the Reset Window Position button to restore the side-by-side view. Click the Close Side By Side button when you're through with your comparison.

Figure 6.10

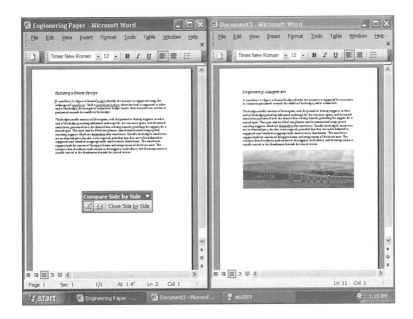

This option is ideal for occasional work with multiple documents. But if you regularly find yourself needing to arrange Office documents side by side, we have an even better suggestion: Get a second monitor (you might need a second display adapter as well, although many computers will support a second monitor with an inexpensive splitter cable). Windows XP supports multiple monitors, and with careful shopping you can find the extra hardware for a relatively low cost. With two monitors, you can devote one full monitor to each window, without having to worry about squinting or painstakingly arranging windows on a single screen.

USING OUTLOOK

CHAPTER 7

GETTING STARTED WITH OUTLOOK

In this chapter

THE FIVE FACES OF OUTLOOK

Microsoft Outlook is, first and foremost, an excellent e-mail program, and for some people that's all it will ever be. Too bad they'll miss out on all the other useful features in this large and complex program. Outlook 2003, as it turns out, presents five distinct faces, each of which helps you manage a different type of personal information:

- **Mail** is, of course, where you send and receive electronic mail. You can have as many different e-mail accounts as you can manage. Outlook takes care of the business of sending and receiving messages, discarding junk mail, and helping you organize incoming messages into folders.

- **Calendar** is where you keep track of meetings, appointments, and other items that are tied to a specific date and time. You can add a reminder to any item and Outlook will pop up an onscreen note so you don't forget.

- **Contacts** is where you keep information about people and organizations. You can store up to three e-mail addresses for every contact, along with their instant messaging information, web addresses, phone numbers, home and work addresses, business and personal details, and free-form notes.

- **Tasks** allows you to maintain a to-do list, with due dates, start and end dates, priority and status reports, and reminders.

- **Notes** is the simplest view of all—each item in this folder is a free-form snippet of text that looks like the sticky notes that litter most desktops, even down to the yellow color.

A sixth option, Journal, is designed to automatically track activities and associate them with individual contacts, e-mails, and other data types—useful if your job requires you to track tasks related to a specific project. This feature is disabled by default, it's difficult to use, and it doesn't work all that well anyway, which is why we don't cover its use in this book.

Using Outlook, you can create links between different types of information. You can link an appointment to one or more people in your Contacts folder, for example. You can also drag items from one folder and drop them in another to create new items.

In this chapter, we introduce the basic concepts you need to know to put these five features to work for you and your family. We explain where data is stored, how to create different views, and how to work with items. We show you how to take advantage of features that are common to all the different Outlook modules, such as flagging items for follow-up. In the remaining chapters in this section, we go into greater detail about each of the five main Outlook folders.

USING AND CUSTOMIZING THE OUTLOOK INTERFACE

Outlook stores all information in a single database file. The format of this database is a simple list. In Outlook parlance, each record is an *item*, and the type of item—e-mail message, contact, appointment, and so on—defines which fields are available for entering and displaying information. Each of Outlook's default folders displays items of a single type, and you can create new folders as well.

In previous versions of Outlook, the left side of the program window was reserved for a pane that showed either the Outlook Bar (a list of folder icons) or an Explorer-style folder list. In Outlook 2003, the left side of the screen now consists of a customizable *Navigation pane*, the contents of which change dynamically based on which of seven navigation buttons you've selected from the bottom of the pane. Figure 7.1 shows all these interface elements.

Navigation pane

Figure 7.1
In the Mail view, the Navigation pane shows a list of all folders containing mail; drag shortcuts for favorite folders to the box on top.

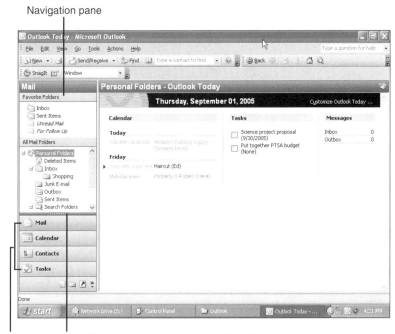

Navigation buttons

Drag this handle to expand or shrink the button list

CUSTOMIZING THE NAVIGATION PANE

As we noted earlier, the contents of the Navigation pane change, depending on which button you've clicked from the list at the bottom of the pane. Click the Mail button and you'll see all mail folders plus a short list of user-definable Favorite folders. Click the Calendar button, and the top of the Navigation pane displays a month calendar for the currently selected date, with clickable links below it to add shared calendars from other users on a corporate network.

TIP FROM

Ed & Woody

To show or hide the Navigation pane, you can use the pull-down menus—View, Navigation Pane. A much quicker alternative is the keyboard shortcut, Alt+F1. For most configurations, you'll have best results leaving the Navigation pane visible. If you use Outlook at a resolution of 800×600, though, you might want to hide the pane to give yourself more room.

7

By default, as you can see in Figure 7.1, these buttons are arranged in individual rows. At common resolutions, this arrangement uses much of the space on the Navigation pane, potentially cutting into space you might prefer to use for viewing and switching between folders. The more folders you create to keep your Outlook data organized, the more obvious this problem becomes. Although you can't make these buttons disappear completely, you can tweak the button list so that it takes up only a single row. You can also change the order of buttons and hide buttons for views you never use. Use any or all of the following techniques to tweak the Navigation pane:

- To expand or shrink the list, click and drag the handle just above the topmost button. As you shrink the list, buttons that previously had their own row appear in a button bar across the bottom of the Navigation pane.

- To add or remove buttons from the list, right-click on any visible button (or click the chevron and arrow at the right side of the list) and choose Navigation Pane Options. Select or clear the check boxes to the left of each item to show or hide that button.

- In the same dialog box, select any item and click Move Up or Move Down to change the order of buttons.

- Click and drag the separator bar to the right of the Navigation pane to make the pane larger or smaller.

Figure 7.2 shows the Navigation pane after shrinking the button bar to a single row. The large, bold labels for each button are gone, although clicking the icon for each button in the list still switches to that folder. This view is especially useful if you have a large number of mail folders and you want to avoid constantly having to scroll through the folder list.

Figure 7.2
Shrink the buttons at the bottom of the Navigation pane to a single row to reclaim space for use at the top of the pane.

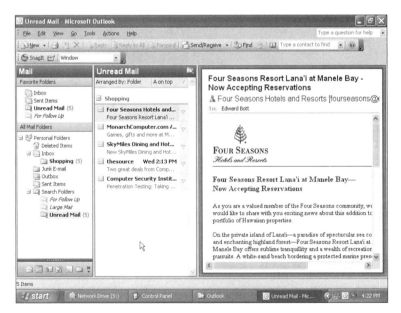

Five of the buttons at the bottom of the Navigation pane correspond to different types of data: Mail, Calendar, Contacts, Tasks, and Notes (the Journal button is disabled by default). The Folder List button displays all available folders, regardless of their data type; select this view if you prefer to navigate between folders using a no-frills, Explorer-style interface. The Shortcuts button is unlike any other, as we explain in the next section.

ADDING CUSTOM SHORTCUTS TO THE NAVIGATION PANE

Some people prefer the Folder List as their primary way to get around in Outlook 2003. If you have multiple e-mail accounts and you use lots of subfolders for organizing mail, the full list of folders can become overwhelming. One good alternative is to build a pane filled with only those folders that you use the most. That's the idea behind the Shortcuts button. In this view, you can build a custom list of shortcuts and arrange them in any order. Initially, the Shortcuts pane includes only shortcuts to the Outlook Today page and to Microsoft's Outlook Update. You can add shortcuts to any or all of the following items:

- **Outlook folders**—Click the Add Shortcut button to choose an existing folder containing any type of item. Use this same technique to select a search folder, such as Unread Mail.

→ For more information about Search Folders, see "Creating and Using Search Folders," **p. 251**.

  - **Web pages**—Drag any Internet shortcut and drop its icon on the bold Shortcuts label at the top of the pane. Clicking any web shortcut opens the web page in the contents pane of the Outlook program window. Outlook isn't a particularly good environment for heavy-duty web browsing; reserve this option for sites where you're not likely to navigate to other web pages.

  - **Programs**—Drag any program shortcut onto the Shortcuts list to give you one-click access to that program. The program opens in its own window, just as if you had clicked a shortcut on the Start menu or the desktop.

  - **Files or folders**—Drag a file or folder shortcut from Windows Explorer and drop it onto a group heading. Clicking a file shortcut opens the file in the program with which it's associated; clicking a folder shortcut opens Windows Explorer in its own window (not in the Outlook program window) and displays the contents of the folder.

TIP FROM

Ed & Woody

> When you drag an Internet shortcut into the Shortcuts pane, Outlook creates the new shortcut using the web page address, complete with http://. To make the shortcut easier to identify, right-click its entry in the list, choose Rename Shortcut, and give it a more descriptive name.

7

At any time, you can click the Add New Group link. Give the group a name, and then drag existing shortcuts into the group to reorganize the list. Figure 7.3 shows a customized shortcut.

Figure 7.3
A custom Shortcuts pane can include Outlook folders, web pages, and shortcuts to programs, files, and folders.

CUSTOMIZING THE OUTLOOK TODAY PAGE

Outlook Today is a web-style view of selected items in your primary store; it shows upcoming appointments, current tasks, and unread messages in a single convenient web view. If you like this "day-at-a-glance" style, you can make Outlook Today your default view. You can also customize this template, but only in limited ways.

To customize the Outlook Today page, click the icon at the top of the Outlook hierarchy in any folder view (by default, this icon is called Personal Folders if you use an uncustomized PST file). Click the Customize Outlook Today link on the page itself (the exact location of this link varies depending on the style you've selected). You can set startup options, define which folders appear on the page, and customize Calendar and Task lists.

> **NOTE**
>
> The Outlook Today layout is based on an HTML template. At one time, Microsoft provided tools that programmers could use to customize the Outlook Today page using a technology called Digital Dashboards. For the most part, this technology is obsolete, and you're stuck with the basic Outlook Today look.

USING CUSTOM VIEWS TO DISPLAY INFORMATION

Outlook uses *forms* to display the data in individual items. To see groups of items within a folder, you use *views*. By default, every Outlook folder includes a selection of built-in views available to all folders containing that item type. If none of the ready-made views matches the way you work, you can create custom views to sort, filter, and group items as required.

You don't have to be a programmer to create, customize, and use views. In fact, you don't even have to use menus to switch views; you can select any available view for the current folder by clicking an option button in the Navigation pane. Using the Arrange By option on the View menu, you can quickly choose from more than a dozen predefined arrangements for folders based on Table views, such as those that contain e-mail messages or tasks. This option allows you to instantly sort and group the items in the current view—by date, size, or importance, for instance.

USING VIEWS TO DISPLAY, SORT, AND FILTER ITEMS

Every folder starts with a default view. For example, when you first open the Calendar folder, you see today's appointments, with a clickable calendar at the top of the Navigation pane; you can switch to Recurring Appointments view to see a list of all recurring items, grouped according to whether they repeat Daily, Weekly, Monthly, or Yearly. Likewise, items in the Contacts folder appear by default as address cards with minimal details, but you can choose to see more detailed cards or a simple Phone List view with one contact per row instead, as we've done in Figure 7.4.

Figure 7.4
Click any view in the Navigation pane to instantly switch to that view.

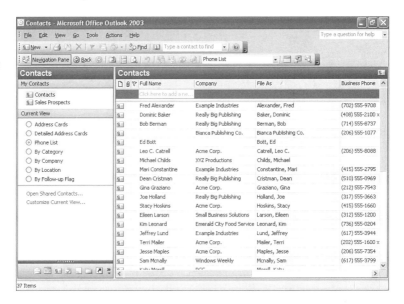

To switch between views, select an entry from the list of defined views in the Navigation pane, or in the drop-down list on the Advanced toolbar; if neither of these interface elements is visible, choose View, Arrange By, Current View. Outlook remembers the view you used most recently and reapplies that view whenever you return to that folder.

TIP FROM

If you can't see the list of available views on the Navigation pane for a particular folder, choose View, Arrange By, and click Show Views in Navigation Pane.

7

ARRANGING ITEMS IN A VIEW

When you're working with folders that contain mail or task items, Outlook 2003 includes a menu choice that allows you to apply one of 13 predefined *arrangements* of grouping and sorting options. These choices appear at the top of the View, Arrange By menu. You can group e-mail messages by date, for instance, to see today's messages in one group, yesterday's messages in another group, and so on.

The groupings are logical and in many cases contain preset groupings. For example, when you view the contents of your Inbox and choose Size from the Arrange By menu, the contents are grouped into distinct "buckets" (see Figure 7.5)—Enormous (>5MB), Huge (1–5MB), Very Large (500KB–1MB), Large (100–500KB), Medium (25–100KB), Small (10–25KB), and Tiny (<10KB).

Figure 7.5
Choices on the Arrange By menu automatically group items by the categories you select.

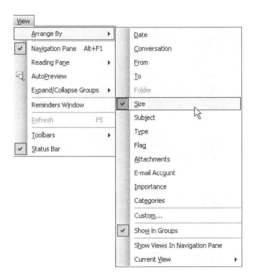

Using any of these Arrange By options has the same effect as if you had customized the current view, using the techniques described in the next section.

If your e-mail messages no longer appear in the grouping you select, see "Restoring Groups to an Arrangement" in the "Troubleshooting" section at the end of this chapter.

TIP FROM

Ed & Woody

In table-based views, you can click any column heading to quickly sort by that column. Click again to sort in reverse order. If the Show in Groups option on the View menu is selected, clicking a column heading changes the grouping, just as if you had clicked the corresponding choice on the Arrange By menu.

7

CUSTOMIZING AN EXISTING VIEW

If none of the built-in views offers the arrangement of data you're looking for, you can customize the current view. As you'll learn shortly, you can change some aspects of a view directly, without using dialog boxes. To see all your customization options, click Customize Current View in the Navigation pane (if this option isn't visible, choose View, Arrange By, Current View, Customize Current View). The Customize View dialog box appears, as shown in Figure 7.6.

Figure 7.6
Use this dialog box to customize all available options for the current view. Depending on the view type, some options may be unavailable.

The sections that follow explain how to modify each characteristic of the selected view. Note that some of these options will not be available for specific view types. For example, you can group items or adjust column formats only in a table-based view; these options are grayed out if you attempt to modify a Card-based view, such as the Address Cards or Detailed Address Cards options in the Contacts folder. In table-based views, you can also apply changes to the current view interactively. The Format Columns button gives you control over the display of non-text data types, such as icons and dates. The Reset Current View button offers the capability to instantly roll back to the default settings for a predefined view.

 If you've customized a built-in view and you need to undo your settings, see "Resetting the Standard Views" in the "Troubleshooting" section at the end of this chapter.

TIP FROM

The most effective way to create a custom view is to start with a built-in view and then modify it. If you prefer the modified view to the built-in one, leave your changes in place. If you want to switch between your custom view and the original built-in view, save the changes under a new name, as we explain later in this chapter.

7

CUSTOMIZING FIELDS

You can add fields to or remove fields from the current view. If most of your contacts are personal, for example, you might want to include the Personal Home Page and IM Address fields in the Address Cards view of the Contacts folder and remove the Business Fax, Company Main Phone, and Car Phone fields.

Using the Customize View dialog box, click the Fields button to display the Show Fields dialog box (see Figure 7.7). Select fields from the list on the left and click the Add button to add them to the current view. Select fields from the list on the right and click Remove to eliminate them from the view. (Hold down Ctrl as you click to select multiple fields from either list.)

Figure 7.7
Use this dialog box to control exactly which fields appear in a custom view.

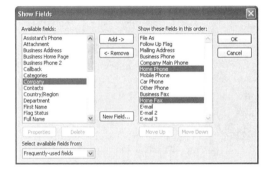

If you're customizing a table-based view, such as the Messages view of the Inbox or the Phone List view of the Contacts folder, you can drag and drop to add or remove fields. Click the Field Chooser button on the Advanced toolbar or right-click the field headings and click Field Chooser to display a list such as the one shown in Figure 7.8. Drag fields onto the headings in the current view to add them to the view; to remove fields, drag column headings down onto the list itself, and release when you see the large X. Drag headings from side to side to change their left-to-right order in the list.

Figure 7.8
The Field Chooser lets you add fields to a view by dragging and dropping.

TIP FROM

> When you add fields to a view using either the Customize View dialog box or the Field Chooser, Outlook displays only its limited selection of frequently used fields. To see a broader list of available fields, use the drop-down list in either dialog box. For example, if a folder contains Contact items, you can see all Name fields, all Phone Number fields, or an enormous list of all Contact fields.

GROUPING ITEMS

Outlook's grouping options allow you to arrange the contents of a folder in outline style, with each main item in the outline corresponding to unique values in a field you select. Some folders include ready-made views with grouping already enabled—the Contacts folder, for instance, includes a By Company view that sorts your list by the contents of the Company field and then groups individual items according to Company. As you can see in Figure 7.9, the resulting list allows you to collapse or expand each grouping.

Figure 7.9
Use the plus and minus signs to the left of each group to expand or collapse the list of items in that group.

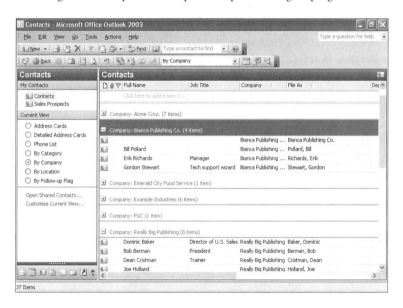

Whenever possible, you should use the options on the Arrange By menu to do grouping. But the Group By box can come in handy for specialized tasks, such as grouping by multiple fields or by fields that are not represented in the predefined arrangements. To add grouping to a view, click the Group By button in the Customize View dialog box. This displays the Group By dialog box shown in Figure 7.10.

You can group by multiple fields; for example, if you're planning a meeting for a national organization with a number of different interests, you might want to group by State and then by Category to see all the contacts in a particular area organized according to categories you've defined.

7

Figure 7.10
Use this dialog box to define grouping levels; note that you can choose whether the view starts with all items expanded or collapsed.

In any table-based view, you can change grouping on the fly. To group by any field that's visible, right-click its column heading and choose Group By This Field. You can also drag headings into or out of the Group By box, which appears just above the column headings. Click the Group By Box button or right-click the column heading and choose Group By Box from the shortcut menus to show or hide this area. To move an item between groups in this type of view, just drag it out of its old group and drop it under the new group heading.

SORTING ITEMS

In any view, you can *sort* your data in a specific order—tasks by Due Date, contacts by Last Name, e-mail messages by Subject, for example. In the Customize View dialog box, click the Sort button to choose up to four fields for sorting.

TIP FROM

> Normally, the Messages view of your Inbox shows all mail sorted by the date and time it was received. Want to find mail from a specific person in a hurry? Click the From heading to sort the folder's contents by the sender's name, and then quickly type the first few letters of the sender's name as it is displayed in this list. Outlook jumps immediately to the first message in the list, and you can scroll to see all other messages from that person, sorted by date received.

FILTERING ITEMS

Filters show a subset of the items in any folder, based on criteria you define. The Overdue Tasks view in the Tasks folder, for example, displays only those tasks that you should have completed by now; if you inspect this view, you'll see that it uses a filter consisting of two items: Complete equals no, and Due Date on or before Yesterday. Likewise, the Annual Events view of the Calendar folder shows all the birthdays and anniversaries you've defined, using a custom filter that shows only all-day events that recur yearly.

In combination with custom views, filters are a powerful way to manage information. In the Contacts folder, for example, you can define filters that show you only people who live in your city or who belong to a category you define. If you have a large family, you can create a filtered view of your Contacts folder that includes only people who share your last name or who belong to the Family category.

➔ When working with e-mail folders, Search Folders are often more useful than filtered views, as we explain in "Creating and Using Search Folders," **p. 251**.

To define a filter for any view, open the Customize View Summary dialog box, click the Filter button, and select the criteria you want to use in your filter. This dialog box is identical to the one used in the Advanced Find dialog box.

➔ For more information about how to define filters and searches, **see** "Advanced Search Techniques," **p. 199**.

FORMATTING

Two formatting options allow you to control the display of fields used in a specific view. For table-based views, click the Format Columns button to open the dialog box shown in Figure 7.11. As this example shows, you can adjust the display format of columns that contain date/time information. You can also change the label used in column headings and change the width and alignment of data in selected columns.

You can also tell Outlook to automatically apply a specific color or font to an item based on conditions you define. In the Calendar folder, you can automatically apply color-coded labels to appointments that meet specified conditions. Some formatting options are preset; unread messages and group headers in e-mail folders, for instance, appear in bold. You can also add your own conditions, such as one that applies bold italic

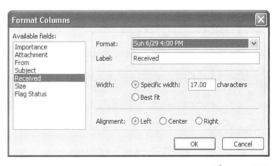

Figure 7.11

font formatting in red to any message from your boss, or applies the Important label to any appointment that includes your boss in the list of attendees.

To define automatic formatting, follow these steps:

1. In the Customize View dialog box, click the Automatic Formatting button. The Automatic Formatting dialog box (see Figure 7.12) shows all existing rules.

2. Click the Add button to create a new rule. Outlook gives it the default name Untitled. Replace this text with a descriptive name.

3. Click the Font button and select the formatting you want to use for items that match the condition. In the case of Calendar items, choose a color and matching text label from the Label list.

7

4. Click the Condition button and define the criteria that an item must match to be subject to automatic formatting. This dialog box works exactly the same as the Advanced Find dialog box.

5. Click OK to save the rule and apply it instantly to the contents of the current folder.

Figure 7.12

Note that rules are applied according to their order in the Automatic Formatting dialog box. Rules that are higher on the list prevail over those beneath them. Note, too, that manual formatting always overrides automatic formatting. Finally, be aware that automatic formatting is applied only in the current view. If you switch to a different view, you need to create a new set of automatic formatting conditions.

Other View Settings

You can define custom display formats for many items in many views. In general, these options are available from shortcut menus. For example, in a table view, you can right-click any column heading to set its alignment (left, right, or center), change its column size to automatically fit the widest entry in the view, or change the column heading.

From the Customize View dialog box, you can also set a variety of other options, including font sizes. Most adults have trouble with the tiny 8-point fonts used in default table views; bumping this size up to 9 or even 10 points can make a world of difference. Just remember that font changes apply to all fields in a section (card body or a row in a table); you can't pick out one field and format it separately.

Click the Other Settings button to see a dialog box like the one in Figure 7.13. The specific options vary by the type of view selected; in table views, as shown here, you can control whether or not it's permitted to edit in rows and whether gridlines appear.

The AutoPreview option is a useful way to see additional information about items that contain details. In your Inbox folder, it shows the first three lines of each message so you can tell at a glance what's inside without having to open and read each message. In other folders, you can use it to see details—notes about each person in your Contacts folder, for example, or the beginning of an appointment's description.

To add the AutoPreview option to a view's settings, use the Other Settings tabs of the Customize View dialog box, or click the AutoPreview button on the Advanced toolbar to hide and show this information on the fly.

7

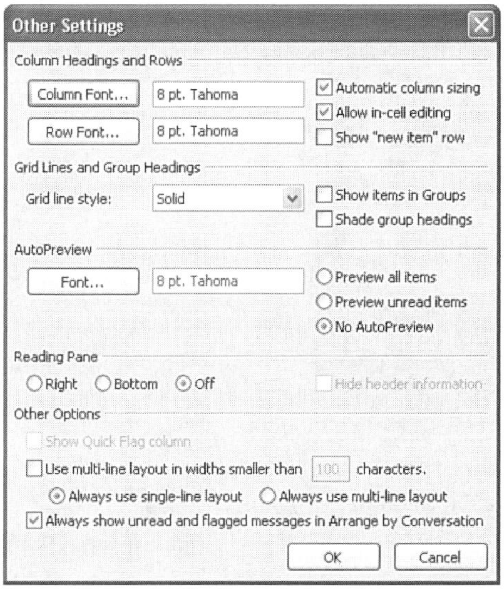

Figure 7.13
Use this dialog box to set overall formatting options for a table or other type of view.

NOTE Don't confuse AutoPreview with the Reading pane. When the Reading pane is visible, you can view the contents of any Outlook item—an entire mail message, or a contact item, or an appointment—in a window just below or to the right of the contents pane; by contrast, enabling the AutoPreview feature shows only the first three lines of an item, and in the case of e-mail messages the preview disappears after you've opened and read the message. If you use AutoPreview in other folder types, the text remains visible at all times.

CREATING A NEW CUSTOM VIEW

Sometimes the fastest and surest way to create the view you're looking for is to start from scratch. To begin defining a new custom view, switch to the folder that contains the items you want to view, and then choose View, Arrange By, Current View, Define Views. Click the New button to display the dialog box shown in Figure 7.14.

NOTE You can't change a view's type after you create it—you can't convert a Card-style view to a Table-style view, for example. When you first create a new view, you have one, and only one, opportunity to make this choice.

7

Figure 7.14
When defining a new view, you must start by defining a view type.

All views start with one of the following arrangements.

Type of View	Description
Table	Default view for Tasks folder and Inbox, although you can use it with any folder. Displays data in worksheet style, with each item in its own row, each field in its own column, and headings for each column. Useful for displaying simple lists.
Timeline	A bar along the top displays days or hours; tiny icons underneath show all the items in the folder according to when they were created, received, or started. Especially useful with Tasks folder.
Card	Displays item title in bold, with selected details underneath. Most useful in Contacts folder, which includes two built-in Card views.
Day/Week/Month	Available for all folders, but appropriate only for the Calendar folder. Options determine how many days you can see at once; more days mean less detail for each entry.
Icon	Displays each item as a large or small icon with title text underneath, as in an Explorer window. You can't add fields or group by different fields. Default view for Notes folder is inappropriate for other item types.

After you select a view type, choose where you want to use the view from the set of three options at the bottom of the dialog box. If you want the custom view type to be available for all folders containing the same type of items as the current folder, choose All *<Item Type>* Folders. In general, this is your best choice; make an exception when you've defined a view that is relevant only to a specific folder.

Choose This Folder, Visible to Everyone or This Folder, Visible Only to Me if you do not want the view to be available from the list of named views in other folders that contain the same type of data.

7

NOTE

> This Folder, Visible to Everyone is applicable only if you're creating a view for a public folder on a business network using the Microsoft Exchange e-mail server software, or if you've chosen to share a particular personal folder with other Exchange users. This option has no effect if you're not connected to an Exchange Server. If you're using Outlook at home or in a small office without an Exchange server, you can ignore this option.

After completing this step, the process of creating a new view is identical to the procedure for customizing an existing view. Add fields, set grouping and filter options if necessary, and save the view under a new name.

MANAGING CUSTOM VIEWS

Outlook gives you a complete set of tools for managing custom views you create. Choose View, Arrange By, Current View, Define Views to display a dialog box listing all views available for the current folder. Select any entry in this list and use the following buttons to work with that view:

- Click Copy to make a copy of the selected view. Give the view a new name to add it to the list. This technique lets you experiment with view options without worrying that you'll mess up a view you've carefully constructed.

- Click Modify to edit any available view setting for the selected view. Note that you cannot change the view type, and some settings are unavailable for certain views.

- Click Rename to give a view a different name; the name you enter is the one that appears in the drop-down list on the Advanced toolbar.

- Click Delete to remove a custom view completely. Note that you cannot remove or rename Outlook's built-in views, although you can edit their settings.

- Click Reset to remove all customizations from a built-in Outlook view. This option is not available for custom views.

OPENING A FOLDER IN A SEPARATE WINDOW

If you open a single Outlook window, you'll notice after switching to a new folder that the Back button is no longer grayed out. If you switch folders a few more times and use the Back button, you'll see that the Forward button is now available as well. These buttons are identical in function to those on the Internet Explorer toolbar: Click the drop-down arrows to the right of either button to see a list of previously viewed folders.

On a fast PC with sufficient memory, Outlook is quick to switch the display of information between folders. However, if you use Outlook regularly, you might prefer to open multiple windows—for example, one window to show your e-mail, another for your Calendar, and a third for Contacts. (This arrangement also makes it easier to move or copy items between windows.) Outlook lets you open an unlimited number of windows at any time, and each can display any folder using any view.

7

To open an Outlook folder in its own window, right-click its button at the bottom of the Navigation pane or in any folder list and choose Open in New Window. Each window gets its own Navigation pane and taskbar button.

TIP FROM

If you inspect the properties of the Outlook shortcut that the Office 2003 installer creates on the Quick Launch toolbar, you'll see that it includes the command-line switch `/recycle`. This switch tells Windows to switch to any existing Outlook window instead of opening a new window. If you plan to create any shortcuts to open specific folders in new windows, omit the `/recycle` switch.

CREATING, EDITING, AND MANAGING OUTLOOK ITEMS

When you create, view, and edit items, Outlook uses a variety of standard and custom forms to control which fields are visible. When you double-click any item, it opens using the default form for its type. The basic techniques for managing items are the same, regardless of the item type.

MOVING, COPYING, AND DELETING ITEMS

To move or copy items between Outlook folders, you can use many of the same techniques you use to manage files in an Explorer window. After switching to the Folder List view in the Navigation pane, you can move an item by dragging it out of the contents pane and dropping it on the icon for another folder; hold down the Ctrl key while dragging to make a copy. Or use shortcut keys to cut (Ctrl+X), copy (Ctrl+C), and then paste (Ctrl+V) the item into the destination folder. Curiously, although Outlook's pull-down Edit menu includes all three choices, the shortcut menus available when you right-click on any item (such as a mail message) don't allow you to cut, copy, or paste.

 If you try to move an item into a folder and it opens a new item instead, see "Dragging Doesn't Always Move an Item" in the "Troubleshooting" section at the end of this chapter.

→ The Office Clipboard lets you copy and paste up to 24 Outlook items at a time; for details, **see** "Using the Office Clipboard," **p. 146**.

Although it's possible to create multiple folders for any type of Outlook items, you'll most commonly use subfolders to manage e-mail messages. To do major message management, click the Mail or Folder List button at the bottom of the Navigation pane and then drag messages out of the message list and drop them onto destination folders as you would in Windows Explorer.

To move one or more selected messages into folders without using the Folder List, click the Move to Folder button on the Standard toolbar. This displays a menu showing the folders you've used most recently. If the folder you want isn't listed, choose Move to Folder from the bottom of the menu. (This option is also available if you right-click one or more items to display the shortcut menu.) Click the New button to create a new folder in any open Personal Folders file.

TIP FROM

E_Q & Woody

You can drag any item onto the Windows desktop or into a folder to create a copy of that item. This is a convenient way to keep a contact's personal information at hand or to keep a copy of a mail message available for ready reference. When you create a copy using this technique, you create a new file containing only that item. Be careful when using such a copy, however: Because there is no link between the item you create on the desktop and the one that remains in Outlook, any changes you make in either place are not reflected in the other.

To delete items in any Outlook folder, first make a selection, and then click the Delete button on the Standard toolbar, use the keyboard shortcut Ctrl+D, press the Delete key, or drag the item and drop it on the Deleted Items icon in the Folder List.

By default, Outlook saves the contents of the Deleted Items folder until the next time you archive. To empty this folder manually, right-click its shortcut in the Navigation pane and choose Empty "Deleted Items" Folder. If you prefer to empty this folder automatically every time you close Outlook, choose Tools, Options, click the Other tab, and click the Empty the Deleted Items Folder Upon Exiting check box.

To create a new folder at any time, choose File, New, Folder. In the Create New Folder dialog box (see Figure 7.15), enter the name of the new folder and specify the type of items you want to store in the folder (if you're creating a subfolder within an existing folder, the default setting is usually correct). Select the folder in which you want to store the new subfolder, and then click OK.

Figure 7.15
When creating a new folder, be sure you specify the correct type of item you want to store in the folder.

To move, copy, delete, or rename a folder, click the Folder List button at the bottom of the Navigation bar and use the right-click shortcut menus.

7

ENTERING DATES AND TIMES AUTOMATICALLY

One of Outlook's most impressive time-saving features is its capability to interpret dates using almost any text you enter—a feature known as AutoDate. Knowing how to use this shortcut can be a real time-saver because it spares you from having to do date-based calculations on the fly. To enter a date in any date field in any type of Outlook item, use any of the following techniques:

TIP FROM

Ed & Woody

> These techniques are useful throughout Outlook, not just in appointments or meetings. For example, you can use AutoDate shortcuts to define the dates for follow-up flags on e-mail messages, or to specify the due date for an upcoming task.

- Type the date in a format that Outlook recognizes, such as 9-29-05, 9/29, or Sep 29. If you omit the year, Outlook automatically fills in this year's date if that date is in the future; if appending the current year to the date results in a date that has already passed, Outlook uses next year's date instead.

- To pick dates from a calendar, click the drop-down arrow to the right of the date field and use the control showing the current month (see Figure 7.16). Use the arrows to scroll backward or forward, and click to insert any date in the current field. Clicking the Today button quickly returns you to the current date.

- When you enter dates and times for appointments, you can also use words and phrases and let Outlook use its AutoDate feature to interpret your meaning.

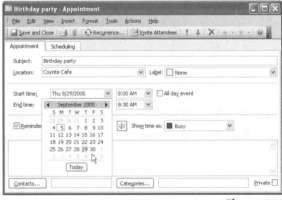

Figure 7.16

Outlook can recognize text such as next Thursday, one week from today, or tomorrow, substituting the correct date for you. To schedule a study group meeting for next Wednesday at 2:00 p.m., for example, click in the Start Time box, enter next wed, and then press Tab and type 2 (Outlook assumes that times you enter are during the default workday unless you specify otherwise).

AutoDate understands dates and times that you spell out or abbreviate, such as 6a (for 6:00 a.m.), or first of jan. If you type 30 days in the Start Time box, Outlook converts it to the date 30 days from the current contents of that field; if you enter that same text as the end time, Outlook adds 30 days to the start date you specified. AutoDate recognizes holidays that fall on the same day every year, such as Halloween, New Year's Eve, and

Christmas. It can also correctly interpret dozens of words you might use to define a date or an interval of time, including the days of the week (spelled out or abbreviated), now, yesterday, today, tomorrow, next, and following.

CAUTION

> You can't use AutoDate to define a recurring appointment. If you enter every other Wednesday in the Start Time box, for example, Outlook will appear to accept your entry, but it will ignore the first two words, setting the appointment for the coming Wednesday and ignoring your attempt to create a recurring appointment.

ASSIGNING ITEMS TO CATEGORIES

You can assign most Outlook items, including e-mail messages, contacts, appointments, meetings, and tasks, to *categories*. Using categories can be a powerful way to extract groups of information from a list of contacts or to categorize e-mail messages by project.

TIP FROM

> Categories work exceptionally well in conjunction with Word's mail-merge feature. In fact, you can even use categories to ease the drudgery of one dreaded annual task. Go through your Contacts folder and assign close friends and family members to a Holiday Cards category. You can then use that category to extract address information to print address labels or personalized letters.

By default, Outlook includes a Master Category List containing 20 entries. You can add your own categories to this list, and then assign items to categories individually or in groups. In the case of e-mail messages, you can assign categories automatically, by defining *rules*.

→ For more details on how to create rules for handling incoming mail, **see** "Using E-mail Rules to Sort and Process Mail," **p. 244**.

TIP FROM

> You can assign a single item to multiple categories. This flexibility lets you work with the same item in multiple contexts—for example, you might assign your mother-in-law's contact to the VIP, Gifts, and Holiday Cards categories to make sure that her name is included each time you pull together a list based on any of these categories.

To assign a single item to a category, open the item and click the Categories button; you can also select one or more items, right-click, and choose Categories from the shortcut menu. Either action displays the Categories dialog box shown in Figure 7.17.

7

Figure 7.17
To assign categories to Outlook items, use the check boxes in this list.

Select the check box to the left of the categories to which you want to assign the item(s). To add a new category and make it available to all items, click the Master Category List button; in the Master Category List dialog box, type the name of the new category and click Add. A category name can contain up to 255 characters, including spaces, but in practice you should keep category names much shorter.

CAUTION

> It's possible to assign categories directly by typing in the box to the right of the Categories button in each item. We recommend avoiding this practice, however, because even a slight difference in spelling or style (VIPs instead of VIP, for example) will result in inconsistent categories and will cause errors when you try to filter or group by category.

HOW OUTLOOK STORES DATA

As we mentioned earlier in this chapter, Outlook is, at its core, a flat-file database. When new mail arrives, or when you create and save a new item in one of Outlook's default folders (Contacts, for example), Outlook adds the new item to the location specified as the *primary store*. If you're using Outlook at home or in a small office, that location is almost certainly a single file stored on the hard disk of your computer. (If you use Office 2003 Professional on a corporate network with an Exchange Server, your data files are probably stored on the server, in an Offline Store File with an extension of .ost. We do not cover this configuration in this book.)

A *Personal Folders file* is the basic storage format for a single user's data. These files use the extension .pst. When you configure Outlook 2003 for use with one or more Internet-standard e-mail accounts (no Exchange servers), Outlook creates a single Personal Folders file called Outlook.pst and stores it in your user profile, along with a handful of other files that contain settings and preferences. This file holds all Outlook data—messages, attachments, the Contacts and Calendar folder...the works.

Where are your Outlook data files and settings stored? For a remarkably complete listing of these locations, open the Help system and search for the topic "Outlook file locations." Unless you change the default settings, your Personal Folders file is located in `%userprofile%\Local Settings\Application Data\Microsoft\Outlook`. In Outlook 2003, thankfully, it's not necessary to wear out your mouse button to get to this folder. Instead, choose File, Data File Management, and click the Open Folder button.

In this configuration, the Personal Folders file is the primary store: New messages are delivered to the Inbox in that file, and all other default Outlook folders are stored there as well. You never have to explicitly save a Personal Folders file. Outlook takes care of updating the file with changes and additions automatically.

The Personal Folders file used as your primary store must be stored on a local hard drive. You can also create additional Personal Folders files and access them at the same time. In this configuration, the additional Personal Folders files are defined as *secondary stores* and can be saved on a local hard disk or on a shared network location. Outlook does not save new items directly in these files, but you can move items into a secondary store by dragging and dropping them from your primary store, or you can define rules that automatically move incoming messages into the secondary store based on their content.

Outlook's default settings bury data files in your user profile, where they're not always easy to find. Fortunately, in Windows XP you can easily back up everything in your user profile using the Ntbackup program. You don't even need to exit Outlook; a Windows XP feature called the Volume Shadow Copy Service allows NTBackup to archive open files.

In Outlook 2003, you have a choice of two formats for Personal Folders files. You can use a Unicode format, which works only with Outlook 2003, or you can choose the original Outlook 97-2002 format, which preserves the capability to create new files and use existing ones in older versions of Outlook. When you choose File, New, Outlook Data File, you see the dialog box shown in Figure 7.18. What's the difference?

Figure 7.18
The Office Outlook Personal Folders file format has a much larger storage capacity than the Outlook 97-2002 format; choose the latter only if compatibility is a concern.

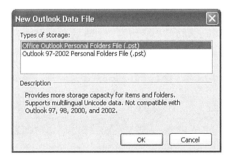

7

- The newer Office Outlook Personal Folders File (.pst) format stores text in Unicode format, which means it supports multilanguage input. It also allows file sizes to exceed 20GB, with an essentially unlimited number of items and folders.

- The older Outlook 97-2002 Personal Folder File (.pst) format supports only ANSI text and allows a maximum file size of 2GB with up to 65,535 items and 65,535 folders per file.

So, which one should you choose? You might not need to choose. When you first set up Outlook, the program chooses the newer file format for you. Unless you think you'll need to share a Personal Folders file with an earlier version of Outlook, choose the newer format. The 2GB limit on file size may sound large, but in practice it's all too easy to hit that ceiling, especially if you send and receive lots of files containing large file attachments. Select the older Outlook 97-2002 format only if you need to open the data file in Outlook 2002 or earlier.

CAUTION

> You might think that 2GB is more storage than any human being could ever use. Trust us, you can use up all that space more quickly than you can imagine, especially if you send and receive lots of movies, pictures, and other attachments. We strongly recommend that you choose the new PST format; if you use the old-style PST format, Outlook is unforgiving when you reach the 2GB limit. Your files won't open, and you'll need sophisticated help to have any prayer of recovering your important information. (If you've bumped into this limit, you can find advice and links to some useful tools at http://www.slipstick.com/problems/repair2gbpst.htm.)

If you subscribe to several active mailing lists, you might want to create a second Personal Folders file to reduce the clutter in your primary store. This strategy allows you to back up your main Personal Folders file containing your important e-mail and copy it to a safe place, without worrying that all those list messages will make it too big to back up properly. To create a second or subsequent Personal Folders file, choose File, New, Outlook Data File. Choose a file format from the dialog box. Give the file a name, choose a location, and click OK. You'll see the dialog box shown in Figure 7.19, which allows you to define the top-level name that appears in Outlook's Folders List and set compression and encryption options.

TIP FROM

Ed & Woody

> There's no relationship at all between the name of the Personal Folders data file and the text label that appears in the Folders List. If you create a second file that you intend to use for messages from mailing lists, for example, you might choose to use a filename such as Lists.pst, and then change the top-level folder name to My Mailing Lists.

7

Figure 7.19
Outlook uses the name you enter here to identify the top-level folder for a Personal Folders file.

After creating the additional Personal Folders file, Outlook automatically opens it. To close the file, right-click its icon in the Navigation pane (you might need to click the Folder List button to see its icon) and choose the Close option from the shortcut menu. You can also use this shortcut menu to adjust the properties of any Personal Folders file.

Working with an Exchange Server

If you connect to a Microsoft Exchange Server, your primary data is stored on the server and is managed by the server's administrator. You can create one (and only one) *Offline Store file* and save it on your computer. This file type, which uses the extension .ost, closely resembles a Personal Folders file.

Items in an Offline Store file can be synchronized with your primary store on a Microsoft Exchange Server. As the name implies, Outlook compares the items on the server with those in your Offline Store file and adds, updates, or deletes items in both places so they always contain the same information. This enables you to read and compose e-mail or other items when the server is unavailable—for example, when you're sitting in an airplane seat reading mail on a notebook computer. When you connect to the server via remote access, or when you return to the office and reconnect your notebook computer to the network, click the Send/Receive button to transfer changes in both directions.

When your primary store is an Exchange Server that synchronizes with an Offline Store file, you can still create and use any number of Personal Folders files. All such files will be secondary stores. You might choose this strategy if you want to save network space or reduce synchronization time by archiving messages to a local file for ready access. In any case, you'll need to coordinate your storage strategy with whoever runs your network.

Mailbox Folders on an Exchange Server Only

If you use Outlook to connect to a Microsoft Exchange Server, you can access mail and create calendar and contact items in your Mailbox folders on the server. If you lose the network connection, you lose all access to your data. This option is typically found in highly managed corporations where administrators are concerned about security and/or local storage space on users' computers.

7

Managing Outlook Data Files

Left unchecked, an Outlook data file can grow to mammoth proportions quickly. If your data file gets too large, you'll encounter trouble trying to back it up, and if you're using the old-style Outlook 97-2002 format, you run the risk of losing data completely if it hits 2GB. In this section, we explain how to keep your mailbox slim and trim. We also list tools and techniques you can use to prevent and recover from Outlook errors.

Cleaning Up and Archiving Outlook Information

By default, Outlook automatically moves items out of your Personal Folders file after a specified amount of time has passed. Using this AutoArchive feature, Outlook checks every item in your Personal Folders file at regular intervals. When it finds appointments, tasks, and e-mail messages that exceed the age limits you specify, it automatically moves them to an *archive file*. Unless you change the settings to specify a different interval, Outlook runs an AutoArchive check every 14 days and looks for any items that are more than 6 months old. The archive file is called Archive.pst, and it's located in the same folder as your primary store (you can change the filename and its location, if you prefer). You can also force Outlook to archive items instead of waiting for its next scheduled archive operation.

TIP FROM

EQ & Woody

> Cleaning up and archiving mail folders is easier if junk mail and other nonessential messages never get there in the first place. Use Outlook's Rules Wizard to create rules that automatically delete specific types of messages and move other types directly into folders as they arrive. The folders you specify as the destination in each rule can be in a different Personal Folders file; if you use rules to move messages into different folders in your primary Outlook data file, you can specify custom AutoArchive options for those folders.

Configuring AutoArchive options in Outlook is a fairly straightforward process. From the AutoArchive dialog box, you tell Outlook how often you want it to scan your Personal Folders file (or files) and perform AutoArchive options. Then, optionally, you can adjust archiving options for individual folders.

To adjust the default AutoArchive options, choose Tools, Options, click the Other tab, and click the AutoArchive button. This action displays the dialog box shown in Figure 7.20.

Use any or all of these AutoArchive settings:

- To enable the AutoArchive option, make sure a check mark appears in the Run AutoArchive Every *nn* Days box. Clear this box if you want AutoArchive to run only when you specifically choose to do so.

- To adjust the AutoArchive interval from its default of 14 days, pick a new number between 1 and 60 here. Choose a smaller number if you want Outlook to aggressively manage your data.

7

- If you want the AutoArchive operation to occur unattended, clear the Prompt Before AutoArchive Runs check box.

- Specify a filename and location in the Move Old Items To box. Unless you change this setting, Outlook creates a new Personal Folders file called Archive.pst and stores it in the default Outlook data files location, along with your main Outlook data file.

Figure 7.20
By default, Outlook scans all Personal Folders files every 14 days. Click Apply These Settings to All Folders Now to change settings for all folders.

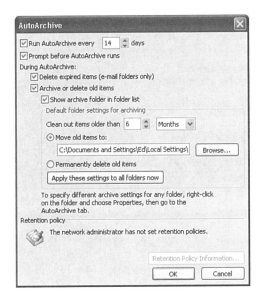

TIP FROM

By definition, the archive file includes data you don't need every day, so it doesn't make sense to keep this file open. Clear the Show Archive in Folder List option to keep Outlook from adding it to your Folder List when AutoArchive runs. If you want to search for an item in this file, choose File, Open, Outlook Data File (.pst), and select the Archive.pst file. Then switch to the Folder List to display the contents of individual folders in the archive file.

CAUTION

Unless you're absolutely positive that you don't want any archives at all, do *not* select the Permanently Delete Old Items check box. If you set this option as the default, any message that is older than the specified interval will be permanently and irretrievably deleted from your e-mail archives when AutoArchive runs. Reserve this option for folders that contain types of messages you know you won't want to keep, such as time-sensitive newsletters.

7

Each time Outlook runs its AutoArchive check, it performs operations on each folder separately, using the default settings. To adjust AutoArchive options for an individual folder, click the Folder List button at the bottom of the Navigation bar, right-click the folder's icon, and then choose Properties. The AutoArchive tab of the Properties dialog box (see Figure 7.21) lets you enable or disable archiving for that folder. (With AutoArchiving disabled, old items hang around until you choose to delete them.) This dialog box also lets you specify an alternative location where you want Outlook to move items (the default is the file you specified in the global AutoArchive options), or you can choose to delete all items that are older than the specified time.

Figure 7.21
Use this dialog box to set alternate AutoArchive options for each folder.

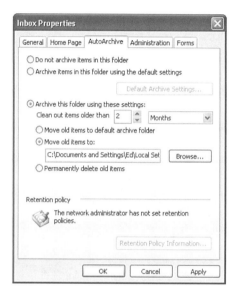

N O T E

Because items in the Contacts folder do not have a date associated with them, there is no AutoArchive tab in this folder's Properties dialog box, and AutoArchive operations do not affect this folder.

In many cases, you'll want to radically adjust the default settings. For example, if you never refer to your Calendar folder to look up old meetings and appointments, you can safely specify that you want to delete these items when AutoArchiving. On the other hand, if you live and die by e-mail, you might want to keep a year's worth of messages in your Personal Folders file so you can search for information easily. In that case, right-click the Inbox folder, choose Properties, and adjust the Clean Out Items Every *nn* Months option to 12; then do the same for the Sent Items folder.

RECOVERING FREE SPACE IN OUTLOOK DATA FILES

Deleting items from your Outlook data files doesn't automatically recover the space the deleted items used. (Old database developers are familiar with the syndrome, in which the database file continues to reserve space long after the data is gone.) In fact, even after you delete every single item from a 200MB Personal Folders (.pst) file, that file continues to occupy the full 200MB.

Outlook 2003 automatically *compacts* files in the background, during times when Outlook is idle. If you want to compact the files manually, start by clearing out the clutter. Delete any unwanted messages, and remove large file attachments (after copying important files to local storage, of course). Empty the Deleted Items folder, and then follow these steps:

1. From the main Outlook menu, choose File, Data File Management.

2. In the Outlook Data Files dialog box, select the file you want to compact and click the Settings button to open the Personal Folders dialog box shown in Figure 7.22.

3. Click the Compact Now button. Depending on the size of the file and your available system resources, this action might take some time.

4. Click OK to close the Personal Folders dialog box.

5. To compact another open Personal Folders file, select it from the list and repeat steps 2–4. When finished, click OK to close the dialog box.

REPAIRING A DAMAGED PERSONAL FOLDERS FILE

If you begin encountering error messages or suspect that a Personal Folders file is damaged, a well-hidden Outlook tool called the Microsoft Personal Folders Scan/Repair Utility can help you set things right in short order. Search your hard drive for a file called Scanpst.exe (in a typical U.S. English installation, you'll find it in `%ProgramFiles%\Common Files\System\MSMapi\1033`). Double-click the file and follow the wizard's prompts to select the Personal Folders file you want to scan; if the utility finds any damage, it asks your permission and creates a backup before attempting to repair the errors. Note that this process might take several hours on a large PST file, so be prepared to wait.

Figure 7.22

TIP FROM

Personal Folders files are remarkably resilient, but they're not indestructible. If you keep irreplaceable information such as important e-mail or contact information in one of these files, back it up regularly—preferably to removable media (an external hard drive or writable CD, for instance) or on a server stored in a different physical location. You must shut down Outlook before you can copy a Personal Folders file.

7

USING REMINDERS AND FOLLOW-UP FLAGS

Do you have an assignment due tomorrow? Did you promise to return a phone call this week? Outlook allows you to attach pop-up *reminders* to any type of item except a note. In the case of appointments and tasks, the default form allows you to define the date and time when you want to see a reminder. For an e-mail message or contact item, you must create a *follow-up flag* before you can set a reminder. You can also attach color-coded flags (in any of six colors) to messages and contact records. You can use these colors any way you want to— you might want to use red flags to indicate high-priority items, green flags to denote financial reminders, purple flags for family, and so on. In table-based views, you can add a follow-up flag with a single click, and a built-in search folder lets you quickly see all messages that are flagged for follow-up.

 In some cases, reminders and follow-up flags simply won't work. For an explanation, see "Alarms Fail to Go Off," and "Alarms Work Only in Four Key Folders" in the "Troubleshooting" section at the end of this chapter.

FLAGGING MESSAGES FOR FOLLOW-UP

Follow-up flags help you keep track of unfinished business. Reminders help you avoid the embarrassment of missing a meeting or a phone call because you forgot to check your calendar. By default, Outlook adds a reminder to all meetings and appointments, set for 15 minutes before the scheduled time. That's appropriate if you're using Outlook at work and you sit in front of your computer all day. But you might want to change this setting if you normally sit down at the computer once a day. To change this setting, choose Tools, Options, click the Preferences tab, and set the preferred interval under the Calendar heading by using the pull-down list (or typing an entry) in the Default Reminder box. Clear the Default Reminder check box if the only reminders you want to see are those you expressly add to an item.

You can enter or edit the reminder for an appointment or meeting by opening the item and selecting or entering a time from the Reminder drop-down list. This time is always relative to the start time of the appointment or meeting; you can request a reminder by entering any number of minutes, hours, days, weeks, months, or years in this box. For example, if you enter 1 week, Outlook pops up a reminder exactly one week before the meeting is scheduled to start. You cannot, however, enter a specific date or time when you want to receive a meeting or appointment reminder.

Outlook automatically includes reminders for tasks as well, using the date you enter in the Due Date field and a default time of 8:00 a.m. If you're an early riser, you can change this default: Choose Tools, Options, click the Preferences tab, and select a new time from the drop-down list in the Tasks section.

TIP FROM

To prevent Outlook from automatically setting a reminder on every new task, choose Tools, Options, and then click the Task Options button on the Preferences tab. Clear the Set Reminders on Tasks with Due Dates check box. Close all open dialog boxes to return to Outlook with your new preferences in place.

To set a reminder for an e-mail message or a contact, you must first assign a follow-up flag for that item. Unlike task and appointment reminders, which display the Subject line of the item, you can define custom text that appears in the pop-up reminder notice.

If you and a fellow student are working on a project together and she sends you some notes via e-mail, you might attach a follow-up flag to the message and set a reminder to follow up on those items tomorrow. Similarly, if you want to call a handful of parents next Monday after your meeting with the school board, you can select each person's item in the Contacts folder, one at a time, and flag each one for a phone call.

- To flag an item in the message list, click the flag icon at the far right. (Click again to mark the item as completed.) This option uses the default red flag, with the generic "Follow up" message and no reminder. Right-click this icon to choose from one of six available colors.

- To flag an open e-mail message or contact, click the Follow Up button on the Standard toolbar.

- To flag a contact in the Contacts folder, click the Follow Up button on the Standard toolbar or select the item, right-click, and choose Follow Up.

If you use either of the last two methods, you'll see the dialog box shown in Figure 7.23.

Figure 7.23
To flag a message or contact, choose one of the canned messages in this drop-down list, or enter a text message of your own.

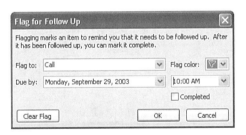

The default text in a flag is Follow Up. You can choose from other alternatives, including Call, Read, or Review. If none of the canned alternatives is suitable, you can enter your own text. For example, if you're planning a school picnic for next weekend and you want to make sure parents get a copy ASAP, you can flag a group of contacts with the text `Call About Picnic` and set a reminder for Thursday.

The reminder date and time are optional parts of a follow-up flag. Enter a value here if you want a reminder to pop up at a specified date or time. By default, if you enter a date,

7

Outlook sets the time to 12:00 a.m. You can enter a specific reminder time for any follow-up flag by using the exact date and time or any text that Outlook's AutoDate feature recognizes. If you received an e-mail that you need to act on first thing next week, for example, enter **next mon** in the date portion of the Due By box and **6am** in the time box. Outlook translates the date and time for you.

MANAGING FLAGGED ITEMS

In table views, flagged items include a flag icon; overdue items appear in red text. The follow-up message text and date appear in the information header at the top of a flagged message or contact item, whether you open it in its own window or use the preview pane.

TIP FROM

Ed & Woody

> You can use follow-up flags in mail you send to other people as well; while composing a message, click the Follow Up button on the Standard toolbar to add your follow-up flag (unlike in older versions, flags you add to an existing message are not included when you forward a message). If the recipient uses Outlook, he'll see the flag text and due date in the info bar at the top of the message when he reads it. (Sending a flagged message with a due date does not set a pop-up reminder for the recipient, however.) Several of the choices in the Flag for Follow Up dialog box, in fact, are available precisely for this purpose. While composing a message, click the Follow Up button and choose For Your Information or No Reply Necessary to alert the receiver that he needn't act on the message. Or choose Review and add a due date; even if the text of your message includes a request to reply by a certain time, this technique adds emphasis.

Regardless of how you set a reminder, when the specified time rolls around, Outlook plays a sound (if you selected that option) and pops up a reminder message. If you have several reminders, Outlook consolidates them in a single window, as shown in Figure 7.24.

Figure 7.24
This Reminder dialog box can stay open while you work with items in Outlook folders. Click each item to see its details at the top of the dialog box.

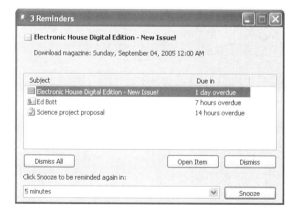

When you see a reminder, you can dismiss it so you don't see it again, or open it so you can view the item itself. This option is especially useful when you want to review notes for an upcoming appointment or look up the phone number of a contact you plan to call.

Use the Snooze button to hide the reminder for a while. The default setting is five minutes, but you can use the drop-down list to select a new reminder time as much as one week later.

 If reminders don't appear when you expect them to, see "Alarms Fail to Go Off" in the "Troubleshooting" section at the end of this chapter.

TIP FROM

To see all flagged e-mail messages from all folders, display the Inbox and then choose the For Follow Up search folder. To see all flagged contacts, open the Contacts folder and switch to the built-in By Follow-up Flag view. This table view shows all items that include flags at the top of the list.

After you've finished working with a flagged item, you have two choices to remove the flag. Flag the item as complete if you want it to show in views that include flags, or clear the flag completely. Either option is available from right-click shortcut menus or in the Flag for Follow Up dialog box.

FINDING OUTLOOK ITEMS

If you use Outlook regularly, your collection of personal data might eventually become so large that you won't be able to find individual items simply by browsing through folders. Outlook offers two tools to help you track down items based on their content. The Find pane, accessible via a button on Outlook's Standard toolbar, is fast and simple. The Advanced Find dialog box requires much more work, but it allows you to pinpoint a single item or snag an entire group of items with precision. (A third option is to use a desktop search program, as described in the sidebar at the end of Chapter 2, "Making Office 2003 Work Your Way.")

For some tasks, using built-in or custom Outlook views and arrangements is faster and easier than performing a search. For example, if you use categories in the Contacts, Calendar, and Tasks folders, switching to the built-in By Category view makes it easy to locate all related items. Likewise, try the By Sender view in the Inbox folder to see all messages from a specific person, or the By Company view in the Contacts folder to organize all contacts based on the companies they work for.

FINDING CONTACT INFORMATION FAST

By far, the fastest way to open any Contact's record is with the Find a Contact text box at the right of Outlook's Standard toolbar. Enter a part of any person's name or e-mail address, and then press Enter. If only one item matches the text you entered, Outlook opens that record. If more than one contact's name includes the text you specified, you'll have to pick from the full list of matching names in the Choose Contacts dialog box. If multiple matches appear in the e-mail address field, you'll see the Check Names dialog box from the Outlook Address Book; pick a name and click OK to open that contact's record.

7

TIP FROM

Ed & Woody

This tiny text box is far more powerful than it looks. It's especially useful if you want to find a whole group of people who have e-mail addresses in the same domain. Enter aol, for instance, to see all your contacts who have addresses at aol.com. This technique is especially useful when you need to change a group of e-mail addresses in your Contacts folder after one Internet provider swallows up another and forces its current customers to change domains.

USING THE FIND PANE FOR SIMPLE SEARCHES

To use the Find pane, first switch to the folder in which you want to search, and then click the Find button on Outlook's Standard toolbar, or press Ctrl+E, or choose Tools, Find, Find. The Find pane in Outlook 2003 occupies a single row just above the Contents pane, as shown in Figure 7.25.

Figure 7.25
Use the Find pane to search for items in the current Outlook folder.

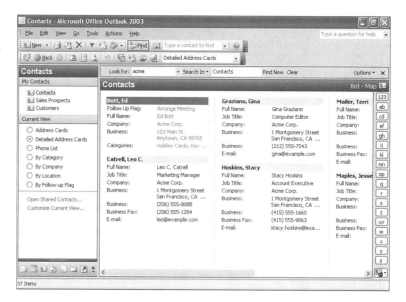

Enter a word, phrase, or a string of characters in the Look For box. By default, the current folder is selected; click the arrow to the right of the Search In box to choose a different folder. To search through all text in all items in the folder, click the Options arrow and choose Search All Text in Each Message. Click the Find Now button to begin the search.

NOTE

How do you stop a search in progress if you realize you typed the wrong name or number? While a search is under way, a Stop button appears just to the right of the Find Now button. After the search is complete, this button changes to read Clear.

7

Outlook searches for the exact text you enter in the Look For box; if you enter two or more words separated by a space or punctuation, all the words you entered must appear in the same field. The search results replace the contents below the Find pane. You can change the view of the search results to make them easier to scan; click the Clear button to the right of the Find Now button to restore the full view.

TIP FROM

> Searches are not cumulative. Each time you click the Find Now button, Outlook searches the entire folder and replaces the results of your previous search. If you want to perform a series of searches to narrow down a large group of items, use the Advanced Find dialog box instead.

ADVANCED SEARCH TECHNIQUES

If the Find pane doesn't turn up the information you're looking for, use the more sophisticated (and complex) Advanced Find dialog box. This option lets you find items that contain specific types of information; you can also use it to search for virtually unlimited combinations of *criteria*. For searches you run regularly, you can save and reuse any set of Advanced Find criteria. For searches in folders that contain e-mail messages, Outlook 2003 adds the capability to save your search as a *search folder*.

The Advanced Find dialog box is most useful when you want to search using multiple criteria or within specific date ranges. If you're preparing a year-end report about the swim club's activities, you might search for Calendar items that include the word "swim" in the description and that occurred in the current year. If you need to do a round of follow-up calls about an upcoming meeting, you might search for contacts that you've assigned to the Swim Club category who are located in your area code.

TIP FROM

> If you regularly use Advanced Find, learn its keyboard shortcut–Ctrl+Shift+F–or add an Advanced Find button to the right of the Find button on Outlook's Standard toolbar.

→ For more details on how to add buttons to Office toolbars, **see** "Customizing Toolbars," **p. 33**.

To open the Advanced Find dialog box, press Ctrl+Shift+F, or choose Tools, Find, Advanced Find. If the Find pane is visible, you can click the Advanced Find link on the Options menu. In any case, you'll see the dialog box shown in Figure 7.26.

Follow these steps to use the Advanced Find dialog box:

1. Use the Look For drop-down list to specify the type of items you want to search for—messages or appointments, for example. By default, this value is set to the type of item stored in the current folder. For the widest possible search, choose Any Type of Outlook Item—this option is useful if you want to search for all messages, contacts, appointments, and tasks related to a specific company, for example.

Figure 7.26
Use this dialog box to search for Outlook items using a combination of criteria.

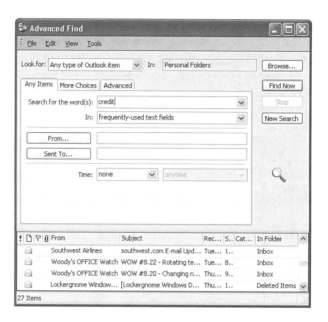

2. By default, your search covers only the current folder. To change that folder or select more than one folder, click the Browse button and select or clear check boxes as needed.

NOTE

> You can search multiple folders within only a single Personal Folders file. Thus, to search for related messages in current and archived folders, you'll need to perform two searches. Open a second copy of the Advanced Find dialog box if you want to see all search results simultaneously.

3. Fill in your search criteria using one or more of the three tabs in the Advanced Find dialog box.

  • The most common options appear on the first tab; the name of this tab and the exact choices available vary slightly, depending on the type of item you're looking for. For example, when searching through mail messages you can look for text in the subject field only, in the subject field and message body, or in frequently used text fields.

  • Click the More Choices tab to see additional options that are specific to the type of item you're looking for. When searching for Outlook items, this tab always lets you select from the Categories field or find items based on their size. As Figure 7.27 demonstrates, you can use this tab to recover space in your Inbox by selecting messages that contain file attachments over a specified size, and then deleting them or moving them to a new location.

- Use the Advanced tab (see Figure 7.28) to define criteria based on any Outlook field. Click the Field button to select a field, and then enter a Condition and (if necessary) a Value. Click the Add to List button to insert the criteria in the box above the button. Repeat this step to use multiple criteria.

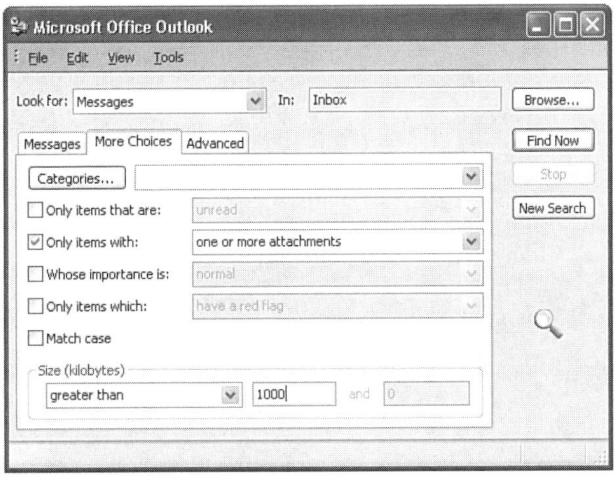

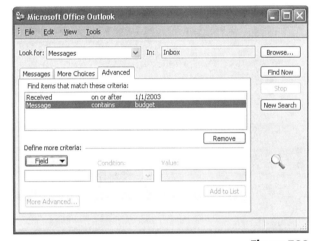

Figure 7.27

4. Click the Find Now button to begin the search, using the criteria you entered. The results of the search appear in a simple list below the Advanced Find dialog box. Click the Stop button to interrupt the search at any point.

Double-click to open any item in the search results list. You can move, copy, delete, or edit items in this folder as well, using right-click shortcut menus (or

Figure 7.28

click and drag to folders in the Outlook window). You can't choose a view other than the Table view; however, you can customize the fields that appear in the search results, change the sort order, and apply grouping. Right-click any column headings in the search results and use the Field Chooser to add or remove columns; you can also group messages in this display. When you save the search, these settings are saved also.

7

> The settings in the Advanced Find dialog box are identical to those in the Filter dialog box that you use to define a custom view. Unfortunately, you can't transfer settings between these two dialog boxes. When you use the Advanced Find dialog box, you can view the results only as a simple list; if you want to see the search results in a different view, such as Address Cards, define a new view and create a filter for it. For searches that start in folders containing e-mail items, you can also choose File, Save Search as Search Folder and change the view or arrangement in the search folder.

Click the New Search button to clear all previously defined criteria and start from scratch.

→ To learn how to save and reuse complex searches, **see** "Extra Credit: Building a Library of Saved Searches," **p. 207**.

IMPORTING AND EXPORTING OUTLOOK INFORMATION

The simplest way to transfer data between Outlook and other programs is with the help of the Import and Export Wizard. The most common use of this feature is to help you migrate your data between Outlook and a web-based address book program. You can also use this feature with a contact-management program such as Act! Before going to the trouble to do a one-time transfer of data, however, check to see whether your program can read Outlook data files directly, as recent versions of Act! can. If the Import and Export Wizard doesn't include the specific name and version number of the program you use, you can usually export the data to a delimited text file or a database format and then import the converted file into Outlook or your other program.

> If you use multiple Personal Folders files to maintain your mail, use the Import and Export Wizard to effortlessly move items from one file to another. Choose File, Import and Export, and then select Export to a File or Import from Another Program or File. In either case, you'll find a Personal Folder File (.pst) option. Follow the wizard's prompts to select the folder or folders you want to move—defining a filter if necessary, so you move only items that match criteria you specify—and choose the name of the destination file.

IMPORTING DATA FROM EXTERNAL PROGRAMS

Outlook makes it relatively easy to import personal information, including contacts and appointments, from other software. Using the Import and Export Wizard, choose Import from Another Program or File, and then select one of the following supported file formats. Outlook 2003 recognizes data files created by a number of modern contact-management programs.

If Outlook can't work directly with the native format of the program that contains the data you want to import, you'll have to first export the data to a supported format. Comma Separated Values and Tab Separated Values are the most common, but the import utility can also read Excel lists.

NOTE

> Both delimited text formats (*Comma Separated Values* and *Tab Separated Values*) offer DOS and Windows alternatives. The DOS version uses the ASCII character set, while the Windows versions incorporate the *ANSI character set*, which includes international and publishing characters. When in doubt, always choose the Windows option.

To import data, follow these steps:

1. Choose File, Import and Export.

2. In the Import and Export Wizard, choose Import from Another Program or File; then follow the wizard's prompts to select the specific data format and the file that contains the data.

3. In the Import a File dialog box (see Figure 7.29), specify how you want Outlook to handle items that duplicate those in the current folder. You can replace the existing item with the imported one, ignore the duplicate item, or allow Outlook to create duplicates. When in doubt, allow Outlook to create duplicate items and manually resolve the differences later.

Figure 7.29
Specify whether you want to create duplicate items (based on the title) when importing information. Regardless of your choice, Outlook does not warn you whether it created or rejected any duplicates.

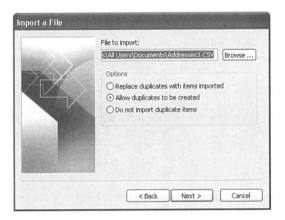

TIP FROM

EQ & Woody

> When you import data, Outlook doesn't give you any feedback as to how many new items it created, or whether it dealt with any duplicate items. If you want to know how many new items were created, open the destination folder before importing and check the status bar (just below the Navigation pane) to see how many items the folder contains. After completing the import, check the new count to see how many items were added.

→ Under some circumstances, Outlook can help you merge duplicate items that creep into your Contacts list so that you don't inadvertently keep outdated information; **see** "Merging Duplicate Contact Items," **p. 285**.

7

4. Select the *destination folder* into which you want to import the data, and then click Next.

5. In the last step of the Import and Export Wizard, click the Map Custom Fields button if you want to verify that Outlook plans to stuff information from the source file into the correct folder. The Map Custom Fields dialog box (shown in Figure 7.30) reads the *field* names from the *source file* and makes its best guess at matching them in the destination file.

Figure 7.30
The pane on the left shows the field names from the source file; drag names into the pane on the right to match them with Outlook field names.

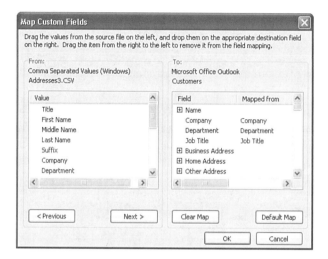

TIP FROM

EQ & Woody

> Whenever you import any amount of data, large or small, into your primary Outlook data file, we strongly recommend that you first create a new, temporary folder. Give the folder a name that describes the data, such as "Imported Addresses," and then start the import. This precaution lets you inspect the imported items for errors and correct any information that was damaged during the import. When you're satisfied that the new items are correct, drag them into the proper destination folder.

6. Outlook displays the field names from the source file in the left pane. Scroll through the list of mappings on the right to see how Outlook has matched the field names in the source file to Outlook fields. Drag field names from the left pane and drop them on the corresponding fields in the right pane to create a mapping. For example, if your source file includes a field called Full Name, drop it onto the Name field in the right pane.

7. Click Finish to import the data.

7

You don't need to map all the fields from your source file to Outlook. If your original database includes hundreds of fields for each record, but all you want to import is the name and mailing address so that you can send out a newsletter, click the Clear Map button to eliminate all mappings. Then drag just the handful of fields you want to use into the destination pane.

EXPORTING OUTLOOK DATA

When you need to export data, Outlook offers fewer options than on the corresponding import side. In most cases, you'll need to export the data from one or more folders into a file using a standard data-interchange format.

Outlook enables you to export to an Excel worksheet or a Microsoft Access database; choose the Excel option if you want to manipulate the data using Excel's list-management features.

→ To learn more about working with Excel's list-management features, **see** Chapter 20, "Working with Lists and PivotTables," **p. 629**.

If you plan to export the data into a non-Office program, choose one of the comma- or tab-delimited text formats. To export data to a file, choose File, Import and Export. In the Import and Export Wizard, choose Export to a File, and then follow the prompts to select the folder you want to export from, the file format you want to create, and the name and location of the resulting output file. As with the import version of this wizard, you can map custom fields. This is an excellent way to quickly export selected information from your Contacts folder into a format that other programs (including Word and Excel) can readily use.

 If your exported data contains stray characters that cause problems when you try to open the file in another program, see "Removing Multiline Addresses from Your Contacts Folder" in the "Troubleshooting" section at the end of this chapter.

SYNCHRONIZING OUTLOOK DATA WITH A HANDHELD DEVICE

If you own a handheld computer or another mobile device that stores personal information you can *synchronize* data between your Outlook Personal Folders file and the handheld device. The task is easiest if you use a Pocket PC or a phone that runs Windows Mobile, which includes its own slimmed-down version of Outlook. If you use a handheld device or a phone that has its own data format, you'll probably have to use a special software program to keep the data in both places in sync. If your software can work directly with Outlook data files, you don't need to use Outlook's Import and Export Wizard; you can just sync and go.

To set up and synchronize with a handheld device running Windows Mobile, use the ActiveSync utility, available for download from http://www.microsoft.com/mobile. After installing this software on your main computer, you connect the handheld device (usually with a USB cable) and the software automatically synchronizes your calendar and contacts

7

list, downloads a limited selection of e-mail messages, and moves files between your hand-held device and a desktop or portable PC. You can also configure space-saving options, such as restricting the size of messages on the handheld device and ignoring attachments.

If you have a handheld device running the Palm OS and you purchased it in 2004 or later, its utility software probably already includes the Palm Outlook Conduits. With older devices, you must first install Chapura's PocketMirror software. This software adds a button to Outlook's Standard toolbar and also makes a PocketMirror Settings option available on the Tools menu. (Download the latest version from http://www.palmsource.com.)

Note that this option only synchronizes the Calendar, Contacts, Tasks, and Notes folders. If you set up e-mail on your Palm device, only the Outlook Inbox is synchronized. In addition, some information is lost during synchronization. For instance, recurring appointments are typically split into individual appointments on the handheld device.

TROUBLESHOOTING

RESTORING GROUPS TO AN ARRANGEMENT

In my Inbox, I chose the Size option from the View, Arrange By menu, but I got one long list instead of the logical groupings I usually see. What happened?

You must have inadvertently cleared the Automatically Group According to Arrangement option on the Group By dialog box for the current view. This can easily happen if you tinker with view settings. To restore the groups, choose View, Arrange By, and click Show In Groups.

ALARMS FAIL TO GO OFF

I set a reminder on an Outlook item, but I never received a pop-up reminder.

It sounds obvious, but Outlook must be running if you expect to receive reminders. Outlook displays past-due reminders the next time you start the program, but these reminders don't do you much good if you've already missed an important meeting or appointment. To ensure that Outlook runs every time you start your computer, place a shortcut to the program in your Startup group. And if you use reminders, avoid shutting down Outlook except when you plan to turn off your PC.

ALARMS WORK ONLY IN FOUR KEY FOLDERS

Outlook was running, but I still never received a pop-up reminder for an item.

Check the folder the item is stored in. This problem is most common when you use rules to automatically move incoming messages to a folder other than the Inbox. Outlook monitors only four specific folders for reminders and follow-up flags: Inbox, Calendar, Contacts, and Tasks. And it monitors only the data store that is designated as the one to receive incoming messages. If an item is in another folder, even if it's a subfolder to one of these folders, Outlook will allow you to set the reminder, but it won't pop up the notice when you expect it. When you move the item back to one of these four folders, you'll see an Overdue reminder immediately.

RESETTING THE STANDARD VIEWS

When I view information using a built-in Outlook view, some fields are missing, or the sorting and grouping options aren't what I want.

Outlook makes it too easy to customize the built-in views, which is usually the cause when fields disappear from standard views. Fortunately, it's also easy to return a built-in Outlook view to its original settings. If you've messed up the Messages view of the Inbox or the Address Cards view of the Contacts folder, for example, just choose View, Current View, Define Views, and then select the view name and click Reset. This option is not available for custom views.

REMOVING MULTILINE ADDRESSES FROM YOUR CONTACTS FOLDER

When I open the Outlook data I exported to another program, the file contains stray characters that I didn't put there. What's happening?

Your exported data contains stray characters that cause problems when you try to open the file in another program. The culprit might be multiline addresses from your Contacts folder. In some export formats, Outlook includes carriage return characters with each line of the address, and the program you're using to import the data interprets these as end-of-record markers. Try exporting your data again, this time using the Comma Separated Text format, which adds carriage returns only at the end of a line.

DRAGGING DOESN'T ALWAYS MOVE AN ITEM

I tried to move an item from one folder to another, but Outlook opened the form for a new item instead.

You can move items only to folders capable of storing that type of item. If you try to move one type of item (such as an e-mail message) to a folder intended for a different item (such as the Contacts folder), Outlook assumes you want to create a new item, just as if you had dropped the original icon on the folder's shortcut in the Navigation pane. Choose a different destination folder.

EXTRA CREDIT: BUILDING A LIBRARY OF SAVED SEARCHES

One way to make it easier to find Outlook items is to build a library of saved searches that you can reopen easily. Even if you need to modify one or two details of a saved search, it's usually much easier to do so than to start from scratch.

For searches that target folders containing e-mail messages, Outlook 2003 allows you to create a special type of shortcut called a search folder. When you click one of these shortcuts, Outlook runs the saved search and displays the results in the contents pane. For searches in other folders, you can save the search settings in an Office Search shortcut file, with the extension .oss. To keep track of these saved searches, create a subfolder in My Documents or on the Start menu and call it Saved Outlook Searches. Whenever you create and save a search, store the shortcut here so you can access it again.

Initially, Outlook includes a handful of search folders that help you identify unread mail, messages that are flagged for follow-up, and larger-than-normal messages. To begin building a library of useful searches, open the Advanced Find dialog box and start with the list shown here. For each search, establish the type of item to look for: Messages, Contacts, or Tasks, for example. Specify which folders you want Outlook to search. If you've set up rules to process incoming messages into multiple folders, be sure to select all those folders; remember to create separate searches to cover archived messages in separate PST files.

After selecting all search settings in the Advanced Find dialog box, click Find Now and then choose File, Save Search As Search Folder. Give each saved search a descriptive name—you could use the bold text at the beginning of each item in the following list—and click OK. (For non-mail searches, choose Save Search, select the location you set up for your saved searches, and click OK.)

- **Messages Received Since Beginning of Last Month**—Choose Messages from the Look For list, and then choose the Inbox and any other folders you use for incoming messages, especially those included as part of rules. Click the Advanced tab and add two criteria: Received This Month and Received Last Month.

- **Messages Received Since Beginning of Last Week**—Same as the previous item, but use Received This Week and Received Last Week as the criteria on the Advanced tab.

- **Messages Sent Since Beginning of Last Month** and **Messages Sent Since Beginning of Last Week**—Same as previous two items; specify the Sent Items folder as the location in which to search.

- **Company Mail**—Choose Messages from the Look For list. Choose the Inbox, the Sent Items folder, and any other commonly used message folders as the locations in which to look. On the Advanced tab, use criteria that search for a specific domain name in the To and From fields. For example, if you work for Que Publishing and your e-mail address is at quepublishing.com, add the criteria To contains quepublishing.com and From contains quepublishing.com; this will find all messages to or from other people in that domain. Use the Field Chooser to remove unnecessary icon fields and show both the To and From fields in the results pane; then group the results by the In Folder field.

Use these ideas as a jumping-off point for your own selection. You can add criteria to any of these searches; for instance, you might filter the Received Since Beginning of Last Month search to show only mail sent by someone in your company's domain. Save the search folder as Recent Company Mail, and you'll be able to cut through Inbox clutter quickly.

KEEPING YOUR E-MAIL UNDER CONTROL

In this chapter

8

MAKING THE MOST OF E-MAIL

How did we ever get along without e-mail? In the past decade, e-mail has progressed from a curiosity to a necessity. Today, the question isn't whether you use e-mail—it's how you manage multiple e-mail accounts and keep up with the flood of incoming messages.

Earlier versions of Outlook were frequently criticized as too big, too hard to configure, too insecure, and too unstable. None of those criticisms apply to Outlook 2003. And it's not just for use on corporate networks, either. If you get a few messages a week by way of a single e-mail account, you can set up Outlook with a few clicks and use it effortlessly. Adding a second or third e-mail account is also simple, and you can customize the process of retrieving, reading, sorting, and deleting messages.

In this chapter, we'll help you sort out the alphabet soup of e-mail acronyms, including POP3, SMTP, and IMAP. We'll also show you the difference between Outlook's message formats and explain how to use rules to keep incoming messages filed automatically.

SWITCHING FROM OUTLOOK EXPRESS OR ANOTHER E-MAIL PROGRAM

The first time you run Outlook 2003, it scans your system for compatible e-mail client software. If it finds a previous version of Outlook (97/98/2000/2002), Outlook Express, Netscape Mail or Netscape Messenger, Eudora Pro or Light, it offers to import your account settings (server information, username, and so on) and any existing mail messages. If you accept this option, you're done—Outlook creates a default profile, sets up mail accounts, and copies all your messages to your Inbox. You might be asked to reenter passwords the first time you connect to a mail server, but otherwise you shouldn't have to jump through any extra hoops to complete your configuration.

If you use Outlook Express or Eudora and you skip this option the first time you run Outlook, you can do it later. Choose File, Import and Export, and then choose Import Internet Mail Account Settings or Import Internet Mail and Addresses. (To run both options, you'll need to first choose one, and then restart the import utility.)

SETTING UP E-MAIL ACCOUNTS

In Outlook 2003, you can have as many mail accounts as you like. If you're like most people, you'll have a combination of Internet-standard accounts and Web-based accounts, such as Hotmail and MSN accounts. Exchange Server mailboxes are uncommon in homes and schools, but if you occasionally check your work mail from your home computer you can take advantage of this option using Outlook 2003. Your account settings are saved in a *user profile*.

→ Most users need only a single Outlook user profile; to learn when multiple profiles may be necessary and how to create them, see "Setting Up Alternative E-mail Profiles," **p. 220**.

8

When you first run Outlook on a computer with no existing e-mail settings, you jump straight to a wizard that offers to set up an e-mail account and create a default profile. If you skipped this wizard the first time you ran Outlook, or if you have a new e-mail account to add to your existing profile, you'll need to go through a fairly painless setup process. Choose either of the following methods to open the E-mail Accounts dialog box:

■ Click the Mail icon in Windows' Control Panel, which opens the dialog box shown in Figure 8.1, and then click the E-mail Accounts button.

■ If Outlook is already running, choose Tools, E-mail Accounts.

Figure 8.1
To configure Outlook accounts, data files, or profiles, you can use the Mail icon in the Control Panel, which opens this dialog box.

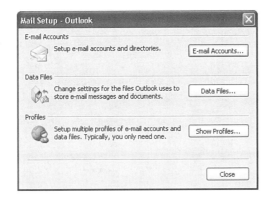

Choose Add a New E-mail Account and click Next to display the dialog box shown in Figure 8.2.

Figure 8.2
When setting up a new e-mail account, Outlook gives you these options. For typical Internet e-mail accounts, POP3 is the correct choice.

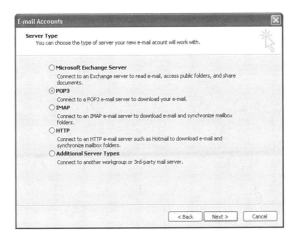

8

N O T E

> Like all previous Outlook versions, Outlook 2003 doesn't directly support AOL e-mail accounts. However, you can send and receive messages using an AOL account in Outlook, using one of two techniques.
>
> A third-party program, eMail2Pop, can help bridge the gap between the two worlds by converting the traffic from AOL's e-mail servers into standard SMTP and POP3 formats for use with Outlook. Visit `http://www.email2pop.com` for more details.
>
> If you're willing to jump through a few configuration hoops, you can access your AOL e-mail account using the IMAP standard. You'll find detailed instructions in an Office Online Help article entitled "Use Outlook with AOL E-mail," which is available at http://office.microsoft.com/en-us/assistance/HA010936921033.aspx.

In Outlook, you can configure multiple e-mail accounts, but you must designate one of those accounts as your default account. You can configure each account's connection options individually, so that you check for new mail automatically, or only on demand.

In the remainder of this section, we'll explain how to configure the different types of e-mail accounts.

CONFIGURING INTERNET STANDARD E-MAIL ACCOUNTS

Before you can send or receive e-mail over the Internet, you have to configure Outlook to communicate with incoming and outgoing mail servers. Outside of the corporate world, the most popular e-mail configuration by far is an Internet-standard SMTP server that supports POP3 connections.

N O T E

> In the course of setting up your e-mail accounts, you'll run across three widely used acronyms. Here's your secret decoder ring.
>
> SMTP stands for *Simple Mail Transfer Protocol*, which is the most widely used method for transferring outgoing mail to its ultimate destination. After you compose an e-mail message and click Send, your e-mail program typically connects to an SMTP server at your Internet service provider, which accepts the message on your behalf and makes contact with the SMTP server that handles mail for the recipient. The recipient's SMTP server stores the message in a *mailbox*.
>
> To retrieve messages from a mailbox at most Internet service providers, you use a mail client that supports *Post Office Protocol 3* (POP3, for short). A much less popular option for retrieving mail is *Internet Message Access Protocol 4 (IMAP)*. When you set up Outlook for use as a POP3 client, it downloads headers, message bodies, and attachments to your Personal Folders file. With IMAP, messages are stored on the server itself rather than in your Personal Folders file. If you set up an IMAP account, you will see an additional tab (IMAP) on the *<Account>* Properties dialog box, and the account name will appear in your folder list as a new icon at the same level as your Personal Folders file.

You can only set up IMAP if your server supports it. Some ISPs do, but most don't. As we noted earlier in this chapter, AOL allows you to use IMAP to access your e-mail using Outlook. The IMAP protocol offers options that are especially useful over slow connections, but it also creates some configuration headaches when using Outlook. You can't automatically save copies of sent messages, for example, and in some circumstances you won't receive notifications of new mail, even if you've set up Outlook to do so.

When you choose POP3 or IMAP as the account type, you enter information on the Internet E-mail Settings dialog box shown in Figure 8.3.

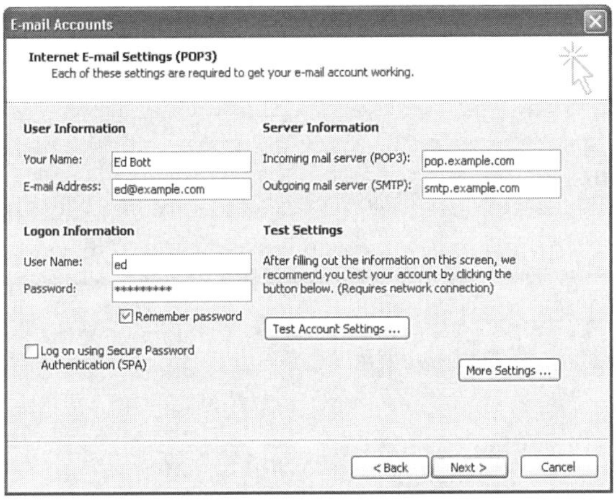

Figure 8.3
Fill in the basic information here and click the Test Account Settings button to set up a POP3 account in Outlook.

The Internet E-mail Settings dialog box requires that you fill in information such as the names of mail servers and the username and password you use to log on. Fill in the information exactly as it's provided to you by your Internet service provider or mail system administrator. In the User Information section, enter your name and e-mail address, exactly as you want mail recipients to see these details in the From: line on messages you send.

TIP FROM

Ed & Woody

If you use more than one mail account, enter slightly different information in the Name field for each one. For example, in the account you use to send and receive mail for your small business, add your company name in parentheses after your username. When you receive replies to messages you sent through that account, you'll usually be able to spot them quickly just by looking at the name in the To field.

In the Server Information section, you must specify fully qualified domain names for both incoming and outgoing mail servers. At some Internet service providers, both names are identical, usually in the form `mail.example.com`. Other common configurations use `smtp`, `pop`, or `pop3` as part of the full server name, with separate server names for incoming and outgoing mail servers. Most ISPs provide this information when you establish an account, and those that care about their customers also make it easily available on the Web. (Browse to your ISP's home page and look for a Support or Setup link.)

Outlook automatically fills in the User Name box in the Logon Information section, using the first part of the e-mail address you entered earlier. If your logon name is different, change this text. If you want Outlook to supply your password automatically each time you connect to the server, enter it in the Password field and select the Remember Password check box.

NOTE

> Leave the Password box blank if you want to reduce the possibility that someone else can send mail from your computer using this account; in that configuration, Outlook prompts you for your password the first time you connect to the server after starting Outlook.

On mail systems that use *Secure Password Authentication (SPA)*, a separate security package prompts the user for credentials when logging in to a server. This option is extremely rare at ISPs; older versions of MSN (POP3 accounts created before November 2000 and never converted to web-based format) and CompuServe used SPA. If your ISP tells you to select this check box, do so; otherwise, leave it blank.

After you use this dialog box to create a new account, click the More Settings button and adjust the information on the General tab (see Figure 8.4). In particular, give the account a friendly name (the default is the name of the incoming mail server); you can choose to fill in the optional Organization and Reply E-mail fields here as well.

Figure 8.4
If you have multiple e-mail accounts, be sure to change this default account name to something more descriptive.

After you've entered all the details, click the Test Account Settings button. This option logs on to the POP3 server and sends a test message using the SMTP server. If you receive an error message, check your username, password, and server names carefully. If the test succeeds, click the Next button to add the newly created account to your profile.

 If your outgoing mail keeps getting rejected, see "Solving SMTP Snags" in the "Troubleshooting" section at the end of this chapter.

CONFIGURING YOUR SMTP SERVER TO SEND MAIL

In the never-ending battle against junk mail, Internet service providers are increasingly installing locks on their outgoing mail servers, to keep them from being taken over by spammers intent on illicitly relaying bulk messages to an unwilling audience. In the good old days, you could simply enter the name or IP address of your SMTP server and start sending mail. Today, some ISPs allow access to SMTP servers only when you can prove your identity. Still others block access to all traffic on port 25 (the port normally used by SMTP servers) unless it's going to their SMTP server. In this situation, for each account you will need to specify that account's incoming (POP3) server and then enter your ISP's outgoing (SMTP) server. You'll also need to adjust the authentication settings as described in the following section.

If the owner of your e-mail server has enabled extra security precautions on the SMTP server you use to send messages out, you might need to take extra steps to prove that you're an authorized user before you can successfully send messages to the outside world.

To set up custom authentication options for an account, click the More Settings button on the Internet E-mail Settings dialog box and click the Outgoing Server tab. You'll see the dialog box shown in Figure 8.5. Select the My Outgoing Server (SMTP) Requires Authentication check box and then use one of the following options:

Figure 8.5
For networks that restrict access to SMTP servers, use this dialog box to adjust authentication options.

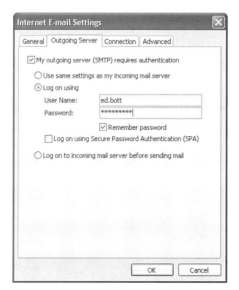

8

- In the simplest scenario, the server requires you to log in with the same credentials as you use for your incoming POP3 server. Select the Use Same Settings As My Incoming Mail Server option.

- In some cases, you may have to log on with a specific username and password that is different from the one specified for the incoming server. This is true if you're receiving mail from a remote server on one network while sending messages out through your ISP's SMTP server. Click the Log On Using option and then fill in the User Name and Password boxes.

- Some SMTP servers require that you log on to your incoming POP3 server (authenticating yourself with your username and password) before you're allowed to send mail. Choose the final option, Log On to Incoming Mail Server Before Sending Mail.

An increasing number of ISPs block all traffic outside their own network on port 25 (the default port used by SMTP servers). This prevents spammers from using their network to relay junk mail through distant servers. If this is the case on your network, you have three options:

- Use the ISP's SMTP server for all outgoing mail and customize the Outgoing Server options as noted previously in the second option.

- If you have access to another ISP's SMTP server that accepts incoming connections on a nonstandard port, you can configure your account to use that server. AOL, for example, allows members to send mail on its SMTP servers using port 587. Specify the correct port number on the Advanced tab of the properties dialog box for that account.

- You can send e-mail messages through a Web-based account, such as Hotmail or MSN, from within Outlook. You can also send messages through other Web-based services using the browser's interface. Using this technique doesn't allow you to save a copy of the sent message in Outlook or to use Outlook's editing tools.

HOTMAIL AND OTHER HTTP ACCOUNTS

If you have a free Hotmail or MSN account that you normally access via the Web, you can read and send messages from within Outlook. Choose Tools, E-mail Accounts, select Add a New E-Mail Account, click the HTTP option, and select Hotmail or MSN.

NOTE

> Microsoft disingenuously offers an "Other" option that allows you to enter the URL of an HTTP server from a non-Microsoft provider. As of this writing, no other Web-based e-mail providers are compatible with this option. But as we explain in this section, you still might be able to make your Web-based e-mail service work with Outlook.

As with a POP3 account, you need to specify your username and password for an HTTP account. However, the server details are filled in automatically for you and you have limited connection options.

8

You can set up multiple HTTP-based Hotmail and MSN accounts in a single Outlook profile. If you have more than one Hotmail account, use the technique described in the previous section to give each account a descriptive name so you can identify it easily.

Hotmail accounts work differently from POP3 accounts, as described in the following section.

MANAGING MULTIPLE E-MAIL ACCOUNTS

How many e-mail addresses do you use? These days, it's not unusual for even a casual e-mail user to have 3 or more accounts to check. If you're an e-mail addict, you could easily have more than 10 e-mail addresses to keep track of.

Outlook includes a variety of tools and features that you can use to manage multiple e-mail accounts effectively:

■ From within Outlook, you can send and receive messages using accounts on Microsoft's Web-based mail services, Hotmail and MSN.

■ You can define multiple Send/Receive groups with separate connection settings for each mail account. This allows you to check your favorite mail accounts regularly while downloading from infrequently used mail accounts only when you want to do so.

■ You can define rules to process incoming and outgoing mail automatically—moving it to folders, color-coding it, or assigning a message priority, for example.

Later in this chapter, we'll explain how to use each of these options most effectively.

If you experience problems sending mail through multiple accounts from a single connection, see "Working Around Anti-Spam Filters" in the "Troubleshooting" section at the end of this chapter.

MANAGING CONNECTIONS TO E-MAIL SERVERS

For each Internet e-mail account you set up, Outlook allows you to specify separate connection options. These options are most useful when you have a full-time dial-up connection or a network connection that is sometimes not available—on a portable PC, for example. To change settings for an Internet e-mail account, choose Tools, E-mail Accounts, and select View or Change Existing E-mail Accounts. In the E-mail Accounts dialog box, select the account name, and then click the Change button. Click More Settings and select the Connection tab of the Internet E-mail Settings dialog box. Then adjust any of the three options shown in Figure 8.6:

■ **Connect Using My Local Area Network (LAN)**—The LAN option assumes you have a full-time connection to the Internet through a *local area network*. Unless you choose to work offline, Outlook checks for mail every 10 minutes. If you have an "always on" broadband Internet connection, such as a DSL line or cable modem, this is the option for you.

Figure 8.6
Use the Connection page to specify connection options for each account separately.

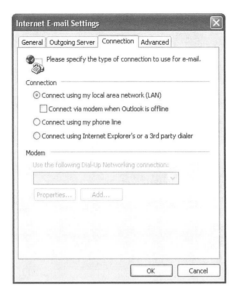

- **Connect Using My Phone Line**—This option uses an existing dial-up Internet connection every time you send or receive e-mail. Choose a connection from the list at the bottom of this dialog box (the list is grayed out and unavailable unless this option or the check box under the LAN option is selected), or click the Add button to create a new one. When Outlook attempts to connect with your mail server, Windows displays the dialog box for the connection you selected.

- **Connect Using Internet Explorer's or a 3rd Party Dialer**—In this configuration, Outlook does not dial or disconnect automatically. This option is your best choice if you use the same phone line for voice calls and Internet access and you want to control exactly when you connect to the Internet. To adjust settings, double-click the Internet Options icon in the Control Panel and click the Connections tab.

On a computer that is permanently connected to the Internet through a broadband connection, you can set all accounts for LAN access; this option allows you to receive mail from any Internet account.

On a notebook computer that is occasionally connected to the Internet via a broadband connection and at other times uses a dial-up connection, choose the LAN option, and then select the Connect via Modem When Outlook Is Offline box (refer to Figure 8.6). This sets up a hybrid LAN/Dial connection option; if you attempt to check your mail and Outlook cannot find the specified server, you see a dialog box that offers to make a dial-up connection for you.

On a computer that uses more than one dial-up connection, you can configure a variety of dial-up options. Choose Tools, Options, and then click the Mail Setup tab to display the dialog box shown in Figure 8.7. Use these options to control whether Outlook dials and hangs up automatically after it finishes sending and receiving mail. Note that these options apply to all dial-up connections; you cannot apply separate dial-up options to individual accounts.

Figure 8.7
Use the options shown here to create a hands-free connection for checking Internet mail.

ADVANCED OPTIONS

For POP3 and IMAP accounts, click the Advanced tab of the Internet E-mail Settings dialog box to adjust any of the following options:

CAUTION

> Do not adjust any of the options listed in this section unless you are certain of the consequences. Most of these advanced options have the potential to completely shut off the flow of e-mail if set incorrectly.

■ If your mail server uses nonstandard *TCP/IP* port numbers or requires a *Secure Sockets Layer (SSL)* connection to send or receive mail, use the boxes in the *Server Port Numbers* section. Outlook's default settings use widely accepted Internet standards, and the overwhelming majority of configurations use these default settings; one noteworthy exception is AOL, which requires that you connect to your SMTP server on port 587 instead of the standard port 25. Change these settings only if your mail server administrator provides specific instructions.

■ Use the Server Timeouts slider to control how long Outlook attempts to connect to the server before timing out and displaying an error message. The default is 1 minute; you can adjust this setting in 30-second increments to any value between 30 seconds and 5 minutes. Set a longer value if you get frequent error messages when trying to send or retrieve mail over a slow connection or a poor-quality phone line.

■ Select the Leave a Copy of Messages on Server check box when configuring a copy of Outlook to retrieve mail from a location other than the one at which you normally receive mail. For example, if you occasionally check your office mail from a home PC, but you want to maintain a complete archive of messages on your office computer, select this check box on the home PC and leave the check box cleared on your computer at the office. Any messages you download at home will remain on the server; when you return to the office and retrieve your messages, they will be available for you.

SETTING UP ALTERNATIVE E-MAIL PROFILES

In Outlook 2003, your main profile is configured automatically during the initial setup process; you can set up additional profiles later, although this is rarely required. For most people, a single profile containing all accounts is the correct configuration.

When you set up a new profile, you associate e-mail accounts and data files with that profile. This option allows you to use one profile to access mail directly from an Exchange server, with another profile set up for remote access synchronized to an Offline Folders file. You might want to set up separate profiles if you work with highly sensitive or confidential information in a particular e-mail account—the finances or personnel decisions for a non-profit organization that you chair, for example—and you want to avoid any possibility of mixing messages between that account and your personal e-mail.

To set up an Outlook profile, double-click the Mail icon in the Control Panel and click the Show Profiles button. This option displays the dialog box shown in Figure 8.8.

Figure 8.8
Use the options at the bottom of this dialog box to select a profile when you start Outlook.

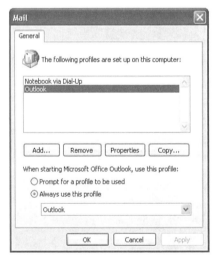

Click the Add button to create a new profile. A wizard will prompt you to add e-mail accounts and specify a data file. Click the Remove button to eliminate an existing profile. To work with a profile without opening Outlook, choose the profile and click the Properties button.

8

Normally, Outlook creates a single profile and uses it automatically each time you start. Choose the Prompt for a Profile to Be Used option if you want to select from a list of available profiles every time you start Outlook.

CHECKING YOUR MAIL AND READING NEW MESSAGES

How often do you need to check e-mail? That's a matter of personal preference. You might want to leave your computer and Outlook running around the clock, checking for new messages every few minutes. That way, you know you'll never miss a message—as long as you're near your computer. Or you can check for messages manually, each time you sit down at your computer. Depending on your preferences, you can have Outlook do as much or as little of the work as you wish. You have a variety of manual and automatic choices that control how you check messages.

SETTING UP SEND/RECEIVE GROUPS

By default, Outlook assigns the same mail-checking options to all your e-mail accounts. Messages you create are sent out as soon as you click the Send button. When you press F9 or click the Send/Receive button, Outlook sends any messages in the Outbox and then checks each account for new messages, going through the accounts in the order in which they appear in the E-mail Accounts dialog box. To adjust the settings for this All Accounts group, or to create additional groups, choose Tools, Options; click the Mail Setup tab; and click the Send/Receive button. This opens the Send/Receive Groups dialog box (see Figure 8.9).

Figure 8.9
Using offline settings is especially helpful for notebook users; in this configuration, for instance, Outlook checks for new mail every three hours when online and never when offline.

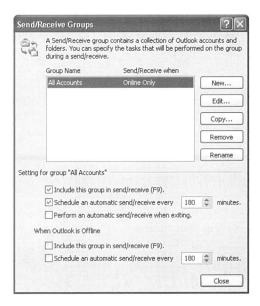

Most of the options here are fairly self-explanatory. You can create a new group; edit, copy, or rename a group; or remove a group from the list. Note that you can also define separate online and offline settings, which are controlled by the Work Offline choice on Outlook's File menu. These options are especially useful if you have a dial-up connection; users with always-on broadband connections can safely ignore offline settings.

To add a Send/Receive group, click the New button. Give the group a name and click OK to display the dialog box shown in Figure 8.10.

Figure 8.10
Adjust settings for each mail account in a Send/Receive group.

In each Send/Receive Group, you can define whether to send or receive mail items and whether you want to download headers only or retrieve complete items. In the case of Web-based mail accounts, you can specify which folders to download—typically, this is the Inbox only.

Each Send/Receive Group you create appears on the Tools menu, under the cascading Send/Receive list. Using this menu, you can select all accounts, choose a group you've defined, or check messages for a single account.

CHOOSING WHICH MESSAGES TO DOWNLOAD

With any Internet e-mail account (including Hotmail and MSN accounts), you can specify that you want Outlook to download only the headers of messages—a small block of data that includes the Subject, the sender's name, the date and time it was sent, and its size—rather than the full message bodies. This option is a lifesaver when you have a slow connection, especially when you're paying by the minute. It's more of a nuisance than a benefit if you have a high-speed Internet connection, however, as it prevents junk e-mail filters from operating properly.

To tell Outlook you want to work with message headers from a specified account, open the Send/Receive Settings dialog box as described in the previous section, click the icon in the Accounts pane at left, and select Download Headers Only. If you want to receive regular text messages but leave larger messages on the server while you decide what to do with them, select the Download Only Headers for Items Larger Than *nn* KB box (where *nn* is a value you set in KB). See Figure 8.10 for an example.

When you connect to an e-mail account that is configured to download headers only, Outlook downloads the envelope information (subject, sender, size, and so on) to your Inbox. An icon to the left of the item indicates that it hasn't yet been downloaded. Select one or more items and right-click to see a shortcut menu that lets you choose what to do with each message, as shown in Figure 8.11.

Figure 8.11
From the list of message headers, right-click to indicate whether you want to download or delete the message the next time you go online.

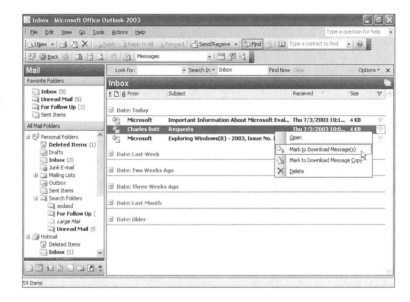

If you double-click the message header, Outlook displays a dialog box offering the same choices that are available from the shortcut menu.

The next time you connect to the server, Outlook processes the marked headers. If you mark a message to be deleted, Outlook tells the server to delete it immediately, without ever downloading it to your Inbox.

> **NOTE**
>
> When you work with message headers, Outlook's Junk Mail filters don't have a chance to kick in until you actually download the message. If you have an account that receives a lot of spam, you'll have to decide whether to mark the messages to be deleted without downloading, or to download the messages and let the Junk Mail filters do their work.

CHECKING FOR NEW MESSAGES

By default, Outlook checks messages at startup, or when you press F9, or when you click the Send/Receive button. If you have an always-on Internet connection, you can configure

8

Outlook to check for new messages automatically by choosing options on the Send/Receive Groups dialog box.

Under several circumstances, you might prefer to check your e-mail manually rather than setting an automatic option:

- If you're on vacation and using Outlook on a notebook computer, you can't predict when you'll have an Internet connection. Configure Outlook's Send/Receive Groups to skip automatic mail checking when you work offline.

- For secondary mail accounts that you use only sporadically, you might choose to check your e-mail once every few days or even less frequently. When setting up a mail account in this configuration, clear the Include the Selected Account in This Group check box.

- If you're expecting an important message and your next scheduled automatic connection is hours away, make a manual connection.

- If you have only one phone line at home, you probably want to check for mail only when you're certain other family members aren't on the phone.

When you click the Send/Receive button on the Standard toolbar, Outlook uses the settings from the All Accounts group. To check a single account, choose Tools, Send/Receive; then select the correct account or group from the cascading menu.

SETTING NOTIFICATIONS

Outlook offers to notify you in several ways when you've received new mail. To change notification settings, choose Tools, Options; click the E-mail Options button on the Preferences tab; and click the Advanced E-mail Options button. As Figure 8.12 shows, all of the following options are enabled by default, but can be disabled by clearing a check box.

- The two most subtle options play a sound and briefly change the mouse pointer when you receive new mail. To adjust either setting, you need to burrow several dialog boxes into the Outlook interface. If you're not at your computer, you'll completely miss both these cues.

- A more persistent but still subtle reminder is the icon that appears in the notification area to the right of the Windows taskbar (this area is also sometimes called the tray). An envelope icon here means you've received new mail; double-click the icon to open the Inbox and read the messages.

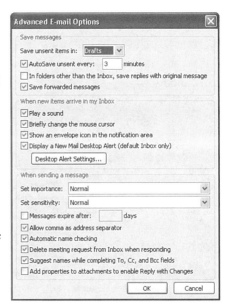

Figure 8.12

8

- The final notification option is the *desktop alert*, a small window that fades in to show you the subject and sender when a new message arrives in your Inbox, and then fades out after a few seconds. Click the Desktop Alert Settings button in the Advanced E-mail Options dialog box to adjust its behavior. (See Figure 8.13.) To make the alert window more or less visible, drag the Transparency control to the right or left; to control how long alerts stay on screen, use the Duration slider.

Figure 8.13

 If some of your messages are mysteriously missing from desktop alert windows, see "Forcing Outlook to Show Desktop Alerts" in the "Troubleshooting" section at the end of this chapter.

SPEED-READING NEW MESSAGES WITH THE READING PANE

How many e-mail messages do you get every day? If you have a busy social or civic life or an active business, you may get hundreds of messages a day, and you can waste hours just sorting those that are trivial from the ones that really matter. To save time, use the Reading pane; as you can see in Figure 8.14, turning on the Reading pane shrinks the message list to a still-readable display that shows the sender, date, and subject of each message. As you select items in the list, the contents appear in the pane to the right.

Figure 8.14

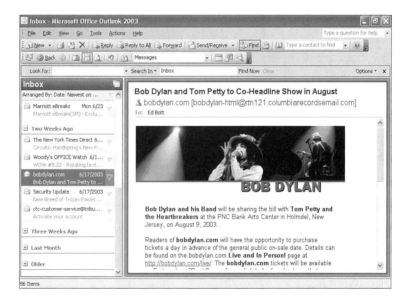

TIP FROM

Ed & Woody

> If you prefer, you can arrange the screen so the Reading pane appears below the message list. Choose View, Reading Pane, Bottom to select this configuration.

8

Here's how to use the Reading pane to blast through messages at lightning speed:

1. Click the Mail or Folder List button on the Navigation pane and click the Unread Messages search folder. (If this search folder doesn't exist, you'll have to create it using the techniques described in "Creating and Using Search Folders," later in this chapter.)

2. If you can't see the contents of a message when you click its entry in the message list, click the Reading Pane button. Using this pane lets you quickly scan any message without having to open it.

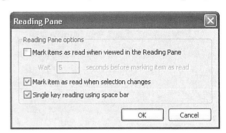

Figure 8.15

3. Choose Tools, Options; click the Other tab; and click the Reading Pane button to display the Reading Pane dialog box shown in Figure 8.15. Select the middle check box (Mark Item As Read When Selection Changes) to mark mail as read when you view it in the Preview pane; if you want to be able to skip over some messages and leave them marked as unread, select only the check box at top (Mark Items As Read When Viewed in the Reading Pane) instead, and leave the wait time at least 5 seconds.

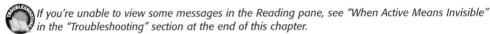 *If you're unable to view some messages in the Reading pane, see "When Active Means Invisible" in the "Troubleshooting" section at the end of this chapter.*

4. Begin reading your mail. Use the spacebar to move through the contents of each message, one screen at a time. (Don't use the arrow keys.) As you finish with each message, press Ctrl+R to compose a reply, Ctrl+Shift+R to reply to all. Press the Delete key to send the current message to the Deleted Items folder and move to the next one in the list, or press the spacebar to mark the previous message as read and jump to the next unread message.

CREATING, MANAGING, AND USING E-MAIL ADDRESSES

In terms of complexity, Outlook's address-book structure falls somewhere between baseball's infield-fly rule and the U.S. tax code. What looks simple on the surface quickly becomes baffling, thanks to the many locations in which Outlook can store e-mail addresses and other contact information, and two completely different interfaces for viewing and editing that information. The configuration is relatively easy to understand if you install a clean copy of Outlook 2003 and enter or import your contact information. Things get more complicated, however, if you've upgraded from a previous edition of Outlook, or if you connect to a corporate network running Microsoft Exchange.

In this book, we assume that you've started fresh with a clean copy of Outlook 2003, and that no Exchange Server is in your configuration. (Exchange Server is commonly used in large corporations; most home and small business users do not access email via an Exchange Server). In this setup, here's what you need to know:

8

- The Contacts folder is the default location for addresses in your primary store; you can create additional folders containing Contact items and make them available for use with e-mail messages as well.

- The Windows Address Book is included with Outlook Express and all versions of Windows since Windows 98; it stores addresses in its own file format (using the .wab extension). Normally, its collection of names and addresses is completely separate from those in the Contacts folder. You can import and export information between the two locations or, if you're willing to make a Registry hack, you can use the WAB to view information stored in Outlook's Contacts folder.

- Outlook's Address Book (accessible by choosing Tools, Address Book or by pressing Ctrl+Shift+B) represents an important alternative method for viewing the contents of the Contacts folder and any other folders that contain Contact items. In Outlook 2003, the Address Book does not point to a physical location for storing addresses. Instead, you use this simpler alternative view when addressing new messages or replies. It shows only four fields: Name, Display Name, E-mail Address, and E-mail Type.

CONFIGURING THE OUTLOOK ADDRESS BOOK

The best way to enter or manage contact information is to start in the Contacts folder. Its default data-entry form is the most flexible way to enter new items, and its support for custom views and filters makes it the best choice for quickly viewing information. But Outlook also offers another view of the Contacts folder; click the Address Book button on the Standard toolbar (or choose Tools, Address Book or press Ctrl+Shift+B) to display a window on your Contacts like the one shown in Figure 8.16.

Figure 8.16
If you've configured Outlook correctly, the Address Book view shows information that's stored in your Contacts folder.

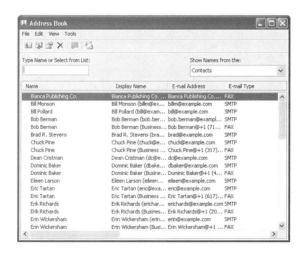

→ For full details on how to use the Contacts folder, **see** "Managing Your List of Contacts," **p. 276**.

Normally, the Contacts folder in your primary Personal Folders (*.pst) file is designated as your Outlook Address Book. If you've made any changes to your profile, if you've used more than one Personal Folders file, or if you've created multiple folders for contacts, you might experience problems with the Outlook Address Book. Here's how to check and, if necessary, repair your Address Book configuration:

1. Choose Tools, E-mail Accounts. Select View or Change Existing Directories or Address Books and click Next.

2. If the Outlook Address Book is not in your profile, click the Add button in the Directories and Address Books dialog box and install it. Close and restart Outlook if prompted.

3. Make sure the Contacts folder is visible in the Navigation Pane (choose Go, Contacts or Go, Folder List, if necessary). Right-click the Contacts icon and choose Properties. On the Outlook Address Book tab, select the Show This Folder As an E-mail Address Book check box. Click OK to close the dialog box. Repeat this step for any other folders that contain contact items with e-mail addresses.

TIP FROM

Ed & Woody

> You don't have to designate all contact folders as address books. Reserve this honor for folders filled with items that have e-mail addresses or fax numbers. If you create one or more secondary folders with contact items that you don't use for e-mail, such as a membership roster where you keep mailing addresses for an organization, or a folder full of phone numbers for restaurants, hotels, airlines, and other travel-related institutions, don't designate these folders as address books.

4. Open the Directories and Address Books dialog box again. Select Outlook Address Book from the list of address books and click the Change button. Make sure the Contacts folder and any other folders you specified in step 3 are listed here (see Figure 8.17).

NOTE

> If you receive e-mail through an Exchange Server, your profile might also include an Offline Address Book. Do not remove this entry from your profile.

5. By default, all names are shown in the Address Book using First Name/Last Name format (John Smith). If you prefer to display names using Last Name/First Name format (Smith, John), click File As and choose it from the drop-down list.

6. Close all dialog boxes and choose Tools, Address Book. Click the Show Names From list to verify that the folders you specified are the only ones available in the Address Book.

INTEGRATING OUTLOOK WITH THE WINDOWS ADDRESS BOOK

Figure 8.17

The Windows Address Book was originally designed to store e-mail addresses for Outlook Express. You can configure the WAB so that it draws addresses from your Outlook Contacts folder instead of from a WAB data file; this allows you to use your Outlook Contacts folder from within Outlook Express, without having to worry about keeping two address books in sync. If you never use Outlook Express, we recommend that you enable this integration, because it allows you to access information from your Contacts folder quickly, even when Outlook is not running.

In older versions of Windows, this option could be selected from a menu. In Windows XP, you must edit the Windows Registry to make this option available.

CAUTION

As always, we recommend extreme caution when working with the Registry. A misplaced edit can cause programs to stop working properly and can cause Windows to refuse to start up. Registry hacking is for experts; if you're uncomfortable working with your system's innards, skip this section.

Open Registry Editor (Regedit.exe) and select the following key in the left (tree) side:

`HKEY_CURRENT_USER\Software\Microsoft\WAB\WAB4`

In the right pane, look for UseOutlook in the list of existing values. If this value isn't present, right-click any empty space in the right pane and choose New, DWORD Value. Replace the default name with UseOutlook; then double-click the newly created value and set it to 1 (Hexadecimal). Close Registry Editor.

NOTE

To remove the option to share information between the Windows Address Book and Outlook, delete the UseOutlook value, or set it to 0.

Once you've made this change, click the Start button, choose Run, type **WAB**, and press Enter. The Windows Address Book opens, with your Outlook Contacts on display in the Windows Address Book. This allows all contact managers to share address book data stored in the Contacts folder.

Some people find it easier to use the Windows Address Book to edit e-mail addresses and other personal information, such as the name of a contact's spouse and children, as well as

8

birthdays and anniversary dates. If you've configured the Address Book and Contacts folder to share information, entering or editing an item in either window changes the information in the Contacts folder.

THOSE OTHER ADDRESS BOOKS

Depending on your configuration, Outlook might store addresses in any of several alternative locations:

- The *Global Address List* is the master address book on a network running Microsoft Exchange Server. Everyone who has an e-mail account on that server is listed in this directory.

- The *Offline Address Book* is your personal version of the Global Address List, which typically contains a subset of the Global Address List and is designed to be used when you're not connected to the Exchange server. This file is updated automatically every 24 hours when you're connected to an Exchange Server. To force Outlook to create or update an Offline Address Book, connect to the Exchange Server and choose Tools, Send/Receive, Download Address Book.

- The *Personal Address Book* (stored as a file with a .pab extension) is the original address-book format for Exchange clients and Windows Messaging. This option is still available in Outlook 2003, primarily for backward compatibility. If you have a PAB file on your computer, we recommend that you import its contents into the Contacts folder and delete it.

- Finally, third-party software developers can hook into Outlook as services, using their own file formats to store address information. Most modern programs in this category can access information directly from the Contacts folder.

TIP FROM

EQ & Woody

When you install other programs, they might take over functions you expect Outlook to handle, including e-mail and address-book management. To specify that you want to use Outlook as your default e-mail, calendar, and contact manager, choose Tools, Options; select the Other tab; and select the Make Outlook the Default Program check box.

Outlook includes the Contacts folder as a default store for contact information, but you might find it useful to create additional contact folders. Why would you want to do this? Primarily to keep your data organized. For example, if you maintain the membership list for a large organization, you might want to keep these details in their own folder and reserve your main Contacts folder for friends and family. If you're a frequent traveler or an amateur concierge, put listings for hotels, airlines, restaurants, and other on-the-road resources in a Travel folder. If you intend to subdivide your collection of contacts this way, we recommend you do so by creating additional subfolders under the Contacts folder.

8

ADDRESSING AN E-MAIL MESSAGE

When addressing an e-mail message, you have several options:

- The most reliable way to make sure you address each message correctly is to reply to an e-mail message you've received. In this situation, you can almost always be certain that the address is accurate. (If it turns out to be wrong, you can blame the original sender.)

 If you reply to a message and get a delivery failure, see "When Your E-mail Bounces" in the "Troubleshooting" section at the end of this chapter.

TIP FROM

Although it's not immediately obvious, all address information in the header of a message you receive is "live." Right-click any address to display a shortcut menu. Choose Add to Contacts to create a new item in your Contacts folder using the name and e-mail address displayed in the header, or choose Look Up Contact to search your Contacts folder for an item that contains a matching e-mail address. You can also use the shortcut menu to copy the address and paste it in the To or CC box in another message.

- For addresses you don't plan to reuse (such as a request for information from a merchant), enter the full e-mail address in the To, Cc, or Bcc box.
- Open the Address Book, select one or more names, and click the New Message button.
- Open the Contacts folder, select one or more names, and choose Actions, New Message to Contact.
- Start a new message and click the To, Cc, or Bcc buttons to display the Select Names dialog box, which is actually a different view of the Address Book (see Figure 8.18). Select one or more names and then click the buttons in the Message Recipients area to add addresses to any of the three envelope fields. This is the easiest way to add a large number of addresses to a message quickly and accurately. Click OK to return to the message window.

Figure 8.18
Select one or more names from this list; then click one of the three buttons to add the selected addresses to the fields on the right.

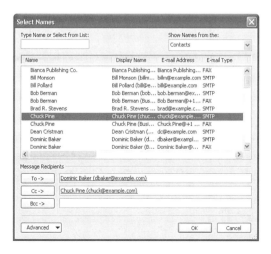

8

■ For people you send mail to most frequently, enter any portion of the recipient's name in any envelope field (To, Cc, or Bcc) and let Outlook's AutoComplete feature resolve the address for you. (To enter multiple names this way, separate each name with a comma or semicolon.)

AutoComplete is a power user's dream. It searches in your Contacts Folder and other Address Book locations; it also remembers addresses you've recently entered manually or by replying to a message. If Outlook finds one and only one matching item, it completes the name automatically, using the default email address. If Outlook finds multiple matching names, it shows a drop-down list of matching names so you can select one.

CAUTION

> AutoComplete can also cause nightmares if you're unaware of how it really works. Because the list of AutoComplete possibilities includes addresses you've entered manually, Outlook may "remember" a name and suggest it to you. The name looks all right in the To field, so you accept it; unfortunately, you don't realize that the message is going to a rarely used e-mail account for that contact, rather than the address she checks 10 times a day. To avoid this possibility, double-click the name in the To field to display a dialog box that shows the Display Name and E-mail Address fields.

 If you find that AutoComplete has "memorized" some incorrect addresses, see "Cleaning Up the AutoComplete List" in the "Troubleshooting" section at the end of this chapter.

To configure AutoComplete options, choose Tools, Options, click the E-mail Options button on the Preferences tab, and click the Advanced E-mail Options button. To turn off AutoComplete, clear the Suggest Names While Completing To, Cc, and Bcc Fields choice at the bottom of the dialog box.

How do you deal with contacts that have multiple e-mail addresses? Don't create multiple Contact items, each with a different address; that will cause a mess when Outlook tries to resolve the addresses for you. Instead, enter each different e-mail address as part of the same Contact item. When you use the Contacts folder, you can enter up to three e-mail addresses; the first is the default address that Outlook uses when sending mail to that person.

→ If you've inadvertently created multiple Contact items for the same person, you might be able to merge them into a single record; for details, **see** "Merging Duplicate Contact Items," **p. 285**.

SENDING E-MAIL TO GROUPS OF PEOPLE

Outlook enables you to create an alias called a *Personal Distribution List* that represents a group of e-mail addresses. Use this option to avoid having to repeatedly enter a slew of addresses when you routinely send mail to the same group of people. For example, if you're on the board of a local charity, you can create a Personal Distribution List that includes all the other members of the board, and then name it Board of Directors. When you type that name in an envelope field on a message form, Outlook recognizes the list and resolves it for you. When you send the message, Outlook substitutes all the individual names so that your message is delivered correctly.

To create a Personal Distribution List in the Contacts folder, choose File, New, Distribution List. From the Address Book, choose File, New Entry, and then select New Distribution List and click OK. Both methods lead to the dialog box shown in Figure 8.19.

Figure 8.19
Use this dialog box to add names to a Personal Distribution List.

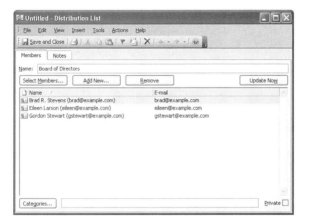

Enter the name you want to use for the list in the Name field. Click the Select Members button to add names from the Address Book. Click the Add New button to open a dialog box where you can enter a new name that isn't currently in your Contacts folder; select the Add to Contacts check box to store that new item in the Address Book as well as in the Personal Distribution List. After you finish adding names to the list, click the Save and Close button to save the list.

Personal Distribution Lists appear in the Address Book as boldfaced entries; in the Contacts folder, they appear as one-line entries with a distinctive icon. If you need to change the lineup of names that make up the list—if a member of the board quits and another takes her place, for example—double-click the item to reopen this dialog box, and then use the Remove button to get rid of the names you no longer need.

TIP FROM

EQ & Woody

If you routinely send messages to a large number of recipients—more than 10, for example—think carefully about how to address the message. If it's not necessary for any of the recipients to respond to all others on the list, leave the To field empty and add the other recipients' names (individually or as part of a distribution list) to the Bcc field. Outlook automatically addresses the message to you and suppresses the display of all other addresses. Your message is far more likely to be read in this format, especially by people using mail software that displays the entire message header—a list of 20 or so names can take up the entire screen and push your message completely out of sight otherwise.

8

USING WORD AS AN E-MAIL EDITOR

By default, Outlook 2003 uses Word as the default editor for composing new messages. In this configuration, you have to deal with the following tradeoffs:

- On the plus side, you get to use Word's much more sophisticated editing tools to compose messages. That means you can take advantage of AutoText and AutoCorrect in messages, and you can use macros and templates to automate message creation. If your default format is HTML, you'll appreciate Word's editing tools, especially because you can use Word tables and text boxes to organize an HTML message. You can use themes to add personality to your messages. And Word's unlimited undo feature is a godsend when composing messages.

- On the downside, you must load Word to compose a new message. (Outlook starts Word automatically if it isn't already running; this instance of Word doesn't appear in the taskbar.) In theory, the Word-Outlook combination slows down performance initially, uses more memory than Outlook alone, and could impact your system's stability. In practice, on a modern PC with at least 256MB of RAM, you're unlikely to notice any performance degradation associated with loading and unloading Word with Outlook.

To enable or disable the use of Word as the default editor for all new messages, replies, and forwards, choose Tools, Options, click the Mail Format tab, and select the Use Microsoft Office Word 2003 to Edit E-Mail Messages check box. (A second check box, unselected in a default configuration, allows you to use Word to read messages you receive in Rich Text format. This option is meaningless unless you are connected to an Exchange server.)

If you'd prefer not to configure Word as your full-time mail editor, you can still get most of the benefits of this configuration and choose exactly when you want to use it. Instead of using Outlook to compose a new message, open a new Word document instead, and then click the E-mail button on the Standard toolbar. This adds the E-mail toolbar and message headers to the document, enabling you to create and send a message in HTML format. You can't use this option for replies or forwards, however.

CREATING AND SENDING MESSAGES

After you successfully fill in the address block in a message window, composing the message itself is a reasonably straightforward process that varies slightly depending on the message format you choose. If you've chosen Plain Text format, enter text and add attachments (you can drag any file from an Explorer window into the message window to attach it, or choose Insert, File to choose items from a dialog box). For Rich Text messages, you can also use font and paragraph formatting. HTML messages give you the option to add pictures, background colors and graphics, and other Web-style formatting. Depending on the message type you've selected, you can also choose several advanced options.

CHOOSING A MESSAGE FORMAT

When you compose a new message or click the Reply button, Outlook lets you choose from three distinct message formats. In some circumstances, Outlook chooses the message format for you. If you're picky about which message format you send out, you may have to specifically override that decision. Pay attention to the fine details in this section, because the options that seem so obvious do not always behave as you expect.

- **Plain Text**—When you use this format, your message contains nothing but letters, numbers, and symbols in the character set you use to create the message. Outlook strips any formatting, including colors, fonts, and inline pictures, when it sends the message. The recipient sees the text of your message displayed in the default font for his or her mail program.

- **Outlook Rich Text**—This format, the default on most Exchange servers, was developed by Microsoft years ago, before HTML became popular. Using Rich Text format enables you to specify fonts, colors, bullets, and other text attributes, with one major caveat: Only recipients who use Outlook or another Exchange client will be able to correctly view that formatted information. If you send a Rich Text message to a recipient who is using an older e-mail client program, he will see most of the text in your message as well as an attachment called Winmail.dat, which contains useless information. Outlook automatically creates messages in Rich Text format when you use any group-oriented features such as meeting invitations and task requests. We strongly advise against deliberately using this format to send e-mail over the Internet.

TIP FROM

Ed & Woody

> The default settings for Outlook 2003 make it nearly impossible to send a Rich Text message over the Internet; instead, any such message is automatically converted to HTML or Plain Text. If you send and receive some e-mail through an Exchange Server but also through an Internet-standard SMTP/POP3 account, you can override this decision. Choose Tools, Options; click the Mail Format tab; and click the Internet Format button. Choose a format from the drop-down list.

- **HTML**—Offers text-formatting options similar to those available using Rich Text format, plus the capability to specify styles, automatically number lines, and add horizontal rules. Because the underlying format is the same as a web page, you can also define background graphics and insert images into a message. Most modern Internet mail client programs are capable of reading HTML-formatted messages. If your recipient uses any e-mail program that is less than seven years old, he or she should have no trouble reading your HTML-formatted messages. If the recipient's mail client software can't interpret HTML, the recipient sees a plain-text version of the message with an attachment that can be viewed in any web browser.

Which of these three formats will Outlook use when you create a message? As with so many configurable settings throughout Office, the correct answer is: It depends.

TIP FROM

Ed & Woody

> The name of the current message format always appears in parentheses in the title bar of an open message.

When you create a new message from scratch, Outlook uses the default message format. To change the current message format, choose Tools, Options; then click the Mail Format tab and select HTML or Plain Text from the Compose In This Message Format list. (Don't choose the Rich Text option.)

When you reply to a message, Outlook ignores the preferences you specified as your default and uses the format of the original message. This isn't as rude as it sounds: If you receive a message that was composed in HTML or Rich Text format, you can be certain that the sender is capable of reading messages in that format. On the other hand, when you receive a message in Plain Text format, the most conservative response is to assume that the sender either can't work with other formats or chooses not to use formatted mail, and respond in kind.

You can switch on the fly to a new message format. From the Format menu in Outlook's editor, choose Plain Text, HTML, or Rich Text. The same options are available as a drop-down list on the E-mail toolbar in Word. Note that when using Outlook's built-in editor you can't switch directly from HTML to Rich Text or vice versa; in either case, you have to first convert the message to Plain Text format, losing all formatting, and then choose the other format. Using Word as your editor, you can freely switch among all three formats.

FORCING OUTLOOK TO USE PLAIN TEXT FORMAT

In one specific circumstance, Outlook uses Plain Text format, regardless of whether you are creating a new message or replying to an existing one. This option is useful when a particular contact has made it clear that he absolutely despises HTML-formatted messages.

To ensure that you never send HTML messages to a particular recipient over the Internet, you need to set an additional option. Open that person's Contact item and double-click the e-mail address you want to configure. This opens the E-mail Properties dialog box (see Figure 8.20). In the Internet Format box, choose the Send Plain Text Only option instead of the default (Let Outlook Decide the Best Sending Format). Repeat this process for other e-mail entries in the same Contact item, if necessary, and then close the item, being sure to save your changes.

When you set this option, Outlook automatically converts messages to Plain Text format when you send to the specified recipient. You do not see any confirmation dialog boxes or warning that the message format has changed. In fact, if the original message was in HTML format, the copy in your Sent Items folder remains in that format.

Figure 8.20
Setting this option guarantees that you won't accidentally send an HTML-formatted message to a recipient.

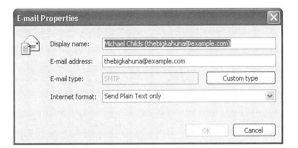

ADVANCED MESSAGE FORMAT OPTIONS

Both Plain Text and HTML formats include advanced settings that can make your messages easier to read. (If you mess with these options too much, you can also turn outgoing text into garbage, so be careful.) To see and adjust these settings, choose Tools, Options; then click the Mail Format tab. In the Message Format section, choose your default format for outgoing mail, usually Plain Text or HTML. Click the Internet Format button to set other options, as shown in Figure 8.21.

Figure 8.21
In general, most Outlook users should leave these settings at their defaults.

USING A SPECIFIC ACCOUNT TO SEND A MESSAGE

Normally, Outlook sends replies using the same account with which you received the original message. On new messages and forwards, Outlook uses the account specified as the default in your E-mail Accounts list. If you have set up more than one e-mail account, you can choose which account to use for sending a specific message. Open the message and use the drop-down Accounts button on the Standard toolbar (just to the right of the Send button) to select a different account.

CREATING, EDITING, AND MANAGING SIGNATURES

Outlook allows you to create a *signature*—a short block of text (and, optionally, graphics or HTML code) that identifies you and perhaps supplies some information about you.

8

Signatures are typically inserted at the end of a message. When you use Word as your e-mail editor, you can specify a different default signature for each account—a businesslike signature for your work account, say, and a more playful one for your personal mail. If you use Outlook as your message editor, you can create one or more signatures for use with all outgoing messages. In this configuration, Outlook maintains separate signatures for plain text, Rich Text, and HTML messages.

1. Choose Tools, Options, click the Mail Format tab, and then click the Signatures button. The Create Signature dialog box (see Figure 8.22) shows all the signatures you've created so far.

Figure 8.22
Create multiple signatures for use with different accounts.

2. Click the New button. In the Create New Signature dialog box (see Figure 8.23), enter a descriptive name for your signature and specify whether you want to create it from scratch or base it on an existing signature or file. Click Next to continue.

3. In the Edit Signature dialog box (see Figure 8.24), enter the text you want to use for your signature.

4. Click the Font and Paragraph buttons to add formatting to selected text. To add advanced formatting using an HTML editor such as FrontPage, click the Advanced Edit button.

5. Click Finish to save your signature.

Figure 8.23

Figure 8.24
Your signature can include just your name and title, your e-mail address, or complete contact information.

8

You'll search in vain for a button that lets you rename an existing signature, but it's easy to accomplish the same goal with a simple workaround. Select the signature you want to rename and click the New button. In the Create New Signature dialog box, enter the name you want to use, and then select the Use This Existing Signature as a Template option. Click Next to continue, and then click Finish to save the signature under the new name without editing it. Finally, select the original signature and click Remove.

On the Mail Format tab of the Options dialog box, you can specify a default signature to use when you create a new message for each e-mail account you've set up. (A second check box lets you specify whether you want to include a signature with replies and forwards.) Outlook automatically adds your signature to the end of every new message you create.

When you work with Word as your e-mail editor, you can change signatures on the fly by right-clicking the signature in an e-mail message. The shortcut menu lets you choose from all defined signatures; you can also open the E-mail Signatures dialog box and add or edit a signature.

TIP FROM

If you delete the signature from a message created using Word as your e-mail editor, or if you create a new message with no signature, you'll find that it's impossible to insert one of your defined signatures. The solution? Create a new, blank message with an account that has a signature associated with it. Copy that signature to the Clipboard and paste it into the first message.

8

To insert a signature on a message that you're editing in the Outlook editor, choose Insert, Signature; then select an entry from the list of available signature files. Note that if you use a default signature, you must delete that text before you insert a new one; this routine dumps the new text into your message body without deleting the old signature.

USING STATIONERY AND FONTS IN FORMATTED MESSAGES

Want to impress some message recipients and annoy others—sometimes even in the same message? Use a graphic image and predefined fonts as *stationery* for an e-mail message. Like a web page theme, stationery adds consistent formatting to an e-mail message that you compose in HTML format. If you stick with a simple color and font selection, the effect can subtly enhance your message; if you go too far, it adds unnecessary distraction and can make message text nearly impossible to read. Outlook's stunningly inconsistent collection of built-in stationery choices offers plenty of examples of both.

The procedures for using stationery are slightly different, depending on whether you use Outlook or Word as your e-mail editor.

If you use Outlook as your message editor, you can make a particular stationery selection your default for every new message. Choose Tools, Options; select the Mail Format tab; and click the Stationery Picker button. Select a background image from the Stationery Picker dialog box and click Edit to adjust stationery options (see Figure 8.25).

Figure 8.25
You can adjust fonts and backgrounds for Outlook's stationery selections.

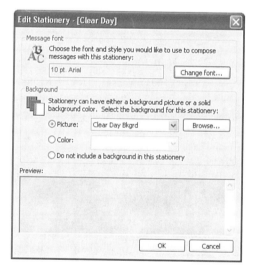

If you use Word as your e-mail editor, personal stationery is tied to your collection of web themes. You can choose one of Outlook's themes or choose from a much larger list of default background images, colors, and matching fonts for messages you create using Word. Open Word and then choose Tools, Options; click the E-mail Options button on the General tab; and set options on the Personal Stationery tab.

SETTING MESSAGE OPTIONS

When you click the Send button after composing a message, you tell Outlook to deliver the message using all your default settings: The message goes to your default mail server, a copy is saved in your Sent Items folder, and that's about it. If you want the message to have special handling, click the Options button and adjust any of the settings in the Message Options dialog box shown in Figure 8.26.

Figure 8.26
Several options in this dialog box, such as the capability to defer sending a message, can be extremely useful in business.

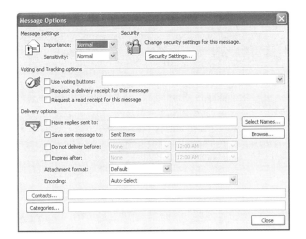

In the Message Settings section, use the Importance and Sensitivity drop-down lists to change these fields from their default setting of Normal to Low or High. Other Outlook users will see a blue down-arrow in the message list for Low Importance messages, and a red up-arrow for High Importance messages.

TIP FROM

Ed & Woody

If you encourage your regular correspondents to use the Low and High Importance settings for messages, you can use e-mail rules to automatically highlight or file messages based on this setting. Skip the Options button and use the High and Low Importance buttons on the Standard toolbar when composing a message.

The choices in the Delivery Options section of the Message Options dialog box are probably the most useful:

- Select the Have Replies Sent To check box and enter an alternative Reply-to address. This option is especially useful when you want an outgoing message to go out under your name, but you want to redirect replies to a different address. As the president of a club or civic organization, for example, you might want to introduce a new membership director; if you specify that person's e-mail address in this box, recipients can reply directly to her with congratulations or requests for more information.

■ Clear the Save Sent Message To box if you don't want to save a copy of the current message, or click the Browse button to select a different folder.

■ Select the Do Not Deliver Before check box and enter a date if you want to compose a message and send it automatically at a time you specify. This option can be extremely useful when the timing of a message is crucial but you won't be physically present to send the message. For example, say you're planning an important announcement for Monday at 10 a.m.; go ahead and prepare the press release, and then enter `Monday 10am` in this box. Make sure to leave Outlook running with the option to automatically send and receive mail every 10 minutes or so, and your message will go out within 10 minutes of the time you specify, even if you're out of the office.

NOTE

If you use the deferred delivery option to schedule messages far in the future, be prepared for an annoying side effect of this option. Every time you close Office, you'll see a dialog box warning you that there are still messages in your Outbox and asking whether you want to exit anyway. If you know you'll restart Office before the message is due to be sent out, click OK.

→ For more details on how to enter dates using plain-English equivalents in any Outlook item, **see** "Entering Dates and Times Automatically," **p. 184**.

■ The Expires After box is effective only if you use Exchange Server and your message has a time element to it. For example, if you're sending a reminder of a meeting that starts in an hour, add an expiration time that matches the start of the meeting. Recipients who check their e-mail before the start of the meeting will see the message. In the case of recipients who haven't picked up the message by its expiration time, the Exchange Server automatically deletes it, and you avoid cluttering up their Inboxes.

Are you tempted by the check box in the Voting and Tracking Options section that enables you to request a receipt when your message is delivered or read? Temper your expectations. This is yet another option that works when you send a message on an Exchange Server to another user on the same server: The server can send you a delivery notice when the e-mail lands in the recipient's Inbox, and another when it's opened. If your message is going out over an Internet-standard account, however, it's extremely unlikely you'll see a receipt—support for this feature is hit-or-miss on the Internet, and the recipient can choose to ignore the request for a receipt. In our experience, most people find requests for read receipts annoying and even insulting, as if you're insinuating that they might be ignoring them. We don't recommend using this feature unless it's absolutely necessary.

SETTING REPLY AND FORWARD OPTIONS

When you reply to a message, it's customary to include some or all of the original message to give the recipient a context for your answer. Outlook lets you choose from several formatting options to help make the original message text stand out. You can also define how

Outlook identifies the original message text when you forward a message to someone else. Regardless of which option you choose, the insertion point appears at the top of the message window, with the original message below it.

To set either or both options, choose Tools, Options; click the Preferences tab; and click the E-mail Options button. If you routinely use HTML format, you can include the original message, or include and indent the original message. If you use Plain Text as your default format, we recommend that you choose the Prefix Each Line of the Original Message option and select the default quote character, a greater than (>) sign, as shown in Figure 8.27.

Figure 8.27
If you send mostly Plain Text messages, use the options shown here to prefix the original message in replies and forwards.

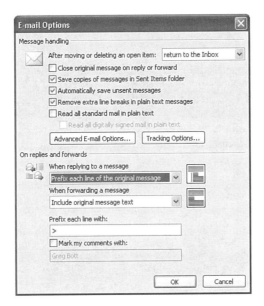

Avoid two options available in this dialog box. Specifying Do Not Include Original Message for replies makes it difficult (and sometimes impossible) for recipients to figure out what you're responding to. (It is good etiquette, however, to try to trim extraneous matter from replies and forwards.) The Attach Original Message option sends the message as an attached file instead of incorporating it into the message you're sending; this forces recipients to go through the additional step of detaching and opening an attachment to read the original message. They won't thank you for the extra work.

ORGANIZING YOUR E-MAIL

Some people receive hundreds of e-mail messages daily. Some people get only a dozen or so per day. In either case, it's just a matter of time—days, weeks, a few months—before your Inbox becomes so cluttered you can't find a thing.

8

Search utilities help you find stuff, and using the Delete key to get rid of trivial mail that doesn't need to be archived also helps keep clutter down. But some messages deserve to be saved for posterity, and for that task, creating and managing a system of e-mail folders is essential.

You can drag messages into folders to keep them organized, but it's smarter still to create Outlook rules that process messages automatically. In less than the time it takes to read a day's e-mail, you can create a set of rules that can easily help you avoid wasting time on low-priority messages, file e-mail by category or project, and also ensure that you never miss an important message because it was buried in your Inbox. Outlook 2003 has an easy-to-use interface for creating and managing e-mail rules. The combination of well-crafted rules, Junk Mail filters, and search folders can go a long way toward eliminating e-mail overload.

TIP FROM

Ed & Woody

Two built-in shortcuts are especially useful for locating related messages or for finding all messages from the same sender. From the message list, right-click any message and then choose Find All. Choose Related Messages to find all messages that are part of the same conversation (the original message and all replies); choose Messages from Sender to display a list of all messages in the current folder from the sender of the selected message. In either case, Outlook opens the Advanced Find dialog box and displays the results there.

➔ For an in-depth explanation of how to set up and use Junk Mail filters, see "Stopping Spam and Other Unwanted E-Mail," **p. 263**.

NOTE

Outlook offers a beginner-level message-processing tool called the Organize pane. When you choose Tools, Organize, it slides into position just above the message window. The Organize pane is a bare-bones tool that allows you to move a selected message to a folder, apply basic color coding, and change views. If you've read even half of this chapter, you've already outgrown any conceivable need to mess with this feature.

USING E-MAIL RULES TO SORT AND PROCESS MAIL

Outlook's single most powerful mail-handling option is its ability to define *e-mail rules* and *alerts*. When you define a rule, you tell Outlook to examine each incoming message as it hits your Inbox (or to look at each outgoing message when you click the Send button) to see whether it matches *conditions* that you define. If Outlook detects a match, it performs one or more *actions* you defined for that rule. *Alerts* are small messages that slide up from the bottom of your desktop to inform you when an important message has arrived. You define the rules for displaying alerts as part of a rule.

The following list includes a few examples of how you can use e-mail rules to sort and organize messages:

- **Urgent mail**—If you sometimes receive messages from key contacts who need immediate assistance, you want to know ASAP. You can create a rule that pops up a dialog box as soon as messages containing hot-button words—urgent or problem, for example—arrive from particular senders.

- **Personal mail**—Move personal messages from family members and good friends into a designated folder, away from work-related messages or those from more casual acquaintances, when they arrive in the Inbox.

- **Messages you receive as a member of a mailing list**—If you receive daily digests from the Doberman Fanciers list, you can instruct Outlook to sort them into their own folder automatically.

- **Mail from other accounts**—Move all mail you receive from a particular account (a personal account you check at work, for example) into a special folder so you can clearly segregate it.

- **Commercial mail**—Identify commercial e-mail from companies that you truly want to hear from. If your favorite online bookstore, music dealer, bank, broker, or travel agent occasionally sends you notices of deals you might be interested in, you can move these messages out of your Inbox and into a folder where you can examine them at your leisure.

- **General clutter**—You can create a set of cleanup rules to be run before you perform major cleanup operations on a Personal Folders file. For instance, you might define a rule that identifies messages with large attachments and moves them to a special folder. Set these rules so they don't run automatically on new messages you receive in the Inbox; instead, use the Run Rules Now button in the Rules and Alerts dialog box to apply them to selected folders, including your archive folders, when they're needed.

TIP FROM

Ed & Woody

> Outlook stores all rules you define in your Personal Folders file. If you want to share your mail-handling rules with other people, or transfer a set of e-mail rules to a new Personal Folders file, click the Options button in the Rules and Alerts dialog box and click Export Rules. To restore rules or to add rules that a friend or co-worker defined and sent to you, click Import Rules and browse to the file containing the previously exported rules. After importing a set of rules, open the Rules and Alerts dialog box and verify that everything is working as expected. In particular, you'll need to re-create the folders that any custom rules use for sorting messages.

CREATING A NEW E-MAIL RULE

The simplest way to create a new e-mail rule is to use an existing message as a template. If you have a message that matches one or more of the conditions you want to use in your rule, right-click the message in Outlook's message list and choose Create Rule from the shortcut menu. The Create Rule dialog box offers a simplified set of three conditions and three actions, as shown in Figure 8.28.

Figure 8.28
For simple rules, you can click one or more check boxes to define conditions and actions based on an existing message.

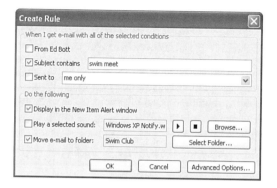

Select one or more of the three options in the top half of the dialog box to define the condition. You can edit the text in the Subject Contains box, but the From and Sent To boxes can't be edited. Next, click one more check boxes in the bottom of the dialog box to define the associated action. The most common action is to move the message to a folder, with or without a desktop alert or sound. Click OK to save the rule using a default name. Outlook gives you the opportunity to run the rule immediately against the contents of the current folder.

NOTE

Note that e-mail rules do not apply to HTTP (Web-based) accounts such as Hotmail or MSN.

If none of these combinations is exactly right, click the Advanced Options button and use the Rules Wizard to create exactly the rule you want. The wizard walks you through four dialog boxes, each consisting of a dialog box with check boxes in the top half and an editable rule description in the bottom. As you select options in the top of the dialog box, the details of the rule appear in the bottom pane; when you see underlined text in the condition or action, click to pop up a dialog box to add more details. (Editing a rule works the same way; choose Tools, Rules and Alerts to open the Rules and Alerts dialog box, select a rule, and click the Edit button.)

 If you've defined a rule and it doesn't work properly on incoming messages, see "A Rule Isn't Working As You Expect" in the "Troubleshooting" section at the end of this chapter.

CHOOSING CONDITIONS

As you can see in Figure 8.29, the opening screen of the Rules Wizard offers a list of 27 options you can use to define almost any combination of conditions. Your range of options is impressive:

Figure 8.29
Combine conditions to identify specific types of messages for further processing.

TIP FROM

EQ & Woody

> You can enter multiple data items for any condition that requires you to specify items. Enter each item individually and click the Add button after each one. Outlook will add them to the list, separated by a logical "or." (In other words, the rule will work if any of the conditions you create are true.)

- Select messages depending on the account through which they were received (choose the Through the Specified Account option).

- Is an incoming message addressed specifically to you? Rules can determine whether your name is or is not in the To or Cc box, for example, or when a message is sent only to you. Fine-tune combinations of conditions to highlight mail that is indisputably for you (Sent Only to Me, especially when you add conditions that test who sent the message) or identify less important mail (Where My Name Is Not in the To Box).

- Attach conditions that test for a specific sender or recipient: From People or Distribution List or Sent to People or Distribution List. These conditions depend on Outlook's capability to resolve an address in your Address Book.

→ To learn more about handling Personal Distribution Lists, **see** "Sending E-mail to Groups of People," **p. 232**.

- Use two extremely powerful conditions to fine-tune rules that search for mail from a specific person or group of people, regardless of whether they're in your Address Book. Check With Specific Words in the Recipient's Address or With Specific Words in the Sender's Address, and then enter any part of the e-mail address you want to test for.

8

TIP FROM

Ed & Woody

> Use this option to identify all mail that arrives from anyone in a particular organization or domain. While working on this book, for example, we created a rule and applied special handling to any message that arrived from any recipient whose address contained quepublishing.com.

■ Search for specific words in the subject or body, or in the message header. Use this condition in combination with those that search for messages from a specific person to look for hot-button words: With quepublishing.com in the Recipient's Address and With deadline in the Subject or Body, for example.

■ To create cleanup rules, or to identify messages that might bloat your mail file on a system with limited storage, use the conditions that test whether a message has an attachment or has a size in a specific range.

SPECIFYING ONE OR MORE ACTIONS

After you specify the conditions to test for, click the Next button to move to the dialog box shown in Figure 8.30. Outlook applies actions you choose here to messages that meet the conditions you specify.

Figure 8.30
Click the underlined text in the description pane at the bottom of this dialog box to specify details such as folder names.

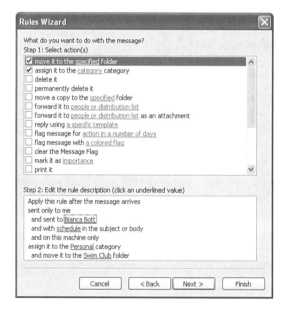

■ One of the most powerful options available is Display a Specific Message in the New Item Alert. Using this option, you can tell Outlook to interrupt whatever you're doing and display an alert that alerts you to important incoming messages. If you're willing to drop everything when you hear from a special friend or family member, for example,

8

you might define this type of rule for messages from that person's e-mail address. If your stockbroker uses e-mail to alert you to important developments in the stock market, you can tell Outlook you want to know immediately whenever you receive a message from that address.

- One of the most interesting options available here is the Stop Processing More Rules choice. Use this option to avoid unintended consequences when rules collide. For example, if you want to be notified when you receive a message sent only to you from your boss, select the proper conditions and actions; then scroll to the bottom of this dialog box and click this option. Make sure rules using this option are high on your list.

- You can move messages that match your defined conditions to a specified folder, copy them to a folder, delete them (move to Deleted Items folder), or permanently delete them.

CAUTION

Never, ever use the Permanently Delete It action on rules that apply to incoming messages. No matter how carefully you define a rule, it's possible that the Rules Wizard will inadvertently apply it to a message you didn't expect it to; use the Delete It condition to move messages to the Deleted Items folder instead, where it's possible to recover messages moved by mistake. Reserve the permanent option for cleanup rules only.

- Forward messages to an address you select, either as an e-mail message or as an attachment. Use the latter option if you want the recipient to see the message exactly as it was received.

- The Reply Using a Specific Template option is powerful and potentially dangerous. You might be tempted to use this option to send a message automatically to anyone who sends you mail, alerting them that you've gone on vacation. Unfortunately, if you apply that option to all incoming messages, you risk creating an e-mail loop with some automated message senders. If you receive a message from a mailing list and Outlook replies automatically to the list, for example, the list server might send a message telling you that you're not authorized to post to the list; if Outlook replies to that message, the loop begins. Outlook is smart enough to send only one such message per day, but that's still enough to annoy other list members seven times while you're away for a week's vacation. Craft this type of rule carefully and test it before using it.

- Flag a message for action in a specified number of days (or clear a flag, useful in a cleanup rule), assign it to a category, change its Importance setting, play a sound, or start an application.

NOTE

Most Outlook users can safely ignore the Perform a Custom Action option, which applies only when you have a third-party add-in that defines special actions for incoming messages.

ADDING ANY EXCEPTIONS

After defining actions, click Next to move to the list of exceptions. In general, the 25 built-in categories here mirror the conditions you specify in Step 2 of the wizard. Defining exceptions is a powerful way to fine-tune rules: "Delete all messages from John Smith except if my name is in the To or Cc box" will squelch posts from particularly annoying senders who post to mailing lists you receive.

SAVING THE RULE

In the Rules Wizard's final step, give the rule a name and check all conditions, actions, and exceptions in the dialog box shown in Figure 8.31. Use the check boxes here to specify whether you want to run the rule on the contents of the current folder immediately and whether you want to enable the rule. Clear the second check box for "cleanup" rules that you want to run only when needed.

Figure 8.31
The final step of the Rules Wizard lets you confirm all the steps in your rule and run it on the current folder.

Click Finish to save your rule. Outlook adds the new rule to the top of the Rules and Alerts list. In some cases, you may need to open this dialog box and move the new rule down the list to ensure that more important rules have a chance to work first.

MANAGING E-MAIL RULES AND ALERTS

To edit, delete, rename, or run e-mail rules, choose Tools, Rules and Alerts. The Rules and Alerts dialog box (see Figure 8.32) shows you all the rules you've previously defined and lets you create new rules and manage existing ones from a central location.

Figure 8.32
The new Rules and Alerts dialog box lets you manage existing e-mail rules and create new ones.

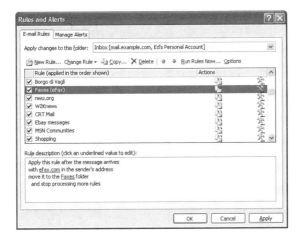

8

For starters, you can select any entry in this list and click Change Rule to quickly adjust its actions or rename it. When you click New Rule you can choose from eight templates (see Figure 8.33), most of which are predefined combinations of options available in succeeding steps. If your rule doesn't fit into any of these predefined categories, choose the Start from a Blank Rule option and choose one of the two general-purpose rules: Check Messages When They Arrive and Check Messages After Sending.

Figure 8.33
Use any of these templates to get started quickly. Click Next to continue using the Rules Wizard or click Finish to build a simple rule using default settings.

CREATING AND USING SEARCH FOLDERS

Search folders, a new feature in Outlook 2003, represent virtual folders that gather messages matching conditions you specify and display them in the contents pane, just as if they were in a single folder.

Initially, Outlook creates search folders that let you see all Unread Mail in one place, even when you've used rules to sort the new messages into multiple folders. You don't have to worry about jumping from folder to folder in search of unread messages; Outlook does the work for you.

Other built-in search folders let you click to see all messages that have been flagged for follow-up and those that are especially large. To create new search folders, click the Mail or Folder List button in the Navigation pane, right-click Search Folders, and choose New Search Folder. The New Search Folder dialog box, shown in Figure 8.34, lets you quickly build simple search folders that cover common searches.

Figure 8.34
Build a generic search folder using the settings in this dialog box.

To build more complex search folders, you could scroll to the bottom of the list in the New Search Folder dialog box, click Create a Custom Search Folder, and then drill through a half-dozen dialog boxes to build a search folder from scratch. But there's a much easier way. Use the Advanced Find dialog box to build a search, using the techniques we described in Chapter 7, and then use the Save As Search Folder menu choice.

→ For details on Using the Advanced Find dialog box to create custom search folders, see "Advanced Search Techniques," **p. 199**.

TROUBLESHOOTING

SOLVING SMTP SNAGS

I have several Internet e-mail accounts that I use for different purposes. I have no trouble sending e-mail from one account, but all the others give me an error message when I try to send e-mail.

The most likely explanation is that your Internet service provider has blocked port 25 as an anti-spam measure. This configuration prevents you from using any outgoing mail servers except those that your ISP provides. You'll need to customize each e-mail account to point to that SMTP server. Don't forget to click the More Settings button for each account and adjust the authentication settings on the Outgoing Server tab.

WORKING AROUND ANTI-SPAM FILTERS

I have two Internet service providers. One is a local provider I use at home, because I like its speed and service. For business trips, I use an account with a national Internet service provider, to avoid having to access the Internet via a long-distance call at exorbitant hotel rates. While on the road, I have no trouble receiving mail from my regular ISP, but when I try to reply to e-mail, I get an error message that says something like This server does not allow relaying.

Most ISPs restrict access to SMTP servers for sending outgoing mail—typically, the mail server checks your IP address before allowing you to connect to the SMTP server. This step verifies that you are an authenticated user on the network, as is the case when you dial in directly. If you connect from another ISP, the server doesn't recognize your IP address and blocks your attempt. This configuration prevents unauthorized users from hijacking the mail server to unleash a flood of spam, but it also prevents you from connecting to the outgoing mail server to relay messages. If your ISP allows it, you may be able to use the SMTP server remotely by supplying authentication details. If not, you'll need to set up another Internet mail account for use on the road, and adjust your configuration so you send mail through the SMTP server that belongs to the account you dialed in with. To make sure that recipients send replies to the right address, be sure to specify your regular (home) mail account as the Reply-To address on this new account.

FORCING OUTLOOK TO SHOW DESKTOP ALERTS

When I receive new messages, the desktop alert window doesn't always appear. Sometimes it shows up, but other times I get no notice.

There are three possible explanations for missing desktop alerts. First, desktop alerts don't appear if you check for new mail manually, by pressing F9 or clicking the Send/Receive button.

Second, if you've defined a rule that moves incoming messages to another folder, you need to specifically enable the Display a Desktop Alert action for that rule. Choose Tools, Rules and Alerts, double-click the rule you want to modify, click Next to move to the actions page, and select the Display a Desktop Alert check box. Click Finish to save the edited rule.

Finally, Outlook is programmed to show no more than five alerts in a row. If you've received a flood of new mail, the sixth alert should simply say "You have new messages."

WHEN ACTIVE MEANS INVISIBLE

The Reading pane says it can't display the message because it contains active content.

That's Outlook's maddeningly roundabout way of telling you the message is in HTML or Rich Text format and contains a script. Open the message to read it.

WHEN YOUR E-MAIL BOUNCES

I replied to a post on an Internet newsgroup via e-mail, but my mail server bounced the message back to me, saying the recipient doesn't exist.

More than anywhere else, people who post to public newsgroups are likely to disguise their true e-mail address. The reason is to prevent bulk-mail artists—spammers—from harvesting their address and reselling it to scam artists. Check the header on the message carefully to see whether the true e-mail address is hidden. Sometimes the solution is as simple as removing the phrase no.spam from an address such as bianca@no.spam.example.com.

CLEANING UP THE AUTOCOMPLETE LIST

Every so often, I mistype an e-mail address when composing a new message. Unfortunately, Outlook has a memory like an elephant and won't forget my mistakes! It keeps "suggesting" my typos as legitimate e-mail addresses. How do I clean up this list?

Outlook keeps track of names you've typed in address boxes, saving these settings in a hidden file called the *nickname cache*, with the extension .nk2. To eliminate a single incorrect entry from this cache, start a new message, click in the To box, and begin typing until the unwanted AutoComplete entry appears. Press the down arrow to select the name and press Delete to remove it. For step-by-step instructions on how to clear the entire nickname cache, see Knowledge Base article 287623, "How to Reset the Nickname and Automatic Completion Cache," at http://support.microsoft.com/?kbid=287623.

A RULE ISN'T WORKING AS YOU EXPECT

I used the Rules Wizard to define a mail-processing rule, but Outlook isn't processing the message as I expected it to.

This problem is almost always the result of conflicting actions from multiple rules. First things first: Check the order of rules, and pay special attention to any rule that contains the Stop Processing More Rules action. You might have defined two rules that apply to the message in question (it's from a specific person and it contains a certain phrase, for example), and each rule wants to move the message to a different folder. When the actions in two or more rules conflict in this way, the one that's higher in the list wins. Try changing the order of the rules, using the Move Up and Move Down buttons. Finally, be especially careful with rules that create message flags with reminders; if another rule also moves that message to a different folder, you'll never see the reminder, because Outlook monitors flags only on messages in the Inbox. Rules that attach message flags should always be high in the list, and they should include a Stop Processing More Rules action.

EXTRA CREDIT: EXPERT STRATEGIES FOR OUTLOOK RULES

Outlook rules follow a rigid set of logical standards. Knowing how rules work can help you troubleshoot problems:

- When rules contain multiple conditions, they are always treated as logical AND statements: The subject contains "homework" AND the sender is "Bill Green." You must create separate rules to apply OR logic.

- Within a condition, items you specify are always treated as though they are joined with a logical OR: The sender is "Woody Leonhard" or "Ed Bott" or "Bill Green."

In general, you'll get best results from Outlook rules when you follow these guidelines:

- Deal with your most important messages first. Identify messages you definitely want to receive and handle them with rules at the top of the list, ending each such rule with the Stop Processing More Rules condition. This guarantees that a less important filter doesn't inadvertently catch a message that you want to keep.

- Try to combine similar rules to reduce clutter. For instance, if you subscribe to daily updates from several online newspapers or mailing lists, you can create a single rule that moves all those messages to a Daily News folder. Use AutoArchive options to clean all messages out of this folder after a week or two. This strategy also helps you deal with the limit on the number of rules you can create.

- Give each rule a meaningful name. A descriptive name can help you sort through a list of rules more quickly.

- Your rules are saved in your Personal Folders file, so be sure to back up regularly. The more work you put into constructing them, the more you'll appreciate being able to recover them in the event of a problem.

CHAPTER 9

STOPPING VIRUSES, SPAM, AND OTHER SECURITY THREATS

In this chapter

WHY SHOULD YOU CARE ABOUT E-MAIL SECURITY?

It's a dangerous world out there. Every time you check for new e-mail messages, you run the risk that a hostile intruder will try to take over your computer, steal your identity, or invade your privacy.

An entire software industry has sprung up to defend Internet users against outside attackers—antivirus and software, personal firewalls, and spam-blocking solutions, for instance. Outlook 2003 includes an assortment of features that should be part of an overall security strategy to help defend yourself against the following threats:

- *Attachment-borne viruses* get the most publicity, especially in mainstream media. Outlook includes severe restrictions that prevent most executable attachments from running; this protection has been so effective that the people who write viruses have been forced to change their tactics, with most current viruses contained in compressed (Zip) files. In this chapter, we explain how these restrictions work and how you can work most effectively with them.

- *Script-based attacks* exploit security flaws in Windows that allow hostile programs to be embedded in a message and automatically executed when you open or preview that message. Outlook protects against all such attacks by blocking execution of any automatic scripting or ActiveX controls.

- *Spam*, the popular term for unwanted commercial e-mail, isn't a security threat on its own. But some types of spam can hoodwink a naïve or careless user into visiting a hostile website or responding to a scam. In addition, legitimate messages can get lost in the clutter of junk mail or swept away by indiscriminate spam-blocking solutions. Outlook 2003 includes a customizable, highly effective junk mail filter that is vastly improved over the crude filters in previous versions.

- *Phishing attacks* are a relatively new form of threat, in which an attacker sends an e-mail message that appears to be from a trusted source, such as a bank or a popular online merchant. The goal is to fool you into visiting a spoofed website and entering your username, password, and other personal details that the attacker can then use to make unauthorized charges, transfer funds from your bank account, or steal your identity. Office 2003 Service Pack 2 introduced some anti-phishing features to Outlook.

- *Web bugs*, also known as *Web beacons*, are links to external graphics embedded in HTML-formatted e-mail messages. The link that retrieves an image can contain tracking codes that allow the message sender to see when you have opened or previewed a message, even if you would prefer to protect your privacy by not disclosing this information. If a spammer can confirm that you have opened or previewed a message, he knows that your e-mail address is valid and may start sending you more unwanted e-mail. Outlook 2003 automatically prevents Web bugs from functioning by blocking the retrieval of all external images in e-mail messages unless you specifically approve.

BLOCKING E-MAIL VIRUSES

Viruses, typically spread through e-mail messages, have garnered plenty of publicity in recent years, and for good reason. Although some are simple pranks, most viruses that have spread in recent years have horrifying consequences. They can destroy or corrupt data files and typically install Trojan horse programs that allow outsiders to take over your computer. Cleaning up after a virus is time-consuming and often requires technical skills that are beyond those possessed by average users. In the fight against viruses, your best strategy is to prevent them from reaching your computer in the first place.

Your first line of defense, of course, is effective, up-to-date antivirus software. As viruses in recent years have proved time and again, even the most disciplined and vigilant user can fall prey to new types of attacks. Office 2003 includes an integrated antivirus interface that allows third-party software to hook directly into the File Open dialog box in Office and scan e-mail messages as they arrive.

NOTE

> To verify that your currently installed antivirus program is compatible with Office 2003, open Word or Excel and choose Tools, Macro, Security. On the bottom of the Security Level tab, look for the message "Virus scanner(s) installed." Oddly, this message is not displayed in the Outlook version of this dialog box.

CONFIGURING ATTACHMENT OPTIONS

Outlook 2003 is ruthless with file attachments. With some file types, in fact, it simply refuses to allow you to access attachments at all. This is not a bug; it's a security feature designed to protect you from possibly dangerous attachments.

Every time you receive an e-mail message that has an attached file, Outlook checks the file extension for that attachment. If the attachment's extension is on its blacklist of 38 potentially dangerous file types, Outlook might force you to save the file before opening it, or it might forbid you to access the attachment in any way.

The attachment security list divides potentially dangerous files into two levels. So-called Level 1 files—executable files, shortcuts, scripts, Access databases, and other objects that can conceivably carry viruses or other harmful content—are considered the most dangerous. When Outlook finds a Level 1 file, it displays a banner in the Info pane that tells you it has blocked access to a file; the message includes the full name of the attached file. (To see a full list of the blocked attachment types, search the Help files for the topic, "Attachment File Types Blocked by Outlook.")

You can't remove a file type from the blacklist, but you can lower it from a Level 1 file type to a Level 2 file type. (There are no Level 2 file types on the default blacklist.) In that case, when Outlook detects that file type, it forces you to save the file to your hard disk where, presumably, it will be scanned for known viruses using the antivirus software you have installed.

TIP FROM

Ed & Woody

> You *do* have antivirus software installed, right? It has been updated recently, hasn't it? Do yourself a favor—if you don't have an up-to-date antivirus program installed, download one now (we'll wait right here) and protect yourself. Windows users have dozens of choices in antivirus software, including some that are absolutely free. For an excellent list of available alternatives and links to useful information, look through the list of certified products at the ICSA Labs Anti-Virus Community (`http://www.icsalabs.com/antivirus`). If you have installed antivirus software, make sure you keep its definition files up to date so you're not bitten by fast-spreading new viruses.

9

If you have an e-mail account on an Exchange Server, your administrator can change any file type from Level 1 to Level 2. If you're using Outlook with an Internet-standard e-mail account, however, there is no easy way to tweak these settings using the Outlook interface. If you're brave (and you know exactly what you're doing) it's possible to change a file type from Level 1 to Level 2 by editing the Registry. Look for this key:

```
HKEY_CURRENT_USER\Software\Microsoft\Office\11.0\Outlook\Security
```

Under that key, add a new string value, name it `Level1Remove`, and fill in its value using a list of file extensions, separated by semicolons. Entering `url`, for instance, changes this extension to a Level 2 file type, which allows you to send and receive Internet shortcuts through Outlook. After making the Registry change, restart Outlook to make your changes take effect.

TIP FROM

Ed & Woody

> You don't need to hack the Registry to fix this Outlook annoyance. Outlook MVP Ken Slovak has written a free add-in program that adds a new tab to the Tools, Options dialog box. You can pick and choose file extensions that are included or excluded from the Level 1 category or click one button that tells Outlook that you want to be able to make your own decisions about *all* file attachments (but we don't recommend that latter strategy for anyone!). Get Ken's program from `http://www.slovaktech.com/attachmentoptions.htm`.

When you add a file type to the Level 2 list, it's no longer blocked when Outlook detects it as an attachment in an e-mail message. But that doesn't mean you can double-click an attachment of that type directly from an e-mail message and expect it to run. Instead, when you double-click the attachment icon in the mail message, Outlook displays the stern Attachment Security Warning dialog box shown in Figure 9.1 and prompts you to save the file.

Attachments that Outlook deems safe (including Word documents, Excel workbooks, and Zip files) appear in the Preview pane and in message windows, where Outlook displays an icon and filename for each attached file. These details appear in the Attachments line, just below the Subject. You can drag and drop attachments into Windows Explorer or onto the desktop; be sure to click the filename and not the icon to its left when clicking and dragging. You can also right-click any icon and use shortcut menus to open, print, save, or remove that attachment. To quickly save an attached file in an open Explorer window, for instance, right-click on the attachment icon and choose Copy. Then right-click in the Explorer window and choose Paste. The same technique works for copying attachments between e-mail messages.

Figure 9.1
Potentially dangerous attachments cannot be opened directly from an e-mail message.

9

TIP FROM

EQ & Woody

If you regularly send around attachments and you don't want to worry about attachment blocking, get in the habit of sending your files in compressed (Zip) format. You can use a third-party program such as WinZip (http://www.winzip.com) or just right-click one or more files in Windows Explorer and choose Send To, Compressed Folders. Outlook waves Zip files right through, without stopping and without checking the archive file's contents. Unfortunately, virus writers noticed this loophole as well, and in the past few years virtually all new viruses have consisted of executable files embedded in Zip files and attached to e-mail messages. Be suspicious of any Zip file you receive unexpectedly. If in doubt, don't open it!

If you receive a message that contains one of the banned attachment types and you're unable to open it using Outlook, don't despair. The attachment is still within the message. Outlook's restrictions *block* access to it without actually removing it. Edit the Registry to change the file type to Level 2 (or use Ken Slovak's Attachment Options utility), as described earlier in this chapter, and you'll be able to save the attachment.

CONTROLLING EXECUTION OF SCRIPTS

Like most modern e-mail programs, Outlook can create and display e-mail messages written in HTML—the same language used to create web pages. To accomplish this task, it uses the same program code that Internet Explorer uses to display web pages. That's a great way to add fonts, images, and other formatting to a message. Security problems arise, though, when e-mail messages contain scripts, which can attempt to perform hostile actions such as running a program or exploiting a known, unpatched vulnerability in Windows to install a program on your computer without your knowledge or consent. The problem is especially severe for e-mail messages, because anyone who knows or can guess your e-mail address can send you a message containing hostile script.

Several years ago, script-based viruses were a serious problem. Today, this problem is practically nonexistent. Outlook 2003 prevents virtually all scripts from being executed. It accomplishes this task by configuring your system using a security feature originally designed for Internet Explorer. All e-mail messages are viewed using the settings from Internet Explorer's Restricted Sites zone. This is the most secure of all five zones, with settings based on the assumption that all sites you visit are potentially dangerous. In this zone, active scripting is disabled by default and ActiveX controls are also prevented from opening.

NOTE

For more information on security zones, see the Microsoft Knowledge Base article 174360, "How to Use Security Zones in Internet Explorer," which is available at `http://support.microsoft.com/default.aspx?scid=kb;en-us;174360`.

When you open a message that contains a potentially dangerous script, Outlook displays the message shown in Figure 9.2. After you click OK, the message opens, with the script or ActiveX item disabled.

Figure 9.2
Outlook blocks HTML e-mail messages containing scripting, showing this error message instead.

What should you do when you receive a message from a known trusted source that contains script or attempts to execute a file? You're highly unlikely to get any message matching this description from a friend or classmate. You might, however, receive a message containing script or ActiveX content from a commercial site that wants to show you some fancy presentation. If you're certain the message is safe, you can view it with a few extra clicks. Don't adjust Outlook's security zones to lower your level of protection; instead, open the message and choose View, View in Internet Zone. This option displays a warning dialog box like the one shown in Figure 9.3. After you click OK, the message displays properly.

Figure 9.3
When you're certain that the contents of a message are safe, you can choose to view it in the Internet zone, where scripts are permitted.

RESTRICTING ACCESS TO THE OUTLOOK ADDRESS BOOK

All programs in Microsoft Office are designed in such a way that other software developers can create scripts, macros, and external programs to take advantage of functions within Office programs. That's a tremendously convenient feature. It means you can install a piece of software and allow your mobile phone or your handheld computer or a fax program to share phone numbers and e-mail addresses stored in the Outlook Address Book. This feature is also a potentially huge security risk; if a virus sneaks into your your PC and gets into your address book, it can spread itself far and wide without your knowledge.

Outlook 2003 no longer allows third-party programs to automatically access your Address Book or Contacts list or to send messages on your behalf. Instead, the default settings require your explicit permission before allowing access to address information.

If an external program attempts to access your Outlook Address Book, you might see the warning dialog box shown in Figure 9.4. You can allow access just for this instance, or you can select the Allow Access For check box and choose an amount of time (up to 10 minutes). If you don't want the program to access your Address Book, click No. Your decision remains in force until you close and restart the program.

Figure 9.4
Programs that want to tap into Outlook address data need your explicit permission.

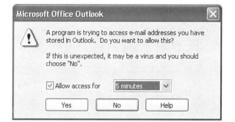

NOTE

> Outlook add-ins that you install can access the Outlook Address Book without permission if they use proper techniques. If you have an Outlook add-in that's giving you problems when you try to import addresses, check with the software developer and see if a newer, Office 2003–compatible version is available.

STOPPING SPAM AND OTHER UNWANTED E-MAIL

What was once a trickle of junk mail has now become a flood. According to one reliable source, more than 70% of all e-mail messages sent and received in the first half of 2005 were unsolicited commercial e-mail, better known as spam. That's up from 50% in 2003 and a mere 8% in 2001, and the trend continues to go in the wrong direction.

You can't stop spammers from barraging you with unwanted e-mail. But you can prevent most of those messages from ever reaching your Inbox. The most effective filtering strategy is one that bounces unwanted email before it reaches your inbox. If you control the server through which your email passes, you can install sophisticated filtering software that will do the job. If your e-mail accounts are hosted by an Internet service provider, check to see whether they offer a server-side spam-filtering option. Finally, for every message that gets past the server and reaches your computer, you need to separate the messages you want from those that belong in the trash.

Outlook 2003 has a junk mail filter that is remarkably effective and is updated as new techniques and technology become available.

FINE-TUNING OUTLOOK'S JUNK MAIL FILTER

The junk mail filter in Outlook 2003 examines every piece of email as it arrives, looking at the content of the message, when it was sent, and other factors to determine whether it is likely to be junk.

NOTE

> The precise techniques that Outlook uses to identify junk mail are classified as a trade secret and are very closely guarded. And for good reason: In the constant battle between spammers and spam-busters, learning how filters work gives the bad guys an edge.

By default, Outlook's junk mail filters are enabled and set to catch only obvious junk mail and shunt it into a Junk E-mail folder. You can adjust these settings to make the filters more restrictive. In doing so, you need to balance your desire to be protected from spam against the risk that legitimate messages will be caught up in the filters. To change the defaults settings, choose Tools, Options, and click the Junk E-mail button on the Preferences tab. The Junk E-mail Options dialog box, shown in Figure 9.5, lets you choose your spam-busting strategy.

Figure 9.5
The default Low setting allows many junk messages to hit your Inbox. Choose the High protection level to block more junk.

Outlook's Junk E-mail filters are extremely effective at the default Low setting, with little risk of false positives. As a result, the only reason to select No Protection is if you rely heavily on your own filters or on third-party spam-catching software.

At the High setting, Outlook catches virtually all junk mail (in our tests, the success rate is well over 95%). This setting also inevitably captures some legitimate messages. If you choose the High setting, you'll need to monitor the Junk E-mail folder carefully at first and set up lists of safe senders and recipients, as we'll explain shortly.

The strictest anti-spam setting is the Safe Lists Only option. In this configuration, the Junk E-mail filters assume that all e-mail is junk unless you've specifically designated the sender (or recipient) as safe. This option is most useful when you have a serious spam problem and virtually all of your legitimate messages are from people you already know.

The first check box at the bottom of the Junk E-mail Options dialog box allows you to choose whether you want Outlook to permanently delete any messages it identifies as junk e-mail. For most people, this option is unacceptable, because it gives you no chance to identify false positives and deal with them.

CAUTION

> Deleting suspected junk e-mail automatically is a bad strategy if you receive any important news via e-mail. Every year, a significant percentage of your friends, family, and neighbors will change Internet service providers and get new e-mail addresses. Banks, Internet service providers, and other businesses change names and addresses as a result of mergers and acquisitions, and sometimes companies change e-mail domains for no apparent reason. If someone who's important in your life changes the details of how they send e-mail to you, you'll have no way of knowing if its change-of-address notices are automatically deleted as junk.

The second check box at the bottom of this dialog box appears only after you install Office 2003 Service Pack 2. With this option enabled (its default setting), Outlook watches for messages that appear to be "phishing" attempts—fraudulent e-mail messages designed to fool you into giving up personal or financial details to a would-be identity thief. When Outlook determines that a message contains one or more suspicious links, it does one of two things:

- Messages that appear to be spam are moved to the Junk E-mail folder and converted to plain text. All links within the message are disabled. To convert the message back to its HTML format and reenable the links, move the message back into the Inbox (or any folder other than the Junk E-mail folder) or click the message in the Info bar and choose Display As HTML.

- When a message contains suspicious links but doesn't appear to be junk e-mail, Outlook leaves it in its original format and location but disables all links. If you're certain the message is safe, click the Info bar and choose the option to turn on links.

→ For more details on how scammers use e-mail for identity theft attacks, **see** "Extra Credit: How to Avoid Being Victimized by a Phishing Attack," **p. 273**.

If you choose one of the more aggressive spam-fighting options, you will almost certainly need to do some fine-tuning to weed out false positives and to block junk senders who sneak through the filters. Initially, Outlook warns you each time it moves a message to the Junk E-mail folder, displaying the dialog box shown in Figure 9.6.

Figure 9.6
After you're comfortable with Outlook Junk E-mail filters, select the check box to stop showing this warning message.

To fine-tune the filters, you need to manage three lists, each of which has its own tab on the Junk E-mail Options dialog box:

- The Safe Senders list includes e-mail addresses that you want Outlook to always recognize as legitimate e-mail. This list can include individual e-mail addresses (*someone@example.com*) or entire domains (*@example.com*). Figure 9.7 shows a typical Safe Senders list. Note that the Always Trust E-mail From My Contacts check box at the bottom of the dialog box is selected; with this option enabled, every address in your Contacts folder is considered "safe."

Figure 9.7
Add addresses to the Safe Senders list to avoid having messages from those recipients mistaken for spam.

- The Safe Recipients list works almost exactly the same as the Safe Senders list. Add names to this list to identify mailing lists and other messages that you want to receive but that are not addressed specifically to you. For instance, if you are a member of the Ferret Fanciers of West Wenatchee mailing list, you might add the group alias, *ferret-fanciers@example.com*, to your Safe Recipients list. Regardless of who sends a message to the list, you can be sure it will arrive in your Inbox.

- Blocked Senders are individuals or domains that you want Outlook to identify as junk mail, no matter how legitimate the content may seem to be. This option is especially useful for filtering out junk from direct e-mail marketers that refuse to acknowledge your unsubscribe requests.

 Is Outlook blocking a domain that you've added to your Safe Senders or Safe Recipients list? See "What's in a Domain Name?" in the "Troubleshooting" section at the end of this chapter.

You can add addresses and domains to any of these three lists manually by opening the Junk E-mail Options dialog box, selecting the appropriate tab, and clicking the Add button. It's much easier, though, to build this list by example. If a piece of spam lands in your Inbox, right-click the message, choose Junk E-mail, and click Add Sender to Blocked Senders List. When you see a legitimate message that has been mistakenly moved to the Junk E-mail folder, right-click the message and choose Junk Mail, Mark As Not Junk. Outlook gives you the opportunity to identify the sender or recipient as a trusted address. For messages in other folders, right click and choose Junk Mail; then select Add Sender to Safe Senders List, Add Sender's Domain to Safe Senders List, or Add Recipient to Safe Recipients List from the shortcut list.

TIP FROM

> Over time, your lists of Blocked Senders, Safe Senders, and Safe Recipients become an indispensable part of your Outlook configuration. We recommend backing up both lists to a safe location every so often. Open the Junk E-mail Options dialog box, click the Export button, specify a filename, and click OK.

Here are a few details you need to know about Outlook's Junk E-mail filters:

- Junk e-mail filtering does not apply to Web-based (HTTP) accounts such as Hotmail and MSN. To adjust junk filtering options for a Web-based account, you need to visit the web page for that service.

- Filters work only after the message body is fully downloaded. If you've configured Outlook to download headers only, junk e-mail headers will show up in your Inbox and will be filtered only after you mark items for downloading and then retrieve the body. For many spam messages, this gives you an opportunity to mark obvious spam for deletion before it ever arrives.

- Junk e-mail filters are processed independently of rules. If you set up a rule that moves messages containing a word or phrase to a folder and you receive an e-mail message containing that phrase that Outlook identifies as spam, you'll end up with two copies of the message—one in the Junk E-mail folder, another in the folder designated by your rule.

Finding organizational strategies that mesh well with Outlook's junk e-mail filters can take some creative thinking. If you receive e-mail through multiple accounts, for instance, you might be tempted to use rules to sort mail from each account into its own folder. However, this strategy clashes with Outlook's Junk E-mail filters because the rules move copies of each incoming message, including suspected spam, to those folders!

The solution? Forget using rules and take advantage of other features in Outlook 2003. The simple approach is to create a view that groups messages by e-mail account. (Choose View, Arrange by, E-mail Account, and then choose View and click the Show In Groups box). Better yet, use Search Folders. Instead of creating a rule to move e-mail from each account into its own folder, create a Search Folder for each account. Here's how:

1. Make a note of the exact names of each e-mail account you use (as listed in the E-Mail Accounts dialog box or on the Send/Receive list), and then select the Inbox and choose Tools, Find, Advanced Find.

2. Click the Advanced tab.

3. Click the Field button and select All Mail Fields, E-mail Account from the drop-down list.

4. Change Condition to is (exactly). Fill in the exact name of the first e-mail account in the Value box and then click Add to List.

5. Click Find Now to run the search. After verifying that the results are as expected, choose File, Save Search As Search Folder. Give it a descriptive name and click OK.

Repeat the preceding steps for all your other e-mail accounts. When you're finished, you'll have a collection of Search Folders, one for each e-mail account. From now on, new messages come into the Inbox, as usual, and Outlook's Junk E-mail filters eliminate the spam. The Search Folders do the work of "sorting" the messages into virtual folders, one for each account.

USING E-MAIL RULES TO BLOCK JUNK E-MAIL

Spammers are sneaky and most are smart enough to figure out how to worm their way past even the most sophisticated filters eventually. As a result, trying to fight spam by constructing your own set of rules is a losing battle. Here are just a few of the obstacles you face:

- If you try to identify words or phrases commonly used in spam, you'll be foiled by the creative misspellings and unique turns of phrase that junk senders use. (Would you like to r3f|n4nce your m0rt_gage?)

- Want to block individual senders? It's a losing battle, because most spammers use forged headers and return addresses. Even with a list of 50,000 "known spammers," most junk mail would get through.

■ Blocking domains belonging to known spammers will cut out only a fraction of the junk e-mail. Semi-legitimate spammers who send torrents of e-mail using their real domain name (a minority among spammers, sadly) are notorious for changing domains every few days or weeks. By the time you block a domain, it's usually been abandoned.

The biggest obstacle to using e-mail rules to fight spam is the ironclad limit that Outlook imposes on custom mail-handling rules. Your list of active rules can be no larger than 32KB in size. In practice, that means you can have somewhere between 30 and 70 e-mail rules. That sounds like a lot, but if you're trying to build a spam-filtering system, it's just a start.

Using Third-Party Spam-Fighting Software

In just the past few years, a thriving industry has grown up around software designed to eliminate spam. The number of choices is dizzying, although most use one of a small handful of technologies. The most promising spam-fighting software uses *Bayesian analysis*, which relies on the users of the software to forward spam to a central database. The software "trains" itself by examining the messages and formulating rules based on their content.

Most third-party spam-filtering solutions communicate directly with your e-mail server and then feed their output into Outlook. If you decide to experiment with one of these programs, you should disable Outlook's Junk E-mail filters.

Protecting Your Privacy

Everyone who markets products and services—legitimate or otherwise—via e-mail wonders the same thing: Are my messages actually being opened and read? To answer that question, some enterprising marketers devised the *Web bug*. In its sneakiest form, a Web bug is an image file that consists of a single pixel and is literally invisible on the HTML-formatted page. Using standard mail merge techniques, the sender composes an HTML-based e-mail message and attaches a unique identifier (a serial number, perhaps, or your e-mail address) to the link that retrieves the Web bug. When you open or preview the message, your e-mail client connects to the server and requests the image. Using the server logs, the sender can build a database of people (like you) who opened the message he sent. He now knows that your e-mail address is valid, and that you aren't blocking his address, and he's emboldened to send you more messages. The result is more junk in your Inbox.

Outlook 2003 includes a default setting that automatically blocks all external content from being retrieved when you open or preview an HTML e-mail message. The effect can be disconcerting at first, because every image that would normally appear in the message is replaced with a message box containing a red X, an explanation from Microsoft, and the alternate text associated with the image (which normally appears in the ScreenTip for the image). Figure 9.8 shows a message in which images have been blocked.

Figure 9.8
In HTML e-mail messages, Outlook does not download external content such as images unless you specifically approve.

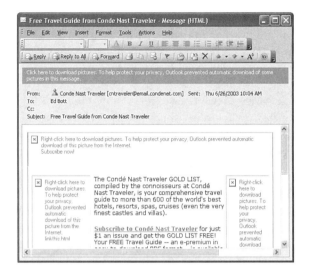

NOTE

Outlook blocks external links to sound files as well as images, so you don't have to worry that an unsolicited message will begin playing music when you open it.

If you know that the message is one you don't want to see, just delete it. If, on the other hand, you're confident that the sender is trustworthy and the blocked content is both acceptable and something you want to see, right-click any image (or click the info bar at the top of the message window) and choose one of the options in the shortcut menu shown in Figure 9.9.

Figure 9.9
Right-click to download blocked external content for the current e-mail message and to set options for future messages from that sender.

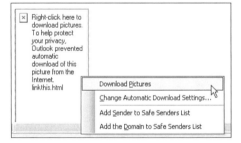

Choose Download Pictures to see the full contents of the current message. The next time you receive a message from this sender, its content will be blocked.

Click either of the bottom two choices on the menu to add the sender or the sender's domain to your Safe Sender list. This action causes Outlook to download all external content for the current message and tells Outlook that you want to download external content for any future messages from that sender or that domain.

CAUTION

When you choose to download external content for a message, Outlook downloads *all* external content. You can't click a single blocked item and choose only to download that image. Also, if you click on any blocked image that is associated with a hyperlink, Outlook activates the link and takes you to that external site.

Finally, click Change Automatic Download Settings to adjust the options Outlook uses for all HTML messages that contain external content. (This dialog box is also available when you choose Tools, Options, and click the Change Automatic Download Settings button on the Security tab.) In the Automatic Picture Download Settings dialog box (see Figure 9.10), you can allow all external content to get through by clearing the check box at the top.

Even if you're not concerned about the privacy effects of Web bugs, disabling external content has one salutary effect that makes it well worthwhile: It prevents spammers from assaulting your senses with images that try to lure you to adult-oriented sites. The graphic images that appear in pornographic spam messages can be shocking, and in some settings simply allowing them to be shown on your PC, especially when kids are present, can actually constitute grounds for legal action. When image blocking is enabled, the only images you'll see are those that are embedded in the message itself.

Figure 9.10
These default settings provide maximum protection from Web bugs.

If some offensive images are sneaking into spam messages you receive, see "Outlook Doesn't Block Embedded Images" in the "Troubleshooting" section at the end of this chapter.

DISABLING HTML-BASED E-MAIL

If you're concerned about the risks of viruses and other problems that can be spread by HTML-based e-mail, one radical solution is to strip all graphics and formatting out of HTML-based e-mail messages and read them as plain text. For highly security-conscious

Outlook users who want nothing to do with HTML content of any sort, this option is welcome.

To use this configuration, choose Tools, Options, click the E-mail Options button, and select the Read All Standard Mail in Plain Text check box.

When you view an HTML message in this fashion, Outlook does not download any external content. Instead, all images and hyperlinks are converted to text-based links within angle brackets. Colors, fonts, tables, lines, and other formatting are also ignored, and the text of the message is displayed in the default plain-text font—10-point Courier New, unless you changed this setting. Any scripts or ActiveX controls are also ignored. Figure 9.11 shows a side-by-side view of an HTML message displayed in its original format (left) and with the plain-text option (right).

Figure 9.11
When you configure Outlook to display HTML messages as plain text, graphics appear as clickable links and all formatting is stripped away.

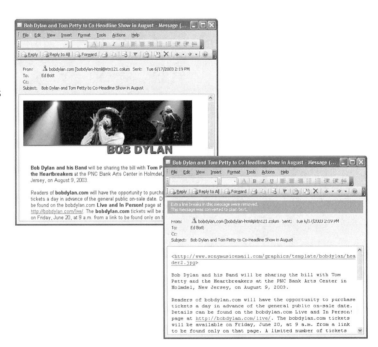

TROUBLESHOOTING

WHAT'S IN A DOMAIN NAME?

I added a domain to my Safe Senders list, but some messages coming from that domain are still being blocked. What's wrong?

As you can see when you examine the Safe Senders and Blocked Senders list, Outlook considers a domain to be everything after the @ sign. In your case, it's likely that the sender is using subdomains, such as *marketing.example.com* and *travel.example.com*. Look at the sender's address carefully and you should be able to see the full domain. Add each subdomain to your Safe Senders list and your filters will work properly again.

OUTLOOK DOESN'T BLOCK EMBEDDED IMAGES

I can see offensive images in an Outlook message I received recently, even though I have image blocking enabled and the sender is not on my Safe Senders list. Other messages display the red X that indicates a blocked image. What's the problem with this message?

The most likely answer is that the sender has embedded the image directly into the message, using MIME encoding. Because the image is not being downloaded from an external server, Outlook doesn't block it. The good news is that this sort of image doesn't represent a threat to your privacy. The bad news is there's no truly effective way to prevent these images from displaying. If you're plagued by a particular sender, you may be able to block that sender or create a rule that identifies messages based on the message header.

EXTRA CREDIT: HOW TO AVOID BEING VICTIMIZED BY A PHISHING ATTACK

It's not exactly spam, and it isn't exactly a virus. In fact, your garden-variety phishing attack isn't new at all. It's the online variation of an age-old confidence game.

The scam works like this: You get an e-mail message that seems to be from a bank, or an online merchant, or a credit card company. It seems there's been a problem with your account—irregular activity, maybe, or a problem with your credit card. All you have to do is click the link, log on to your account, and fill in a few details.

Of course, when you click that link, you actually go to a site owned by the phisher. If he'd done his job well, it looks just like the real thing, and when you enter your logon details, the phisher has enough information to tap into your account or even steal your identity.

So how do you avoid a phishing attack? The most important thing you can do is to install Office 2003 Service Pack 2 and the latest Junk E-mail filters from Office Update. They add a series of new options to the Junk E-mail filter feature that automatically disable links in any suspicious message.

Don't rely only on filtering, however. These common-sense precautions are essential:

- Be suspicious of any unsolicited e-mail that warns of problems with an online account. Be especially suspicious if the message is not personalized in any way except via your e-mail address or other publicly available information.

- Look carefully at any link in an e-mail message. The text in the message may look legitimate, but let your mouse pointer hover over the link and you'll see the actual hyperlinked destination. If the domain doesn't match the one you expect to see, and especially if the address begins with an IP address in numeric format, assume it's a scam and delete the message. The anti-phishing features in Office 2003 SP2 make this task much easier because suspicious messages are converted to plain text and any links they contain are immediately visible.

■ Enter sensitive information only on an encrypted connection. Look for the padlock icon in the lower-right corner of your browser window.

■ Don't click a link in a suspicious e-mail message. Outlook's SP2 anti-phishing features help in this respect by disabling suspicious links.

■ When in doubt, check it out. Open your browser and visit the website by typing in the address or using a shortcut you created yourself. If you're still suspicious, pick up the phone and call the contact number for that merchant or financial service provider.

■ Educate every member of your family on how to spot and avoid

■ Consider installing additional software that can block phishing attacks. Internet Explorer 7 (which was scheduled for release around the same time as this book) includes anti-phishing features. You can also install SpoofStick (www.spoofstick.com), a browser add-in that displays the true location of a web page even if the designer has tried to disguise its address.

CHAPTER 10

ORGANIZING YOUR CONTACTS LIST

In this chapter

MANAGING YOUR LIST OF CONTACTS

Outlook's Contacts folder serves a dual purpose: For Internet mail users, it's the primary storage location for e-mail addresses. It's also a useful place to store names, addresses, phone numbers, and other important information about friends, family members, and business associates. If you use the Contacts folder only to manage e-mail addresses and occasionally print an address book, it will certainly be worth the minimal effort it takes to enter and update contact information. But if you're willing to learn Outlook's secrets, you can make it do much more. For example, you can do any or all of the following tasks:

- Quickly add addresses to letters and envelopes you create with Word. After you master the quirks of the Outlook Address Book, you can configure each entry so names and addresses appear in the correct format.

- Build lists of related contacts for use in mail merge projects.

- Flag one Contact item or a group for a follow-up reminder.

- Synchronize the contents of your Contacts folder with the address book in your mobile phone or handheld computer.

- Use categories to print specialized phone books. If you're a member of a civic group or school club, you can assign the members of that group to a category and then print a list of just those names for up-to-date handouts at the next meeting.

→ The Contacts folder and the Outlook Address Book offer different views of the same information; for full details, **see** "Configuring the Outlook Address Book," **p. 227**.

By default, the Contacts folder opens in Address Cards view, shown in Figure 10.1. This view includes the contact's name (as defined in the File As field), plus the mailing address and as many phone numbers as you've defined for the contact. This view lets you see a fairly large number of records at one time, but it doesn't display company or job title information.

Figure 10.1
The default Address Cards view packs the maximum number of records onto the screen by displaying only essential address and phone information.

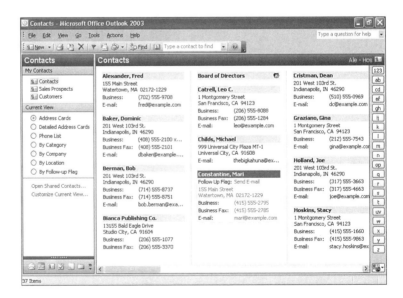

To see more information about each contact, switch to the Detailed Address Cards view, which displays virtually all fields in each contact record.

→ Outlook provides a variety of options for sorting and filtering your Outlook items; **see** "Using Views to Display, Sort, and Filter Items," **p. 171**.

ENTERING AND EDITING CONTACT INFORMATION

To begin creating a new contact from scratch, use any of the following techniques:

- Click the New Contact button.
- Press Ctrl+Shift+C.
- Select File, New, Contact.

Outlook's form for creating a new item in the Contacts folder includes a number of smart features that help you enter properly formatted information quickly and accurately. Start in the Full Name field and use the Tab key to jump from field to field. After you've entered all the information, click the Save and Close button at the top of the dialog box to store the new item. Figure 10.2 shows a filled-in Contact form.

Figure 10.2
Outlook automatically fills in some of the blanks when you create a new item in the Contacts folder, and it checks the rest to make sure that you left nothing out.

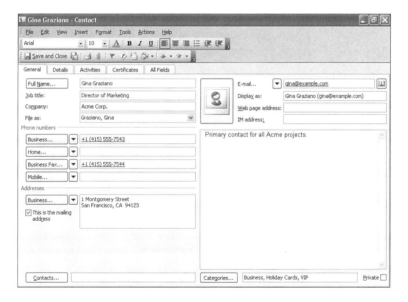

In all, each Contact item includes more than 140 fields of information. Most of the time, however, you'll use only a small fraction of these fields—those that are visible on the General tab of the default Contact form. To see more information, click the All Fields tab. Use the drop-down list to filter the collection of fields so you see a manageable subset, such as all Address fields, all Name fields, and so on. Select All Contact fields to see (and edit) the entire list of available fields, in alphabetical order, as shown in Figure 10.3.

Figure 10.3
The last tab of the default Contact form lets you scroll through (and edit) more than 140 fields in each item.

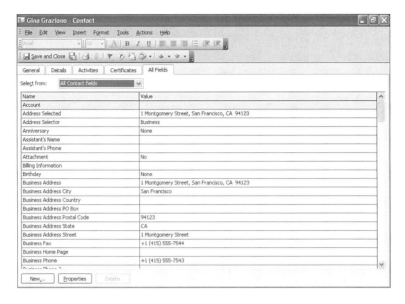

If you're having trouble selecting or deleting a field's contents, see "Selecting and Deleting Field Contents" in the "Troubleshooting" section at the end of this chapter.

ENTERING AND EDITING NAMES

When you enter a new contact's name in the Full Name field (or change an existing one), Outlook slices and dices your entry into as many as nine separate fields. You will rarely see most of these fields, but knowing how Outlook *parses* names—that is, breaks them into their component parts—lets you control the process. This will pay off later when you use items from the Contacts folder as the source for e-mail, letters, envelopes, and mail merge projects.

TIP FROM

> Don't bother with the Shift key when you enter Contact names. If you enter a name in all lowercase letters, Outlook automatically capitalizes each name as soon as you Tab out of the field.

As soon as you enter the full name, in any order, Outlook attempts to break it into five subfields: First Name, Middle Name, Last Name, Title (Ms. or Dr., for example) and Suffix (Jr. or M.D., for instance). To view (and edit) the contents of these fields, click the Full Name button, which opens the Check Full Name dialog box, shown in Figure 10.4. If any information is incorrect, edit it here.

How do you include a courtesy title such as Mr., Ms., or Dr. in each new Contact item? Get in the habit of entering the title at the beginning of the Full Name field. Outlook recognizes the following titles, which are also on the Title drop-down list in the Check Full

Name dialog box: Dr., Prof., Mr., Mrs., Ms., and Miss. Even if a title is not available on the drop-down list, it still might work. For example, beginning a name with Sir, Herr, Fraulein, Monsieur, Madame, or Signore will correctly fill in the Title field. If you're not sure a prefix will work, try it in a new, blank Contact form.

Figure 10.4
When you enter a full name, Outlook automatically breaks it into these subfields; if any information is incorrect, edit it here.

Based on what you type in the Full Name field, Outlook also fills in two additional fields automatically:

- **The File As Field**—Controls the order in which the Contacts folder displays items when you switch to Address Cards or Detailed Address Cards view. Although Outlook automatically fills in this field using its default format, Last Name first, you can easily change it.

- **The Subject Field**—Does not appear on any built-in forms but is accessible on the All Fields tab. It defines how each Contact item appears when you display the Address Book. By default, Outlook fills in this field with the First Name field first.

→ To learn more about how Outlook files your Contact items, **see** "Changing the Way a Contact Item Is Filed," **p. 282**.

 If you don't want Outlook to automatically (and incorrectly) split company names in your Contacts Folder into first and last names, see "Using Company Names in Your Contacts" in the "Troubleshooting" section at the end of this chapter.

WORKING WITH ADDRESSES

Just as with name fields, when you enter a mailing address in the Address field on the default Contact form, Outlook splits the address into component parts and stores the information in as many as 31 separate fields. You can store up to three addresses per contact; click the drop-down list just below the Address button to select Business, Home, or Other.

When you enter an address, Outlook parses the address into separate fields for the street, city, state, and other fields. If you enter information in a format Outlook doesn't recognize—if you omit the city or state, or if you accidentally leave a digit off the ZIP Code—Outlook pops up the Check Address dialog box shown in Figure 10.5 (you can also click the Address button to display this dialog box). This display shows how Outlook proposes to divide the information into subfields. Click OK to save the record as typed, or edit the contents of any field.

Figure 10.5
This dialog box shows you how Outlook proposes to parse the address you entered into subfields.

When you select the This Is the Mailing Address check box, Outlook copies this address to the fields that are used when you create letters, envelopes, or mail merge lists in Word.

→ To learn more about using Word's mail merge capabilities, **see** "Using Mail Merge to Personalize Form Letters," **p. 483**.

Entering Job and Company Details

On the General tab of the default Contact form, you'll find two boxes for entering work-related information about a contact: Job Title and Company. Click the Details tab to enter other work-related information, such as Department and Manager's Name.

Although the Details tab includes a field for Assistant's Name, the field for Assistant's Phone Number is buried in the full list of fields on the last tab of the dialog box. There's a much easier way to enter this information, however: Click the drop-down arrow to the left of any of the four phone number boxes and select Assistant, and then enter the number. After you enter the number, it is visible in both Address Card views.

Managing Phone, Fax, and Other Numbers

The General page has room to enter up to four phone numbers—by default, you can fill in Business, Home, Business Fax, and Mobile numbers. You're certainly not limited to those options, however; you can actually enter as many as 19 separate phone numbers, using the drop-down lists at the left of each number to select different fields.

NOTE

Both default Address Card views display as many phone numbers as you've defined for a contact. These appear in an order determined by this form, with most business-related numbers at the top. Curiously, the Business Fax field appears at the bottom of each list, and we can't find any way to change this order.

You can enter phone numbers any way you like, with or without punctuation; when you exit the field, Outlook automatically reformats the numbers using its standard punctuation scheme—parentheses around the area or city code and a hyphen after the first three digits of the phone number. If you omit the area code, Outlook assumes the number is in your local dialing area and adds your area code to the entry. If Outlook parses this information incorrectly, or if you need to add a country code to the number, click to select the phone number field and then click the button to the right of the field. This action opens a dialog box that allows you to enter or edit this information.

If a contact's phone number includes an extension, add this information at the end of the phone number, preceded by a space and the letters x or ext. Outlook ignores this information when formatting the phone number or using the AutoDial feature. You can also add text before or after a phone number; for example, if someone listed in your Contacts has an office in two cities, you might enter a number in both the Business and Business 2 fields, and then label them LA and NY.

TIP FROM

Ed & Woody

Are you sick of seeing both an e-mail address and a fax number appear in the AutoComplete list when you enter a contact's name in a new e-mail message? Tell Outlook to stop automatically suggesting fax numbers by adding the text label FAX at the beginning of the fax number field. You can still read the number, but Outlook no longer recognizes it as a legitimate address and stops suggesting it.

10

ENTERING AND EDITING E-MAIL AND WEB ADDRESSES

You can store up to three e-mail addresses per contact. Click the drop-down arrow next to the E-mail box to select any of these three blanks, and then enter the address. Click the Address Book button at the right of this box to view e-mail addresses in the Outlook Address Book, which uses a different form to display information.

→ For an authoritative explanation of how the Outlook Address Book works, **see** "Configuring the Outlook Address Book," **p. 227**.

→ To find out how Outlook uses Address Book information to fill in addresses on e-mail messages, **see** "Creating, Managing, and Using E-mail Addresses," **p. 226**.

When you send or receive an e-mail message, Outlook lets you see and change the text displayed in the To and From fields of message windows for each address. When you enter an e-mail address in any of the three boxes on the Contact form, the Display box beneath it shows how the name will appear in messages you send to that address. By default, the Display value is set to the value of the Full Name field, followed by the e-mail address in parentheses. Edit this address to show whatever you want—you might want to replace the e-mail address with a Company name or the word *Personal* in parentheses, for instance.

The General tab of the default Contact form also includes input boxes where you can enter a web page address; if you enter a recognizable URL here, Outlook converts it to a hyperlink so you can jump to a personal or corporate web page directly from the contact's record.

NOTE

If you use Windows Messenger or MSN Messenger, enter the Instant Messaging address for the contact in the IM Address field. This field does not work with other instant-messaging services, such as those from AOL or Yahoo.

➜ For more information on how Outlook integrates with MSN Messenger, **see** "Using Windows/MSN Messenger to Communicate with Contacts," **p. 287**.

ENTERING PERSONAL INFORMATION AND OTHER DETAILS

Click the Details tab to add some personal information about each contact. Fields on this tab include Nickname, Spouse's Name, Birthday, and Anniversary. You can see still more fields in this category (including one in which you can enter the names of children or specify a contact's hobbies) by clicking the All Fields tab.

As in virtually all Outlook items, the Notes area at the bottom of the Default Contact form lets you add extensive notes and comments, as well as shortcuts to other Outlook items, files, or file attachments. Click the Categories button to assign each entry to one or more categories; the long list of built-in categories includes a Holiday Cards choice that lets you quickly print a list of friends, family, and business associates to whom you'll send season's greetings.

If you click the Contacts button, Outlook pops up a dialog box that lets you link one Contact item to another. You might want to do that with business partners, for example, or to link the individual Contact items for a married couple to a third item that contains their family details. Assign that last item to the Holiday Cards category.

➜ To learn more about categorizing Outlook items, **see** "Assigning Items to Categories," **p. 185**.

WORKING SMARTER WITH CONTACT ITEMS

Most Outlook users are perfectly content to enter one item at a time in the Contacts folder. If you have a bulging address book, though, you'll want to employ the secrets and shortcuts described in this section.

CHANGING THE WAY A CONTACT ITEM IS FILED

In both built-in Address Card views, the field used for sorting and displaying information is the File As field. By default, Outlook fills in this field by using the information you type in the Full Name field, displaying it last name first. If you don't enter a name here, Outlook assumes the record refers to a business and uses the information from the Company field. You can accept the default, or you can change the information displayed here.

Although organizing an address book by last name is traditional, you might choose to mix different filing orders within the Contacts folder. For example, when you enter a record for a person who serves as your main contact with a school, business, or organization, file the record under the company name, with the person's name in parentheses. In some cases, you might even use simple generic descriptions such as Drugstore or Travel Agent.

If you can't remember how you filed a Contact item, click the Find button on the Standard toolbar. A simple search looks through all Name, Company, and Address fields. Click the Options drop-down arrow and select Search All Text in Each Message to look for specific information in a Contact's Notes field.

To change the way a specific Contact item is filed, double-click to open the item. In the File As field, click the drop-down arrow. If both the Full Name and Company fields contain data, Outlook offers the following five choices:

- Full name, first name first
- Full name, last name first
- Company name
- Full name, last name first, followed by company name in parentheses
- Company name, followed by full name, last name first, in parentheses

To file the item using any other text, replace the contents of the File As field. Whatever you type appears in alphabetical order in all views of your Contacts folder.

To change the default order for all new contacts, select Tools, Options, click the Preferences tab, and click the Contact Options button. Two drop-down boxes let you select a default for the Full Name field and the File As field—they don't have to be the same. When you do this, remember that the change does not affect existing contact records—only new ones.

ENTERING SEVERAL NEW CONTACT ITEMS AT ONCE

You've just returned from a meeting with a thick bundle of business cards or a membership roster that runs for several pages. How do you speed up the process of typing those details into Outlook? Here are three time-saving shortcuts to help make shorter work of that tedious job:

- Enter data by using a table-based view (such as the built-in Phone List view) instead of the default Contact form. Click in the empty box in the top line to begin entering a new item. Press Tab to move from field to field. When you press Enter, Outlook stores the record and moves the insertion point back to the beginning of the first line, where you can begin a new item immediately.

  If you just want to get a few crucial names, phone numbers, and e-mail addresses into Outlook, create a custom Table view that contains only the fields you need and no more. Be sure to include the Categories field so you can identify the meeting or place where you met this person (PTSA Kickoff 2006, for example).

- If you prefer to use a Contact form, enter the information for the first card in the stack; then select File, Save and New. This hidden menu option saves the item you just entered and clears the form so you can begin a new contact immediately. After you enter the last card in the stack, press Esc to clear the blank form.

- When you have two or more cards from people who work in the same office, let Outlook copy key information to the new Contact item. Open the item, click the Actions menu, and select New Contact from Same Company. Outlook creates a new item, entering the company name, address, and phone number from the previous item, but clearing all other fields.

10

EXCHANGING CONTACT INFORMATION

It's extremely easy to exchange items with other Outlook users. For example, if a neighbor sends you an e-mail message asking how to contact a mutual friend, you can forward a copy of that person's item from your Contacts folder. If you're certain the other person uses Outlook, the procedure is easy: Drag the item from the Contacts folder and drop it in the message window to send it as an attachment. Your neighbor can add the item to her Contacts folder by opening the message and dragging the attached item onto the Contacts icon on the Outlook Bar.

To exchange information with someone who doesn't use Outlook, use the *vCard* format (short for virtual business card) to translate standard name, business, address, and phone fields into a simple text file that other compatible programs can import. When you send your vCard to another person via e-mail, that person can easily add your address information into Outlook, a mobile phone or handheld computer, or any compatible contact-management program. You can also turn any item from your Contacts folder into a vCard and attach it to an e-mail message.

TIP FROM

Ed & Woody

Unless you're absolutely certain the person to whom you're sending a mail message uses Outlook, you should send contact information in vCard format. In fact, because this card uses plain text, your recipient can read its contents even without a compatible contact manager—just open the file in a text editor, such as Notepad.

EXPERT EDITING TECHNIQUES

If you want to change an address or phone number or edit a misspelled name, you don't need to open a Contact item. You can edit directly in any Card view (Detailed Address Cards, for example) or Table view (such as Phone List). Click the letter along the right side of the window that matches the first letter of the item you're looking for; use the scrollbars, if necessary, to find the name you're looking for and then just click and start typing.

TIP FROM

Ed & Woody

Do you find yourself inadvertently editing contact records? You can turn off the capability to change records unless you open them. Choose View, Arrange By, Current View, Customize Current View. Click Other Settings and clear the Allow In-cell Editing box.

It's also possible (although difficult) to update the same field in a group of records, all at one time. Let's say XYZ Corp. merges with ABC Industries to form a new company, A to Z Industries. If your Contacts folder includes a few dozen records for people who work at XYZ and ABC, you can change the company name for all those records in one operation, instead of having to open and edit each one individually.

Unfortunately, this technique has some serious limitations. It will not allow you to update phone numbers when an area code changes, for example—an increasingly common situation in the United States—because the area code is not stored in a separate field from the rest of the number. Nor can you sort and update using fields based on formulas.

1. Switch to a view that shows all Contacts grouped by the field you want to change. In this example, you can use the built-in By Company view; to change another field, you might need to create a custom view.

→ To learn more about using Outlook's built-in view or to create your own custom views, **see** "Using Views to Display, Sort, and Filter Items," **p. 171**.

2. Select View, Expand/Collapse Groups, Collapse All Groups. Find the group that contains the items you want to change and click the plus sign to expand only that group.

3. Select one item in the group and edit the Company field so it contains the correct information—in this example, change XYZ Corp. to A to Z Industries. As soon as you save the change, you'll see a new group in your list, containing the item you just changed.

4. Drag the Group bar from the group of records with the old Company name and drop it onto the Group bar for the item you just changed. As you drag the Group bar, a ScreenTip will alert you that you're about to change the Company name to A to Z Industries.

You don't need to use this technique to assign multiple contacts to categories, however. Instead, select a group of records, either individually or by using filters; then right-click and select Categories from the shortcut menu.

MERGING DUPLICATE CONTACT ITEMS

How do you deal with duplicate Contact items? This problem is particularly prevalent if you use incoming e-mail as the basis for a Contact item. When you drag a message from the Inbox and drop it in the Contacts folder, Outlook creates a new Contact item using the sender's name as it appears in the From box. If one person occasionally sends messages using a different display name, eventually you'll wind up with two, three, or more Contact items for a single person—most consisting of just an e-mail address.

In some cases, Outlook can combine duplicate records for you. If you attempt to enter a record using exactly the same name as an existing Contact item, Outlook displays the dialog box shown in Figure 10.6.

If you intended to create a duplicate record, or if this is a new contact that happens to have the same name as another item in your Contacts folder, select Add This As a New Contact Anyway. If you select the default option, Update New Information from This Contact to the Existing One, Outlook replaces every field in the existing item if the new item contains information in that field. If you're not sure whether to update the record, click the Open Existing Contact button and compare the contents of the two items.

Figure 10.6
When you try to enter a new Contact item with the same name as an existing one, Outlook offers to merge the two records.

CAUTION

Think before you automatically update a contact record. Outlook does not show you what it's going to do before you merge items, and there's no record afterward of which fields changed and which stayed the same. If you enter even a single character in the Notes field for the new record, for example, it will completely erase any notes and file attachments or shortcuts in the existing record. If you inadvertently delete important information by merging contact records, look in the Deleted Items folder, where Outlook keeps a copy of the original item when you use the merge option.

The merge function is smart about e-mail addresses. Each contact item can contain a maximum of three e-mail addresses. If the original item contains one or two e-mail addresses, Outlook will add e-mail addresses to the unused address field rather than replacing an existing address.

Outlook offers to merge items only when the name you enter in the Full Name field is absolutely identical to an existing item, and the offer is good only when you create the duplicate item. If you've added several items to your Contacts folder that refer to the same person with slightly different names—William Gates and William H. Gates, for example—you can use a sneaky workaround to merge the data:

1. Open the master item—the one that contains the record you want to merge other information into. Copy the contents of the Full Name field to the Clipboard and close the item.

2. Open the second item—the one that contains information you want to merge into the master item. Paste the contents of the Clipboard into the Full Name field in the second record, and then click the Save and Close button.

3. Select the second item and press the Delete key.

4. Select Edit, Undo Delete. Outlook restores the contact item from the Deleted Items folder. Because this has the same effect as creating a new item, Outlook displays the Duplicate Contact Detected dialog box. Select the option to merge information.

You can also merge information from two or more records manually. Open each contact item in its own window, and then drag information such as e-mail addresses from one item to another.

TIP FROM

If you never, ever want to be prompted to merge contact items, turn off this feature. From the main Outlook window, select Tools, Options, and select the Preferences tab. Click the Contact Options button and clear the Check for Duplicate Contacts box.

USING WINDOWS/MSN MESSENGER TO COMMUNICATE WITH CONTACTS

Outlook 2003 integrates with Microsoft's instant messaging utilities, MSN Messenger and Windows Messenger, enabling you to communicate with contacts immediately, in a Messenger window, rather through e-mail. (The younger you are, the more likely you are to use instant messaging as a primary means of communication, but instant messaging is not just for kids!)

Outlook looks for a value in the IM Address field for any Contact item. When you open an e-mail message from a contact whose address is listed in your Contacts folder, Outlook checks to see whether that person is listed in the Contacts folder as having a Messenger ID. If so, you'll see a small name icon to the left of his or her name in the From line at the top of the message. The message appears green if the contact is online, gray if she's currently offline. Click to display a menu like the one shown in Figure 10.7.

Figure 10.7
If you'd prefer a quick online chat to an extended session of e-mail tag, use this menu to open MSN/Windows Messenger.

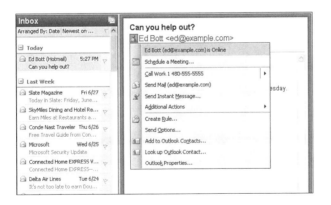

ADDRESSING LETTERS AND ENVELOPES USING YOUR CONTACTS LIST

Word and Outlook can work together with varying degrees of success to help you generate properly addressed letters and envelopes. Outlook's Actions menu, in fact, includes a New

Letter to Contact choice that ostensibly does exactly that. What it actually does, however, is kick off Word's Letter Wizard—an option that always works better when started from within Word. We don't recommend that you select this option from Outlook; instead, always start with Word when you want to create a letter or envelope with the Letter Wizard.

→ For full details on the only effective way to use Word's Letter Wizard, **see** "Creating and Editing Letters," **p. 472**.

You can, however, kick off a Word mail merge from Outlook. This process can be surprisingly effective, especially if you're willing to create a custom view and filter your Contacts list first. Start by opening the Contacts folder, and then select View, Arrange By, Current View, Define Views. Click the New button and define a Table or Card view that contains all the fields you need for your merge. For example, if you're planning to mail holiday letters to everyone in your Holiday Cards category, be sure the list of fields includes First Name, Last Name, Suffix, and all the Home Address fields. Don't use the Full Name or Mailing Address fields, which might contain business addresses or names that are formatted incorrectly. Save the view with a name such as Holiday Letter Mail Merge.

→ For instructions on how to create a new view, **see** "Creating a New Custom View," **p. 179**.

1. If you want to send the mailing to a subset of your list, select the individual items manually, using Ctrl+click, or right-click any empty space in the contents pane, choose Filter from the shortcut menu, and define a filter.

→ For details on how to create a filter in Outlook, **see** "Customizing an Existing View," **p. 173**.

2. Select Tools, Mail Merge. The Mail Merge Contacts dialog box opens, as shown in Figure 10.8.

Figure 10.8
Use these options, combined with a custom Outlook view, to quickly create a Word mail merge document.

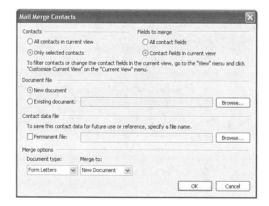

3. From the Contacts section, choose whether you want All Contacts in Current View or Only Selected Contacts. From the Fields to Merge section, choose whether you want All Contact Fields or Contact Fields in Current View. If you've created a custom view as we recommend, select the Contact Fields in Current View option.

TIP FROM

You can merge using the entire list of fields from the Contacts folder. If you do that, how-ever, the list of merge fields will include all 140-something fields from Outlook, and scrolling through the list will be a chore. Trust us—creating a custom view will save you a lot of time.

4. From the Document File section, choose whether you want to use a New Document or an Existing Document. Use the Browse button to select a file. If you want, you can pause here, create your document in Word, save it and close it, and return to the dialog box to continue.

TIP FROM

Using an existing document is a great way to print custom envelopes easily, using a return address of your choosing. Run this mail merge routine and create an envelope that contains the First Name, Last Name, and appropriate Home Address, Business Address, or Mailing Address fields. Add a text box containing your return address (with a logo, if you want), and save the file using a name such as My Envelope.doc. The next time you want to create an envelope, select one or more items from your Contacts folder, and use Outlook's mail merge features with the document you just created. The results are nearly foolproof—and you can use the same technique for letters as well, pro-ducing much better results than the Letter Wizard.

5. In the Contact Data File section, select the Permanent File box if you want to save the filtered data from your Contacts folder in a separate file for reuse later. If you've defined a custom view, this step is not necessary; it's most applicable if you want to share the data file with another Word user who doesn't have access to your Contacts folder. This file is static and doesn't update if a contact's details are updated.

6. Select a Document Type from the Merge Options section of the dialog box; normally, you'll use the Form Letters option, but you can also select Mailing Labels, Envelopes, or Catalog. These options are the same as those available using Word's Mail Merge Wizard. Select one of three Merge To destinations as well: a new document, the printer, or e-mail.

7. Click OK to launch Word with the document and data you specified ready to merge. If you started with a new document, you must add merge fields and text; if you began with an existing document that already contained merge fields and text, you're ready to go.

→ For more details about how to use Word's mail merge capabilities, **see** Chapter 16, "Letters, Mail Merge, and "Smart Documents," **p. 471**.

PRINTING PHONE LISTS FROM YOUR CONTACTS LIST

You can print contact lists in a variety of styles and formats, using all the items in your Contacts folder or only a subset of them. You can even turn your address list into a booklet printed on both sides and small enough to fit in a shirt pocket—although you must be willing to hover over the printer while it spits out pages. (You also must resign yourself to wasting many sheets of paper while you figure out the precise order in which to perform each step.) This feature can be useful if you've entered the contact details for every member of a school group or civic organization you're involved in, for example, and you want to print the addresses and phone numbers of the entire membership roster to hand out at a meeting.

The steps required to print an address book or phone list containing items from your Contacts folder are nearly identical to those for printing a calendar. If you want to print a subset of the folder's contents, use one of the following techniques:

- To select a contiguous block of items, click the first item; then hold down the Shift key and click the last item in the group.

- To select individual items that are not adjacent, hold down Ctrl while clicking each one.

- To show only items that match specific criteria, use the Find button or the Advanced Find dialog box.

- Customize the current view or switch to another view and filter the list.

→ To learn more about using views to control how you work with Outlook items, **see** "Using Views to Display, Sort, and Filter Items," **p. 171**.

→ To learn more about Outlook's search capabilities, **see** "Finding Outlook Items," **p. 197**.

→ For an explanation of the techniques for printing calendars, **see** "Printing a List of Appointments and Tasks," **p. 313**.

1. Switch to any Card view and select the items to be printed. If you want to print the entire list, you do not need to make a selection.

2. Click the Print button. Outlook displays the Print dialog box shown in Figure 10.9.

3. Select one of the five page formats from the Print Style list.

Figure 10.9
Select the Phone Directory Style option to print all the names and phone numbers in your Contacts folder, with no company or address information.

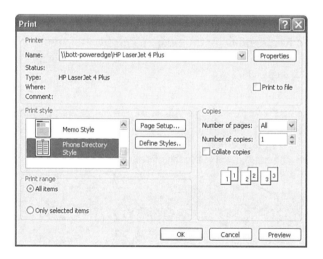

Are you having problems seeing all the Print Style choices in the Print dialog box? If so, see "Setting Print Styles" in the "Troubleshooting" section at the end of this chapter.

4. In the Print Range box, choose whether you want to print All Items or Only Selected Items.

TIP FROM

Ed & Woody

> Have you used the Notes field to keep track of a lot of information about some contacts? To extract the maximum amount of information when printing, select Memo Style, check the options to start each item on its own page, and print all attachments. Be careful, however; this option can chew through a ream of paper faster than you can say, "Save the rainforest."

5. Click the Preview button to see what your page will look like when printed. Use the Page Up and Page Down keys (or the corresponding toolbar buttons) to see additional pages in the Preview window, as shown in Figure 10.10.

Figure 10.10
Preview an address book or phone list before printing to ensure the format matches what you expect.

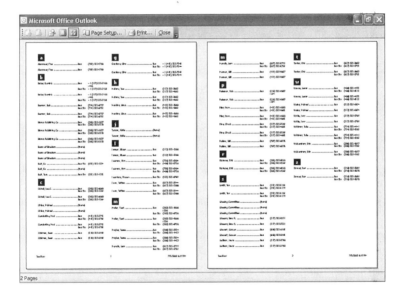

6. Click the Page Setup button in the Preview window or in the Print dialog box to adjust layout options, paper sizes, fonts, headers, footers, and other settings.

7. Click Print to send the job to the printer.

When you print your phone book, select from the following five formats:

- **Card Style**—Shows all the details from the underlying Card view. Switching to Detailed Card view adds more fields to each item but also extends the size of your printed book.

- **Small Booklet Style**—Prints in Card view, with each page shrunk to 1/8 normal size. Default settings suggest you should print this booklet using both sides of the paper. If you don't have a printer capable of handling two-sided printing, you can get the same effect, tediously, by using the manual feed option in your printer and feeding each sheet through individually.

- **Medium Booklet Style**—Also prints a two-sided booklet, but each page in this style is only 1/4 the size of the printed page. Experiment with a four-page sample before printing your entire phone book.

- **Memo Style**—Prints every bit of information about a contact, including all notes. To print a single contact in Memo Style, bypassing all dialog boxes, open the item and click the Print button.

- **Phone Directory Style**—Prints the name and all phone numbers for each contact in a two-column format that takes up the full width of an 8 1/2×11-inch sheet of paper. Although you can change the number of columns and the fonts used in this style, you can't add new fields.

→ If none of the built-in print formats is exactly right, try creating a custom format using the same techniques as with a calendar; **see** "Printing a List of Appointments and Tasks," **p. 313**.

TROUBLESHOOTING

SELECTING AND DELETING FIELD CONTENTS

When working with the All Contact fields list on the last tab of a Contact form, Outlook won't let you edit the File As field, the names of e-mail entries, and several other fields. So, how do you select or delete the contents of these fields?

Outlook won't let you edit a handful of fields in this list; most of these are fields Outlook generates automatically based on the contents of other fields. Use the General tab of the Contact form to change this information.

USING COMPANY NAMES IN YOUR CONTACTS

You've entered a company name in the Contacts folder, but Outlook insists on splitting it into first and last names—so that Acme Industries becomes Industries, Acme.

When entering a new Contact item for a company, leave the Full Name field blank and instead press the Tab key twice to jump to the Company field. Whatever you type in that field also appears in the File As and Subject fields, exactly as you typed it.

SETTING PRINT STYLES

You clicked the Print button, but you see only one print style choice in the Print dialog box. Naturally, it's not the one you want.

This occurs when you click the Print button while displaying the Contacts folder in a Table view, such as Phone List view. Exit the Print dialog box and switch to a Card view, such as Address Cards or Detailed Address Cards, and then try again.

EXTRA CREDIT: PUTTING A FACE WITH EACH NAME

One of the coolest features in Outlook 2003 is so subtle that you might not notice it, even after using Outlook for a few months. The form for a contact item includes a placeholder for a photo, just above the Notes box and to the left of the E-mail field.

To add a photo to a contact, click the placeholder icon, or choose Actions, Add Picture. Browse to the picture file and click OK. Don't worry about the size or location of the original picture, either. Outlook converts the file to a JPEG image less than 2KB in size and attaches it directly to the contact record.

Figure 10.11

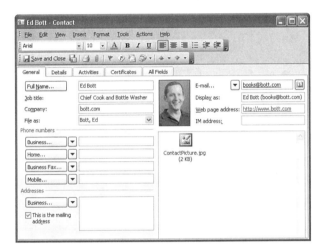

CHAPTER 11

MANAGING APPOINTMENTS, MEETINGS, AND TASKS

In this chapter

MANAGING YOUR PERSONAL CALENDAR

Outlook's Calendar folder can keep track of any number of appointments and meetings, whether they're one-time-only events or recurring appointments that repeat on a regular schedule. Outlook's calendaring features are best suited to people whose duties keep them close to a computer screen most of the time, or those who have a handheld device (such as a Palm or Pocket PC or a SmartPhone) that can synchronize data from Outlook's Calendar, Tasks, and Contacts folders. If you're not near your computer all day, you can still get in the habit of reviewing and updating your calendar each morning, before beginning your day's planned activities. You can then print a daily or weekly calendar, complete with notes, and update it throughout the day with changes and new meetings or appointments. Then, when you return home at the end of the day, you can input the changes into your calendar and bring your schedule up to date.

The default view of the Calendar folder displays appointments for the current day; you can change this view to show multiple days, a full week, or a full month. A calendar control called the Date Navigator appears at the top of the Navigation pane. As an alternative to this view, you can enable the TaskPad (choose View, TaskPad). In this configuration, the Date Navigator moves to the right of the contents pane, above a short list of tasks. Figure 11.1 shows the two alternative views side by side.

Figure 11.1
The Date Navigator changes position depending on whether the TaskPad is hidden (left) or visible (right).

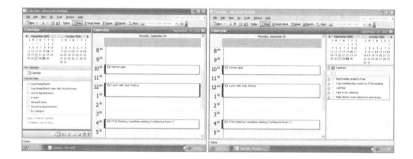

TIP FROM

Want to see more than one month in the Date Navigator? Drag the border between the Navigation pane and the contents pane to the right (or, if the TaskPad is visible, drag its border to the left and/or down). Outlook shows as many months as will fit in the space you allot.

In the Date Navigator, boldfaced numbers indicate days on which you currently have at least one scheduled appointment or meeting. Click any date (past or future) to quickly show that day's items in the contents pane. Use the left- and right arrows to move backward and forward a month at a time. For long-distance jumps, there's a secret, undocumented short-cut. Click the name of a month above the Date Navigator and hold down the mouse button to see a list that includes the three months before and after the current month. Drag the pointer below or above the list to scroll to any month, and then release the mouse button to jump to that month.

CREATING A NEW APPOINTMENT OR EVENT

You can create three similar types of items in the Calendar folder. *Appointments* have starting and ending times blocked out in your schedule; *all-day events*, such as vacations and business trips, are measured in full days and don't have specific start or end times; and *meetings* are appointments to which you invite other people.

→ To see how Outlook can help you coordinate meetings, **see** "Planning a Meeting with Outlook," **p. 315**.

If you want to add a new item to your personal calendar and you know the date and time of the appointment or event, you can open a new appointment form with those details already filled in. Open or switch to a window displaying the contents of the Calendar folder, and then use any of these techniques:

- From any Day view (including multiday views), use the Date Navigator to select the correct date, and then double-click a time slot to open a new appointment. Outlook uses the default appointment interval of 30 minutes. To use a different interval, click and drag the mouse pointer from the start time to the end time, and then right-click and choose New Appointment.

- In Week or Month view, select the date of the appointment, and then right-click and choose New Appointment; this creates an appointment with a start time that is the default starting time for the day. If you select multiple dates, Outlook creates a new event on the selected dates, with no start or end times.

- To open a new event form from any view, right-click and choose New All Day Event.

You can also create an appointment instantly by dragging an e-mail message from your Inbox and dropping it on the Calendar icon in the Outlook Bar. This shortcut can be a true time-saver when you receive a message that includes essential details about an upcoming event. The subject of the mail message becomes the subject of the appointment, and the message text appears in the Notes area of the appointment form. You'll probably need to adjust the date and time, however, because by default Outlook uses the next available block of time in today's schedule.

TIP FROM

EQ & Woody

> The drag-and-drop technique is especially useful for creating appointments after you've made an online purchase of tickets for a concert or a play, or electronic tickets for an upcoming flight. When you receive the confirmation e-mail message containing details of the event or the flight, drag the message from your Inbox and drop it on the Calendar icon. Adjust the event details as needed. All the details, including ticket numbers and confirmation codes, will be saved as part of the appointment.

If you've looked up a name in your Contacts folder and you want to create an appointment that includes a link to that person, don't just drag the item onto the Calendar icon—that action creates a meeting request addressed to the selected person. Instead, hold down the

11

right mouse button and drag the item from the Contacts folder, drop it on the Calendar icon, and then choose Copy Here As Appointment with Text. If you drag two or more Contact items into the Calendar folder, Outlook assumes you want to include all the information in a single appointment.

To see the maximum amount of information in an appointment you create by dragging and dropping a Contact item, switch to Detailed Address Cards view in your Contacts folder first.

You can create a new appointment from scratch by using any of the following techniques:

- Click the New Appointment button.
- Press Ctrl+Shift+A.
- Choose File, New, Appointment.

Enter a name for the appointment in the Subject field, and then tab from field to field and add more details. Add details about the meeting in the Notes area just below the Reminder field. You can also add attachments here, including files, copies of Outlook items, or shortcuts to files or Outlook items. Click the Save and Close button when you're finished. Figure 11.2 shows a filled-in appointment form.

Figure 11.2
Like most Outlook items, appointments can include file attachments and links to Contacts.

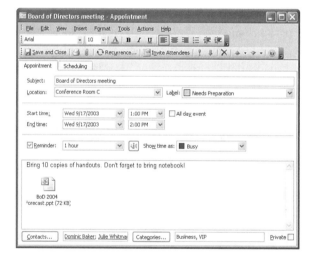

Table 11.1 describes the type of information you can include in each field of an appointment item.

→ To learn how Outlook will fill in times and dates for you, **see** "Entering Dates and Times Automatically," **p. 184**.

→ To learn how to organize Outlook items using categories, **see** "Assigning Items to Categories," **p. 185**.

→ To learn more about instructing Outlook to remind you of important activities, **see** "Using Reminders and Follow-Up Flags," **p. 194**.

TABLE 11.1 STANDARD APPOINTMENT FIELDS

Field Name	Description
Subject	Enter the text you want to see in Calendar view. Although you can enter up to 255 characters, you should keep the Subject line much shorter—referably 30 characters or fewer. Subject lines over about 150 characters will not print correctly in Tri-fold format.
Location	Enter a location; the drop-down list lets you choose from among the 10 locations you entered most recently (you can't customize this list or change its order).
Start Time, End Time	Enter starting and ending times and dates by using any common date and time format or an AutoDate description; click the arrow to the right of a date or time field to select from a calendar control or a list of preset times.
All Day Event	Clicking this box removes the Start Time and End Time fields from the form; when you enter an event, Outlook's default settings show the time in your shared schedule as Free.
Reminder	Appointments can pop up reminders at times you define; unless you change the defaults (as described in Chapter 7, "Getting Started With Outlook"), Outlook adds a reminder 15 minutes before every appointment.
Show Time As	This option is useful only in an office where you share calendars on an Exchange Server. It specifies how others view your calendar by designating the time an appointment takes as Busy, Free, Tentative, or Out of Office. Each of these four descriptions uses a different color in Calendar views. You cannot add new descriptions to this list.
Label	This option allows you to color-code appointments using one of 10 labels. You can apply a label manually or use rules to color-code appointments on the fly.
Contacts	Click this button to link an appointment to one or more items in your Contacts folder.
Categories	Assign appointments to categories, just as you do contacts and tasks. See "Assigning Items to Categories" (page 185) for instructions on how to view the list of standard categories and create new ones of your own.
Private	Designate an appointment as private so no one who looks at your shared schedule will know that you've gone to the ballgame. This option is most useful in an office with an Exchange Server, but it also allows you to hide details in printed calendars.

11

ENTERING A RECURRING APPOINTMENT

Some appointments and events are one-shot deals, but others—like it or not—happen over and over again. If you have a class that meets every Tuesday and Thursday at 10:00 am, that's a recurring appointment. So is a scheduled parent-teacher conference that occurs on the third Thursday of each month, or a committee meeting that ruins every other Saturday for you. When you enter details for a recurring appointment, Outlook manages the entire series from a single appointment form. You can specify recurring patterns on a daily, weekly, monthly, or annual basis. The options for recurring appointments are surprisingly flexible.

→ To learn more about setting up recurring tasks, **see** "Entering Recurring Tasks," **p. 311**.

To set up a *recurring appointment* or event, create the item from scratch or open an existing item, and then click the Recurrence button to display the Appointment Recurrence dialog box (see Figure 11.3).

Figure 11.3
Use this dialog box to schedule even complicated recurring appointments, like this one every Thursday at 10:00 a.m.

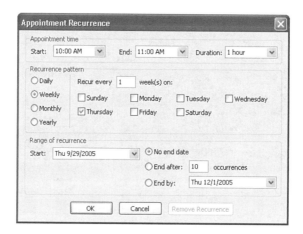

Adjust the options as needed to match the schedule of your event. Enter an ending date or a fixed number of occurrences, if appropriate, and click OK. Then click Save and Close to add the recurring appointment or event to your Calendar folder. Outlook adds a recurrence icon to the left of the event description in all Calendar views.

To edit a recurring appointment or event, open the item. A dialog box lets you specify whether you want to change the entire series or just the selected instance. If your study group moves this week's get-together from its regular slot of Wednesday at 2:00 p.m., you can change the times for that occurrence without affecting the rest of the items in the series. On the other hand, if the entire group agrees to move the weekly sessions to Thursday evenings, you can edit the entire series, and you need to change the details only once to reschedule all future occurrences.

To see a list of all recurring appointments and events (and edit one or more of them, if necessary), switch to Outlook's predefined Recurring Appointments view. Note that this list includes birthdays and anniversaries, which Outlook treats as recurring annual events.

RESCHEDULING AN APPOINTMENT OR EVENT

The most labor-intensive way to change the date and time of an appointment or event is by opening the item and manually adjusting the entries in the Start Time and End Time fields. Try these time-saving shortcuts instead:

- To change the scheduled starting time for an appointment in any Day view (including multiday views), point to the left border of the item until the pointer turns into a four-headed arrow, and then drag the item to its new time.

- To move an item to a different day, point to the left border until the pointer turns into a four-headed arrow; then drag the item and drop it on the selected day in Week or Month view or in the Date Navigator. (If the date you want is not visible in any of these places, you must use the Cut, Copy, and Paste options on the Edit menu instead.)

- To copy an item to a new date and time, hold down the Ctrl key and drag the item to the new date by using the Week or Month view or the Date Navigator. This technique is particularly useful when scheduling a follow-up appointment with your doctor or dentist; because copying the original appointment item also copies all its details, you eliminate the need to search for your notes from the earlier meeting when it's time for the follow-up.

If you want to edit the description of an event or appointment, without adjusting its date, time, or details, click its listing in any daily, weekly, or monthly Calendar view and edit the text directly. As soon as you click the text to begin editing, the location (in parentheses after the description text) disappears; the only way to edit location information is to open the form.

VIEWING A DAILY, WEEKLY, OR MONTHLY CALENDAR

When you first click the Calendar icon in the Outlook Bar, you see today's schedule in Day/Week/Month view. The default view of your appointments shows just one day at a time, but you can expand the view to cover appointments that span multiple days, one or more weeks, or a full month at a time.

SWITCHING BETWEEN DAY, WEEK, AND MONTH VIEWS

Four buttons on the Calendar folder's Standard toolbar let you quickly switch between Outlook's built-in views.

Click the Day button to display one day's events. Use the Date Navigator to show another day's schedule, or click the Go to Today button to jump back to today's calendar. Click in the contents pane and then press the Page Up and Page Down keys to scroll through meetings and appointments for the selected day; use the left- and right-arrow keys to move through the Calendar folder one day at a time.

TIP FROM

In any Day view (including the built-in Work Week view and others that include multiple days), pressing Home takes you to the beginning of the workday and End jumps to the end of the workday—8:00 a.m. and 5:00 p.m., unless you adjust these defaults. Press Ctrl+Home or Ctrl+End to jump to the beginning or end of the day—midnight in either direction.

Click the Work Week button to show a side-by-side view of five days at a time, leaving off weekends, as in the example in Figure 11.4. Because the display for each day is extremely narrow, don't expect to read the full description of each event; point to any item to see a ScreenTip that includes its time, subject, and location.

Figure 11.4
Use the Work Week view to see five days at a time (customize the display if your work or school week is different).

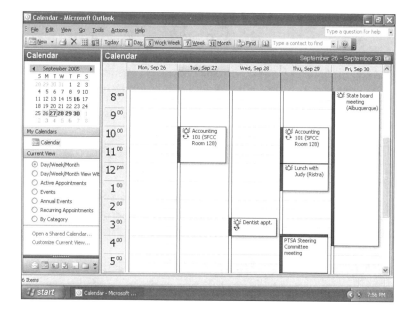

Click the Week button to display a full week's schedule (see Figure 11.5), with each day's appointments in a box; Saturday and Sunday listings are half the size of other days. As in other views, all-day events appear in a banner at the top of each day, with multiday events extending over the tops of several days. Press Page Up and Page Down to move through the calendar a week at a time.

Figure 11.5
Unlike daily views, the Week view shows only scheduled items and events in the block for each day.

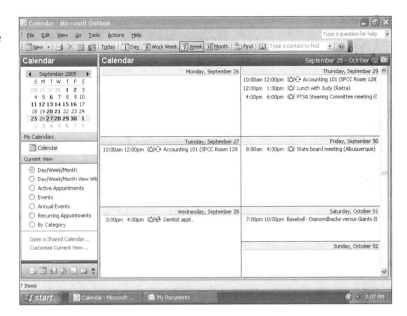

Click the Month button to see a month-at-a-glance calendar (see Figure 11.6), with event descriptions truncated to fit. To jump a month at a time in either direction in this view, use the Page Up and Page Down keys, or the vertical scrollbar at the right of the window. The Home and End keys jump to the beginning and end of the current week.

Figure 11.6
In this monthly view, as in all other views, clicking an appointment selects it, and double-clicking opens it.

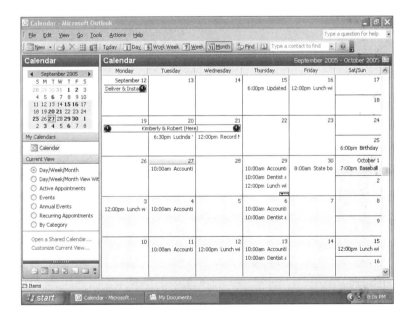

TIP FROM

ED & Woody

> In any Day/Week/Month Calendar view, press Alt+Page Up to go back to the first day of the current month or Alt+Page Down to jump forward to the last day of the current month. Each time you press either key again, you'll move one month in that direction. If you start on March 15, for example, pressing Alt+Page Down repeatedly takes you to March 31, April 30, May 31, June 30, and so on.

Use the Date Navigator to create a custom view of your calendar that's different from the standard day, week, and month views. Hold down the Ctrl key while you click two or more dates (they don't have to be adjacent), and the display changes to show you a side-by-side view of the schedules for the selected days. This technique is especially useful when you want to copy a meeting or appointment from one day to another. It's also handy if you're checking your schedule to see which day works best for a meeting or appointment. A multi-day view can display up to 14 days at a time, side by side, although with more than 5 days visible it's nearly impossible to see details because each day's display is so narrow.

COLOR-CODING IMPORTANT APPOINTMENTS

If you use Outlook's Calendar to track large numbers of appointments and meetings, it's easy to lose track of individual items. Because each one looks the same on the screen, you might have trouble distinguishing between important meetings (with your boss or your most important client, say) and trivial ones.

The solution? Use color codes to highlight items in the Calendar folder. Outlook includes 10 predefined and color-coded text labels. When creating or editing an appointment or meeting item, use the Label drop-down list (see Figure 11.7) to apply a color coding. By default, for example, red means Important and gray means Vacation.

Figure 11.7
Use this drop-down list to assign any of the 10 colors to appointments in your Calendar folder.

You can't add to this list, which is hard-wired to exactly 10 entries. But you can change the text associated with each color. For instance, you might change the label on red from Important to High Priority or change Business to School. To work with the list of labels, choose Edit, Label, Edit Labels. Make your changes in the Edit Calendar Labels dialog box shown in Figure 11.8.

Figure 11.8
Be careful—changes you make here apply to all items, past and present, to which you've assigned that color.

CUSTOMIZING THE CALENDAR DISPLAY

To change options for Outlook's built-in Day, Week, and Month views, right-click any unused space in the calendar display and choose Other Settings. The resulting dialog box (shown in Figure 11.9) lets you change the fonts and font sizes used in each of the three views:

11

Figure 11.9
Adjust these options to change the way Outlook's default Day/Week/Month views display your schedule.

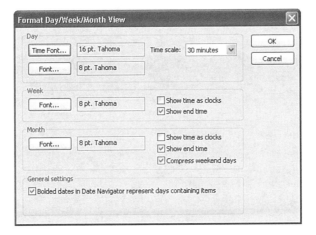

- In the Day view settings, you can adjust the Time Scale from its default setting of 30 minutes. The shorter intervals of 5-, 6-, 10-, or 15-minute increments are most appropriate for professionals who bill for their consulting time. Most people will either accept the default or use the drop-down list to adjust this value to its maximum of 60 minutes and see their entire schedule without scrolling.

- By default, appointments displayed in Week view include only a starting time. Select the Show End Time check box to display end times for each appointment as well. If you want to see more text, select the Show Time as Clocks option, which uses icons to display each time—light clocks represent a.m. and dark clocks are for p.m.

TIP FROM

Ed & Woody

> If your vision is less than 20/20, we recommend that you pass on the option to use tiny clocks to show appointment times in Week and Month views. Trying to identify the position of the microscopic hands, especially against the dark background for p.m. times, is difficult at best, and possibly a painful cause of eyestrain.

■ Options for the Month view are the same as those for the Week view, with one addition. Select the Compress Weekend Days option to show each week in a row of six boxes, beginning on Monday, with Saturday and Sunday sharing a box. Clear the check box to display each day in its own box, resulting in a row of seven boxes for each week. The latter option makes sense if you routinely schedule appointments or meetings on weekends and you're willing to surrender some screen real estate for weekdays to see a full display for each day of the weekend.

CUSTOMIZING OTHER CALENDAR OPTIONS

Outlook includes another batch of calendar options that allow you to adjust the basic look and feel of this folder. Choose Tools, Options, and then click the Calendar Options button on the Preferences tab to display the dialog box shown in Figure 11.10.

Figure 11.10
If you don't follow a Monday-to-Friday schedule, use these options to redefine your work week and its starting date.

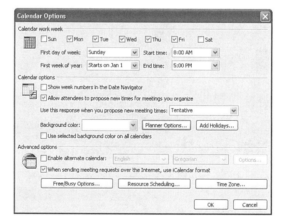

■ In the Calendar Work Week section, click to select or clear the days that correspond to your work week. In the First Day of Week drop-down list, select the day you want to see at the beginning of Week and Month views. You can also define the Start Time and End Time for your typical work day here.

NOTE

When you double-click to add an appointment in Week or Month view, Outlook opens a new appointment form using the starting time as defined in this dialog box.

- Check the Show Week Numbers in the Date Navigator box if you want to see small numbers to the left of each week. This specialized option is most useful for people who work in retail and other industries that measure performance by week numbers. It also corresponds to the schedule used in the timeshare industry. If you own one or more timeshare weeks, be sure to check your ownership documents to confirm that your calendar corresponds to the one Outlook uses.

- The Background Color option lets you choose from a limited selection of pastel colors to use behind Day and Work Week views. The default Light Yellow is the most readable.

- If you regularly travel across time zones, or if you coordinate your calendar with friends, family members, and associate in another part of the world, you can also specify a second time zone to display in daily views of the Calendar folder. That option lets you see at a glance whether you're trying to call Moscow at midnight or Hong Kong at 3:00 a.m., when you're likely to wake someone from a sound sleep (if they answer the phone at all). Click the Time Zone button to open the dialog box shown in Figure 11.11, and then check the Show an Additional Time Zone box. Select the second time zone and give each one a label, and then click OK. (Be sure to read the sidebar that follows this section before changing your time zone, however!)

11

Figure 11.11
Frequent flyers can click the Time Zone button to add a second time zone along the left side of a Daily calendar view.

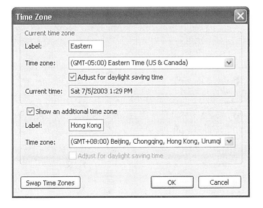

- Click the Add Holidays button to incorporate a list of common holidays into your Outlook calendar. Surprisingly, this feature doesn't use a sophisticated set of calculations to determine when Easter, Thanksgiving, and Yom Kippur fall each year. Instead, Outlook looks at the contents of a text file called Outlook.hol; in a U.S. English installation, this file is stored in `C:\Program Files\Microsoft Office\Office11\1033`. The Add Holidays to Calendar dialog box lets you choose which country's holidays should be added to your calendar—a handy option if you routinely travel around the globe or deal with folks in other countries.

TIP FROM

Ed & Woody

> Through the years, Microsoft has screwed up the list of holidays on more than one occasion. To customize the holidays list or fix errors, open this text file in a text editor such as Notepad. Each group of holidays (organized by country) starts with a name in square brackets; each item in the list includes a name, followed by the date in yyyy/mm/dd format. If your community or school district has its own list of special days, put the community or district name in brackets to treat it as if it were a country. Then double-click Outlook.hol, choose the custom name from the list of countries, and click OK to add the custom holidays to Outlook.

- The Resource Scheduling button is used in offices that have an Exchange Server. It allows resources, such as conference rooms and slide projectors, to be scheduled using meeting requests.

- The Free/Busy Options button contains settings that allow you to publish information about your calendar to an Internet location for other people to use when scheduling meetings. This option is difficult to set up, unreliable, and in our opinion more trouble than it's worth.

→ If you want to coordinate schedules with other people, consider using meeting requests; **see** "Planning a Meeting with Outlook," **p. 315**.

JUGGLING MULTIPLE TIME ZONES

Microsoft's engineers designed Outlook so that when you change time zones on your computer, Outlook adjusts all appointments, past and present, to match the new time zone.

That decision might sound logical, but it causes problems if you and your notebook or Outlook-synchronized handheld computer travel across time zones. Let's say you live in Los Angeles and travel to New York for a few days of vacation. You're scheduled to depart on Thursday at 8:51 a.m. and your return flight is at 5:00 p.m. on Tuesday. On Friday, you're scheduled to participate in a conference call with your local homeowners association at 10:00 a.m. You enter all these details in your calendar and synchronize with your handheld computer.

You bring your notebook or PocketPC with you to New York. What happens next depends on what you do with your computer's clock:

- If you change your computer's clock to match New York time (three hours later than Pacific time), Outlook changes the entry for your conference call to 1:00 pm. Unfortunately, it adds three hours to the start time of your return flight as well. When Tuesday rolls around, you'll miss your flight if you rely on Outlook's reminder instead of your ticket.

■ If you don't adjust the time zone, Outlook leaves your appointments at the time you entered. When you phone in for the conference call at 10:00 a.m., it will actually be 7:00 a.m. in New York and no one will be there to take the call. But you'll be right on time for your return flight.

Confusingly, Outlook is working exactly as intended. You're expected to adapt by adding a second time zone to your Calendar, using this simple shortcut: Switch to Day view, right-click the time display along the left edge of the calendar, choose Change Time Zone from the menu, and check the Show an Additional Time Zone box. Enter a label for each time zone, click OK, and you'll see two time displays at the left side of the Day view. Whenever you enter an appointment or meeting, make sure you choose the correct time scale.

This solution is cumbersome, but it works well enough if your trip takes you to only two time zones. When you reach your destination, open the Time Zone dialog box again and click the Swap Time Zones button. The time on the system clock changes, but you can still stay on time as long as you don't succumb to jet lag and look at the wrong scale. If your trip takes you to three or more time zones, however, using this technique is a one-way ticket to hopeless confusion. If you can't handle this date arithmetic—especially with jet lag—leave Outlook's time zone alone and add a note about the time zone in the Subject of every appointment.

Oh, and if you move to a different time zone, all your records of previous appointments will be changed as soon as you change your computer's time zone. So if you consult the Calendar folder to determine exactly when you had a particular meeting, you'll discover that Outlook's records are off by several hours. Outlook is irritatingly insistent on making these changes, too. If you move from New York to Los Angeles, every holiday, birthday, and anniversary will be shifted three hours earlier on your calendar; to set each of these recurring events right, you'll have to open and edit each one individually. A more confusing option (but much easier if you have lots of entries in your calendar folder is to do the following:

1. Make a backup copy of your PST file first!

2. Export all appointments and meetings, past and present, to a file using the Comma Separated Values format. (See "Importing and Exporting Outlook Information," p. 202, for details.)

3. Open Outlook's Calendar and switch to By Category view. Because this is a table-based view, you can see and edit all appointments. Click to select any item, press Ctrl+A to select all items, and press Delete.

4. Change your computer's time zone.

5. Import the appointments and meetings to your Calendar folder.

This option destroys the recurring option for any appointments. You'll need to delete and re-enter any recurring appointments manually. It also eliminates attachments that you might have included in the Notes field, so be careful!

11

MAINTAINING A PERSONAL TASK LIST

In Outlook, *tasks* are essentially to-do items. They can be as simple as a note to yourself ("Pick up milk on the way home") or you can add start dates, due dates, and detailed notes, and then track your progress on a complex task over time. Outlook lets you define *one-time tasks* or *recurring tasks*, such as weekly status reports. A list of current tasks appears on the *Outlook Today* page.

→ To learn how you can modify the Outlook Today page to meet your needs, **see** "Customizing the Outlook Today Page," **p. 170**.

ENTERING TASKS

The absolute simplest way to create a task is to view the Tasks folder in Simple List view. Click the Tasks button at the bottom of the Navigation pane, and then click where you see the gray letters Click Here to Add a New Task. Enter a short description of the task; if you want to associate a deadline with the task, press Tab to move to the Due Date field and enter a date. Press Enter to record the task.

To create a new task with more details, click the New button in the Tasks folder, or choose File, New, Task, or press Ctrl+Shift+K. In the Task form (see Figure 11.12), enter the task text in the Subject box and fill in any of the additional fields, all of which are optional.

Figure 11.12
The only required field for a Task item is the Subject line; enter date and status information if you plan to produce status reports.

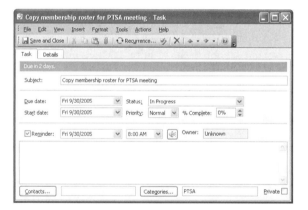

Enter the Due Date first, and then fill in the Start Date. Fill in the Status, Priority, and % Complete boxes only if you want to be able to sort a complex list of tasks using this information. By default, Outlook creates a *reminder* for every task on its due date; if you don't want to set reminders automatically, choose Tools, Options, and click the Preferences tab. Then click the Task Options button and clear the Set Reminders on Tasks with Due Dates check box.

Add details, notes, and file attachments (including document shortcuts) for the task. Click the Contacts button at the bottom of the form to link to one or more persons in your Contacts list. Click the Categories button to assign the task to *categories*. Don't bother clicking the Private box unless you're on a corporate network with an Exchange Server or you plan to print out your schedule for someone else and you want to hide details of private appointments.

→ Sorting your Outlook items by category is essential to managing your appointments, contacts, e-mail, and so on; **see** "Assigning Items to Categories," **p. 185**.

If you need to keep track of the time you spend on certain tasks (for reimbursement by a business or volunteer organization, for example, or for tax purposes), click the Details tab. Boxes on this region of the Task form let you enter the amount of time you spend on a task, as well as Mileage details and additional notes in the Billing Information box. Click the Save and Close button to add the new item to your Tasks folder.

TIP FROM

> To create a billing statement with Outlook, create a custom Table view that includes the fields you want to use on your billing report. Sort or filter the list to show only the clients or companies for whom you want to generate the report. Select the rows and press Ctrl+C to copy them to the Windows Clipboard; then open a new Excel workbook and paste the copied rows into a blank worksheet range. Use formulas to translate hourly rates and mileage allowances into totals.

Items on your task list show up in red when they're overdue, and in gray, with strikethrough formatting, when you click the Mark Complete button.

 If the due dates on some task items mysteriously change, see "You Need It When?" in the "Troubleshooting" section at the end of this chapter.

ENTERING RECURRING TASKS

For tasks that repeat at regular intervals, enter the data just as you would for a one-time task, but before you save, click the Recurrence button. With one noteworthy exception, the technique for specifying how often a task recurs is essentially the same as for a recurring appointment or event. You specify whether the task repeats at daily, weekly, monthly, or annual intervals, and then enter the recurrence pattern—every other Tuesday and Thursday, the second Wednesday of each month, and so on. You can define recurring tasks that occur a set number of times—once a week for the next three weeks while a co-worker is on vacation, say—or click the End By box and enter a specific date when the task ends.

→ If you must complete the same task at the same time on a regular basis—such as preparing the agenda for a weekly meeting—use Outlook's recurring appointment feature; **see** "Entering a Recurring Appointment," **p. 300**.

Unlike recurring appointments, you can define an interval for recurring tasks that are based on completing the previous instance. Let's say you're the president of a national organization. You want to stay in touch with the executive director by calling roughly once a month, but you don't want to wear out your welcome by calling too often. If you define a recurring task to call on the 5th of each month, and you don't actually connect until the 20th, you'll end up making your next call only 15 days later.

Instead, use the dialog box shown in Figure 11.13 to specify that you want to generate a new task 30 days after you complete the previous instance. Click the Regenerate New Task box, and then fill in the number of days, weeks, months, or years you want between instances. Each time you mark a task complete, Outlook creates a new Task item using the specified settings. So if you make a call on September 19, your next reminder occurs a month later, on the 19th of October.

Figure 11.13
Use the Regenerate New Task check box to specify that you want the due date of the next recurring task to be based on the date the previous one was completed.

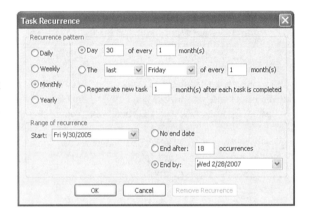

11

Outlook adds recurring tasks to your task list one at a time. When you mark one occurrence of the task complete, the next occurrence appears in the list. If you look at your task list for the next month, you'll see only one instance of a recurring task, even if it recurs daily or weekly. When you mark each task complete, Outlook creates a new item with a new due date. If you try to delete a recurring task, you can delete just the specified instance or all recurrences.

SORTING AND FILTERING THE TASK LIST

Outlook's built-in views for the Tasks folder include table views—Simple List or Detailed List—that let you see all tasks regardless of due date and status. You can create custom filters and views for items in the Tasks folder as well. The following views are built-in:

- Switch to the Active Tasks view to see all tasks except those where the Status is Complete or Deferred.

- The Next Seven Days view shows all tasks due in the next week. It does not include overdue tasks.

- Choose Overdue Tasks to see only those items for which the due date has passed. This view excludes tasks that have no due date.

- Click the By Category view to see an outline style view of tasks organized according to categories you assign.

You can assign a single task to multiple categories; switch to By Category view, and then hold down the Ctrl key and drag to assign an item to a new category.

- The Assignment and By Person Responsible views are relevant only if you assign tasks to other persons.

- Choose the Completed Tasks view to see only those tasks you've marked as completed.

→ Use Outlook's Views settings to organize your Outlook data; **see** "Using Views to Display, Sort, and Filter Items," **p. 171**.

If you scrupulously update the Due Date, Start Date, Status, and % Complete fields, you can use the Tasks folder to perform rudimentary project-management tasks. But when we say rudimentary, we mean it. Outlook's Task Timeline view shows start and end dates for individual tasks, but it doesn't enable you to do full-fledged project management tasks. If you need to manage a big project with dependencies, a large staff, and significant budgets, look at a product such as Microsoft Project instead.

PRINTING A LIST OF APPOINTMENTS AND TASKS

Outlook's calendar works best for those who sit at a desk all day long. It's not much help if you leave the computer on your desk at home as you go to work, school, or just out and about every day. If you're not willing or able to carry around a portable computer or a hand-held Outlook-compatible organizer, then do the next best thing and put your schedule on paper.

You can print Outlook calendars and task lists in a variety of styles and formats. What's the easiest way to keep the paper and electronic versions in sync? If you get in the habit of printing out a daily or weekly calendar, you can jot notes and record new or revised appointments on that printout. When you return to your desk, transfer the handwritten notes to Outlook so that they'll appear the next time you print out your calendar.

To print your schedule for one day or for multiple days, weeks, or months, first switch to the Calendar folder, and then follow these steps:

1. If you plan to print one day, week, or month, select the corresponding view for the period.

2. Click the Print button. Outlook displays the Print dialog box shown in Figure 11.14.

3. Choose one of the five page formats from the Print Style list:

   • **Daily**—Shows appointment and event descriptions for 7:00 a.m. to 6:00 p.m., a two-month calendar resembling the Date Navigator, the TaskPad, and room for you to write notes. Only a few lines from the Notes field for each appointment are visible.

Figure 11.14
Choose the Calendar Details Style option to print all the notes you've added for individual appointments and events on your calendar.

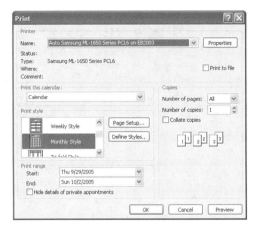

11

- **Weekly**—Shows one week per page, with the Subject field only. This format includes a two-month calendar that resembles the Date Navigator, but no Notes field and no TaskPad.

- **Monthly**—Shows an entire month's events and appointments, with Subject lines truncated at approximately 50 characters. If the print range spans two or more months, Outlook prints a calendar for each month in the range.

- **Tri-Fold**—Prints a three-paned view in landscape mode on 8 1/2×11-inch paper. The left pane shows today's appointments, the middle includes the TaskPad and room for handwritten notes, and the right shows a compressed view of the week's schedule.

- **Calendar Details**—If you've added detailed notes such as driving instructions or agenda items to an appointment, choose this format so your printed pages include all details, not just the description, time, and location. This style uses the full width of the page.

4. In the Print Range area, adjust the Start and End dates, if necessary. If you're printing the paper version for someone else, you might want to click the check box that lets you hide details of private appointments and show only that those times are booked.

5. Click the Preview button to see what your page will look like when printed. Use the Page Up and Page Down keys (or the corresponding toolbar buttons) to see additional pages.

6. Click the Page Setup button to adjust layout options, paper sizes, fonts, headers, footers, and other settings.

7. Click Print to send the schedule to the printer.

If none of the built-in print formats is exactly right, try creating a custom format. The safest way to explore print formats is to choose File, Print, and then click the Define Styles button. Choose the format that you want to modify, and click Copy. In the Page Setup dialog box (see Figure 11.15), enter a name for your new layout, and then adjust options on the three tabs of the dialog box:

Figure 11.15
Instead of designing a new print format from scratch, modify an existing layout and give it a new name.

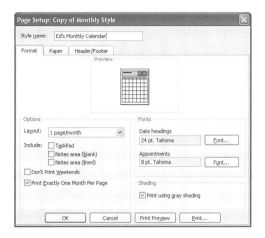

- Use the Format tab to set options that are specific to the layout you started with. For example, in a Tri-fold format, you can choose which parts of the calendar go in each of the three panes. In Daily and Weekly styles, you can define the starting and ending times for the day's appointments. This tab also lets you select fonts and shading options for all views.

- Use the Paper tab to define the dimensions, paper source, margins, and orientation for each page. Scroll through the Size list in the Page box to see a collection of layouts intended for use with Day-Timer, Day Runner, and Franklin Planner products.

- Click the Header/Footer tab to customize the text at the top and bottom of each printed page. You can add literal text, or click any of the five buttons to add fields that insert the page number, number of pages, date printed, time printed, and username.

TIP FROM

If you regularly print out monthly calendars, visit the list of Outlook add-ins at Slipstick Systems (`http://www.slipstick.com/addins/calendar.htm#print`). The selection includes several Word document templates that produce good-looking printable calendars using Outlook data.

PLANNING A MEETING WITH OUTLOOK

In the world according to Outlook, there is a crucial difference between an *appointment* and a *meeting*. When you create an appointment, you set aside a block of time on your own personal calendar. Although an appointment might involve other people, it's your responsibility, not Outlook's, to coordinate your schedule with theirs.

An Outlook meeting, on the other hand, consists of identical items in the Calendar folders of two or more people. Although these items closely resemble appointments—with a subject, start and end times, and the option to set a reminder—there are several crucial differences:

- Every meeting has an *organizer*, who is responsible for setting the time, location, and other details.

- The organizer fills in a meeting request form that includes details of the meeting as well as the names and e-mail addresses of all required and optional attendees; Outlook sends the invitations automatically when the organizer saves the meeting request.

- When you receive a meeting request, you can accept, tentatively accept, or decline the invitation. If you accept, Outlook adds the meeting to your calendar; Outlook sends all responses to the meeting organizer and tracks the meeting's status automatically.

In an office where all meeting attendees have shared access to an Exchange Server, you have access to some additional features, including the ability to schedule resources such as conference rooms and to automatically pick available dates and times from shared calendars. These features are unavailable if you're using Outlook on a home PC where an Exchange Server isn't handy.

TIP FROM

Ed & Woody

> Meeting requests are an incredibly useful feature, even if you only use them to keep your schedule in sync with that of your spouse or children. As long as everyone uses Outlook's calendar with their own account, you can coordinate items on the calendar easily. Expand your definition of a "meeting" to include dinner reservations, specific household chores, vacations, even Little League games, and think of "attendees" as family members. With these expanded definitions you can begin to see more uses than might be immediately apparent.

You can begin scheduling a meeting by opening a meeting request form directly, using any of the following four techniques:

- Choose New, Meeting Request; or press Ctrl+Shift+Q to open a blank meeting request form.

- If you've already selected the exact date and time of the meeting, switch to a Calendar view of that date and select the block of time; then right-click and choose New Meeting Request from the shortcut menu. This option opens a meeting request form with the date and time already filled in.

- To open a meeting request form with the invitees' names already filled in, select one or more names in the Contacts folder. With a single contact selected, you can right-click and choose New Meeting Request to Contact; with multiple contact selected, choose Actions, New Meeting Request to Contact.

- If you've already created an appointment in your Calendar folder and you want to turn it into a meeting, open the item and click the Invite Attendees button. This option uses all details you defined previously, adding a field in which you can enter the names of other attendees.

As Figure 11.16 shows, a meeting request form closely resembles an appointment form, with the crucial addition of the To field. Fill in the prospective attendees' names, and then add the remainder of the meeting details—Subject, start time, end time, notes, and so on—as you would for an appointment, and click Send to deliver the invitations.

Figure 11.16
A meeting request form resembles a cross between an e-mail message and an appointment form.

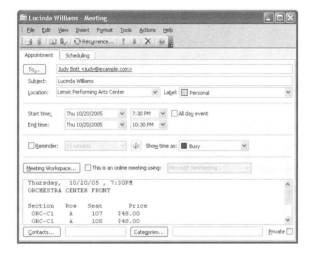

TIP FROM

Because the meeting request form is delivered via e-mail, you can use any of Outlook's addressing shortcuts, including automatic name checking. Click the To button to open the Address Book and select names directly.

Don't forget to include details in the Notes box at the bottom of the Appointment tab. Text you enter here appears in the Meeting item added to each attendee's Calendar folder after your invitation is accepted; it also serves as the text of the e-mailed invitation.

TIP FROM

If you're planning a meeting that requires preparation, you might want to send one or more files with the invitation—an agenda or a background memo in Word format, for example. Drag a file icon directly into the Notes box on the meeting request form, or choose Insert, File, and select the file from the Insert File dialog box.

After you've finished entering all details in the meeting request form, click the Send button. Outlook delivers the requests via e-mail to all prospective attendees.

TIP FROM

Outlook 2003 automatically sends all meeting requests delivered via Internet mail in *iCalendar* format, which ensures that the request will work with all compatible contact-management programs. To change this global option, choose Tools, Options, click the Calendar Options button on the Preferences tab, look under the Advanced Options heading and select or clear the When Sending Meeting Requests over the Internet, Use iCalendar Format box. Outlook recipients will still see all meeting requests exactly as they normally do, but users of other contact management programs will be able to deal with them as well.

RESPONDING TO MEETING REQUESTS

When you receive a meeting invitation via e-mail, it resembles an ordinary message, with the following key differences:

- The Meeting Request icon to the left of the invitation in the message list is different.

- The message header shows the sender's name, Required and Optional attendees, and the location and time of the meeting.

- Special-purpose toolbar buttons are visible in the message window and in the Reading pane, as shown in Figure 11.17. Using these buttons, you can accept the invitation, decline it, or propose a new time. Click the Tentative button when you want to reserve the right to change your mind later.

Figure 11.17
Use these buttons to accept or decline a meeting invitation. Click the Calendar button to open your Calendar folder and check details of your schedule.

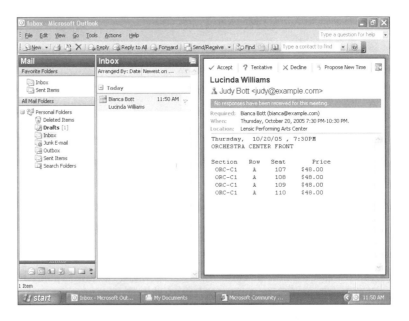

If you accept the invitation, Outlook adds the item to your calendar. You can add a note to your response or send a default notification to the meeting organizer.

If you're not the meeting organizer, you can propose an alternative date or time for the meeting. Choosing this option opens a form in which you can respond to the meeting organizer. As the organizer, you can see all proposed changes in a single window and choose the one that works best for you.

If a meeting organized by someone else is on your calendar, you can change its time—for that matter, you can delete it outright. There's nothing wrong with this course of action if the meeting organizer sends an e-mail message or calls on the phone to cancel or change the time. If you change the item in your calendar, Outlook does not update the original item on the meeting organizer's calendar.

CAUTION

> If you attempt to change the time of a meeting organized by someone else, be sure to click the Propose New Time box. If you click Accept or Tentative, the Office Assistant displays a warning dialog box urging you to send a message to the meeting organizer, but Outlook's response-handling script ignores the changes and marks the original item on the organizer's calendar to show that you've accepted.

To decline an invitation after you have already accepted the meeting request and added it to your calendar, open the item and click the Decline button. Outlook offers to send a message to the organizer; add text explaining that your schedule has changed, and click the Send button.

If you are the meeting organizer, you can also cancel a meeting at any time by deleting it from your calendar. Outlook offers to send a cancellation message on your behalf to all the attendees you previously invited.

CHECKING THE STATUS OF A MEETING YOU'VE ARRANGED

Outlook uses special scripts embedded in meeting invitations to process responses. As the invitees accept or decline the meeting request, they return a message to you; when it arrives in your Inbox, Outlook uses the script commands to update the status of the list. As the meeting organizer, you can check a meeting's status at any time by opening it. Look at the information bar at the top of the Appointment tab to see a running tally of the number of prospective attendees who have accepted, declined, or failed to respond.

 If you continually fail to receive updates from specific people, see "The Case of the Missing RSVP" in the "Troubleshooting" section at the end of this chapter.

For a more detailed view of responses, click the Tracking tab. This list lets you see at a glance which invitees have failed to respond to your invitation, allowing you to send a follow-up message quickly, if necessary.

RESCHEDULING OR CANCELING A MEETING

Handling changes to Outlook meetings requires a delicate balancing act. After the initial round of invitations and responses, each prospective attendee has a separate meeting item on his or her calendar. Communication of any changes is crucial.

As the organizer, you can change the date or time of a meeting, change other details (such as its location), or cancel it outright. To make any changes, open the item in your Calendar folder, click the Appointment tab, and change the meeting details; then click the Send Update button. To cancel the meeting, open the meeting item and choose Actions, Cancel Meeting, or click the Delete button on the Standard toolbar. If you change the date, time, or other details, Outlook prompts you to send an Update message to everyone on the list; if you cancel a meeting, Outlook generates a cancellation request.

An Update message looks exactly like the original request. Everyone who receives it will see the Accept, Decline, and Tentative buttons, just as if it were an original meeting request.

TIP FROM

When you send an Update message, be sure to include text in the Notes box that explains the changes you've made—that text becomes the body of the update message. If you omit this step, attendees who don't read the message carefully might assume they're receiving a duplicate of the original meeting request and fail to notice the change in date or time.

TROUBLESHOOTING

RESETTING THE FORMATTING OPTIONS

I customized a built-in calendar layout without making a copy first. How do I start over with the default form?

Choose File, Print, click the Define Styles button, and click the Copy button. Give the layout a descriptive name. Next, select the built-in format from the Print Styles list. Click the Reset button to return all formatting options to their default settings. This option does not affect your custom layout.

YOU NEED IT WHEN?

The due dates of some Task items changed, even though I never touched the Due Date field.

That's not a bug; it's a design decision. Did you change the value in the Start Date box at any point? If so, Outlook automatically changed the value in the Due Date field by the

exact same interval. By design, Outlook assumes that tasks take a fixed amount of time, and delaying the start date delays the finish as well, even if you know you can meet your original deadline. Always check the Due Date field—and adjust it if necessary—after you change the Start Date.

THE CASE OF THE MISSING RSVP

Every time I plan a meeting involving a specific person, I fail to receive a response from that person.

Make sure the recipient is receiving your e-mailed invitations. If there's a problem with her e-mail address, the invitations might not be arriving. If she doesn't use Outlook, you might need to send the invitations in iCalendar format. Outlook should choose this format automatically; to verify that this option is selected, open the meeting request form and choose Tools, Send As iCalendar. It's also possible that the recipient is consistently choosing the Don't Send a Response option when acting on meeting invitations. If you can't break recipients of this habit, you'll have to follow up (preferably by phone) and manually update their status on the Attendee Availability tab of the Meeting item.

EXTRA CREDIT: PUBLISHING A CALENDAR AS A WEB PAGE

Outlook can help you maintain an events calendar for a busy organization. Instead of mixing the items in with your personal calendar, choose File, New, Folder and create a folder that contains Calendar items. Give the folder a descriptive name so you can tell at a glance what it contains. Enter details of the organization's activities as appointments in this folder.

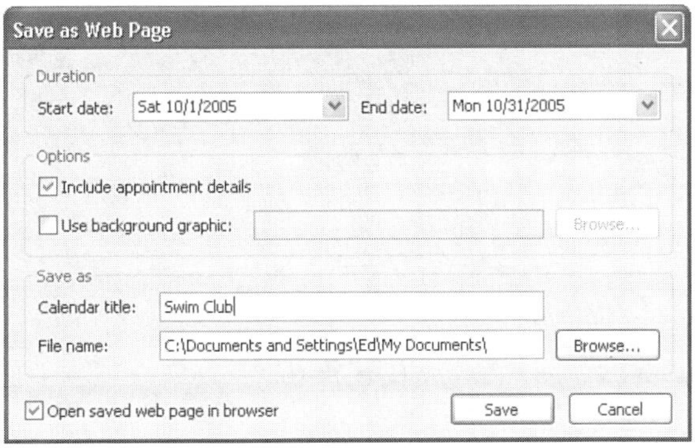

How do you share that information with other members of the club or organization? Publish the contents of the calendar periodically as a web page.

Switch to the Calendar folder and choose File, Save As Web Page. Outlook opens the following dialog box.

Figure 11.18

Choose the start and end dates you want to publish and specify whether you want to include details about each appointment from the Notes box. Give the calendar a title, specify a file location, and click Save. If you have access to a web server, you can publish the page directly to the server so that recipients can view it over the Internet. The result, as shown in Figure 11.19, is a slick, frame-based page that lets you click individual dates in the month view at left and see details in the frame on the right.

Figure 11.19

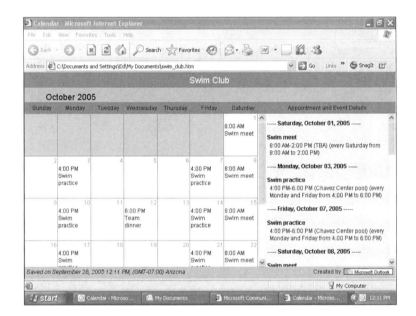

Using Word

CHAPTER 12

GETTING STARTED WITH WORD

WORD ESSENTIALS

When most people begin working with Microsoft Word, they open a new document and just start typing. Although that strategy has the advantage of producing immediate results, it doesn't allow you to take advantage of the power of Word. In fact, many of the most useful features of Word aren't immediately obvious, a failing we try to remedy in this chapter. Give us a few minutes of your attention and we'll explain why Word has so many different views, how to navigate effectively through even the longest documents, what you should know about printing, and how to enter and edit text using some of Word's most effective (and occasionally well-hidden) techniques.

We also show you how to customize the Word interface so you can be more effective, and in the Extra Credit section at the end of this chapter we introduce a useful tool that can protect you from accidentally publishing personal or private information in a Word file.

CHOOSING THE RIGHT DOCUMENT VIEW

The View menu offers at least five different ways to display the text, graphics, and other contents of the current document. The same menu allows you to show or hide an array of useful editing tools and features. Depending on the task at hand, you'll want to choose the view that provides the most appropriate mix of these features. Most experienced Word users find themselves switching views as they work on documents—particularly more complex documents—depending on what they're trying to accomplish.

TIP FROM

> If the horizontal scrollbar is visible at the bottom of the document window, you'll see icons for each of the five main views—Normal, Web Layout, Print Layout, Outline, and Reading Layout—to the left of the scrollbar. If you've hidden the scrollbar, these buttons are hidden, too.

NORMAL VIEW

Normal view (see Figure 12.1) shows section breaks, fonts and other character attributes, page breaks (shown as a dotted line), and, optionally, the names of paragraph styles. Normal view simplifies page layouts, hiding some elements to make editing easier.

Normal view has three advantages that appeal to advanced users:

- You can see section breaks. If you have more than one section in a document, you should seriously consider working in Normal view when formatting or entering text.
- You can see style names for all paragraphs in a column to the left of the document. Normally, this area is hidden; to make it visible, choose Tools, Options, click the View tab, and use the Style Area Width spinner control to set a width greater than 0. With the style area visible, you can quickly scroll through a document to ensure that style standards are being observed. (This option is also available in Outline view.)

Figure 12.1
Normal view shows most formatting, but reduces overhead by not showing pictures in their ultimate location.

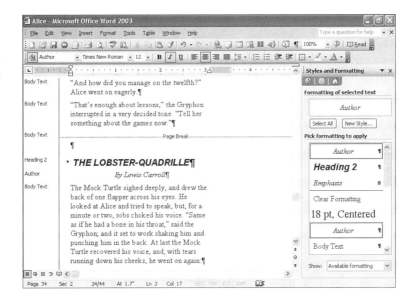

After you make the style area visible, you can use the mouse to drag it to a new width. If you drag the style area back to 0 width, the only way to make it visible again is with the Options dialog box.

- Normal view hides certain layout elements, including headers and footers, background images, drawing objects, and any picture that doesn't use the In Line with Text wrapping style. As a result, you can scroll through complex documents much faster in Normal view than in Print Layout view. When editing an exceptionally large file on a computer with limited resources, the difference in scrolling speed can be considerable.

WEB LAYOUT VIEW

If your document's ultimate destination is not paper but a website, it's important to see how the document will look when viewed as an HTML file. That's where Web Layout view comes in.

In Web Layout view, Word wraps text to fit the window, shows backgrounds, and places graphics on the screen the same way they would appear in a browser.

If you want to see how the document will appear in your default web browser—after all, each browser shows pages differently—choose File, Web Page Preview. Word saves a temporary copy of the file in HTML format, and launches your browser with the page loaded.

PRINT LAYOUT VIEW

Print Layout view (see Figure 12.2) shows the document precisely as it will be printed, with page breaks, headers and footers, and pictures arranged correctly onscreen. (In previous Office versions, this view was called Page Layout view.)

Figure 12.2
Print Layout shows a true WYSIWYG (What You See Is What You Get) view of your document.

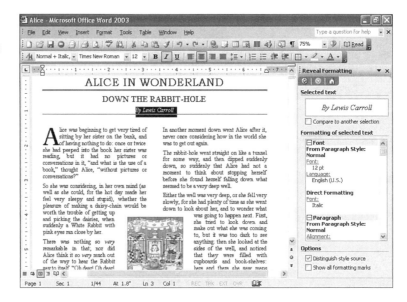

Picky Word users work in Print Layout view unless they specifically need one of the tools available in the other views because there are no surprises: The rendition on the screen closely mimics what will appear on paper.

OUTLINE VIEW

Outline view (see Figure 12.3) allows you to see an outline of your document while you're working on it. This view can be particularly helpful for rearranging sections of large documents, or promoting and demoting headings.

TIP FROM

EQ & Woody

If you use Word's default Heading styles, outline levels are maintained for you. Otherwise, you can set your own outline levels in the dialog box that appears when you choose Format, Paragraph. If you use the built-in Heading styles, Word changes the style applied to a given heading as you promote or demote it, using the buttons in Outline view.

Of course, all the normal editing techniques are available in Outline view: You can select, drag, copy, cut, and paste, as you would in any other view.

Master Documents are generally maintained in Outline view.

Move selected text up/down

Promote/Demote
one outline level

Expand/collapse
selected headings

Show second-level
headings and above

Figure 12.3
Outline view shows
the document's
structure and lets you
freely move elements.

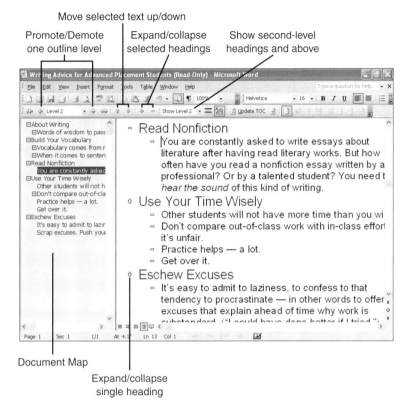

Document Map

Expand/collapse
single heading

READING LAYOUT VIEW

Word 2003 introduces a view not found in previous versions of Word. In Reading Layout view, Word uses the same fonts as in the original document; however, the display uses ClearType technology to make text easier on the eyes, and you can easily increase or decrease the size of the fonts without changing the formatting of the document itself. Unlike the Web and Print Layout views, which are designed to display pages exactly as the designer intended them to be viewed (in a browser or on paper), pages in Reading Layout view are rearranged to fit well on the screen, as shown in Figure 12.4. What you see, in other words, is not at all what you'd get on paper.

To switch to Reading Layout view, click the Read button on Word's Standard toolbar, or use the small button just to the left of the horizontal scrollbar at the bottom of the document window. In Reading Layout view, you can show the Document Map and the Thumbnails pane (both of which are described in the next section). Word hides all toolbars except the Reading Layout and Reviewing toolbars. To change the size of text in this view, click the Increase Text Size or Decrease Text Size buttons. To see the page as it would appear when printed, click the Actual Page button.

Figure 12.4
Reading view alters the arrangement of text so that pages are easier to read on the screen.

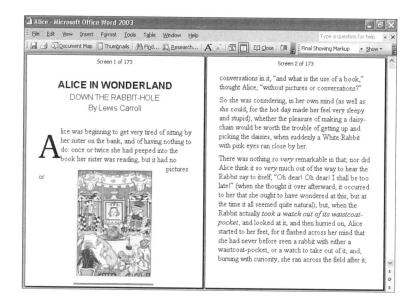

Although this view is designed for reading, you have full access to editing tools, and you can track changes and add comments as well. To exit Reading Layout view, click the Close button.

TIP FROM

When you open a Word document you received as an attachment to an Outlook e-mail message, Word automatically opens it in Reading Layout view. To change this default setting, choose Tools, Options, click the General tab, and select the Allow Starting in Reading Layout check box.

NAVIGATING WITH THUMBNAILS AND THE DOCUMENT MAP

Word provides two tools for keeping track of a document's navigation structure while you edit it. In all views, you can display a Thumbnails pane that appears along the left side of the document window. This pane gives you a big-picture look at long documents and provides clickable links you can use to jump to a specific page. To make this pane visible, choose View, Thumbnails. To resize the Thumbnails pane, click and drag its right edge; to make it disappear quickly, double-click the right edge.

The Document Map (see Figure 12.5) shows an alternate view of the document's outline, using the same outline levels employed in Outline view. It occupies the same space as the thumbnail pane, and in fact you cannot configure Word to show both elements at once.

To view a Document Map, click the Document Map icon on the Standard toolbar, or choose it from the View menu. Right-click the empty space below the currently visible Document Map or right-click the plus or minus sign to the left of a heading to expand or collapse a specific heading or to hide headings below a selected outline level.

Figure 12.5
If you have enough room on the screen, Document Map offers one-click navigation to any heading in a document.

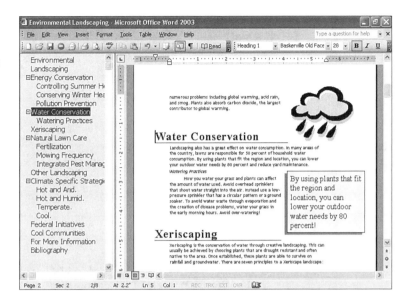

The Document Map is "hot" in the sense that you can click anywhere in the map and be transported to that location in your document. Unlike Outline view, it is not designed to offer interactive editing features—you can't promote or demote headings in the Document Map—but experienced Word users who commonly deal with long documents can readily navigate with it.

→ For more details on how to use the Document Map to get around in a long document, **see** "Navigating with the Document Map," **p. 335**.

ZOOM OPTIONS

Word lets you "Zoom" a document, making it appear larger or smaller on the screen, by choosing View, Zoom (see Figure 12.6), or the Zoom button on the Standard toolbar.

Figure 12.6
Zoom in (higher percentage number) to see more detail; zoom out to see more of the page.

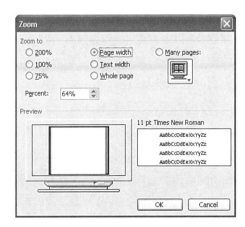

12

TIP FROM

> Fine-tune the Zoom percent to make your fonts more legible. For day-to-day use, you want the largest zoom factor that lets you see your most commonly used fonts without straining. Also, double-check to ensure that your zoom setting lets you easily distinguish, visually, between normal, bold, and italic characters.

In Print Layout view only, you can use the Zoom dialog box or the Zoom control on the Standard toolbar to choose automatic scaling options: Zoom the display to the width of a page, fit just the text on the page, view an entire page, or see two pages side by side. The Zoom dialog box includes one additional control that you can use to view multiple pages. If your mouse is equipped with a wheel, you can zoom in 10% increments by holding down the Ctrl key as you rotate the wheel up or down.

FULL SCREEN VIEW

Full Screen view temporarily hides virtually the entire Word interface, giving you more room on the screen to see your document without changing screen resolution. This option is particularly useful for people working at relatively low display resolutions.

When you choose View, Full Screen, Word removes most interface elements from the screen—including the title bar, menus, toolbars, status bar, rulers, and scrollbars—showing you only the document along with a lone toolbar that contains the Close Full Screen button.

In Full Screen view, you can reach the pull-down menus by sliding your mouse to the top of the screen or tapping the Alt key, but toolbars that were previously visible are hidden. If you lose the Close Full Screen button, you can restore the normal Word interface by pressing Esc.

12

TIP FROM

> To display other toolbars in Full Screen view, right-click the Close Full Screen button and choose from the list of available toolbars. After making one or more toolbars visible, you can dock them to any edge of the screen or allow them to float. The Close Full Screen toolbar is also fully customizable. If you regularly work in Full Screen view, consider adding buttons to this toolbar for common tasks.

SPLITTING A DOCUMENT WINDOW

Word allows you to split the document window, giving you two independently scrollable panes looking in on the same document, one over the other (see Figure 12.7). Although each of the panes operates independently—you can even have Normal view in one pane, and Outline view in the other—it's important to realize that you have just one copy of the document open: Changes made in one pane are reflected immediately in the other. This can be useful because it allows you to compare parts of a document directly, even when they're widely separated in the document.

Figure 12.7
Split the document window into two separately maintained panes to view different parts of the same document simultaneously.

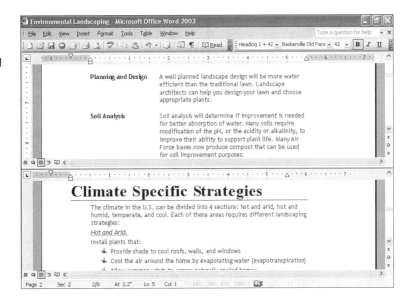

To split the document window, choose Window, Split, and click where you want the split to appear. Click and drag the split bar to resize the document panes. Double-click the split bar to restore the window to a single pane.

NOTE

You cannot split the document window if the Document Map or Thumbnails pane is active.

NAVIGATING THROUGH A WORD DOCUMENT

Word offers an enormous number of ways to move through a document, and most people can increase their productivity by learning some of the shortcuts.

You needn't memorize dozens of key combinations or obscure mouse tricks to boost your productivity, and the amount of time you need to invest is negligible. If you concentrate on reducing the effort you expend on the two or three navigational techniques you use most, your productivity will soar.

Not all the best navigation tricks are well known, either. Some of them aren't even documented. In this chapter, we promise we won't just throw lists of shortcuts at you; instead, we'll teach you some tricks for memorizing the most important ones.

USING THE KEYBOARD TO MOVE THROUGH A DOCUMENT

Aside from the obvious up, down, left, and right arrows, the most useful keyboard shortcuts for navigating around a document are listed in Table 12.1.

TABLE 12.1   NAVIGATION KEYS IN WORD

To Move	Press
Next word to right	Ctrl+Right Arrow
Next word to left	Ctrl+Left Arrow
One paragraph up	Ctrl+Up Arrow
One paragraph down	Ctrl+Down Arrow
To beginning of line	Home
To end of line	End
Up one screen	Page Up (PgUp)
To beginning of first line of current screen	Alt+Ctrl+Page Up
Down one screen	Page Down (PgDn)
To end of last line of current screen	Alt+Ctrl+Page Down
To beginning of document	Ctrl+Home
To end of document	Ctrl+End

Most experienced Word users would benefit from memorizing three groups of shortcut keys from those in Table 12.1, and they're all based on the Ctrl key. Here are the combinations, and the way the Ctrl key changes the keys you're probably accustomed to:

- **Ctrl+Home/Ctrl+End**—Go to the beginning/end of the document (instead of beginning/end of line)
- **Ctrl+Left/Right Arrow**—Move by words (instead of characters)
- **Ctrl+Up/Down Arrow**—Move by paragraphs (instead of lines)

TIP FROM

EQ & Woody

> Possibly the most useful, but obscure key combination in Word is Shift+F5. Word keeps track of the last three locations where you edited text. Pressing Shift+F5 cycles through those three locations. This setting is persistent, too. When you open a document, if you want to return to the last location you were editing, press Shift+F5.

USING THE MOUSE TO MOVE THROUGH A DOCUMENT

Word follows most of the standard Windows mouse navigation techniques, with a few interesting twists. All of them are based on proper use of the scrollbars and the scroll box (the rectangular element within the scrollbar that defines which portion of a document is visible within the window) as described in Table 12.2.

TABLE 12.2	MOUSE NAVIGATION TECHNIQUES IN WORD
To Scroll	**Do This**...
Up one screen	Click above the scroll box
Down one screen	Click below the scroll box
To a specific page	Drag the scroll box and watch the ScreenTips for page numbers
In Normal view, scroll left, into the margin	Press Shift and click the arrow at the left of the horizontal scrollbar

If you have a mouse with a scroll wheel or extra buttons, additional mouse navigation options might be available. See the documentation that came with your wheel mouse for more details.

NAVIGATING WITH THE DOCUMENT MAP

By far the most powerful way to navigate through a long document with the mouse is via Word's Document Map. It's particularly valuable for advanced Word users who have to navigate through documents that are more than, say, five pages in length.

The Document Map is a "hot" outline of the document's contents—similar to a Table of Contents—which appears in a pane to the left of the document itself. If you take a little care in applying heading styles, the entire structure of your document appears in the Document Map, and each important point is directly accessible.

Because the Document Map table is "hot," you can click a heading and jump immediately to the corresponding point in the document. You can use section headings or chapter numbers, for instance, to navigate using the Document Map pane.

Word constructs the Document Map based on outline levels, as defined in paragraph styles. If you stick to the standard Word heading styles—Heading 1, Heading 2, and so on—the outline levels are automatically applied by Word (level 1, level 2, and so on). If you use your own styles, they can have whatever outline level you want to apply.

➔ For more details on styles, **see** "Formatting Documents with Styles," **p. 451**.

➔ For details on changing the outline level and other paragraph format settings, **see** "Adjusting Paragraph Alignment and Outline Level," **p. 388**.

TIP FROM

EQ & Woody

Want to change the look of the text in the Document Map? No problem, as long as you know where to look. This setting is controlled by a hidden style; if you make it visible, you can adjust it. Open the Styles and Formatting task pane and choose Custom from the Show list at the bottom of the pane. In the Format Settings dialog box, select All Styles from the Category list, and then select the check box next to Document Map in the Styles to Be Visible List. Close the dialog box, saving your changes. The Document Map style should now be visible in the task pane, where you can change the font, font size, color, and other settings.

USING THE KEYBOARD AND MOUSE TO SELECT TEXT

In general, Word parallels the rest of Office in methods for selecting blocks of text. The wonders of Extend mode, however, remain unique to Word.

→ Think you know all there is to selecting text? Think again…and while you're at it, **see** "Selecting Text," **p. 92**.

Word allows you to select multiple, noncontiguous blocks of text. Hold down the Ctrl key as you drag across the text you want to select, and then repeat the process to select the second and subsequent blocks (or double- or triple-click as you would with a single selection).

TIP FROM

> You can change one single selected block of text without deselecting everything. Hold down the Ctrl key and click once inside a previously selected block. That specific selection, and only that selection, is deselected.

In addition, Word enables you to extend the current selection:

1. Click once at the beginning of the text block you want to select.

2. Double-click the grayed-out EXT box on Word's status bar (or press F8; see later in this section). This puts you in *Extend* mode.

3. Click again at the end of the text block you want to select. If you make a mistake, continue clicking until you get it right.

4. Double-click the EXT again, or press Esc, to leave Extend mode.

This technique can be particularly useful if you need to select large blocks of text. Although you can always click and drag across the text you want to select, Word sometimes scrolls so quickly that it's hard to stop. Use Extend mode or hold down the Shift key as you drag with the left mouse button to scroll at your own pace.

TIP FROM

> You can even use Word's Find feature while in Extend mode. To select everything from the insertion point to the next occurrence of the word "Foundation," for example, double-click EXT, click Edit, Find, type `Foundation`, and click Find Next. The selection is extended automatically for you.

If you hold down the Alt key and drag to select text, you'll find that Word selects a rectangular block of text without regard for sentences and paragraphs. This feature comes in handy in oddball circumstances—for instance, when you want to trim leading spaces from an imported text list. Click at the beginning of the text block, hold down Alt, and drag down to select the "column" of spaces. Then press Delete. Mastering this technique may take some practice; if you don't get it right the first time, press Ctrl+Z to undo your work and start over.

Word has one additional keyboard-related method for selecting text that doesn't have a parallel in any other Office program: the F8 key.

Press the F8 key once, and Word goes into Extend mode. Press it a second time to select the current word. Press it a third time and you select the current sentence. Press it a fourth time, and you highlight the current paragraph. Press it a fifth time to select the current section, if your document is divided into sections, and then once more to select the whole document.

Conversely, at any point in the F8 expansion process, you can press Shift+F8 to shrink one level: If a paragraph is selected and you press Shift+F8, the selection shrinks to include only the current sentence.

TIP FROM

Ed & Woody

> F8 has one more trick up its sleeve. Say you want to select all the text from the current insertion point location up to and including a specific letter. Press F8, and then that letter. To extend the selection from the insertion point to the next *r* in the document, for example, press F8+r.

BOOKMARKS

In the classroom or the den, a *bookmark* is a piece of paper that marks a location in a document. In Word, a bookmark is a selection—a piece of text, a picture, or just an insertion point—with a name.

Bookmarks come in handy in two different situations:

- They provide a location to which you can navigate. For example, you can put a bookmark in a document called "StartOfChapter17." Then you can tell Word "go to the bookmark called StartOfChapter17" and you're transported to that location. Similarly, you can use bookmarks as the destination for hyperlinks setting up a link, say, to the bookmark called PopulationTable in a document saved as Economic History of Florence.doc.

- Word provides several tools for retrieving the text covered by a bookmark. For example, if you create a bookmark called MemberName in a form letter you're creating for the Swim Club, you can sprinkle {REF MemberName} fields throughout the contract, and everywhere the field appears, that person's name will show up.

To set a bookmark, do the following:

1. Select the text you want to have bookmarked, or click in your document to position the insertion point at the location you want to bookmark.

2. Choose Insert, Bookmark (or use the keyboard shortcut Ctrl+Shift+F5). The Bookmark dialog box appears (see Figure 12.8).

12

Figure 12.8
Bookmarks can cover text, pictures, paragraph marks, and almost anything else in a document—or they can be as small as an insertion point.

3. Type a bookmark name. Names must start with a letter and can include letters, numbers, or the underscore character (_), but not spaces.

4. Click Add. Word establishes a bookmark with that name at the indicated location.

How can you spot existing bookmarks in a document? Normally, bookmarks are invisible. You can configure Word to display bookmarks with a subtle (maybe too subtle) indicator. Click Tools, Options, click the View tab, and select the Bookmarks check box. Word displays bookmarks as faint gray brackets surrounding the bookmarked text or location. You may need to squint to see these indicators, and you will look in vain for any further help—Word offers no ScreenTips or other indications that could help identify the bookmark.

If you move a block of text that includes a bookmark, the bookmark goes along. If you delete a block of text that includes a bookmark, the bookmark is deleted. If you copy a block of text that includes a bookmark, the bookmark stays in its original location, and the copy does not contain a bookmark.

Word has no built-in method for renaming bookmarks. You must take the long way around: Use the Bookmark dialog box to select the existing bookmark, create a new bookmark with a new name, and then delete the old bookmark.

Be careful when adding or deleting text near a bookmark. Text you enter at the beginning of a bookmark is added to the bookmark. Text you enter at the end of a bookmark is not added, unless the bookmark ends with a paragraph mark.

NAVIGATING THROUGH DOCUMENTS WITH THE SELECT BROWSE OBJECT MENU

In the lower-right corner of the Word window—down below the vertical scrollbar's down arrow—you'll find a remarkable collection of three buttons that allow you to browse through your document by jumping from object to object. In this case, the "objects" can be any of a dozen common types of Word data, including fields, comments, pictures, pages, and headings.

Browsing by object generally works best if you use it this way:

1. Click the circle in the middle (the Select Browse Object button, shown in Figure 12.9) and select one of the 12 "browse by" boxes.

Figure 12.9

Browse by Graphic

2. Click the Next button (the double down arrow, just below the Select Browse Object button) to search toward the end of the document for the next occurrence (the next picture, for instance, if you chose Browse By Picture). Click the Previous button (the double up arrow just above the Select Browse Object button) to search toward the beginning of the document. If you have trouble clicking these undersized buttons, use the keyboard shortcuts instead: Ctrl+Page Up and Ctrl+Page Down.

You can search for the following "objects":

- **Fields**—Word moves from field to field, although it skips hidden fields (such as {XE}, the field that creates entries for a document's index).

→ To learn how you can empower your documents with fields, **see** "Using Fields Intelligently," **p. 494**.

- **Endnotes**—An endnote is typically used to cite sources in a research paper or other formal document; it consists of a *note reference mark*, which is embedded in text, and the note itself, which appears at the end of the document. If you start in the body of the document, Word jumps through the document, stopping at each note reference mark. If you start in an endnote, Word cycles through each of the endnotes.

- **Footnotes**—Footnotes are constructed like endnotes, except that the note portion appears at the bottom of the page containing the note reference mark. If you start in the body of the document, Word jumps from one note reference mark to the next. If you start inside a footnote, each click selects the next footnote.

- **Comments**—The Next button works differently, depending on whether comments are visible on the page (as they are when you choose View, Markup). If you position the insertion point inside a comment and click the Next button, you'll go to the next comment. If comments are hidden, clicking the Next button goes to the next comment marker. Using the Previous button jumps through the body of the document, from one comment marker to the next, regardless of whether comments are visible.

- **Sections**—Word moves from the beginning of one document section to the next.

→ Ever used sections before? Many Word users haven't, at least knowingly. **See** "Page/Section Setup Options," **p. 374**.

- **Pages**—Word moves to the top of the next or previous page.

12

- **Go To**—This is the most interesting of the "browse by" options. When you click the Go To box on the Select Browse Object menu, Word opens the Go To dialog box, as shown in Figure 12.10. Go To includes most of the other options on the Select Browse Object menu (Page, Section, Field, and so on), as well as Line, Bookmark, Equation, and a confusingly named "Object" option, which goes to the next embedded object.

Figure 12.10
Use the Go To box with the Select Browse Object menu to navigate in unconventional ways; these settings jump forward 10 lines at a time when you press Ctrl+Page Down.

Using the Go To box and the Select Browse Object menu together make it easy to navigate through a document in creative ways. To see all the bookmarks in a document, one after the other, click the Select Browse Object menu, and then click Go To (or choose Edit, Go To or press the keyboard shortcut Ctrl+G). In the Go to What box, select Bookmark. Click the Go To button. From that point on, each time you click the Previous button or press Ctrl+Page Down, you'll go to the next bookmark in the document. If you want to review all the second-level headings in an important term paper, you can choose Heading from the Go to What box, type *2* in the Enter Heading Number box, and begin browsing. Choose Line and enter +10 to move through a document exactly 10 lines at a time.

- **Find**—Same as choosing Edit, Find from the menu bar. We discuss the Find dialog box at length later in this chapter.

    After you've set up a Find or Replace, the easiest way to repeat the Find or Replace is to clear the dialog box away and use the keyboard shortcut Ctrl+Page Down (or Ctrl+Page Up to search backward).

- **Edits**—Word automatically keeps track of the last three locations where you've made changes. This setting lets you cycle among the three edits (the same as the Shift+F5 keyboard shortcut). Note that these changes may be in different documents.

- **Headings**—Cycles to the beginning of each paragraph in the document that is formatted with a "Heading n" style, where "n" is any integer between 1 and 9.

- **Graphics**—Moves to the next or previous picture in the document (whether linked or embedded), or to the next or previous drawing canvas. This option ignores pictures and drawing canvases in the drawing layer.

- **Tables**—Cycles through all the Word tables in the document.

→ To learn more about the intricacies of drawing layers and drawing canvases, **see** "Using Office Drawing Tools," **p. 114**.

Entering Text and Graphics Automatically with AutoText and AutoCorrect

Word has two main features for entering text and graphics automatically: AutoText (the older feature that's available only in Word) and AutoCorrect (newer, and available throughout Office).

→ To learn how to speed up repetitive text entry, **see** "Using AutoCorrect to Type Faster," **p. 98**.

When you type an AutoCorrect entry followed by the Spacebar, Enter key, or any punctuation mark, Word swaps out the text you've typed and replaces it with the indicated text (and graphics) in the entry. For example, you can set up an AutoCorrect entry to change dfre into "The Decline and Fall of the Roman Empire." You see no warning that the change will take place; it just happens.

On the other hand, when you start to type an AutoText entry, after the first four letters Word displays a ScreenTip alerting you that a possible matching entry exists. Type octo, for example, and you'll see a ScreenTip that reads October (Press ENTER to Insert). If you want to accept the AutoText entry—in this case, replace the octo you've typed with the word October—you need to press Enter, or the Tab key, or F3 (they're all equivalent).

In addition, you can insert an AutoText entry into a document by clicking Insert, AutoText. In this case, you have two choices: Choose any entry directly from the cascading menu, where your choices are grouped into categories; or choose AutoText from the top of the cascading menu, select from the list of AutoText entries on the AutoText tab of the AutoCorrect dialog box (see Figure 12.11), and click Insert.

Figure 12.11
The Add button creates a new AutoText entry from the current selection. Click Insert to place the selected AutoText entry into the current document.

The categories for entries on the AutoText menu match the style of the paragraph in which the entry was originally created. If you create a new AutoText entry in a paragraph formatted with the Normal style, the resulting AutoText entry will appear in a category called "Normal."

TIP FROM

Ed & Woody

> If you use AutoText entries regularly—and any productivity-obsessed Word user should—we suggest that you add the AutoText toolbar to your standard editing screen. Right-click any blank spot on any toolbar or menu and choose AutoText.

The current date, days of the week, months of the year, your company name, your user name, and your initials are all picked up automatically by Word and turned into AutoText entries.

AutoText entries are stored in templates, so you can have separate "global" entries stored in the Normal document template (Normal.dot), and "local" entries that apply only to documents based on specific templates.

The AutoText menu (available on the Insert menu and on the AutoText toolbar) changes depending on the style of the paragraph you're working on. In paragraphs formatted with the Normal style, or with a style that contains no custom AutoText entries, the full AutoText list is available. For paragraphs formatted with a style that does contain custom AutoText entries, the AutoText menu shows only entries associated with that style.

NOTE

> You can get at all available AutoText entries by clicking Insert, AutoText, AutoText. If you've added the AutoText toolbar to your editing screen, click the AutoText button. If you can't find a specific AutoText entry in the list, chances are good it's stored in a template that isn't currently accessible.

In most cases, you'll find AutoCorrect easier to use than AutoText, thanks to the following advantages:

- Unformatted AutoCorrect entries are available to all Office programs.
- After AutoCorrect makes a change, if you hover your mouse pointer over the AutoCorrected entry, the AutoCorrect action menu (the lightning bolt icon) gives you access to the full array of AutoCorrecting options, both for this individual entry and for AutoCorrect in general. That's handy.
- It takes an extra keystroke—Enter, Tab, or F3—to put an AutoText entry into a document. Many typists, especially fast typists, find that distracting.

However, in some circumstances AutoText is preferred:

- You can create AutoText entries for words without fear of accidentally triggering a replacement. For example, you could create an AutoText entry called `pater` that expands into `The Paternal Order of Ornery Fellows`. If you had an AutoCorrect entry with the same name and you typed the Latin phrase `pater familias`, you would end up with `The Paternal Order of Ornery Fellows familias`.

- AutoText ScreenTips warn you about the contents of the replacement. AutoCorrect gives no warning.

- AutoCorrect entries are global. Super-global, in fact, in that they take effect throughout Office. AutoText entries can be localized to specific templates.

To create an AutoText entry:

1. Type and, optionally, format the replacement text (or graphics) that you want.
2. Select the text. Include the paragraph mark, if you want to include it and the paragraph's formatting in the AutoText entry.
3. To save the AutoText entry in the default template, click Insert, AutoText, New (or click the New button on the AutoText toolbar, or press Alt+F3). To save the AutoText entry in a different template, choose Insert, AutoText, AutoText, and select the template from the Look In box. Give the new AutoText entry a name and click OK.

Word includes tools for copying and moving AutoText entries in the template organizer (choose Tools, Templates and Add-Ins, Organizer, AutoText).

USING HYPHENS AND DASHES

A hyphen is a character on any standard keyboard. Dashes are longer than hyphens and are used for specific purposes in keeping with rules of typography and grammar. Word automatically changes some hyphens into em and en dashes (an em dash, as the name implies, is the width of a lowercase m, and an en dash is the width of a lowercase n). For example:

- Type a letter, followed by two hyphens, followed by another letter, and Word changes the hyphens to an em dash. It's nicely done, because the em dash has a little bit of space to the left and right, and a line can break before or after an em dash.

- Type any letter, followed by a space, a hyphen or two, and any other letter, and Word transforms the hyphen(s) into an en dash.

This behavior is controlled by Word's AutoFormat As You Type feature.

→ For instructions on how to disable this and other AutoFormat options, **see** "Disabling AutoFormat Settings," **p. 363**.

In addition, you can always type an em dash into a document by pressing Alt+Ctrl+- (minus) on the Number pad. An en dash is Ctrl+- (minus) on the Number pad.

CAUTION

Don't use the - (minus, or hyphen) that's located on the top row, to the right of the zero, on most keyboards.

→ For instructions on how to customize keyboard shortcuts for dashes and other characters, **see** "Bypassing Menus with Keyboard Shortcuts," **p. 46**.

When you use narrow columns, good hyphenation becomes crucial. On a term paper or letter that uses the full width of a letter-sized page, hyphenation isn't necessary. But in a highly formatted document where you use all of Word's designer-level typographical tricks—columns, text boxes, and so on—you need to pay close attention to line length. Unhyphenated or poorly hyphenated text is easy to spot—just look for the vast expanses of white space in the right margin. Word offers three different methods for hyphenating:

■ **Automatically**—Most experienced Word users who work in Print Layout view avoid this method because the constant sliding of lines makes it hard to concentrate on the screen; choose this option when you're copying text from another source into a formatted document. To turn on automatic hyphenation, choose Tools, Language, Hyphenation. In the Hyphenation dialog box (see Figure 12.12), click the Automatically Hyphenate Document box. Hyphenation takes place immediately when you click OK, and Word continues to automatically hyphenate as you type or edit text. The Hyphenation Zone is the maximum allowable white space at the end of a line; the Limit Consecutive Hyphens To box specifies the maximum number of consecutive lines that can be hyphenated.

Figure 12.12

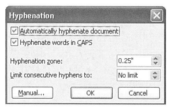

■ **Manually, Whole Document**—Choose Tools, Language, Hyphenation, and then click the Manual box. Word steps you through each hyphenation, allowing you to accept or reject each.

NOTE

Generally, you'll want to undertake a manual hyphenation only after the text is in its final form. Making any changes to the text will probably throw off the hyphenation, at least in any changed paragraphs.

- **Manually, One Word at a Time**—You needn't turn on automatic hyphenation to have Word hyphenate an occasional word. Instead, use a "soft" or "optional" hyphen: Click where you want the soft hyphen to appear and then press Ctrl+-. Word uses the hyphen if it's required to balance out the line; if not, the hyphen won't appear.

Sometimes you want to prevent Word from breaking a line at a hyphen. For example, you decide in a paper on computer storage technology that the word CD-ROM should never be broken. Tell Word that you don't want it to break at that point by using a "hard" or "non-breaking" hyphen: Ctrl+Shift+-.

TIP FROM

EQ & Woody

> Do you want to tell Word not to hyphenate a particular paragraph? You can accomplish that goal by using one of two formatting options. You'll find the more explicit under paragraph formatting: Choose Format, Paragraph, click the Lines and Page Breaks tab of the Paragraph dialog box, and then select the Don't Hyphenate check box. For a more indirect option, open the Language dialog box (choose Tools, Language, Set Language), and select the Do Not Check Spelling or Grammar check box. Although it isn't immediately obvious, this option also prevents hyphenation.

FINDING AND REPLACING TEXT AND OTHER PARTS OF A DOCUMENT

If you want to find something simple, the standard Find features used throughout Office should suffice. You can look for literal text by typing any word or phrase into the Find What box on the Find dialog box. After selecting the Use Wildcards check box, you can have Word perform fuzzier searches: `m?ne` matches `mane` and `miner`, but not `manner`, and `bo*t` matches `boats` or `bought`, but not `bat`.

→ To sharpen your text-finding skills with techniques that work in any Office program, **see** "Finding and Replacing Text," **p. 93**.

Sometimes you need even more powerful search capability. Perhaps you're looking for all the words in a document that end with "ing." Or you can get complex—say you have a list of license plate numbers and need to find the ones starting with the number 1 through 9, followed by the letters "QED," and then four numbers ending in "9."

Word contains a flexible, powerful mini-language, a close cousin of the widely used *regular expression* syntax, that lets you specify precisely what to find. To begin creating your own search expressions, choose Edit, Find, click the More button, and select the Use Wildcards check box (see Figure 12.13).

As detailed in the next section, this search string will find all those license plates:

```
<[1-9]QED[0-9]{3}9
```

12

Each part of the search string is explained below:

- The < signifies that the following characters have to start a new word (in this case, a *word* is a license plate number).
- The [1-9] matches any single number between 1 and 9.
- The QED forces an exact match on the letters QED.
- [0-9] matches any single number.
- The {3} that immediately follows [0-9] means that the previous element is repeated three times; thus, you must have three consecutive numbers to match this search term.
- Finally, the 9 on the end will match only a 9.

Figure 12.13
The search string shown here uses wildcards and expressions to solve the license plate number problem described in the text.

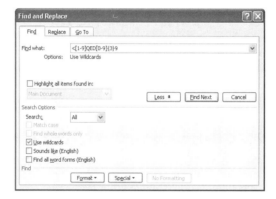

Finding Text

In addition to the ? and * wildcards, Word recognizes the symbols in Table 12.3. (See the preceding section for a detailed example using this syntax.)

Table 12.3 Wildcards for Find

Symbol	Meaning
[xyz]	Matches exactly one of the listed characters. b[aioe]g matches bag and bog, but not bug.
[A-Z]	Matches any single character in the range. Case sensitive. b[A-W]g matches bAg and bUg, but not bug or bARge.
[!xyz]	Matches any single character except the ones listed. b[!au]g will match big and bog, but not bag or bug or bring.
[!A-Z]	Matches any single character that doesn't lie in the range. Case sensitive. b[!a-m]g matches bog or bug, but not bag or big.
<	The character(s) that follow this symbol must appear at the beginning of a word. <[a-c] matches act and cat, but not react. <bl matches blue and blech, but not able.

Symbol	Meaning
>	The character(s) that precede this symbol must appear at the end of a word. ing> matches hiking and writing but not singer. [a-c]> matches Alma and tab but not read.
{n,m}	The preceding character or expression must appear between "n" and "m" times. If the "m" is omitted, the character must appear "n" or more times. Thus, blec{3,7}h matches blecccch and bleccccccch, but not blecch, and b[an]{2,}g matches bang but not bag.
@	Same as {1,}: the preceding character must appear one or more times. bo@t matches bot and boot, but not bat or boat.
\	Search for the literal character that follows the backslash, even if it's a wildcard. wh[ae]t\? matches what? and whet? but not whether or whatever.

Word also includes a handy list of special symbols—tab characters, em and en dashes, page and section breaks, and so on—under the Special button of Figure 12.13, shown previously.

All this wildcard-matching business can be confusing, but it gets worse: Word supports two different kinds of pattern matching. All the wildcard matching discussed so far in this chapter applies when you select the Use Wildcards check box, as shown in Figure 12.13. A different set of symbols is available if you do not check the Use Wildcards box.

Perhaps the easiest way to illustrate the difference is with the paragraph mark. If you leave the Use Wildcards box unselected and then type ^p in the Find What box, Word will dutifully find the next paragraph mark.

However, if the Use Wildcards check box is selected, there is no apparent way to tell Word to find the next paragraph mark! If you type ^p in the Find What box, and the Use Wildcards box is checked, Word will stop only if it finds a literal match in the document—that is, a caret followed by a p.

It's difficult to tell, offhand, whether a particular character or symbol is included in one group or the other. If you're trying to match a character that you can't type directly, the best approach is to start by clicking the Special button on the Find and Replace dialog box. If the character is on the drop-down list, click to select it and add the code to the Find What box. If that doesn't work, select the Use Wildcards check box, click Special, and look again.

Although the online documentation encourages you to paste text from a document into the Find What box, in fact, some characters (most notably paragraph marks) can't be pasted.

There are two more search options that you should use with caution:

- Sounds Like catches some simple homonyms (new, gnu, knew, for example, or fish and fiche), but it also makes odd matches (rest, according to Word, sounds like reside) and bizarre mistakes (oh sounds like a, according to Word, but not owe). It also fails the Woody test: According to Word, Leonard does not sound like Leonhard. Woody's parents would beg to differ.

■ Find All Word Forms is supposed to catch noun plurals, adjective forms, and verb conjugations: Tell Word to replace heavy with light and, with Find All Word Forms checked, heavier will be replaced by lighter, heaviest will be replaced by lightest. This, too, has problems. For example, tell Word to replace bring with take and, with Find All Word Forms checked, "I have brought it" will be replaced by "I have took it."

REPLACING TEXT

Replace behaves much the same as Find, except the entry in the Find What text box is replaced by the entry in the Replace With text box (see Figure 12.14).

Figure 12.14
The Replace tab of the Find and Replace dialog box lets you build expressions using Word's powerful wildcard syntax.

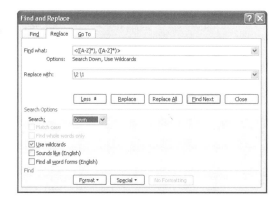

When performing a replace, you can use parentheses in the Find What box to specify groups of characters, which are then referenced in the Replace With box. The contents of the first pair of parentheses in the Find What box becomes \1 in the Replace With box; the second becomes \2; and so on.

This can be handy if, say, you want to replace all the occurrences of American style dates (perhaps 10-20-51) with their European day-first equivalents (20-10-51). Make sure the Use Wildcards box is selected, and then in the Find What box, type

```
<([0-9]*)-([0-9]*)-([0-9]*)>
```

to force Word to recognize the American style date: the day (inside the first set of parentheses) becomes \1, the month (in the second set of parentheses) becomes \2, and the year becomes \3. In the Replace With box, type

```
\2-\1-\3
```

and the dates are swapped around.

Few people realize that you can use Word to change a list of names that looks like this:

```
Lastname, Firstname
```

Into a list that looks like this:

```
Firstname Lastname
```

To do so, click Use Wildcards and in the Find What box, type

```
<([A-Z]*), ([A-Z]*)>
```

and in the Replace With box, type

```
\2 \1
```

TIP FROM

You can tell Word to "Replace With" the contents of the Windows Clipboard. That can be handy if, for example, you want to replace a word, such as STOP, with a picture (perhaps a stop sign) throughout a document. To make it so, clear the Use Wildcards check box, and then type ^c in the Replace With box. Word interprets ^c as being the contents of the Windows Clipboard.

FINDING AND REPLACING FORMATTING

Word doesn't limit you to searching for and replacing text. You can specify formatting, as well—say, replace all occurrences of the italicized words *current annual dues* with the bold number **$100**. Here's how:

1. Choose Edit, Replace. Click the More button to expose the Format selections.

2. In the Find What box, type `current annual dues`.

3. With the insertion point still in the Find What box, click the Format button and choose Font. Under Font Style, click Italic, and then click OK.

4. In the Replace With box type `$100`. With the insertion point still in the box, click the Format button and choose Font. Under Font Style, click Bold, and then click OK (see Figure 12.15).

12

Figure 12.15
In formatted searches, Word tells you that you're searching for formatted text by including the Format: line under the Find What or Replace With boxes.

5. You can now proceed with the replace. Click Replace to verify each match individually, or Replace All to make the update throughout the document.

TIP FROM

EQ & Woody

If you're handy with keyboard shortcuts, you can use them to great effect in the Find/Replace dialog box. Click in the Find What or Replace With dialog boxes and then use any relevant keyboard shortcut to bypass the Format dialog boxes. Click Ctrl+I or Ctrl+B to toggle between italic and bold fonts, for instance. (This option also makes available a third option, Font: Not Italic or Font: Not Bold, where you can search only for matching text that *doesn't* have a particular attribute.) You can also search for paragraph attributes, such as centered or justified text or those with a particular line spacing specified.

If you need to find and replace multiple instances of a particular word or phrase, it's easier to find the first instance, change it if needed, and then close the dialog box. That way, you can click the Next button (just below the Select Browse Object button) or press Ctrl+Page Down or Shift+F4 to find the next instance. Closing the dialog box clears clutter off the screen, and you can better see what you're doing. You can also quickly edit the found text without having to click outside the dialog box, and then press Ctrl+Page Down to continue searching. Press F4 to repeat the previous change, or use the contents of the Clipboard to replace the found text by pressing Ctrl+V.

In addition to Font formatting, you can specify Paragraph formatting, Styles (either character or paragraph), Tabs, Language, Frame type, or Highlight.

If you want to clear the formatting for either the Find What or Replace With boxes, click once inside the box and then click the No Formatting button at the bottom of the dialog box.

Both the Find and Replace formatting settings are "sticky": If you set Find to look for "Heading 1" style paragraphs, for example, the next time you perform a Find or Replace, Word continues looking for "Heading 1" style paragraphs.

NOTE

When you're done looking for a particular kind of formatting—or replacing with a particular kind of formatting—you must manually clear the formatting. Click to position the insertion point in the Find or Replace box and then click the No Formatting button.

INSERTING FOOTNOTES

Footnotes in Word are straightforward, although the terminology can be a bit difficult to fathom.

To put a footnote in a document, click Insert, Reference, Footnote. The Footnote and Endnote dialog box appears, allowing you to choose whether you want a footnote (at the bottom of the page or bunched after the end of the text on the page) or an endnote (at the end of the current section or the end of the document). Word numbers the footnotes (or endnotes) for you, automatically, or you can specify your own footnote reference character.

Word draws a horizontal line between the text on a page and the first footnote. The line is called a Footnote Separator. If the footnote is too long to fit on one page, Word continues it onto the next page and uses a longer horizontal line, called a Footnote Continuation Separator. You can work with the separators by switching into Normal view, choosing View, Footnotes and, in the footnote pane, selecting Footnote Separator or Footnote Continuation Separator.

→ If you need to create two references to the same footnote, **see** "Inserting Cross-References," **p. 50**.

CHECKING SPELLING AND GRAMMAR

Word contains one of the most sophisticated spell-checkers you can find. The spell-checking module, which Word shares with the rest of Office, contains rich tools for custom dictionaries and "exclude" dictionaries, and easy right-click access to suggested spellings for words highlighted with the infamous red squiggly line.

→ To find out how to supercharge Word's spell checker, **see** "Setting Up Spell-Checking Options," **p. 50**.

Some people find the red squiggly lines distracting—as if they're being forced to correct spelling mistakes as they type. Word includes a batch spell-checker, so you can turn off the squiggly lines and run a spell check after you're done typing. To turn off the squiggly lines, choose Tools, Options, click the Spelling & Grammar tab, and then clear the Check Spelling As You Type check box. To run a batch spell check, choose Tools, Spelling and Grammar—or press F7.

TIP FROM

Ed & Woody

> If you don't want Word to spell-check a specific word or paragraph, select the text or paragraph, choose Tools, Language, Set Language, and select the Do Not Check Spelling or Grammar check box.

The grammar checker's advice, on the other hand, can be overly simplistic. Why? Because it's rule-based, and grammar (whether in English or in French, Spanish, or any of the other commonly used languages that also use the Word grammar checker) is far too complex to fit neatly into a small set of rules. If you know you need help with basic (and we do mean basic) grammar issues, you can get a great deal of benefit from the grammar checker. Most advanced users, however, find the squiggly green lines distracting and turn them off (choose Tools, Options, and on the Spelling & Grammar tab, clear the Check Grammar As You Type box).

If you want the grammar checker to help improve specific aspects of your writing (such as flagging sentences that are too long, or those in passive voice, or their/there mistakes), you can customize Grammar Checker to respond only to violations of those rules. To do so, choose Tools, Options and click the Settings button on the Spelling & Grammar tab. There you'll find dozens of different grammatical problem areas, and you can instruct Word to watch for the ones most important to you.

To use Word's built-in Thesaurus, position the insertion point inside the word you want to look up, and choose Tools, Language, Thesaurus. Alternatively, you can bring up the spelling checker by pressing F7, and the Thesaurus with Shift+F7.

PRINTING WORD DOCUMENTS

Most Word documents are destined for the printer. Word offers many features to give you extensive control over how pages print.

PREVIEWING PRINTED PAGES

If you're looking at one page, Word's Print Preview mode offers no advantage over the standard Print Layout view. But there are two situations in which Print Preview is extremely useful. Click the Multiple Pages button and drag to show as few as two pages or several dozen at one time (the maximum number of pages allowed in Print Preview mode depends on your hardware—at $1,280 \times 960$ resolution, we can see 91 pages, arranged in 7 rows of 13 pages each). This view is especially helpful when you want to see at a glance where headlines, graphics, tables, and other nontext elements fall in your document. Although it's possible to edit text and move objects on the Print Preview screen, this screen is most appropriate for getting a bird's-eye view of your entire document.

To enter Word's Print Preview mode (see Figure 12.16), click the Print Preview button on the Standard toolbar, or choose File, Print Preview.

Figure 12.16
Word's Print Preview mode shows you precisely how the printed page will appear—but Print Layout view does almost as well, with none of the limitations.

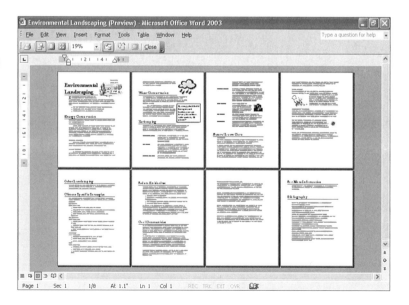

TIP FROM

Ed & Woody

In Print Preview mode, the default mouse pointer lets you toggle between a 100% view of the page you click or back to a view of the number of pages you selected. Click the Magnifier button to toggle between this pointer and an I-beam insertion point you can use for editing.

In Print Preview mode, you also have access to the Shrink to Fit button. Use this feature when the last page of your document includes two or three lines, and you want to force those leftovers to fit on the previous page.

Click the Shrink to Fit button and Word alters font sizes to reduce the number of pages in the document by one. Note that changing the font size sometimes doesn't affect the spacing between paragraphs, so the resulting document might have an inordinate amount of white space. Also, the Shrink operation makes no changes to margins. Word won't reduce font sizes below the range of 6 or 7 points.

CAUTION

While in Print Preview mode, you can click the Undo button or press Ctrl+Z to reverse the Shrink to Fit operation, but after you've closed and saved the document, it's impossible to return the document to its original state.

CHOOSING WHAT TO PRINT

If you want to print one copy of the current document using the defaults established on the Print tab of the Options dialog box (see the Print What Choices table later in this chapter), click the Print icon on the Standard toolbar.

Word also allows you to print the currently selected page(s), or to specify the pages you want to print by page number. To invoke either of those options, choose File, Print, and select Current Page or type in the page numbers in the Pages box (see Figure 12.17).

12

Figure 12.17
Word's Print dialog box allows you to print "thumbnail" images, two or four (or more) to a page, using the Pages Per Sheet box.

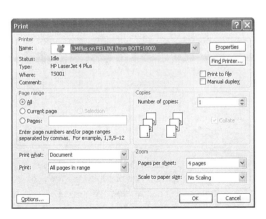

The Print box lets you print all pages, or odd or even pages only. If you know how your printer feeds sheets, you can use this setting to print "duplex"—where pages alternate on the front and back of each sheet.

TIP FROM

If you check the Print to File box in the Print dialog box, Word prompts you for a file-name. If your printer is currently unavailable, but you want to produce a hard copy of a document you're working with now, it can be a good option. Later, when the printer is available, you don't need to reopen Word; just copy the file you created directly to your printer by, for example, dragging it onto the printer icon in Windows Explorer.

Ever wonder what AutoText entries you have set up in a particular document or template? How about the styles, or many other hidden parts of your document, for that matter? Choices in the Print What drop-down list let you find out (see Table 12.4).

TABLE 12.4   PRINT DIALOG BOX'S PRINT WHAT CHOICES

Option	What Prints
Document Properties	Some of the information found in the dialog box that appears when you choose File, Properties: all the Summary information, and some of the General and Statistics
Document Showing Markup	Prints the document with changes, including comments, tracked in the margin; it does *not* print the style area
Styles	All the styles that you can see if you choose Format, Styles, and select Styles in Use
AutoText entries	All AutoText entries available in the document, whether they orig-inate in the document's template or the Normal global document template, Normal.dot
Key Assignments	Only custom keyboard assignments for the current document, template, and global

PRINTING THUMBNAILS

The Pages Per Sheet list in the Print dialog box (shown previously in Figure 12.17) offers you the opportunity to print thumbnails of your documents—2, 4, 6, 8, or 16 pages—on a single sheet of paper.

TIP FROM

If your primary reason for printing is to file away a hardcopy record of your documents, consider printing 2-up or 4-up, duplex if possible. Although you might need a magnifying glass to read the resulting printout, the storage space savings are enormous. If you regu-larly need to print double-sided pages and booklets, we highly recommend a wonderful program called FinePrint (http://www.fineprint.com), which handles those tasks and much, much more with aplomb.

COLLATING

If you choose to print more than one copy of a document, Word's default settings *collate* the copies for you—printing one copy from start to finish, and then printing the next copy from start to finish, and so on. That's convenient if you want to pull the pages right out of the printer and pass them around without any additional work.

SHARING DOCUMENTS

As the co-authors of this book can attest, collaborating on a writing project isn't easy. When two or more people work together to produce a document, disagreements inevitably arise over the right words to use and the best way to communicate concepts. To smooth the bumps in the collaborative process, Word includes a set of workgroup features that make it easier to track changes in a document.

In this section, we discuss Word's traditional collaboration features, all of which entail different people opening and editing a document. In a business setting, the shared document is typically stored in a shared network folder; in this book, we assume that you're most likely to pass around drafts of a document in progress via e-mail.

TRACKING CHANGES TO A DOCUMENT

When more than one person can make changes to a document, pandemonium can ensue. The surest way to maintain the integrity of a document is to ensure that changes—if they're allowed at all—are clearly identified. That way, anyone reviewing the edited document can see each specific change and review the reasons for that change with the person who made it.

When you use Word to track changes made to a document, Word keeps a careful record of insertions, deletions, and changes in formatting, attaching a set of initials to each change. You and your partners can insert comments that aren't included with the text of the document. At the end of the process, you can go through the document one change at a time, accepting or rejecting each change, or you can accept every change with one click of the mouse.

To specify that you want Word to track changes made to the current document, choose Tools, Track Changes, or double-click the grayed-out TRK button on the Status bar. If this is the first time you have enabled this option for the current document, Word displays the Reviewing toolbar; any changes made from that point on are explicitly saved by Word.

The Reviewing toolbar (which can be moved anywhere on the screen) gives you one convenient location for working with all document changes. The drop-down list at the left of the toolbar lets you look at any of the following:

- **Final Showing Markup**—This view shows the final state of the document. In Print Layout, Web Layout, Outline, or Reading Layout views, inserted text appears underlined and in a different color and deleted text appears in balloons in the margin. In Normal view, deletions appear as strikethrough text and insertions appear in color with the underline attribute.

12

- **Final**—The end result.
- **Original Showing Markup**—In all views except Normal view, this option shows the original document, with insertions appearing in the margin and deletions marked with the strikethrough attribute.
- **Original**—What the document looked like before Change Tracking was turned on.

Shifting back and forth among the different views gives you a quick idea of the effect of changes. If you're rewriting a first draft prepared by someone else, for instance, you might prefer to work in Final view, where Word behaves exactly as if you were editing the document without tracking changes. If you're reviewing an edited document, you can switch to Final Showing Markup so that you can see what was deleted. Figure 12.18 shows a document that is currently under revision.

Figure 12.18
Using the Final Showing Markup view, you can see additions in the body of the document, and deletions in the margin.

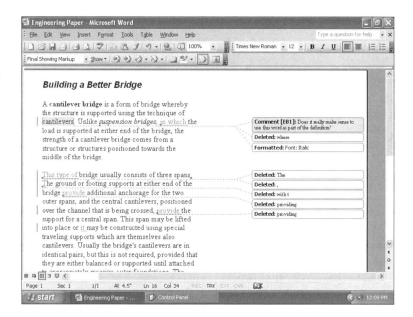

Using the Show menu on the Reviewing toolbar, you can fine-tune which changes Word tracks and how it displays them on the screen. If you find the balloons distracting, click Show, Balloons, and then click Never. Use the Only For Comments/Formatting option to show deletions and additions in the body of the document and comments in the margin. If you'd rather not keep track of formatting changes, clear the check mark to the left of Formatting on the Show menu. (Balloons are only visible in Print Layout and Web Layout view. If you're working in Normal view, changes appear in the document itself, and comments appear in a pane at the bottom of the document editing window.)

When reviewing a document, use the four buttons to the right of the Show menu on the Reviewing toolbar to jump from revision to revision, accepting or rejecting individual changes as you go. There's also a button you can click to add your own comments, in case you need to follow up on a change, another for highlighting text, and another that displays the Reviewing Pane, which lists changes in order. Overall, it's a powerful and useful feature.

What if you didn't turn on change tracking before passing a Word document along to someone else for their input? If the other person saved changes to a new document and you still have the original document, you can have Word compare the two documents and mark the differences between them. Open the original document and choose Tools, Compare and Merge Documents. Select the second document, click the arrow to the right of the Merge button, and choose Merge Into New Document. This feature automatically generates revision marks, noting the pieces that have been added or deleted from the original document, along with formatting changes. Use the buttons on the Reviewing toolbar to view and accept or reject changes.

ADDING COMMENTS TO DOCUMENTS

When you're collaborating on a document with other people, it's helpful to leave comments along the way, explaining why you made a specific change or suggesting places where additional changes might be necessary. When editors or reviewers make changes to a document for which you have final responsibility, it's relatively easy to accept or reject their additions or deletions. Don't fall into the trap of using comments to suggest changes, however; transferring those comments into the document requires multiple steps and takes a fair amount of time. Instead, you should make the change in the document itself (highlighting it with a bold color, if necessary) and add a comment inviting the original author to reject the change if he or she disagrees with it.

To enter a comment, highlight the text that pertains to the comment and choose Insert, Comment. (If you don't make a selection, Word attaches the comment to the word immediately preceding the insertion point.) Type your comment in the comment box.

To cycle through all the comments in a document, use the Next button on the Reviewing toolbar.

You can print all the comments attached to a document by choosing File, Print, and selecting Document Showing Markup in the Print What drop-down box.

SAVING DOCUMENT VERSIONS

If you're working on an especially important document that involves large amounts of revision over a long period of time, such as a doctoral dissertation, you might find it useful to keep a collection of drafts as you work. If you decide that a section you wrote, reviewed, and discarded weeks ago was a keeper after all, you can restore it to the current version by copying it from a saved draft. Keeping backup copies and early versions of important documents should be a regular part of your daily Office routine. In addition to the normal backup cycle, Word enables you to keep multiple versions of a document in a single file.

If you're sharing documents and need to keep track of who made changes to what, you should consider saving versions of the document from time to time. Word makes version

12

saving automatic, if you choose File, Save As, and then choose Tools, Save Version. The Save Version dialog box (which is also accessible by choosing File, Versions) lets you make comments about each specific version. Three caveats with Save versions:

- All the versions are stored in a single file. Word keeps file sizes from growing too large by saving only the changes between versions (it's all invisible to you, of course). However, file size can become a significant issue in documents where version tracking is enabled.

- The Save Version dialog box lets you delete versions as they become obsolete. Use it.

- Be extremely careful when using versioned files with sensitive information. If you're not extremely careful, you run the risk of allowing someone to see embarrassing or confidential information contained in intermediate drafts.

RESTRICTING CHANGES TO A SHARED DOCUMENT

For change tracking to work, all the people working on a document have to keep this option turned on. Otherwise, their changes won't be explicitly shown, and you'll have to go through the additional step of comparing your original document with their modified versions to figure out what has changed. In addition, you might want to pass around a document so that other people can read it without making any changes. To handle either of these scenarios, you can *protect* the document from unwanted changes. Word 2003 uses a special task pane to help you specify editing restrictions.

To set editing restrictions for the current document, follow these steps:

1. Choose Tools, Protect Document. This opens the task pane shown in Figure 12.19.
2. Under Editing Restrictions, click to select the Allow Only This Type of Editing in the Document check box.
3. Select an editing option from the drop-down list. To force everyone making changes to a document to have Word track their changes, choose Tracked Changes. To prevent any changes to the document, select No Changes (Read Only).
4. Click Yes, Start Enforcing Protection.
5. In the next dialog box, enter an optional password if you don't want people to be able to override this setting. Click OK to finish.

From that point on, anyone who opens the document has to abide by the restrictions you specified. To remove the restriction, choose Tools, Unprotect Document; or open the Protect Document task pane again and click Stop Protection.

STRATEGIES FOR NON-WORD ENVIRONMENTS

Do other people in your circle of co-workers use non-Microsoft word processors? Although Word is still the most popular word processor by a huge margin, WordPerfect has a loyal base of users, thanks to widespread bundling on inexpensive new computers. In addition, the free StarOffice and OpenOffice suites have attracted fans who are either on a tight budget or want to make an anti-Microsoft statement. To exchange documents with people who use these and other word processors, the simplest solution is to save your files in a format the other person can open. (Choose File, Save As and select from the Save As Type list.) The Word file format is now the de facto standard for formatted business documents. Most modern word processors can read and write files using Word 97 format, and the latest versions can work directly with documents created in Word 2000/2002/2003 format. If none of these options is satisfactory, consider Rich Text Format as an option.

Figure 12.19
Use the Protect Document task pane (backed up with a password, if necessary) to force other team members to track changes to the current document.

If the persons you want to share a document with don't need to edit the file you send, have them use the Word Viewer 2003. Although this free utility doesn't allow changes to a document, it does allow anyone who uses a Windows-based PC to see documents as you intended and cut or copy text to other programs. The free viewer is available from the Microsoft Office website, http://office.microsoft.com/downloads. Knowledge Base article 891090 includes a detailed description of this utility and installation instructions and has a download link as well (http://support.microsoft.com/kb/891090).

CUSTOMIZING THE WORD INTERFACE

Many components of the Word interface—menus, toolbars, keyboard shortcuts, and the like—work precisely the same way as the other Office programs.

→ For the Office-wide overview, **see** "Point, Click, Customize," **p. 30**.

In this section, you learn how to take control of features that are specific to Word.

Much of the rest of the way in which Word works can be customized, as well. If you find that a specific "feature" in Word gets in your way, more often than not there's a simple check box that will disable the feature—or enable an alternative that might work better for you.

Word's customizing settings fall into two main groups: Options settings and AutoCorrect settings. You'll find both menu choices on the Tools menu; in addition, the action menu (the "lightning bolt" icon that appears whenever AutoFormat makes a change) allows you to delve directly into the AutoCorrect settings, by choosing the Control AutoCorrect Options item. Although most of the settings are quite obvious, we cover the most important (and confusing) ones in the following sections.

TIP FROM

Take a few minutes to review your settings, with these advanced user suggestions in mind. Then save the settings with the Save My Settings Wizard so you can restore them if you have to reinstall Office or switch to a new computer. To get to the Save My Settings Wizard, open the Programs menu and find the Save My Settings Wizard shortcut in the Microsoft Office Tools group. Run the wizard and follow the instructions to store your settings in a convenient location.

CONTROLLING HOW WORD DOCUMENTS APPEAR ON THE TASKBAR

Word 2003 uses the Single Document Interface (SDI), which produces one taskbar icon for each open document. If you would prefer to see a single window for Word, with each open document appearing within that window, you can choose the Multiple Document Interface (MDI) instead. Choose Tools, Options, click the View tab, and clear the Windows in Taskbar check box. (To restore the SDI interface, repeat these steps and select the check box again.)

TIP FROM

If you routinely work with more than one document on the screen at a time, making side-by-side comparisons, you'll probably prefer to stick with SDI. Give it a try.

OPTIONS SETTINGS

The View tab controls what appears on the screen. When you create a new document, it takes on the View tab settings in effect when it was created. You can subsequently change View tab settings for the document, and they "stick" when you open and close the document. These are the main considerations for making View tab options more useful:

- Consider showing tab characters, so you can see why and how text lines up on tab stops.

- Some people prefer to see paragraph marks when they're copying, moving, and deleting blocks of text. If paragraph marks aren't shown on the screen, it's difficult to tell when you have selected one.

- If you have trouble with drawing layer items moving around on a page, show object anchors to see where the drawings are tethered.

SETTING OPTIONS ON THE GENERAL TAB

The General tab contains a hodgepodge of settings:

- If a specific document has links that you want to update only manually (perhaps because the updating takes a long time), clear the Update Automatic Links at Open check box.
- There is no penalty in rolling the Recently Used File list to nine, aside from a little lost screen space when you display the File menu.

SETTING OPTIONS ON THE EDIT TAB

The Edit tab controls how Word reacts when you edit text:

- If you select Typing Replaces Selection, Word overwrites any selected text whenever you press a key on the keyboard. Many advanced users turn off this option, to avoid accidentally deleting text.
- Normally, the Insert key toggles Word into and out of Overtype mode (where characters you type at the keyboard overwrite characters on the screen). You can turn off that behavior by telling Word to use the Insert key to paste, although the side effect might be just as bad: If you press the Ins key by accident, Word dumps the contents of the Clipboard at the insertion point.

TIP FROM

If you find yourself pressing the Insert key accidentally all the time, there's a much better way to disable the key entirely. Choose Tools, Customize, then click the Keyboard button. On the left, choose All commands. On the right, pick Overtype. Click Insert and then the Remove button. Click Close twice to permanently prevent Insert from shifting you into Overtype mode.

12

- The Use Smart Paragraph Selection option drives many advanced Word users nuts. If you select this check box, and you select only part of a paragraph but include the paragraph mark, Word drops the paragraph mark automatically and without warning.
- Select the Use Ctrl+Click to Follow Hyperlink check box to ensure that you never accidentally chase a hot link by inadvertently clicking it.
- By default, the When Selecting, Automatically Select Entire Word setting is on. It forces Word to select an entire word plus the following space when only part of a word is actually selected. For most people, this is a usability improvement. If you routinely select portions of words and sentences, clear this check box (or learn to hold down Ctrl+Shift as you drag the mouse pointer).

SETTING OPTIONS ON THE PRINT TAB

The Print tab contains default printer settings:

- Consider selecting the Update Fields check box if you want Word to automatically update all the fields in a document before it's printed. In some cases, it's beneficial to update all the fields so they have the most recent information (times, dates, and so on). But in other cases, you might want Word to skip the updating—for example, if you've gone in and modified several field results (perhaps Table of Contents or Index entries), manually.

→ To learn about fields in depth, **see** "Using Fields Intelligently," **p. 494**.

- Specify whether hidden text should appear on the printout by selecting or clearing the Hidden Text check box.

TIP FROM

Printing hidden text can come in handy if you need to print two different versions of a document. For example, a teacher might set up an exam so the questions are in regular text and the answers are marked as hidden. Printing hidden text would produce a key for graders.

SETTING OPTIONS ON THE SAVE, USER INFORMATION, AND FILE LOCATIONS TABS

The Save tab includes settings for both saving and AutoRecover:

- Select the Allow Fast Saves check box only if you have huge documents that take enormous amounts of time to save. Even so, you should weigh the time you might save against the potential risks of losing data.

CAUTION

Fast saves are the single greatest source of corrupt Word documents. If something goes wrong in the middle of a fast save—the power goes out or your hard drive controller hiccups—the entire file can be rendered illegible. Fast saves also preserve deleted text and other remnants of documents; a sufficiently motivated snoop could see data you've deleted from a document by using a file viewer to inspect the hexadecimal text. In Word 2003, the Fast Save option is disabled by default. We recommend that you make sure this setting is off.

- Word can automatically save an AutoRecover backup copy of the currently active document—a so-called *.wbk file—at time intervals you specify in this dialog box. If Word crashes or freezes, the next time it starts, it automatically looks for and opens any *.wbk files. With a little luck, the automatically recovered file will contain all your edits, up to the most recent AutoRecover time. This protection is in addition to the built-in crash protection. If you're a fast typist, consider setting the interval to as little as two or three minutes.

Don't disable AutoRecover unless you find the backup process terribly onerous. And if you do disable it, make sure you periodically save the current file. Word *does* crash–it isn't a question of whether, only of when.

The User Information tab contains the user's name, initials, and address. These settings are used for identifying tracked changes, comments, envelope return addresses, and much more. Take a moment to make sure they're correct.

The File Locations tab lets you change the location of all Word's key data files: My Documents, templates, AutoRecover files, and more.

DISABLING AUTOFORMAT SETTINGS

Advanced Word users should also periodically examine their AutoCorrect settings to ensure they aren't getting in the way. To open this dialog box, choose Tools, AutoCorrect Options. You'll find five tabs in the AutoCorrect dialog box:

- The AutoCorrect tab consolidates all AutoCorrect entries.

→ For an overview of how AutoCorrect works, **see** "Using AutoCorrect to Type Faster," **p. 98**.

- The AutoFormat As You Type tab contains several settings that advanced users, in particular, might want to disable, per Table 12.5. This tab also contains the setting Word uses to automatically detect web addresses and e-mail addresses and turn them into hyperlinks. If you're planning to publish your document on the Web or share it in electronic format with other people, that can be useful. In the case of printed documents, it isn't necessary. To turn off this intrusive setting, clear the Internet and Network Paths with Hyperlinks check box.

TABLE 12.5   GETTING RID OF AUTOFORMATTING

To Disable This Kind of AutoFormatting	Uncheck This Box
* - - - > -> => symbols or pictures to create bulleted paragraphs	Automatic Bulleted Lists
0 1 I i A a to create numbered lists	Automatic Numbered Lists
Three or more - _ = * ~ # to put a border on a paragraph	Borders
+- - - -+- - - -+ to create a table	Tables
1st, 2nd, 3rd, and so on converted to 1st, 2nd, 3rd	Ordinals (1st) with Superscript
1/4, 1/2, 3/4 converted to $^1/_4$, $^1/_2$, $^3/_4$	Fractions (1/2) with Fraction Character ($^1/_2$)

- The AutoText tab controls all AutoText entries.

→ For the full story on AutoText, **see** "Entering Text and Graphics Automatically with AutoText and AutoCorrect," **p. 341**.

■ The AutoFormat tab controls what Word does when you choose Format, AutoFormat.

→ To learn more about Word's AutoFormatting features, **see** "Formatting All or Part of a Document Automatically," **p. 398**.

■ The Smart Tags tab controls whether Word looks as you type for something that appears to be an Outlook Contact. The only downside to enabling the full look-up capability is the performance hit: If you feel that Word is unnecessarily sluggish, try disabling these settings to see if performance perks up.

WORD STARTUP SWITCHES

You can control how Word starts with *command-line switches*. These switches work from a command line, the Start/Run box, and as switches in Windows shortcuts. For example, to start Word with the /a switch enabled, click Start, Run, type **winword /a** in the Open box, and press Enter.

The available switches are listed here:

■ /a keeps Word from running any Auto macros stored in the Normal document template, Normal.dot. It also keeps Word from loading any add-ins in the Startup folder. Use this switch if you are having trouble getting Word to start.

■ /n starts Word normally, but doesn't load the usual "Document1" first document.

■ /mMacroname starts Word, and then runs the specified macro. (Note that there is no space between the "m" and the macro name.) For example, the following line starts Word and runs the macro File1, a built-in macro which loads the most recently used document:

```
c:\Program Files\Microsoft Office\Office\winword.exe /mFile1
```

Similarly, you can use /mFile2 to open the second file in Word's most recently used list, and so on. This line

```
"c:\Program Files\Microsoft Office\Office\winword.exe " /mFile1 /mFile2
```

starts Word and opens both the #1 and #2 files on the most recently used list.

NOTE

The Word documentation says that the /t switch opens a document as a template, but actually that startup switch opens the specified file as a document. Unfortunately, this is a bug that has been around in Office for some time.

Of course, you can always put the name (or names) of one or more documents on the command line, and Word will load them when it starts:

```
"c:\Program Files\Microsoft Office\Office\winword.exe " "c:\My Documents\some.doc"
```

TIP FROM

> If the filename—including the path—includes any spaces, be sure to put quotes around the entire filename. Otherwise, Word won't interpret the command line correctly.

EXTRA CREDIT: PROTECT YOUR PRIVACY WHEN SAVING AND SHARING DOCUMENTS

Do you know what's hidden in your Word documents? The answer might surprise you. Every document you create using Word contains your name, for starters. It might contain the names of other people who reviewed the document. It might also contain comments, annotations, changes from previous versions (including text that had been deleted), data about your computer and network, e-mail headers, and even text from other documents that might have been open at the same time. If you're the only person who will ever see this document, or if you intend to print it out and pass the printed copies around at a meeting, then your secrets are safe. But as soon as you send the document file to someone else via e-mail or publish the document file on a website, your secrets become accessible.

In some cases, the results can be embarrassing, to say the least. In recent years, several high-level government officials have been embarrassed when Word experts took a closer look at documents that had been made publicly accessible on a website; in at least one case they discovered comments from an earlier draft that contradicted the public statements being made by the affected agency!

Even if you're not creating top-secret documents, you should be careful with any document that you plan to make publicly available. We recommend that you download the free Remove Hidden Data tool from Microsoft and use it on any document you plan to publish. (Get the full details and a download link at http://support.microsoft.com/kb/834427.)

After you install this tool, you'll notice a new Remove Hidden Data option on the File menu. When you've finished editing a document and you're ready to publish it, choose this option. The Remove Hidden Data tool displays the dialog box shown in Figure 12.20.

12

Figure 12.20

Remove Hidden Data

Remove Hidden Data creates a new version of your document without comments, revisions, file properties, or other data that you might not want others to see. You should only use this feature when you are ready to publish your document.

Enter a file name for the new version of your document.

File name: [   ] Browse

Recommended: Use a different file name from the source file name. The source file will save in its original state with its original name.

Cancel   Next >

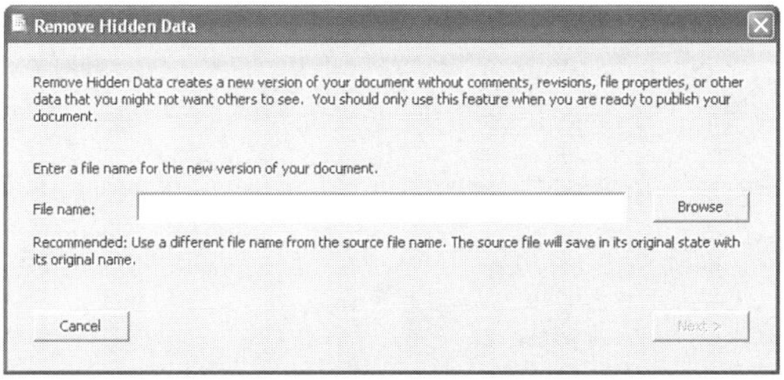

After you enter a name for the new version of the current document, the tool strips away all hidden data, including comments, tracked changes, and personal information stored with the document's properties. After it finishes its work (a job that typically takes only seconds), it displays a text file showing what was removed. The new document is saved with the read-only attribute turned on, to reduce the risk that you'll accidentally save it with personal information included.

One word of warning: Be sure to specify a new name for the scrubbed document, because this tool is ruthlessly effective at its job, and if you save a document under its current name you'll find that what's been removed cannot be recovered!

CHAPTER 13

CREATING GREAT-LOOKING DOCUMENTS

In this chapter

UNDERSTANDING YOUR FORMATTING OPTIONS

The point of formatting is to make documents look good for printing (or onscreen viewing). This attention to design details also has an impact on readability; a carefully designed document, with bold headings, well-laid-out pages, and proper typography, is also easy to read or scan. Word's formatting toolkit includes options for specifying pages (paper size and orientation), margins, fonts, paragraph formatting, tab stops, bullets, and numbering. But before you click any of those buttons, you need to understand how formatting works.

Every Word document consists of components arranged in a strict hierarchy that is unrelated to the way you create a document. Inside a Word document, data is stored in one or more *sections*, which in turn contain one or more *paragraphs*, each of which consists of one or more *characters*. Although it's possible to select an entire document and apply formatting to it, Word doesn't actually format at the document level; instead, it applies your changes individually to characters, paragraphs, and sections within the document.

Word enables you to apply formatting directly, by making a selection and then using the Styles and Formatting task pane, the Format menu, or the Page Setup dialog box. You can also re-use formatting that appears elsewhere in your document via the task pane in an ad hoc fashion. Or you can define collections of character or paragraph formatting choices, save them as named styles, and then apply the style to selected characters or paragraphs.

CHARACTER FORMATS

Character formats apply to letters, numbers, and punctuation marks. The most common formatting options that apply to characters are font-related: the font name, size, and color, for example, as well as attributes such as bold, italic, underline, and strikethrough. If you copy or move a formatted character from one part of a document to another, the formatting travels with it.

→ To learn more about formatting, **see** "Common Formatting Options," **p. 106**.

Three special characters merit close attention:

- Each space is a character. Although you can't see its color, you can easily note its size: A 10-point space takes up much less room on a line than a 48-point space.

- Within a Word document, a tab is a character. When Word encounters a tab character, it shifts to the next tab stop before continuing to lay down text.

- A paragraph mark is technically a character as well, although you can't print a paragraph mark. By default, Word does not show paragraph marks on the screen, but they're always there. You can select, copy, move, or delete paragraph marks.

To make paragraph marks and other formatting characters visible, you can select the Show All Formatting Marks check box at the bottom of the Reveal Formatting task pane or click the Show/Hide button.

13

→ You can also selectively show or hide spaces, paragraph marks, tabs, and other special characters, as we explain in "Options Settings," **p. 360**.

The most common character treatment options are available via toolbar buttons and keyboard shortcuts. For example, you can click the Bold, Italic, or Underline buttons on the Formatting toolbar, or use the shortcut key combinations Ctrl+B, Ctrl+I, Ctrl+U, respectively, to toggle these formatting options for selected text.

TIP FROM

Here's a formatting shortcut even many experienced Word users don't know about. If you position the insertion point within a word and click a formatting button or key combination, the formatting applies to the entire word. In this case, a "word" is any series of characters delimited on each end by a space or punctuation mark. Use this option to change the font, size, or attributes of a word without selecting it first. Another, related quirk is worth noting: If you place the insertion point within a word and choose a paragraph style, Word applies the style to the entire paragraph; but if you select the entire word and change the style, the style is applied only to that word.

When you start typing in a new, blank document, Word's default setup uses 12-point Times New Roman. To change the default font and size, choose Format, Font, select the font you want to use as a default, and click Default (see Figure 13.1).

Figure 13.1
Change the default font for all documents by selecting the font you prefer and then clicking the Default button (bottom left).

For normal correspondence, consider changing the font—Garamond, for example, is much more striking visually—and reducing the point size down to 11, or even 10. Although 12-point is the Word default, many people find it too large for ordinary correspondence. In our opinion, 11-point type is an excellent compromise.

TIP FROM

Ed & Woody

If you usually share documents with other users instead of printing them, make sure you pick a default font that others are likely to have, such as one of the default Windows or Internet Explorer fonts. Don't select an exotic custom font that you've installed specially.

Character spacing can be changed in any number of ways: moving characters above or below the baseline (superscripting and subscripting); magnifying or reducing selected groups of characters (scale); and even squishing together predefined pairs of letters that fit well together—such as VA—to minimize the white space between them (a process called *kerning*). All these techniques are discussed in the next chapter.

→ To learn more about fonts and character formatting, **see** "Using and Managing Fonts," **p. 105** and "Changing Character Attributes," **p. 106**.

Word also supports *highlighting*, a method of changing the background color of selected text much as you would mark up a paper document with a highlighting pen. Although highlighting is rarely used in final documents, it's a handy way to draw attention to text that you want someone else to review closely, or to emphasize pieces of text that are incomplete or need additional editing.

If you're exchanging drafts of a document with a co-worker, for example, use a yellow highlighter to flag sections where you have questions or comments. If several people are reviewing the same document, each one can use a different color so others can see at a glance who marked up specific sections. Although you can formally track changes to a document, highlighting comes in handy in informal situations.

→ To work with documents in a group, **see** "Sharing Documents," **p. 355**.

Although highlighting isn't, strictly speaking, a character format (because it really affects the character's background), it behaves much like a character format: If you copy or move highlighted characters, for example, the highlighting travels with the character.

CAUTION

Highlighting is *not* removed when you use the Clear Formatting option on the Styles and Formatting task pane or when you press the Ctrl+Shift+N shortcut to restore the Normal character style to selected text. Internally, Word does not treat highlighting as if it were character formatting.

13

To apply highlighting to characters within a document, you can either make a selection and then click the Highlight button on the Formatting toolbar, or click the Highlight button, and then "paint" the highlighting on characters. Click the drop-down arrow to the right of the Highlight button to choose one of 15 available colors. The pointer changes to a highlighting pen with an insertion point; to turn off highlighting and return to normal editing, click the Highlight button again, or press Esc. To turn the tool into an eraser that removes highlighting from existing text, click the drop-down arrow to the right of the Highlight button and choose None as the highlight color.

→ For advanced formatting tips, **see** "Changing Text Formatting," **p. 384**.

If you open a document that contains fonts that are not installed on your computer, Word provides a way to specify which fonts should be substituted for the missing ones. Choose Tools, Options, Compatibility, and then click the Font Substitutions button. In the Missing Document Font box, select the font you want to change. Then, in the Substituted Font drop-down list, choose the font to replace it.

TIP FROM

Ed & Woody

Normally, the fonts you specify in the Font Substitution dialog box are not literally substituted for the missing ones. The document file itself isn't changed; Word uses the fonts you pick to display the document onscreen and to print it. If you want to make the substitution final, replacing all references to a particular font with a font of your choosing, click the Convert Permanently button after specifying the substitutions.

PARAGRAPH FORMATS

Each time you press Enter, Word inserts a paragraph mark and starts a new paragraph. By definition, a paragraph in Word consists of a paragraph mark, plus all the characters before the paragraph mark, up to (but not including) the preceding paragraph mark. Paragraph marks are a crucial part of Word, because they contain all paragraph formatting. When you copy, move, or delete a paragraph mark, the paragraph formatting goes with the mark.

Paragraph formatting includes alignment (left, center, right), indenting, bulleting, numbering, and spacing—both between lines within a paragraph and between paragraphs. It also covers background colors and shading, as well as boxes and lines drawn around and between paragraphs. Tab stops are also considered paragraph formatting—you don't specify a set of tab stops for each line on a page; instead, tab stops remain uniform throughout an entire paragraph.

When you press Enter to create a new paragraph, the new paragraph usually takes on the formatting of the paragraph immediately preceding it. For example, if you position the insertion point within a right-justified paragraph and press Enter, the new paragraph will also be right-justified. (The exception to this rule is if the style of the first paragraph specifies that a new style is to be used for following paragraphs; this setting is stored in the Style for Following Paragraph property.)

13

DIRECT FORMATTING VERSUS STYLES

For simple, short documents, it's often easiest to apply formatting directly to paragraphs and characters, either through the Format menu, or by using the Style list on the Formatting toolbar, or by selecting options from the Styles & Formatting task pane. But when a document extends beyond a few pages, or when consistent formatting is crucial, you should use styles instead. Styles have one great advantage over manually applied formatting: When you change a style, your changes ripple throughout the document and are applied to all other text formatted with the style of the same name.

Word supports two kinds of styles: *character styles*, which include only character formatting; and *paragraph styles*, which combine paragraph formatting information with character formatting.

→ To learn more about styles, **see** "Formatting Documents with Styles," **p. 451**.

For example, while working on a thesis or dissertation you might establish a paragraph style called ChapterTitle, defining the style as Arial 24-point bold (that's the character formatting part), with 6 points of space after the heading (the paragraph formatting part). As you're typing, every time you start a new chapter, you type in the title of the chapter and apply the ChapterTitle style. The day before you're supposed to hand in your thesis, you decide it will be easier to read if you change the chapter titles to Garamond 20-point italic with 12 points of space after the heading.

Because you carefully formatted every chapter title in the thesis with the ChapterTitle style, you can change all the chapter titles in a matter of seconds, by changing the settings for the ChapterTitle style. On the other hand, if you had applied formatting manually, you would have to scan the entire document and change the formatting of each chapter title manually; in doing so, you run the risk of missing a chapter title, which results in a sloppy look for your document—and could have an effect on your final grade.

→ Line and page breaks, indents, tabs, and other paragraph formatting are covered in depth in "Changing Paragraph Formatting," **p. 387**.

APPLYING AND MODIFYING FORMATS

Word includes two nifty task panes that make it easy to understand why and how formatting has appeared in your document, and to apply formatting quickly and reliably.

REVEALING FORMATTING WITHIN A DOCUMENT

Word 2003 includes a feature that's meant to mimic the "reveal codes" capability found in WordPerfect.

After selecting any text—from a single character to an entire document—choose Format, Reveal Formatting (or use the keyboard shortcut Shift+F1) to display the Reveal Formatting task pane. Word responds with a comprehensive list of all formatting applied to the current selection (see Figure 13.2).

The more you use the Reveal Formatting task pane, the more you're likely to discover what a tremendous help it can be in troubleshooting formatting problems. Here are three ways to squeeze extra information out of the task pane:

■ Select the Distinguish Style Source check box at the bottom of the Reveal Formatting task pane. When you do so, Word shows you the source of each specific type of formatting in the selection. For example, in Figure 13.2, you can see that the base font for the paragraph is 12 point, as defined in the Normal style, and the font (Univers Condensed) has been applied directly to the selection. This kind of detail can be useful if you're trying to sort through exactly why and how text appears in a particular format.

- Hover the mouse pointer over the Selected Text box at the top of the task pane to reveal a drop-down arrow on the right side of the box. Click this arrow to reveal a menu that lets you select similarly formatted text elsewhere in the document, clear all formatting from the selection, or change the formatting of the selection to match the surrounding text.

- After selecting some text, click the Compare to Another Selection check box. When you select this option, a second box opens beneath the original Selected Text box. You can now navigate to another part of the document and make a second text selection. The contents of the Reveal Formatting task pane change to show just the differences in formatting between the two selections.

Figure 13.2
Word can show you full formatting information for any part of a document.

COPYING FORMATS

There are three ways to copy specific formatting from one place in a document to another:

- Set up a style to reflect the formatting, and apply the style (either character or paragraph) to the text you want to change. This is the most consistent and reliable approach, and it enables you to change formatting throughout a document by modifying the style.

- Use the Format Painter icon on the Standard toolbar. You select the text (or paragraph) that includes the text that's formatted to your liking, click the Format Painter icon, and then "paint" the formatting elsewhere in your document. This process is most effective when copying character formatting to a very limited selection. If your hand-eye coordination is less than perfect, the process can be cumbersome and error-prone, especially if you accidentally select a paragraph mark prior to "painting."

13

■ Use the Styles and Formatting task pane. If your document already contains the formatting you want, select the text you want to format, and then click the formatting in the Pick Formatting to Apply box on the task pane. Note that the Styles and Formatting task pane isn't limited to formally defined styles: It also includes entries for all the manually applied formatting that exists in your document.

The Styles and Formatting task pane also makes it easy to set up formal styles, and then modify and apply them.

REMOVING TEXT FORMATTING

Novice users can make a thorough mess of a document by randomly applying direct formatting to characters and paragraphs. To remove all manually applied formatting from a selection so you can start fresh, bring up the Styles and Formatting task pane and choose Clear Formatting. Doing so removes all manually applied formatting, both at the character and the paragraph level.

TIP FROM

Although the key combination is a bit arcane, you can also remove manually applied formatting using keyboard shortcuts: First, select the text, and then press Ctrl+Q to remove manually applied paragraph formatting, and finally press Ctrl+Spacebar to remove character formatting.

PAGE/SECTION SETUP OPTIONS

Most simple Word documents contain just one *section*. Usually, you'll add sections to a document when you want to use a different header or footer on certain pages of a document, or to alter the number of columns—perhaps to print a long list. You can also change sections to switch from one paper size or orientation to another—for example, to print a table in landscape orientation in the middle of a document.

Each section in a document has its own headers and footers, page size, margins, number of snaking newspaper-like columns, and paper source—a designated paper bin on your printer.

→ To properly format sections, **see** "Formatting Documents by Section," **p. 423**.

Sections are separated by section break marks, which are visible only in Normal view (see Figure 13.3).

Section formatting is stored in the section break mark; the formatting for the final section in a document is in the document's final paragraph mark. When you select a section break mark and copy, move, or delete it, the section formatting stored in the mark goes with it.

The safest way to add a new section to a document is to insert a new section break manually—choose Insert, Break and choose from the list of available section break types:

■ Next Page starts the next section on a new page.

■ Continuous enables the new section to follow the current one, without a page break.

- Even Page forces the next section to start on an even-numbered page.
- Odd Page forces the next section to start on an odd-numbered page.

Figure 13.3
To see section breaks, switch to Normal view.

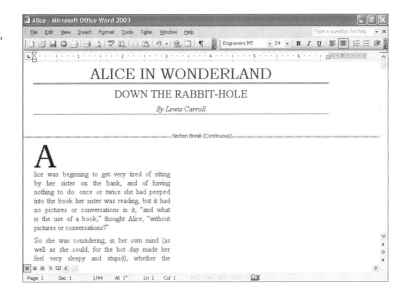

Word automatically inserts section break marks in a document if you choose File, Page Setup, click the Layout tab, and choose This Point Forward (see Figure 13.4). Word adds the section break as a consequence of changing the layout. Similarly, if you choose Format, Columns and choose This Point Forward from the Apply To drop-down list, Word automatically inserts a section break to mark the point where the number of columns changes.

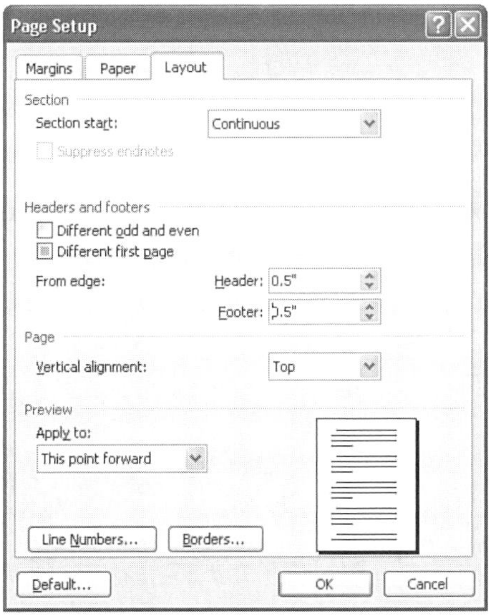

Figure 13.4
Choosing This Point Forward inserts a section break mark in the document, and then formats the newly created section.

13

TIP FROM

Ed & Woody

> Editing and formatting documents with multiple sections can be extremely confusing. If you inadvertently move or delete a section break mark, you can make a mess of the document's headers and footers, for example, and it's nearly impossible to recover except by starting over. When you work on documents with more than one section, we strongly recommend that you work only in Normal view, and that you insert section break marks manually by choosing Insert, Break.

The most common reason for using multiple sections in a document is to alter headers and footers. Each section in a document has its own headers and footers, although you can specify that a section "link to" the preceding section, and carry forward the preceding section's headers and footers.

→ To customize headers and footers, **see** "Creating and Editing Headers and Footers," **p. 431**.

Sections also enable you to organize snaking newspaper-like columns, whether they're for an entire document or for a list of items you want to appear in the middle of a document.

→ If you need to change the number of columns, **see** "Formatting a Document with Columns," **p. 430**.

FLOATING VERSUS INLINE OBJECTS

Like other Office applications, Word includes a *drawing layer*, which can contain pictures, text boxes, and other drawing objects. When you specify that text should wrap around a picture, for example, Word places the picture in the drawing layer.

→ To change text-wrapping options when you use floating objects in the drawing layer, **see** "Working with the Drawing Layer," **p. 114**.

NOTE

> When you place a picture inline in the document itself, Word treats it as though it were a single character. Thus, you can choose Format, Font and use the resulting dialog box to place an animated border—say, Marching Black Ants—around a picture.

Word also enables you to insert an object called a Drawing Canvas onto the drawing layer. The canvas constitutes a "sanctuary" for drawings: Everything you place on a canvas sticks together; objects on the canvas stay in the same relative location, and the canvas as a whole is not allowed to break across a page. To place a canvas on a page, choose Insert, Picture, New Drawing. A canvas also appears the first time you select an AutoShape on the Drawing toolbar. (To access this setting, choose Tools, Options and click the General tab on the Options dialog box. Then select the Automatically Create Drawing Canvas When Inserting AutoShapes check box.)

AUTOMATIC FORMATTING

Unless you make a special effort to turn them off, Word applies automatic formatting in a wide variety of situations, sometimes for no apparent reason. The effect is guaranteed to annoy anyone except a Microsoft marketing manager, for whom these automatic changes are a trademarked feature called IntelliSense. The most obvious paragraph AutoFormatting options are listed in Table 13.1.

TABLE 13.1   PARAGRAPH AUTOFORMATTING

If You Type Any of These...	Followed by This...	You'll Get...
* ---- > -> =>	A space or tab, and then text, and Enter	A paragraph formatted as bulleted
A symbol from a symbol font such as WingDings (Insert, Symbol)	Two or more spaces, or a tab, followed by text, and Enter	A paragraph formatted as bulleted, using the symbol as the bullet character
A picture (Insert, Picture) slightly larger than the height of the line	Two or more spaces, or a tab, and then text and Enter	A paragraph formatted as bulleted, using the picture as the bullet character
0 1 I i A a	A period, hyphen, closing parenthesis, or > sign, then a space or tab, and then text and Enter	A paragraph formatted as numbered, using standard, Roman, or alphabetic numbers
Three or more - _ = * ~ #	Enter	Applies a border to the paragraph above (or below)
Series of plus signs and hyphens, ending in a plus sign; for example, +----+----+	Enter	Creates a one-row table, with columns defined by the plus signs

As soon as Word applies AutoFormatting, you're presented with an action menu (indicated by a "lightning bolt" icon) that gives you quick access to various options for undoing what Word hath wrought (see Figure 13.5).

Figure 13.5
Word's action menu lets you undo AutoFormatting as soon as any piece of text has been changed.

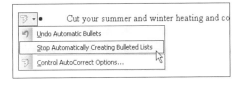

TIP FROM

To undo automatic paragraph formatting promptly, press Backspace or Ctrl+Z immediately after Word applies the AutoFormatting.

13

In the case of AutoFormatted numbered or bulleted lists, if you press Enter twice, the bulleting/numbering is removed from empty paragraphs. To turn on bullet/numbering formatting again, either start the list numbers over or go back to the end of the last bulleted or numbered paragraph where you left off, and press Enter. Auto bulleting and numbering can also be turned off by clicking on the appropriate icon on the Formatting toolbar.

The most obvious types of character AutoFormatting:

- If you type an ordinal, such as 1st, 2nd, 3rd, 4th, 30th, 175th, and so on, Word superscripts the characters: 1st, 2nd, 3rd, 4th, 30th, 175th.

- The specific fractions 1/4, 1/2, and 3/4 are changed into $\frac{1}{4}$, $\frac{1}{2}$, and $\frac{3}{4}$.

- Internet addresses such as `www.quepublishing.com` and `ed@example.com` are automatically converted into hyperlinks. The hyperlinks are "hot," so Ctrl+clicking a web address brings up your web browser and takes you to the site; Ctrl+clicking an email address invokes your default email program and creates a blank message addressed to the name in the mail link.

In all three of these cases, if you click the Undo button or press Ctrl+Z immediately after Word performs its AutoFormatting, the formatting returns to normal. In addition, automatically created hotlinks come with full drop-down instructions on various means of their removal.

→ To turn off this kind of character AutoFormatting, see "Disabling AutoFormat Settings," **p. 363**.

LOCKING A DOCUMENT'S FORMATTING

Few tasks are more frustrating than having to undo someone else's formatting follies. The syndrome is all too common: You carefully format a Word document, crafting styles and applying them consistently throughout a document. Then you send it to a friend for comments and discover, to your horror, that the returned document contains a mishmash of mangled styles and haphazard direct formatting.

In one of its most useful new features, Word 2003 offers a solution. You can lock formatting options in a document so that it can't be accidentally undone. This capability is a welcome add-on to the capability to restrict a document so that it can't be changed at all.

To turn on this option, choose Tools, Protect Document, or press Ctrl+F1 and choose Protect Document from the list of available task panes. As Figure 13.6 shows, this option involves a simple three-step process.

In Step 1, select the Limit Formatting to a Selection of Styles check box. Click the Settings link to open a dialog box that lets you choose which, if any styles are available. Choose one of the following three options from the Formatting Restrictions dialog box (see Figure 13.7):

- **All**—Allows anyone editing the document to choose from currently defined styles but eliminates their ability to add new styles or modify existing ones.

- **Recommended Minimum**—Selects standard Word styles. Use this option as a starting point and select additional styles from the list, if you wish.

- **None**—Clears all selections from the list of styles. With this option selected, users cannot modify any formatting.

Figure 13.6
Use this task pane to prevent other people from tampering with document formatting.

Figure 13.7
Styles you select in this dialog box can be applied to a protected document, but cannot be modified.

After setting formatting restrictions, you can restrict available editing options in Step 2. When your changes are complete, click the Yes, Start Enforcing Protection button in Step 3. You'll be offered the option to remove any existing direct formatting or any style-based formatting that does not match the restrictions you just specified. When you enable the Formatting Restrictions option, you eliminate the ability for anyone (including you!) to make any direct formatting changes. When this document is opened, the Protect Document task pane appears, warning the person viewing the document that formatting restrictions are in effect. Clicking a link in this task pane opens a customized version of the Styles and Formatting task pane, containing only those styles that are available for his use.

CHANGING PAPER SIZE AND ORIENTATION

The Paper tab on the Page Setup dialog box (see Figure 13.8) enables you to choose from several common paper sizes (Letter, Legal, or A4, for example). The Margins tab lets you pick whether you want the printing to run from left to right along the short edge of the paper (Portrait orientation) or the long edge (Landscape orientation).

Figure 13.8
Word gives you complete control over paper size and the printer bin.

As with margins, the settings for paper size and orientation apply to sections. If your document has only one section, the size and orientation you choose applies to the entire document.

By judiciously choosing the page size, you can use a few tricks for special effects.

TIP FROM

Ed & Woody

Word can print to within 1/8 inch of the bottom of the sheet on a Hewlett-Packard LaserJet printer—an important discovery if you're trying to print labels that extend to the bottom of the sheet. To fool Word into using the full space at the bottom of the page, open the Page Setup dialog box and, on the Paper tab, select a Paper Size of Legal 8 1/2×14 in. Then in the Paper Source box, pick Manual Feed. If you manually feed a regular letter-sized sheet, the print nearly touches the bottom of the sheet.

13

Other effects are possible as well. For example, when printing envelopes, adjust the page size to extend beyond the borders of the envelope, and you can frequently print all the way up to the edge, or even "bleed" over the edge. Experiment a bit. Remember that envelopes can often be fed either short-end first or long-end first.

ADJUSTING MARGINS

In the world of pen and paper, margins are lines that define white space at the left, right, top, and bottom of each page; if your penmanship is neat, you avoid crossing over those lines and thus preserve the pristine appearance of the page.

Word's margins appear similarly straightforward in concept, but some of these settings work in strange and deceptively complex ways—in particular, the interaction between paper size, margin, and header and footer areas gets quite complex. If you've been having trouble with margins, follow along closely.

To view and change the margin settings for a document with a single section, choose File, Page Setup, and click the Margins tab. Word responds with the Page Setup dialog box shown in Figure 13.9.

Figure 13.9
Margins appear to be simple, but they're not.

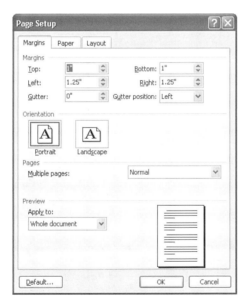

The Left margin setting works as you would expect: It specifies the distance from the left edge of the paper to the left margin of text. So, if you set a left margin of 1 inch, any left-aligned paragraph with an indent of 0 inches will start precisely 1 inch from the left edge of the paper. Similarly, the Right margin setting gives the distance from the right edge of the paper to the rightmost character in right-aligned or fully justified paragraphs, with 0 right indent.

→ For an explanation of how indents work, **see** "Indenting Paragraphs for Emphasis," **p. 389**.

If you're going to print on both sides of each sheet of paper (called *duplex printing*) and bind the sheets in a book or some kind of binder, you might want to allow extra room along the bound side—the left side on odd-numbered pages, and the right side on even-numbered pages. If you look at this book, you'll see how the additional white space, alternating left and right, improves the balance of the pages. To allow extra room, alternating left and right, choose Mirror Margins from the Multiple Pages drop-down list. Word adjusts the Page Setup dialog box—instead of Left and Right margins, you now see Inside and Outside margins, with the inside margin being the one closer to the binding (see Figure 13.10).

Figure 13.10
Use mirror margins when you create a bound document with printing on both sides of each sheet of paper.

Similarly, you can choose the 2 Pages per Sheet option from the Multiple Pages drop-down list to print two half-size pages on a sheet (if your original pages are in portrait mode, be sure to select Landscape orientation for the new layout, so that the pages maintain their original orientation).

Choose the Book Fold option to print in booklet sequence so the pages can be stapled down the middle. If you choose Book Fold for a document, the pages print in landscape orientation, two to a page. If you change your mind and choose Normal from the Multiple Pages drop-down list, Word leaves your document in landscape orientation. You'll have to change it back to portrait manually.

13

TIP FROM

Ed & Woody

> Although Word's capability to arrange multi-page documents in booklet form is somewhat useful, it requires a lot of careful preparation on your part, and if you miscount the number of pages your booklet can be unreadable. For maximum control over printed pages, we recommend a marvelous third-party program called FinePrint. It handles booklets, double-sided pages, and other fancy printing options from any Windows program, not just Word, and its ease of use is unparalleled. If you print a few hundred pages a month, we predict you'll save enough in paper alone to pay the software's modest cost in a few months. Check it out at `http://www.fineprint.com`.

A *gutter* is the additional amount of space left on each sheet for binding pages. If you're going to print on only one side of each sheet of paper, the Gutter distance is added to the left edge of each sheet. If you're going to print on both sides of each sheet of paper, and have chosen Mirror Margins in the Multiple Pages drop-down list, Word adjusts the gutter accordingly—adding it to the left margin on odd-numbered sheets and the right margin on even-numbered sheets.

NOTE

> Word also has a provision for gutters at the top of each sheet; just choose Top in the Gutter Position drop-down list. This is a rather odd setting because it won't be "mirrored" if you plan to print on the front and back of each sheet. (You might expect the gutter to appear at the top of odd-numbered pages and at the bottom of even-numbered pages, but it doesn't work that way.) You might use it for legal briefs that are bound at the top, or for single-sided pages that are destined for flip-top binders.

To control the amount of white space at the top of each sheet, you must juggle three different settings: the Top setting on the Margins tab in the Page Setup dialog box, the Header setting on the Layout tab, and the contents of the header itself. After exhaustive testing, we have determined that Word lays out the top of each document by using the following rules:

- Word takes the Header measurement in the Layout tab of the Page Setup dialog box and goes down that far from the top edge of the page, placing the top of the first line of the header (if a header exists) that distance from the top of the paper.

- Word then lays out the rest of the header, including pictures, before and after spacing, and the like. So, for example, if the last paragraph of the header has an After spacing of 24 points, Word reserves an additional 24 points of space at the bottom of the header.

- Finally, Word assembles the first line in the body of the document, placing it below the header in the location it would normally occupy if there were no distinction between header and body text. Word then measures the distance from the top of this first body line to the top of the paper. If that distance is less than the Top value on the Margins tab of the Page Setup dialog box, Word moves the line down so at least the Top amount of space is between the top of the first line and the top of the sheet.

13

Using the terminology commonly associated with paragraph distances, the Header distance is an "exactly" measurement; and the Top distance is an "at least" measurement.

Bottom margins work the same way, in reverse, with the bottom of the last line of the footer "exactly" the Footer distance from the bottom of the sheet, and the bottom of the last line of body text "at least" the Bottom distance.

Click the Default button at the bottom of the Page Setup dialog box, and Word offers to alter the template attached to the current document, giving it all the page-formatting options specified on the three tabs in the dialog box.

You can also change margins for individual sections within a document.

➔ For more information about your options when setting up a document, **see** "Page/Section Setup Options," **p. 374**.

CHANGING TEXT FORMATTING

When you're typing, each new character you type takes on the formatting of the character before, unless you do something to change it (such as pressing Ctrl+I to turn on italic formatting). The first character you type in a paragraph takes on the formatting of the paragraph mark.

To remove all manually applied character formatting—that is, to make it match the formatting of the current paragraph style—bring up the Styles and Formatting task pane, select the text, and click Clear Formatting. (Equivalently, you can press Ctrl+Spacebar.)

Select a character or characters, click Format, Font (or right-click and choose Font), and you will see Word's main font formatting options (see Figure 13.11). Most of the character (Word says "font") formatting you'll commonly encounter is applicable to all the Office applications.

➔ To learn more about character formatting, **see** "Changing Character Attributes," **p. 106**.

Word has a few formatting options that aren't quite so straightforward. On the Font tab:

- Superscript reduces the size of the characters about four points, and moves them above the baseline by about three points; Subscript also reduces about four points, and moves the characters below the baseline about two points.

- Small caps shows and prints lowercase letters as capitals, reduced about two points (so, for example, a lowercase letter in 11 point will print as a cap in 9 point). Some fonts have specific small caps characters, in which case those will print.

- Hidden text is displayed onscreen and/or printed only when you specifically request it (choose Tools, Options, and then either the View or Print menu).

Figure 13.11
Most of the Font dialog box's options match up with options in other Office applications.

Hidden text can be useful when you want to keep details handy but show them only occasionally. For example, teachers frequently type exams in Word and place the answers inside the document as hidden text. That way, they can print the exam normally for distribution to students, but then print a second copy with answers for graders.

The Hidden Paragraph Mark

Sometimes Word forces you to have a paragraph mark, whether you want one or not. For example, if you have a document that ends in a table, Word insists on placing a paragraph mark after the table. Sometimes those extra paragraph marks get in the way—in the worst case, Word might print an extra, blank page at the end of the document to accommodate the invisible paragraph mark.

If that should happen to you, remember that the paragraph mark is just like any other character. In particular, you can format it as Hidden. A Hidden paragraph mark won't print and won't show on the screen, and one at the end of a document won't force Word to print an extra, blank page.

13

Formatting options on the Character Spacing tab (see Figure 13.12) include the following:

- Scale applies a zoom effect to the selected text. This option is particularly useful when you're trying to squeeze a headline into a tight space and it just won't quite fit. Adjust the scale to 95% or so and see if the problem goes away.

- Spacing controls the distance between characters. In particular, it allows you to add a uniform amount of space after each of the selected characters (Expanded) or uniformly reduce the amount of space between characters (Condensed). Use this option to unobtrusively expand lines that need to be longer, or shorten lines that are too long.

Figure 13.12
Character spacing enables you to squish, elevate, lower, and push together fonts.

- Position controls how far above or below the baseline of text the selected characters will appear. This is similar to Superscripting and Subscripting, discussed earlier in this section, except it doesn't change the font size, and this box gives you fine control over the positioning.

- Kerning squishes matched pairs of letters together. The most dramatic example in English is AV. If AV is not kerned, there's a considerable amount of white space between the letters. If it is kerned, they're squished together so the leftmost part of the V appears to the left of the rightmost part of the A. Kerning is best used sparingly, with display type such as headlines. It doesn't have much effect at smaller point sizes and, for letters smaller than 10 points or so, it even inhibits your ability to read the type. If you want to kern letters, select them and tell Word the point size at which you want kerning to begin.

 Are you having trouble getting kerning to work? See the "Troubleshooting" section, "When You Can't Kern," at the end of this chapter.

Word has one more automatic character-formatting capability that some people love, and others hate: If you type an asterisk, followed by text, followed by another asterisk, the text between the asterisks is made bold. Similarly, if you type an underscore, text, underscore, the text between the underscores is made italic. This feature exists for compatibility with long-standing formatting conventions in text documents exchanged over the Internet. In Word 2003, this option is off by default. If you upgraded from an earlier version of Word, however, you might find that it is enabled. To turn this feature on or off, choose Tools, AutoCorrect Options. Click the AutoFormat As You Type tab and select or clear the *Bold* and _italic_ with Real Formatting box.

In fact, this option is a bit more complex than it first appears. When Word detects the asterisk-text-asterisk combination, it formats the text between the asterisks using the formatting defined by the Strong character style. (The text remains in Normal style—it isn't turned into Strong—but the formatting defined by the Strong style is applied to it.) The underscore combination is formatted with the formatting of the Emphasis character style.

TIP FROM

The Strong and Emphasis styles exist for compatibility with the corresponding HTML tags, <strong> and <em>. If you don't use Word to create web pages that use these tags, you can change the characteristics of the Strong and Emphasis styles; for example, you can change the style so that *text* makes the text red, or _text_ makes the text Arial 14 point.

If you select the *Bold* and _italic_ with Real Formatting box and then use asterisks to create bold text, the style Strong suddenly appears on the Styles and Formatting task pane. From that point, it's easy to change the style definition. This works similarly for Emphasis.

→ To learn more about working with styles, **see** "Saving Formats as Named Styles," **p. 457**.

CHANGING PARAGRAPH FORMATTING

Word enables you to change the indenting and spacing of paragraphs. Word also gives you control on a paragraph-by-paragraph basis over whether to keep entire paragraphs together or to force one paragraph to "stick to" the next, so they both appear on the same page.

The key concept: Paragraph formatting is stored in the paragraph mark. When you copy or move a paragraph mark, the formatting goes with it. When you delete a paragraph mark, any text following the paragraph mark becomes part of the current paragraph, and the new, combined paragraph takes on the formatting of the deleted paragraph mark.

TIP FROM

It's almost impossible to tell whether you've selected a paragraph mark unless you have paragraph marks showing on the screen. Some Word users (Woody, for instance) keep paragraph marks and tabs visible at all times. Others (like Ed) find these marks distracting and keep them hidden except when working with paragraph formats. To make these marks visible temporarily, click the Show/Hide ¶ button on the Standard toolbar. To make them visible at all times, choose Tools, Options, click the View tab, and select the Tab Characters and Paragraph Marks check boxes.

13

To restore default paragraph formatting—that is, the formatting mandated by the paragraph's style—select the paragraph and click the style name on the Styles and Formatting task pane.

ADJUSTING PARAGRAPH ALIGNMENT AND OUTLINE LEVEL

Word includes simple tools for aligning your paragraphs to the left, center, or right, or "justifying" paragraphs so they line up neatly along both left and right margins. If you click inside a paragraph, or select one or more paragraphs, and click Format, Paragraph (or right-click and select Paragraph), you'll see the Indents and Spacing tab of the Paragraph dialog box, as shown in Figure 13.13. Set the Alignment box to reflect the alignment you like.

Figure 13.13
Use the Paragraph dialog box to set a paragraph's relative outlining level, for both Outline View and Document Map. Body Text is the lowest level; Level 1 is the highest.

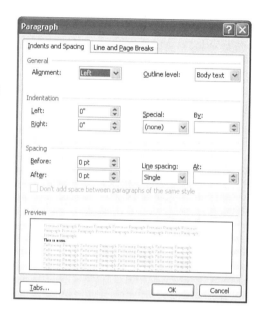

→ Word helps you navigate through large documents by using headings. To learn more, **see** "Outline View," **p. 328** and "Navigating with the Document Map," **p. 335**.

Equivalently, you can use the Align Left, Center, Align Right, or Justify buttons on the Formatting toolbar to set alignment.

TIP FROM

To justify the last line in a justified paragraph, click just before the paragraph mark and press Shift+Enter. Use this technique sparingly; the results can be unappealing if the last line is significantly shorter than the rest of the paragraph.

Word has another text-aligning technique called "Click and type," which allows you to click anywhere on the screen and start typing text. Although it should be called "Double-click and type," the paragraph alignment part of the concept is straightforward:

- If you double-click somewhere near the middle of an empty line (that is, halfway between the left and right margins), Word converts the line to Center alignment. You can tell the area is "hot" because Word puts centered lines below the usual I-beam pointer.

■ If you double-click somewhere near the right end of a line (that is, near the right margin), Word converts the line to right-justified. Again, you know the area is hot because Word changes the I-beam pointer so it has lines to the left. This feature makes it especially easy to put left- and right-justified text on a single line.

CAUTION

> Unless you're careful and watch the lines around the I-beam closely, Word might insert tabs and tab stops instead of changing the entire paragraph's alignment. Although the tab stops might fool a novice, paragraphs with tabs don't act like aligned paragraphs, as a few moments' work will demonstrate. This is yet another reason for showing paragraph marks and tab characters on the screen.

Normally, the outline level is set along with the paragraph style. In fact, if you select one of the built-in heading styles (Heading 1, Heading 2, and so on), the Outline Level option will be grayed out and unavailable. Adjust this level manually for a paragraph if you want that specific paragraph to be visible in Outline view or in the Document Map without affecting other paragraphs that use the same style.

INDENTING PARAGRAPHS FOR EMPHASIS

You might think of it as a margin change, or a way to set off quotes or other material for emphasis. In Word terminology, an "indent" moves the left edge of a paragraph to the right or the right edge of a paragraph to the left. The paragraph shown in Figure 13.14 has been indented on the left and the right.

Hanging indent

First-line indent

Right indent

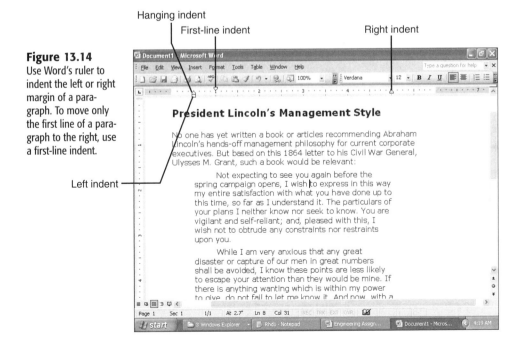

Figure 13.14
Use Word's ruler to indent the left or right margin of a paragraph. To move only the first line of a paragraph to the right, use a first-line indent.

Left indent

13

Left and right indents are often used to set off blocks of quoted text. Another common type of indenting, typically used in informal letters, moves only the first line of a paragraph; not surprisingly, this is called a *first-line indent*. Its counterpart—where the first line juts out to the left—is called a *hanging indent*. Used sparingly, this is a good way to emphasize the first few words of a paragraph. (It's also common for bulleted and numbered paragraphs, which are discussed later in this chapter.)

Although it takes a bit of practice, Word's ruler offers the fastest, most accurate way to control indents. Learn what each of the four widgets on the ruler does, and you're well on your way. The downward-pointing triangle at the left controls the first-line indent for the current paragraph; the upward-pointing triangle just below it controls the hanging indent. Click the rectangle (below both triangles) to adjust the left indent by moving both the first-line indent and the hanging indent simultaneously. The triangle at the right controls the right indent.

TIP FROM

EQ & Woody

As you drag these widgets, a faint dotted line appears on the document to show where the indented text will end up. And if you absolutely can't remember which widget is which, let your mouse hover over each one and read the ScreenTips.

You can also use the Paragraph dialog box to set indents. To adjust the left and/or right indent, use the Left and Right boxes of the Paragraph dialog box. To change the left indent only, in half-inch increments, you can also use the Increase Indent and Decrease Indent buttons on the Formatting toolbar. To create a first-line indent, select the paragraphs you want to indent, choose Format, Paragraph, and select First Line in the Special box.

When you press Tab at the beginning of a new paragraph, Word adds a tab character. However, when you position the insertion point at the beginning of an existing paragraph and press Tab, Word adds a first-line indent. If you actually wanted a tab instead, you can use the AutoCorrect action menu (the lightning-bolt icon just below the indented text) to cancel the change.

To create a hanging indent, select the paragraphs you want to indent, choose Format, Paragraph, and in the Special box select Hanging.

ADJUSTING LINE AND PARAGRAPH SPACING

Word has controls for three kinds of spacing:

- The amount of blank space before the first line of a paragraph
- The amount of blank space after the last line of a paragraph
- The amount of space internally, between the lines of a paragraph

The spacing between paragraphs adds up just as you would think: The "after" from the first paragraph is combined with the "before" of the second paragraph. Word ignores the "after" space if a paragraph will fit at the end of a page; but it includes the "before" space when a paragraph starts on a new page.

Internal line spacing isn't so simple:

- If you set Line Spacing to Exactly (say, Exactly 12 points), Word makes the distance between all the lines in the paragraph equal to whatever measurement you choose. If you put a large character on a line—say, an 18-point character—the top of the character might be cut off.

- If you set Line Spacing to Single, 1.5 lines, Double, or some other Multiple, Word calculates the distance between each line of the paragraph separately. It takes the tallest character (or graphic) on each line and adjusts to single, 1.5, or double spacing, as appropriate. If you have one 18-point character in the middle of a paragraph consisting of 12-point characters, the distance to the line containing the 18-point character will be 50% greater than the distance between the other lines.

> **NOTE**
>
> Normally, the height of "invisible" characters—spaces, paragraph marks, tabs, and the like—is not taken into account when calculating Single, 1.5, Double, or Multiple spacing. The exceptions: If the paragraph is empty, the calculation is based on the size of the default font for that paragraph; if it contains only invisible characters, the height of those characters counts.

- If you set Line Spacing to At Least (say, At Least 12 points), Word treats it the same as single spacing but sets spacing to a minimum of the height you specified, even if all characters in a given line are smaller than that size.

Generally, you'll want to use Exactly spacing if you use two or more fonts in a paragraph: By setting the internal spacing to Exactly a given figure (typically one or two points more than the largest font used in the paragraph), all the lines will be equally spaced, even if the different font normally calls for more white space.

CONTROLLING PAGE BREAKS

Each paragraph can also be formatted to control the way Word breaks pages. The Line and Page Breaks tab in the Paragraph dialog box (see Figure 13.15) holds these settings:

- Widow/Orphan Control, when selected, keeps Word from printing *widows* (the last line of a paragraph all by itself at the top of a new page) and *orphans* (the first line of a paragraph all by itself at the bottom of a page). It's on by default.

- Keep Lines Together ensures that all the lines of the paragraph appear on a single page.

- Keep with Next forces Word to put this paragraph and the next paragraph on the same page.

- Page Break Before makes Word start the paragraph on a new page.

13

Figure 13.15
You can control each paragraph, individually, to determine whether it flops onto a new page.

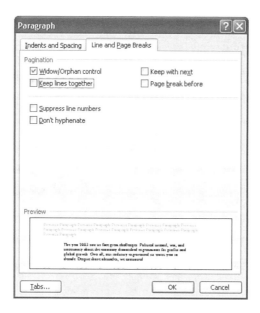

NOTE

Word can't always follow your instructions, of course: If you format all the paragraphs in a long document to Keep with Next, the pages have to break somewhere. Word makes a valiant effort to follow your instructions but, if they're impossible, lays out the pages as best it can.

In almost all cases, you'll want to enforce widow and orphan control. If you have a paragraph in a report whose visual impact depends on the whole paragraph appearing on one page (a mission statement, for example, or a quotation), you will probably want to keep the lines together. And headings should generally be formatted Keep with Next so they don't get separated from the text they head.

USING DROP CAPS FOR EMPHASIS

Drop caps add emphasis and distinction to a paragraph. Used sparingly, they make a good visual break at the beginning of major sections in a report. Word makes drop caps easy: Click once inside the paragraph that's to have its initial letter turned into a drop cap, and then choose Format, Drop Cap (see Figure 13.16).

The default height of the drop cap is three lines, which is about right for most paragraphs. If the drop cap appears to be crowding the text that follows it, increase the value in the Distance from Text box. You're not limited in your selection of fonts, either. Some "fancy" fonts are particularly well suited to drop-cap treatment. Take a look at the Algerian font, which is installed with Office, or Old English Text MT.

To remove a drop cap, click to the left or right of the drop cap and choose Format, Drop Cap; then select None from the Position box.

Figure 13.16
Drop caps work best in decorative fonts. Fonts that you wouldn't normally use in a business report make eye-catching drops.

The year turmoil, diminish enges. Political he economy d global growth. Over a s worst year in decade. Despite ed to gain market share a

If anything, the new economy, in a new centur rces can and will coexist. This is the hallmark of the global economy.

POSITIONING TEXT WITH TABS

To fully understand the way tabs work in Word, you first must realize that a "tab" consists of two parts. First, there's the tab character—which, like any other character, is placed in a document when you press the Tab key. Second, there's the tab stop, which is a location, or series of locations, on the page. In Word, you set up tab stops for each paragraph, not for each line; in other words, every line in a paragraph has identical tab stops.

TIP FROM

Ed & Woody

> It's nearly impossible to work with tabs unless you make them visible on the screen. To do so, click the Show/Hide ¶ button on the Standard toolbar; or choose Tools, Options and select the Tab Characters check box on the View tab of the Options dialog box.

When Word encounters a tab character in a document, it advances to the next defined *tab stop*. Tab stops come in four different varieties: left-aligned, right-aligned, centered, and decimal-aligned (which aligns numbers so the decimal point appears at the tab location). In addition, you can specify a *leader* character (pronounced "leeder")—a character that will appear, repeated, in the blank area leading up to the tab stop. You've no doubt seen them in tables of contents.

```
This is a leader of periods........<Tab393 stop>
```

When working with tabs, it's always much easier to plan on having just one line per paragraph, and one paragraph per line. You'll see how that makes a big difference in the example in the next section.

To set a tab stop, do the following:

1. Select the paragraph(s) where you want to set new tab stops.
2. Choose Format, Tabs. You'll see the Tabs dialog box as shown in Figure 13.17.
3. Type the location of the first tab stop in the Tab Stop Position box. (The "location" is the distance from the left margin of the document to the position of the tab stop, regardless of where the left edge of the paragraph might fall.)

13

Figure 13.17

NOTE

The default Normal paragraph style starts out with no explicitly defined tab stops. In this case, Word uses the Default Tab Stops setting of 0.5 inches, which treats the paragraph as if it contained a left-aligned tab stop every half-inch. As soon as you specify one or more tab stops, Word stops using the default tab stops preceding the ones you create. So, if you set a tab stop at 3 inches and another at 4 inches, pressing the Tab key once advances to 3 inches from the left margin; pressing Tab again goes to the right another inch. After it reaches the last user-defined tab stop, Word goes back to its default setting of left-aligned tab stops—in this case, at 4.5, 5.0, 5.5, 6.0, and so on, until you reach the right margin. You can change the Default Tab Stops setting to any value between 0.01 and 22 inches.

4. Choose the alignment and leader you want for the tab stop. Click the Set button and Word establishes a tab stop at the location you specify.

CAUTION

The Bar tab type in the Tabs dialog box creates a vertical rule—an up-and-down line—in the paragraph at the indicated tab location. This setting is a throwback to an early version of Word that didn't have borders. If you need a vertical line, use tables or borders, but avoid this setting.

13

The next section contains a detailed example, showing how leaders can be used to create a fill-in-the-blanks form.

The tab stops you create are stored in the paragraph mark along with other paragraph format settings; copy or move a paragraph mark, and the tab stops go with it. If the insertion point is in a normal paragraph with custom tab stops and you press Enter, the new paragraph inherits the same tab stops. Many Word users—even advanced Word users—find that confusing. To restore a paragraph to the default (left-aligned tab stops every half inch), select the paragraph, bring up the Styles and Formatting task pane, and click the original style's name.

USING THE RULER TO SET TAB STOPS

Although the Tabs dialog box (refer to Figure 13.17) gives you much greater control over the location and characteristics of tab stops, many people use the Word ruler to set and move tab stops. To set a left-aligned tab stop at 2 inches using the ruler, you might try this approach:

1. Select the paragraphs that need tab stops. (You'll be able to see the results of setting tab stops immediately if you've already put the tab characters in the paragraphs.)

2. Bring up the ruler at the top of the screen by choosing View, Ruler. (If you want the ruler invisible most of the time, just "hover" your mouse directly below the Formatting toolbar.)

3. The icon on the far left of the horizontal ruler tells you what kind of tab is available: left-, center-, right-, or decimal-aligned. Click the icon to cycle through each of these tab types until you get the one you need.

4. Click the ruler where you want the new tab to appear. All default tabs to the left of the new tab are destroyed in the process. Click and drag the tab icon left or right to position it precisely where you want it. To get rid of a tab, click it and drag it off the ruler.

It's impossible to set the leader character directly from the ruler. For that task, you need to use the Tabs dialog box. Skip the menus, though; if the ruler is visible, just double-click on any tab stop to open the Tabs dialog box and fine-tune the settings.

USING TABS TO CREATE A USER-INPUT FORM

Suppose you want to create a fill-in-the-blanks form, with room for respondents to write (or type) information such as their name and address.

If you've used Word for any time at all, you have probably tried to create just such a form, most likely by typing underscore (_) characters and trying to line up columns that never look right. By far the easiest way to create such a form is by using tabs, with the underscore leader. Here's how:

1. Type the text, including tab characters, which will comprise the final form. In this case:

    `Last Name <tab> First Name <tab>`

    `Address <tab>`

    `City <tab> State <tab> Zip <tab>`

2. Position the insertion point inside the first paragraph, and choose Format, Tabs. Set two tab stops—a left-aligned tab at 3 inches, with underscore leader (Type 4); and a right-aligned tab at 6 inches with underscore leader.

13

TIP FROM

EQ & Woody

> The default Word page layout—8.5-inch paper width, with 1.25-inch margins left and right—places the right margin at 6 inches, using the tab-measurement method.

3. Position the insertion point inside the second paragraph, and set a right-aligned tab at 6 inches, with underscore leader.

4. Position the insertion point in the third paragraph and set three tabs: left-aligned at 3 inches, left-aligned at 4.5 inches, and right-aligned at 6 inches, all with underscore leader.

5. If you want to fine-tune individual lines, click inside the line and then drag tab stop icons on the ruler to whatever position you like.

Word also enables you to double-click a "hot" spot on a line and insert a tab stop at the double-click location. This variant of click and type is notoriously inaccurate and much harder to use than either the Tabs dialog box or the ruler.

→ To learn more about Click and Type, **see** "Adjusting Paragraph Alignment and Outline Level," **p. 388**.

FORMATTING SIMPLE LISTS WITH BULLETS AND NUMBERS

By far, the simplest way to create a bulleted or numbered list is to use one of the many shortcuts for starting and continuing such lists. For example, if you type a number or letter, followed by a period, a space, and then text, Word begins a numbered list, provided that you haven't disabled the options on the AutoFormat As You Type tab in the AutoCorrect dialog box. Dozens of combinations are available.

→ To have Word handle some of the formatting chores for you, **see** "Automatic Formatting," **p. 376**.

Numbering and bulleting are paragraph properties. As such, they're stored in the paragraph mark and travel along with other paragraph settings if the paragraph mark is copied or moved. Position the insertion point inside a numbered or bulleted paragraph and press Enter, and the bulleting or numbering is "inherited" by the new paragraph.

NOTE

> AutoNumbered and AutoBulleted lists are slightly different because Word lets you bail out of bulleting or numbering by pressing Enter twice in succession. In other words, if the insertion point is inside a bulleted or numbered paragraph, and the paragraph is empty, when you press Enter, Word removes the bulleting and formatting from both the old and new paragraphs.

13

Bullets and numbers maintained by Word aren't "real" characters. You can't select them, much less delete or change them. Instead, they are generated automatically by Word, as a consequence of their paragraph formatting. That's a big help when you're working on a document and want the freedom to add new items to a list or reorder existing items without having to worry about renumbering or manually applying bullet characters.

Many advanced Word users disable Word's AutoBulleting and AutoNumbering feature and apply bullets or numbers to lists by using simple toolbar buttons or—in more complex situations—using the dialog box.

→ AutoFormat driving you crazy? The good news is that you can disable it. **See** "Disabling AutoFormat Settings," **p. 363**.

You can always create a simple bulleted or numbered list by selecting the paragraphs you want to bullet or number, and then clicking the Bullets icon or Numbering icon on the Formatting toolbar.

To take advantage of Word's extensive bulleting and numbering options, select the paragraphs you want to bullet or number and then choose Format, Bullets and Numbering (or right-click and choose Bullets and Numbering). You'll see the Bullets and Numbering dialog box shown in Figure 13.18.

Figure 13.18
From simple bullets to complex outline-style numbering schemes, Word has a solid (but far from complete) array of options.

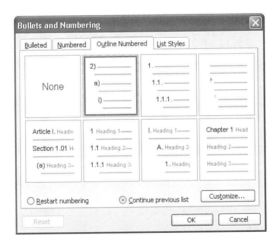

Select from the prebuilt bullet or numbering schemes, or click the Customize button to establish your own.

Consecutive paragraphs need not be numbered consecutively. For example, you could have paragraphs numbered 1, 2, and 3, then two paragraphs with no numbering, and pick back up at 4, 5, and so on. To stop the numbering sequence, select the paragraph(s) you don't want to have numbered, choose Format, Bullets and Numbering and, on the Numbered or Outline Numbered tab, click the None box in the upper-left corner. To continue numbering where you last left off, select the first paragraph after the break, and on the Numbered or Outline Numbered tab, click the Continue Previous List button. You can get the same effect by right-clicking on a paragraph and choosing Restart Numbering or Continue Numbering.

TIP FROM

Ed & Woody

You can associate numbering with a specific paragraph style, making Word put a sequential number in front of each paragraph formatted with that style. If your chapter headings are formatted with a custom ChapterTitle style, for example, associating numbering with the ChapterTitle style automatically generates chapter numbers. To make the association, choose Format, Bullets and Numbering, click the Outline Numbered tab, click a numbering style, and then click Customize, More. In the Link Level to Style box, choose the ChapterTitle style.

Because bulleting and numbering is a paragraph property, if you place the insertion point inside a bulleted or numbered paragraph and press Enter, the newly created paragraph "inherits" the bulleting or numbering.

It also means that you can move, drag, or rearrange numbered paragraphs at will, and Word renumbers them, on-the-fly, as appropriate.

FORMATTING ALL OR PART OF A DOCUMENT AUTOMATICALLY

If you feel intimidated by all of Word's formatting options, you can leave your document's destiny in the hands of Word's occasionally useful, but frequently awful, batch AutoFormat capability.

When you run it, AutoFormat scans your document, identifies the "AutoFormat As You Type" kinds of changes—changing straight quotes to curly ones, creating headings, AutoNumbering and AutoBulleting lists, and the like—and adds some general formatting changes (changing paragraphs that use the Normal paragraph style to Body Text, for instance). You can simply let the process happen, or you can tell Word you want to review each suggested change and decide whether to apply it or ignore it.

→ To learn more about the perils and pitfalls of AutoFormatting, **see** "Automatic Formatting," **p. 376**.

Because you have the option to review the changes onscreen and vote yea or nay on each, you really have nothing to lose by running AutoFormat. An AutoFormat run can be useful if you've just opened a plain-text document and need to format it quickly, or if you're having trouble getting the hang of Word's formatting capabilities. If you select a portion of a document, AutoFormat works only on your selection.

Word's built-in AutoFormat choices include settings designed for cleaning up email messages. Using AutoFormat removes extra carriage returns and emphasize marked reply text.

It's also an ideal way to read mailing lists sent in digest format, where many consecutive messages appear in a single message body. After using AutoFormat on an email message that contains many replies or embedded messages, you can turn on the Document Map to jump through the message quickly and easily.

TIP FROM

Using AutoFormat with email messages requires jumping through a few hoops. Within Outlook, the option is available only when you use Word as your email editor, and only when forwarding or replying to a message in HTML format. To take advantage of AutoFormat capabilities when reading a long message, you need to first save the message (in HTML or Text Only format), and then open the saved file in Word.

Before using AutoFormat, save a copy of the file. If anything goes wrong, you can restore your backup copy and be right back where you started. To run AutoFormat, follow these steps:

1. To format the entire document, make sure no text is selected. To format a portion of the document, select that portion first.

2. Choose Format, AutoFormat. If you want to review changes, select the AutoFormat and Review Each Change option.

3. Tell Word whether you're AutoFormatting a plain document, a letter, or an email message. Slightly different rules are applied in each case.

4. To see which AutoFormat rules will be applied to your document, click the Options button. If necessary, select or clear any options.

5. Click OK to perform the AutoFormat. If you chose the option to review changes, you can accept or reject any or all of them (see Figure 13.19).

Figure 13.19

Out of the box, AutoFormat can cause as many formatting headaches as it cures. However, you can tame the AutoFormat beast and actually make it useful by following these tips:

- Try to "clean up" documents before using AutoFormat. Headings should be separated by line spaces, if possible, so that they aren't mistaken for short paragraphs.

- If you have any custom styles you want to use, apply those first. The default AutoFormat settings preserve manually applied styles.

- AutoFormat automatically applies heading styles, list styles, and paragraph styles (using the Body Text style for anything that isn't a heading or a list, for instance). To suppress any of these changes, click the Options button and clear the appropriate check box under the Apply section.

■ If you don't like the results, press Ctrl+Z to undo them immediately and then try again using different options. Word treats AutoFormat as a single, undoable action.

When you review AutoFormat changes, Word offers you access to the Style Gallery, which allows wholesale (and frequently disastrous) substitution of styles. Unless you know what you're doing, we strongly recommend that you avoid the Style Gallery. Using one of Word's canned templates (Professional Fax, for instance) on an AutoFormatted document usually doesn't produce acceptable results. The Style Gallery is most useful if you have created a library of standard templates based on the default Word templates, using different fonts and format settings for identically named styles. In that case, you can safely experiment with the Style Gallery to adjust the look of a document to match your styles. Most Word users, even advanced users, don't take this much care with templates, of course, making the Style Gallery a hindrance rather than a help.

TROUBLESHOOTING

WHEN YOU CAN'T KERN

When I select a block of text and use the Font dialog box to set kerning options, nothing seems to happen.

Kerning must be defined in the font itself—the people who design the font have to set up pairs for kerning and tell Windows how much space can be squeezed out between each pair. Most common text fonts have defined kerning pairs; many fonts do not.

If you tell Word to kern selected text, and you can't see any effect on obvious kerning pairs such as AV, first check to make sure the type size is equal to or larger than the "points" setting on the Character Spacing tab. If it is, chances are good that the font you're using doesn't support kerning.

EXTRA CREDIT: STRAIGHT QUOTES OR CURLY QUOTES?

One of the most useful AutoFormat As You Type options is the default setting that changes straight quotation marks to curly quotes (referred to as *smart quotes* in Word) as you type.

The effect gives printed documents a more professional look, as the figure here shows.

"That's incredible!"

"That's incredible!"

The straight quotes at the top are exactly what you'd see if you used an old-fashioned typewriter. The curly quotes are typographic characters used for centuries by professional printers and publishers.

If your goal is to produce a printed page, you'll want to use the default option to automatically replace straight quotes with curly quotes. But there are a few cases where straight quotes are more appropriate. If you need to save a Word document as a plain text file, for example, you'll have better results with straight quotes. Also, some email programs and desktop publishing programs can't process curly quotes properly.

When you know that the ultimate destination of your document is more suited to straight quotes, disable this feature by choosing Tools, AutoCorrect Options. On the AutoFormat As You Type tab, clear the Straight Quotes with Smart Quotes check box under the Replace As You Type heading. Select this check box to reenable the setting.

What do you do if you've created (or inherited) a document whose contents need to be converted from straight to curly quotes, or vice versa? Simple. First, make sure that the straight quotes setting on the AutoCorrect Options dialog box matches the result you want to achieve in your final document. Then press Ctrl+H, enter a single quote character in both the Find What and Replace With boxes, and click Replace All. Repeat this process with double quotation marks.

CHAPTER 14

TABLES, SECTIONS, AND OTHER ADVANCED FORMATTING OPTIONS

In this chapter

GOING BEYOND BASIC FORMATTING

Word isn't a full-fledged desktop publishing program, but that doesn't mean you're limited to dull paragraphs of text with an occasional heading and graphic sprinkled in to relieve the tedium.

As we explain in this chapter, you have a rich set of options available when you want to create professionally designed pieces using Word. For starters, you can use tables to arrange words and numbers in neat rows and columns. You probably didn't know, however, that you can also use tables to perform some sophisticated page layout tricks. We show you how to coax more out of plain old tables than you ever dreamed possible.

Want to add some zing to a flyer or brochure? Use lines, borders, shading, and background graphics to add an extra dimension to the page. You can even divide text into newspaper-style columns to create a quick, easy-to-read newsletter.

Word also has a collection of features that are tailor-made for working with longer documents. If you're working on an epic research paper, you can chop the project into sections, add headers and footers to make navigation easier, create a table of contents and index by tagging text, and even add cross-references that update themselves automatically.

USING TABLES TO ORGANIZE INFORMATION

You might take one look at the neat row-and-column arrangement of Word tables and dismiss them out of hand as a pale imitation of Excel worksheets. Big mistake.

In fact, Word tables are at their weakest when pressed into service as repositories for rows and columns of numbers. Word has a paltry selection of tools for working with numbers. If you want to do any sort of arithmetic in a Word document—anything more complex than an occasional sum or product on a small handful of data—you're far better off embedding or linking an Excel range inside your Word document, even if you have to learn Excel to do it.

So, what are Word tables good for? Obviously, they're tailor-made for organizing and presenting price lists, feature comparisons, schedules, and other orderly arrangements of text. But Word tables are also excellent page layout tools that can help you precisely place words, numbers, and pictures on a page. In Figure 14.1, it might be obvious to you that we used a table to create the list of school holidays—after all, each cell has a line around it and the data is classically tabular. But it might not be so obvious that the Word template for this fax uses a table to organize the header. (Choose Show Gridlines from the Table menu to reveal the non-printing gridlines around the table.)

You should consider using tables when you need to perform any of the following tasks:

- Line up paragraph headings on the left with text on the right. This type of formatting is especially useful if you're preparing a résumé or a curriculum vitae.
- Draw intersecting horizontal and vertical lines. Using tables is generally much simpler than trying to add borders around words or paragraphs.

- Create fill-in-the-blanks printed forms.
- Place text in a fixed location on a page. Anytime you're thinking about using tab stops to arrange text or graphics on a page, consider using tables (without gridlines) instead. In general, tables are faster and easier to set up, and much simpler to maintain.

In Word 2003, you can draw one table inside another—a very handy trick if you use tables for page layouts. Each "nested table" appears, in its entirety, within a single cell in the larger outer table.

Figure 14.1
A table, without the gridlines, makes it easy to create and maintain the "To/From/Re/Date" part of this fax.

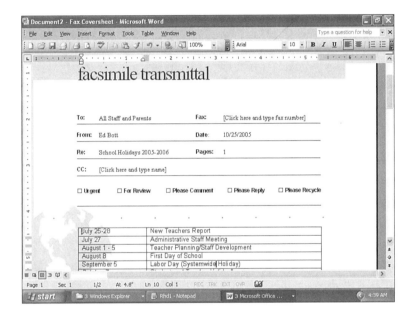

ADDING A TABLE TO A DOCUMENT

When creating a new table, you have two basic choices: Either Word can draw the table for you, or you can draw it yourself. When Word draws the table for you, you are subject to the following restrictions:

- You specify the number of columns (to a maximum of 63) and rows (up to 32,767).
- You define how the table fits on the page, using one of three options: the table can fill the width of the page; or each column can have the same width; or each column can automatically expand to accommodate the contents of the widest cell.
- Rows start out one line tall but automatically get taller, if necessary, to hold text or graphics.

If you can live with those restrictions, Word will make your table quickly. If you want more control over the initial table design—if you want the table to occupy only part of the page width, for example, or if you have complex cell patterns—you can draw your table freehand.

14

CREATING QUICK TABLES

To have Word draw a table for you, follow these steps:

1. Click in an empty paragraph where you want the upper-left cell of the new table to be located.

2. Choose Table, Insert, Table. The Insert Table dialog box appears (see Figure 14.2).

Figure 14.2

3. In the Table Size section, choose the number of columns and rows. (If you're not sure how many columns or rows you'll need, don't worry; you can easily increase either number later.)

4. In the AutoFit Behavior section, tell Word how to determine the width of the table and its columns.

5. By default, every new table uses the generic Table Grid style. Click the AutoFormat button to choose from dozens of prefab formats for this table. Click OK and Word creates the table (see Figure 14.3).

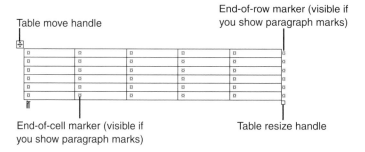

Figure 14.3
Quick, cookie-cutter tables are easy with the Insert Table dialog box.

Table move handle

End-of-row marker (visible if you show paragraph marks)

End-of-cell marker (visible if you show paragraph marks)

Table resize handle

14

If you routinely create tables of a certain size, shape, and format, you can save those settings for reuse. After defining your preferred table settings in the Insert Table dialog box—including the AutoFormat option—click the Remember Dimensions for New Tables check box. From now on, you can use the Insert Table button on the Standard toolbar to add a table with those settings in a single click.

Although you can use Word's Table menu and the right-click context-sensitive menu to manipulate tables and cells, you'll find that most common table-editing tasks are much easier if you use the Tables and Borders toolbar. To do so, click the Tables and Borders button on the Standard toolbar.

DRAWING A COMPLEX TABLE

Unless you specifically want a table that conforms to Word's Insert Table restrictions, drawing one by hand is the best option. To do so:

1. Choose Table, Draw Table, or click the Draw Table button on the Tables and Borders toolbar. The mouse pointer turns into a pencil.

2. Click where you want the upper-left corner of the table to appear. (You can even click inside a table cell, to create a *nested table* within that cell. For details, see "Nesting Tables Within Tables," later in this chapter.)

3. Drag the pencil down and to the right, to the lower-right corner of the new table. Word creates a table with a single, large cell.

4. Using the pencil, click an existing table line and drag to the opposite edge to form a row, column, or individual cell. You can even click a cell corner and drag to the opposite corner to create a diagonal line.

If you don't like the position or size of a line you've drawn, use the Erase button on the Tools and Borders toolbar to remove it. Position the "eraser" mouse pointer on the line you want to erase and click. To restore your usual mouse pointer, press Esc or click the Erase button again.

Don't worry about being neat when drawing rows and columns within a table. Just concentrate on getting the number of rows and columns right. You can use Automatically Equalize Row Spacing and move column borders later.

14

CONVERTING TEXT TO A TABLE

As you type text into a Word document, you might decide that what you've been typing would work better as a table. You might be tempted at that point to create a new table and then cut and paste the text into it—before you go through that labor-intensive exercise, consider doing the job in a few clicks with Word's built-in text-to-table converter.

For the conversion to work properly, your text must include a *delimiter* (paragraph mark, tab, comma, or some other character) so that Word can figure out what data goes in which cell. The number of delimiters must be consistent, too, or Word will be unable to figure out how many columns to use in each row. The lines shown in Figure 14.4, which include a single tab character delimiting cells, will work fine.

Figure 14.4
If you're careful about using delimiting characters (such as the tab here), Word will readily convert text to a table.

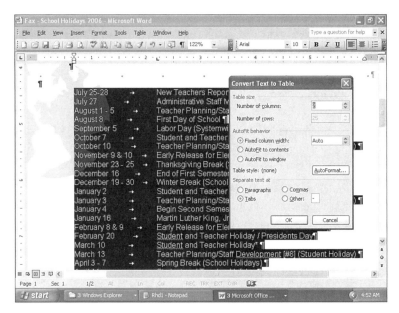

TIP FROM

By far the simplest and most reliable way to delimit text for easy conversion to a table is with tabs separating the values that will go in each column, and paragraph marks at the end of each row. Although you can use commas, hyphens, or just about any other character, you're more likely to run into problems when these characters appear in the data and throw off the conversion.

To convert properly delimited text to a table, follow these steps:

1. Select the text you want to convert.
2. Choose Table, Convert, Text to Table. Word presents the Convert Text to Table dialog box shown previously in Figure 14.4.
3. Choose the delimiter in the Separate Text At section at the bottom of the dialog box. If the number of rows and columns doesn't match your expectations, take another careful look at your selected text. Chances are you picked up a stray line along the way.
4. Click the AutoFormat button if you want to use something other than the default Table Grid. When everything is to your liking, click OK.

If you can't make the last row of your table match the last row of your data, see "Check for Stray Delimiters" in the "Troubleshooting" section at the end of this chapter.

TIP FROM

Ed & Woody

> One of the hardest characters to find is a Tab character that's "squished" between two pieces of text—or, worse, two or more tab characters in succession that aren't entirely visible because text surrounds them. You can select the text and use Find to search for single or double tabs—look for ^t or ^t^t.

You can convert a table back to text using the Table, Convert, Table to Text menu. As part of the conversion, you can choose which character you want to use as a delimiter.

NESTING TABLES WITHIN TABLES

Word lets you create tables within tables. These *nested tables* can be handy if you're using tables to perform advanced formatting tricks, such as creating side-by-side headings in a résumé) in which you need to put a table inside one of the cells.

NOTE

> You can move a table anywhere on a page by clicking and dragging the table move handle (at the upper-left corner of the table). To put two tables side by side, for example, you don't need to create a table inside a table. Just drag the two tables into position.

To create a table within a table, click in the desired cell and use the menu or freehand drawing tool as explained earlier in this section.

For an example of nested tables and their application in a common business document, see the "Extra Credit" section at the end of this chapter.

WORKING WITH TABLES

Table cells behave much like Word paragraphs: Text within a cell can be formatted, centered, indented and spaced, bulleted and numbered, with borders and shading, and each cell can have its own tab stop settings. All cell formatting is stored in the end-of-cell marker, which you can see only when paragraph marks are showing (click the Show/Hide ¶ button on the Standard toolbar, or choose Tools, Options, and select the Paragraph Marks check box on the View tab).

SELECTING CELLS, ROWS, AND COLUMNS

Select data within a cell just as you select data in a paragraph; if you want to transfer cell formatting, make sure you pick up the end-of-cell marker. Alternatively, you can select everything in a cell (including the end-of-cell marker) by letting the mouse pointer hover

14

over the left side of the cell. When it turns into a thick arrow pointing up and to the right, click to select the whole cell. Or you can click inside the cell and choose Table, Select, Cell.

Other selection techniques include the following:

- To select an entire row, including the end-of-row marker, move the mouse pointer to the left of the row. When it turns into the shape of a hollow arrow pointing to the upper right, click. Equivalently, click once inside the row and choose Table, Select, Row.

- To select an entire column, let the mouse pointer hover near the top of the column. When it turns into a black solid arrow pointing down, click. Or you can choose Table, Select, Column.

- To select the whole table, let the mouse pointer hover over the table move handle at the upper-left edge of the table until the pointer turns into a four-headed arrow, and then click to select the table. Alternatively, choose Table, Select, Table.

ENTERING AND EDITING DATA

You can type in a table cell precisely the same way you would type in a paragraph. If you press Enter, Word creates a new paragraph for you—in the same cell. Single cells can contain text, graphics, linked and embedded items—basically anything you can put in a document.

To move from one cell to the next, press Tab. To move back one cell, press Shift+Tab. To move backward or forward one character at a time, jumping from cell to cell at the beginning and end of each cell's contents, use the left- and right-arrow keys. To move up or down one cell, press the up- or down-arrow keys.

TIP FROM

Ed & Woody

> To enter the Tab character in a table cell, press Ctrl+Tab.

If the insertion point is in the last cell in a table, pressing Tab creates a new row, formatted the same as the current row, and moves the insertion point to the first cell in that row.

Many of the special navigation key combinations described in Chapter 4, "Entering, Editing, and Formatting Text," work inside tables. For example, Shift+Right Arrow selects text one character at a time, Ctrl+Shift+Right Arrow picks up a word at a time, and so on.

→ To learn about Word's extensive text-selection techniques, **see** "Selecting Text," **p. 92**.

14

TIP FROM

> You can add text above a table at the top of a document. With the insertion point in the first row of the table, press Ctrl+Shift+Enter to insert a paragraph above the table, and then move the insertion point into that new paragraph. Use this same shortcut to split a table in two; position the insertion point in the row you want to use as the first row of the new table and then press Ctrl+Shift+Enter.

MOVING AND COPYING PARTS OF A TABLE

All the usual copy, cut, and paste routines you're accustomed to in Word work equally well within tables and cells. If you've placed cells on the Clipboard, Word responds by adding new entries in the Edit menu: Paste Cells, Paste Columns, Paste Rows, and Paste as Nested Table.

Paste Cells replaces the existing cells with the contents of the copied cells; the table itself is expanded only if there are too many copied rows or columns to fit in the existing table. If you choose Paste Columns, Rows, or Paste as Nested Table, Word creates a new column, row, or table as needed and fills it with the contents of the Clipboard. If you click inside a cell, and then insert directly from the Clipboard task pane, Word assumes you want to insert the columns, rows, or table on the Clipboard as a nested table, within the current cell.

CAUTION

> When you paste cells, Word overwrites the contents of the current cells—without warning, and without giving you an opportunity to change your mind. If that happens, click the Undo button (or press Ctrl+Z or choose Edit, Undo), and try again.

You can click and drag cells, columns, and rows, just as you do elsewhere in Word—with one exception. If you're going to move an entire row, you must select the end-of-row marker.

If you copy or move a cell, including the end-of-cell marker, to an area outside a table, Word creates a new table on the spot. The new table consists of a single cell, whose contents match those of the cell being copied or moved.

 If you are frustrated with cell contents or the row markers disappearing, see "Disappearing Cell Contents and Row Markers" in the "Troubleshooting" section at the end of this chapter.

CHANGING COLUMN WIDTHS AND ROW HEIGHTS

To adjust a column's width, you have four choices:

- **Eyeball it**—Move your mouse pointer so it's near a vertical line in the table. When the pointer changes into a double-headed arrow, click and drag the line. If you move left, the column to the left gets narrower and the column to the right gets wider. If you move right, the column to the right gets narrower and the column to the left gets wider.

14

TIP FROM

If you want to change the width of the column only on the left (shrinking or expanding the size of the entire table as you go), hold down the Shift key as you drag.

■ **Measure it**—Right-click inside the column you want to change, and then choose Table Properties from the shortcut menu. In the Table Properties dialog box, click the Column tab (see Figure 14.5). From that point, you can precisely specify the width of each column.

Figure 14.5
To get precise column measurements, nothing beats the Table Properties dialog box.

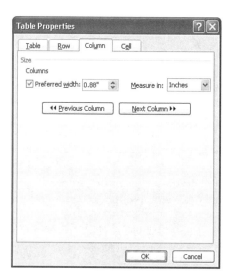

■ **Fit the contents**—If you want the column width to grow or shrink, depending on the width of the contents, right-click in the row, and then choose AutoFit, AutoFit to Contents from the shortcut menu.

TIP FROM

To AutoFit a single column, select the entire column and then double-click on its right border.

■ **Fit the margins**—You can also have Word automatically calculate how wide a specific column must be to have the table extend all the way from the left to the right margin. To do so, right-click inside the column, and then choose AutoFit, AutoFit to Window from the shortcut menu.

If you need to restore some uniformity to the table, you can always make all the columns the same width by choosing Table, AutoFit, Distribute Columns Evenly.

TIP FROM

Yes, you can use the ruler to adjust column widths, as you'll discover with some experimentation (try dragging each little widget left and right, and then try the same operation while holding down the Shift, Ctrl, or Alt keys, for instance). You can also use the vertical ruler to rejigger row heights, and if you double-click on any of the markers that denote breaks between columns you'll open the Table Properties dialog box. In our experience, though, trying to figure out and remember the exact function of each little slider and triangle is more trouble than it's worth. It's much easier to manipulate a table directly.

By default, rows expand and contract to hold the tallest item in the row. Row height can be adjusted in much the same way as column widths: Eyeball it with a click and drag; measure it in the Table Properties dialog box (click the Row tab, select the Specify Height check box, enter a height in inches, and select "At least" or "Exactly"); or make each row height the same to fill up the space occupied by the table (choose Table, AutoFit, Distribute Rows Evenly).

TIP FROM

If you're creating a Word form for data entry, using "Exactly" for the row height prevents the cell from expanding if the user types in too much text. That prevents entries from pushing information from one page onto the next.

To change the width of individual cells, select the entire cell (including the end-of-cell marker), and then click and drag. As long as you've selected an entire cell (or group of cells), only those cells are resized.

 If you can't see all the contents of a table cell, see "Properly Setting the Row Height for Word Tables" in the "Troubleshooting" section at the end of this chapter.

ADDING AND DELETING ROWS AND COLUMNS

Sometimes, you want to keep your table formatting intact, but replace existing data in the table. For example, if you create a monthly status report showing the progress of your school's fund-raising efforts, you can copy the table from last month's report into a new document, and then delete the old data and replace it with this month's numbers. Here are a few tricks you need to know:

- If you select a cell and press Delete, the cell contents are deleted. If you include the end-of-cell marker and press Delete, the end-of-cell marker *with its formatting* stays intact.

- If you select a column or row and press Delete, the contents of all the cells in the column or row are deleted—but the column or row itself stays and, again, the end-of-cell markers and their formatting remain. It doesn't matter whether you select the end-of-row marker or not.

- If you select an entire table and press Delete, the contents of all the cells in the table are deleted, but the table skeleton remains, formatting intact.

14

- If you select an entire table plus one or more characters after the table (including, for example, a paragraph mark) and press Delete, the entire table and selected character(s) are deleted completely. No skeleton remains.

To truly delete a cell, row, column, or table, click in the cell, row, column, or table that you want to delete, and choose Table, Delete, and then select either Cells, Rows, Columns, or Table.

NOTE

All of these options are also available from right-click shortcut menus and from buttons on the Tables and Borders toolbar.

To insert a cell, row, or column (or a table, for that matter), click in the cell, row, or column to the left, right, above, or below the place you want to put the new cell, row, or column, and then choose Table, Insert, and the appropriate entry.

ROTATING TEXT

It's easy to rotate text in a table by 90 degrees, clockwise or counterclockwise. To do so, select the cell(s) you want to rotate, and then choose Format, Text Direction. The Text Direction–Table Cell dialog box enables you to choose orientation (see Figure 14.6).

Figure 14.6
As long as you want your text aimed straight up or straight down, Word can accommodate.

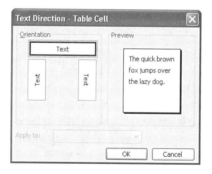

If you want table headings at any other angle than 90 degrees, consider embedding or linking an Excel range. It's much easier to rotate text to any desired angle in an Excel worksheet.

MERGING AND SPLITTING CELLS AND TABLES

If you insert a table into a cell, you have two tables, one inside the other, which are nested tables. Most of the time you don't need—or want—two separate tables; usually, when you run out of room in a table, what you really need is the capability to split an existing cell into two, four, or six cells.

There are only a few subtle differences between, say, nesting a four-column one-row table inside a cell and manually splitting the cell into four smaller cells. The main difference is in spacing—unless you change the spacing settings, nested tables take up an additional amount of space inside the cell to accommodate the outside of the table itself, whereas split cells require no additional spacing. Use a nested table when you want to manipulate the contents of a portion of the table as a unit: You can click and drag a nested table outside its confining cell, for example, but moving four subcells is considerably more complex.

→ To learn more about using nested tables, **see** "Nesting Tables Within Tables," **p. 409**.

The easy way to split a cell into multiple cells is to use Word's table-drawing tools. Click the Draw Table button on the Tables and Borders toolbar (to display this toolbar, right-click any visible toolbar or the main menu bar and check the Tables and Borders box). Use the pencil-shaped pointer to draw horizontal or vertical lines inside the cell(s) you want to split.

Use the Table, Split Cells menu command if you want to rearrange a group of selected cells and their text—converting four cells in one column into four cells in a single row, for example.

In some cases, you might want to merge cells. In a table that has one or more rows that function as headings, as in Figure 14.7, merging the cells from that row makes the heading easier to see. To merge two cells together, use the Eraser icon on the Tables and Borders toolbar. To merge cells in a row that contains many columns, select the cells and choose Table, Merge Cells, or use the Merge Cells button on the Tables and Borders toolbar.

Figure 14.7
You might want to merge the cells in one row of a table to accommodate a heading, as shown here.

Electricity	
Production	261.6 billion kWh
Consumption	293.9 billion kWh
Exports	900 million kWh
Imports	51.5 billion kWh
Natural gas	
Production	15.49 billion cu m
Consumption	71.18 billion cu m
Exports	61 million cu m
Imports	54.78 billion cu m
Proved reserves	209.7 billion cu m
Oil	
Production	79460 bbl/day
Consumption	1.866 million bbl/day
Exports	456600 bbl/day
Imports	2.158 million bbl/day
Proved reserves	586.6 million bbl

To split a table horizontally—between two rows—click once in the row that will become the top row in the new table. Choose Table, Split Table. A paragraph mark appears between the two tables. (As we noted earlier, you can also press Ctrl+Shift+Enter to split a table.)

TIP FROM

You can easily split a table vertically as well. Select the columns you want to split away from the original table. Cut them (choose Edit, Cut or press Ctrl+X). Move the insertion point to wherever you want the new table to appear, and paste. You can then place the two tables side-by-side, if you want, by using their drag handles.

SORTING DATA WITHIN TABLES

Although it doesn't hold a candle to Excel's sorting capabilities, Word can sort up using as many as three keys, including dates—within a table that contains student records, for instance, you can sort by Grade, and then by Last Name, and then by First Name. Word can also handle case-sensitive sorts as well as nonstandard sorting sequences (for languages other than English).

Sorting in Word can come in handy in all sorts of situations. You might want to sort a table of names, to put it in alphabetical order by last name, and then copy the table and sort it again by grade point average or test score. Or perhaps you created a table with the data sorted by last name, but you later decide that it would be more useful if sorted by first name. That kind of sorting is easy in Word.

NOTE

In fact, you needn't put data in a table to sort it. Word does just fine if you have clean data with delimiters—precisely in the same way that's required for converting text to a table. You can also sort simple lists (say, a list of state names, each in a single paragraph) because the paragraph mark is a delimiter.

TIP FROM

Entire chapters and sections can be sorted (using their headings) in Outline view.

→ To learn more about automatically converting your text into a Word table, **see** "Converting Text to a Table," **p. 407**.

You can also sort by individual words within cells—for example, if you have a row with names in FirstName LastName order, you can tell Word to sort by LastName, the second word in the column, followed by FirstName, the first word in the column (see Figure 14.8).

To sort data, do the following:

1. Click once inside the table (or data).
2. Choose Table, Sort. You see the Sort dialog box shown in Figure 14.8.

Figure 14.8
Although not as comprehensive as Excel's sorting capabilities, Word does rather well—it even has a LastName FirstName sorting capability—and you needn't convert your data to a table to sort it.

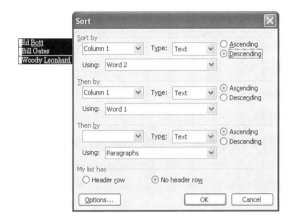

3. If your table (or data) has a header row—that is, if the first row describes the data below it—start by clicking the My List Has Header Row option. That way, Word uses the names from the header row instead of the generic "Column 1," "Column 2," and so on.

4. Choose your sort conditions. If you're planning to sort by LastName FirstName, you need to click Options and enter a space as the field delimiter. (You will also use this dialog box for nontable data, when specifying a case-sensitive sort, or when choosing a sorting sequence other than standard English.)

5. When you're ready to perform the sort, click OK.

TIP FROM

Ed & Woody

In unusual circumstances, you might want to sort just one column of a table, while leaving the other columns untouched. A teacher might construct a table with two columns, one containing scientific terms, the other containing definitions. By sorting just one column, the teacher could create a "connect the definitions" test, in which the students have to associate terms with definitions. To sort just one column of a table, select the column prior to choosing Table, Sort. Click Options, and check the Sort Column Only box. Click OK, and the single column is sorted independently.

POSITIONING TABLES ON THE PAGE

Although you might think that tables exist in the drawing layer—click the dragging handle to move them around—in fact, they are in the main part of the document. Thus, you can put captions inside tables and reference them via the Cross-reference dialog box, which appears when you choose Insert, Reference, Cross-reference; paragraphs can be numbered and the numbering continues from the main part of the document, through the table, and into the rest of the document; and entries in tables are picked up for indexes and tables of contents.

Although you'll most often want a table to appear flush left with text above and below it (not wrapping around), from time to time, you might want the table to appear flush right or

14

centered. You also might want main body text in the document to wrap around the table, especially with smaller tables. Follow these steps to make it happen:

1. Create the table by using any of the methods explained in this chapter.

2. Click once inside the table, and then choose Table, Table Properties. You see the Table Properties dialog box (see Figure 14.9).

Figure 14.9
The Table Properties dialog box lets you align tables on a page and specify whether you want text to wrap around.

3. Click the Table tab and set Left, Center, or Right alignment in the Alignment section. If you want to control the distance from the left edge of the box to the left margin of the page, use the Indent from Left spinner.

4. Allow document body text to flow around the table by clicking the Around box. If you want finer control over text wrapping—for example, the distance from text to the table edges—click the Positioning button.

ADVANCED TABLE FORMATTING OPTIONS

A properly formatted table helps the reader absorb and understand the contents. You know your table hasn't been formatted well when a reader has to pull out a ruler to tell which numbers belong on what rows.

LETTING WORD DO THE WORK WITH AUTOFORMAT

Word provides more than three dozen AutoFormat options that give you a good start on your way to table perfection. To use AutoFormatting, click once inside the table, and then choose Table, Table AutoFormat. (You can also bring up the AutoFormat dialog box when you create a table by choosing Table, Insert, Table.)

Table AutoFormatting comes in handy when you want to make your tables stand out—give them a personality, beyond the standard font—but you don't want to go to a lot of trouble creating and applying your own custom formatting. AutoFormatting is a good first choice when creating any type of table that includes rows or columns of numbers, such as a price list or a financial statement.

The Table AutoFormat dialog box (see Figure 14.10) contains dozens of predefined formats, with a preview of each.

Figure 14.10
Although Table AutoFormat might not have the design you want, it does provide a good starting place for creatively formatting your own tables.

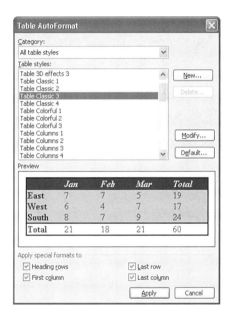

If your data doesn't match the preview's format, don't worry; AutoFormat gives you a lot of options. For example, all the previews assume that column headings appear in the first row. If your table doesn't have headings, clear the Heading Rows box.

TIP FROM

Ed & Woody

Tables of numbers on web pages can be particularly challenging. Take a look at the three Web AutoFormats for some interesting ideas.

You can create your own Table AutoFormat style by clicking the New button and assembling the formatting you want.

14

TIP FROM

The styles that Word uses to create its built-in AutoFormat tables are available for your use, too. Bring up the Styles and Formatting task pane, in the Show box choose All Styles, and then scroll down to the lengthy list that begins with the word "Table." When you pick a "Table" style, it's applied to the entire current table—all the rows and all the columns—even if you haven't selected the table.

USING BORDERS AND SHADING

Borders, shading, and background colors in table cells are identical to their counterparts in paragraphs. Click once inside a cell to change the border, shading, or background for that cell; select cells, rows, columns, or the entire table to change them.

→ To learn more about the common drawing tools used throughout Office, **see** "Adding Lines, Borders, Shading, and Backgrounds," **p. 426**.

Word normally displays a faint gray gridline on the screen, corresponding to cell borders, even if you format the cells so their borders are invisible.

TIP FROM

If you're creating a table that will be viewed on the screen in Word, you can hide the table gridlines by choosing Table, Hide Gridlines.

Tables viewed by a web browser never show gridlines, regardless of the Show/Hide Gridlines setting.

ALIGNING TEXT IN CELLS

Left-aligned text in cells might work for certain types of text tables, or tables where the columns are narrow. Frequently, however, you'll want to right-align numbers or center text. Right-aligned numbers are much easier to read and compare. If you're using a two-column table to simulate columns (in a résumé, for example), right-align the text in the left column to help show the connection with the matching blocks of text in the right column. For small amounts of text, centered text—even if it's just centered headings over a column—looks better than left-aligned almost anywhere in a table, except the first column.

You can click once in a cell, or select a series of cells, and change the alignment from left-justified to centered to right-justified by clicking the Align Left, Center, and Align Right buttons on the Formatting toolbar. Because end-of-cell markers behave much like paragraph marks, that formatting travels with the end of cell marker when it's copied or moved.

Word also allows you to center text vertically inside the cell. To do so, select the cells you want to format, choose Table, Table Properties, and then click the Cell tab. There you can choose from Top, Center, or Bottom positioning. Click the Options button and you can even tell Word how much white space you want between the cell edge and the text inside the cell.

14

You can combine the actions of horizontal and vertical alignment in one easy step: Select the cells you want to align, right-click, and choose Cell Alignment from the context menu. All nine combinations appear (see Figure 14.11), ready for you to apply.

Figure 14.11
All nine combinations of left, right, center, and top, middle, bottom appear on the cell's context menu.

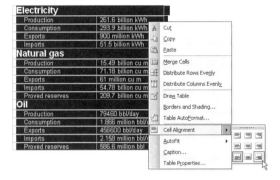

TIP FROM

If you click and drag on the horizontal bar above the nine alignment pictures shown in Figure 14.11, it turns into a tear-off menu (which is basically a floating toolbar that appears in the right-click Tools shortcut menu until closed). You can also drag this menu off the Tables and Borders toolbar.

WORKING WITH BIG TABLES

When you work with large tables, you'll commonly encounter three distinct problems. Fortunately, each has a simple solution:

- **Too wide**—When adjusting column widths or adding columns, sometimes the table extends beyond the page margins. If you're working in Print Layout view, you won't be able to see (or work with) the rightmost columns.

 If you lose the final column, refer to "Can't See Final Column(s) in a Table" in the "Troubleshooting" section at the end of the chapter.

- **Repeating titles**—If your table will print on more than one page, you might want the title row(s) to appear at the top of each page. Select the row(s) you want to repeat, and choose Table, Heading Rows Repeat.

- **Page breaks in cells**—By default, Word keeps all of a cell's contents on one page, allowing a page to break only when a new cell starts. If you're writing a résumé using a table, for example, you might want to relax that restriction, so page breaks can fall more naturally.

 If you want to relax the way Word breaks cells in a table, see "Allow Page Breaks in a Table Cell" in the "Troubleshooting" section at the end of the chapter.

14

TAKING CONTROL OF PAGE BREAKS

We cringe every time we see a Word beginner try to control pagination by clicking at the beginning of the paragraph that should start a new page and then pressing the Enter key—over and over again—until the text appears at the top of a new page. The result is almost always a mess that spirals out of control with even the simplest changes.

In long, highly formatted documents, the best way to control page breaks is through the use of paragraph styles—set a page break before each paragraph with the Chapter Heading style, for example, or force all the text in a Quote style paragraph to appear on one page. That kind of page break setting belongs in the paragraph style—choose Format, Style, and select the style you want to adjust; then click the Modify button, choose Format, Paragraph, and click the Line and Page Breaks tab. Even with well-designed paragraph styles, however, sometimes you'll want to force Word to start a new page at a location of your choosing.

If you want to force Word to start a new page in a specific place, don't use the Enter key. Instead, click once where you want the new page to begin; then choose Insert, Break, Page Break, and click OK. (Alternatively, you can press Ctrl+Enter.) In Normal view (see Figure 14.12), each page break appears as a dotted line. In other views, the break markers are visible only if you click the Show Hide ¶ button on the Standard toolbar.

Figure 14.12
Manually inserted page breaks are visible as dotted lines in Normal view.

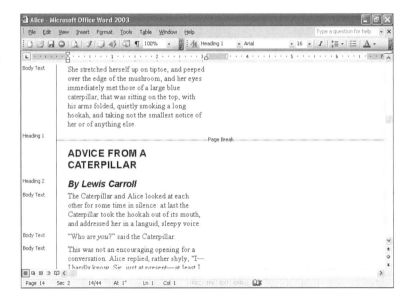

The problem with manually inserted page breaks, of course, is that they don't change when the text changes: If you add or delete a few lines in several places in a document, you might need to adjust every manual page break—a dreary prospect indeed.

To delete all manual page breaks, follow these steps:

1. Choose Edit, Replace (or press Ctrl+H).

2. Clear the Find What and Replace With boxes, if necessary, and then click the More button. Clear all check boxes and all formatting.

3. Click the Special button and choose Manual Page Break. Word adds the ^m character to the Find What box. Leave the Replace With box empty.

4. Choose Replace All to remove every manual page break in the document.

FORMATTING DOCUMENTS BY SECTION

Although most Word documents contain only one section, if you want to change headers or footers, page size or orientation, margins, line numbers (used in some legal documents), page borders, or the number of newspaper-like columns in different parts of a document, you have to use sections.

Perhaps the most common situation arises when you want to change headers or footers in the middle of a document. In that case, you have to add a new section; there's no alternative. Likewise, you might need to add a section if you have a wide table in the middle of a long report. Most of your pages will be printed in portrait orientation, but you'll need to add a section break before and after the table so that you can print it in landscape orientation. You could print the table separately and collate it by hand, but using section breaks removes your layout hassles with just a few clicks.

→ For a description of other page setup settings, **see** "Page/Section Setup Options," **p. 374**.

TYPES OF SECTIONS

Word recognizes four different types of section breaks:

- **Continuous**—Defines a new section but does not force a page break. Continuous section breaks are used almost exclusively for changing the number of newspaper-like columns in a document or resetting line numbering (typically in legal documents).

- **Next Page**—The most common type of section break, a Next Page section break not only defines a new section, it forces Word to start the section on a new page.

- **Odd Page**—Like the Next Page break, except Word can add one additional blank page (if necessary) to force the new section to begin on an odd-numbered page.

- **Even Page**—Like the Odd Page break, but Word starts on an even-numbered page.

Section breaks are visible in all views when you click the Show/Hide ¶ button to make special formatting characters visible.

Just as paragraph formatting is stored in the paragraph mark at the end of a paragraph, Word stores section formatting in the section break mark at the end of the section.

14

Formatting for the final section in a document is stored in the last paragraph mark in the document. If a document has only one section, the document's final paragraph mark holds the section formatting for the entire document.

Inserting and Deleting Section Breaks

To insert a new section break into a document:

1. If the document does not yet include one, we strongly recommend that you put a dummy manual section break at the end of the document. To do so, click once in front of the final paragraph mark in the document. Press Enter a few times. Then choose Insert, Break. In the Break dialog box (see Figure 14.13), choose Continuous, and click OK.

Figure 14.13
Before you insert that first section break, you can save yourself hours—days!—of trouble by placing a dummy section break at the end of the document.

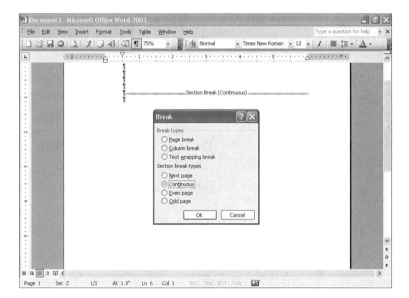

2. If all the headers and footers in the document will be the same, you'll find it much easier to establish them now. Follow the instructions in the "Creating and Editing Headers and Footers" section later in this chapter.

3. Carefully determine what section breaks you'll need in your document, what type they should be, and where they will occur. In particular, if you plan to change the number of newspaper-like columns for a short run in the middle of the document, you'll want Continuous section breaks both before and after the change.

4. Starting at the beginning of the document, create the section breaks, one at a time, by using the Break dialog box (choose Insert, Break).

The dummy section break at the end of the document can help you salvage important formatting information, because you can copy or move the section break, although copying or moving the final paragraph mark won't have any effect on section formatting. See the next section for details.

After establishing all sections, carefully go back into each section and apply the section formatting you require.

TIP FROM

You'll find it much easier to work with sections if you plan ahead and then go through each section in order, from beginning to end, applying the section formatting. By working from beginning to end, you simplify problems—massive problems—associated with changing headers and footers, and whether a section is linked to the previous one or not. If you start at the beginning, you can see the effect each change has on subsequent sections. If you start in the middle, it can be infuriatingly difficult to see why or how a header or footer has changed.

If you must delete a section break, select the break and press Delete. The newly merged section takes on the settings of the section break at the end. Immediately examine the document for odd formatting changes. If you find any unwelcome formatting, press Ctrl+Z or click the Undo button to restore the section break.

COPYING FORMATTING BETWEEN SECTIONS

Section breaks store the settings for the section. You can select, delete, copy, or move these settings at will.

By far, the simplest way to copy section formatting from one section to another is by copying the section break. If you want to copy the section formatting from, say, section number 6 to section number 3, follow these steps:

1. Select the section break at the end of section 6 and press Ctrl+C to copy it to the Clipboard.
2. Click just in front of the section break at the end of section 3.
3. Press Ctrl+V to paste the section break you copied previously.
4. Press Delete to delete the old section break at the end of section 3.

TIP FROM

If you created an extra dummy section break at the end of the document, all the document's original section formatting is stored in that section break. To restore a specific section to the document's original formatting, copy that dummy section break to the end of that specific section.

14

ADDING LINES, BORDERS, SHADING, AND BACKGROUNDS

Word lets you draw border lines and apply colors and other forms of shading to specific pieces of text, cells in tables, paragraphs, entire tables, or entire pages. When you draw a line around a page, it's called a *page border*. When you apply colors or shading to an entire page, it's called a *background*. And when you place a picture or text "behind" the text on a page—say, to print DRAFT diagonally across the page or to brand the page with the word CONFIDENTIAL—that picture or text is called a *watermark*.

TIP FROM

To add a watermark to a document, choose Format, Background, Printed Watermark. The watermark is inserted as part of the document's (actually, the section's) header. By working directly with the header (View, Header and Footer), you can manually change the watermark—move it, resize it, or even delete it.

QUICK WAYS TO CREATE LINES

The easiest way to draw a horizontal line across a page is to type any of the horizontal line AutoFormat characters (see Table 14.1) three or more times and press Enter. The line will appear above the characters you typed.

TABLE 14.1 AUTOFORMAT CHARACTERS FOR HORIZONTAL LINES

Character	Type of Line
- (hyphen)	Light single line
_ (underscore)	Heavy single line
= (equal)	Heavy double line
# (number sign)	Thick line with thin lines above and below
~ (tilde)	Wavy line
* (asterisk)	Horizontal line of small squares

The horizontal line (also called a *rule*) is actually a lower border for the paragraph above the one where you typed. If you click once on that paragraph, and then choose Format, Borders and Shading, you'll see what formatting has taken effect. If you find this behavior annoying, you can turn it off in the AutoFormat dialog box.

→ To eliminate unwanted AutoFormat behaviors, **see** "Automatic Formatting," **p. 376**.

You can also use the tools on the Drawing toolbar to draw lines, or choose Table, Draw Table, and use Word's table drawing tool; however, neither of these approaches quickly creates lines that extend all the way across a page and move with their associated text.

14

BORDERS AND BOXES

You can draw borders—essentially rectangles—around characters, paragraphs, table cells, or pages. To create a border for characters, paragraphs, or cells, follow these steps:

1. Select the character(s), paragraph(s), table cell(s), or table(s) you want to format.

2. Choose Format, Borders and Shading. On the Borders tab (see Figure 14.14), make sure the Apply To box shows the correct setting: Paragraph, Text, Cell, or Table.

Figure 14.14
The Borders and Shading dialog box lets you draw lines around characters, paragraphs, or cells.

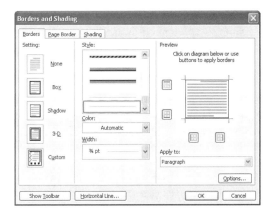

3. Choose from the common settings along the left, or draw your own border in the Preview pane on the right. You might want to use the Preview pane if, say, you want to have lines appear to the left and above a paragraph but not to the right or below. Choose the line style, color, and width in the center pane.

TIP FROM

EQ & Woody

> If you want borders of different types (to add double lines on the top and bottom but single lines at the left and right, for example), start by clicking the Custom box. Then build the first border type by selecting from the Style, Color, and Width boxes. Finally, tell Word where you want this particular border type to appear by selecting the location(s) in the Preview pane. Go back and build your second border type, apply it in the Preview pane, and repeat as needed.

4. To set the distance between the text and the border, click Options and fill in the amounts. Click OK and the border appears.

NOTE

> If the Tables and Borders toolbar is hidden, click the Show Toolbar button in the Borders and Shading dialog box to quickly display it.

14

The procedure for applying page borders is similar:

1. If you want only a specific page (or pages) in your document to have a border, set up section breaks at the beginning and end of the page (or pages). Then click once inside the section you want to have page borders.

2. Choose Format, Borders and Shading, and click the Page Border tab.

3. To choose from a fairly large selection of border options, click the down arrow in the Art box. Page Border formatting options are similar to general Border formatting, except pages can also use artwork for their borders.

NOTE

Unfortunately, you can't add your own page borders to Word's collection.

4. If you don't want the border to encompass the header or footer, click the Options button, choose Measure from Text, and clear the Surround Header and Surround Footer boxes. Click OK and the border will be visible in Print Layout view.

To understand how borders can move around a document and appear suddenly as if out of nowhere, it's important to know where the formatting is stored:

- Character borders are stored in the characters themselves. If you move or copy a character with a border, the border goes along with it.

- Paragraph borders are stored in the paragraph mark. If you copy, move, or delete a paragraph mark, the border goes with it. If you press Enter while inside a paragraph with a border, the new paragraph "inherits" the border settings from the previous paragraph.

- Table cell borders are stored in the individual cell's end-of-cell marker. Borders that apply to the entire table are in the final end-of-row marker.

- Page borders are stored in the section break mark. If your document has only one section, page borders are stored in the final paragraph mark in the document.

→ For an explanation of how to format cells, rows, and tables, **see** "Working with Tables," **p. 409**.

SHADING CHARACTERS, PARAGRAPHS, AND PAGES

A little shading goes a long way. Black text on a light shade of gray (or a pale yellow) can be quite legible. On forms, in particular, a little shading can actually enhance the appearance of text and make the form easier for users to fill in. White text on a very dark background makes a striking visual impression. But avoid the middle ground: Dark shading with dark characters can be virtually illegible, even if you never print the document—colors vary widely from monitor to monitor, as well.

14

Character, paragraph, table cell, and entire table shading works much like borders. Select the item(s) you want to shade, choose Format, Borders and Shading, and then click the Shading tab. You see the Shading options shown in Figure 14.15.

Figure 14.15
Color and shading are both applied from the Shading tab.

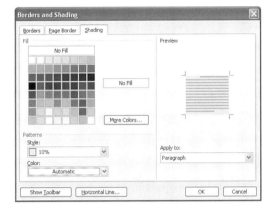

The interaction of the various parts of the Shading dialog box can be confusing. Think of it this way: If you want to apply a solid color, use the Fill box at the top of the dialog box. If you want to apply a shade—say, a 5% gray background—use the Pattern box at the bottom.

"No Fill" in the Fill box on the top means there's no solid background color. "Clear" in the Style box near the bottom means there's no shading.

If you absolutely must have a background color, with a shade of gray on top of the color, pick the color in the Fill box and the shade in the Pattern box. Finally, just to guarantee that you stay thoroughly confused, shades aren't confined to shades of gray. In fact, you can "shade" with any color; choose it in the Color box at the bottom.

If you want to apply a shade or a fill color to the entire page, you're in the wrong place. You'll have to go back to your document, and then choose Format, Background. At that point, you can choose a solid color background, or you can choose Fill Effects to bring up the Fill Effects dialog box shown in Figure 14.16.

Using fill effects, you can perform one- or two-color gradient fills; use a repeating picture called a "texture" to give your document a background that looks like stone, wood, or fabric; create cross-hatched patterns in a wide variety of styles and any color; or bring in your own picture, which will be repeated like a tiled Windows wallpaper.

NOTE

Page backgrounds are intended for use on web pages and have virtually no other uses. They show up onscreen only in Web Layout view, and they do not appear if you print the document. If you choose a page background, Word automatically shifts to Web Layout view.

14

Figure 14.16
Word has an extensive collection of fill effects, but they can be applied only to pages, and all the pages in a document must have the same effects.

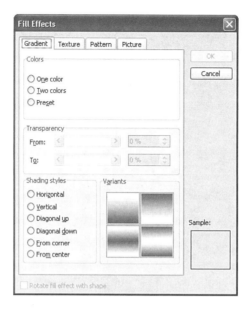

Page backgrounds apply to the entire document; they cannot be changed from section to section, like page borders. In addition, the fill effects available on pages are not available to characters, table cells, or paragraphs.

FORMATTING A DOCUMENT WITH COLUMNS

Another section-formatting option controls the number of newspaper-like snaking columns within the section. You might be tempted to use multiple columns for laying out newsletters and brochures, or (not surprisingly) newspapers. Text arranged in relatively narrow columns is often easier to read than the same text that uses the full width of a letter-size page; the human eye can take in a narrow column all at once and allow the reader to scan down quickly, whereas the eye has to move from left to right and back again for a wide column.

Before you begin using columns, take a closer look at the pluses, minuses, and gotchas.

Snaking newspaper-like columns might not work the way you're expecting: They run from top to bottom, and there's no rebalancing for a page break. If you have, say, 12 items in a section that's set up with 3 columns, they'll appear arranged as in Table 14.2.

TABLE 14.2   SEQUENCE OF SNAKING COLUMNS

Item 1	Item 5	Item 9
Item 2	Item 6	Item 10
Item 3	Item 7	Item 11
Item 4	Item 8	Item 12

However, if you add a page break between, say, the second and third lines in Table 14.2, items 2, 6, and 10 will appear on the first page, and items 3, 7, and 11 will end up on the second page.

If you need greater control over the appearance and layout of snaking columns, use tables instead of column formatting. Place each item in its own table cell and hide the table's gridlines. With Word's capability to draw custom tables with any number of cells, including nested cells, it makes little sense to work with columns if the layout is complicated.

To set up snaking columns in the middle of a document, follow these steps:

1. Switch to Normal view, click to position the insertion point where you want the columns to begin, and then choose Insert, Break. Add a Continuous section break immediately before the beginning of the text or the first item in the list.

2. Add another Continuous section break immediately after the end of the text block or the last item in the list.

3. Click once between the two section break marks, choose Format, Columns, and choose the column layout you like (see Figure 14.17). Note that you can set column widths and inter-column white space manually.

Figure 14.17
To avoid confusion, set up the "before" and "after" section breaks manually: Click inside the area you want to format in snaking columns, and choose This Section from the Apply To box.

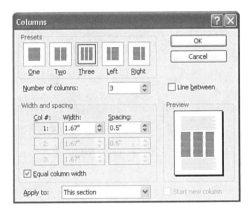

CREATING AND EDITING HEADERS AND FOOTERS

Headers appear at the top of each page; footers at the bottom. Word lets you specify "first page only" headers and footers, so the first page of a report or letter can have headers and footers that are different from those in the body of the report. That's useful if your first page is a decorative title page and you don't want it to contain a page number or the title. In addition, Word enables you to set up different headers and footers for odd-numbered and even-numbered pages. That comes in handy if you're going to be printing on the front and back of each sheet of paper and then binding the final document into a book format. (Look at the headers in this book for an example.)

14

CREATING HEADERS AND FOOTERS

Headers and footers exist on every page in a Word document. Until you put something in them, however, they're invisible. Word reserves room for them but doesn't print anything (or show anything on the screen) in the reserved area.

To create a header, follow these steps:

1. Choose View, Header and Footer. Word switches to Print Layout view (if necessary), displays the Header and Footer toolbar, turns the body text of the document gray, and highlights the header area of the page (see Figure 14.18).

Figure 14.18
You "view" a header, in Word parlance, because the header already exists—even if you haven't put anything into it.

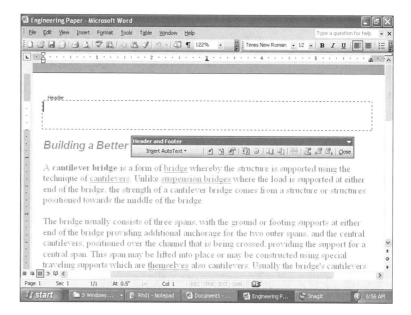

2. Enter anything you want in the header. Note that the paragraph is formatted with the Header style, which includes two tab stops: a centered stop at the middle of the page and a right-aligned stop on the right margin. (If you've changed margins, you also need to change the locations of these tab stops.)

3. When you're finished with the header, click the Switch Between Header and Footer button on the Header and Footer toolbar. Word moves the insertion point to the footer for the current page.

4. Enter text, graphics, or whatever else you want in the footer.

5. Click the Close button on the Header and Footer toolbar to return to your document.

If you have created a header or footer for a page, you can see it when you're in Print Layout view, as a grayed-out shadow of how the header or footer will appear on the final printed page. To edit a header or footer that you can see on the screen, double-click it.

To force Word to use a different header and footer on the first page than the one in the rest of the document, or to alternate headers and footers for odd- and even-numbered pages, click the Page Setup icon on the Header and Footer toolbar. That displays the Layout tab in the Page Setup dialog box (see Figure 14.19), where you can select the Different Odd and Even and Different First Page check boxes.

Figure 14.19
Specify whether you want different headers for the first page and odd/even pages in this dialog box.

After selecting the Different First Page check box, you can navigate to the first page in your document, choose View, Header and Footer, and customize the first page header and footer as you like.

With the Different Odd and Even check box selected, any changes you make in the header or footer of any even-numbered page will appear on all even-numbered pages; thus, if you change the header on page 6, your changes appear on all even-numbered pages. Similarly, changing the header or footer on any odd-numbered page changes all the odd-numbered pages, with the possible exception of page 1, which remains unaltered if you've selected the Different First Page check box.

The actual locations of a header or footer on the page are determined by the margins.

→ For an explanation of how headers and margins work together, **see** "Adjusting Margins," **p. 381**.

NUMBERING PAGES

By far the most common use for a header or footer is to show the page number. Word gives you several options:

- To place a plain page number in the header or footer, with no additional text (a simple 14 instead of Page 14), choose Insert, Page Numbers. You'll see the Page Numbers dialog box (see Figure 14.20) which allows you to position the number at the top or bottom of the page—left, middle, or right. This approach has one noteworthy gotcha, as we explain shortly.

Figure 14.20

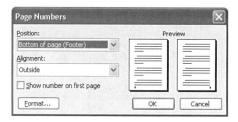

- While editing the header or footer, use the Header and Footer toolbar buttons to insert the current page number, or the total number of pages. Use the Insert Page Number and Insert Number of Pages buttons, or click Insert AutoText and choose Page x of y from the predefined AutoText list.

- Type any text or use fields to create a completely custom page numbering scheme. The Insert Page Number button actually places a {Page} field in the header or footer; the Insert Number of Pages icon adds a {NumPages} field. By inserting your own fields, you can create and edit custom page number formats—to track sections, chapters, or other divisions, for example.

TIP

> If you choose Insert, Page Number, Word actually puts a {Page} field *inside a frame*, and tucks that frame into the header or footer. Frames (a leftover design element from early Word versions and largely supplanted by text boxes) can cause all sorts of problems, especially when you're formatting other header or footer entries. For example, if you select the entire footer and apply some sort of font formatting, the formatting will not "take" inside the frame. Unless you're in a big hurry, it's smarter and cleaner to use the icons on the Header and Footer toolbar. To get rid of a frame, click to select the {PAGE} field, double-click the frame border, and click the Remove Frame button in the Frame dialog box.

ADDING DATES AND DOCUMENT DETAILS

The Header and Footer toolbar also includes icons that let you insert the current date or time. You can accomplish the same result manually by choosing Insert, Date and Time, or by creating your own fields to show, say, the document's filename or the date and time it was last printed. Both of these options are available from the Insert AutoText list on the Header and Footer toolbar.

One of the most important fields—called {StyleRef}—allows you to put text from the document into a header or footer. You can use {StyleRef} to add the title or number of the current chapter to a header, for example, or to produce "Able–Autry" page indexes in the header, as in a telephone book.

➡ For step-by-step instructions on how to create custom headers and footers for catalogs and other long documents, **see** "Referring to Document Contents," **p. xxx. (ch 16)**

HOW SECTION BREAKS AFFECT HEADERS AND FOOTERS

Headers and footers are section-level settings; if you have more than one section in a document, each section can have its own set of headers and footers. Headers and footers are stored in the section break marks. If a document has just one section, the headers and footers are stored in the final paragraph mark in the document; that is an important detail if you find yourself trying to unravel inscrutable headers and footers in a multi-section document.

➡ To decipher the mysteries of sections, **see** "Formatting Documents by Section," **p. 423**.

To format a section so that it uses the same headers and footers as the preceding section, you don't need to do anything more than insert a section break. Word automatically formats the headers and footers in the new section by using the Same As Previous option.

If you want to break the Same As Previous link between the current section and the preceding section, click the Same As Previous button on the Header and Footer toolbar.

When you break the Same As Previous link, you effectively break the document into two separate pieces. With this setting in effect, any changes to a header or footer in the first section affect pages only in that section. Likewise, changes to a header or footer in the second section affect only that section.

CAUTION

> When you break and restore the Same As Previous link, or add, delete, move, or copy section breaks on-the-fly, the effects on existing headers and footers can be extremely unpredictable. It's always best to lay out your document and establish section breaks first, before you begin modifying text, headers, or footers.

Sometimes you need to restart the page numbers in a section. Perhaps you want to start the numbering at 1 once again, as many books do following the introduction. Maybe you need to advance a handful of numbers to accommodate sheets you plan to print and interleave manually.

To restart page numbers, follow these steps:

1. Switch to Normal view and choose Insert, Break, Next Page to create a section break where you want the new page-numbering sequence to begin.

➡ For an explanation of how each type of section works, **see** "Types of Sections," **p. 423**.

2. The insertion point should be positioned immediately after the Next Page section break. Choose Insert, Page Numbers.

3. In the Page Numbers dialog box, click the Format box.

14

NOTE

The Format Page Number icon also appears on the Header and Footer toolbar.

4. In the Page Numbering section, select the Start At option and specify the section's starting page number. Close the dialog box to save your changes.

KEEPING LONG DOCUMENTS UNDER CONTROL

Effectively using Word to handle long documents—100 pages or more in length, or more than a megabyte or two in size—requires forethought and planning. If you *can* break a very long document into several smaller ones, you probably should. If you need some of Word's advanced features, such as a table of contents or page numbering, use some of the strategies we outline in this section.

ONE FILE OR MANY?

As your documents get larger, you have several choices:

- **Continue to work with a single large file**—An effective backup strategy is always valuable, but it's especially important when working with large files, where a single misstep can wipe out huge amounts of work.

- **Cut the large file down to size**—If your file contains multiple graphics, save the pictures in separate files and create links instead of embedding them.

→ To learn more about when embedding is better than linking, **see** "Embedding Versus Linking," **p. 154**.

- **Use fields to include the contents of one file in another**—Choose Insert, Insert File, select the name of a second file, click the down arrow to the right of the Insert button, and then choose Insert Link. Word adds an {INCLUDETEXT} field to your document that automatically reads in the contents of the second file. This technique is especially useful for boilerplate text. For example, if you have a legal disclaimer that you are required to use in all documents you create on behalf of your homeowners association or nonprofit group, you can use an {INCLUDETEXT} field to ensure that this block of text always contains the latest version.

- **Break the large document down into smaller files**—The best way to perform this task is manually, employing techniques described in this chapter to keep everything together.

CAUTION

All the approaches that involve linking pictures or using multiple documents depend on hard-coded filenames that include the full path name. That can pose problems when moving a large document from one machine to another. Replicating folder structures is almost a prerequisite for moving large documents from one machine to another.

> Word also includes a feature called *master documents*, which allow you to create a single large document made up of links to smaller documents. We know very few Word users who take advantage of this feature, which is complex and has a checkered history. To work with long documents, you have simpler, easier options, and we don't recommend using master documents.

USING BOOKMARKS

One of the largest problems facing those who maintain large documents is maintaining the integrity of references. For example, the title of Chapter 3 in your dissertation might be "The Birth of the Industrial Revolution." When you refer to Chapter 3 in other parts of the document, you might be tempted to type that text. But if you later change the title of Chapter 3, you'll have to search through your document and change every reference. For a long, complex document that undergoes many changes, keeping cross-references synchronized manually is a nightmare.

The simplest way to keep text in sync is to use bookmarks.

→ To create and work with bookmarks, **see** "Bookmarks," **p. 337**.

In this example, you could select the text "The Birth of the Industrial Revolution" and give the bookmark the name Chapter3Title. Then, anyplace you wanted to refer to the title of Chapter 3, you could choose Insert, Field, click the REF field, and add Chapter3Title to tell Word you want to insert the field {Ref Chapter3Title}.

→ For details on the {Ref} field, **see** "Using Fields Intelligently," **p. 494**.

That way, anytime the title changes—that is, anytime the contents of the Chapter3Title bookmark changes—all the {REF} field references to the title will change, too, automatically.

You can maintain page number references in the same way, using the {PAGEREF} field. For example, the field {PAGEREF Chapter3Title} gives the page number of the bookmark Chapter3Title. So a line such as "See {Ref Chapter3Title} on page {PageRef Chapter3Title}" will yield a valid reference, no matter what the bookmark Chapter3Title might contain, or where it might be located, as long as the bookmark, {Ref} field, and {PageRef} field are all in the same document.

If you break a long document into multiple files, the bookmark options aren't quite as good: You can reference bookmarks in other documents, by using the {IncludeText} field, but the references will retrieve only the contents of the bookmarks; you can't get at the page number.

For example, this field

```
{INCLUDETEXT "D:\\My Documents\\Annual Report.doc" Chapter3Title}
```

will retrieve the contents of the Chapter3Title bookmark in the indicated file and place it in the current document.

14

INSERTING CROSS-REFERENCES

Word includes extensive support for *cross-referencing*—everything from "See Figure x-y above" kinds of references to "as defined in paragraph IV.B.7.a." Each type of cross-reference has its own requirements and quirks, so a little bit of planning goes a long way.

These references persist even if the document changes. That's what makes them so powerful and useful. Say you have a reference in your homeowners association agreement that says "as defined in paragraph IV.B.7.a." Then, after reviewing the draft, the board of directors adds an additional numbered paragraph, and that new paragraph has to go ahead of the current paragraph IV.A. All you need to do is insert the paragraph, select the document, and press F9 to update fields. Automatically, the old paragraph IV.B.7.a becomes paragraph IV.C.7.a, and the old reference to it turns into "as defined in paragraph IV.C.7.a."

Many kinds of cross-references interact with captions (see the next section for details on how to set up the captions correctly). Say you have a picture in a document with a caption that says "Figure 17," and a reference to it such as "See Figure 17." You decide to add a figure immediately before figure number 17. If you used cross-references and captions correctly, the next time you update fields, the old figure number 17 will get the caption "Figure 18," and the old reference will be updated so it says "See Figure 18." The connections persist even in the face of complex restructuring in the document. So, if you moved this new Figure 18 to the beginning of the document, for example, it would get the caption "Figure 1" and the reference would change to "See Figure 1." Captions and references throughout the document would change to match the new numbering scheme—and all you have to do is update fields.

To see Word's Cross-reference dialog box (see Figure 14.21), click Insert, Reference, Cross-reference.

Figure 14.21
Word's cross-reference capabilities key off of precisely defined styles, bookmarks, and sequences located inside the document.

Choices in the Reference Type drop-down list are linked to specific elements in the document.

Reference Type: Numbered item refers exclusively to paragraphs formatted with Word-applied numbering. (If you number your paragraphs manually, they won't appear here.)

There's a fair amount of native intelligence in the cross-reference: For example, if you refer to paragraph IV.B.7.a from inside paragraph IV.B.6.c, you can tell Word to use the reference "7.a."

NOTE

> For a detailed discussion of these "full context" and "no context" numbering references, see the online Help topic "Paragraph number options in cross-references."

Reference Type: Heading choices include only those paragraphs marked with the built-in Word heading styles: Heading 1, Heading 2, Heading 3, and so on.

Say you're preparing an itinerary for an upcoming group excursion. You've created a document in which the name of each destination appears in a paragraph formatted as Heading 2. You've written a description of the glorious beaches and resorts of Thailand that appears on page 17. Throughout your document, you would like to insert references that follow the format "For more information about *destination*, see page *nn*" (where *nn* is the actual page number on which that content appears). No problem. Follow these steps to add cross-references:

1. Click once where you want the reference to appear. Type your introductory text—in this example, **For more information about** (don't forget the trailing space)—and then choose Insert, Reference, Cross-reference. Choose Heading from the Reference Type drop-down list and Heading Text from the Insert Reference To list (see Figure 14.22).

Figure 14.22
It's easy to insert a reference to a heading, if you use the built-in tools.

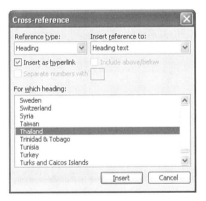

2. In the For Which Heading box, choose the item for which you want to create a cross-reference—Thailand, in this example. Click Insert, and then Close.

3. Type **, see page** (with a comma, a leading space, and a trailing space) and then choose Insert, Reference, Cross-reference again.

4. In the Reference Type drop-down list, choose Heading; in the Insert Reference To drop-down list, choose Page Number. In the For Which Heading list box, choose the same item you selected in step 2. Click Insert, and then Close.

14

The cross-reference in your document now reads, "For more information about Thailand, see page 17."

Reference Type: Bookmark includes any bookmarks you've defined in the document. By using the Insert, Cross-reference feature, you can put the bookmarked text or the bookmark's page number in the document, and it will be updated should the contents of the bookmark—or its location—change.

Reference Type: Footnote, Endnote are tied to footnotes and endnotes in the document. If you want to create an additional reference to an existing footnote, choose Insert, Cross-reference, and in the Reference Type drop-down list, choose Footnote.

→ To work with footnotes in general, **see** "Inserting Footnotes," **p. 350**.

Reference Type: Figure refers exclusively to paragraphs in the document that contain the {SEQ Figure} field. When you choose Insert, Cross-reference, and select Figure from the Reference Type drop-down list, Word scans the document for {SEQ Figure} fields and puts the paragraphs containing those fields in the For Which Heading list. See the next section ("Wrapping Text Around Graphics") for several examples of how to use figure cross-references. In particular, when you use Word's built-in Insert, Caption feature, it can generate an {SEQ Figure} field that's picked up by the Insert Cross-reference feature.

Reference Type: Equation, Table similarly refers exclusively to {SEQ Equation} and {SEQ Table} fields.

CAUTION

> Captions that appear in the drawing layer aren't detected by Word's Insert Cross-reference feature. If you place a caption in a text box, or if your figures "float over text" with an attached caption, you must first move the caption into the document itself before your cross-references will work properly.

Cross-references work only on references inside the current document, or inside a master document.

CREATING INDEXES

Creating an index for your document is a straightforward two-step process:

1. Mark index entries in the document by using Insert, Reference, Index and Tables (see Figure 14.23), and then click Mark Entry. Proceed through the entire document, marking index entries where they occur.

2. When you're done marking the entries, generate the index by placing the insertion point where you want the index to appear, bring up the Index and Tables dialog box (refer to Figure 14.23), and click OK.

Like so many other advanced Word features, indexing is driven by field codes. In this case, the {XE} field code, generated previously in step 1, marks the location of index entries. The index itself, generated in step 2, is really just an {Index} field. To understand how indexes are built, you first must understand Word fields.

→ To learn more about fields, **see** "Using Fields Intelligently," **p. 494**.

Figure 14.23
The Index tab allows you to both mark index entries and generate the index itself.

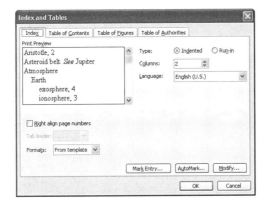

Unfortunately, Word's indexing feature is not as intuitive as one might hope. Although it appears that indexes built with the Standard Mark Index Entry dialog box can run only two entries deep, there is a workaround. Although the Mark Entry dialog box has only two boxes for entry levels (Main Entry and Sub Entry), you can enter up to seven levels in either of these boxes by separating your entries with colons—for example, you could enter Flowers:Roses:Red.

With that caution in mind, there are a few tricks you can use to make indexing faster and easier.

To create an index entry for a particular word in a document, double-click the word to select it, and then press Alt+Shift+X. If you want to use the word as the main (highest level) entry, press Enter. If you want to use something different for the main entry, press Ctrl+X to cut the selected word, type in your main entry, press Tab, and then press Ctrl+V to make the selected word a subentry.

For example, if you see the word Rose in a document and want to create an entry for Flowers:Rose, here's a quick way to do it:

1. Double-click Rose to select it.
2. Press Alt+Shift+X to bring up the Mark Index Entry dialog box.
3. Press Home to move the insertion point to the beginning of the Main Entry box.
4. Type the word **Flowers:** (note the colon).
5. Press Enter twice (or click Mark and then click Close). Word inserts an {XE "Flowers:Rose"} field into your document.

Although the key sequence is a bit convoluted, you'll quickly master it with practice.

14

{XE} fields are hidden. If you insert them via the Mark Index Entry dialog box, Word turns on the Show All feature so you not only can see the fields, but you also get dots for spaces. To turn off Show All, choose Tools, Options, click the View tab, and clear the All box.

If you want to see your {XE} fields, choose Tools, Options, and on the View tab select the Hidden Text check box.

If you're willing to trust the computer to construct your index, consider using a concordance file. You set up the concordance file as a two-column table, with entries you want to index in the first column (say, Roses), and the index you want to use in the second column (say, Flowers:Rose). You apply an index concordance file to a document via the AutoMark button in the Index and Tables dialog box, as shown in Figure 14.23. For more information, see the Word help file entry "Create an index."

Now for the gotcha: When Word updates the {Index} field, you're given two options: Update the page numbers only (in which case new index entries are ignored); or update the entire index (in which case any entries or formatting you've entered manually into the index get wiped out). The lesson to learn is not to make any manual changes to an automatically generated index.

Fortunately, you can pour Word documents into high-end desktop-publishing programs, which include all the tools necessary to generate decent professional-grade indexes.

If you're frustrated because your edits to the compiled index are lost whenever you update the index, see "Updating Index Entries" in the "Troubleshooting" section at the end of this chapter.

If you've spell-checked your index but still find spelling errors, see "Spell-Checking an Index" in the "Troubleshooting" section at the end of this chapter.

CREATING A TABLE OF CONTENTS

If our explanation of the difficulties of creating an index scared you off, take heart. The Table of Contents (TOC) generator in Word works quite well:

1. Make sure you've applied styles to all the heading paragraphs you want to appear in the TOC. You can use Word's default "Heading n" styles, or you can create your own.

2. If you want to add more entries—say, free-form text entries that will appear in the TOC even if they aren't in paragraphs with appropriate styles—use Insert, Field to put {TC} fields in your document.

    {TC} fields can include much more than plain text. For detailed reference information on how to use this type of field, see "Field codes: TC (Table of Contents Entry) field" in online help.

3. Put the insertion point where you want the TOC to appear, and choose Insert, Reference, Index and Tables, Table of Contents. The Index and Tables dialog box appears with the Table of Contents tab in front (see Figure 14.24).

14

Figure 14.24
You can build a table of contents based on any set of styles.

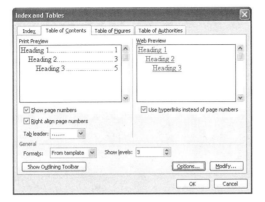

4. If you're using styles other than the standard "Heading *n*" set, click Options and map each style to a TOC heading level. When you're done, click OK and Word builds the TOC.

A table of contents (even a large one) is just a Word field—a {TOC} field, to be precise. To see the field, choose Tools, Options, click the View tab, and select the Field Codes check box.

TIP FROM

> If you regularly work with field codes, memorize the ViewFieldCodes keyboard shortcut, Alt+F9. Or assign the command to a toolbar button so you can toggle it on and off.

{TOC} behaves just like any other field, with one exception. When you update it, Word might ask you whether you want to Update Page Numbers Only, or Update the Entire Table. Although the default response is Update Page Numbers Only, you should accept this choice only if you are absolutely certain that none of the TOC entries has been deleted or changed, and no new entries have been added.

Word generally keeps good track of your headings, and if it detects that a heading has been added or deleted it won't even ask whether you want to Update Page Numbers Only.

Word can also produce TOC-like tables for figures, or any of the special {SEQ} fields. Choose Insert, Reference, Index and Tables, and click the Table of Figures tab.

The entire Table of Figures engine is based on the labels in {SEQ} fields, in a manner similar to the cross-reference hooks described earlier in this chapter. In fact, a Table of Figures is nothing more than a {TOC} field, with switches added to indicate which {SEQ} field should be indexed.

A table of contents, index, or other kind of reference table can be generated only for entries inside the current document.

14

WRAPPING TEXT AROUND GRAPHICS

Word makes it easy to wrap text around a graphic. Insert the graphic into your document (for example, by choosing Insert, Picture), right-click the graphic, and choose Format Picture (or Format AutoShape). Click the Layout tab (see Figure 14.25) and choose how you want the text to wrap. (You'll find additional options when you click the Advanced button.)

Figure 14.25
Word does a decent job of wrapping text tightly around a picture, but you can do better.

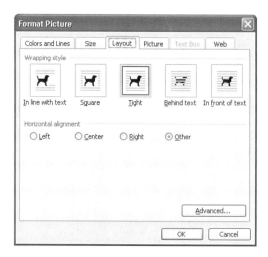

If you want to wrap text tightly around an odd-shaped graphic, start with the Tight option in the Format Picture (or Format AutoShape) dialog box shown in Figure 14.25.

TIP FROM

For complete control over text wrapping, use the Drawing toolbar to adjust the *wrapping points*—the points Word uses to judge how closely it should move text to the graphic. Bring up the Drawing toolbar and click Draw, Text Wrapping, Edit Wrap Points. (Or click the Edit Wrap Points button on the Picture toolbar.) Click and drag any of the text-wrapping points—you can even have text wrap onto the graphic itself. When you're finished, click outside the graphic, and Word rearranges the text.

TROUBLESHOOTING

CHECK FOR STRAY DELIMITERS

When I use Word's Convert Text to Table feature, occasionally it does the conversion incorrectly and the table is off by a cell or two.

Immediately after converting text to a table, look at the last row of the table and verify that it matches the last row of the selected data. If you're off by one or two cells (typically, one or two cells will be dangling at the bottom of the table), you probably have a stray delimiter character somewhere in the selected text. Scan the table to see whether you can locate it. Click the Undo button or press Ctrl+Z, fix the data, and try the conversion again.

DISAPPEARING CELL CONTENTS AND ROW MARKERS

I selected a row and dragged it to a new location, but instead of moving the whole row, as expected, Word replaced the contents of existing cells in the destination row.

Although you thought you selected the entire row, you actually selected all the cells in the rows. To select an entire row, place the mouse pointer in the margin to the left of the row until it turns to an arrow that points up and to the right, and then click. To make sure you select the entire row, configure Word so that you can see the end-of-row markers—which are visible only if you show paragraph marks (choose Tools, Options, click the View tab, and select the Paragraph Marks check box). If you want to click and drag a table row to a new location, select the entire row—including the end-of-row marker—and then click and drag, as you would with any other Word component.

PROPERLY SETTING THE ROW HEIGHT FOR WORD TABLES

When I insert a lot of text (or graphics) in a table cell, I can't see all of it. The bottom is chopped off.

Chances are good you did something to make Word set the row height using the "Exactly" option. To restore the default setting—in which rows grow and shrink to fit the contents— open the Table Properties dialog box (choose Table, Table Properties), click the Row tab, and clear the Specify Height box.

CAN'T SEE FINAL COLUMN(S) IN A TABLE

When I add a column to a table (or adjust the width of a column), I can no longer see the last column.

The table is too wide to fit in the defined margins, and if you try to view the document in Print Layout view, you won't see the portion that falls off the page. Switch to Normal view (choose View, Normal) and use the horizontal scrollbar to move to the right.

ALLOW PAGE BREAKS IN A TABLE CELL

In one of my documents, Word insists on waiting until the end of a cell before it triggers a page break. As a result, my tables flip-flop all over the page: Some pages have only one row showing, and it looks horrible.

You must have changed Word's default setting, which allows page breaks to occur at logical points. You might want all the data in a row to stay together, especially when the cells all contain fairly modest amounts of text. But in your case, this setting is getting in the way. To get Word to relax a bit, select the entire table and choose Table, Table Properties. In the Table Properties dialog box, click the Row tab, click the Options button, and select the Allow Row to Break Across Pages box.

UPDATING INDEX ENTRIES

After inserting an index, I edited the entries by directly typing over them within the index itself. But when I updated the index, all those edits were lost.

Always make changes to the index entries in the body of the document—that is, change the contents of the {xe} fields themselves. That way, when you update the index (or table of contents), your changes will be reflected in the new index. The process doesn't work in reverse, as you discovered the hard way. If you type over an item in the index itself, you eliminate the reference to matching index fields within the document.

SPELL-CHECKING AN INDEX

Even though I spell-checked my index, there are still spelling errors in the index.

Index entries—that is, {xe} fields—normally are hidden. Word doesn't check hidden text when you run a spell-check. To spell-check your index entries, first display hidden characters (choose Tools, Options, click the View Tab, and click the Hidden Text check box). Next, run the spell-check. Misspelled words in {xe} fields will appear with a red squiggly underline.

EXTRA CREDIT: NESTED TABLES FOR SUPERIOR LAYOUT

Nested tables provide great flexibility in setting page layout. In Figure 14.26, we've modified the standard Word Professional Résumé with a table across from the Education entry, making it easy to enter multiple degrees. The gridlines are visible only when editing; they won't appear on the final, printed document.

A nested 2-row, 2-column table

Figure 14.26

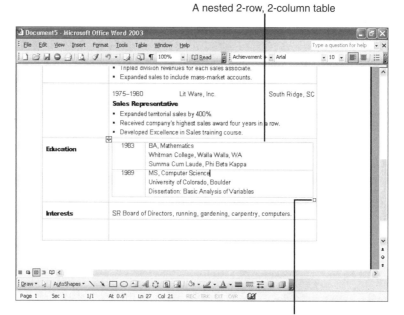

The nested table's drag handle

CHAPTER **15**

MASTERING STYLES AND TEMPLATES

In this chapter

15

MOVING BEYOND MANUAL FORMATTING

Most Word users work too hard. They start with a set of boring default formats for every new document and then manually adjust those formats for every document. Manual formatting works, but at a high price in time and inconsistency. Doing the same work over and over again is unnecessary, especially when you learn how to save formats and reuse them.

To unlock this power, it's important that you understand how Word handles formatting. The secret resides in a handful of key concepts that are not immediately obvious. When you understand how much time and effort you can save with a minimal investment of work, you'll never go back to manual formatting again.

USING STYLES AND TEMPLATES TO MANAGE FORMATS

Word allows you to apply multiple formatting settings at one time by using *styles*. You gather character and paragraph format settings together and give them a name. Then, when you want to use all the formatting at once, you apply the style. For example, you could tell Word that you want the NewsHeadline style to consist of centered paragraphs, with Arial 18-point, italic blue characters. Then, every time you apply the style NewsHeadline to a paragraph, Word formats it as centered, Arial 18 point, italic blue. To work with styles, use the Styles and Formatting task pane; click the Styles and Formatting button on the Formatting toolbar to show or hide this task pane.

Think of styles as an easy and fast way to organize the format settings you see on the Styles and Formatting task pane. Although you can scroll through the task pane's Pick Formatting to Apply list, and ultimately find the Arial 18-point, italic blue entry, it's generally simpler to find a style called NewsHeadline. Styles also tie parts of your document together, to ensure the formatting is consistent: If you decide to change formatting for all your product names to Arial 18 point, bold blue, you can change the style and watch your changes ripple through the document to every piece of text that uses that style. Looking for the old formatting and replacing it by hand is a tedious, cumbersome, error-prone task.

Styles are stored in *templates*. When you create a new document, you must base it on a template. You can use the default Normal document template (Normal.dot) or one of the cookie-cutter prototypes installed with Word, or you can create and save your own custom template and use it as the basis for new documents. Word dutifully copies all the text that resides in the template into the new document—even if the template contains only a single paragraph mark—before it presents the document to you for editing. It also loads all the styles, macros, AutoText entries, and other saved elements from that template.

Behind every document sits at least one associated template. Unless you've taken steps to change it, the main template attached to a document is the same one you used to create the document in the first place. To see the name of the template associated with the current document, choose Tools, Templates and Add-Ins, and look in the Document Template box (see Figure 15.1).

Figure 15.1
Word tells you the name of the template attached to the current document, as well as the names of any "global" templates (other than Normal.dot) that were loaded when Word started.

NOTE

A *global template* is a template that's available to all open documents. Specifying a global template gives you access to styles, special-purpose macros, and AutoText entries throughout Word, without having to change the template for a given document. Because the Normal document template (Normal.dot) is always loaded and made global each time Word starts, it's always available to every open document. You'll hear Normal.dot called "the" global template, but it isn't the only one: You can have multiple global templates available if you wish.

Now say that you apply the style NewsHeadline to a paragraph. Word first checks the document to see whether it includes a style by that name. If the style isn't there, Word looks in the document's template. If the style isn't in the template (or if no custom template is attached to the document), Word looks in a special template, called Normal, which is always available.

The Normal document template includes dozens of predefined styles, including the ubiquitous "Heading 1," "Heading 2," and "Heading 3" styles, the "Normal" paragraph style, and a plethora of styles used for formatting table of contents entries, footnotes, bulleted and numbered lists, index entries, tables, and more.

To make matters even more confusing, sometimes Word takes it upon itself to automatically apply a style to text you've typed. We discuss these automated escapades elsewhere in this chapter, but here are the major culprits:

- Word may apply a Heading style to your short sentences or sentence fragments. To enable or disable this behavior, choose Tools, AutoCorrect Options, and on the AutoFormat As You Type tab, select or clear the Built-in Heading Styles box.

15

- Word may change the properties of styles when you position the insertion point in manually formatted text and then use the Style drop-down box. To stop this behavior, choose Tools, AutoCorrect Options and, on the AutoFormat As You Type tab, clear the Define Styles Based on Your Formatting box.

- If you manually apply formatting to one paragraph, Word may apply that change to your entire document. To prevent this from happening, you need to modify your Normal paragraph style so that it stops automatically updating every time you make a change.

 See "Word Keeps Changing My Entire Document," in the "Troubleshooting" section at the end of this chapter, for instructions on how to make the change.

- Word automatically applies the Hyperlink character style (blue, underlined, and clickable) to text you type that appears to be a web address—say, www.quepublishing.com. To disable this setting, choose Tools, AutoCorrect, and on the AutoFormat As You Type tab, clear the Internet and Network Paths with Hyperlinks box.

NOTE

> In addition to named styles and templates, Word also supports *themes*, which are prepackaged sets of background colors, graphical bullets, and other design elements, suitable only for online viewing (in web pages and email messages, for example). Themes originated with another member of the Microsoft Office family, a distant cousin called FrontPage, which is used for designing and managing websites. Themes aren't so much integrated with Word as they are tacked on. You can't create or change a theme using Word; for that job, you must use FrontPage. In general, themes can cause behavior that many experienced Word users find perplexing. (Themes aren't stored in templates—they're in *.inf and *.elm files; they don't print.)

Styles and templates are a powerful way to manage formatting. You'll have best results if you follow these basic guidelines:

- Change global preferences and styles—those you want to use in all documents, all the time—in the Normal document template, Normal.dot.

- If you plan to reuse custom styles, store them in their own templates, not in individual documents or in the Normal document template.

- Be extra careful when creating custom styles in individual documents. In particular, avoid customizing any styles that use the same names as Word's built-in styles—the Normal and Heading 1 paragraph styles, for instance. It's too easy to accidentally replace your customized styles with the default style, wiping out your careful formatting work. If you must create a custom, one-off style, use a descriptive name that is unique to that document.

- Develop a consistent naming strategy for custom styles, especially those that use inheritance to pick up attributes from other styles.

■ Back up every custom document template you create. At a minimum, you should have safe copies of your customized Normal.dot file and any special-purpose templates you've created. Be sure to update these backup copies whenever you make changes.

→ To learn where Word and other Office programs store your customized files, **see** "Where Should You Keep Your Files?," **p. 62**.

FORMATTING DOCUMENTS WITH STYLES

A style is nothing more or less than a shorthand for formatting: Put a bunch of formatting specifications together, give it a name, and you have a style. If you find yourself applying the same formatting to text throughout a document, styles can help ensure a consistent and professional appearance that's easily modified. Use styles to control the formatting of the following:

■ **Heading paragraphs**—Whether the headings are chapter titles, section names, class numbers, departments, committee and subcommittee names—it doesn't matter. If your documents include multiple paragraphs that are used for a specific purpose and are always formatted the same way, create a style for that type of paragraph.

■ **Repeating body text**—If your document includes multiple blocks of text that require formatting different from normal body text, use a style to format it. For example, if your school district name always appears in Arial 12 point, bold, create a style for it. If your homeowners association documents consistently apply bold formatting to **Acme Homeowners Association**, use a style. Similarly, you can use a style to format italicized telephone numbers in a phone directory, to highlight student names in an article for the yearbook or the school paper, or to call attention to negative numbers in a report on fund-raising activities.

Defining and using styles consistently provides two great benefits. First, it ensures that all similar items in a document are formatted consistently—say, all the student names will appear in Garamond 12 point, bold. Second, if you need to make a change to the appearance of a style—say, you decide that all the student names should appear in 14 point instead of 12 point—changing the style (which requires just a few clicks) changes the appearance of everything formatted with that style, all the way through the document.

→ To learn when you should use direct formatting from the Styles and Formatting task pane's list and when you should choose styles, **see** "Direct Formatting Versus Styles," **p. 371**.

PARAGRAPH VERSUS CHARACTER STYLES

Paragraph styles control all the characteristics of a paragraph. Settings available as part of a paragraph style include centering, spacing, widows (that is, whether a single line that begins a paragraph should be allowed to appear at the bottom of a page), orphans (whether a single line that ends a paragraph should be allowed to appear alone at the top of a page), and other settings in the Paragraph dialog box that appears when you choose Format, Paragraph.

15

Paragraph styles also dictate bullets and numbering, borders and shading, tab stops, and the language Word uses for proofing tasks such as checking spelling and grammar.

TIP FROM

> One well-hidden check box in the settings for a paragraph style allows you to tell Word to skip over all text formatted with that style when using the spelling checker. This option is a time-saver in documents that contain lots of proper names and other words that normally trip up the spelling checker.

In addition, paragraph styles define *character formatting* for all characters within the paragraph. When you establish a paragraph style, you must also specify the default character format for the paragraph. Unless you specifically override the default character format with direct formatting or a character style, all text within a paragraph will appear in the paragraph's default character format.

Say you have a paragraph style called NewsHeadline that specifies centered paragraphs, with Arial 18-point, italic blue characters. If you apply the NewsHeadline style to a paragraph, all the characters turn Arial 18-point, italic blue. But if you then select the last word in the paragraph and make it red, the formatting you applied manually—the red—takes precedence over the default character formatting specified in the NewsHeadline style.

Character styles behave similarly, except they carry only character formatting. That includes the font, font size and style, color, super/subscript, underscore, and other attributes available in the Font dialog box that appears when you choose Format, Font. Character styles can also define borders and shading and proofing settings.

Say you have a character style called PhoneNumber that specifies the Courier New font in 10 point. If you apply the PhoneNumber style to some text, that text loses its previous formatting (which probably originated as the default character formatting of the underlying paragraph style) and picks up the formatting defined by the character style—Courier New 10 point.

TIP FROM

> How can you tell the difference between a character style and a paragraph style? You can look at the Style Type property on the Modify Style dialog box, but here's a faster way: In the Styles and Formatting task pane, look for the little symbol to the right of the style's name. A paragraph mark (¶) indicates a paragraph style, and an underlined lowercase a points out a character style.

When it comes to character formatting, Word's hierarchy is strict. First comes the paragraph style, which you can modify by applying formatting directly (for example, you can format a Normal paragraph to be right-aligned, without changing its style). Then comes the character style, which takes precedence over the paragraph style settings. Finally, you can apply formatting directly to a character. That formatting takes precedence over both the character and the paragraph styles.

You can see the hierarchy at work by bringing up the Reveal Formatting task pane as shown in Figure 15.2, and then selecting the Distinguish Style Source option at the bottom of the pane. The full hierarchy of formatting applied by both the paragraph and character styles, and by directly applied formatting is shown.

Figure 15.2
Using the Distinguish Style Source option on the Reveal Formatting task pane gives you all the formatting details about the selected text, along with an explanation of where the formatting originated.

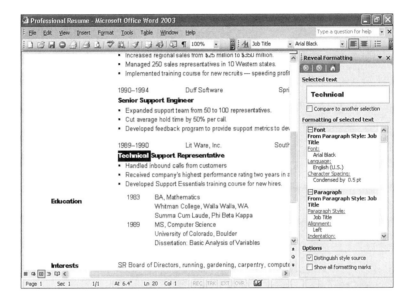

Every paragraph has exactly one paragraph style. Every character has exactly one character style. If no character style is defined for a particular piece of text, the style is "Default Paragraph Font," in which case Word applies the character formatting defined in the paragraph style. If you don't explicitly define a paragraph style when you begin a new paragraph, Word uses the default paragraph style for the document. Typically, this is the Normal style, but you can set any paragraph style as the default. To do so, format at least one paragraph in the current document using the style you want to set as your new default; then choose Tools, Options, click the Edit tab, and select that style from the Default Paragraph Style list in the Click and Type section.

LIST AND TABLE STYLES

Word has two built-in sets of styles that you might find useful when applying complex formatting:

TIP FROM

To see all the built-in styles available to you, bring up the Styles and Formatting task pane, and in the Show box, select All Styles. This setting also controls which styles are available from the drop-down Style list on the Formatting toolbar.

15

- List styles let you directly specify the level of a list item by choosing the style and applying it to your selected paragraph. For example, if you want a bulleted list item that appears at the third indent level, you can apply the List Bullet 3 style, and Word takes care of the details. List styles are available for standard indented lists with no bullets or numbering (called, simply, "List"), standard lists with extra space inserted below the list item ("List Continue"), bulleted lists ("List Bullet"), and numbered lists ("List Number").

- Table styles, which include all the formatting options available in Word's Table AutoFormat dialog box. There are dozens of styles, all with names beginning with the word "Table."

CAUTION

Word makes some effort to apply selected "Table" styles to all the rows in a table, whether they've been selected or not. That's not what you would expect from Word, and it trips up even experienced users. Make sure you review formatting changes made by the "Table" styles before moving on to other parts of a document, making liberal use of the Undo button, if necessary. To remove all table formatting (a drastic step), select the entire table and apply the Table Grid format.

APPLYING STYLES MANUALLY

To apply a paragraph style, follow these steps:

1. Click once inside the paragraph whose style you want to change, or select one or more paragraphs.

2. Choose the paragraph style from the Styles and Formatting task pane or from the drop-down Style list on the Formatting toolbar.

To apply a character style, follow these steps:

1. Select the characters whose style you want to change.

2. Choose the character style from the Styles and Formatting task pane.

If you select text and apply a paragraph style, Word looks at what you've selected before applying the style. If you have chosen all the text in a paragraph (with or without the paragraph mark), Word applies the paragraph style, just as you would expect. If one or more paragraph marks are in the selection, all the selected paragraphs have the chosen paragraph style applied.

You can assign styles to a selection manually, if you prefer, by clicking in the Style box on the Formatting toolbar and typing the style name. Word AutoCompletes this entry for you, so you might need to enter only a few characters. When you see the correct style name, press Enter to apply it to the selection.

You also have the option of assigning styles to toolbar buttons, to the right-click context menu, or to keyboard shortcut keys. If you regularly use a collection of styles for a specialized task, consider creating a custom toolbar with a button for each style; you can show or hide the toolbar as needed. For styles you use on all types of documents, keyboard shortcuts are the ticket. On a default installation, Word includes the keyboard shortcuts shown in Table 15.1.

→ To learn how to create customized buttons for frequently used styles and place them on toolbars, **see** "Customizing Toolbars," **p. 33**.

→ For instructions on how to assign keyboard shortcuts to frequently used styles, **see** "Bypassing Menus with Keyboard Shortcuts," **p. 46**.

TABLE 15.1	DEFAULT KEYBOARD COMBINATIONS FOR STYLES
Style	**Shortcut Key**
Normal	Ctrl+Shift+N
List Bullet	Ctrl+Shift+L
Heading 1	Ctrl+Alt+1
Heading 2	Ctrl+Alt+2
Heading 3	Ctrl+Alt+3

TIP FROM

The slow, predictable way to assign keyboard shortcuts in Word is to choose Tools, Customize, click the Keyboard button on the Commands tab, and then scroll through the list of available styles. Here's a much faster way: Open the Styles and Formatting task pane, click the arrow to the right of the style, and choose Modify. Click Format, Shortcut Key. The insertion point is already positioned in the Press New Shortcut Key box; all you have to do is hold down the key combination you want to assign to the style. Click Assign to save the new shortcut key.

USING THE STYLES AND FORMATTING TASK PANE

The Formatting and Styles task pane is much more than a static list of available styles. It represents both a window on your document's formatting and a central place from which to apply, modify, and manage styles in your documents and templates.

The most basic information appears in the Formatting of Selected Text box at the top of the task pane, which shows the source of the character formatting for the current selection (if no text is selected, this box shows the formatting at the insertion point). This will display direct formatting first; if no direct formatting is applied to the selection, this box shows the style that is the source of the character formatting.

15

TIP FROM

Ed & Woody

When you edit a document in Normal view, you can set an esoteric option to show the Style Area, which displays the current paragraph style in the margin to the left of every paragraph. For details on how to show or hide the Style Area, see "Normal View," **p. 326**.

Using the Styles and Formatting task pane, you can select all the text in a document that shares a particular type of formatting—whether it's direct or applied by a style. To select all text that matches the formatting of the current selection, click the Select All button under the Formatting of Selected Text box. To select all text that's formatted with a particular style, or with a combination of a style and direct formatting, find the formatting entry in the list, click the arrow to its right, and choose Select All *nn* Instance(s) (conveniently, Word tells you exactly how many times that particular bit of formatting is used in the current document).

This technique is the preferred way to change styles applied to a particular type of text. If you've used direct formatting to make all headlines appears as Arial 18-point, italic blue, you might decide you want to apply the NewsHeadline style instead. No problem. Select all text with the direct formatting (as shown in Figure 15.3), and then click the NewsHeadline style to instantly reformat every instance.

Figure 15.3
Use the Styles and Formatting task pane to select all instances of a particular type of manual formatting so that you can apply a named style instead.

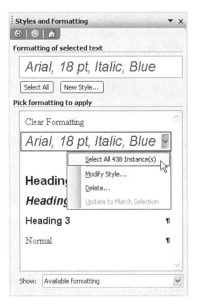

As we'll see in the following section, you can also use this task pane to create a new style, modify an existing style, or delete a custom style that's no longer needed. (You cannot, however, delete any of the built-in styles in the Normal document template, such as Normal, Heading 1, and Body Text.)

TIP FROM

> If you find the formatting lists overwhelming, click Custom, and then select and clear check boxes to limit the display of styles to those you know you want to use and no others.

SAVING FORMATS AS NAMED STYLES

Although Word ships with more than 100 defined styles—they're built in to the Normal template—you'll quickly find that they don't always apply to your documents and your specific needs.

If your needs are simple, you can set up a paragraph style by formatting a paragraph the way you want and telling Word the name of the style to be based on that formatting. To do so:

1. Format an entire paragraph to have all the attributes you want—both character and paragraph formatting apply.

2. Click once inside the paragraph. If you've used multiple fonts or font styles in the paragraph, the new paragraph style will use the font formatting at the point where you click.

3. Click New Style in the Style and Formatting task pane, and type in a name for the new paragraph style in the Name box (see Figure 15.4).

Figure 15.4
Creating a new style can be tricky. Make sure you understand what all the options mean before using them.

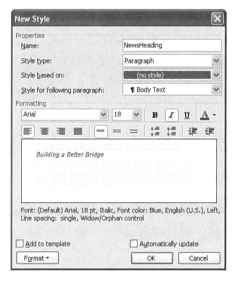

4. In the Style Type box, choose Paragraph to create a paragraph style, or Character for a character style. (You can also choose a table or list style, although it would be inappropriate in this example.)

15

5. In the Style Based On box, choose the style you want your new style to be based on. Any changes you make to the style listed here will also apply to your new style. If you want your style to stand on its own, choose (no style) from the top of the list.

TIP FROM

EQ & Woody

> Managed properly, an inheritance scheme is a wonderfully effective way to help you keep a complex design in perfect order with styles. You can create hierarchies of styles that are all based on a small number of base styles, and then change the overall design of your publication by adjusting just the base font. For example, you might define a Catalog Base style that contains only the basic font formatting—Arial 12 point, with single line spacing. You can then define styles for Catalog Headings and Catalog Product Descriptions and Catalog Captions, varying the size, color, and weight of the font. Using this organization, you can change the font used throughout your publication—from Arial to Arial Narrow, say—just by modifying the Catalog Base style. If you decide to create a highly structured style scheme like this one, be sure to document it thoroughly!

6. The Style for Following Paragraph box lets you tell Word which style it should use for the next paragraph when you press Enter.

TIP FROM

EQ & Woody

> By defining a chain of styles in your document, you can automate a lot of routine formatting. After using the Illustration style, for example, you might want the next paragraph to be formatted with the Caption style, and the paragraph after that to be formatted with the Body Text style. By adjusting the Style for Following Paragraph settings for each style, you can format a paragraph as Illustration and then apply the following styles effortlessly, just by pressing Enter.

CAUTION

> The Style for Following Paragraph setting kicks in only if the insertion point is immediately in front of a paragraph mark when you press Enter. If you leave even a single space between the insertion point and the paragraph mark when you press Enter, Word gives you a new paragraph with the same formatting and style as the current paragraph.

7. Select or clear the Add to Template check box. If this box is cleared, the new style is saved only in the current document. If the Add to Template check box is selected, however, the style is added to the document's template and is available for use with any other document based on the template.

8. Select the Automatically Update box if you want every change you make to a paragraph formatted with this particular style to be automatically applied to every paragraph in the document with that style. Clear this check box if you want the style's formatting to remain fixed as you define it.

CAUTION

> In almost all circumstances, Automatically Update is a disaster waiting to happen. You should use this option only on those rare occasions when you are absolutely certain that you never want to apply any direct formatting to text formatted with a particular style without changing all other paragraphs that use the same style.

9. Click the Format button to apply any additional formatting options. For a paragraph style, you can adjust virtually any type of formatting; for a character style, you can adjust font, border, and language settings only. You can also assign a shortcut key from this menu.

10. Click OK. If no style with that name exists, a new one is created for you and placed in the document. Click the style name in the Styles and Formatting task pane to apply the newly created style to the current paragraph or any other existing paragraphs.

TIP FROM

EQ & Woody

> To create a new paragraph style based on a selected paragraph's attributes, you can just type a new name into the Style box on the Formatting toolbar and press Enter.

If you want to modify a style's definition, click the drop-down button next to the style's name in the Styles and Formatting task pane, and then choose Modify. You'll have all the foregoing formatting options at your disposal. For simple changes, such as changing the font, font size, or spacing of a paragraph style, you can modify a style by example: Format some text using the style you want to modify and make your changes; then click the arrow to the right of the style name in the Styles and Formatting task pane and choose Update to Match Selection.

 If your custom styles disappear when you open a document, see "Automatically Updating Styles" in the "Troubleshooting" section at the end of this chapter.

CUSTOMIZING THE NORMAL DOCUMENT TEMPLATE

When you create a new, blank document—either by clicking the New Blank Document icon on the Standard toolbar or by choosing Blank Document in the New Document task pane—Word creates a new document based on the Normal document template, Normal.dot. The Normal template is always available when Word is running.

As we noted at the beginning of this chapter, Word looks for styles, starting with the document, moving up to the document's template and, if the style name can't be found there, looking inside the Normal template.

NOTE

> If the document is based on the Normal template, there's no intermediate step—the search progresses directly from the document to Normal.

15

Actually, the Normal document template is no more "normal" than any other template. A more accurate name would be the default document template, the one Word uses when you create a new blank document without specifying a template. Normal.dot is frequently called the global template, because it's always available. Although other templates can be global in the sense that they're loaded when Word starts (refer to the Templates and Add-Ins dialog box, Figure 15.1 at the beginning of this chapter), no other template is tied directly to the New Blank Document icon on the Standard toolbar or the Blank Document choice in the New Document task pane.

By default, Word 2003 starts new blank documents with the Times New Roman 12-point font, and no paragraph indenting or spacing. If you open Normal.dot, you'll see why: It contains a single paragraph mark formatted in the Normal style, and the Normal style is defined as Times New Roman 12 point, with no paragraph indenting or spacing. When Word creates a new document based on Normal.dot, it copies everything in the template into the new document—just as it does when creating a document from any template—and you end up with a new document with a single paragraph mark, with Normal style formatting.

TIP FROM

> If you want to change the default font for new blank documents, you don't need to mess with Normal.dot. Instead, use this hidden shortcut: Create a new blank document, and then choose Format, Font. Choose the font you want (say, Garamond 11 point), and click the Default button. From that point on, any new blank document you create will use the Garamond 11-point font for its Normal style.

If you want to change more than the default font on new blank documents, the simplest way is this:

1. Create a new blank document by clicking the New Blank Document icon on the Standard toolbar.

2. Choose Format, Styles and Formatting. In the Styles and Formatting task pane, you should see Normal highlighted. Click the down-arrow to the right of Normal, and then click Modify to change the Normal style.

3. Make whatever changes you want to make to Word's defaults for new blank documents. Click the Format button to adjust more advanced formatting options: You can change the font, paragraph formatting, tabs, borders and shading, proofing language, bullets, and numbering.

4. When you've made all the changes you want to make, select the Add to Template check box, and click OK. All the modifications you made to the Normal style are reflected in this document's template—which just happens to be the Normal document template, Normal.dot.

If you've made a colossal mess of your Normal document template and want to start over, see "Restoring the Default Normal Template" in the "Troubleshooting" section at the end of this chapter.

USING WORD'S BUILT-IN TEMPLATES

Word ships with scores of templates, and hundreds more are available for download from Microsoft's Office Online website. Choose Help, Microsoft Office Online to search for additional templates not included on the Office CD-ROM.

Although the generic "click here and type" templates can come in handy in a pinch, you'll want to customize any generic template that you expect to use more than a few times. It's well worth your while to replace the "click here" instructions with text appropriate to your particular situation—your name, phone number, and so on. Here's how to customize Word's Professional fax template and make it your own. You can use the same basic techniques with any of Word's "canned" templates.

1. Choose File, New, and click On My Computer... in the Templates section. On the Letters & Faxes tab, double-click Professional Fax.

2. Fill out the appropriate portions of the fax template—the information that won't change from fax to fax—such as the company name, address and phone number, and possibly the From: entry.

3. Choose File, Save, and in the Save as Type box, choose Document Template. Give the template a descriptive name and click the Save button.

4. The next time you want to use the template, open the Templates dialog box and select the template name you assigned from the offerings on the General tab.

Many of the built-in Word templates contain interesting examples of techniques discussed elsewhere in this book. The following are the ones you're likely to learn from, starting with the most instructive:

- The Manual template (Publications tab) contains dozens of excellent hands-on examples that apply to any document more than a few pages long.

- The Résumé templates and wizard (Other Documents tab) use tables, as you might expect. They show you how to set up text on a line so some is left-aligned, some centered, and some is right-aligned. (Hint: Use two tab stops, the one in the middle centered, the one on the right margin right-aligned.)

- The Pleading Wizard (Legal Pleadings tab) shows you how to use tables to construct and control horizontal and vertical lines.

- The various Report templates (Reports tab) contain several unusual examples of graphic elements in longer documents. These templates are also well worth studying.

- The various Fax templates (Letters & Faxes tab) all use tables to good advantage, with different kinds of borders. They also have macros you can use called CheckIt and UncheckIt that allow you to select and clear check boxes in a document.

- The Brochure template (on the Publications tab) contains an interesting example of three-column section formatting, used to create a tri-fold brochure. Work with it long enough and you'll become convinced that Publisher handles simple tri-fold brochures much more easily.

- The Directory template (Publications tab) gets you started with a membership roster, or directory of organizations. This template is well worth examining closely for its deft use of styles. Unfortunately, it doesn't include a demonstration of the {styleref} field, which is an indispensable part of most rosters.

- If you have to prepare a thesis to complete your MBA, the Thesis template (Publications tab) comes in handy, providing your university conforms to the styles used in the template.

If you intend to use any of the built-in Letter templates, be sure to read the indispensable discussion of the Letter Wizard before you go any further. You'll find it in Chapter 16, "Letters, Mail Merge, and 'Smart' Documents."

CHANGING DOCUMENT FORMATS GLOBALLY

When Word creates a new document, it copies the entire contents of the template to the new document—text, pictures, headers and footers, and so on—and then establishes a link between the document and template (so, for example, styles in the template become available in the document). With one possible exception, after a document is created, nothing from the template gets copied into the document. So, for example, if you change the Normal template so its default font is Garamond 11 point, all new blank documents will have Garamond 11 point—but all old documents based on the Normal template will stay just as they are.

TIP FROM

EQ & Woody

> There's one huge exception to this rule: If you choose Tools, Templates and Add-Ins, and then click the Automatically Update Document Styles check box in the Templates and Add-Ins dialog box, Word "updates" a document style if one exists in the template with the same name. This option is good news if you always, without exception, want template styles to control the look of a document, as you might in a corporate environment, where maintaining a standard design is essential. But if you sometimes create styles within a document, avoid this option.

So unless the Automatically Update Document Styles box is checked, you can make all the changes you want to a template, and the documents associated with that template won't change a bit. Changes to the template affect only new documents based on the template.

How do you make global paragraph and character formatting changes to a document—that is, make global changes to the appearance of a document—without going into each style, each paragraph, and making the changes manually? Word gives you three options:

- Allow Word to make changes for you, either piece-by-piece (in the AutoFormat feature) or wholesale (by using the Style Gallery). Neither of these options is likely to improve the appearance of the document.

→ To learn how you can put Word's AutoFormatting features to work for you, **see** "Automatic Formatting," **p. 376**.

- Change the template applied to the document, and then force Word to update all the styles in the document so they conform to the styles in the new template. You might want to do this if, for example, you're updating an old document with a new template that handles all the styles you commonly use.

- Apply a theme. Because themes include background colors, and background colors rarely appear in professional documents, this approach is virtually unusable unless you're working with a web page.

To attach a new template to a document and update the document's styles, follow these steps:

1. If the document has any styles defined inside it (that is, at the document level), save a copy of the document. This process can completely overwrite styles in the document, and you can't bring them back.

2. Choose Tools, Templates and Add-Ins. Click the Attach button, navigate to the template you want to attach to the document, and click Open.

3. Select the Automatically Update Document Styles check box. Click OK.

4. Close and reopen the document. With the Automatically Update Document Styles check box selected, the act of opening the document flushes out any styles with identical names in the document—overwriting the document's formatting with the new template's formatting.

5. If you don't want to update the document with future style changes in the attached template, immediately go back into the Templates and Add-Ins dialog box (choose Tools, Templates and Add-Ins) and clear the Automatically Update Document Styles check box.

CAUTION

The Word documentation says you can leave that box selected "to ensure that your document contains up-to-date style formatting." That's true for documents based on standard corporate templates, where you absolutely, positively want the template to dictate every style choice. It's also the right choice if you fully understand the relationship between the document you're working with and the template to which it's attached, and you want to use only the styles in the template. If you're experimenting with styles in a document, however, leave this box cleared. You'll avoid headaches caused by disappearing document styles.

Before you consider applying a theme to change the appearance of a document, make sure you understand what a theme entails. A theme contains the following elements:

- A background pattern (few of the themes that come with Word have solid-color backgrounds)

- Style definitions for Heading 1, 2, 3, 4, 5, and 6, as well as the Normal style

- A graphic for bullets

- A graphic for horizontal lines
- AutoText entries specifically designed for web pages—the "created by" entry puts the originator's name on the page; "created on" inserts the date

Themes can be handy if you're trying to create a web page that matches the formatting generated in a different program—FrontPage or PowerPoint, for example. They're also reasonably useful if you're developing a web page from scratch or designing a colorful template for use with HTML-formatted email messages. But they're effectively unusable for most documents you intend to print out.

When you apply a theme to a document (choose Format, Theme, per Figure 15.5), Word does the following:

- Changes the background of the document (choose Format, Background) to match the pattern in the theme.

Figure 15.5
Apply a theme to a Word document by choosing Format, Theme, and choosing from the list.

- Replaces the document's (not the template's) style definitions for Normal and Heading 1, 2, 3, 4, 5, and 6.
- Sets up default bullets and horizontal lines to match the graphic in the theme.
- Puts the AutoText entries in the template (not the document).

CAUTION

> At the beginning of this chapter, we warned you to avoid customizing the standard styles in a document (Normal, Heading 1, and so on). This advice is especially relevant if you decide to tinker with themes. When you apply a theme to a document, it replaces those standard styles with those from the theme. You can use the Undo option to immediately remove the them and restore your customized styles. However, if you save the document and then remove the theme by opening the Themes dialog box and setting it to (No Theme), Word replaces the standard styles with those from the Normal document template. Unless you saved a backup copy first (always a good strategy), the custom styles you defined in the original document are gone for good.

15

You should expect a lot of additional anomalies if you decide to work with themes. Animated graphics appear in themes, but they won't be animated in Word—you have to use your web browser to see them move. You can't create or modify a theme in Word. You have to use FrontPage. They don't print.

MANAGING STYLES AND TEMPLATES

As you can see from the discussion in this chapter, styles and templates are inextricably related. Because many of the styles you use are stored in templates, managing styles boils down to managing the templates that contain them.

CREATING A NEW TEMPLATE FROM SCRATCH

To create a new template choose File, New. In the New Document task pane, click On My Computer… and select the file you want to use as the starting point for your new document (use the default, Blank Document, to start from scratch). Select the Template option under Create New, and then click OK.

Look in the title bar and you'll see that the newly created file uses the default name Template1 instead of Document1. A Word template is nearly identical to a Word document, except that it also contains AutoText entries. (The Normal template also contains formatted AutoCorrect entries.) That's the only difference. By default, Word templates are identified with the filename extension *.dot. Although you can use a different file extension, only files with the *.dot extension appear in the Templates dialog box.

WHERE DOES WORD STORE TEMPLATES?

When you save a new template, Word attempts to save it in your User templates folder— that's the location marked User Templates in the File Locations tab of the Options dialog box (choose Tools, Options), as shown in Figure 15.6.

Unless you specifically change the location on the File Locations tab, custom templates you create are stored in a standard location within your personal documents folder. As we noted in Chapter 3, "Keeping Track of Your Files and Settings," you can open this folder directly by typing `%appdata%\Microsoft\Templates` in the Run box on the Start menu or in the Address Bar of Windows Explorer. If you want to create a new tab for the Templates dialog box and place your template on that tab, choose File, Save As, choose Document Template from the Save As Type list, and then click the Create New Folder icon. Give the new folder the name you want to appear on the new tab, and then choose Save. Follow these same steps if you want to add a custom template to one of the existing, predefined tabs on the Templates dialog box. To add a template to the Letters & Faxes tab, for instance, you need to create a new folder called Letters & Faxes and save your template to that folder.

When you bring up the Templates dialog box, Word combines the templates in the User Templates folder, the Workgroup Templates folder, and any predefined (possibly uninstalled) templates that ship with Office (in the U.S. English version of Word, those are stored in `%programfiles%\Microsoft Office\Templates\1033`).

Figure 15.6
The User Templates and Workgroup Templates folders should hold all the templates you intend to use.

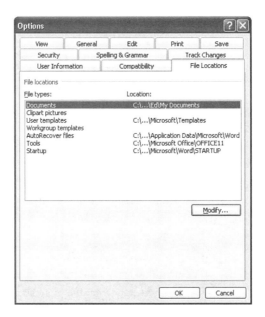

→ To learn the tricks of the trade when it comes to creating new files throughout Office, **see** "Creating New Files," **p. 66**.

Templates stored in the \Startup folder (shown at the bottom of Figure 15.6) are automatically loaded by Word when it starts. If you have any VBA macros that you want to be available every time you run Word, they should be placed in templates located in the \Startup folder. We recommend this strategy instead of using the Normal document template (Normal.dot).

NOTE

The Word documentation would have you believe that styles defined in templates in the \Startup folder are available in every open document. That isn't true. Macros, AutoText entries, toolbars, and other saved items in the \Startup templates are available in all documents. Styles are not.

CUSTOMIZING WORD TEMPLATES

When you open a template (as opposed to creating a new document based on a template), you can modify it in precisely the same ways as you would change a document: You can add text, pictures, headers and footers, hyperlinks, macros—in short, everything that goes in a document (plus AutoText entries).

Remember, however, that any text you place in the document itself is considered to be "boilerplate," and is copied into any new documents you create based on that template. If you attach a template to an existing document, however, saved items in that template are available, but the boilerplate text is ignored.

COPYING STYLES AND SETTINGS BETWEEN TEMPLATES

Word includes a handy tool called the *Organizer* that allows you to copy styles, toolbars, and macro projects between documents and templates. The Organizer also lets you copy AutoText entries, but these can move only from template to template.

To make use of the Organizer, follow these steps:

1. Choose Tools, Templates and Add-Ins. Click the Organizer button. You see the Organizer dialog box (see Figure 15.7).

Figure 15.7
The Organizer copies, deletes, or renames styles, AutoText entries, custom toolbars, and macro projects.

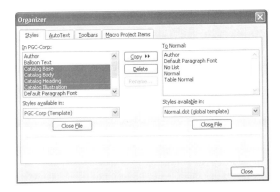

2. Make sure the "from" and "to" files—documents or templates—are referenced in the Styles Available In boxes. If you have the wrong files, click Close File, then Open File, and select the correct ones.

3. Select Styles, AutoText, Toolbars, or Macro Project Items, depending on which settings you want to manipulate. Note that AutoText items can reside only in templates.

4. Select the individual items and click Copy, Delete, or Rename, as appropriate.

TROUBLESHOOTING

WORD KEEPS CHANGING MY ENTIRE DOCUMENT

Every time I select a paragraph and make even the tiniest change to it, Word changes my entire document. If I want to boldface a paragraph, my entire document turns bold. If I add a bullet character, every paragraph in the document gets a bullet. I figured out that I can press Ctrl+Z to undo the global change, but this is getting ridiculous. What's going on?

Word is only following orders. Somewhere along the line, you told Word that you wanted it to automatically update the Normal paragraph style every time you made a change to it. When you select a paragraph formatted using the Normal style, Word dutifully applies the change to every other paragraph using that style. Although this option is incredibly useful for custom styles you create, we can't think of a single good reason to have this option turned on for the Normal style. To turn it off, open the Styles and Formatting task pane, click the arrow to the right of the Normal style entry, and choose Modify. Clear the Automatically Update check box and click OK.

REVEALING CHARACTER FORMATTING

As a former WordPerfect user, I'm accustomed to WordPerfect's "reveal codes" command, which displays formatting directives hidden in a document, much like HTML tags. When I search through online help, however, there's no mention of Word's reveal codes command.

Word's native document format doesn't use WordPerfect-style codes to apply formatting. Instead, it stores formatting for each character with the character itself, and it stores paragraph formatting in the paragraph mark. The Reveal Formatting task pane displays the names of styles and direct formatting applied to any character. If you save a document in Extended Markup Language (XML) format, Word saves formatting instructions as XML tags, but these bear no resemblance to WordPerfect codes.

AUTOMATICALLY UPDATING STYLES

When I opened a document that contained a number of custom styles, the formatting changed unexpectedly, and clicking the Undo button didn't bring them back.

Styles in the document template are overwriting styles in the document itself. If you create a set of formats in named styles and save them in a document, you might find that your styles get wiped out by styles of the same name stored in the document template every time you open the document. To make sure you don't encounter this problem with a specific document, choose Tools, Templates and Add-Ins, and clear the Automatically Update Document Styles box. To avoid the problem in the future, do not use standard style names (Normal, Heading 1, and so on) when creating custom styles within a document.

RESTORING THE DEFAULT NORMAL TEMPLATE

I've made a mess of the Normal template, and every new document I create inherits formatting I don't want.

You have three choices. The easy (but drastic) option is to exit Word, rename Normal.dot to something else (for example, Old-normal.dot), and start Word again. When Word can't find Normal.dot, it creates a new Normal document template; in the process, however, you'll lose all your toolbar customizations, keyboard shortcuts, formatted AutoCorrect entries, and much more.

If you just want to reset the Normal paragraph style and other standard styles to their defaults, you can use the Modify Style dialog box to work through each style in the template until you have the Normal style back to where it started. For U.S. installations, that includes the following defaults: Times New Roman, 12-point, English (U.S.), Flush left, Line spacing single, Widow/orphan control. Make sure you click Add to Template when you're done. It's more work, but you won't lose any of your customizing.

If that sounds like too much work, then combine the two strategies. Create a fresh copy of Normal.dot using all Word's defaults, and then use the Organizer to selectively move custom styles, toolbars, macros, and other items from the backed-up Old-Normal.dot to your new file. Just don't overwrite the standard styles!

EXTRA CREDIT: STYLES AND MANUALLY APPLIED FORMATTING

To understand the interplay between styles and manually applied formatting, consider the character highlighted in Figure 15.8. Using the techniques discussed in the section, "Direct Formatting Versus Styles," in Chapter 13, "Creating Great-Looking Documents," we created a paragraph style called ChapterHeading and applied to the heading, "*Cool Communities.*"

Consider what Word goes through to display the letter C properly. First, it picks up the paragraph formatting from the ChapterHeading paragraph style—flush left, page break with Auto space before, and so on. Second, it picks up formatting that's been applied manually to the entire paragraph—in this case, a 5% gray pattern that appears in back of the letter C.

Third, Word picks up the font formatting defined in the paragraph's style—here, that's Baskerville Old Face 20 point bold, kern 2ed at 16 point. Fourth, Word applies any formatting associated with a character style. Because the letter C does not have a character style applied to it, there's nothing new at that level.

Finally, Word looks for font formatting that's been applied directly to the character. In this case, the letter C is italic because it's been formatted manually this way.

Figure 15.8

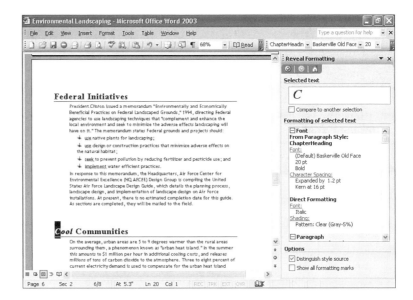

Every time Word displays a character, it goes through a complex process just like this, to sort out exactly how the character should appear. You can see precisely how Word came up with the formatting of any specific character by following along closely in the Reveal Formatting task pane, particularly if the Distinguish Style Source box is checked. Shift+F1 will bring up the task pane.

LETTERS, MAIL MERGE, AND "SMART" DOCUMENTS

PUTTING WORD TO WORK

In previous chapters, we've discussed how you use Word to create documents, generally starting from a blank page. In this chapter, we explain how to get Word to do some of the work for you, starting with letters and advancing to documents that can literally fill in the blanks on your behalf.

One of the most common uses of Word is to create letters. This chapter starts by explaining how to create simple letters using the Letter Wizard. The process isn't as simple as it sounds. In fact, if you use the Letter Wizard incorrectly, you might wind up creating more work for yourself! We also explain how to use Word to print matching envelopes and labels.

What if you need to create multiple letters to a long list of recipients, all based on the same basic text? For that task, use Word's mail merge (a topic known to cause migraine headaches even for experienced Word users). Mail merge isn't just for junk mail; we explain how to use its features to create directories, mass e-mail campaigns, sheets of labels and postcards, and other unconventional outputs.

The secret weapon that makes mail merge possible is a complex Word feature called fields. After we explain how to create basic mail merge projects, we end with a detailed discussion of more advanced uses of fields.

CREATING AND EDITING LETTERS

It sounds so easy: In theory, the Letter Wizard walks you step-by-step through the process of addressing, writing, and formatting a personal or business letter, with perfect results. In practice, the Letter Wizard and its connection to the Outlook Contacts list suffer from dozens of frustrating flaws—unless you know the secrets.

TIP FROM

Ed & Woody

> Although you might think the Letter Wizard is just another ho-hum step-by-step helper, you might be surprised at what you don't know about this seemingly innocuous wizard. The more you know, the more you can get out of it!

USING THE LETTER WIZARD

The key to making the Word Letter Wizard generate decent-looking letters lies in understanding what it can and cannot do, and how it interacts with the letter itself.

The least effective way to use the Letter Wizard is to start with a blank document and choose Tools, Letters and Mailings, Letter Wizard. The results, as shown in Figure 16.1, will surely be unsatisfactory—even if you choose a superb custom template in the Choose a Page Design box.

Figure 16.1
When you run the Letter Wizard on a blank document, the wizard throws away almost all the contents of the template you choose, generating an amateurish-looking letter.

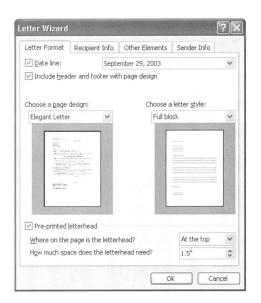

Be vigilant: Word can trick you into running the Letter Wizard on a blank (or nearly blank) document in any number of ways. If you select an item in Outlook's Contacts folder and choose Actions, New Letter to Contact, you'll end up running the Letter Wizard on a blank document. If you choose File, New, choose General Templates, and pick the Letter Wizard from the Letters & Faxes tab, once again you'll end up running the Letter Wizard on a blank document. Regardless of how you get there, this approach dooms you to a poorly constructed, amateurish letter.

TIP FROM

> The only way to get a professional-looking letter out of Word's Letter Wizard is to start with a document that's been specifically designed to work with the Letter Wizard. The three templates on the Letter Format tab include all the right elements, but you need to replace generic text and graphics with your own content for best results.

The fundamental trick to using the Letter Wizard is this: Create a new document first—one that is specifically designed to work with the Letter Wizard. *Then* run the Letter Wizard.

Word ships with three templates that produce documents for use with the Letter Wizard. To see what they'll do, choose File, New. In the New Document task pane, click On My Computer (in the Templates section). In the Templates dialog box, click the Letters & Faxes tab and pick Contemporary Letter, Elegant Letter, or Professional Letter. Click OK to create the new document, and then click anywhere within the document itself and choose Tools, Letters and Mailings, Letter Wizard.

As you can see from the Letter Wizard's Recipient Info tab shown in Figure 16.2, the Letter Wizard actually picks up information from the letter itself—in this case the Dear Sir or Madam: salutation found in the Professional Letter template—and presents that information in the Letter Wizard dialog box.

Figure 16.2
The Letter Wizard picks up text from the letter template, such as the salutation shown at the bottom of this dialog box.

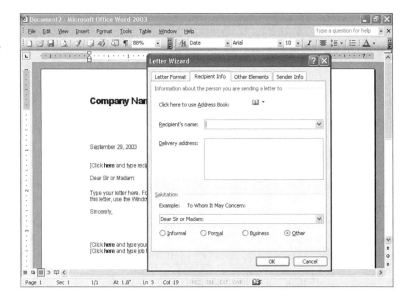

CUSTOMIZING LETTER TEMPLATES

The easiest way to make a template that will generate documents designed to work with the Letter Wizard is to start with one of Word's three built-in letter templates—Contemporary Letter, Elegant Letter, or Professional Letter—and save the modified template under a new name.

→ For details on how to work with Word templates, **see** "Customizing Word Templates," **p. 467**.

If you prefer to create a new template from scratch or modify an existing letter template, follow these guidelines to ensure that the documents it creates are compatible with the Letter Wizard:

- Use a {CreateDate} field for the date. The Date line box (shown previously in Figure 16.1) automatically finds the field and changes its formatting, based on the sample you choose from the drop-down box.

→ For a detailed explanation of how date and time fields work, **see** "Showing Dates and Times," **p. 502**.

- If you're printing on letterhead paper, draw an empty text box around the area where a logo or other graphic appears. The Letter Wizard adds the text box and flows the letter text around it. This technique is much simpler than trying to guess the exact settings to use in the Pre-printed Letterhead section on the Letter Format tab.

- Build your letter template any way you want, but be sure to use the style names listed in Table 16.1. The Letter Wizard relies heavily on named styles, and any deviation from this list will prevent the wizard from doing its magic.

In some cases, the Letter Wizard retrieves text from the letter and displays it on the wizard tabs. It identifies the text it needs based on the paragraph styles in the letter itself. For example, if you enter the text Ed Bott and format it with the Signature style, and then run the Letter Wizard, it places that text in the Sender's Name box on the Sender Info tab, as shown in Figure 16.3.

16

Figure 16.3
If you format a paragraph using the Signature style, the Letter Wizard picks up the text from that paragraph and uses it as the Sender's Name on the Sender Info tab.

The process works in reverse, too: if you type the name Woody Leonhard in the Sender's Name box on the Letter Wizard's Sender Info tab, and then click OK, the Letter Wizard removes any line in the letter that is formatted in the Signature style, and replaces each such line with one containing the text Woody Leonhard.

NOTE

If you use the Letter Wizard on a blank document, it remembers the settings you used most recently for the return address and fills in your name and address by default. These settings are stored in the Registry.

In short, the Letter Wizard picks up data from the letter based on certain predefined styles, and it puts data back into the letter using those styles. The styles are listed in Table 16.1.

TABLE 16.1   STYLES RECOGNIZED BY THE LETTER WIZARD

Style in Letter	Tab in Wizard	Box in Wizard
Inside Address Name	Recipient Info	Recipient's Name
Inside Address	Recipient Info	Delivery Address
Salutation	Recipient Info	Salutation
Reference Line	Other Elements	Reference Line
Mailing Instructions	Other Elements	Mailing Instructions
Attention Line	Other Elements	Attention
Subject Line	Other Elements	Subject
Cc List	Other Elements	Cc:
Signature	Sender Info	Sender's Name
Return Address	Sender Info	Return Address
Closing	Sender Info	Complimentary Closing
Signature Job Title	Sender Info	Job Title
Signature Company	Sender Info	Company
Reference Initials	Sender Info	Writer/Typist Initials
Enclosure	Sender Info	Enclosures

In addition, the main part of the letter should appear in a style called Body Text. The Letter Wizard modifies the Body Text, Closing, Signature, Signature Job Title, and Signature Company styles on-the-fly, depending on the option you select in the Choose a Letter Style box (Full block, Modified block, Semi-block) on the Letter Format tab.

If you construct your own templates using these styles, you should be able to use the Letter Wizard with excellent results.

TIP FROM

EQ & Woody

> The three prebuilt letter templates contain a number of "click here" placeholders. You can add your own placeholders using the same simple trick. Create a new macro that contains no code, name it NoMacro, and save it in your custom letter template. In the boilerplate text that makes up the body of the letter template, click to position the insertion point where you want the placeholder to appear. Choose Insert, Field, and select MacroButton from the list. In the Display Text box, enter the text for the "click here" prompt as you want it to appear in your document. From the Macro Name list, select NoMacro. Click OK to save your changes. Finally (and this step is crucial), format the paragraph that contains the prompt text using one of the named styles used by the Letter Wizard, as described in this section. Because your prompt text appears in the document as part of a field, you can select it with a single click; because the associated macro does nothing, you can simply replace the selected text.

ADDRESSING LETTERS WITH THE OUTLOOK CONTACTS LIST

On the Letter Wizard's Recipient tab, you can click the Address Book icon to open a dialog box that contains a list of all names in your Outlook Address Book. After you select a name and click OK, Word inserts the contact's name and address into your document. (If the contact has no address defined, this function inserts the contact's name only.)

TIP FROM

Ed & Woody

> You can customize Word so that it imports names and addresses directly from your Outlook Address Book into any document, without requiring the Letter Wizard. To add an Insert Address button to a toolbar, choose Tools, Customize, and click the Commands tab. From the Categories list on the left, choose Insert. Scroll through the list on the right until you find the Address Book command, and then click and drag it onto a convenient toolbar.

16

You can also use a record from the Contacts folder to fill in information about the sender of a letter. In the Letter Wizard, click the Address Book button on the Sender Info tab and select your own contact record. Word fills in your name, return address, job title, and company (if any of those details are missing, it leaves the corresponding fields blank).

Although we don't recommend it for standard letters, you can change the layout that Word uses for Address Book imports. This technique might come in handy if you want to use the Letter Wizard to create memos or other types of documents that don't follow the conventions of a standard letter. To customize the format of names and addresses imported with the Insert Address icon:

1. Start with a new blank document. Carefully type these three lines in the document:

```
<PR_DISPLAY_NAME>
<PR_TITLE>, <PR_COMPANY_NAME>
<PR_STREET_ADDRESS>
<PR_LOCALITY>, <PR_STATE_OR_PROVINCE> <PR_POSTAL_CODE>
```

2. Select all four lines. Choose Insert, AutoText, New, and create a new AutoText entry with the name AddressLayout (all one word).

The next time you click Word's Insert Address button and choose a name, it will use the codes from the new address layout AddressLayout as the template for the imported name and address.

If you use the four-line AutoText entry codes in step 1 in the previous list, you'll start getting names and addresses that look like this:

Bill Gates
Chief Software Engineer, Microsoft Corporation
One Microsoft Ave
Redmond, WA 98052

Word and Outlook recognize all the formatting codes defined in Table 16.2.

TABLE 16.2   VALID FORMATTING CODES FOR THE ADDRESSLAYOUT AUTOTEXT ENTRY

Code	Corresponding Field from Contact Form
PR_DISPLAY_NAME	Full Name
PR_GIVEN_NAME	First name
PR_SURNAME	Last name
PR_STREET_ADDRESS	Street address (one or more lines, from the designated mailing address)
PR_LOCALITY	City
PR_STATE_OR_PROVINCE	State or province
PR_POSTAL_CODE	ZIP or postal code
PR_COUNTRY	Country
PR_TITLE	Job title
PR_COMPANY_NAME	Company name
PR_DEPARTMENT_NAME	Department name (Details tab)
PR_OFFICE_TELEPHONE_NUMBER	Business number
PR_BUSINESS_FAX_NUMBER	Business fax number
PR_OFFICE2_TELEPHONE_NUMBER	Business 2 number
PR_HOME_TELEPHONE_NUMBER	Home number
PR_CELLULAR_TELEPHONE_NUMBER	Mobile number
PR_BEEPER_TELEPHONE_NUMBER	Pager number
PR_EMAIL_ADDRESS	First listed e-mail address
PR_COMMENT	Text in the Notes box

CREATING ENVELOPES AND LABELS

Word includes an extensive set of features that allow you to address and print a single envelope, use mail merge to generate a large number of properly addressed envelopes, or format single and multiple labels using addresses from a variety of sources.

PRINTING ENVELOPES

To print an envelope, choose Tools, Letters and Mailings, Envelopes and Labels. Fill in the Envelopes and Labels dialog box shown in Figure 16.4, and then click the Print button. Insert a blank envelope in your printer's manual feed, and you should get the results you expect.

Figure 16.4
To pull a delivery or return address for an envelope from the Outlook Address Book, click the Insert Address icon.

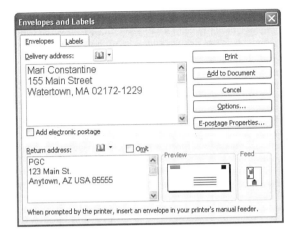

The first time you print an envelope, make sure you click the Options button to set up the proper envelope size, fonts, paper source, and other printing options.

TIP FROM

Although Word usually does a good job of figuring out what kind of printer you're using—and thus how to orient an envelope so it prints properly—it rarely (if ever) correctly identifies an envelope paper tray. If you have an envelope tray for your printer, you'll need to click the Options button and specify that your printer includes this tray.

If you select an address before choosing Tools, Letters and Mailings, Envelopes and Labels, that address appears in the Delivery Address box. In addition, Word is frequently smart enough to identify an address, if it appears near the beginning of the document.

When you click the Add to Document button in the Envelopes and Labels dialog box, Word creates a new section at the beginning of the document and stores the envelope in that section, numbered as Page 0. When you subsequently print the letter, both the letter itself and the envelope will print (unless you manually specify that you want to print only Page 1 and later). That can be helpful if you aren't ready to print the letter, but want to set the envelope up ahead of time. It can also be helpful in creating a template with an envelope attached to the document. Finally, you can use this technique to place a logo, text box, or other graphic element on the envelope prior to printing.

→ For more details on how to merge addresses with envelopes, **see** "Merge Envelopes," **p. 491**.

TIP FROM

Want to automatically add graphics to an envelope? Word recognizes two AutoText entries, EnvelopeExtra1 and EnvelopeExtra2, which it uses exclusively for this purpose. Define one or both of these entries and they'll be added automatically to the return address portion of your envelopes when you click Print (or when you click Add to Document) on the Envelopes tab. You might add a logo and return address (in a text box) and define it as EnvelopeExtra1—you don't need to set up custom templates, and you can use the Envelopes dialog just as you normally would.

Printing Labels

For mass mailings, labels are often easier to work with than envelopes. Typically, "peel and stick" labels are sold in sheets that match a standard paper size. You can also buy heavier stock that is perforated rather than adhesive-backed; this type of label is used for business cards, postcards, and so on. When you choose Tools, Letters and Mailings, Envelopes and Labels, and then click the Labels tab, Word displays the dialog box shown in Figure 16.5, which allows you to create single labels or an entire sheet of labels. Click the Options button to tell Word what kind of label position (row and column) you're using. (If you use standard labels, you can let Word set these options automatically. The dialog box includes settings for virtually all Avery labels, for example.) Then fill in the label number if you want to print only one label, and click Print.

Figure 16.5
Word's label format includes grids for all the major label (and business card) sizes.

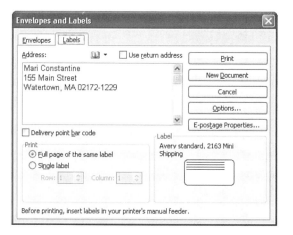

You can also generate mailing labels for an entire list of recipients, via a mail merge.

→ For details on how to merge data and labels, **see** "Merge Labels," **p. 493**.

Customizing Labels

The major shortcoming in Word's bag of labeling tricks is its inability to let you customize what gets printed on labels. If you're running standard Avery 5260 labels, with 3 labels per row and 10 rows per sheet, there's no room on the label to print anything interesting. But if you have larger labels (or business cards), you don't have to limit yourself to a plain-vanilla name and address.

TIP FROM

Ed & Woody

> If you have an odd-sized label, Word makes it easy to add it to the list of available labels, with extensive tools to help you get the layout just right. On the Labels tab of the Envelopes and Labels dialog box, choose Options. Then on the Label Options dialog box, choose New Label. Use a ruler that can handle fine measurements, and you should have no trouble filling in the details.

For example, the Avery 8154 (and related) labels run six to the page. More than enough room is available on a label that big to include your return address and a picture or logo.

If you want to print larger, fancier labels, your best choice is to create a template that includes all the design elements—logo, return address, and so on—except the addressee's name and address. If you have such a template handy, you can create a new document based on the template, then copy the addressee's name and address into it, and print. If you want to get even fancier and let yourself print just one label at a time, you can create a collection of templates, each with the design elements for just one label. Give the template a descriptive name ("AV5164 lower-right label") and you can generate precisely the right document for the right location.

The easiest way to make a template for a specific type of label is to use the Envelopes and Labels dialog box. In Figure 16.5 (shown previously), leave the Address box blank, choose the Full Page of the Same Label option, and click the Options button. Pick the manufacturer and product number from the Label Information section and click OK to return to the Envelopes and Labels dialog box. Finally, click New Document. Word creates a grid of labels for you, completely blank and ready for your customizing. Add your return address, logo, and other custom details, then choose File, Save As, and save it as a Document Template.

TIP FROM

Ed & Woody

> Because the labels are just a table, you can use all the table formatting tricks, including dividing the label into "sub cells" to better place graphics and text.

→ To read more about how to create and modify templates, **see** "Customizing Word Templates," **p. 467**.

MERGING DATA TO CREATE CUSTOM REPORTS AND LETTERS

Most Word users think of *mail merge* as a synonym for "form letters" or "junk mail." Although it's true that Word can churn out form letters and bulk mailings until the cows come home, the term *mail merge* only hints at what you can do with this capability.

At its most basic, a mail-merge operation consists of two parts—a database and a document—and the "merge" just brings the two together. The database can contain just about anything—names and addresses are the most common contents, of course, but you can also stuff the database with product names, court case citations, serial numbers, website addresses, test scores, or anything else you can fit into a database record.

The document, too, can take just about any imaginable form—yes, the first thing you think of is likely to be a form letter, but you can also add fields from your database to an envelope, catalog, e-mail or fax message, telephone book, web page, financial report, stock inventory, or time log. For that matter, the "document" could simply be a text file, enabling you to use a mail merge to create a new database from an old one.

Word doesn't have the extensive merging capabilities of a full-strength database manager (such as Microsoft Access, which is included in Office 2003 Professional). But it's the best tool to choose when you need to produce a document or series of documents based on data in a reasonably clean list.

Word's mail-merge features come in handy in a variety of circumstances. When you're working with form letters going out to a mailing list, Word allows you to sort and/or filter the incoming data, removing records according to field-level criteria you establish (for example, you could specify "Only include people in my ZIP Code"). You can also force the merge process to pause at each record, to enable you to type in custom information. Use this technique if you're producing a holiday newsletter, for example, and you want to add some unique content for each recipient.

When you move beyond basic form letters, Word's mail-merge capabilities let you

- Send similar, but customized, e-mail messages or faxes to a large number of people.
- Create a product catalog, parts list, or price sheet from a list (or database) of individual products.
- Create an organization membership roster or telephone book from a list (or database) of members.

TIP FROM

EQ & Woody

> Most Office users tend to think of mail merge as producing one page (or form letter) per data record, but Word isn't so constrained. As long as you tell Word that you want to create a "directory," it will place data records on a page until the page gets full, and then go on to the next page. Thus, if you have a data file for your coin collection, home inventory, paid checks, office carpool, VIP donors, or best-selling books, you can use Word's mail merge to create a professional-looking, well-formatted report. Just call it a directory.

Word contains extensive support for running mail merges, embodied in the Mail Merge Wizard (which looks just like a task pane). To get to it, click Tools, Letters and Mailings, Mail Merge Wizard. The wizard handles almost every merge problem you're likely to encounter (see Figure 16.6).

Figure 16.6
The Mail Merge Wizard—the first wizard Microsoft ever created—appears as a task pane.

16

Although the wizard has its share of idiosyncrasies, it makes perfect sense after you've learned how to use it.

TIP FROM

The first few times you run a mail merge, keep a detailed log of the steps you take—especially problems you encounter with Word or your printer. Chances are good you'll hit similar problems when using mail-merge capabilities sometime in the future, and good notes can save you precious troubleshooting time.

Each of the major types of mail merge is a bit different—Letters, E-mail messages, Envelopes, Labels, and Directories—so we're going to deal with each one separately.

USING MAIL MERGE TO PERSONALIZE FORM LETTERS

By far the most common mail merge scenario involves a form letter, a database, and a printer. You have a database of names and addresses, most likely in an Outlook Contacts list, but possibly in the form of an Excel list or a simple text file in tab- or comma-delimited format. And you have a form letter (or at least an idea of what you want to write). That's all you need: In Word-speak, you have a data source and a main merge document. The rest is just juggling.

The Mail Merge Wizard walks you through six steps, each of which is neatly labeled at the bottom of the Mail Merge task pane (we provide additional details and useful suggestions for each of these steps later in this chapter). The following six descriptions match up with each of the numbered steps in the Mail Merge task pane.

1. In the wizard's first step, choose the type of document you're working on. For this example, select Letters.

2. Pick an existing document, or create a new one, to use as the "merge document"—the boilerplate skeleton that will drive the merge.

3. Attach a data source—the list or database to be merged—to the form letter. The wizard lets you create a new list from scratch, draw from an Outlook Contacts folder, or use an existing list.

4. Use the Mail Merge Wizard to place merge fields in the form letter. They'll appear something like this: <<Address Block>>, or <<First Name>> <<Last Name>>.

> **NOTE**
>
> You can't just type the << and >> marks: Word has to insert them for you, via buttons in the Mail Merge Wizard.

5. Use the wizard to preview how the first few merged letters will appear. If you want to exclude certain records from the merge, or sort them so that the letters print in a particular sequence (ZIP Code order, for example), use the Mail Merge Wizard's Edit Recipient List option to set them up.

6. On the Mail Merge Wizard's final pane, click the Edit Individual Letters option so Word will merge the form letters to a new file, and save the new merged file. Before you print the file, go through it and make sure it doesn't contain any surprises. When you're satisfied that everything is correct, start printing.

> **TIP FROM**
>
> Long merge print jobs can pose all sorts of mechanical challenges, from toner cartridges running down to buffer overflows to massive paper jams. If the merged file contains more than a few hundred pages, consider printing a hundred or two at a time (choose File, Print, and enter a range in the Pages box).
>
> For important mailings, keep the merged file handy until the mailing has been delivered to the post office—or better yet, until you're certain that most addressees have received their copies.

The merged document consists of multiple sections—one section per input record. That can cause unexpected problems if you try to use an advanced technique to get particular pages to print.

→ If you get stuck working on multiple sections, **see** "Formatting Documents by Section," **p. 423**.

CREATING THE FORM LETTER

When creating a main merge document, all Word's tools are at your disposal. You can adjust formatting, insert pictures, create headers and footers, add tables and fields, and work with objects in the drawing layer. For example, you might choose to insert your company's logo in the letter (see Figure 16.7), or use a callout AutoShape to draw attention to a specific selling point.

Figure 16.7
In the second step of the Mail Merge Wizard, for form letters, you put together a main merge document.

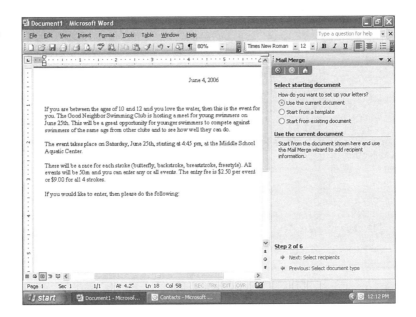

When you're satisfied with the content of your form letter, choose Next: Select Recipients at the bottom of the task pane, and begin adding merge data.

SPECIFYING A SOURCE FOR NAMES AND ADDRESSES

After you have the static part of the form letter complete, you have to tell Word where to pick up the data that will be merged. In fact, at this point, Word just needs the data field names—last name, first name, address, and so on—but the Mail Merge Wizard takes advantage of the moment to have you select the data source.

TIP FROM

> It's an often-overlooked point, but the biggest problem you're likely to encounter at this juncture is the lack of a specific data field, or a poorly defined field. For example, if your form letter demands an "Amount Due" in each letter, you'd better have a data file handy that includes an "Amount Due" for each customer.

The Mail Merge Wizard gives you three choices:

- **Use an Existing List**—If you have an existing data source, whether it's a table in a Word document, a list in an Excel workbook, or an Access database, use this option. If the first row of the Word table or Excel list includes field names (Last Name, First

Name, and so on), you'll be able to merge immediately. Click Browse and retrieve the list.

- **Select from Outlook Contacts**—Make this choice and Word imports the data directly from Outlook. Click Choose Contacts Folder and pick the Contacts list that you want to use (see Figure 16.8).

Figure 16.8
The Mail Merge List of Recipients is generated from your Outlook Contacts list. Click the appropriate column heading to sort the list.

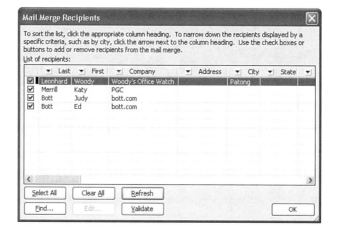

- **Type a New List**—Select this option and click Create... to bring up a useful Data Form (see Figure 16.9) that allows you to create your own merge database and add names and addresses on-the-fly. If you want to modify the field names and their order, click the Customize button.

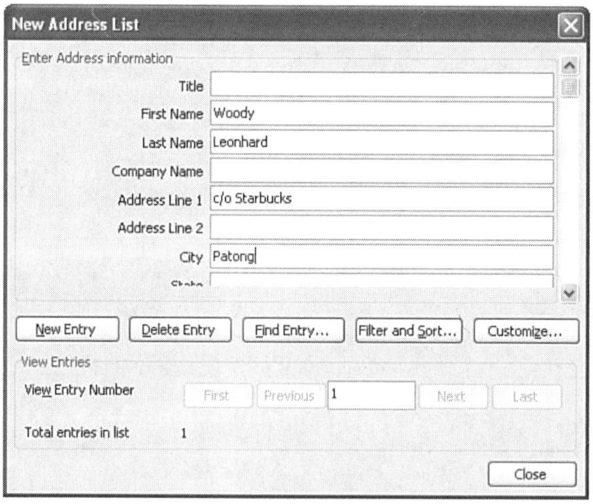

Figure 16.9
The New Address List allows you to build a merge data document on-the-fly. The address list is stored in Access database format using a *.mdb extension.

PLACING DATA FIELDS WITHIN YOUR DOCUMENT

Now that Word knows what data you're going to use, it can help you put merge data into your document. Data fields represent the link between your form letter and the data source. For example, if you have a data source field called Last Name, Word replaces every occurrence of the field <<Last Name>> in the form letter with the Last Name data in the current record of the data source.

The easiest way to insert data fields into your form letter is via step 4 of the Mail Merge Wizard. Place the insertion point wherever you want a data field to appear, click Insert Merge Field, and choose the field you need. Instead of entering every single element of the name and address, click the Address Block link to display the dialog box shown in Figure 16.10. This dialog box inserts an especially helpful merge field called Address Block, which does a graceful job of importing Outlook Contacts data into Word.

Figure 16.10
This dialog box adds the Address Block field to your merge document.

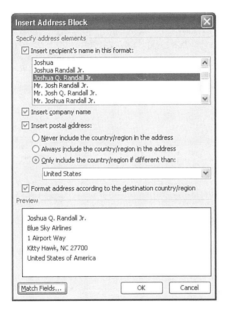

From the Mail Merge Wizard, click the Greeting Line… link to add an opening to your letter. Click the More Items… link to insert other fields throughout the letter. Remember that you have to provide the punctuation if it isn't included in the data source. A typical letter opening might look like this:

<<AddressBlock>>

Dear <<Title>> <<LastName>>:

TIP FROM

Ed & Woody

You can put the same data field in the form letter as often as you like. If you're preparing a letter to parents in a specific school district, for example, you might include the <<City>> field in the text of the letter as well as in the address block: "This meeting will discuss issues that are of particular interest to families of school age children who live in <<City>>."

PREVIEWING MAIL MERGE RESULTS

To see how the merge will progress, start by having Word show you what the result will be when you merge live data with your form letter. To do so, go on to step 5 of the Mail Merge Wizard, and click the Next Record button repeatedly to see how the records appear (see Figure 16.11).

Figure 16.11
Word lets you preview your form letter with live data, stepping through each data source record.

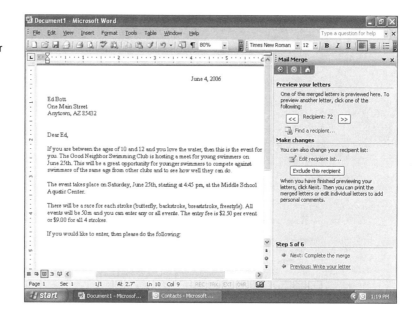

Use this preview to check for gross errors:

- Look for incorrect fields—for example, those using <<First>> where you really wanted <<Last>>.

- Identify unreliable data source information; if half of your data source records don't have an entry in the <<Title>> field, for example, you need to find a way to work around the problem.

- If you see any parts of the merge that just don't look right—if some of the merged letters flop over to two pages, for example—click Edit Recipient List and try to tweak the data so it fits.

When all looks well, go on to step 6 in the wizard, and click Edit Individual Letters. Before you print the resulting document, which has all the merged letters head-to-toe, examine it closely for any unexpected and unwelcome merge results.

TIP FROM

In general, you should avoid merging directly to the printer. Creating a merge file first lets you easily recover from mechanical disasters—you can reprint letters 1378 to 1392, for example, if the printer runs out of toner or the person carrying the envelopes to the post office drops them in the mud.

16

MASS E-MAILING AND FAXING WITH OUTLOOK AND MAIL MERGE

If you use Outlook 2003, creating personalized mass e-mailings and faxes is almost as simple as creating and merging a form letter. Here's how:

1. For either mass e-mail or faxes, choose E-mail messages in the first step of the Mail Merge Wizard. Complete the e-mail message or fax as if it were a form letter, using the instructions in the preceding section.

2. Attach a recipient list and preview the messages or faxes with live data in step 5 of the wizard.

3. In the final step of the Mail Merge Wizard, choose to merge to Electronic Mail. In the Merge to E-mail dialog box (see Figure 16.12), choose which Outlook Contact field you want to merge to. Most often, you'll either choose E-mail_Address or Business_Fax. Type a subject, if you like, and click OK.

Figure 16.12
If you want to send the same fax to many people, tell the Mail Merge Wizard that you want to create e-mail messages, and then choose Business_Fax in this very last step.

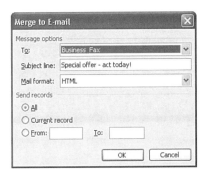

4. Word performs the merge, and transfers the merged e-mail messages or faxes to your Outlook outbox.

The next time you use Outlook to send mail, the e-mail messages or faxes will be sent in the usual way.

TIP FROM

High-volume unsolicited e-mail—better known as spam—is almost universally detested, even when it's personalized. Sending unsolicited e-mail might violate local and federal laws. If you're going to use Word to automate mass e-mailings or fax blasts, make absolutely certain that your recipients have given their approval first.

CREATING DIRECTORIES

The only real difference between the way Word handles form letters and the way it handles merged "directories" (in previous versions of Word, they were called "catalogs") lies in the way Word uses page breaks. In a form letter, Word inserts a page break (actually, a "next page" section break) after it finishes processing a record from the data source. In a directory, Word doesn't add page breaks; as a result, one record follows another in the finished document.

→ You can also use Outlook's built-in printing capabilities to produce phone lists, even on Day-Timer sheets; for details, **see** "Printing Phone Lists from Your Contacts List," **p. 289**.

Say you want to print a custom report of all the people in your Outlook Contacts list, in which several records appear on a page in a format like those used by a paper-based personal organizer. Here's how you do it:

1. Start a new document as described in the preceding sections, but in the first step of the Mail Merge Wizard, choose Directory. That tells Word you want to put more than one record on a page.

2. Add the fields by using step 4 of the Mail Merge Wizard, as before. A typical page might look like Figure 16.13.

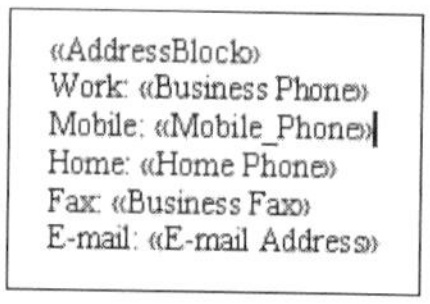

Figure 16.13
Custom Outlook Contacts reports are much easier to config-ure in Word than in Outlook itself—if you know how to merge.

```
«AddressBlock»
Work: «Business Phone»
Mobile: «Mobile_Phone»
Home: «Home Phone»
Fax: «Business Fax»
E-mail: «E-mail Address»
```

3. Adjust the document any way you see fit. In the case of Day-Timer-like reports, you might want to create multiple columns, change the page size, and/or set the paper source to print on special drilled sheets.

TIP FROM

To control page breaks in directory-style merges such as this one, use the paragraph for-matting property Keep with Next. In this case, you might put an empty paragraph mark at the end of all the data lines. Then select the data lines (*not* the final paragraph mark); choose Format, Paragraph; click the Line and Page Breaks tab; and select the Keep with Next check box to ensure records don't break across pages.

4. Have Word merge to a new document. You'll probably want to print in duplex style—that is, using both sides of each sheet of paper. To do so, choose File, Print, and select the Manual Duplex check box in the Print dialog box.

ADVANCED MAIL MERGE TECHNIQUES

Mail merge works by using Word fields specially designed for implementing a merge. To see those fields, open a main merge document and press Alt+F9, or choose Tools, Options; click the View tab; and select the Field Codes check box (see Figure 16.14).

Figure 16.14
Main merge documents contain fields that dictate how the merge should happen.

```
{ ADDRESSBLOCK \f "<<_TITLE0_ >><<_FIRST0_>><< _LAST0_>><<
_SUFFIX0_>>
<<_COMPANY_
>><<_STREET1_
>><<_STREET2_
>><<_CITY_>><<,_STATE_>><< _POSTAL_>><<
_COUNTRY_>>" \l 1033 \c 2 \e "United States" \d }
Work: { MERGEFIELD "Business Phone" \m }
Mobile: { MERGEFIELD "Mobile_Phone" }
Home: { MERGEFIELD "Home Phone" \m }
Fax: { MERGEFIELD "Business Fax" \m }
E-mail: { MERGEFIELD "E-mail Address" \m }
```

In many cases, you'll be able to get satisfactory results with a merge by using the Mail Merge toolbar to manipulate these fields. In some more advanced cases, however, you might find yourself operating on the fields directly.

→ To learn how to manually manipulate fields, **see** "Some Useful Custom Fields," **p. 501**.

MERGE ENVELOPES

Running a merge to generate envelopes that match one-for-one with a form letter run isn't difficult, as long as you go to great pains to ensure that the data source doesn't change between the time you run the form letters and the time you print the envelopes, and that the filters you specify are identical.

TIP FROM

Ed & Woody

Beware of paper jams, because one missing or one extra letter or envelope can throw off the entire sequence. If a jam should occur, mark that point in the run—with a paper clip or a sticky note, for example. After you've finished running both letters and envelopes, go back to the marked points and ensure you have one—and only one—letter for each envelope.

To start an envelope run, use the Mail Merge Wizard and select Envelopes as the document type in the first step. If you use the Envelope Wizard and tell it you want to create envelopes for a mailing list, it launches the Mail Merge Wizard automatically. To start this wizard, choose File, New. On the New Document task pane, click On My Computer, and then on the Letters & Faxes tab, double-click Envelope Wizard.

You can take advantage of an alternative (and undocumented) method for generating envelopes at the same time you do the main form letter run. This method creates envelopes interleaved with the form letters—you get an envelope and its letter, the next record's envelope and its letter, and so on. As long as you have a printer with separate feeders for the form letter paper and the envelopes—most laser printers pull envelopes from a different location than the standard paper trays anyway—the technique works, and it could save you a great deal of frustration with mismatched envelopes and form letters. Here's how to do it:

1. Create your form letter, following the instructions in the preceding sections.

2. At the end of the Envelope Wizard's step 2 (before you click Next to move on to the Select Recipients step), choose Tools, Letters and Mailings, Envelopes and Labels. On the Envelopes tab, set up the return address the way you want it. Then click Options and make sure the correct paper tray has been set up for your envelopes. *Do not click Print.* Instead, click Add to Document. The envelope appears above your form letter on the Word screen.

3. Attach the data source and place fields in your form letter as usual. When you're finished with the letter, move up to the envelope and insert merge fields in the envelope, wherever you want them to appear (see Figure 16.15).

Figure 16.15
Merge data fields go into the envelope, just as they would in the form letter itself.

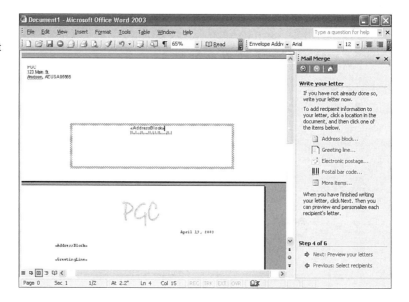

4. Merge to a file, as usual. When you print the file, envelopes appear before form letters, interspersed throughout the merge run.

MERGE LABELS

Word's features for creating mailing labels work well enough for small labels—that is, labels that are specifically designed to comfortably accommodate a name and address. But if you're using preprinted labels, or if you have larger labels and want to print your return address or logo on them, or if you want to change the default font, you'll probably run into a few common problems (unless you know these tricks, of course).

To run a mail merge and generate labels the usual way:

1. Start the Mail Merge Wizard by choosing Tools, Letters and Mailings, Mail Merge Wizard, and then selecting Labels as the document type.

   or

   Choose File, New, and click On My Computer in the New Document task pane. On the Letters & Faxes tab of the Templates dialog box, select Mailing Label Wizard and click OK.

2. In the first step of the wizard, choose the Create Labels for a Mailing List option and click OK.

3. In the wizard's next step, click Label Options… in the Change Document Layout section. Supply the details for your mailing labels in the Label Options dialog box. In most cases, you can select a manufacturer and product number; most common label products, including those from Avery, the 800-pound gorilla of the industry, are among the built-in formats listed here (see Figure 16.16).

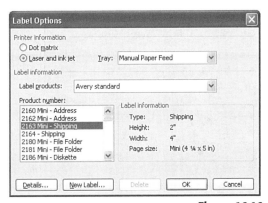

Figure 16.16

4. Follow Word's prompts to select a recipient list. Place the data merge fields in the first label position.

> **NOTE**
>
> Word automatically causes text in the label to "float up and down"—to be centered vertically. If you want the printing on your labels to always appear at the same location, choose Table, Properties, click the Cell tab, and choose Top or Bottom.

5. When you're happy with the first label, click the Update All Labels button at the bottom of the Mail Merge task pane. Finish the merge by using the techniques described earlier in this chapter. Preview the merge, merge to file, and print.

TIP FROM

EQ & Woody

> Because the label form is just a table, you can divide the existing cells to better position text, graphics, a return address, or anything else on the label.

See "Extra Credit: Professional Labels, Big Time" at the end of this chapter for an example of how Word's mail merge features can be used to create slick-looking mailing labels.

USING FIELDS INTELLIGENTLY

As mentioned earlier in this chapter, the secret of mail merge, as with many of Word's other powerful features, is a peculiar document element called a *field*. Word fields are placeholders whose contents change dynamically; they are normally invisible and work in the background, displaying the correct data onscreen and in print, based on information within the current document, in other documents, or from external sources such as a database used for a mail merge. For example, if you put a {Date} field in your document, Word displays the current date in that location each time you open the document.

Word supports more than 70 different types of fields. Use them when you want to accomplish tasks such as these:

- Show the current day in a document ({date}, {time}), or the time the document was last printed ({printdate}).

- Refer to the contents of bookmarked text. For example, you can place a bookmark on a chapter title and refer to that title throughout your document by using the {Ref} field. If the title changes, all the references change, too.

→ For details on all the nuances of using bookmarks, **see** "Using Bookmarks," **p. 437**.

- Insert information about a document into the document itself ({info})—total number of pages, filename, author, file size, number of words, date when the document was last saved, and so on.

- Perform calculations, comparisons, and even elementary arithmetic. For example, the {Page} field produces the number of the current page, whereas a {{Page}+1} field results in the number of the next page.

There's even a {barcode} field that converts a postal ZIP Code to a USPS bar code!

In addition to mail merges, fields also drive such key built-in Word capabilities as tables of contents, figures, tables, equations, and indexes. Although Word uses layers of wizards and dialog boxes to shield you from the field codes used to implement those features, sometimes the only way to tweak the feature—to limit a table of contents to a part of the document covered by a specific bookmark, for example—is by working with the field code itself.

NOTE

Fields are an enormous topic. In this chapter, we barely scratch the surface and explain how to work with some of the more useful fields. If you need a detailed fields reference, see *Special Edition Using Microsoft Word 2003* (published by Que).

CAUTION

Many fields do not translate well into HTML-formatted files. If you need to use a field on a web page, make sure you test it with all the commonly used browsers to ensure that it works properly.

INSERTING A FIELD INTO A DOCUMENT

By far, the easiest way to put a field into a document is to use one of the built-in Word features to do the dirty work for you. For example, if you choose Insert, Date and Time, and then click the Update Automatically check box, Word inserts a {Date} field into your document, adding a formatting switch for the date format you choose (see Figure 16.17).

Figure 16.17
Selecting the Update Automatically check box here causes Word to insert a {Date} field instead of the date itself.

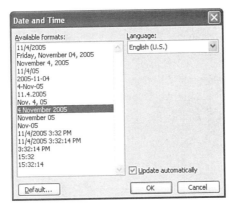

Similarly, putting a page number in a header or footer using the Insert Page Number button on the Header and Footer toolbar will insert a {Page} field, as will inserting a table of contents or index, creating a caption or cross-reference, or inserting merge fields using the Mail Merge Wizard.

If you want to build a field from scratch, you can do it the hard way, by pressing Ctrl+F9 to create the field marks, and then manually typing the field name and any optional or required parameters. If you make even the tiniest mistake, of course, the field won't work as you expect. To be absolutely certain you get the syntax right, choose Insert, Field instead. This Field dialog box (see Figure 16.18) offers context-sensitive help and immediate access to the most common field switches (the terms "properties" and "options" are somewhat arbitrary; don't get hung up on the terminology). If you want to work with the raw field code (or you just want to explore and preview the field's syntax), click the Field Codes button in the lower-left corner.

Figure 16.18
Word provides good support for fields via the Field dialog box.

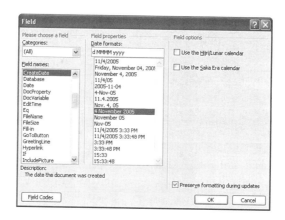

 If you consistently have trouble finding field codes you insert within a document, see "Hiding and Revealing Field Codes" in the "Troubleshooting" section at the end of this chapter.

SHOWING AND HIDING FIELD CODES

Word allows you to flip-flop between seeing the field codes themselves and field code results—for example, between seeing

```
{Date \@ "d-MMM-yyyy"}
```

and

```
1-JAN-2006
```

To show field codes, choose Tools, Options; choose the View tab; and then select the Field Codes check box. To return to showing field code results, clear that same Field Codes box.

TIP FROM

> If you're going to do much serious work with field codes, you might want to add the ViewFieldCodes command as a button on the Standard or Formatting toolbar; or memorize the View Field Codes keyboard shortcut, Alt+F9. Either one toggles between showing field codes and showing their results.

FIELD CODE SYNTAX

Field codes can take on many different forms, but generally they look like this, with the field name and required or optional parameters enclosed in curly braces:

```
{Author \* mergeformat}
```

In this case, the field {Author} has one parameter, called a *formatting switch*. The formatting switch, if present, controls the way the field result is formatted inside the document. We discuss switches in the following section, "Formatting Field Results."

NOTE

In this book, you'll always see field codes as they appear onscreen, surrounded by curly braces—something like this:

```
{Seq Figures \* mergeformat}
```

Field codes are not case-sensitive, so you may see them in all capitals rather than upper- and lower-case as we depict them here. Functionally, there's no difference. And of course, you can't type curly braces into a document and get a field code. There are only three ways to insert field marks (braces): Choose Insert, Field; use one of the built-in Word functions that produces a field code; or press Ctrl+F9.

16

FORMATTING FIELD RESULTS

Unless you add a switch inside the field to change formatting, the field result takes on the formatting of the first nonblank character of the field.

For example, if you have a field that says {*A*uthor}, with the "A" in Times New Roman, 10-point italic, the result of the field takes on that formatting: *Douglas Adams*.

Word has three different field switches that control the appearance and formatting of field code results.

GENERAL * FORMAT SWITCHES

The most common field switch is the general formatting switch:

```
\* mergeformat
```

This switch tells Word to ignore the formatting of the first character of the field, and instead to use whatever formatting you apply to the field itself.

For example, say you're typing along in 12-point Garamond, and you insert a {NumWords} field (which shows the number of words in the document), using the Field dialog box. If you click the Preserve Formatting During Updates check box, Word inserts a * mergeformat switch:

```
{NUMWORDS   \* MERGEFORMAT}
```

With that switch in place, every time you update the field, it takes on the original formatting—Garamond 12 point—unless you apply some different formatting directly on the field result.

By using formatting switches, you can exercise an enormous amount of control and flexibility over how a field appears in your document. For example:

```
\* dollartext
```

converts a number—say, 123.45—into the kind of text you put on a check—one hundred twenty-three and 45/100.

```
\* caps
```

capitalizes the initial letters of each word in the field result. Combine the two formatting switches with the = field, which evaluates numeric expressions, to get the field:

```
{ = 123.45 \* dollartext \* caps }
```

which appears in your document as

```
One Hundred Twenty-Three And 45/100
```

The most useful formatting switches are detailed in Table 16.3.

TABLE 16.3   * FORMATTING SWITCHES

Switch	Action
* mergeformat	Retains the current formatting of the field result whenever it's updated.
* charformat	Uses the formatting applied to the first nonblank character of the field code.
* caps	Capitalizes the first letter of each word.
* firstcap	Capitalizes the first letter of the first word only.
* lower	Makes all letters lowercase.
* upper	Makes all letters uppercase.
* cardtext	Converts a number to text: *12* becomes *twelve*.
* ordtext	Converts a number to the ordinal text: *12* becomes *twelfth*.
* Roman	Displays a number in capitalized Roman numerals: *12* becomes *XII*.
* dollartext	Spells out the whole part of the number, then rounds the fraction and appends "and xx/100": *123.456* becomes *one hundred twenty-three and 46/100*.

NUMERIC \# PICTURE SWITCHES

Word also allows you to specify a numeric "picture" switch to be applied to numbers. This could come in handy if, for example, you calculate numbers in a table or bring them in for a merge, and you want to show negative numbers in parentheses.

The basic building blocks of field numeric pictures are as follows:

- Decimal point
- Thousands separator (in the United States and Canada, this is typically a comma; in Europe, it's a period)

- Zero (digits that always appear)
- # sign (digits that are used only if necessary)
- Various combinations to format negative numbers; and literal text, which appears in the field result.

You could practically write an entire book on the nuances of numeric picture formatting. Rather than dwell on the details, examine the common numeric picture elements shown in Table 16.4.

TABLE 16.4 COMMON \# NUMERIC PICTURE ELEMENTS

Switch	Result
* 00.00	Forces Word to display two digits to the left and two to the right of the decimal point, adding leading and trailing zeros as needed: *1.2* displays as *01.20* and *–1.2* shows up as *–01.20*. Use this format when you want numbers in a column to line up perfectly.
* #0.000	One or more digits might appear to the left of the decimal point, but three must appear after: *1.23* displays as *1.230*, *–12.3456* becomes *–12.346*, and *1234.5* shows *1234.500*.
* $,#.00	Shows a dollar sign, followed by the number with commas grouping each set of three digits, and two decimal places: *.12* appears as *$.12*; *12345.678* shows *$12,345.68*.
* $,0.00	Same as the preceding, but always shows at least one digit for dollars: *.12* displays as *$0.12*.

Unless you specify a different format, Word always displays negative numbers with a leading minus sign. To force Word to show negative numbers in parentheses, you have to provide two formatting pictures, the first for positive numbers and the second for negatives, enclosed in quotes, separated by a semicolon. For example, this format

```
\# "$,#.00;($,#.00)"
```

will show *0.123* as *$.12* and *–1234.56* as *($1,234.56)*.

DATE-TIME \@ FORMAT SWITCHES

The date-time picture switch almost always appears in a {Date}, {Time}, {Createdate}, {Printdate}, or {Savedate} field. (The last three fields show when the document was created, last printed, or last saved.) The switch tells Word how to format the date or time for display in the document. For example, add this field to a document:

```
{Date \@ "MMMM d, yyyy - h:mm:ss AM/PM"}
```

When you open the document on the morning of Bill Gates's 50th birthday, Word updates the field and displays text that looks like this:

```
October 28, 2005 - 8:33:05 AM
```

The most common date-time picture elements are shown in Table 16.5.

TABLE 16.5	\@ DATE-TIME PICTURE ELEMENTS
Element	**Meaning**
M	Month number without leading 0: *August* is *8*
MM	Month number with leading 0: *August* is *08*
MMM	Month as three-letter abbreviation: *Aug*
MMMM	Month spelled out: *August*
d	Day of the month without leading zero
dd	Day of the month with leading zero
ddd	Day of the week as three-letter abbreviation: *Mon*
dddd	Day of the week spelled out: *Monday*
yy	Last two digits of the year: *01*
yyyy	Four-digit year: *2001*
h	Hour on a 12-hour clock without leading zero
hh	Hour on a 12-hour clock with leading zero
H	Hour on a 24-hour clock without leading zero
HH	Hour on a 24-hour clock with leading zero
m	Minutes without leading zero
mm	Minutes with leading zero
s	Seconds without leading zero
ss	Seconds with leading zero
AM/PM	AM or PM (used with h and hh for 12-hour clock)
Text	Appears as literal text in the field result

DISPLAYING FIELD RESULTS CORRECTLY

When you first insert a field code into a document, or when you create a new document with a field code in it, Word calculates the value of the field code and displays its results.

After the first time, however, field codes are never updated automatically, except when a file is opened. So, for example, if you create a new letter based on a template that has a {Date} field code, Word puts the current date in the new document. When you close and reopen the document, Word updates the field if necessary, but if you leave the document open overnight, the date won't change.

When you open a document containing a field, the field is updated automatically. There are two common ways to update a field manually—that is, to have Word recalculate the field's value and display the new value in your document:

- Select the field (or position the insertion point anywhere within the field), and then press F9.
- Select one or more fields, right-click, and choose Update Field.

You can also specify that Word should automatically update all fields in a document immediately before printing the document. To set this option, choose Tools, Options; click the Print tab; and click the Update Fields check box. The setting is global, so it stays in effect for all documents until you change it.

You can permanently eliminate a field, and have it replaced with the text that's currently showing in the document. For example, if you've printed and mailed a letter that you originally wrote using a {Date} field, you might want to replace the field with its results; that way, when you open the letter later, you'll see the date you sent the letter rather than the current date. This process is called "unlinking" a field, although it actually removes the field entirely, replacing it with the current value of the field.

To unlink a field, do the following:

1. If you want to be certain the field result is current, update the field. (In some circumstances, you might choose not to update the field; for example, if it shows an old date and time that you want to preserve.)
2. Click to position the insertion point in the field. It doesn't matter whether field codes or field code results are showing.
3. Press Ctrl+6 (that's the 6 on the keyboard, not on the number pad) or Shift+Ctrl+F9.

TIP FROM

Ed & Woody

> If you regularly work with fields, add an Unlink Fields button to a convenient toolbar, using the procedures described in Chapter 2, "Making Office 2003 Work Your Way."

To lock a field—that is, to prevent a field from being updated—select the field or place the insertion point in it and press Ctrl+F11. To allow the field to be updated again, select the field and press Shift+Ctrl+F11.

SOME USEFUL CUSTOM FIELDS

Word includes a wasp's nest of fields, many of which have become outdated over the years and remain available only so documents created in older versions of Word will still work in Word 2003. These fields and their switches and settings comprise an entire programming language unto itself, buried inside Word, and completely separate from the language used in macros: Visual Basic for Applications.

TIP FROM

Don't let the profusion of fields sway you. In general, if there's a way to accomplish your goal without using fields, that alternative is preferable. Many Word field codes are poorly documented, and you can expect to squander precious time and brain cells trying to make them work properly. Outside of the Help files, the best documentation we've found is online at Microsoft's website:

```
http://support.microsoft.com/support/word/usage/fields/
default.as p.
```

Although you can use the Field properties and Field options lists in the Field dialog box to assemble a field, some options aren't listed at all, and interactions among options are complex and confusing. And because error messages are few and far between, debugging field codes is usually a tedious, repeated trial-and-error process.

SHOWING DATES AND TIMES

If you want to insert the current date and/or time in a document, choose Insert, Date and Time; if the choices in the Date and Time dialog box include the formatting you need, use the menu. Forget the field.

TIP FROM

The date and time formats that appear when you choose Insert, Date and Time are identical to the formats offered when you choose Insert, Field and then choose Date from the Field Names list. If one of the formats listed in the Date and Time menu dialog box is close to the one you want, use the Date and Time entry, and click the Update Automatically check box to insert the field code in your document. Then press Alt+F9 to show field codes and edit the field manually. It's much easier than constructing a field from scratch.

Word's date and time fields are listed in Table 16.6. They're all formatted by using the \@ date-time format switches, discussed earlier in this chapter.

TABLE 16.6 DATE AND TIME FIELDS

Field	Meaning
{Date}	The current date and time
{Time}	The current date and time
{CreateDate}	The date and time the file was created
{PrintDate}	The date and time the file was last printed
{SaveDate}	The date and time the file was last saved

So, for example, the field

```
{PrintDate \@ "d-MMM-yy h:mm AM/PM"}
```

in a document last printed on September 29, 2005, might have a field result that looks like this:

```
29-Sep-05 10:45 AM
```

The only significant difference between {Date} and {Time} is in the default formatting—that is, the format of the field result if no \@ date-time format switch is used:

- For the {Date} field, if you've set a default date format using the Default button on the Date and Time dialog box, Word uses that format. Otherwise, Word looks to the Windows Short Date style; to adjust this format, open Control Panel and adjust the date settings under Regional Options (Windows 2000) or Regional and Language Options (Windows XP).

- For the {Time} field, if you've set a default time format in the Date and Time dialog box, Word uses that format. Otherwise, Word uses the Windows Time style setting; in Windows XP, open Control Panel, double-click Regional and Language Options, click the Customize button on the Regional Options tab, and then click the Time tab to adjust this format.

The {Date} field also takes a \l switch that isn't used in the {Time} field. When Word updates a {Date \l} field, it checks to see which date or time format you last used in the Date and Time dialog box and then applies that format to the field.

 If you enter a time field in your document, but when you update the field it displays a date, see "Time and Date Discrepancies" in the "Troubleshooting" section at the end of this chapter.

If there is no \@ date-time switch in the {CreateDate}, {PrintDate}, or {SaveDate} fields, they will show the date and time, formatted according to Date and Time defaults, as described previously, or the Windows date and time options.

CAUTION

> Be careful using {Date} fields in templates. Date fields are useful in form letters, such as those you might use to reply to a request for information from a potential customer. However, these fields are potentially dangerous in correspondence where the date is an important part of the letter's content. When you create a new letter based on the template, Word puts the {Date} field in the document, and then updates the field so it shows the current day. A week later, when you discover that you need an extra copy of the letter, you open the saved file and Word dutifully updates the {Date} field—leaving you no idea when you actually created the letter.

To avoid allowing Word to insert the current date in a document each time you open it, you should use the {CreateDate} field in templates, and explicitly supply the \@ date-time format switch for it. That way, the date won't change if you open or print a letter sometime after it was originally created.

For example, this field

```
{CreateDate \@ "MMMM d,yyyy"}
```

produces a result reflecting the day the document was created, with formatting like this:

```
May 23, 2003
```

CAUTION

Be careful when using the {PrintDate} field in a template. Word always updates this field immediately prior to printing, regardless of the setting you specify on the Print tab of the Options dialog box.

PAGE NUMBERING

To show the current page number or the total number of pages in a document's header or footer, you don't need to enter the {Page} and {NumPages} fields manually. The Header and Footer toolbar has buttons for each.

If you aren't in a header or footer, however—or you need to use the {SectionPages} field, which displays the total number of pages in the current section—you should start by choosing Insert, Field. You'll find {Page}, {SectionPages}, and {NumPages} in the Field Names box.

DISPLAYING DOCUMENT PROPERTIES

How many words are in your document? When was it last edited? What template does it use? Word allows you to retrieve these and other details and insert them in the current document. These details are also available from the dialog box that appears when you choose File, Properties (see Table 16.7).

TABLE 16.7   FILE PROPERTIES AVAILABLE VIA FIELDS

Field	Meaning
Author*	From the Summary tab.
Comments*	From the Summary tab.
EditTime	Total editing time from the Statistics tab.
FileName	Filename (MS-DOS name) from the General tab. Click the Add Path to Filename check box in the Field dialog box to show the filename with full path.
FileSize	Size of the file from the General tab. Click one of the check boxes in the Field Options section to show the size in KB or MB.
Keywords*	From the Summary tab.
LastSavedBy	From the Statistics tab. Word keeps track of the last person to save the file by using the name in the User Information tab on the Options dialog box (choose Tools, Options to get there).

Field	Meaning
NumChars	Number of characters (excluding spaces) from the Statistics tab. Use DocProperty (described later in this section) to retrieve the number of characters with spaces.
NumWords	Number of words from the Statistics tab. Might or might not match your word count because of the way Word defines a "word."
RevNum	"Revision" number from the Statistics tab. Actually has nothing to do with revisions and instead counts the number of times the document has been saved.
Subject*	From the Summary tab.
Template	Name of the file's template, from the Summary tab. Check the Add Path to Filename box to return full path as well. If the file is a template, returns the name of the file.
Title*	From the Summary tab.

16

CAUTION

> The first time Word updates the NumChars field, it will be low by the number of characters in the NumChars field's result! To see a number identical to the one on the Statistics tab, you must update the field twice.

Fields that appear in Table 16.7 with an asterisk can be set as well as referenced. For example, the field

`{Author}`

yields a field result that's identical to the contents of the Author box on the Summary tab of the File Properties dialog box. However, the field

`{Author "Mark Twain"}`

sets the Author value on the Summary tab to Mark Twain, *and* displays that result in the document.

TIP FROM

> There's a tricky, effective, and thoroughly undocumented (until now anyway) method for prompting the user to fill in any of these modifiable file properties. For details, skip ahead to "Prompting for Input" in the following section.

Several of the values that appear in the File Properties dialog box don't have fields associated with them directly. Most of them can be accessed through the DocProperty field. For example, this field

`{DocProperty "Paragraphs"}`

shows the number of paragraphs in the current document, as it appears on the Statistics tab. (Like the NumChars field, this field must also be updated twice to get an accurate value.)

To get to all the DocProperty settings, choose Insert, Field, and choose DocProperty from the Field Names list.

NOTE

> Word has dozens of operators and functions that let you perform (almost) any kind of mathematical calculation, including the Sum, Round, Count, and Average fields. But just because the capability exists doesn't mean you should use it. In all but the most elementary cases, you're much better off working with a tool more suited to calculations, such as Excel 2003 or your trusty calculator.

Prompting for Input

Word supports two fields that prompt for user input. Typically, you would use the {Ask} and {Fillin} fields in a template or a mail-merge master document to request additional information from the person creating a new document or performing the merge:

- A {Fillin} field in a template can prompt the user to type in keywords or other data that can then be placed in the File Properties dialog box. Each time a new document is created based on the template, the {Fillin} field is updated, and the user sees the prompt.

- An {Ask} field in a mail merge can pause the merge on every record, prompting the user to type in information specific to the record—say, a past-due amount or a personalized message in a greeting card—and have that information repeated several places in the merged document.

When you update an {Ask} field, it stores the results in a bookmark in the document. When you update a {Fillin} field, Word uses the typed text as the field result. So the field

```
{ Ask DueDate "Enter the due date:" }
```

replaces whatever was in the DueDate bookmark with what the user typed. And the field

```
{ Fillin "Enter student name" }
```

displays whatever the user types as the field code's result.

The {Fillin} field, in particular, can be manipulated in many useful ways. For example, the

```
{ KeyWords "new key words" }
```

field can set the value of the Keywords box in the Properties dialog box. Say you have a template that you use all the time, but you often forget to fill out the Keywords box—making it difficult to search for documents. Put this field at the beginning of the template:

```
{Keywords {Fillin "Please enter document keywords:"}}
```

Every time you create a new document based on the template, Word first updates the {Fillin} field by prompting you (see Figure 16.19).

Figure 16.19
When Word updates a {Fillin} field, it prompts the user for input.

Then Word updates the {Keywords} field, inserting the keywords typed by the user into the Keywords box in File Properties. Unfortunately, the result of the {Fillin} field will show in the new document. Fortunately, you can use the {Seq} field to hide it. To prompt the user for keywords in a new document, all you need is this nested field in the template:

```
{Seq \h {Keywords {Fillin "Please provide document keywords:"}}}
```

You can do the same for any of the file properties listed with an asterisk in Table 16.7 earlier in this chapter.

CUSTOMIZING FORM LETTERS WITH FIELDS

As with so many other advanced Word features, merging data and documents occurs through the magic of Word fields. The various merge fields discussed in this chapter are just special types of Word fields—which in turn are a small subset of the fields available in Word. The Mail Merge Wizard simply puts a pretty face on the underlying fields: You get to use the merge fields without getting your hands dirty working with field codes, formatting switches, and the like. The fields themselves control all the nuances of merging. You can use any of Word's extensive collection of fields in mail merge documents.

Two fields come in handy if you want Word to pause the merge at each record, and let you type in custom data. Both {Ask} and {Fillin} request data for each merged record. The former places whatever you typed in a bookmarked location on the form letter; the latter replaces the field with the text you fill in, at the point in the document where you place the field.

A {Fillin} field might be useful in a form letter, when you want the option to add a personalized paragraph at the end of every letter. As each merged letter pops up, you can enter your own customized text or just click OK to use the default text. Here's how:

1. Place the insertion point wherever you want the custom text to appear in the form letter.

2. Click Insert, Field, and then select Fill-in from the Field Name box (see Figure 16.20). Type in a suitable prompt and default text. (You can also use the Insert Word Field button on the Merge toolbar.)

NOTE

Although the input box in the Field dialog box is small, you can type in lengthy default responses, providing they don't include carriage returns. A longer input box is available if you use the Insert Word Field button on the Merge toolbar.

Figure 16.20

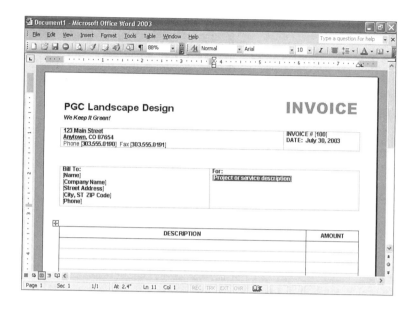

3. Perform the merge as usual. Each time Word encounters a {Fillin} field, once for each data source record, it prompts you for whatever custom text you want to provide. (Needless to say, you do not want to use this trick with databases that include more than a few dozen records!)

For additional information on fields that apply specifically to mail merge, see the Help topic "About mail-merge fields." (To display this topic, choose Offline Help from the Search box at the bottom of the Help task pane and then enter the article title in the Search box.)

MANAGING CUSTOM NUMERIC SEQUENCES

Word supports a variety of built-in paragraph numbering schemes via the Bullets and Numbering dialog box. For custom numbering tasks, there are two fields you can use to create your own numbering schemes and maintain them throughout a document. If you work with legal documents, these capabilities might be the single most important feature in Word:

- The {ListNum} field works wonders in custom-generated paragraph numbering schemes, particularly the type of numbering schemes you'll find in legal documents.
- The {Seq} field, on the other hand, helps you maintain sequences of numbers that are (typically) independent of paragraph numbering.

USING {LISTNUM} TO CREATE SOPHISTICATED NUMBERING SCHEMES

{ListNum} fields can adhere to one of three numbering schemes, per Table 16.8.

TABLE 16.8 {LISTNUM} NUMBERING SCHEMES

Level	Number	Outline	Legal
1	1)	I.	1.
2	a)	A.	1.1.
3	i)	1.	1.1.1.
4	(1)	a)	1.1.1.1.
5	(a)	(1)	1.1.1.1.1.
6	(i)	(a)	1.1.1.1.1.1.
7	1.	(i)	1.1.1.1.1.1.1.
8	a.	(a)	1.1.1.1.1.1.1.1.
9	i.	(i)	1.1.1.1.1.1.1.1.1.

16

The {ListNum} field allows you to build complex and sophisticated numbering sequences, which are sensitive to both other {ListNum} fields and to the position of the {ListNum} field in a sentence. Detailing {ListNum}'s capabilities could take a chapter by itself, but to get a glimpse of its power, try these experiments:

- Put a {ListNum} field at the beginning of a blank paragraph. Select the field, and use the Increase Indent or Decrease Indent buttons to change the level of the field—and thus the format of the number.

- Insert several {ListNum} fields in a paragraph, interspersed with text. Click and drag the text with its associated {ListNum} field. All the fields will be renumbered automatically.

- Put a bookmark on a {ListNum} field, and use a {Ref} field (or Insert, Reference, Cross-Reference) to refer to the field. Then move the {ListNum} field and update the document. The reference will be updated as well. This is the kind of approach you can use to keep references such as "see paragraph III (173) A (3) iii" in sync. If you set up the reference to use a {Ref} field, and the {Ref} field points to a bookmark over a (potentially quite complex) {ListNum} or series of {ListNum} fields, if you move the fields, the reference changes automatically. So if the previously mentioned paragraph is moved and suddenly becomes paragraph III (172) A (3) iii, the reference will be automatically updated to see paragraph III (172) A (3) iii.

- Experiment with two {ListNum} switches. The \s switch tells Word what number to start at (so you can being numbering at any point). Usually, {ListNum} senses its level in the list by its position within a paragraph, and the presence of {ListNum} fields before it. The \l switch allows you to manually override {ListNum}'s level auto-sensing capabilities.

USING {SEQ} TO COUNT AUTOMATICALLY

By contrast, {Seq} fields are straightforward. You have to make up an "identifier" (or use one of the built-in identifiers provided by Word) to keep the various sequences in a document straight. For example, you might add this text with field codes at the start of a document:

```
Refer to folders {Seq FolderNumber} and {Seq FolderNumber}
```

The field results will look like this:

```
Refer to folders 1 and 2
```

NOTE You cannot use {Seq} fields in headers or footers.

The next time Word encounters a {Seq FolderNumber} field, it will display the value 3, then 4, and so on. This technique can be extremely useful if, for example, you want to number illustrations in a manuscript sequentially. If you use a field such as

```
Illustration Number {Seq IllustrationNo} - Monet
```

in the caption above or below each illustration, Word numbers the illustrations sequentially:

```
Illustration Number 77 - Monet
```

Then if you reorder the illustrations—move a few around, delete some, and add some others throughout the document—all you have to do is press Ctrl+A to select the entire document, and then press F9 to update the fields. Word renumbers the illustrations, starting at 1 and continuing sequentially throughout the document.

Moreover, if you use one of the three identifiers that Word recognizes—Figure, Table, or Equation—your {Seq Figure}, {Seq Table}, and {Seq Equation} fields can dovetail into Word's built-in features for generating cross-references, such as (See Figure 17 on page 22), and tables of figures.

{Seq} fields recognize five switches; the three you'll commonly use are shown in Table 16.9.

TABLE 16.9 COMMON {SEQ} FIELD SWITCHES

Switch	Meaning
\c	Repeat the previous sequence number; don't increment the counter
\h	Hide the field and its results
\r val	Reset the sequence number to val

So, for example, this series of {Seq} fields starting at the beginning of a document:

```
{Seq MyId} {Seq MyId \c} {Seq MyId} {Seq MyId \r 8} {Seq MyId}
```

produces this as the field result:

```
1 1 2 8 9
```

TIP FROM

ED & Woody

If you have a long document, with more than one chapter, and you want to reset the Figure sequence so it starts at Figure 1 at the beginning of each chapter, put a field that looks like this at the beginning of each chapter:
{Seq Figure \h \r 0 }

TABLE OF CONTENTS AND INDEX FIELDS

Word creates Tables of Contents and Indexes using fields, as well. There's a wealth of information about those fields—{tc}, {toc}, {ie}, {xe}, and the like—in the online help.

In general, the Table of Contents options are handled so well with the built-in TOC tools (choose Insert, Reference, Index and Tables, and click the Table of Contents tab) that dealing with individual fields is time-consuming and won't buy you much.

By contrast, Word's indexing tools (Insert, Reference, Index and Tables, and click the Index tab) are so woefully inadequate that all the field codes in the world won't accomplish much. Avoid them if you possibly can. If you're serious about indexing, buy an add-on package that can read Word files.

TROUBLESHOOTING

HIDING AND REVEALING FIELD CODES

My document is filled with field codes, but I sometimes have a hard time locating them. On more than one occasion, I've accidentally wiped out a crucial field code while editing some other text because I didn't know the code was there.

Normally, field codes are hidden onscreen, and their locations are invisible except for a gray shading that appears when you select the code's location. You can show all field codes in a document by pressing Ctrl+A and then pressing Alt+F9. To make the location of field codes visible at all times without showing the codes themselves, choose Tools, Options, click the View tab, and change the Field Shading option from its default When Selected to Always. Note that this shading will appear in printed copies of pages that contain fields; you'll probably want to turn field shading off before sending a document to the printer.

TIME AND DATE DISCREPANCIES

I entered a {Time} field in my document, but when I update it, the field displays a date.

To solve the problem, remove the \l switches in your {date} and {time} fields. If you don't understand how the \l switch works, bizarre consequences like this are nearly inevitable. If you use the Date and Time dialog box to insert a time in a document, all the {Time \l} fields will show a time when updated. If you then use the same dialog box to insert a date in your document, all the {Date \l} fields will show a date when updated.

EXTRA CREDIT: PROFESSIONAL LABELS, BIG TIME

Use all the tricks in this chapter to create professional-looking mailing labels, and then add a few embellishments to create the ultimate label.

Use pictures, logos, or other catchy material in the upper part of the label.

Word creates a one-cell table for labels. Use Word's Tables and Borders toolbar to add cells for a return address and other elements.

Figure 16.21

For large mailings, insert a POSTNET bar code. By following USPS guidelines, you can cut costs significantly.

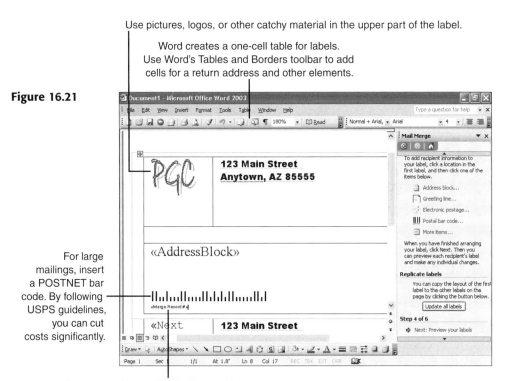

Save yourself some headaches on big merge runs by placing the record number in some inconspicuous spot. In this example, we've placed it at the bottom of the label and formatted it using 4-point Arial.

USING EXCEL

CHAPTER 17

GETTING STARTED WITH EXCEL

In this chapter

WORKING WITH WORKSHEETS AND WORKBOOKS

Before you begin working with Excel, it helps to understand its basic building blocks.

Excel's default file format is the *workbook* (file extension .xls). When you create or save a file in Excel, this is the format you normally use.

Each workbook can hold multiple *worksheets*. A worksheet is the equivalent of a single two-dimensional sheet of paper containing rows and columns. By default, each new Excel workbook starts out with three blank worksheets; an index tab at the bottom of each worksheet identifies the sheet by name. You can add a new worksheet, delete an existing worksheet, and rename or rearrange worksheets to suit your needs.

Every worksheet consists of rows and columns. At the intersection of each row and column is a *cell*, and a selection of multiple cells is called a *range*. (We discuss cells and ranges in much more detail later in this chapter and in Chapter 19, "Using Formulas and Functions.")

Multiple worksheets help keep complex projects organized within a single workbook. In a consolidated annual budget for a school district, for example, you might create a separate worksheet for the numbers reported by each individual school. In this case, you would use identical templates to make sure each sheet is formatted identically: Each budget category appears in the same row and each month is in the same column. You would then use an identical template to create a summary worksheet that totals each row and column for the entire district.

Placing related data tables on different sheets makes it easier to view, format, and print each type of data separately—for example, if you're researching loans for a new house, you might create a loan analysis form on one worksheet, and then generate an amortization table on a separate sheet. When you create new charts or *PivotTable* reports from a list, it's often convenient to give each of these elements its own sheet. That way, you can rearrange the data in the underlying list without having to worry about whether deleting a row or column will mess up the design of a PivotTable report.

TIP FROM

Ed & Woody

> In workbooks with a large number of worksheets, you won't be able to see all the sheet names without using the four arrow buttons to the left of the sheet names to scroll. Unless, of course, you know this secret: right-click any of those arrow buttons to display a pop-up list containing the names of all the worksheets in the current workbook. Click any name to jump straight to that worksheet.

MOVING, COPYING, INSERTING, AND DELETING WORKSHEETS

In many cases, the easiest way to construct a workbook containing multiple sheets is to create the first sheet and then copy it. Although each new workbook starts with three blank worksheets (a setting you can change), you can add, copy, delete, and rearrange worksheets at will.

To add a new worksheet to an existing workbook, right-click any sheet tab and choose Insert, click the Worksheet icon in the Insert dialog box, and click OK. The new worksheet appears to the left of the sheet tab you clicked, with a generic name and a number one higher than the highest numbered sheet in the current workbook—Sheet4, Sheet5, and so on.

If that process feels too cumbersome, point to the sheet tab you want to copy, hold down the Ctrl key, and drag the sheet tab left or right. (This Ctrl+drag technique is the same one you use to copy files in Windows Explorer.) As you drag, the mouse pointer changes shape and a small triangular marker with a plus sign appears above the sheet tab. When you release the mouse button, Excel creates a copy of the sheet you dragged, using its name followed by a copy number in parentheses: Sheet3 (2), for example.

CAUTION

When you copy a sheet that contains data, either within a workbook or to another workbook, Excel truncates the contents of any cell that contains more than 255 characters. If Excel detects that any cell in the sheet you're about to copy contains more than 255 characters, it displays a warning message; when you click OK, it copies the sheet anyway. To fix the copy, press Ctrl+A to select all cells in the original worksheet, and then press Ctrl+C to copy them to the Clipboard. Then, click cell A1 in the copy and press Ctrl+V to paste the Clipboard contents, replacing the truncated data.

To delete a worksheet from a workbook, right-click the sheet tab of the worksheet you want to delete, and then choose Delete from the shortcut menu.

TIP FROM

Ed & Woody

In some workbooks, you might want to hide a worksheet rather than remove it. This technique is especially useful when a worksheet contains static data you use in formulas on other worksheets but rarely need to edit. Hiding a sheet also makes it slightly more difficult for other users to examine (and possibly change) the data on one of these sheets. (But don't even think about using hidden sheets as a true security measure—anyone interested in unhiding the sheet can do so with a few clicks.) To hide a sheet, choose Format, Sheet, Hide. To display a list of hidden sheets in the current workbook so you can make them visible again, choose Format, Sheet, Unhide.

To move a worksheet within a workbook, point to its sheet tab, click, and drag the triangular pointer along the sheet tabs until the black marker is over the location where you want to move the worksheet. Release the mouse button to drop the worksheet in its new location. Although it's possible to drag and drop worksheets between workbooks, it's much quicker and more accurate to use shortcut menus for this task. Follow these steps to move or copy a worksheet from one workbook to another:

1. Open the target workbook into which you plan to move or copy the worksheet. (Skip this step if you plan to move or copy the worksheet to a brand-new workbook.)

2. Switch to the workbook that contains the worksheet you want to move or copy. Point to the worksheet tab and right-click.

3. Choose Move or Copy from the shortcut menu.

4. In the Move or Copy dialog box (see Figure 17.1), select the name of the target workbook from the To Book drop-down list. To move or copy the sheet to a new, empty workbook, choose (new book) from the top of the list.

5. By default, Excel moves or copies sheets to the beginning of the target workbook. To select a different location, choose a sheet name from the Before Sheet list.

6. By default, using this dialog box moves the selected worksheet to the target workbook. To leave the original worksheet in place, select the Create a Copy check box.

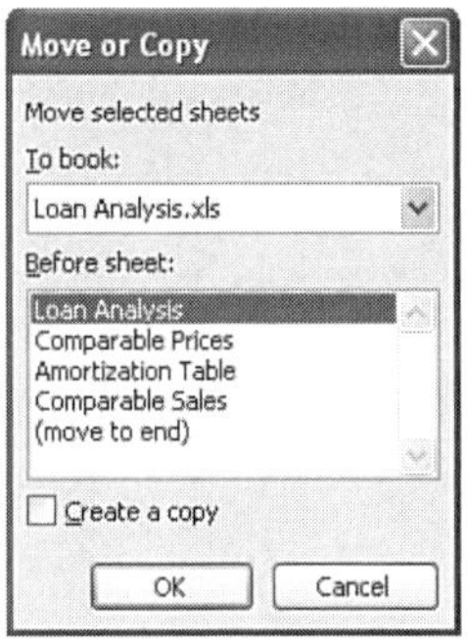

Figure 17.1

7. Click OK.

RENAMING A WORKSHEET

To navigate more easily through workbooks with multiple worksheets, replace the generic default worksheet labels (Sheet1, Chart2, and so on) with descriptive names such as "November Expenses," "Industrial Output," or "PivotTable." To rename a worksheet, double-click the worksheet tab (or right-click the tab and select Rename). Type a new name and press Enter.

Names you enter on worksheet tabs must conform to the following rules:

- Maximum length is 31 characters.

- Spaces are allowed.

- You can use parentheses anywhere in a worksheet's name; brackets ([ ]) are also allowed, except as the first character in the name.

- You cannot use any of the following characters as part of a sheet name: / \ ? * : (slash, backslash, question mark, asterisk, or colon). Other punctuation marks, including commas and exclamation points, are allowed.

If you plan to use references from one worksheet in formulas on another sheet, choose worksheet names carefully. Create names that are as short as possible without being needlessly cryptic; long names can make formulas particularly difficult to troubleshoot and edit.

NOTE

> Worksheet tabs automatically resize to accommodate the name you enter.

TIP FROM

EQ & Woody

Excel 2003 allows you to color code worksheet tabs (right-click the worksheet tab and choose the Tab Color option). This option is best used sparingly. Colorizing each worksheet tab doesn't help organize data. Instead, try using colors to identify sheets that are part of the same group (yellow for East, green for West), or use colors to highlight summary sheets while leaving data input sheets with the default gray background.

NAVIGATING IN A WORKBOOK WITH KEYBOARD SHORTCUTS

For touch typists, Excel includes a wealth of keyboard shortcuts. Some are obvious, but a few are less than intuitive, and some represent unusual ways to move through a worksheet and select cells with precision:

- Ctrl+Home returns to the top-left corner (cell A1) of the current sheet.
- The Home key moves to the beginning of the current row.
- The Page Up/Page Down keys take you one window in their respective directions.
- Ctrl+End jumps to the bottom-right corner of the data-containing part of the worksheet—a useful technique when navigating through a lengthy list.
- If you've selected a range, you can move clockwise through all four corners of the range by repeatedly pressing Ctrl+period. If you've highlighted multiple ranges, this shortcut works only in the currently selected range.
- To move through the current workbook, one worksheet at a time, press Ctrl+Page Up or Ctrl+Page Down.
- Pressing the End key turns on *End mode*, an unusual (and somewhat confusing) way to move through the current worksheet. Most of the End mode shortcuts are alternatives to Ctrl+*key* shortcuts that are appropriate for people who are unable to press two keys simultaneously (or just don't want to). Press End followed by an arrow key to jump along the current row or column in the direction of the arrow, to the next cell that contains data, skipping over any intervening empty cells. Press End and then Home to go to the cell that is at the intersection of the furthest data-containing row and column in the current worksheet. Press End and then Enter to move to the last cell in the current row, even if there are blank cells within the row—this is the most useful of the End mode shortcuts, because it has no matching Ctrl+*key* alternative. If you press the End key by accident, press End again to turn off End mode.

TIP FROM

EQ & Woody

Don't forget all of the common shortcuts that Excel shares with Windows and other Office programs. In particular, F2 (Edit) positions the insertion point in the active cell and makes it available for editing, F4 repeats the previous action, and F6 switches between panes in a worksheet where you've used the Window, Split command.

17

WORKING WITH MULTIPLE WORKSHEETS

Working with multiple sheets simultaneously is how power users quickly create and format a complex workbook with a minimum of wasted effort. Use the following techniques to make working with multiple sheets easy:

- To select multiple worksheets, hold down the Ctrl key as you click each tab.

- To select a contiguous group of worksheets, click the first one in the group and then hold down the Shift key and click the last one in the group.

- To select all the worksheets in the current workbook, right-click any worksheet tab and choose Select All Sheets from the shortcut menu.

- To quickly make any sheet active, click its index tab; to remove a sheet from a group, hold down Ctrl and click its tab.

- To remove the multiple selection and resume working with a single sheet, click any un-selected sheet; if you've selected every sheet in the workbook, right-click any worksheet tab and choose Ungroup Sheets.

- If you've selected more than one sheet, you see the word Group in brackets in the title bar, and any data you enter appears in the corresponding cells on each worksheet in the group. So, if you have grouped Sheet1, Sheet2, and Sheet3, entering text in cell A1 on Sheet1 also enters the same text in the corresponding cells on Sheet2 and Sheet3.

- Likewise, any formatting choices you make—resizing columns, for example, or applying a numeric format—affect all the grouped worksheets identically. If you're building a master workbook with identically formatted sheets for each division or department, you can use these techniques to quickly enter the budget categories in the first column and months along the top of each sheet.

- You can't use the Clipboard to enter data into multiple sheets simultaneously. When you paste data, it appears only in the active sheet, not in any other sheets you've selected. To quickly copy formulas, labels, or formats from a single worksheet to a group of sheets within a workbook, follow these steps:

  1. Select the sheet that contains the data you want to appear in each sheet.
  2. Use Ctrl+click or Shift+click to select the group of sheets to which you want to add the data.
  3. Select the data itself and choose Edit, Fill, Across Worksheets. An additional dialog box lets you choose whether to copy the formatted cell contents, just the data, or just the formats.

NOTE

Watch out for one gotcha if you exchange workbook files with anyone who uses Microsoft Works. Although the Spreadsheet module in Works 7.0 can open Excel workbooks, it treats multi-sheet workbooks as though each sheet were a separate file.

USING CELL REFERENCES AND RANGE NAMES TO NAVIGATE IN A WORKBOOK

Excel's Name box (the combo box to the left of the Formula bar) lets you jump straight to a specific cell or named range. Click in this box, enter a cell reference (H4, for example), and press Enter to jump straight to that cell. To pick from a list of all named ranges in the current workbook, even on different worksheets, click the drop-down arrow to the right of the Name box.

Excel's Go To dialog box offers the same capabilities, with a few extra twists, including the capability to return to a cell you previously selected, or to select all cells on a worksheet that match criteria you specify.

To open the Go To dialog box shown in Figure 17.2, choose Edit, Go To, or use the keyboard shortcuts F5 or Ctrl+G. To jump to a specific cell or range, type its address or name in the Reference box. In general, it's easier to use the Name box to jump around a worksheet in this fashion. The advantage of the Go To dialog box is that Excel keeps track of the four most recent cell addresses you enter here, including the cell you started from. To return to any of these addresses, open the Go To dialog box and double-click the entry in the Go To list.

17

Figure 17.2
The Go To dialog box lets you jump to cells or named ranges you've visited recently.

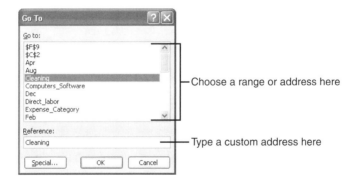

Choose a range or address here

Type a custom address here

The list of references in the Go To dialog box also includes any named ranges in the current workbook. To jump to one of these ranges, select its name from the list and click OK. Because Excel saves range names with the workbook, that list is always available when you open the Go To dialog box. On the other hand, Excel discards the list of recent addresses each time you close the workbook.

TIP FROM

Ed & Woody

Using the Go To dialog box to jump to a specific cell or a named range is needlessly complex. Whenever possible, use the Name box instead. It's also easy to create a macro that jumps to a specific named range or cell address. Use the following code, for example, to jump to a range with the name ZipCodes (the Scroll parameter positions the window so that the top-left cell in the range is at the top-left corner of the window):

```
Sub GoToZipCodes()
Application.Goto
Reference:=Worksheets("Sheet1").Range("ZipCodes"),
➡scroll:=True
End Sub
```

→ For an explanation of how range names work in formulas, **see** "Using Range Names and Labels in Formulas," **p. 602**.

→ For details on the incredibly useful Special button, see "Selecting Ranges of Data with the Go To Dialog Box," **p. 523**.

USING RANGES TO WORK WITH MULTIPLE CELLS

Any selection of two or more cells is called a *range*. You can dramatically increase your productivity by using ranges to enter, edit, and format data. For example, if you highlight a range and click the Currency Style button, all the numeric entries in that range appear with dollar signs and two decimal places. Assigning a name to a range makes it easier to construct (and troubleshoot) formulas, and ranges make up the heart and soul of charts by defining *data series* and labels for values and categories.

The most common way to select multiple cells is to highlight a *contiguous range*—a rectangular region in which all cells are next to one another. But cells in a range don't have to be contiguous. You can also define a perfectly legal range by selecting individual cells or groups of cells scattered around a single worksheet.

Excel uses two addresses to identify a contiguous range, beginning with the cell in the upper-left corner and ending with the cell in the lower-right corner of the selection. A colon (:) separates the two addresses that identify the range—such as A1:G3. Commas separate the parts of a noncontiguous range, and you can mix individual cells and contiguous ranges to form a new range, as in the example A3,B4,C5:D8.

SELECTING RANGES

To select a contiguous range, click the cell at any corner of the range and drag the mouse pointer to the opposite corner. To select a noncontiguous range, select the first cell or group of cells, hold down the Ctrl key, and select the next cell or group of cells. Continue holding the Ctrl key until you've selected all the cells in the range. To select an entire row or column, click the row or column heading. To select multiple rows or columns, drag the selection or hold down the Ctrl key while clicking.

To select all cells in the current worksheet, click the unlabeled Select All button in the upper-left corner of the worksheet, above the row labels and to the left of the column labels.

TIP FROM

EQ & Woody

Use this shortcut to select a contiguous range that occupies more than one screen: Click the top-left cell in the range, and then use the scrollbars to move through the worksheet until you can see the lower-right corner of the range. Hold down the Shift key and click to select the entire range.

Moving from Cell to Cell Within a Range

To enter data into a list in heads-down mode, select the range first. As you enter data, press the Enter key to move the active cell down to the next cell within the range, or press Tab to move to the right. (Press Shift+Enter or Shift+Tab to move in the opposite direction.)

When you reach the end of a row or column, pressing Enter or Tab moves the active cell to the next column or row in the selection. When you reach the lower-right corner of the range, pressing Enter or Tab moves you back to the upper-left corner.

Entering the Same Data in Multiple Cells

Occasionally, you'll want to fill a range of cells with exactly the same data in one operation, without using the Clipboard. For example, you might want to enter zero values in cells in which you intend to enter values later; you can also use this technique to enter a formula in several cells at once. To enter a formula in several cells at once, follow these steps:

1. Select the range of cells into which you want to enter data. The range need not be contiguous.

2. Type the text, number, or formula you want to use, and then press Ctrl+Enter. The data appears in all cells you selected.

TIP FROM

> When you enter a formula using this technique, Excel inserts *relative cell references* by default. If you want the formula to refer to a constant value, select the cell reference and press F4 to convert it to an absolute reference before pressing Ctrl+Enter.

→ For a discussion of the differences between absolute and relative cell references, **see** "Using Cell References in Formulas," **p. 595**.

→ For instructions on how to automatically fill in data using Excel's AutoFill feature, **see** "Automatically Filling In a Series of Data," **p. 634**.

Selecting Ranges of Data with the Go To Dialog Box

The Go To dialog box is especially useful when you're designing or troubleshooting a large worksheet and you want to quickly view, edit, format, copy, or move a group of cells with common characteristics. In fact, mastering this dialog box can make it possible to do things even most Excel experts swear can't be done, such as copying a range of data while ignoring hidden rows and columns. Open the Go To dialog box as usual, and then click the Special button to display the Go To Special dialog box shown in Figure 17.3. When you select one of these options and click OK, Excel selects all the cells that match that characteristic.

Figure 17.3

When you select cells using the Go To Special dialog box, the effect is the same as if you had selected a range by pointing and clicking. If you select all constants, for example, you can use the Tab and Enter keys to move through all the cells in your worksheet that contain data, skipping over any cell that contains a formula.

The following list describes the options available in the Go To Special dialog box:

- **Comments**—Selects all cells that contain *comments*. Use this option, and then press the Tab key to move from comment to comment instead of using the Previous Comment and Next Comment buttons on the Reviewing toolbar. This option is also useful if you want to remove all comments from a worksheet. Select all comments, and then right-click any of the selected cells and choose Delete Comment from the shortcut menu.

- **Constants**—Selects all cells that contain text, dates, or numbers, but not formulas. The Numbers and Text check boxes let you restrict the selection by data type (although the Logicals and Errors boxes are available, using these settings when searching for *constants* will always return an empty set). Select just text, for example, if you want to change the formatting of row and column labels while leaving the data area alone. Select all numbers and clear their contents to turn a worksheet into a template that contains only text labels and formulas.

- **Formulas**—The opposite of the Constants choice, this option selects only cells that begin with an equal sign. The Numbers and Text check boxes let you restrict the selection by data type. Use the Logicals check box to find cells that contain a TRUE or FALSE value. Click the Errors check box to quickly select all cells that currently display an error value, and then use the Tab key to move from cell to cell and fix the misbehaving formulas.

- **Blanks**—A straightforward option that searches all cells between the top of the worksheet and the last cell that contains data, selecting those that do not contain data or formatting. This option is useful when you want to enter a default value (such as 0) or assign a default format to these cells.

- **Current Region**—Selects all cells around the active cell, up to the nearest blank row and column in any direction.

- **Current Array**—If the active cell is within an *array*, this option selects the entire array.

- **Objects**—Choose this option to select all charts, text boxes, AutoShapes, and other graphic objects on the current worksheet. This option is particularly useful when you want to change formatting for borders and shading, or when you want to group objects.

- **Row Differences**—Selects cells whose contents are different from those in a comparison cell. This is a challenging option to master: You must make a selection first, and then use the Tab or Shift+Tab key to position the active cell in the column you want to use for comparison. If you select multiple rows, Excel compares each row independently to the value in the column that contains the active cell. The example in Figure 17.4 shows what happens when you select C2:I12 and then position the active cell in column C and use the Go To Special dialog box with the Row Differences option. The highlighted result helps you readily identify two rows where expenses are different each month, but it also pinpoints one out-of-the-ordinary value in cell E10. Press Tab to move through from one highlighted cell to the next within the results.

Figure 17.4
Using the Row Differences command identifies values that are out of the ordinary; a cost-conscious manager might ask why the March cleaning bill was $275 higher than usual.

Select this range first...

...then position the active cell in this column.

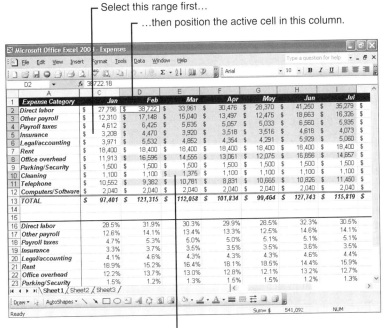

The Row Differences option selects the cells in gray because they contain values that are different from those in the same row in the comparison column.

- **Column Differences**—Like the previous option, except it works on a column-by-column basis. This option is extremely useful for finding unexpected differences in a list. Use a calculated column that determines whether a particular set of columns is within a normal range and returns a TRUE or FALSE result, and then use this option to find all cells that are FALSE.

- **Precedents**—Selects all cells to which the current selection refers. Use the Direct Only and All Levels options to find only direct references or all references. This option is useful when you're trying to trace the logic of a complex worksheet by working through a series of formulas.

- **Dependents**—Similar to the previous option, except it selects all cells that directly or indirectly refer to the active cell or range.

- **Last Cell**—Jumps to the last cell on the worksheet that contains data or formatting.

- **Visible Cells Only**—Easily the most useful of all the options in the Go To Special dialog box. Use this type of selection to avoid the common problem of pasting more data than you expect. For example, if you copy a range of data that includes a hidden row or column, and then paste it into a new sheet, Excel pastes the hidden data as well. To avoid this problem, select the range you want to copy, and then use the Go To Special dialog box to select only visible cells. Copying and pasting that selection will have exactly the result you intend.

- **Conditional Formats**—Selects all cells that use any form of *conditional formatting*. Use the All option when you want to quickly find all cells that contain conditional formatting. Use the Same option if you just want to edit these options for cells that match the current cell.

→ For a detailed explanation of how and when to use conditional formatting, **see** "Using Conditional Formatting to Identify Key Values," **p. 584**.

- **Data Validation**—Similar to the previous option, except it selects cells with *data validation* rules.

 If choosing the Last Cell option in the Go To Special dialog box causes you to jump to a blank cell far below your actual worksheet range, see "Resetting the Last Cell" in the "Troubleshooting" section at the end of this chapter.

HIDING ROWS AND COLUMNS

On some worksheets, you need to use rows or columns to hold data used in calculations, but you don't need to clutter up the rest of the worksheet by showing it. Click any cell within the row or column you want to hide (you don't need to select the entire row or column) and choose Format, Row, Hide or Format, Column, Hide.

To make a hidden row visible again, select cells in the row above and below the hidden row, and then choose Format, Row, Unhide. To display a hidden column, select cells in the columns to the left and right and choose Format, Column, Unhide.

If the first row or column of a worksheet is hidden, press F5 to open the Go To dialog box. Type **A1** in the Reference box and click OK; then choose Format, Row (or Column), Unhide.

FINDING, REPLACING, AND TRANSFORMING DATA

Just as in other Office applications, you can use simple drag-and-drop techniques to move or copy the contents of a cell or range. Using the Windows Clipboard and the Paste Special menu, you can also change the format of information or perform mathematical transformations as you move or copy it. Most of the options are self-explanatory, but a handful are unique to Excel and truly useful.

→ For an overview of standard Clipboard techniques you can use within and between Office programs, **see** "Using the Office Clipboard," **p. 146**.

FINDING AND REPLACING THE CONTENTS OF A CELL OR RANGE

You can use the Find and Replace dialog box to search for and replace strings of text. You can also find and change formatting, or use options to search across all sheets in a workbook or to restrict the search and subsequent changes to the current worksheet.

As in other Office programs, you use the Find and Replace options on the Edit menu (or the corresponding Ctrl+F and Ctrl+H shortcuts) to open the respective dialog boxes. Figure 17.5 shows the Replace dialog box with formatting options selected. (If the additional settings aren't visible, click the Options button.)

Figure 17.5
The Find and Replace dialog boxes let you change formatting globally across an entire workbook.

17

If you leave the Find What or Replace With boxes blank, Excel finds or replaces formatting in all cells where it finds a match. To enter formatting criteria using dialog boxes, click the Format button to the right of the Find What or Replace With text boxes. To find cells where formatting matches the settings of an existing cell, click the drop-down arrow to the right of the Format button and select the Choose Format from Cell option. After you select this option, the Find and Replace dialog box disappears and the mouse pointer changes to an eyedropper shape. Click the cell that contains the formatting you want to match.

DRAGGING AND DROPPING TO CONVERT DATA

As is true elsewhere in Office, you can take control of the options available when dragging cells from one place to another. For instance, if you hold down the right mouse button and drag a cell or range of cells, a shortcut menu with paste options appears when you release the button. Two of these options are worth special note:

- Use the Copy Here as Formats Only option to quickly transfer cell formatting (fonts, shading, borders, and so on) without copying the contents of the cells.

- Choose Copy Here as Values Only to convert formulas to their results and paste the Clipboard contents as constants—numbers or text—rather than as formulas.

This technique is especially useful when you want to quickly convert a cell or range from a formula to a value. Say column A contains a list of ISBN numbers and book titles (all books use these; just look at the back cover of this one), imported from an external database. All you really need from each cell is the 10-digit ISBN number it starts with, so you've filled column B with a range of formulas, each of which uses the LEFT() function to extract the first six characters from the original cell—for example, =LEFT(A2,10).

So far, so good. But if you now delete column A, your list of part numbers will shift to the left and turn into a column full of error messages. Before you can safely delete column A, you must convert column B to its results. To do so, select the entire range that contains the formula, right-click the border of the selection and drag it a short distance in any direction (without releasing the mouse button), and then drag it back and release it over the original cells. Choose Copy Here as Values Only from the shortcut menu. The column now contains just the part numbers, and you can safely delete column A.

NOTE

You cannot use the Clipboard or drag-and-drop techniques to copy or move a noncontiguous range that consists of multiple selections.

TRANSFORMING DATA WITH PASTE OPTIONS

One of the most powerful ways to manipulate data on a worksheet is to copy it to the Clipboard first. Using the Clipboard, you can strip some or all formatting or manipulate values in the copied cells or range; you can then paste the data into the new location so it appears exactly as you want it.

The Paste Options Smart Tag allows you to quickly apply some common transformations. When you copy data to the Clipboard and then use Edit, Paste or the Ctrl+V keyboard shortcut to paste the data, you see a Smart Tag in the lower-right corner of the pasted area. Click the Smart Tag to choose from the menu shown in Figure 17.6.

Figure 17.6
Smart Tag options let you tweak the appearance of data after pasting it; the Keep Source Column Widths option, for instance, fixes this common problem when pasting into a new worksheet.

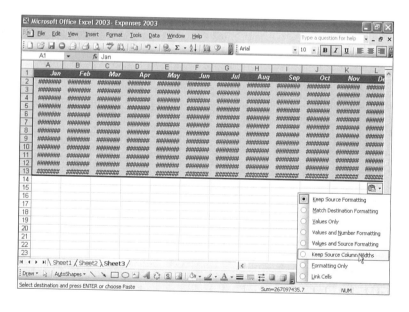

By default, data pasted from another Excel worksheet brings along its own formatting. If the data appears incorrectly when you paste it, click the Smart Tag and change the display of the pasted data in any of these ways:

- Choose Match Destination Formatting to strip all formatting but preserve formulas.

- Use one of the three Values options to convert formulas to their resulting values and paste them into the new location, with or without formatting.

- Click Keep Source Column Widths to copy all formulas, number formatting, and cell formatting along with column widths. This option is most useful when pasting a highly formatted table into a new worksheet, where all columns are the standard width.

- Choose Formatting Only when you want to copy the format of a table to a new worksheet and then enter data manually in the new location.

- Click the Link Cells option to convert the pasted data into a link to the other worksheet.

→ For more details on how to use links between worksheets and workbooks, **see** "Using Links to Automatically Update or Consolidate Worksheet Data," **p. 533**.

Choices available through the Paste Options Smart Tag are convenient for quick, uncomplicated transformations. But they have several limitations, most notably that each change undoes the changes from other Smart Tags. So if you paste in a range of formulas, you can use Smart Tags to convert formulas to values *or* to adjust column widths, but not both.

For more control over the results of a paste operation, use the Paste Special menu. Copy the contents of one or more cells to the Clipboard and choose Edit, Paste Special—you'll see the Paste Special dialog box shown in Figure 17.7. A handful of these options are also available using the Paste Options Smart Tag, but Paste Special offers a much broader range of capabilities.

Figure 17.7
Use the Paste Special dialog box to add or subtract two columns of numbers, or to multiply or divide a range of numbers by a value you copy to the Clipboard.

Within or between workbooks, you can selectively paste in the following ways:

- The Formulas option is hopelessly misnamed, and the Help text does a terrible job of describing its actual function. Use this option when you want to copy all the data from one range to another, including formulas, without copying any formatting. This option is most useful when you're trying to copy data from another worksheet without destroying the formatting of your existing worksheet. Use the Formulas and Number

Formats option to copy number formatting without carrying over other cell formatting, such as borders and colors.

- Select Values to convert formulas to their results and paste them as constant numbers or text. This has the same effect as the drag-and-drop technique described in the previous section. Use this option when you need to convert a noncontiguous range of formulas to its results. This option does not copy any formatting. Use the Values and Number Formats option to preserve number formatting without affecting other cell formatting.

- Click Formats to copy all formatting from one cell or range to another. Use the All Except Borders option to skip cell borders, and the Column Widths option to duplicate column widths, especially from one worksheet to another.

TIP FROM

Using Excel's Paste Special options can test your creativity. It's often possible to save a ton of work by combining several operations in consecutive Paste Special actions. For instance, choose All Except Borders to copy formulas and cell formatting without adding underlines and table borders from the original data; then repeat the Paste Special option and choose the Column Widths option. This duplicates an entire table on a new worksheet, leaving out only borders and underlines.

- Choose the Comments option to transfer comments from one location to another.

- Use the Validation option to duplicate data-entry rules, especially between different worksheets or workbooks.

The options in the Operation area are some of the most interesting of all, because they allow you to perform mathematical transformations on a group of numbers without having to tamper with your existing worksheet structure. To use this technique, enter a number in one cell and copy it to the Clipboard, select the range you want to transform, and use the Paste Special dialog box to add or subtract the value on the Clipboard from each entry in the selection or to multiply or divide the selection by that number. This technique might come in handy if you're beginning to plan next year's budget and you want to start by increasing this year's numbers by 6%. Follow these steps:

1. Click in any blank cell (even on another worksheet) and enter the value you want to use when transforming the existing data. In this case, enter **1.06** because you want to increase the values by 6%.

TIP FROM

You can also use this technique to add or subtract two ranges of numbers, or to multiply one range of numbers by another. If you have two departmental worksheets formatted in exactly the same way, you can copy all the numbers from one worksheet and use this option to add them to the data in the other sheet, for example. Just make sure that the range you copy is the same size as the range you paste to.

2. Press Ctrl+C to copy the value to the Windows Clipboard.

3. Select the range of data you want to increase.

4. Click Edit, Paste Special. In the Paste Special dialog box, choose the Multiply option.

5. Click OK. Excel multiplies the selected range by the constant on the Clipboard, increasing each number by exactly 6%.

The final two check boxes in the Paste Special dialog box work with other options:

- Click the Skip Blanks option if you're performing a mathematical operation using two ranges of data. This setting skips pasting data for any cells that are blank in the original copy area.

- Click the Transpose check box to flip the contents of a row into a column, or vice versa. You can use this option to change the orientation of an entire region as well.

TIP FROM

Changing the orientation of an entire region is a trick that is especially useful when working with imported data. If your list has months along the side and categories along the top, for example, choose the Transpose option to rearrange the list so that each month's data appears in its own column and each category gets its own row.

CUSTOMIZING THE WORKSHEET WINDOW

Changing the size and configuration of a worksheet window can make it easier to work with data, especially in large worksheets. Zoom out or in to show more or less data, lock a row or column in place to maintain titles and headings, work in multiple panes, or open a new window on the same workbook.

USING THE ZOOM CONTROLS

Use the Zoom button on the Standard toolbar to change the view of your worksheet. Most of the options are self-explanatory: You can shrink the worksheet to as small as 10% of normal size for an overview of the sheet's design, or enlarge it to as much as 400% of normal. (This option is inappropriate for entering numbers but is especially useful for close editing of complex grouped objects on a sheet.) If you choose a Zoom level of 39% or lower, your gridlines disappear. That's not a bug—at the lower magnification, the lines get in the way of your ability to edit, so Excel hides them on the screen.

The most useful option on the Zoom control is one that even some expert users don't know about. You can resize and reposition the editing window so that it includes the current selection; Excel chooses the proper Zoom percentage automatically. After you make a selection, choose Selection from the bottom of the Zoom drop-down list (or choose Zoom from the View men and then choose Fit Selection). Excel resizes the selection automatically. To return to normal view, click the Zoom button again and choose 100% from the drop-down list.

17

TIP FROM

EQ & Woody

> If your mouse includes a wheel, you can use it to zoom in and out of your worksheet. Hold down the Ctrl key and spin the wheel down to zoom out; spin the wheel up to zoom back in.

LOCKING ROW AND COLUMN LABELS FOR ONSCREEN VIEWING

In a typical worksheet, labels identify the type of data in each column or row. For example, a common design for budget worksheets arranges data into one row for each budget category, with values for each month appearing in columns from left to right. In this model, a label at the left edge of each row identifies the category, and a label at the top of each column identifies the month. If the data in your worksheet occupies more than a single screen, row and column labels can scroll out of view, making it difficult to identify which data goes in each row and column. The lack of labels also makes it difficult to enter data in the correct rows and columns, unless you want to continually scroll to see the heading labels.

To keep the row and column labels visible at all times, *freeze* them into position. In Figure 17.8, for example, notice that you can see the row titles in column A at the left, as well as the columns for July, August, and beyond at the right (starting at column H). As you click the horizontal scrollbar, columns on the left of the data area scroll out of view, but the labels in the first column remain visible.

Figure 17.8
When you freeze rows or columns in place, you can scroll through the worksheet without losing identifying labels.

	A		I	J	K	L	M	N
1								
2								
3	Amount							
4	Budget Category	▾	Aug	Sep	Oct	Nov	Dec	Grand Total
11	Entertainment		2,401	13,941	4,052	4,133	1,341	102,090
12	Equipment		9,922	10,666	5,345	2,745	10,868	71,554
13	Computer Equipment		2,143	3,510	3,604	11,686	9,229	92,006
14	Office Supplies		755	911	1,402	992	1,010	11,451
15	Printing and Copying		2,075	1,472	1,224	1,686	780	17,862
16	Telephone and Fax		15,036	14,142	11,624	6,562	8,339	147,205
17	Postage and Delivery		10,937	21,332	18,763	14,054	18,522	181,236
18	Rent		19,500	19,500	19,500	19,500	19,500	234,000

To freeze rows, columns, or both, click in the cell below the row and to the right of the column that you want to lock into position. To freeze the first two columns and the first row, for example, click in cell C2. Choose Window, Freeze Panes. A solid line sets off the locked rows and columns from the rest of the worksheet.

TIP FROM

EQ & Woody

> If your worksheet consists of a long list, lock in the labels for columns only. Click in column A, one row beneath the row that contains your column labels, and then choose Window, Freeze Panes.

To navigate in a worksheet whose panes are frozen, use the scrollbars to move through the data in your worksheet. The panes are locked only on the screen; if you print the worksheet, rows and columns appear in their normal positions. To unlock the row and column labels, choose Window, Unfreeze Panes.

→ To learn how to add row or column labels on each page of a printed worksheet, **see** "Using Repeating Titles for Multiple Page Printouts," **p. 544**.

SPLITTING THE WORKSHEET WINDOW

Split a worksheet into separate panes when you want to compare data in different regions of a worksheet side-by-side. A *split bar* divides the window into two panes, horizontally or vertically. You can drag both split bars onto the worksheet to create four panes. All changes you make in one pane are reflected in the other. You can drag cells and ranges between panes, and you can scroll and enter data in each pane independently.

To split a worksheet, use either of the following techniques:

- Click to select the cell below and/or to the right of where you want the split to appear, and then choose Window, Split. Select any cell in the column at the left of the current window to create side-by-side panes (also known as a vertical split). Select any cell in the top row to create a horizontal split, with one pane over another. If you choose the cell at the top left of the screen, Excel divides the window into four equal panes.

- Aim the mouse pointer at one of the two *split boxes*, which appear just above the vertical scrollbar and just to the right of the horizontal scrollbar, to create side-by-side panes (vertical split). When the mouse pointer changes to a double line with two arrows, click and drag in the direction of the worksheet to create a new pane. As you drag, the bar snaps into place at a row or column boundary. Release when you reach the right position.

To remove multiple panes and return to a single editing window, you can do any of the following: Choose Window, Remove Split; double-click the split bar; or click the bar and drag it off the worksheet window.

USING LINKS TO AUTOMATICALLY UPDATE OR CONSOLIDATE WORKSHEET DATA

Use *links* to share data between cells or ranges in one worksheet and another location in the same workbook or a different workbook. Just as a formula displays the results of a calculation, a link looks up data from another location and displays it in the active cell.

Links offer a powerful technique for consolidating data from different sources into one worksheet without requiring that you re-enter or copy data. For example, a teacher might use separate worksheets in a single workbook to keep track of test results for each class, with a separate worksheet that organizes results into an alphabetical list by student.

NOTE

You can use *links* (also known as external references) within formulas as well.

After you establish a link, data you enter in one location automatically appears in all linked locations. To create a link, follow these steps:

1. Open all the workbooks you plan to link.

2. In the source workbook (the one that contains the data you want to reuse), select the cell or range to be linked, and press Ctrl+C to copy it to the Clipboard.

3. Switch to the dependent workbook (the one in which you want to insert the link), and select the cell where you want to create the link.

4. Choose Edit, Paste Special. In the Paste Special dialog box, click Paste Link.

In general, you should avoid creating links between cells or ranges that are contained in separate workbooks. If you move or delete the workbook that contains the external reference, you break the link and damage the integrity of your data and formulas. Excel updates linked cells automatically if the worksheet that contains the link is open. If you change the data in the source workbook when the workbook that contains the link is closed, the links do not update automatically. When you reopen the workbook that contains the links, Excel will ask whether you want to update the links. To update or change the source of links manually, choose Edit, Links.

RESTRICTING AND VALIDATING DATA ENTRY FOR A CELL OR RANGE

When designing a worksheet, you'll occasionally want to restrict the type of data users can enter in a specific cell or range. Excel lets you define data-validation rules for cells and ranges to do exactly that. Examples of useful applications include the following:

- In a list of test scores formatted to show only month and date, restrict entry in a specific column to only dates within the last 14 days. This technique lessens the likelihood that you will inadvertently enter a date in the wrong month or year, or in the future.

- On a budget worksheet, require that the user enter a category and restrict allowed entries to a specific list. You can add a drop-down arrow to a cell with this type of restriction so users can pick from a list.

- For your personal budget, check the amount entered in an expenses column against a typical maximum value—say, $500. If the amount is over that limit, display an "Are you sure?" message.

- Ask a user to enter a description of a list item; to keep data to a manageable length, restrict the total number of characters the user can enter and display a warning message if the description exceeds that length.

- On a form that you send to club members requesting payment of annual dues, allow the option to enter a discount, but only if the member first joined more than five years ago. Compare the entry in the Discount field with a formula that calculates the member's start date to validate the entry.

DEFINING DATA-VALIDATION RULES

Each *data-validation* rule has three components: the criteria that define a valid entry; an optional message you can display to users when they select the cell that contains the rule; and an error message that appears when users enter invalid data. To begin creating a data-validation rule, first select the cell or range for which you want to restrict data entry, and then choose Data, Validation. You'll see a Data Validation dialog box similar to the one in Figure 17.9.

Figure 17.9
When defining data-validation rules, you can enter values or formulas that evaluate to the correct data type. This example restricts valid entries to dates within the last 30 days.

On the Settings tab, enter the criteria that define a valid entry. First, choose the required data type in the Allow drop-down list; then define specific criteria. The available options in the Allow drop-down list (described in Table 17.1) vary depending on the type of data you select. Keep in mind that the options shown in the Data Validation dialog box change depending on the criteria you've selected in the Allow drop-down list. The dialog box shown in Figure 17.9 represents just one example.

TABLE 17.1   DATA-VALIDATION SETTINGS

Data Type	Allowed Restrictions
Any Value	Default setting; no restrictions allowed. Select this option if you want to display a helpful input message only, without restricting data entry.

continues

TABLE 17.1   CONTINUED

Data Type	Allowed Restrictions
Whole Number, Decimal	Choose an *operator* (between, for example, or greater than) and values or formulas. The Whole Number data type produces an error if the user enters a decimal point, even if it's followed by zero. The Decimal choice allows any number after the decimal point.
List	In the Source box, enter the address or name of the range that contains the list of values you want to allow. The range can be on another worksheet (a hidden worksheet in the current workbook is your best choice) or in another workbook. For a short list, enter the valid items directly in this box, separated by commas (East, West, North, South). If you want users to be able to pick from a list, select the In-cell Dropdown check box.
Date or Time	Choose an operator and appropriate values. You can enter formulas here as well; for example, to allow only dates that have already occurred, choose Less Than from the Data box and enter `=TODAY()` in the End Date box.
Text Length	Choose an operator and then specify numbers that define the allowed length; you can also enter formulas or cell references that produce numbers as values for use with the selected operator.
Custom	Enter a formula that returns a *logical value* (TRUE or FALSE). Use this option when the cell that contains the rule is part of a calculation, and you want to test the results of that calculation rather than the cell value itself. On an order form with multiple items that you total in a cell named Total_Order, for example, enter `=Total Order < 500` as the rule for each cell used in the SUM formula; that prevents the user from exceeding a $500 total limit even though each individual item is under the allowance.

DISPLAYING HELPFUL INPUT MESSAGES

Rules that stop users from entering invalid data are good, but helpful error messages are even better. As part of a data-validation rule, you can display messages that appear every time the user enters the cell that contains that rule. These messages appear in small pop-up windows alongside the cell. Use *input messages* to help users (including yourself!) understand exactly what type of data they should enter in the cell, especially if you are designing a data-entry sheet for less-experienced Excel users or one that you use infrequently.

To create an input message, choose Data, Validation. Click the Input Message tab (see Figure 17.10) and enter the title text and message you want to appear. Your message should be as helpful and brief as possible; if you've restricted the user to a particular type of data, make sure they know exactly what they're allowed to enter.

ALERTING THE USER TO ERRORS

How do you want Excel to respond when users enter invalid data? In all cases, you can display an error alert. If the data type is wrong, or if the date or value is not appropriate, you can refuse to accept the input and force users to enter an acceptable value. You can also choose to accept the value; this can be an effective way to force users to double-check values that might be valid but are outside of a normal range. On a report listing contributions to your annual fund drive, for example, you might define valid entries as being below $100. If the amount users enter is over that amount, you could display a message that asks them whether they're sure the amount is correct. If they accidentally added an extra zero, the message will give them a chance to correct their mistake; if the amount was from an exceptionally generous donor, the user can click OK and allow Excel to accept the input.

To define an error message and set options for handling data that is outside the defined range, choose Data, Validation and click the Error Alert tab (see Figure 17.11).

Figure 17.10

The message you enter here can explain the purpose of the cell and warn the user of data restrictions.

Figure 17.11

You define the error message users see when they enter invalid data; you can reject the data or allow them to enter it with a warning.

Check the Show Error Alert After Invalid Data Is Entered box. Enter a title and text for the message you want users to see when they enter an invalid value. As with the Input Message, try to be as informative as possible so that the user knows exactly what he or she must do to correct the error. Then select one of the following choices from the Style box to define how Excel should handle the input:

- **Stop**—Displays a Stop dialog box and lets the user choose Retry or Cancel.

- **Warning**—Displays the error message and adds `Continue?`. The user can choose Yes to enter the invalid data, No to try again, or Cancel.

- **Information**—Displays the error message. The user can click OK to enter invalid data or Cancel to back out.

DELETING, MOVING, OR COPYING DATA-VALIDATION RULES

To remove all validation rules from a cell or range, first select the cell(s) containing the validation rule; then choose Data, Validation, and click the Settings tab. Click the Clear All button and click OK. This option erases the input message, error alert, and validation settings.

When should you select the Apply These Changes to All Other Cells with the Same Settings check box? If you originally create a set of validation rules for a range of cells, Excel stores those settings with the range. If you later adjust the settings for an individual cell in that range, you break the link to the range. Check this box while editing data-validation settings for a single cell, and Excel extends the selection and applies your changes to the entire range you originally selected. The check box has no effect on other cells for which you defined rules individually, even if the rules are absolutely identical.

TIP FROM

When you copy or move a cell or range, data-validation rules travel with the cell's contents. To copy only data-validation rules from one cell to another, without affecting the contents or formatting of the target cell, use Paste Special. Select the cell whose rule you want to copy, and then choose Edit, Copy. Select the cells where you want to copy the rule, and choose Edit, Paste Special. Click the Validation option and click OK.

Are you still finding invalid data in a user form in which you've created validation rules to protect data? See "Data Validation Limitations" in the "Troubleshooting" section at the end of this chapter.

TROUBLESHOOTING DATA ERRORS

Data-validation rules are not perfect. Users can bypass the rules and enter invalid data by pasting from the Clipboard, or by entering a formula that results in an invalid value. Also, Excel does not check the existing contents of a cell or range when you create or copy a validation rule. When you *audit* a worksheet, Excel finds cells that contain values that are outside the limits you defined with data-validation rules. This technique is the only way to find incorrect values on a worksheet.

These auditing tools are not available from any menu. The only way to identify invalid data is to click a button on the Formula Auditing toolbar. To display the Auditing toolbar, right-click any visible toolbar and choose Formula Auditing from the list of available toolbars (or choose Tools, Formula Auditing, Show Formula Auditing Toolbar). Click the Circle Invalid Data button to show any cells that are outside the rules, as shown in Figure 17.12; click the Clear Validation Circles button to clear the highlights.

NOTE

The Circle Invalid Data button will find a maximum of 255 cells. If you have more invalid entries, you'll need to correct the data in some of the invalid cells, and then click the Circle Invalid Data button again.

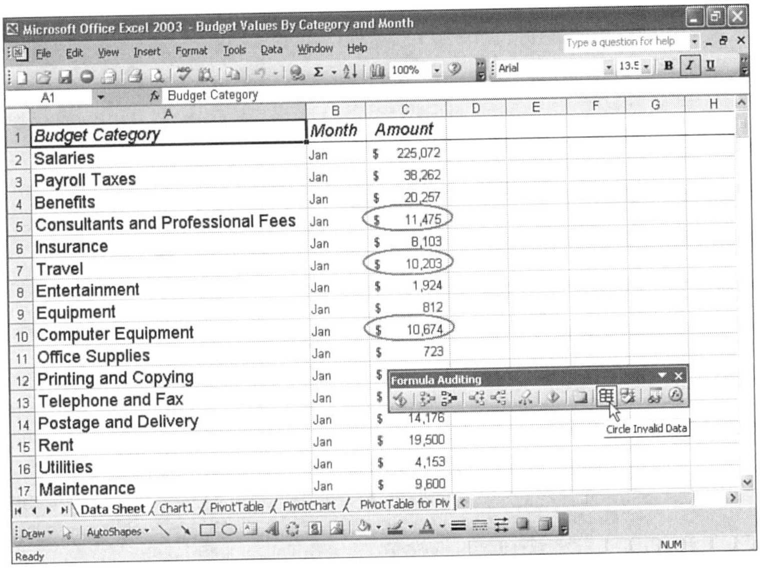

Figure 17.12
Click the Circle Invalid Data button to add these bold highlights around any cell whose contents violate a validation rule.

→ For an overview of other tools you can use to track down problems in formulas, **see** "Troubleshooting Formulas," **p. 618**.

PRINTING WORKSHEETS

Unlike Word documents, which typically are designed to fit on specific paper sizes, Excel worksheets are free-flowing environments that sprawl in every direction. If you click the Print button and leave the formatting to Excel, you'll end up with page breaks that appear at arbitrary locations in your worksheet, with no regard to content. To properly translate a large worksheet into printed output takes planning and a fair amount of creative formatting.

If you don't specifically define a print area, Excel assumes that you want to print all the data in the currently selected worksheet or worksheets, beginning with cell A1 and extending to the edge of the area that contains data or formatting. If necessary, you can divide a worksheet into smaller sections and print each region on its own page. As explained in this section, you can also shrink the print area to fit in a precise number of pages, and you can repeat row and column headings to make the display of data easier to follow.

TIP FROM

EQ & Woody

Don't overlook other techniques for rearranging data on a worksheet for the purpose of producing great printouts. On lists, AutoFilters can help you select and print only data that matches criteria you specify (see Chapter 20, "Working with Lists and PivotTables," for more details). Hiding rows and columns temporarily can help cut a large worksheet down to size. To print this quarter's grades without printing the grades from prior quarters, for example, hide the details before printing the selection. In some cases, the best way to print a complex selection from a worksheet is to translate it into another worksheet, using linked ranges or PivotTable reports (also covered in Chapter 20).

USING RANGES TO DEFINE THE DEFAULT PRINT AREA

You can force Excel to use a defined print area as the default for a worksheet. (Excel bypasses all dialog boxes and uses this region when you click the Print button.) This technique is especially useful if you regularly print a complex worksheet that contains a number of nonprinting regions. On a worksheet that contains a list and a criteria range, for example, you'll typically want to print only the list. On a budget worksheet that includes monthly data by category and an executive summary region, you might want to define the summary as the default when you click the Print button.

TIP FROM

EQ & Woody

The Print button bypasses all dialog boxes and prints the default print area without allowing you to review any options. The results can be tremendously frustrating (and waste reams of paper, if you can't stop the print job fast enough). For that reason, we strongly recommend replacing the Print button with the Print… button (note the three dots to the right of the Print command). The Print… command uses an identical icon, but displays the Print dialog box when clicked instead of sending your job to the printer with current settings. Use the techniques described in Chapter 2, "Making Office 2003 Work Your Way," to make this switch. You'll use one extra click every time you print, but you'll significantly reduce the number of times you accidentally print the wrong selection.

Start by selecting the range you want to print. The range need not be contiguous, but if you select a noncontiguous range, keep in mind that each selection will print on its own page, and the results might not be what you intended. All parts of the range to be printed must be on the same worksheet; each worksheet in a workbook gets a separate print area.

To define the selection as the default print area, choose File, Print Area, Set Print Area. Excel creates a named range called Print_Area in the current worksheet.

TIP FROM

EQ & Woody

If you define a print area on each worksheet, you can preview or print the defined print area on all sheets in the current workbook. Choose File, Print (or press Ctrl+P) and select Entire Workbook from the Print What area of the Print dialog box.

To delete the current print area selection and start over, choose File, Print Area, Clear Print Area.

When you define a specific print area, Excel prints only that area when you click the Print button. If you define a print area and then add rows at the bottom or columns to the right of the data, the new data won't appear on the printed pages. Whenever you redesign a worksheet, make a special point to recheck the print area.

INSERTING YOUR OWN PAGE BREAKS

When you attempt to print a worksheet, Excel automatically inserts page breaks to divide it into sections that will fit on the selected paper size. (To see a dashed line that represents each break as you edit a workbook, choose Tools, Options, click the View tab, and check the Page Breaks box.) Excel doesn't analyze the structure of your worksheet before inserting page breaks; it simply adds a page break at the point where each page runs out of printable area. To make multipage worksheets more readable, you can and should position page breaks by hand.

To insert a manual page break, select the cell below and to the right of the last cell you want on the page; then choose Insert, Page Break. To remove the page break, select the same cell and choose Insert, Remove Page Break. To remove all manual page breaks from the current worksheet, select the entire sheet, and then choose Insert, Reset All Page Breaks.

TIP FROM

Ed & Woody

> To add only a horizontal page break, select any cell in column A; to add only a vertical page break, select any cell in row 1.

Excel includes an unusual view option called Page Break Preview that lets you see all page breaks and adjust them by clicking and dragging. To switch to this view from a worksheet-editing window, choose View, Page Break Preview; from the Print Preview window, click the Page Break Preview button on the toolbar. As Figure 17.13 shows, this view lets you see your entire worksheet, broken into pages exactly as Excel intends to print it, with oversize page numbers laid over each block. (The numbers and lines don't appear on printed pages, of course.)

Dashed lines represent automatic page breaks inserted by Excel; solid lines represent manual page breaks. To adjust page breaks in this view, point to the thick line between two pages and drag it in any direction. To adjust the print area, drag the solid lines on any edge of the print area; cells that are not in the print area appear gray in Page Break Preview.

When using Page Break Preview, you'll have best results if you start at the top of the worksheet and work in the order it will print—normally from top to bottom and left to right, unless you've used the Page Setup dialog box to specify that you want to go across the worksheet before you work your way down. Move page breaks up or to the left only;

moving them down or to the right can cause unpredictable results if you drag past the size of the page. In that case, Excel adds its own page breaks, undoing the effects of your painstaking page-breaking efforts.

Figure 17.13
The page numbers show the order in which pages will print; drag the thick lines to adjust the print area and page breaks.

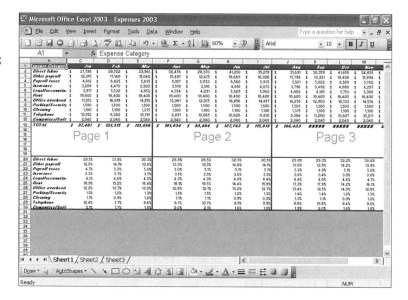

EXTRA ITEMS YOU CAN PRINT

Use Excel's Print dialog box to specify that you want to print additional parts of a worksheet, such as comments, gridlines, and row or column headings. You can also control the way Excel translates colors into shades of gray. To see these additional printing options, choose File, Page Setup, and click the Sheet tab.

Table 17.2 lists the options available for each worksheet.

TABLE 17.2   WORKSHEET PRINT OPTIONS

Print Option	What It Does
Gridlines	It's okay to show gridlines on draft worksheets; for final output, however, turn off gridlines and use borders to set off data areas.
Comments	By default, comments are not printed; select this check box to print them on a separate sheet or as they appear onscreen.
Draft Quality	This option, which prints cell contents but skips gridlines and graphics, is unnecessary when using a laser printer but might be useful for speeding up printing on color output devices or slow inkjet printers.
Black and White	Excel translates color backgrounds to shades of gray on the printed page. This option removes most gray shades; it can also speed up print jobs on color printers. Use Print Preview to print a small test page to check results before printing a large sheet with this option.

Print Option	What It Does
Row and Column Headings	Prints letters and numbers to help identify cell addresses. Use in combination with the option to view formulas (choose Tools, Options, click the View tab, and select the Formulas check box under Window Options) when you want to print out the structure of a worksheet so you can study it.
Print Titles	If the data in your worksheet spans several pages, you might lose your points of reference, such as the headings above columns of data or to the left of each row. Identify the Rows to Repeat at Top of each page or the Columns to Repeat at Left of each page. (See the following section for more details.)
Page Order	The graphic to the right of this option shows whether your sheet will print sideways first, then down, or the other way around. Adjust this order if necessary to make page numbering work properly.

LABELING PRINTED PAGES WITH HEADERS AND FOOTERS

Any worksheet that spans more than one page should include a header or footer (or both). An assortment of preconfigured headers and footers lets you number pages, identify the worksheet, specify the date it was created, list the author, and so on. Choose File, Page Setup, and then click the Header/Footer tab to add or edit a header and footer. Click the Custom Header or Custom Footer button to build either of these elements with text of your choosing. Buttons on both dialog boxes let you add fields, such as the name of the current workbook or sheet or the current date and time. You can also use rich text formatting to adjust fonts, font sizes, colors, and other attributes of the custom header or footer.

Using the Custom Header or Custom Footer dialog box also allows you to include graphic images, such as a company logo, in a header or footer. Click the Insert Picture button and browse to any graphic file whose format is supported by Office. You can insert one and only one graphic in each section—left, center, and right. Click the Format Picture button to crop, compress, resize, or scale a picture file in a header or footer.

→ For general-purpose advice on how to work with graphics in Office, see "Adding Pictures to Office Documents," **p. 126**.

By default, Excel allows a half-inch for a worksheet's header or footer. If you want to maximize the amount of data on each page and you're not using a header or footer, open the Page Setup dialog box, click the Margins tab, and set the Header, Footer, Top, and Bottom boxes to 0. (On some printers, you might need to adjust the top and bottom margins to match the unprintable area on the page.)

 If your custom header or footer doesn't look right on the page, see "Adjusting Header and Footer Margins" in the "Troubleshooting" section at the end of this chapter.

> If you want a custom header or footer to appear on every worksheet you create, add headers and footers to each sheet in the template Excel uses when you create a new workbook. (The specific instructions for creating and saving this template appear later in this chapter.) Remember that each sheet has its own header and footer; if you want the same header to appear on each sheet in the template, you must create each one individually.

USING REPEATING TITLES FOR MULTIPLE PAGE PRINTOUTS

For worksheets that span multiple pages, you can repeat one or more rows or columns (or both) as titles for the data on each new page. On a typical budget worksheet, for example, the first column might contain income and expense categories, with columns for each month's data extending to the right across several pages. In this case, follow these steps to repeat the entries in a particular column or row as titles at the left of each page:

1. Choose File, Page Setup, and click the Sheet tab.

2. To specify a column for titles, click in the Columns to Repeat at Left box. To use a row as titles on each new page, click in the Rows to Repeat at Top check box.

3. Click in any cell in the column or row you want to specify as the title. You need not select the entire row or column. If you select multiple cells, Excel uses all selected rows or columns as titles. If necessary, use the Collapse Dialog button to move the dialog box out of the way as you select.

4. Click the Print Preview button to ensure that you've configured the titles correctly. Click Print to send the worksheet to the printer immediately.

FORCING A WORKSHEET TO FIT ON A SPECIFIED NUMBER OF PAGES

Just as you can use the Zoom control to change the size of cells in a worksheet window, you can also reduce the size of data on a printout. Making the scale smaller lets you squeeze more rows and columns onto each page. If you want your printed worksheet to fit in a specific number of pages, Excel can calculate the *scaling percentage* for you:

1. Click File, Page Setup, and click the Page tab.

2. To scale the page to a fixed percentage, enter a value between 10 and 400 in the Adjust to % Normal Size box.

> Choosing a number that's too low can result in a completely unreadable printout. In general, you should choose a scaling percentage lower than 40 only when you want to see the overall structure of your worksheet, not when you want to actually read and analyze data.

3. To adjust the printout to a fixed height or width, select the Fit To option. Use the spinner controls to adjust the number of pages you want the printout to occupy; leave one number blank if you want Excel to adjust only the width or height of the printout. The settings in Figure 17.14, for example, will scale the worksheet to no more than one page in width but allow the sheet to print additional rows on multiple pages.

Figure 17.14
These settings force Excel to scale the current worksheet to one page wide for printing.

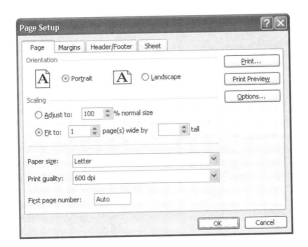

4. Click Print Preview to verify that your worksheet's print settings are correct.
5. Click Print to send the worksheet to the printer.

PROTECTING A WORKSHEET

If you store Excel workbooks only on your own PC, you can control exactly how and when you change the data and structure of each worksheet. But what if you need to share a workbook with other people? How do you maintain the confidentiality of sensitive data? How do you allow others to view the contents of a workbook without changing crucial data or formulas, either deliberately or by accident?

Excel's assortment of security options includes the following:

- You can set passwords that restrict access to the entire workbook. Excel allows you to specify separate passwords to open the workbook in read-only mode and to edit the workbook's contents.
- You can lock parts of a worksheet—such as cells that contain formulas—so that no one can make any changes to those cells without unlocking the entire worksheet.
- You can designate certain ranges as protected and allow editing only by individuals you specify.
- You can restrict access to specific elements of a worksheet, including sorting and AutoFiltering of lists, PivotTable reports, graphic objects, and chart sheets.

■ You can protect a shared workbook so that it can't be returned to exclusive use or have its change history deleted. This prevents a user from deliberately or accidentally deleting a record of changes he or she made to the shared workbook.

USING PASSWORDS TO RESTRICT ACCESS TO A WORKBOOK

The simplest form of protection uses passwords to prevent unauthorized users from opening and/or modifying a workbook. You can specify this option at any time: Choose File, Save As, click the Tools menu, and choose General Options.

By setting up two passwords and carefully restricting access to them, you can allow access to information while maintaining the integrity of data in a workbook. For example, you might assign different Open and Modify passwords to a budget workbook, and then give other members of your committee the Open password, so they can see your calculations, but allow only the organization's Treasurer to have the Modify password. If anyone wants to make a change to the budget, they'll have to talk to you or the Treasurer.

TIP FROM

Ed & Woody

> If you leave the Open password blank but assign a Modify password, anyone with access to the folder in which the workbook file is stored can view, but not change, its contents.

Anyone who attempts to open a password-protected workbook will first have to enter the correct password. If the workbook is protected by a Modify password, you'll see a second dialog box, like the one shown in Figure 17.15.

Figure 17.15
If you don't know the password, click the Read Only button to view the workbook's contents. Without the password, you cannot save changes to the workbook unless you give it a new name.

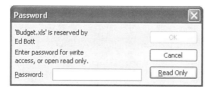

Workbook passwords are an all-or-nothing proposition. After entering the correct Modify password, a user can make any changes. That unrestricted freedom can be disastrous in the hands of a sloppy or untrained user if you've carefully designed a worksheet and entered complex formulas. You can even do irreparable damage to your own workbooks or worksheets if you're distracted or you simply don't notice that you're working with an original when you meant to create a copy. The following two sections describe how to protect yourself.

PREVENTING CHANGES TO A WORKSHEET

Excel allows you to exercise fine-grained control over what other people can do with a workbook or worksheet. You can prevent cell formatting, stop users from inserting or deleting rows and columns, and ensure that no one enters a hyperlink in a worksheet, for example.

To apply protection options to the current worksheet, select Tools, Protection, Protect Sheet. In the Protect Sheet dialog box (see Figure 17.16), select options you want to apply to all users (including yourself). The Protect Worksheet and Contents of Locked Cells check box (at the top of this dialog box) turns protection on or off for the current sheet.

Figure 17.16
Use these options to restrict access to specific worksheet features.

You can require users to enter a password before entering data in specified ranges. To impose this level of control on a worksheet, select Tools, Protection, Allow Users to Edit Ranges. The resulting dialog box (see Figure 17.17) lists currently protected ranges and allows you to specify which users can edit those ranges.

Figure 17.17
Click the Permissions button to specify which users (including yourself) can edit data without a password.

To add a new range to this list, first unprotect the worksheet, if necessary, and then follow these steps:

1. From the Allow Users to Edit Ranges dialog box, click the New button.

2. In the New Range dialog box (see Figure 17.18), replace the generic description (Range1) in the Title box with a descriptive name.

3. Adjust the range shown in the Refers to Cells box, if necessary. By default, this box shows the address of the current selection.

Figure 17.18

4. Enter a password if you want only specific users to be able to enter data in the locked cells.

5. Click the Permissions button to choose the names of users who can enter data without supplying a password. For files stored on an NTFS-formatted drive in a Windows 2000/XP network, this option hooks directly into file system permissions.

The biggest advantage of setting data-entry protection by range is that you can assign varying levels of protection to a worksheet. Lock especially important data with a supervisors-only password while opening the data-entry ranges with a password that's more widely distributed. After defining ranges that are locked for editing, you must protect the worksheet (Tools, Protection, Protect Sheet).

You can also use cell formatting to protect cells. The Protection tab on the Format Cells dialog box includes two check boxes, which you can use, separately or in combination, to prevent changes to data and formulas in individual cells.

■ Click the Locked option to lock a cell. This action prevents all users from deleting or changing the contents of that cell.

■ Click the Hidden box to hide formulas within a cell. In a *hidden cell*, any user can see the results of the formula without being able to see the formula that produced that result. This option lets you protect proprietary calculations and prevent users from being confused by particularly long and complex formulas.

→ To learn more about formatting numbers and text in your worksheets, **see** "How Cell Formatting Works," **p. 560**.

By default, all cells in a worksheet are formatted as locked but not hidden. So why can you enter data on a new worksheet? Because this formatting is disabled unless you specifically enable protection for a worksheet. To unlock a cell or range and allow editing, or to hide formulas within a cell or range, you first must make a selection and adjust its cell formatting. Because the Locked and Hidden formats are independent, you can lock a cell that contains a formula while still allowing the user to see that formula.

CAUTION

> Although you can hide a formula without locking the cell in which it's stored, it's hard to imagine a scenario in which this option makes sense; with this formatting, the user could inadvertently wipe out the formula by typing in another value.

To protect the contents of the current worksheet, follow these steps:

1. Select the cells you want to unlock for editing, typically those used for data entry or notes. (Remember that all cells are locked by default on a worksheet.)

2. Select Format, Cells, click the Protection tab, and clear the check mark from the Locked box.

3. Select all cells that contain formulas you want to hide.

4. Select Format, Cells, click the Protection tab, and click the Hidden check box.

5. Repeat steps 1–4 for other worksheets you want to protect. Click OK to close the dialog box, and then save the workbook.

To enable protection for the current worksheet, select Tools, Protection, Protect Sheet. The Protect Worksheet and Contents of Locked Cells box is selected by default. Add an optional password and click OK. Repeat this process for any other worksheets that you want to protect.

PROTECTING THE STRUCTURE OF A WORKBOOK

After you've assigned a password to a workbook, locked important cells, and turned on worksheet protection, your worksheet is perfectly safe, right? Wrong. A malicious or clumsy user can destroy all your careful work by deleting a worksheet from a workbook, even when it's otherwise fully protected. In fact, you can damage your own workbook if you forget the rules, and the results can be painful if you don't have a backup copy. To keep your data out of harm's way, you need to add one more level of protection.

To prevent users from changing the design of your workbook, select Tools, Protection, Protect Workbook (see Figure 17.19), and then select one or all of these options:

Figure 17.19
Use workbook protection options to prevent users (including yourself) from deleting a worksheet or closing a window.

■ By default, the Structure option is checked. This setting prevents users from adding or deleting worksheets, renaming sheets, or displaying sheets you've hidden.

- Click the Windows check box if your worksheet contains more than one sheet and you've arranged the individual sheets as windows in a particular size and position. When you select this setting, the Minimize, Maximize, and Close buttons on each worksheet window disappear. Any attempt to move or resize a window fails, and although users can select Arrange from the Window menu, this option has no effect.

- Add a password to prevent users from removing protection.

To restore the capability to make changes to a workbook, select Tools, Protection, Unprotect Workbook.

PUBLISHING EXCEL DATA IN WEB PAGES

Like Word and PowerPoint, Excel allows you to save files in HTML format so that you or anyone else can view them in a web browser. You can save a simple range of data, a chart, a worksheet, or an entire workbook in HTML format; when opened in a web browser, the resulting file will closely resemble the worksheet as seen in an Excel window. Some differences in formatting and appearance are inevitable because of the way that browsers display HTML code.

→ For an overview of some of the compatibility issues you'll face with different browsers, **see** "Browser Compatibility Issues," **p. 845**.

When saving a workbook as a web page, you must deal with the following noteworthy restrictions:

- HTML pages represent a static snapshot of the worksheet data; if you view worksheet data in a browser, you can't edit or rearrange cells or their contents unless you use *interactive Web components*.

- Gridlines and row or column headings do not appear in the browser window.

TIP FROM

> To set off rows and columns in an Excel-generated web page, don't rely on gridlines; instead, use borders to separate cells within the data area. Use shading and font formatting to set off headings, totals, and other distinctive elements.

- Some advanced features don't translate properly to HTML pages; for example, if you've saved multiple scenarios in a workbook, they'll be lost in translation, as will rotated text and some other forms of custom formatting.

You'll see an error message if you try to publish a password-protected workbook as a web page; see "Passwords Don't Work on Web Workbooks" in the "Troubleshooting" section at the end of this chapter.

- The first cell that contains data in your workbook always moves to the top-left corner of the HTML page, even if you've left blank rows or columns as part of the design.

■ When you save a workbook, all sheets from that workbook appear on the resulting web page, even those containing no data; the sheet tabs are visible in browsers that support *dynamic HTML*.

To save an entire workbook as an HTML page, choose File, Save As Web Page. Give the page a name, choose a destination folder (on a local hard drive, a network server, or a web server), and click Save. If you want the web page to be updated automatically whenever you update the underlying worksheet, choose File, Save As Web Page, and then click the Publish button. Select the AutoRepublish Every Time This Workbook Is Saved check box and click Publish to save the web page.

TIP FROM

Ed & Woody

> Don't forget the title. In the Save As Web Page dialog box, just above the File Name box, you'll see a space for the page title, which appears in the browser title bar and on the page itself. Excel doesn't add a title by default; click the Change button to add or edit the title.

17

To save a chart or a range from a worksheet, make a selection first, and then click the Selection option in the Save As Web Page dialog box. To save a single sheet instead of an entire workbook, make sure only a single cell is active before you choose Save As Web Page, and then choose Selection: Sheet from the resulting dialog box.

To select multiple named items from a workbook, such as two sheets, a sheet and a chart, or multiple named ranges, click the Publish button in the Save As Web Page dialog box. That in turn displays the Publish As Web Page dialog box shown in Figure 17.20.

Figure 17.20
To save individual items from a workbook to a web page, select them by using this dialog box.

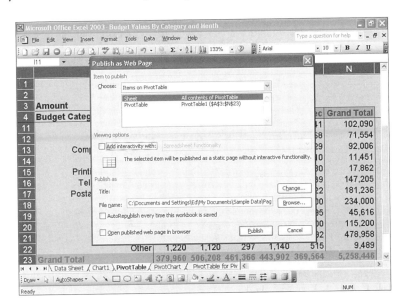

Choose a sheet name or another category, such as Range of Cells or Previously Published Items, from the Choose drop-down list. Then click an item from the list below your selection.

To give viewers of HTML pages the ability to manipulate data, including PivotTables and *AutoFilter lists*, select the Add Interactivity With check box; then choose any of the available options. Note that only viewers using Internet Explorer 5.01 or later are able to manipulate data in pages you create this way. These pages will not be viewable or editable by anyone using a non-Microsoft browser unless that browser specifically supports the Office 2003 Interactive Web Components.

If your worksheet includes any external elements, such as graphics, the Save as Web Page option saves those elements as files in a separate subfolder that is linked to the HTML file containing the Excel data. If you intend to share the resulting file with someone else, save yourself some headaches and choose Single File Web Page from the Save As Type list on the Save As dialog box. This option embeds all elements of the HTML page in a single file with the .MHT file extension.

CUSTOMIZING EXCEL

You can choose from dozens of options for adjusting the way Excel looks, acts, and works. Most are accessible in the Options dialog box that appears when you click Tools, Options. The settings on the 13 tabs here are virtually unchanged since Excel 2002. In general, these options are self-explanatory, and many of them are variations on common features found in other Office applications. In this section, we highlight only the most useful:

→ For details of Office-wide configuration options, **see** "Configuring Common Office Features," **p. 47**.

- Options on the View tab enable you to hide or show interface elements, such as the Formula bar, status bar, gridlines, scrollbars, and the Startup task pane. Unlike Word, which allows you to set many such options on a document-by-document basis, the settings you check here apply to every workbook you open. You can also select an option to show or hide the Startup task pane each time you open Excel.

- The Calculation tab enables you to change the default settings Excel uses for calculating formulas. On the computer hardware that was in use a decade ago, setting *manual calculation* was a survival tactic, because calculating a large worksheet could literally take hours. In an era when processor speed is measured in gigahertz, this option is necessary only for extraordinarily complex worksheets, in which you need to control the precise order of calculations. Unless you're working on a graduate degree in engineering, you should accept the default options on this tab.

- Most of the options on the Edit tab are the same as those found in other Office programs. If you routinely select a range and fill in list values, consider changing the Move Selection After Enter box from its default selection of Down to Right. If you find Smart Tags annoying, clear the Show Paste Options and Show Insert Options boxes.

TIP FROM

Ed & Woody

When entering currency values, such as entries in a check register, people with an accounting background often prefer to let Excel fill in the decimal point. If you choose the Fixed Decimal option on this tab and leave it at the default setting of 2, entering 14398 will result in a value of 143.98. It's extremely unlikely you'll want to set this option permanently. If you use it frequently, however, create this simple toggle macro and assign it to a toolbar button so that you can switch into and out of fixed decimal mode on demand:

```
Sub ToggleFixedDecimal()
    Application.FixedDecimal = Not Application.FixedDecimal
End Sub
```

- The Transition tab was originally designed years ago as a tool for new Office users who had previously used Lotus 1-2-3. The Lotus Help option is gone in Excel 2003, although you can still choose to access menus Lotus-style, using the slash key. The Save Excel Files As option is primarily for use in organizations where the default file format is something other than Microsoft Excel Workbook. For use at home, you should leave this option at its default setting.

→ For a discussion of the Chart and Color tabs, **see** "Editing and Formatting Chart Elements," **p. 687**.

- Click the General tab to display the options shown in Figure 17.21. The Sheets in New Workbook setting enables you to change the number of blank sheets in each new workbook to any number between 1 and 255. Choose a smaller setting if you rarely use multiple sheets in a workbook or a larger one if you regularly create complex workbooks, such as consolidated budgets. You can also adjust the font that Excel uses for text and numbers in new worksheets from the default of 10-point Arial. Choose a new font from the Standard Font list; specify a new size by using the drop-down list to its right.

Figure 17.21
Use these options to adjust the default font size, number of worksheets per workbook, and other key Excel options.

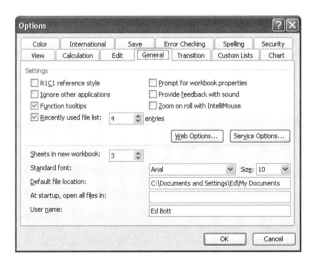

TIP FROM

We recommend you leave the At Startup, Open All Files in the Specified Directory box blank. Templates and workbooks you want to load automatically should go in the Xlstart folder in your personal profile instead. If you specify an alternative location, Excel loads any workbooks stored in that folder as well as those from Xlstart. This feature is typically used in corporate settings to run macros and install Excel add-ins automatically from a network location.

- Options on the International tab let you override system settings for date and currency formats, default paper size, and right-to-left orientation.

- Set AutoRecover options on the Save tab. This feature works similarly to its Word counterpart.

→ For a discussion of Office AutoRecover features, **see** "Setting Up Automatic Backup and Recovery Options," **p. 84**.

- Use the Spelling tab to set spell-checking settings.

- The Error Checking tab includes settings that let you control background checking for common worksheet errors, including those in formulas. These options include check boxes that let you locate numbers stored as text (which can cause problems with formulas) and text dates containing two-digit years (which can result in Y2K-style date arithmetic errors).

→ For more details on how to check for errors in formulas, **see** "Troubleshooting Formulas," **p. 618**.

- Look on the Security tab (see Figure 17.22) for file encryption and file sharing boxes, where you can specify a password that locks a file for modifications or encrypts it so the data can only be seen by authorized users. Click the Macro Security button to access options that affect how Visual Basic macros and scripts work with all workbooks.

Figure 17.22
If you enter a password here, the security option applies only to the current workbook. Click the Macro Security button to set options that apply to all workbooks.

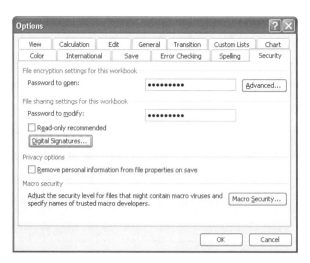

→ Office 2003 includes a broad array of security settings; for a complete overview and important details, see "Setting Security Options," **p. 54**.

CHANGING DEFAULT FORMATTING FOR NEW WORKBOOKS AND WORKSHEETS

Every time you start Excel or create a new workbook without using a custom template, Excel uses its default settings. To change settings for the default workbook, create a new template called Book.xlt and save it in the XLStart folder. Follow these steps:

1. Create or open the workbook whose settings you want to use as Excel's defaults.

2. To change the style of all cells in the workbook, modify the Normal style. Add other named styles, macros, text, and other content or formatting. If you want to change the number of sheets or add headers and footers, go right ahead.

3. Choose File, Save As. In the Save As Type box, choose Template.

4. In the File Name box, enter **Book**. (Excel adds the .xlt extension automatically.) Do not save the file in the Templates folder; instead, save it in the XLStart folder. This folder is stored as part of your Windows profile, which you can reach through Windows Explorer by typing `%userprofile%\Application Data\Microsoft\Excel\XLStart`. (Be sure to include the percent signs around `%userprofile%`; this is a system variable that automatically opens your profile.)

5. Click OK to save the template. Any future workbooks you create will include the formats and content in this template.

> **NOTE**
>
> What's the difference between an Excel template and a worksheet? Structurally, the two file types are identical. Like a workbook, a template can include as many sheets as you want, with or without text, charts, and formatting. The key difference is this: When you open a workbook template, from within Excel or from an Explorer window, Excel leaves the original template file undisturbed and creates a new, unnamed document that is an identical copy of the template.

INSTALLING EXCEL ADD-INS

Excel includes a variety of special-purpose *add-ins*—compiled macros that add new functions beyond those already available. The Analysis ToolPak adds a broad range of worksheet functions to Excel's list of built-in functions, and the Solver add-in offers a wizard-based alternative to trial-and-error formula solving. Both add-ins are described in more detail in Chapter 19. You need to supply the main Office CD (or point to a network install point) to add any of these add-ins.

By default, most of Excel's default add-ins are configured to be installed on first use. If you chose to cache the Office Setup files, this process should be nearly automatic. If you did not select this option, you'll have to hunt down the main Office CD each time you use an add-in for the first time—an annoying distraction, especially if you're in the middle of a deadline and the CD isn't close at hand.

17

If you think you might use any of Excel's add-ins in the future, open Control Panel's Add/Remove Programs option, double-click the Microsoft Office 2003 entry, and launch the Windows Installer in maintenance mode. Go through the list of add-ins under the Excel group and change their status from Installed on First Use to Run from My Computer.

EXCEL STARTUP SWITCHES

When you start Excel, it normally opens a new workbook using the default settings, runs any AutoStart macros in the Personal Macro workbook, and switches to the default location for data files. To change any of these settings, use one of the following startup switches with the Excel.exe command line. You can use any of these switches as part of a shortcut or type them directly at the command line.

Switch	Function
/e	Forces Excel to start without displaying the startup screen or creating a new workbook (Book1).
/p *<folder>*	Sets the active path to a folder other than the default file location; enter the folder name (with its complete path) in quotes.
/r *<filename>*	Forces Excel to open the specified file in read-only mode.
/s	Forces Excel to start in safe mode, bypassing all installed add-ins as well as files in the Xlstart and Alternate Startup Files folders. Use this switch when debugging startup problems.

NOTE

To learn more about using command-line switches with Excel, see *Special Edition Using Microsoft Excel 2003* by Patrick Blattner (published by Que).

TROUBLESHOOTING

RESETTING THE LAST CELL

I pressed Ctrl+End to go to the last cell in my worksheet, but I ended up with the insertion point in a blank cell below and to the right of the actual end of the sheet. How do I convince Excel to jump to the actual end of the sheet?

When you select the last cell in a worksheet, either by using the Go To Special dialog box or by pressing Ctrl+End, Excel actually jumps to the last cell that has ever contained data or formatting. As you've seen, that can produce unexpected results, especially if you've deleted a large number of rows or columns (or both) from a list or worksheet model, or if you once placed a range of data in an out-of-the-way location and then moved or deleted it. In that case, selecting the Last Cell option might position the insertion point in a cell that's far beyond the actual end of the sheet. To reset the sheet so that you can truly jump to the last cell, delete all rows that are between the actual end of the sheet and the location that Excel insists on identifying as the last cell, and then repeat the process for all columns that match that definition.

If this is a common occurrence, you can create a one-line macro that will reset the last-cell location in the current sheet. Press Alt+F11 to open the Visual Basic Editor and enter the following code:

```
Sub ResetRange()
    ActiveSheet.UsedRange
End Sub
```

Be sure to save the ResetRange macro in an easily accessible location, such as your Personal macro workbook; then run it whenever you encounter a worksheet that needs this type of cleanup.

ADJUSTING HEADER AND FOOTER MARGINS

I created a complex custom footer for a worksheet, but when I try to print, the footer runs into data at the bottom of the sheet.

By default, Excel positions headers and footers a half-inch from the edge of the page and another half-inch from the worksheet's data. That's ideal for a one-liner, but if you try to add too much information in either place—for example, if you insert a long boilerplate paragraph required by a government agency at the bottom of each sheet—you'll quickly overrun that margin. If you decrease the Top or Bottom margins without also adjusting the Header or Footer margins, your data might also collide. You can enter an exact measurement for any of these margins by using the Margins tab on the Page Setup dialog box. If you've already created the header and footer, however, it's much easier to set the margins visually. Choose File, Print Preview; click the Margins button, if necessary, to display the margin markers along each edge of the preview window, and drag the indicators up or down until the preview looks right.

PASSWORDS DON'T WORK ON WEB WORKBOOKS

When I try to save a workbook as a web page, I get an error message warning that the workbook or sheet is password-protected.

For security reasons, Excel won't let you save a password-protected workbook or worksheet in HTML format. If the entire workbook is protected, you can still save an individual sheet. If any sheet is protected, however, you cannot publish that sheet or even a selection from it in HTML format. Temporarily remove the password protection by choosing Tools, Protection, Unprotect Sheet. After entering the correct password, you can publish the web page and then restore the protection.

DATA VALIDATION LIMITATIONS

I created a set of validation rules to protect data entry, but when users returned the filled-in worksheet, I found invalid data in those cells. I've triple-checked the data-validation rules, and I'm certain they're working properly. What's the problem?

Validation settings apply only when the user types data into a cell. If the user copies or cuts data from another source and pastes it into the cell via the Clipboard, Excel ignores the rule. There is no workaround for this problem, so you'll have to train your users not to use the Clipboard when filling in forms. Also, if any cell contains a formula as well as a data-validation rule, Excel ignores the rule.

If you want to triple-check the values in cells protected by data-validation rules to make sure they're correct, use the Go To dialog box. Press F5 and click the Special button, and then select the Data Validation option. Click All to see all cells with data-validation rules, or Same to see only cells whose rules match the currently selected cell.

EXTRA CREDIT: BEWARE OF UNDO

Like all Office programs, Excel includes an Undo button and a corresponding keyboard shortcut—Ctrl+Z. Unlike Word, however, which stores an unlimited number of changes, Excel can undo only the 16 most recent actions. When the Undo buffer is full, the oldest entry in the list vanishes to make room for your most recent formatting change, move, copy, data entry, or other action. If you search the Internet, you will find references to a simple change in the Registry that can expand the Undo buffer significantly; however, that Registry hack no longer works in Excel 2002 or Excel 2003.

Excel's Undo feature has other significant limitations. For example, the Undo buffer is disabled for performance reasons whenever you run a macro. If you delete rows from a list and then remove outlining, you cannot undo any changes. Likewise, adding a chart or other object to a sheet clears the Undo history completely. You have absolutely no warning before Excel clears the Undo buffer, and you cannot recover its contents afterwards.

If you're used to working with Word, where the Undo capability gives you a nearly limitless ability to "roll back" a document to a previous version, Excel's considerably less powerful Undo feature might result in a rude surprise. When making extensive changes to the structure or design of an important worksheet, we recommend saving interim versions of the worksheet as you work. This file-saving routine doesn't have to be complex; for instance, you might tack on a version extension—v1, v2, v3, and so on—at the end of the filename each time you save. This simple precaution can make it possible for you to experiment with a worksheet while still preserving the ability to retreat to an earlier version if necessary.

CHAPTER 18

MAKING GREAT-LOOKING WORKSHEETS

In this chapter

HOW CELL FORMATTING WORKS

In an Excel worksheet, what you see in a cell is not necessarily what's stored in that cell. If you enter a formula, for example, Excel stores the formula but displays its result. When entering numbers, dates, and text, you can go as quickly as you want, without too much regard for how they'll look in your worksheet; afterwards, use cell formatting instructions to specify how you want the cells' contents to display, including such details as decimal places, currency symbols, and how many digits to use for the year. Other cell formatting options let you adjust fonts, colors, borders, and other attributes of a cell or range.

A handful of buttons on the Formatting toolbar let you bypass dialog boxes for some common tasks, such as choosing a font or changing a range of cells to bold. If you're building a financial worksheet, click the Currency button to ensure that every number in a given range lines up properly and includes the correct currency symbol. To see the full assortment of Excel formatting options, select a cell or range and choose Format, Cells, or right-click a cell or selection and choose Format Cells from the shortcut menu. All available cell formatting options are arranged on six tabs in the Format Cells dialog box.

USING THE GENERAL NUMBER FORMAT

On a new worksheet, every cell starts out using the General format. When the cell contains a constant value, Excel usually displays the exact text or numbers you entered; in cells that contain a formula, the General format displays the results of the formula using up to 11 digits—the decimal point counts as a digit. (Date and time values follow a special set of rules, as you'll see shortly.) If the cell is not wide enough to show the entire number, Excel rounds the portion of the number to the right of the decimal point, for display purposes only; if the portion of the number to the left of the decimal point won't fit in the cell or contains more than 11 digits, the General format displays the number in scientific notation.

To remove all number formats you've applied manually and restore a cell to its default General format, right-click and choose Format Cells, and then click the Number tab and choose General from the Category list.

> **NOTE**
>
> Although it's not particularly intuitive, there's also a keyboard shortcut that applies the General format instantly to the active cell or current selection: Press Ctrl+Shift+~ (tilde) to reset cells to General format.

CONTROLLING AUTOMATIC NUMBER FORMATS

When you enter data in a format that resembles one of Excel's built-in formats, Excel automatically applies formatting to the cell. In some cases, the results might be unexpected or unwelcome:

- If you enter a number that contains a slash (/) or hyphen (-) and matches any of Windows's date and time formats, Excel converts the entry to a date serial value and formats the cell using the closest matching Date format. If the date you enter includes only the month and date, Excel adds the current year.

→ In some cases, Excel 2003 picks up formatting from your Windows version; for details of how this inter-action works, **see** "Setting Date and Time Formats," **p. 568**.

 If you import data into a worksheet, Excel might convert values that look like dates or times. For suggestions on how to prevent this from occurring, see "Stopping Automatic Conversions" in the "Troubleshooting" section at the end of this chapter.

- If you enter a number preceded by a dollar sign, Excel applies the Currency style, with two decimal places, regardless of how many decimal places you entered. (If you've used the Regional Settings option in Control Panel to specify a different currency symbol, Excel applies the Currency style when you enter data using that symbol.)

> **NOTE**
>
> As explained later in this chapter, the Currency style is actually a variation of the Accounting format.

- If you enter a number that begins or ends with a percent sign, Excel applies the Percent style with up to two decimal places.

TIP FROM

> Excel supports fraction formats as well, but entering data in this format is tricky. If you enter 3/8, for example, Excel interprets your entry as a date—March 8 of the current year—and formats it accordingly. To enter a fraction that Excel can recognize automatically, start with 0 and a space: 0 3/8. Excel correctly enters that number as 0.375 and changes the cell format to Fraction. Although Excel stores the number as 0.375, it is displayed as 3/8.

TIP FROM

> Excel also supports *compound fractions*—fractions that include a whole number and a fractional number, such as 12 1/8. Enter the whole number part (in this case, 12) followed by a space and then the fraction part. Excel displays the entry as 12 1/8 but stores it as 12.125. You'll find this technique invaluable if you ever have to perform calculations involving historical stock market prices; although most major markets have now moved to decimal pricing, some historical data sources still contain data using archaic fractional pricing—16ths, 32nds, even 64ths of a dollar!

- When you enter a number that contains a colon (:), Excel converts it to a time format if possible. If the number is followed by a space and the letter A or P, Excel adds AM or PM to the display format.
- If you enter a number that contains leading zeros (as in part numbers, for example, which might need to fill a precise number of characters), Excel drops the leading zero.

18

- When you enter a number that contains the letter E anywhere in the middle (3.14159E19, for example), Excel formats the cell using the Scientific option, using no more than two decimal places. In this case, Excel would display 3.14E+19.

- If you enter a number that includes a comma to set off thousands or millions, Excel applies the Number format using the default thousands separator as defined in Windows's Regional Settings. If the number you entered contains more than two decimal places, Excel stores the exact number you entered but rounds it for display purposes to no more than two decimal places.

To override any of these automatic number formats, you have four choices:

- After entering the data, choose Format, Cells and select a new format. (Press Ctrl+1 to quickly open this dialog box.) This is your best choice if the underlying data stored in the cell is correct and you just want to use a different display format.

- Enter an apostrophe before entering the number. When you do this, Excel formats the number as text and displays it exactly as entered. Note that this solution might have unintended consequences in formulas that use the value shown in that cell!

- Enter a space character before entering the number. This prefix also tells Excel to format the number as text and display it exactly as entered. Note that this technique will not prevent Excel from converting a number to scientific notation nor will it preserve leading zeros. It will, however, work with all other automatic formatting described in the previous list.

- Format the cell as text (choose Format, Cells, click the Number tab, and select Text) before entering the data. This option might also have unintended side effects, as explained a bit later in this chapter.

AVOIDING ROUNDING ERRORS

It's tempting to assume that because numbers look so orderly in Excel's row-and-column grids, they're also unfailingly accurate. That's not exactly so. To squeeze data so that it fits in a cell, Excel *rounds* numbers and *truncates* cell contents, usually without telling you. And there's an absolute limit on the precision of Excel calculations that affects every calculation you make.

NOTE

What's the difference between rounding and truncating? When Excel rounds a number, it changes the value displayed in the cell without affecting the underlying number stored in the cell. If you enter 3.1415926 in a cell and format it to display two decimal points, Excel displays 3.14. If you later change the display format to show all seven decimal points, your number will appear exactly as you entered it. When Excel truncates data, on the other hand, it chops off digits permanently. If you enter a number with more than 15 decimal places, for example, Excel lops off the 16th and any subsequent numbers to the right of the decimal point. Likewise, if you copy a worksheet that contains cells with more than 255 characters, Excel discards all characters after the first 255.

When Excel alters the display of a number, the most common cause is that the number is too long to fit in the active cell. Excel deals with this sort of data in one of the following three ways:

- When you enter data that is wider than the current cell, Excel automatically resizes the column. It does not resize a column if you have already set the column width manually. If the cell is formatted using General format, this automatic resizing stops when the number reaches 11 digits, at which point Excel converts it to scientific notation. If the cell is formatted using Number format, automatic resizing continues until the number reaches 30 digits.

- In cells using the default General format, Excel uses scientific notation to display large numbers if possible. The General format rounds numbers expressed this way to no more than six *digits of precision* (8.39615E+13, for example).

NOTE

It's no accident that the total number of characters in the preceding example–including the decimal point, plus sign, and E–is 11. Regardless of column width, cells using the General format are always limited to 11 digits.

- In cells using any number format other than General, Excel displays a string of number signs (####) if the column is too narrow to display the number in scientific notation. You must change the cell's number format or make the column wider before Excel can display the number correctly.

18

The second most common cause of apparent errors in a worksheet occurs when the number of decimal cells you specify in a number format doesn't match the number of decimal places stored in that cell or range. Figure 18.1, for example, shows two identical columns of numbers. Because column A uses the General format, each number appears exactly as entered. Column B, on the other hand, is formatted with the Number format to show zero decimal places. When Excel performs the calculation on the numbers in column B, it uses the actual amount stored in the cell, not the rounded version you see here. It then displays the result without any decimal places, exactly as specified in the cell format. Although the sum of the rounded numbers in column B appears to be 16, Excel rounds the actual result to 15 for display purposes. Because of the mismatch between the numbers and their formatting, Excel (and, by extension, the author of this worksheet) appears incapable of basic arithmetic.

That's a simple and obvious example, but subtle rounding errors can wreak havoc in an environment where you require precise results. To prevent rounding from making it look like your worksheet contains errors, always match the number of decimal places displayed with the number of decimal places you've entered in the row or column in question.

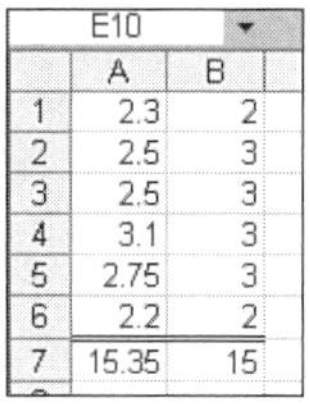

Figure 18.1
The values in these two columns are identical, with different formatting. Because of cumulative rounding errors, the numbers in column B appear to add up to 16, despite what the SUM formula suggests.

	A	B
1	2.3	2
2	2.5	3
3	2.5	3
4	3.1	3
5	2.75	3
6	2.2	2
7	15.35	15

E10

TIP FROM

Ed & Woody

If you must use rounded numbers in a worksheet, indicate that fact in a footnote on charts and reports you plan to present to others. Rounding can cause apparent mistakes, and anyone who sees your worksheet—or a chart or presentation slide based on those numbers—might make unflattering judgments about your accuracy if totals in a pie chart, for example, don't add up to 100%.

THE LIMITS OF PRECISION

There's an overriding limit to the degree of precision you can achieve with Excel. If you enter a number that contains more than 15 significant digits, Excel permanently and irrevocably converts the 16th and subsequent digits to 0. (It doesn't matter which side of the decimal point the digits appear on—the total number of digits allowed includes those on both sides of the decimal point.) Although you can display numbers with up to 30 decimal places, your calculations will not be accurate if Excel has to store more than 15 digits.

Excel includes a useful, but extremely dangerous, option to permanently store numbers using the displayed precision. If you've increased the numbers in a budget worksheet by 8.25%, for example, you might end up with three decimal places for some entries, even though only two are displayed using the Currency format. If you choose Tools, Options, and click the Calculation tab, you can click the Precision As Displayed check box to convert all stored numbers in the current workbook to the values actually displayed.

CAUTION

When you use the Precision As Displayed option, Excel displays a terse dialog box warning you that your data will permanently lose accuracy. Believe it. This option affects every cell on every sheet in the current workbook, and it remains in force until you explicitly remove the check mark from this box. If you forget you turned on this option, even simple formatting choices like changing the display of decimal places will permanently change stored data. Unless you're absolutely certain that using this option will have no unintended consequences, you should treat it like dynamite.

TIP FROM

The Precision As Displayed option affects all cells in the current workbook, and there's no way to apply it just to a selected range. If you want to change the precision of a selection, use the Windows Clipboard to control this option precisely—in the process, you can also avoid any unintended ill effects. Open a new, blank workbook, copy the range you want to change from the original workbook, and paste it into the blank workbook. In the blank workbook, choose Tools, Options, click the Calculation tab, and check the Precision As Displayed box. Click OK when you see the warning dialog box. Now copy the changed data to the Clipboard and paste it over the original data. Close the blank workbook without saving it, and you're finished.

WORKING WITH NUMBERS IN SCIENTIFIC NOTATION

Scientific (or exponential) *notation* displays large numbers in a shorthand form that shows the first few digits along with instructions on where to place the decimal point. To convert a number written in scientific notation to its decimal equivalent, move the decimal to the right by the number that appears after "E+"; if there's a minus sign after the *E*, move the decimal to the left. In either case, add extra zeros as needed. Thus, 8.23E+06 is actually 8,230,000, and 3.82E-07 is .000000382.

Numbers expressed in scientific notation are often rounded. When you see numbers in General format expressed in scientific notation, you'll see a maximum of six significant digits, even if the cell is wide enough to hold more. To display a number in scientific notation using more digits of precision, choose Format, Cells, and choose the Scientific option from the Category list. Use the spinner control to set a fixed number of decimal places, between 0 and 30.

ENTERING NUMBERS AS TEXT

Hands down, the most confusing option on the Number tab of the Format Cells dialog box is Text. Use this format when you want to enter numbers in a cell, but you want Excel to treat them as though they were text. You might use this format, for example, when entering a list of part numbers that you will never use in calculations.

If you apply the Text format to a cell and then enter or paste a numeric value into that cell, Excel adds a small green triangle in the top-left corner of the cell, indicating a possible error. Selecting that cell reveals a Smart Tag that warns you the number is stored as text. Use the Convert to Number option to change the cell's contents to a number format, or click Ignore Error to keep the text and make the green triangle vanish.

→ For more information about Smart Tags, **see** "Common Formatting Options," **p. 106**.

→ To learn how to check an Excel workbook for errors, **see** "Checking for Errors in a Worksheet," **p. 620**.

When you format numbers as Text, Excel ignores them in formulas such as SUM() and AVERAGE(). It also aligns the cell's contents to the left rather than the right. Unfortunately, applying the Text format requires that you work around an admitted bug that still exists in

Excel 2003. If you format the cells first, then apply the Text format, and finally enter the numbers, Excel treats the data as text, just as you intended. However, if you try to apply the Text format to numbers that are already in your worksheet, Excel changes the alignment of the cell, but not the data stored there. After applying the Text format, you must click in each reformatted cell, press F2, and then press Enter to store the number as text. The new error-checking tools in Excel 2003 do not identify cells formatted this way, either.

If you format a cell as text and enter a formula in that cell, you see the formula itself rather than its result. To fix the display, change the cell format back to General, select the cell, press F2, and then press Enter.

CHANGING FORMATTING FOR A CELL OR RANGE

In general, as noted previously, Excel stores exactly what you type in a cell. You have tremendous control over how that data appears, however. Number and date formats, for example, give you precise control over commas, decimal points, and whether months and days are spelled out or abbreviated. And if you can't find the precise format you're looking for, Excel lets you create your own custom format.

SETTING NUMBER FORMATS

How should Excel display the contents of a cell? You have dozens of choices, all neatly organized by category on the Number tab of the Format Cells dialog box. To specify exactly how you want the contents of a cell or range to appear, follow these steps:

1. Click the cell you want to format, or select a range, and then choose Format, Cells. Use the keyboard shortcut Ctrl+1 to open this dialog box instantly.

TIP FROM

Few keyboard shortcuts in all of Office are as useful as Ctrl+1, which opens Excel's Format Cells dialog box. When you're formatting a large or complex worksheet, this key combination can save a startling number of mouse clicks. Even if you generally don't use keyboard shortcuts, this one is worth memorizing. Note that you must use the number 1 on the top row of the keyboard; the 1 on the numeric keypad won't work.

2. In the Format Cells dialog box, choose an entry from the Category list on the left.

3. If the category you selected includes predefined display options, select one from the Type list. Adjust other format options (currency symbol, decimal point, and so on), if necessary.

TIP FROM

To quickly adjust the number of decimal points in a cell or range, make a selection and click the Increase Decimal or Decrease Decimal buttons on the Formatting toolbar. Each click adds or subtracts one decimal point from the selection.

4. Inspect the Sample box in the upper-right corner of the dialog box to see how the active cell will appear with the format settings you've selected. Click OK to accept the settings and return to the editing window.

The following number format categories are available:

- General, the default format, displays numbers as entered, using as many decimal places as necessary, up to a maximum of 11 digits. It does not include separators between thousands. No additional options are available.

Figure 18.2

- Number formats let you specify the number of decimal places, from 0 to 30 (the default is 2), as well as an optional separator for thousands, based on the Windows Regional Settings. You can also choose one of four formats for negative numbers (see Figure 18.2).

- Choices in the Currency category display values using the default currency symbol, as specified in the Regional Settings options of Control Panel. You can adjust the number of decimal places from its default of 2 to any number between 0 and 30 and select a format for negative values (see Figure 18.3).

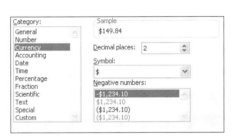

Figure 18.3

- Accounting formats are similar to those in the Currency category, except that currency symbols and decimal points align properly in columns and you can't choose a format for negative values. With Accounting formats, the currency symbol ($ in U.S. English installations) sits at the left edge of the cell. This effect can be odd in wide columns that contain small numbers; in that case, choose a Currency format instead, if possible (see Figure 18.4).

Figure 18.4

- The Date category includes 15 formats that determine whether and how to display day, date, month, and year. All versions of Excel since Excel 2000 include a pair of Year-2000—compatible date formats that use four digits for the year (see Figure 18.5).

Figure 18.5

- The Time category includes eight formats that determine whether and how to display hours, minutes, seconds, and AM/PM designators (see Figure 18.6).

- Applying the Percentage format multiplies the cell value by 100 for display purposes and adds a percent symbol; the only option here lets you specify the number of decimal places, from 0 to 30 (the default is 2).

Figure 18.6

- Fraction formats store numbers in decimal format but displays cell contents as fractions using any of 9 predefined settings; to display stock prices using 8ths, 16ths, and 32nds, click Up to Two Digits in the Type list (see Figure 18.7).

- Choose Scientific to display numbers in scientific notation; you select the number of decimal places, from 0 to 30.

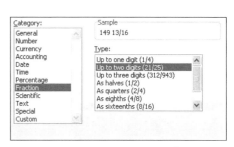

Figure 18.7

- Applying the Text format displays cell contents exactly as entered, even if the cell contains numbers or a formula.

- The four choices in the Special category allow you to select formats for long and short U.S. ZIP Codes, phone numbers, and Social Security numbers. You enter the number without any punctuation, and Excel adds hyphens and parentheses as necessary for display purposes only (see Figure 18.8).

Figure 18.8

- Choose the Custom option to define your own display rules. Start with a built-in format and use symbols in the formatting instructions; see "Custom Number Formats" later in this chapter for more details on custom number formats.

SETTING DATE AND TIME FORMATS

Normally, Excel stores exactly what you type into a cell. That's not the case when you type a recognizable date or time, however; when storing date and time information, Excel first converts the value you enter into *serial date format*. This numeric transformation explains how Excel can perform calculations using date and time information. Understanding the following facts is crucial to working effectively with serial date formats:

- Excel converts the date to a whole number that counts the number of days that have elapsed since January 1, 1900, which has a serial date value of 1. Thus, the serial date value of December 31, 2003 is 37986.

- When you enter a time (hours, minutes, and seconds), Excel converts it to a fractional decimal value between 0 (midnight) and 0.999988 (11:59:59 p.m.). If you enter a time of 10:00 a.m., for example, Excel stores it as 0.416667.

- If you combine a date and time, Excel combines the serial date and time values. Thus, Excel saves December 31, 2003 10:00 a.m. as 37986.416667.

NOTE

When you enter only a date, Excel converts it to a serial value and uses 0 (or 12:00 a.m.) as the time value. If you enter only a time, Excel tacks on a date value of 0; if you later format this cell to show the date and time, Excel displays the nonsense date 1/0/1900.

The transformation to a serial value happens as soon as you enter a date or time value in a cell; at the same time, Excel automatically applies the default Date or Time format to your cell so that the data you enter displays correctly. You can choose a different Date or Time format to change the display format of date or time values. If you change the format of the cell to General or Number, however, you will see the serial values instead of the dates you expect.

Conversely, if you accidentally apply the Date format to a cell that contains a number, the result is likely to be nonsense, especially if the number is relatively low. Choose the General or Number format to display the cell's contents correctly.

TIP FROM

If the display of dates is important to you, be aware of the unusual interaction between Excel's date and time formats and those you define in Windows's Regional Options Control Panel (in some Windows versions, this appears as Regional Settings). These linked formats appear at the top of the Date and Time lists in the Format Cells dialog box, with an asterisk in front of the format. When you change the date format in Windows, the format in your worksheet changes too—if you've used one of these formats.

Excel transforms dates and times to serial values so that you can use them in calculations. Because date and time values are stored as numbers, you can easily enter formulas that calculate elapsed time. If you include a student's birth date as part of a list, for instance, you can use a simple formula to compare that value to today's date and determine whether the student is old enough for a program that is restricted to children who are at least 13 years old. If you enter start and end times for each participant in a road race, you can easily calculate the total elapsed time and determine the top finishers.

After you enter the student's birth date in C1 and your report date in C2, for example, you can calculate the difference between the two dates by using the formula =C1-C2.

TIP FROM

Ed & Woody

Unfortunately, Excel outsmarts itself when you use this type of formula. Because it sees dates in both cells used in the formula, it automatically applies a date format to the cell containing the formula. As a result, the cell contents display as a nonsense date. Reset the cell's format to General or Number to correctly display the difference between the dates.

To use a date directly in a formula, enclose it in quotation marks first: =Today()-"1/1/2003" counts the number of days that have elapsed since January 1, 2003, for instance.

NOTE

Excel's Options dialog box includes a setting for the 1904 date system. This obscure option is necessary only when exchanging files with users of old versions of Excel for the Macintosh, which started the calendar at the beginning of 1904 rather than 1900. Mac Excel versions since Excel 98 handle this conversion seamlessly. Under normal circumstances, you should never need to use this option.

EXCEL AND YEAR 2000 ISSUES

The much-feared global Y2K crisis never happened. Planes continued to fly, power stations hummed along, and banks didn't run out of money. Yes, the world successfully entered the new millennium, but that doesn't let you off the hook when it comes to Year 2000 (Y2K) issues. Excel's default settings correctly handle most formulas that include dates from different centuries. But a few "gotchas" linger for the unwary:

- When you enter a date before January 1, 1900, in an Excel worksheet, the date appears as text. As far as Excel is concerned, dates before the 20th century simply don't exist— that's bad news for students of history and scientists hoping to use Excel to plot dates that go back more than a century.

- On the other hand, dates after December 31, 1999, don't represent a problem. In fact, Excel worksheets will accept any date through December 31, 9999 (that's a serial date value of 2958465, if you want to try it for yourself).

TIP FROM

Ed & Woody

If you need to track timelines and perform calculations for dates before the beginning of 1900 (to chart long-term records of earthquake activities, for example), you'll need to provide some help for Excel. One solution is John Walkenbach's excellent Extended Date Functions Add-in (http://j-walk.com/ss/excel/files/xdate.htm). It handles date arithmetic all the way back to the year 100 C.E. If you're a student of ancient history, you'll need to use another program—or perhaps you can make do with clay tablets.

Because Excel stores dates as serial values, it is unaffected by most garden-variety Y2K problems. In practice, however, you might encounter Y2K problems if you enter or import data that includes only two digits for the year. When Excel encounters dates in this format, it has to convert the year to four digits; in the process, it's possible to select the wrong century. When translating two-digit years, Excel uses the following rules:

- Excel automatically converts dates entered using the two-digit years 00 through 29 to the years 2000 through 2029. Thus, if you enter or import the value 5/23/04, Excel stores it as serial value 38130, or May 23, 2004.

- When you enter the two-digit years 30 through 99 as part of a date, Excel converts the dates using the years 1930 through 1999. Thus, when you enter or import the value 9/29/55, Excel stores it as serial value 20361, or September 29, 1955.

On a new worksheet, Excel automatically displays dates using a four-digit format. However, if you design a worksheet so that some dates display only two years (or if you use an older worksheet that was designed using those formats), you might not realize that Excel has stored the wrong data. In that case, any calculations you make might be off by a full century. To avoid inadvertently entering or importing incorrect data, get in the habit of entering all dates using four-digit formats for the year: 5/23/2004. Excel stores this date correctly regardless of the Date format you've chosen for display purposes.

When importing data that includes dates with two-digit years, check the format of the original data carefully. You might need to manually edit some dates after importing. Pay special attention to worksheets that were originally created using pre-2000 versions of Excel for Windows or the Macintosh, because the algorithms those programs use to convert two-digit years are different from those in Excel 2000 and later versions.

The automatic date conversion routine is a clever workaround, but don't rely on it. Entering or importing two-digit years is guaranteed to cause problems in the following circumstances:

- In the banking industry, in which dates beyond 2029 are common in 30- and 40-year mortgages that begin in the year 2000 or later. If you enter the start date as 2/1/06 and the end date as 2/1/36, your loan will start out 70 years overdue.

- In any group that includes milestone dates—birthdays, graduation dates, and so on—for an older population. If you enter a birthdate of 6/19/27, your worksheet might assume that the person in question isn't born yet.

TIP FROM

Ed & Woody

> This can't be said strongly enough or repeated too often: Get in the habit of using four-digit years whenever you enter or display a date in a worksheet.

CREATING CUSTOM CELL FORMATS

If the exact number format you need isn't in Excel's collection of built-in formats, create a custom format. Custom formats let you specify the display of positive and negative numbers as well as zero values; you can also add text to the contents of any cell.

Excel saves custom number formats in the workbook in which you create them. To reuse formats, add them to the template on which you base new workbooks. To copy cell formats from one workbook to another, copy the cell that contains the custom format, click in the workbook where you want to add the format, and choose Edit, Paste Special, Formats.

The list of 35 custom formats in the Type box includes some that are already available within other categories, as well as a few you won't find elsewhere. It's almost always easier to design a custom format if you start with one that already exists. To create a custom number format, open the Format Cells dialog box and choose the format you want to start with. Then click Custom at the bottom of the Category list. Excel displays the codes for the format you just selected in the Type box, ready for you to modify. The example shown in Figure 18.9, for example, shows the results when we chose a Currency format and changed the symbol from the U.S. dollar sign to the Euro. Although the switches for these codes are undocumented, this technique adds them to the Type box, making it easy to define a new format that uses this symbol correctly.

Figure 18.9
Enter custom format codes here. Note the Sample area, which shows how the contents of the active cell will appear.

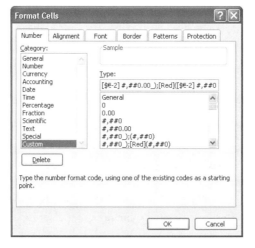

Custom formats use format codes to tell Excel how to display digits, decimal places, dates and times, and other details. Each custom format can include up to four sections, separated by semicolons, as shown in the example in Figure 18.10. Using all four sections defines display formats for positive numbers, negative numbers, zero values, and text, respectively. If you enter only two sections, Excel uses the first set of instructions for positive numbers and zero values and the second for negative numbers. If you enter only one section, that format will apply to all numbers you enter. You don't need to enter a format for each section, but if you plan to skip a format option (specifying formats only for positive numbers and zero values, for example), insert a semicolon for each section you skip.

Figure 18.10
Custom number formats can contain up to four sections.

```
_($* #,##0_);_($* (#,##0);_($* "-"_);_(@_)
```

TIP FROM

ED & Woody

When creating an extremely complex custom format, working with the narrow text box in the Format Cells dialog box can be difficult. To make life easier, select the contents of this box, and then copy them to a friendlier editor, such as Notepad or Word. Edit the format codes, and then use the Clipboard to paste the results back into the dialog box.

Creative use of custom number formats can help you deal with tricky data-entry challenges. For example, how do you make it easy to enter a serial number with leading zeros? Say you are building a list of serial numbers that must be exactly seven digits, with no exceptions. If the number you enter includes fewer than seven digits, you want Excel to pad the beginning of the entry with as many zeros as it takes to reach that magic number. Entering a number like 0001234 won't work, because Excel considers the leading zeros insignificant digits and strips them before storing the value in the cell.

The solution is to create a custom format that includes a zero for each digit you want to include in the displayed result—in this case, 0000000.

TIP FROM

ED & Woody

To guarantee that only correct data appears in the cell, combine this custom format with a data-validation rule. If a valid serial number must be larger than 1000, create a validation rule that restricts data entry to whole numbers (to prevent stray decimal points or text from messing up the list) between 1001 and 9999999. The all-zeros display format guarantees that any data within this range will display as exactly seven digits, with leading zeros if necessary.

CUSTOM NUMBER FORMATS

Custom number formats let you round or truncate numbers, control the number of decimal places or significant digits, and make sure amounts line up properly in columns. Use the codes shown in Table 18.1 to define the display format.

TABLE 18.1   CUSTOM NUMBER FORMAT CODES

Code	What It Does	How You Use It
#	Display significant digit	Using the format #.# displays all significant (nonzero) digits to the left of the decimal point and rounds to one digit on the right of the decimal point; if you enter 0.567, this format displays .6.

continues

TABLE 18.1 CONTINUED

Code	What It Does	How You Use It
0	Display zero if the number has fewer digits than the number to format	The format 0.000 always displays exactly three decimal points; for numbers below 1, it includes a 0 to the left of the decimal point.
?	Align decimal points or fractions	Click any of Excel's built-in Fraction formats, and then choose Custom to see an example of how to use this placeholder.
.	Decimal point	To round the cell's contents to a whole number, leave off the decimal point.
,	Display thousands separator or scale number by multiple of 1,000	Inserting two commas after a number scales it by a million; to display a large number (163,200,000) in an easier-to-read style (163.2 MM), enter this format: #0.0,," MM".
%	Display the number as a percentage of 100	If you enter 8, Excel displays it as 800%. To enter 8, start with a decimal point and a zero: .08.
[color]	Show the cell contents in specified color	Choose one of eight colors—Black, Blue, Cyan, Green, Magenta, Red, White, Yellow—for any section; you must use brackets and enter the color as the first item in each section, like this: [Blue]#,##0;[Red] #,##0;[Black]0.

CUSTOM DATE AND TIME FORMATS

Excel's selection of ready-made date and time formats is extensive, but there are several situations in which you might want to create your own. For example, if you're doing volunteer work for an organization that uses a special date format to identify dates on reports, you can enter a format such as yyyymmdd to display a date as 20050321.

Custom date and time formats are also useful if you need to keep track of time that volunteers spend on a project by the minute or hour, or if you've captured data from time sheets that include starting and ending times for shifts. Table 18.2 includes examples of date and time codes you can add to custom formats.

TABLE 18.2 CUSTOM DATE/TIME FORMAT CODES

Code	What It Does	How You Use It
d, dd m, mm	Day or month in numeric format, with or without columns of dates	Use the leading zero when you want leading zero to line up properly; to add a zero to the date only, use this format: m/dd/yyyy.

Code	What It Does	How You Use It
ddd, mmm dddd, mmmm	Day or month in text format, abbreviated or full	Use ddd or mmm to show abbreviations such as Wed or Jan; use dddd and mmmm for the fully spelled out month or day: January and Wednesday.
mmmmm	Month as first letter only	Potentially confusing because it's impossible to distinguish between January, June, and July, or between March and May.
yy, yyyy	Year, in two- or four-digit format	If you're concerned about possible confusion caused by the year 2000, specify four-digit years.
h, hh m, mm s, ss	Hours, minutes, or seconds, zero	Use a leading zero with minutes and with or without leading seconds; to store precise times, add a decimal point and extra digits after the format: `h:mm:ss.00`.
A/P, AM/PM	Show AM/PM indicator	Insert after time code to use 12-hour clock and display AM or PM (6:12 p.m.); otherwise, Excel displays the time in 24-hour format (18:12).
[h], [m], [s]	Show elapsed time in hours, minutes, or seconds	Add brackets to display elapsed time rather than a time of day. Add decimals for seconds; for instance, for a worksheet containing race times, use this format: [m]:ss.00.

ADDING TEXT TO A CELL

To display text in a cell that contains numbers, Excel includes a selection of special format codes. Use this type of format to add a word like "shortage" or "deficit" after a negative number, for example. Because the format doesn't change the contents of the cell, the number you entered will still work in formulas that reference that cell.

You can add the space character, left and right single quotation mark, and any of the following special characters without enclosing them in double quotation marks:

$ - + / ( ) : ! [ct] & ~ { } = < >

To add other text to a cell, use the codes in Table 18.3.

TABLE 18.3   CUSTOM TEXT FORMAT CODES

Code	What It Does	How You Use It
*	Repeat characters to fill cell to column width	Enter an asterisk followed by the character you want to repeat. Use *- in the third position of a custom format to replace zero values with a line of hyphens, for example.
_ (underscore character)	Add a space the width of a specified character	Enter an underscore followed by the character whose width you want to use. Several built-in formats use _)) with positive number formats, for example, to make sure they line up properly with negative numbers that use parentheses.
\	Display the character that follows the backslash	To add a space and the letter P or L after a positive or negative value, use this format: `#,##0_) \P;[Red] (#,##0) \L`.
"text"	Display the text you enter inside the double quotation marks	Remember to add a space inside the quotes when necessary. For example, to display a negative amount as $514.32 Loss in red, enter this format: `$0.00" Profit";[Red] $0.00" Loss"`.
@	Display the text entered in the cell	Use this code only in the fourth (text) section in a custom format to combine the entered text with other text. If you include a text section without the @ character, Excel hides any text in the cell.

TIP FROM

When creating a custom number format, first click in a cell that contains data you want to see in the new format. As you edit the custom format, the Preview region of the Custom Format dialog box shows you how the active cell's contents will appear in the new format.

ADDING CONDITIONS TO A DISPLAY FORMAT

You can also use *conditions* as part of custom number formats. Conditions use comparison operators and are contained in brackets as part of a format definition. Look at the built-in Phone Number format (in the Special category) to see how this option works:

`[<=9999999]###-####;(###) ###-####`

If you enter a number of seven or fewer digits in a cell that uses this format, Excel treats it as a local phone number and adds a hyphen where the prefix appears. If you enter a number greater than seven digits, Excel uses the second part of the format, displaying the last seven digits as a phone number and any number of digits prior to that number as an area code in parentheses.

The results of this format can be absurd if you enter a number that's smaller than 7 digits or larger than 10 digits. Here's how to use conditions to customize this format. The example shown here assumes you live or work in the 212 area code and want to add that code to the beginning of any 7-digit (local) number; if the number uses more than 10 digits, the default condition at the end kicks in, adding the international dialing prefix (+011) and splitting the digits before the number into country and city codes.

```
[<=9999999](212) ###-####;[<=9999999999](###) ###-####;"+011 "(#-##) ###-####
```

TIP FROM

Ed & Woody

> Don't confuse these custom formats with conditional formatting, which is described later in this chapter. If you want to change the font or color of text based on values displayed in the cell, use the Conditional Formatting option on the Format menu (described later in this chapter). The conditional display formats shown here are most useful when you want to subdivide a number with punctuation marks or change the number of digits displayed. You can effectively combine this type of format with conditional formatting—for example, if the user enters a phone number with six or fewer digits, you might display it in red to help it stand out as a possibly invalid number.

DESIGNING AND FORMATTING A WORKSHEET FOR MAXIMUM READABILITY

If you simply enter data into a new worksheet without adjusting any formatting first, every cell will look exactly the same, and anyone reading the worksheet will be forced to work to pick out the important details. Want to make it easier on your audience? Set off different regions of a worksheet by using custom cell formatting—larger, bolder fonts for headings, for example, plus borders around the data area with a double line to mark where the data range ends and the totals begin. Carefully resetting row heights and column widths, wrapping and slanting text, and adding background shading can make the entire sheet easier to follow.

CHANGING FONTS AND CHARACTER ATTRIBUTES

The default worksheet font (10-point Arial) is fine for basic data entry, but for any worksheet more complex than a simple list you'll probably want to adjust fonts to squeeze more data onto printed pages while beefing up titles, totals, and category headings with larger, bolder fonts.

→ If you're entering data in a list, some cells format themselves automatically; for details, **see** "Speeding Up Repetitive Data Entry with AutoComplete," **p. 633**.

If you select a cell or range, you can apply font formatting to the entire contents of the selection. You can also apply different fonts, font sizes, colors, and font attributes to different words or characters in the same cell. In either case, you can use the Font and font size lists on the Formatting toolbar. Open the Format Cells dialog box and click the Font tab (see Figure 18.11) for access to all font formats, including some options you won't find on the toolbar, such as strikethrough and double underline attributes.

Figure 18.11
Options on the Font tab let you format an entire cell or selected words or characters within a cell.

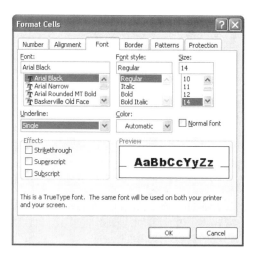

Most of the options on the Font tab of this dialog box are fairly straightforward. One check box deserves some explanation, however. When you add custom font formatting, you automatically clear the Normal Font check box. Check this box again to remove all font formatting from the current cell or selection and restore Excel's default style.

 If you're having trouble restoring default font formatting to a cell, see "Click Twice for Normal" in the "Troubleshooting" section at the end of this chapter.

You'll find countless uses for rich formatting within cells. The range shown in Figure 18.12, for example, uses different font formatting for the ISBN number and title in a list of classic books. This feature is also a useful way to insert trademark and copyright symbols and other special characters within a cell.

Figure 18.12
Mix and match font formatting within a cell to emphasize one type of data over another.

NOTE

To enter a manual line break within a cell, position the insertion point at the spot where you want the break to appear and press Alt+Enter. Unfortunately, there's no easy way to copy rich formatting from one cell to another. If you use the Format Painter or the Clipboard to copy formats, only the first font is copied.

An obscure check box on the Alignment tab of the Format Cells dialog box actually has a major effect on formatting. Click the Shrink to Fit check box when you want Excel to automatically adjust the font size when the contents of a cell are too wide to fit. This option doesn't change the formatting applied to the cell; it changes the scaling instead, going up or down in 1-point increments. If you enter more text or adjust the width of the column, Excel changes the size of the font automatically so that you can continue to see its contents. Use this option with care—if you format an entire column as Shrink to Fit and then fill it with data that varies in length, the results can look like a ransom note.

ALIGNING, WRAPPING, AND ROTATING TEXT AND NUMBERS

When you use the default General format, cells containing text align to the left, and those with numbers align to the right. You can change the alignment of any cell or range by using the Align Left, Center, and Align Right buttons on the Formatting toolbar.

Use the Wrap Text option on the Alignment tab to handle long strings of text that don't fit in a cell. Wrapped text is useful for column headings that are much longer than the data in the column. You can also use wrapped text to create tables, where each cell in a row holds an entire paragraph. Excel wraps text to additional lines automatically, maintaining the column width you specified. To control the location of each break, press Alt+Enter. To use text wrapping, follow these steps:

1. Select the cell or range that contains the text you want to wrap. Right-click and choose Format Cells.

2. Click the Alignment tab on the Format Cells dialog box and check the Wrap Text box.

3. Adjust the vertical alignment if needed. For column headings with long and short entries, for example, choose Center from the Vertical drop-down list. Headings formatted this way seem to "float" instead of sit on the bottom of the cell. For text in a table, choose the Top format so that each paragraph begins at the same point.

4. Click OK to apply the new format. Now, instead of disappearing from view when they reach the right edge of the cell, the text you enter begins filling additional lines in the same cell.

Two other alignment options can help make worksheets easier to read. You can change the orientation of a column heading to any angle, including straight up or down. Slanting column headings can save space and give tables a professional look when you have narrow columns with lengthy titles. To help set off groups of items in a column, indent the cells in second and subsequent levels. (See the before and after worksheets at the end of this chapter for examples of all these alignment options.) This option is especially useful when you want to distinguish subheadings from headings at the beginning of a row.

To indent a cell or range of cells, follow these steps:

1. Select the cell or range you want to format, right-click, and choose Format Cells.

2. Click the Alignment tab. In the Text Alignment section, click the Horizontal drop-down list and choose Indent (Left).

3. Use the Indent spinner to select the indent level for the selection. For each number, Excel adds approximately as much space as a capital M. For the outline levels in column A of Figure 18.13, we used settings of 1 and 2, respectively.

Figure 18.13

	A
1	**Expenses**
2	**Payroll & Benefits**
3	*Salaries*
4	*Payroll Taxes*
5	*Benefits*
6	*Insurance*
7	**Travel & Entertainment**
8	*Travel*
9	*Entertainment*
10	**Capital Budget**
11	*Equipment*
12	*Computer Equipment*
13	**Office Expenses**
14	*Office Supplies*
15	*Printing and Copying*
16	*Telephone and Fax*
17	*Postage and Delivery*
18	**Real Estate Costs**
19	*Rent*
20	*Utilities*
21	*Maintenance*
22	**Consultants and Professional Fees**

4. Click OK to accept the changes and return to the worksheet.

Use the Format Cells dialog box to change the orientation of column headings so that they slant up or down:

1. After entering the text for the headings, select one or more cells, right-click, and choose Format Cells.

2. Click the Alignment tab, and then point to the control in the Orientation section of the dialog box and drag it up or down to the desired angle, as shown in Figure 18.14, or use the spinner to specify a precise angle by degrees.

3. Click OK to accept the changes and return to the worksheet.

TIP FROM

EQ & Woody

Word and PowerPoint don't allow you to position headings using any orientation except horizontal or vertical. If you want to add a table with slanted headings to a Word document or PowerPoint presentation, create the table in Excel, and then use Paste Special and choose Microsoft Excel Worksheet Object to embed the worksheet range, complete with slanted headings.

Vertical headings use little column width, but they can be difficult to read. You have two choices when changing a heading to vertical orientation. Click the skinny box just under the word Orientation to stack letters one over another. This option is most effective with short words in all capitals. You can also change the orientation to 90° to turn the cell on its side, so the contents read from bottom to top.

Figure 18.14
Click the line between the word Text and the red square; then drag it up or down to arrange text at a space-saving angle.

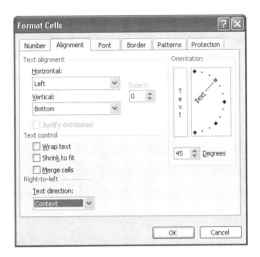

USING BORDERS, BOXES, AND COLORS

You can create a distinctive identity for sections of a worksheet by using borders, boxes, and background colors. Dark backgrounds and white type help worksheet titles stand out. Soft, light background colors make columns of numbers easier to read. Use alternating colors or shading to make it easy for the eye to tell which entries belong in each row, even on a wide worksheet that contains many columns of data.

TIP FROM

EQ & Woody

When preparing a worksheet that you intend to print on a black-and-white printer, test different color combinations. Use the printout to decide which colors are best for you. Sometimes, for example, it's easier to read black type on a light yellow background (which appears gray) than on a background on which you specify a shade of gray.

The Borders, Fill Color, and Font Color buttons on the Formatting toolbar work much as you would expect. After selecting a cell or range, click the arrow to the right of each button to choose a specific option from the drop-down list.

These toolbars don't give you access to every formatting option, however. For maximum control over borders and colors, first select the cells or range you want to format; then right-click and choose Format Cells. Click the Border tab (see Figure 18.15) to add and remove lines around the selection.

To create custom borders, follow these steps:

1. Before you add any lines, choose a line style—thick, thin, doubled, dotted, or dashed— from the Style box at the right.

2. Choose a different border color, if you like, from the Color drop-down list. Colors are most effective with thick lines.

3. Click the Outline button to add lines in the thickness and color you specified on all four sides of the active cell. If you selected a range, click Outline to draw a box around the range, and click Inside to draw borders around every cell in the selection.

4. Click any of the buttons in the Border section to add one line at a time, on the left, right, top, or bottom of the cell, or diagonally. Click again to remove the line. The preview area shows which edges currently have borders.

Figure 18.15
Use borders to distinguish sections of your worksheet. Note that this range includes three different line styles.

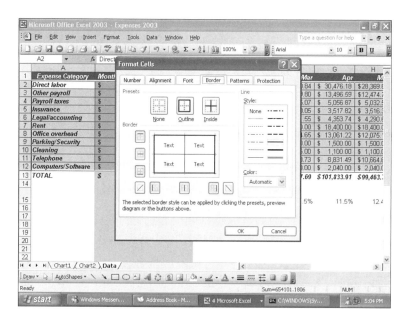

NOTE

You can also click directly on lines in the preview area to add or remove borders.

5. You can mix and match line styles and colors, even on different borders of the same cell. Click the line style or change the color, and then click the button in the Border area to change the style.

6. Click OK to close the Format Cells dialog box and return to the worksheet.

Getting borders just right on a complex worksheet often takes multiple iterations. The trick is figuring out which regions need separate formatting and which have common borders. For example, you might need to select the entire data area first to add a thick border around the outside. Then select the heading rows to adjust their borders, which might be thinner and lighter. Select the data area next, to add, remove, and format interior rules between rows and columns that contain data. Finally, if your data area contains a totals row at the bottom, select that row (or the last row of data) to add a double line between the end of the data range and the totals.

MERGING CELLS

On a highly structured worksheet, merging cells can help you show the relationship between headings and subheadings. In a list where two or three rows have the same value in the first column, for example, you could merge those cells to make the common nature of those rows truly stand out. You can combine adjacent cells in a row, a column, or any contiguous range.

To quickly merge two or more cells, select the cells and click the Merge and Center button on the Formatting toolbar. Excel displays a dialog box warning you that when you merge cells, you will lose all data except the contents of the top-left cell in the selection. Click OK to continue or Cancel if you want to back out and move the data before you lose it.

To edit text in a merged cell, click in the cell and begin typing. You can also change the alignment of the merged cells to left or right, without changing the merge.

You might encounter problems when you try to cut and paste merged cells, or when you attempt to sort a list that contains a merged cell. To restore the merged cells to their normal position on the grid, click to make the merged cell active, and then click the Merge and Center icon on the Formatting toolbar. You can also use Excel's menus: Right-click and choose Format Cells. Click the Alignment tab and clear the check mark from the Merge Cells box.

CHANGING ROW HEIGHT AND COLUMN WIDTH

On a new worksheet, every row is exactly 12.75 points high, and every column is 8.43 characters wide. (If the default font for Normal style is a proportional one such as Arial, Excel uses a lowercase x as the character to measure.) As you design a worksheet and fill it with data, however, you'll need to change the size of rows and columns. A column that contains only two-digit numbers doesn't need to be as wide as one that's filled with category headings, for example.

Some of these adjustments happen automatically. If you change the font size of text in a cell, the row automatically changes height to accommodate it. Likewise, when you enter data that's too wide to fit in the default column width, Excel expands the column.

→ For an explanation of how columns expand to accommodate data you enter, **see** "Avoiding Rounding Errors," **p. 562**.

You can also adjust row heights and column widths manually in any of three ways:

- Use Excel's AutoFit feature to set column widths and row heights automatically. Double-click the right border of a column heading to adjust column width to fit the widest entry in the column. Double-click the bottom border of a row heading to resize a row to accommodate the tallest character in that row. If you select multiple rows or columns, you can adjust them all at once.

- Click and drag any column or row to a new size. Point to the thin line at the right of the column heading or the bottom of a row heading until the pointer changes to a two-headed arrow. Click and drag the column or row to the desired width or height, and release the mouse button.

TIP FROM

EQ & Woody

> When you use the mouse to adjust column widths and row heights, ScreenTips show the exact height and width, in characters (for columns) or points (for rows). Curiously, both ScreenTips also show the measurements in *pixels*—use this scale if you're optimizing a worksheet for viewing in a browser at a specific resolution, say, 800×600 pixels.

- To set a precise height or width, use a dialog box. Choose Format, Row, Height and enter any number between 0 and 409 (points). Or choose Format, Column, Width and enter any number between 0 and 255 (characters).

To adjust more than one row or column, select the group of rows or columns first. Then point to the border of any row or column heading in the selection and drag to the desired size. When you release the mouse button, Excel adjusts all selected rows or columns to the height or width of the column you selected. This technique is especially useful when you're putting together a budget worksheet with 12 columns, one for each month. After entering data, select all 12 columns and drag them to the correct width.

Here are some expert tips to help you when working with row heights and column widths:

- To hide any row or column, set its height or width to 0 (click the right side of a column heading and drag to the left, or click the bottom of a row heading and drag to the top). To make a hidden column or row visible, select the columns or rows on either side of the hidden one; then choose Format, Row or Column, and click Unhide.

- To resize a column according to the contents of one or more specific cells in that column, make a selection and then choose Format, Column, AutoFit Selection.

- To automatically change the size of a group of columns or rows without dragging, use AutoFit from the menus. Select the rows or columns, and then click Format, Row or Column, and choose AutoFit Selection.

- If you've customized column widths and/or row heights and you want to copy this information along with data, copy and paste the entire row or column, not just the individual cells. Use the Column Widths option on the Paste Special dialog box to duplicate the arrangement of columns from one worksheet to another.

- To change the standard width for all columns in the current worksheet, choose Format, Column, Standard Width, and then enter the new column width (in characters) in the dialog box. The new width will not apply to columns whose width you have already reset.

USING CONDITIONAL FORMATTING TO IDENTIFY KEY VALUES

Conditional formatting allows you to set font attributes, colors, and other formatting options that cause data to appear differently based on the value displayed in a cell. Most often, you'll use this feature to set an alarm that highlights data that is outside of an expected range. For example, you might attach conditional formatting to a row of totals on a daily sales report, displaying each cell's contents in bold red letters if it falls below a target level and in bright green if the number is significantly above average. In an employee roster, you might use bold formatting to identify the names of employees who are overdue for a formal evaluation.

TIP FROM

Ed & Woody

Conditional formats are most effective when used sparingly. If every cell in a worksheet has "special" formatting, nothing stands out. The best use of this option is to highlight truly unusual conditions that require action–when you open a worksheet and see one or two items in bright red, they get your full attention.

Some predefined number formats automatically display negative numbers in red, but conditional formatting gives you somewhat greater control. For cells whose contents match one or more conditions you define, you can specify a new font style (bold italic, for example), use the underline or strikethrough attributes, or change the borders and color of the selection. You cannot use conditional formatting to change fonts or font sizes.

To use conditional formatting, select a cell or range, and then choose Format, Conditional Formatting; fill in the dialog box shown in Figure 18.16.

Figure 18.16
Use conditional formatting to change the appearance of certain cells based on comparisons you define.

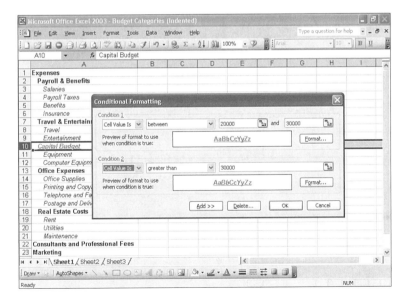

Use drop-down lists in the Condition section to compare the cell values with the contents of another cell, a value, or a formula. For example, you could define a condition Cell Value Is Greater Than or Equal to 20000, and Excel would apply the special formatting if the value is 30,000 but leave the standard format in place if the value is only 15,000. If you enter a formula in this box, it must use a logical function that evaluates to True or False. For most garden-variety conditions, you should choose Cell Value Is.

Formulas in conditional formats can apply to any data on the worksheet, not just the data in the current cell, or even to external data. For example, in a list where Column A contains dates and Columns B, C, and D contain absentee rates for sophomores, juniors, and seniors, you might want to automatically apply shading to each row that contains data for a Monday; this trick helps you pick out each new week at a glance. If headings are in row 1 and the data begins in row 2, create a conditional format using the formula =WEEKDAY($A2)=2, using the shading you want to see. Copy that format to all cells in the data range, using the Paste Special dialog box or the Format Painter (described in the following section), to automatically shade every Monday row in the entire list.

To create a conditional format, follow these steps:

1. In the box labeled Condition 1, use the drop-down lists to define the comparison you want to make.

2. Click the Format button to open a stripped-down version of the Format Cells dialog box, and then define the special format you want to use when the cell's contents match that condition. If you want the highlighted cells to be noticeable on a printed page, use bold italic, underline, or other text formatting rather than color.

3. To create a second or third conditional format, click the Add button and repeat the previous steps for Condition 2 and Condition 3.

 Is conditional formatting producing unexpected results? For possible solutions, see "Working with Multiple Conditions" in the "Troubleshooting" section at the end of this chapter.

4. Click OK to apply the new formatting options to the selected cell or range.

→ To prevent out-of-the-ordinary data from appearing in a worksheet in the first place, use data-validation rules; **see** "Restricting and Validating Data Entry for a Cell or Range," **p. 534**.

COPYING FORMATS WITH THE FORMAT PAINTER

Use the Format Painter button to quickly copy all formats—fonts, colors, borders, alignment...the works—from one cell to another. Select a cell that has the formatting you want to copy, and then click the Format Painter button and click the cell to which you want to copy the formatting. (If you select a range of cells to copy from, Excel repeats the formatting in your selection.)

If you want to copy formatting to multiple cells, select the cell whose formats you want to copy, and then double-click the Format Painter button to lock it in position. Click each destination cell to copy formatting. When you're finished, click the button again or press Esc to turn off the Format Painter.

TIP FROM

If you select an entire column or row, you can use the Format Painter to copy column widths and row heights. After the pointer turns to the paintbrush shape, click the heading of the row or column you want to change. Note that this technique will also copy other formats (fonts, colors, and so on) from the selected row or column.

SAVING FORMATS AS NAMED STYLES

Although Excel's *named styles* are considerably less versatile than their equivalents in Word, you can still use this feature to reuse favorite formats. By default, every new workbook includes a set of predefined formats in the following named styles: Normal, Percent, Currency, Comma, Currency [0], and Comma [0]. (The two styles followed by [0] show whole numbers only rather than two decimal places.)

TIP FROM

The Currency, Percent, and Comma buttons on Excel's Formatting toolbar actually apply the corresponding named styles. If you want to redefine any of these buttons, just redefine that style. The Currency button, for example, applies the Accounting format with two decimal places to the selected cell or range. To change the way the Currency button works, redefine the Accounting named style so that it uses a Currency format, if you want. Likewise, you can change the named Percent style to include one or two decimal places, if you prefer. See Chapter 17, "Getting Started with Excel," for instructions on how to save these changes as part of the default workbook format so that they are available for every new workbook you create.

18

You can create named styles using any format you want. This technique is a great time-saver if you continually find yourself applying the same formatting options to new worksheets:

1. Click to select the cell or range you want to format.
2. Choose Format, Style to display the Style dialog box shown in Figure 18.17.

Figure 18.17
To reuse a complicated cell format, save it as a named style and then apply it when you need it.

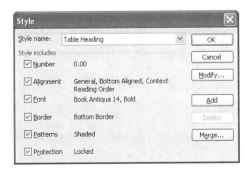

3. Type a descriptive name in the Style Name box. Use any combination of letters, numbers, and spaces; to make sure you can read the full name, keep its total length to 30 characters or fewer.

4. By default, all cell formatting options are included with the style. Clear the check mark from any of the boxes below the style name to remove that option from the style.

5. Regardless of the formatting applied to the current selection, the Style dialog box shows default settings. Click the Modify button to open the Format Cells dialog box and adjust any formatting options, if necessary.

6. Click the Add button to save the style in the current workbook.

To use a named style instead of direct formatting options, choose Format, Style. Choose a style name from the drop-down list and click OK.

Styles are available only to worksheets in the workbook in which you save them. To save named styles so that they're available for all new worksheets, save them in a template. To copy styles between two open workbooks, switch to the workbook you want to copy the styles to, and choose Format, Style. In the Style dialog box, click the Merge button. In the Merge Styles dialog box, pick the name of the workbook that contains the styles you want to reuse, and then click OK.

TIP FROM

EQ & Woody

> If you regularly use named styles in worksheets, you can dramatically increase your productivity by adding the Style list to the Formatting toolbar. You'll find step-by-step instructions for this task in Chapter 2, "Making Office Work Your Way." Make sure you do this with the default workbook template, as defined in Chapter 24, "Adding Sizzle to a Presentation," so the new toolbar is available to all workbooks you create.

→ For more details on how to create and customize toolbars, **see** "Customizing Toolbars," **p. 33**.

→ For step-by-step instructions on how to customize the default Excel workbook template, **see** "Changing Default Formatting for New Workbooks and Worksheets," **p. 555**.

Using AutoFormat

Like the Word feature of the same name, Excel's AutoFormat promises to turn your worksheet into a work of art, instantly and effortlessly. When you apply AutoFormatting to simple worksheet ranges with easily identifiable headings, totals, and other elements, the feature works pretty much as advertised. In fact, the AutoFormat options available with PivotTables are exceptionally useful because the format of a PivotTable is always the same. For more complex worksheets, however, it's likely that you'll need to clean up after AutoFormat. In general, we recommend trying the AutoFormat options (after making a backup copy of your workbook!); you can always undo the results if you don't like them, and in many cases the formatting gives you a good start.

When you use AutoFormat and other table-based options (such as sorting a list), Excel tries to apply your instructions to the current selection. If you don't make a selection, Excel uses the current region, which is the block of filled-in cells that extends in all directions from the insertion point to the next empty row or column or the edge of the worksheet. For that reason, when you design a worksheet, you should always include at least one blank row and column to mark the border of every separate data entry block.

To use AutoFormat, follow these steps:

1. Select a range. If you skip this step, Excel selects the current region.

2. Choose Format, AutoFormat. The dialog box shown in Figure 18.18 appears.

Figure 18.18
AutoFormat is most effective when you use it on small, well-defined ranges. Choose the options at the bottom of the dialog box to determine what types of changes to apply automatically.

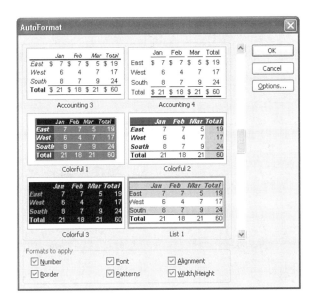

3. Pick one of the built-in formats. Each entry in the list includes a sample that gives you a general idea of the formats you can expect. The Simple and Accounting formats are the most conservative and are best for lists that you plan to include as tables in financial reports. The 3D choices at the end of the list are good for web pages.

4. To enable or disable specific types of automatic formatting, such as borders or fonts, click the Options button and add or remove check marks.

5. Click OK to apply the formats.

→ For an overview of other Office-wide formatting options, **see** "Common Formatting Options," **p. 106**.

TROUBLESHOOTING

STOPPING AUTOMATIC CONVERSIONS

After importing data into a worksheet from text files and databases, I noticed that Excel converts some data to date serial values and other data to scientific notation. I want the information to appear in my worksheet exactly as it did in the database. Is there any way to change it back?

No, unfortunately. When Excel sees a value that looks like a date or time or scientific notation, either when you type a value into a cell or when you import a database, it converts the value automatically as you type or import. There is no way to reverse this conversion. If you have serial numbers that use the format ##X####, where each # is a number and the X is a letter, Excel converts any serial number that contains the letter E in that position to scientific notation. Your best option is to edit the text or database file, adding an apostrophe to the beginning of each field that contains values Excel will try to convert. In that case, Excel imports the data in text format exactly as it appears.

CLICK TWICE FOR NORMAL

I formatted text in a cell using more than one font, and I want to restore Excel's default font format. I opened the Format Cells dialog box, clicked the Font tab, and checked the Normal Font box once, but my formatting stays exactly as it was. What's the secret?

When you have multiple font formats applied to different words or characters in a cell, the Normal Font check box is selected but it's grayed out. To restore the default formatting, click once to clear the box (exactly the opposite of what you normally do), and then click OK to close the dialog box. Now reopen the dialog box and click the Normal Font check box again. This time your change will stick.

WORKING WITH MULTIPLE CONDITIONS

I applied conditional formatting to a cell, but the formatting doesn't appear on some cells, even though the data in those cells meets the conditions I specified.

If you specify multiple conditions and more than one is true for a given cell, Excel applies the formats of the first true condition it encounters and ignores the second and third conditions. If you've defined conditions that have the potential to overlap, arrange them in order so that the most important one (or the one least likely to be true) is first in the list.

EXTRA CREDIT: REDESIGNING A WORKSHEET CLARIFIES THE INFORMATION

When you first create a worksheet, every cell uses the same fonts, every row is the same height, and there's no distinction between headings and the data they describe. With Excel's extensive selection of formatting tools, you can redesign a worksheet to make its organization crystal clear.

When we imported data from a database into a worksheet, the results looked like a data disaster, as the “Before” example in Figure 18.19 illustrates.

Figure 18.19

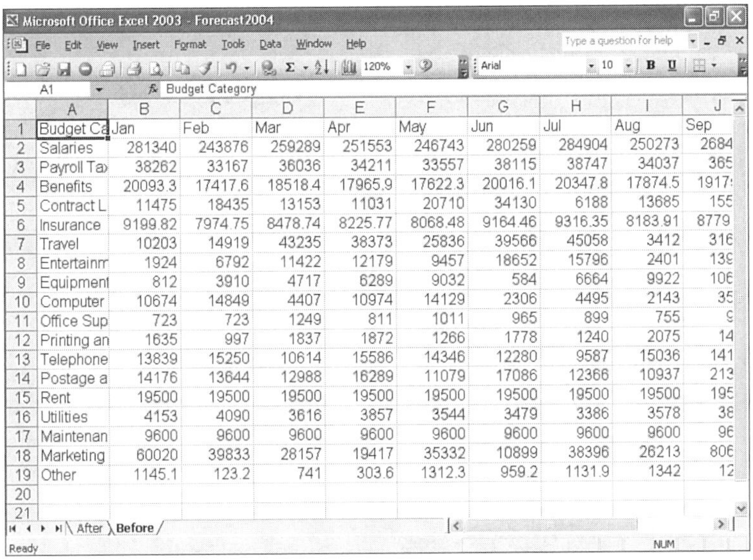

	A	B	C	D	E	F	G	H	I	J
1	Budget Ca	Jan	Feb	Mar	Apr	May	Jun	Jul	Aug	Sep
2	Salaries	281340	243876	259289	251553	246743	280259	284904	250273	2684
3	Payroll Ta	38262	33167	36036	34211	33557	38115	38747	34037	365
4	Benefits	20093.3	17417.6	18518.4	17965.9	17622.3	20016.1	20347.8	17874.5	1917
5	Contract L	11475	18435	13153	11031	20710	34130	6188	13685	155
6	Insurance	9199.82	7974.75	8478.74	8225.77	8068.48	9164.46	9316.35	8183.91	8779
7	Travel	10203	14919	43235	38373	25836	39566	45058	3412	316
8	Entertainm	1924	6792	11422	12179	9457	18652	15796	2401	139
9	Equipment	812	3910	4717	6289	9032	584	6664	9922	106
10	Computer	10674	14849	4407	10974	14129	2306	4495	2143	35
11	Office Sup	723	723	1249	811	1011	965	899	755	9
12	Printing an	1635	997	1837	1872	1266	1778	1240	2075	14
13	Telephone	13839	15250	10614	15586	14346	12280	9587	15036	141
14	Postage a	14176	13644	12988	16289	11079	17086	12366	10937	213
15	Rent	19500	19500	19500	19500	19500	19500	19500	19500	195
16	Utilities	4153	4090	3616	3857	3544	3479	3386	3578	38
17	Maintenan	9600	9600	9600	9600	9600	9600	9600	9600	96
18	Marketing	60020	39833	28157	19417	35332	10899	38396	26213	806
19	Other	1145.1	123.2	741	303.6	1312.3	959.2	1131.9	1342	12
20										
21										

After some careful formatting, however, the results are much easier to read and follow. Here are the basic principles we followed when formatting the “After” worksheet shown in Figure 18.20:

- Adjust the formatting for every cell, especially those that contain numbers, dates, and dollar amounts. Pay particular attention to fonts, font size, and the number of decimal places displayed.
- Enter totals, averages, and other formulas as needed for analytical purposes.
- Make sure that all columns align properly and that rows and columns are the proper width.
- Make headings and titles bigger and bolder so that they clearly define what type of data is in each row and column. Bold white type on a dark background is especially effective in column headings. Excel also uses this formatting to identify headings for sorting purposes.
- Turn on text wrapping and merge cells as needed, especially in headings.
- To unclutter the worksheet, choose File, Page Setup, click the Sheet tab, and clear the check mark from the Gridlines box.
- Use the Borders button to add grid elements as necessary. Notice the double underline above a row of totals and the thin single borders along the bottom of each row of data that help the reader follow along from left to right in each row.

- Use the Fill Color drop-down menu to add light shading throughout the data section. In this worksheet, a soft green shading was added to alternate rows to make long rows easier to follow.

- Freeze worksheet panes to make it easier to scroll through columns and rows without losing track of data.

- Add graphics as needed to give the worksheet a little zing.

Figure 18.20

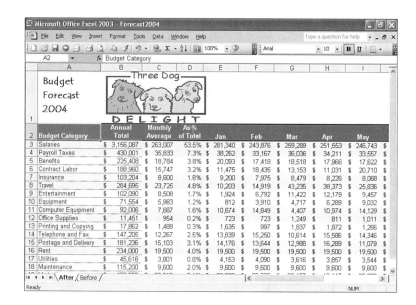

CHAPTER 19

Using Formulas and Functions

In this chapter

ENTERING AND EDITING FORMULAS

Formulas add intelligence to a workbook. Using formulas, you can manipulate values (text, numbers, or dates), perform simple or complex calculations, and display alternative results based on logical tests.

With the help of formulas, you can perform any of the following common tasks:

- Manage home finances by tracking expenses
- Simplify coursework in advanced math and statistics classes
- Create "what-if" worksheets to help make financial decisions such as purchasing a home or leasing a car
- Manipulate text in lists
- Improve your success in hobbies by calculating handicaps from your golf or bowling scores, tracking statistics for players in a fantasy league, and so on

A formula can be as simple as a reference to another cell, or it can go on for hundreds of characters, with as many as seven functions nested within other functions; regardless of its complexity, however, a formula must begin with an equal sign (=). If you start a formula with a plus sign (+) or minus sign (–), Excel adds an equal sign to the beginning of the formula.

Formulas consist of three basic building blocks: *operands* (the elements to be calculated), *operators*, and worksheet functions:

- **Operands**—The data to be calculated in a formula can include any combination of the following: *constant values* (numbers, text, or dates you enter directly in a cell or formula, for example); cell or range references; names that refer to cells or ranges; labels that define the intersection of a specific row and column, used in *natural language formulas*; or worksheet functions. When you use a cell or range reference in a formula, Excel substitutes the contents of that address just as if you had typed it in directly.

- **Operators**—Formulas can use any of six basic arithmetic operators: addition (+), subtraction (–), multiplication (*), division (/), percent (%), or exponentiation (^). You can also use comparison operators to compare two values and produce the logical result TRUE or FALSE. The list of comparison operators consists of equal to (=), greater than (>), less than (<), greater than or equal to (>=), less than or equal to (<=), and not equal to (<>). Use an ampersand (&) to combine, or concatenate, two pieces of text into a single value.

- **Worksheet functions**—Predefined formulas that allow you to perform calculations on worksheet data by entering a constant value or a cell or range reference as the *argument* that a named function transforms. You can use a worksheet function as the complete contents of a cell, or you can use a function as an operand in another formula.

→ For a detailed discussion of how to use natural language formulas, **see** "Using Natural-Language Formulas," **p. 602**.

→ For a full discussion of worksheet functions and arguments, **see** "Manipulating Data with Worksheet Functions," **p. 607**.

USING CELL REFERENCES IN FORMULAS

You can enter any cell or range address directly in a formula. These addresses are not case-sensitive; if you enter a2:b8 in a formula, Excel converts the entry to A2:B8 when you press Enter. You can also point and click to enter any cell or range reference.

One of the simplest Excel formulas is a direct reference to another cell. If you click in cell I24, for example, and enter the formula =A5, Excel displays the current value of cell A5 in cell I24. This technique is most commonly used with worksheets that contain input cells in which you type data that you'll use throughout the worksheet. For example, cell A5 might contain the current interest rate you plan to use as part of a series of loan and payment calculations. If you use custom views to display different portions of your worksheet, this technique lets you see the underlying assumptions at a glance.

To enter a reference to an entire row or column, use the row number or column letter as both halves of the range reference: B:B for column B, 2:2 for row 2. You can also use this syntax for multiple rows or columns—B:K includes every cell in columns B through K, just as 10:13 includes every cell in rows 10 through 13.

USING 3D REFERENCES TO CELLS ON OTHER WORKSHEETS

Sometimes it's helpful to use references to cells and ranges on other worksheets within the same workbook—known as *3D references*. For example, in a worksheet analyzing the economic output of Western Europe since World War II you might include a lookup table that lists industrial output statistics by country and by year on a separate sheet. Using the data from this table to create a series of calculations for each country makes your data accurate, yet keeps the main worksheet uncluttered. Likewise, in a loan worksheet you might want to perform all the data-entry and payment calculations on one sheet, but place the amortization table on its own sheet for display and printing.

To enter a 3D address, preface the cell address with the name of the sheet followed by an exclamation point. (If the sheet name contains a space, enclose it within single quote marks.) If you have a sheet named Amortization Table, for example, you can refer to the top-left cell of that sheet by entering ='Amortization Table'!A1 on any other sheet in the same book. You can also click the appropriate sheet tab and then select the desired cell or range of cells to add references to cells or ranges on other sheets. When you use this technique, Excel automatically enters the sheet name, exclamation point, and cell references.

CONTROLLING THE ORDER AND TIMING OF CALCULATIONS IN FORMULAS

If a formula contains more than one operator, Excel performs calculations in the following order (this list will be familiar to anyone who has taught or studied high school algebra):

- Percent (%)
- Exponentiation (^)
- Multiplication (*) and division (/)

- Addition (+) and subtraction (−)
- Concatenation (&)
- Comparison (=, <, >, <=, >=, <>)

To control the order of calculation, use parentheses; Excel evaluates all items within parentheses first, from the inside out, using the same order as listed previously. If a formula contains operators with the same precedence, such as addition and subtraction or any two comparison operators, Excel evaluates the operators from left to right. The number of levels of nested parentheses you can use within a single formula is not limited, although you are limited to seven levels of nesting for a function.

TIP FROM

EQ & Woody

> When you're trying to figure out the structure of a complex formula with many sets of nested parentheses, let Excel help. Click to make the cell that contains the formula active, and then use the arrow keys to move back and forth through the formula. As you move the insertion point to the right of a left parenthesis or to the left of a right parenthesis, Excel highlights its mate in bold. When you make any change to the formula, Excel displays each matched set of parentheses in a different color, making it easier for you to see which is which.

Normally, Excel recalculates all formulas every time you open or save a workbook. When you change a value in a cell, Excel recalculates all formulas that refer to that cell on any worksheet in the current workbook. Calculation takes place in the background, and on a typical uncomplicated worksheet, the process is essentially instantaneous.

You might want to control when Excel recalculates formulas in at least two circumstances:

- If your worksheet contains a very large number of complex formulas, recalculation can cause annoying pauses when you try to enter data. This is especially noticeable on computers with slow CPUs and low-memory configurations.
- When your formula contains cells that refer to themselves, as in some scientific and engineering formulas, Excel must repeat (iterate) the calculation—by default, each time you recalculate this type of formula, Excel goes through 100 iterations.

Unless you're working with one of these unusual worksheet configurations, you should leave recalculation settings alone. If you must turn off automatic recalculation, follow these steps:

1. Choose Tools, Options, and click the Calculation tab. You see the dialog box shown in Figure 19.1.

2. Choose the Manual option in the Calculation section. (The Automatic Except Tables option is for use with worksheets that include a relatively obscure Excel feature called data tables. If your worksheet includes a one- or two-variable data table, Excel recalculates the entire table every time you edit any cell in the worksheet; checking this option lets you recalculate the table manually.)

3. If you want Excel to recalculate the workbook only when you explicitly choose to do so, remove the check mark from the Recalculate Before Save check box.

4. Click OK to save the setting and return to your worksheet.

Figure 19.1
Adjust recalculation options with care. For most situations, the default automatic options are appropriate.

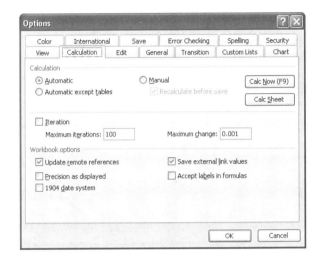

When you turn off automatic recalculation, you need to specify when Excel should recalculate formulas. To calculate all formulas in the current workbook, press F9. To recalculate only formulas in the current worksheet, press Shift+F9.

TIP FROM

> Are you using a worksheet that was prepared by someone else using an older version of Excel? Excel 97, which was very popular in its day and is still used by some diehards, includes several well-documented calculation bugs that can cause incorrect results under some circumstances. Beginning with Excel 2000, Microsoft made major changes to Excel's recalculation engine intended to fix these bugs. The first time you use Excel 2000, Excel 2002, or Excel 2003 to open a worksheet created in Excel 97, the program completely recalculates the worksheet. When you close the worksheet, you'll be asked whether you want to save your changes, even if you've done nothing more than look at the worksheet. We strongly recommend that you click Yes when you see this dialog box to avoid the possibility of being bitten by those old recalculation bugs.

ABSOLUTE VERSUS RELATIVE CELL REFERENCES

Normally, Excel interprets cell and range references within a formula as *relative references*. When you copy or move the formula, Excel automatically adjusts cell references to reflect their position relative to the new location. This capability is useful when you need to quickly copy a formula across several rows or columns. In the worksheet shown in Figure 19.2, for example, the formula in cell B7 totals the contents of column B. When you copy that formula across to the right, Excel assumes you want to total the numbers in the same relative position in each column, so it adjusts the formula accordingly, from =SUM(B2:B6) to =SUM(C2:C6), =SUM(D2:D6), and so on.

Figure 19.2
Relative cell addresses are automatically updated as they are copied from cell to cell.

	A	B	C	D	E	F
		B7	▼	*fx* =SUM(B2:B6)		
1	Year	North	South	East	West	Grand Total
2	2004	5,630	5,880	6,600	4,760	22,870
3	2003	6,120	4,810	6,610	6,790	24,330
4	2002	3,650	5,520	5,870	3,360	18,400
5	2001	6,590	6,470	5,120	4,660	22,840
6	2000	5,600	6,530	4,830	4,180	21,140
7	Total	27,590	29,210	29,030	23,750	109,580

→ The easiest way to copy a row or column of formulas is with the help of Excel's AutoFill feature; **see** "Automatically Filling In a Series of Data," **p. 634**.

In some cases, however, you want to copy a formula so that a cell or range reference in the copied formula points to the same cell or range as in the original. For example, if you enter the current interest rate in a cell near the top of a loan worksheet, you can refer to that cell in any formula that makes an interest-related calculation. To convert a relative reference to an *absolute reference*, which does not adjust when copied or moved, use dollar signs within the cell address. For example, when you copy the formula =B4*$A$5 to the right, Excel adjusts the first cell reference relative to its new location, but leaves the second reference unchanged: =B5*$A$5, =B6*$A$5, and so on.

TIP FROM

Ed & Woody

When you want to include a reference to an input cell in several formulas, you're generally better off using a named range, which is always an absolute reference. If cell A5 contains an interest rate, name the cell Interest_Rate and use that name in formulas— =B6*Interest_Rate, for example. If you move or copy the formula, the reference to the named range will not change.

You can mix and match relative and absolute addresses in a formula, or even in the same address. Using a dollar sign in front of the column portion of the address ($A5) tells Excel to change only the row reference when the formula is moved or copied; likewise, a dollar sign in front of the row (A$5) changes only the column portion of the cell reference. In Figure 19.3, for example, you could enter the formula =B2/$F2 in cell B10 and then copy the formula down and to the right. The *mixed reference* to $F2 adjusts the references so that they always point to the Grand Total formula in Column F for the correct row.

Use the F4 keyboard shortcut to switch quickly between relative, mixed, and absolute references in a formula. Click in the active cell to enable editing; then place the insertion point in a cell or range reference (either in the Formula bar or in the cell itself) and press F4 to convert a relative reference to absolute. Press F4 again to enter a mixed reference. Keep pressing F4 to cycle through all four variations for the selection.

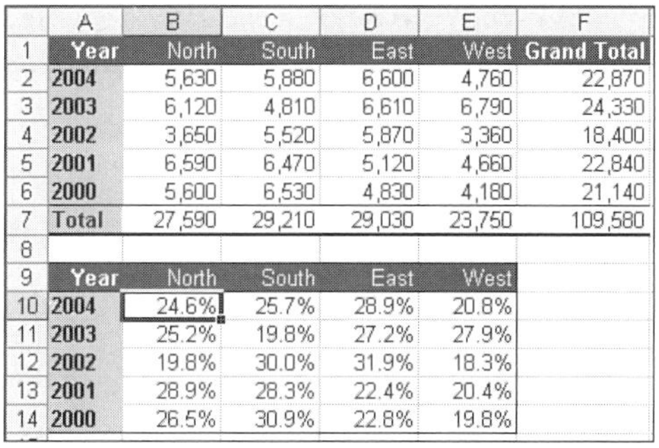

Figure 19.3
Formulas in the bottom table use mixed references; that allows each percentage to be divided by the result in the Grand Total column as you copy the formula down and across.

	A	B	C	D	E	F
1	Year	North	South	East	West	Grand Total
2	2004	5,630	5,880	6,600	4,760	22,870
3	2003	6,120	4,810	6,610	6,790	24,330
4	2002	3,650	5,520	5,870	3,360	18,400
5	2001	6,590	6,470	5,120	4,660	22,840
6	2000	5,600	6,530	4,830	4,180	21,140
7	Total	27,590	29,210	29,030	23,750	109,580
8						
9	Year	North	South	East	West	
10	2004	24.6%	25.7%	28.9%	20.8%	
11	2003	25.2%	19.8%	27.2%	27.9%	
12	2002	19.8%	30.0%	31.9%	18.3%	
13	2001	28.9%	28.3%	22.4%	20.4%	
14	2000	26.5%	30.9%	22.8%	19.8%	

PREVENTING FORMULAS FROM DISPLAYING IN THE FORMULA BAR

When you design a worksheet that you intend other people to use for data entry, you might want to hide the formulas themselves and show their results. This technique can be useful if your formula contains confidential or proprietary information that you don't want to share with others. It's also a useful way to prevent other users from attempting to edit a formula.

To prevent a formula from appearing in the Formula bar, you must first set a specific formatting option for that cell, and then turn on *protection* for the entire worksheet:

1. Right-click the cell that contains the formula you want to hide (to hide multiple formulas, select a range) and choose Format Cells from the shortcut menu.

2. Click the Protection tab and select the Hidden check box.

CAUTION

> Make sure you leave the check mark next to the Locked box as well. If you clear this box and check Hidden, anyone who can open the worksheet can replace the hidden formula with another formula or a constant value, undoing your attempt at protection.

3. Select other cells on the worksheet, if necessary, and adjust whether their contents are hidden or locked.

4. Choose Tools, Protection, Protect Sheet. Make sure the Protect worksheet and contents of locked cells check box is selected.

5. Click OK to close the Protect Sheet dialog box. Users will no longer be able to see hidden formulas in the Formula bar or in the cell itself, nor will they be able to edit formulas. The results of a hidden formula will display in the cell and on printouts.

→ For more details on how to prevent unauthorized changes to a workbook or worksheet, **see** "Protecting a Worksheet," **p. 545**.

USING ARRAY FORMULAS

Array formulas let you perform multiple calculations across a range of cells (an array) by using a function that normally works only on a single cell. To enter an array formula, construct the formula just as you normally would, and then press Ctrl+Shift+Enter. Excel enters the formula in curly braces to indicate that it is an array formula.

An array formula can return either a single result or multiple results. Array formulas are a common way to combine the SUM and IF functions, for example. Under normal circumstances, an IF function compares one cell with another cell or a constant value. An array formula, on the other hand, lets you compare a single value to every cell in an array and return a result you can work with, so you can compare a condition in an IF function and use all matching results in a SUM function, all in one formula.

 If you're having trouble editing an array formula, see "Editing an Array Formula" in the "Troubleshooting" section at the end of this chapter.

For example, say you keep a list of personal spending in an Excel worksheet with header information in row 1 and the first record in row 2, as in the example in Figure 19.4. If column B contains the amount of each purchase and column C contains the category you've assigned to that purchase, you can use an array formula to keep a running total of all purchases by category. Assuming column D is blank, click in cell D2 and type this formula: `=SUM(IF($C$2:C2=C2,$B$2:B2))`. Press Ctrl+Shift+Enter to enter it as an array formula, and then use AutoFill to copy the formula to the remainder of the cells in column D. (Excel automatically adds curly braces at the beginning and end to indicate that this is an array formula. Do not enter the curly braces yourself, or the array formula will fail.)

Figure 19.4
In this example, the array formula allows you to keep a running total of all invoice amounts by salesperson.

D13	▼	fx	{=SUM(IF($C$2:C13=C13,$B$2:B13))}							
	A	B	C	D	E	F	G	H	I	J
1	Trans_Num	Amount	Category	Running Total by Category						
2	1001	$54.23	Groceries	$54.23						
3	1002	$11.56	Entertainment	$11.56						
4	1003	$76.69	Dining Out	$76.69						
5	1004	$79.56	Gifts	$79.56						
6	1005	$63.67	Groceries	$117.90						
7	1006	$46.12	Interest	$46.12						
8	1007	$95.93	Dining Out	$172.62						
9	1008	$25.26	Automobile	$25.26						
10	1009	$1,532.48	Mortgage	$1,532.48						
11	1010	$20.00	Healthcare	$20.00						
12	1011	$57.52	Utilities	$57.52						
13	1012	$88.44	Groceries	$206.34						
14	1013	$76.84	Phone	$76.84						
15	1014	$5.99	Coffee	$5.99						
16	1015	$91.53	Computer	$91.53						
17	1016	$31.48	Dining Out	$204.10						
18	1017	$43.84	Utilities	$101.36						
19	1018	$81.47	Groceries	$287.81						
20	1019	$96.48	Automobile	$121.74						
21	1020	$10.94	Coffee	$16.93						
22	1021	$89.80	Computer	$181.33						

Sheet1 / Sheet2 / Sheet3 /

Ready   NUM

The first argument in this array formula compares each previous cell in column C to the contents of column C in the current row. The second argument returns a purchase amount to the SUM function for each cell in column C if the condition in the IF function is true. The copy of this formula in cell D13, for example, looks like this: `{=SUM(IF($C$2:C13=C13,$B$2:B13))}`. This formula looks in the range from C2 to C13 for cells that match the contents of C13—the category "Groceries." It finds matching contents in C2, C6, C13, and C19, so it adds the purchase amounts in B2, B6, and B13 to produce its result, a running total of all amounts up to and including row 13 for the Groceries category.

USING THE WATCH WINDOW TO MONITOR CALCULATIONS

Normally, as you enter and edit values in a worksheet, formulas that reference those values change as well. If the formula is close to the cells you're editing, you can see the results immediately. But it's more difficult to track formula results when the formulas are widely separated—on the same worksheet or even on linked sheets in a different workbook.

Thanks to a little-known Excel feature, you can keep an eye on the results of specific cells, even when those cells are on different sheets. Use the *Watch Window* to track a list of cells; this window floats above the current worksheet, as shown in Figure 19.5. With this window open, you don't have to continually switch between worksheets to monitor your work.

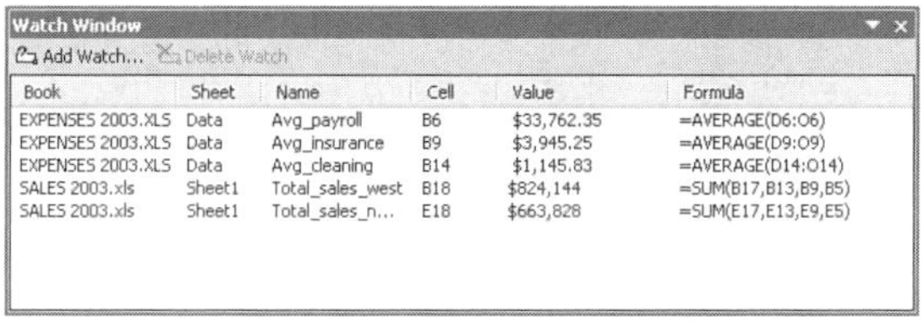

Figure 19.5
The Watch Window lets you track formula results across multiple workbooks. Range names make it easier to identify why you added a cell to the list.

To add a single cell to the Watch Window, select the cell, right-click, and choose Add Watch. (If the selected cell is already on the Watch list, the menu changes to Delete Watch.) As soon as you add a cell address, the Watch Window appears. The Watch Window is resizable. And just as with any list-based control, you can click a column heading to sort by that column, or resize columns by dragging the line between column headings.

In a strange programming decision, Microsoft chose to implement the Watch Window as a toolbar. If the Watch Window is currently hidden, you can make it visible by choosing View, Toolbars, Watch Window. Because it's a toolbar, you can also drag the window to any edge of the screen, where it will dock. (If you want to dock the Watch Window, try the bottom of the screen; that gives you the ability to view information in all columns and doesn't interfere with task panes.) You can't minimize the Watch Window; the down arrow to the left of the Close box in the upper-right corner leads to a basically useless Customize menu.

→ For more details about using and customizing Office toolbars, see "Customizing Toolbars," **p. 33**.

After the Watch Window is open, use the Add Watch button to select a group of cells and quickly add them to the list.

If you use the Watch Window a lot, we recommend that you define names for the cells you include on the Watch list. The Name column appears in the list, and a meaningful name like May_Purchases makes it much easier to identify the value you're tracking than a cell address like B10.

USING RANGE NAMES AND LABELS IN FORMULAS

Understanding the logic of a complex formula can be a challenge, even when you entered the formula yourself. This form of amnesia is especially common when you haven't opened a particular workbook in months or years.

To make it easier for you to understand a formula's purpose just by looking at it, you can enter cell references by using *named ranges*. This technique is especially useful with cells that contain constant values such as interest rates, loan amounts, sales tax rates, and discount formulas, because you can define a handful of input cells and then plug the contents of those cells into formulas on any worksheet within the workbook.

You can define range names explicitly, or you can enter cell references that are defined by the labels on rows and columns.

USING NATURAL-LANGUAGE FORMULAS

If your worksheet includes headings above columns and to the left of rows, Excel allows you to include cell references within formulas by referring to the intersections of rows and columns rather than entering addresses. Microsoft calls this feature a *natural-language formula*, because you describe data by using explanatory labels.

CAUTION

In this section, we explain exactly how to use natural-language formulas. That does *not* mean we recommend using this feature, which has the potential to introduce all sorts of errors into your workbooks. Before you even think about using natural-language formulas in an important worksheet, we recommend reading the section that follows this one, in which we reveal the hidden traps that can cause natural-language formulas to display the wrong result without any warning to you. Fortunately, this feature is disabled in Excel 2003, and you must specifically choose to enable it before using natural-language formulas.

The worksheet in Figure 19.6, for example, uses months of the year as column labels and expense categories as row labels. To refer to the value at the intersection of a row and column, enter the two labels (the order doesn't matter), separated by the *intersection operator*, a space. Thus, =Jan Utilities refers to cell D14, which is at the intersection of the column labeled Jan and the row labeled Utilities.

Figure 19.6
The natural-language formula shown here divides the contents of D14 by D11; using row and column labels makes understanding its purpose much easier.

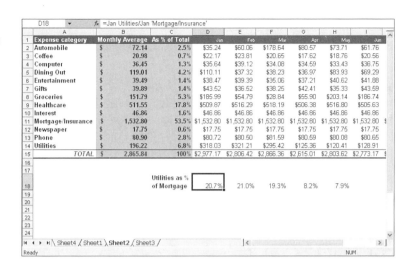

As Figure 19.6 illustrates, row and column labels can contain spaces. To use these labels in formulas, be sure to enclose them in single quotation marks ('). If you use double quotation marks, Excel's Formula AutoCorrect feature offers to correct the entry for you.

→ For a full description of how Formula AutoCorrect works, **see** "How Formula AutoCorrect Works," **p. 618**.

Although it's easy to use a natural-language formula, you should be aware of some quirks in this feature that can affect the results of formulas you enter:

- If your worksheet includes a label that appears to be a cell address (Q4 or FY99, for example), you must enclose the label in single quotation marks in your formula.

- Likewise, you must enclose a label in single quotation marks if it contains a space or a character that might be interpreted as an operator, such as a slash or plus sign: ='Jan 'Mortgage/Insurance', for example, identifies the cell at the intersection of the row labeled 'Mortgage/Insurance' and the column labeled Jan.

- If you move or copy a natural-language formula from one cell to another, the labels change to reflect the relative locations. In the previously shown Figure 19.6, for example, 'Jan Utilities' changes to 'Feb Utilities' if you copy the formula to the right. If you change a row or column label, any formulas that include that label change automatically.

- Numbers used as row or column labels must be between 1900 and 9999.

- If your row or column headings contain duplicate labels and you enter a natural-language formula that could refer to two or more cells, Excel generally uses the one above and to the left of the formula. If your worksheet includes two or more tables that contain the same headings, Excel displays the Identify Label dialog box and prompts you to pick the correct label.

- If you use only one heading for a label, Excel assumes you mean all cells in that row or column. In Figure 19.6, for example, the natural-language formula =Sum(Jan) would total all the entries in the column under the heading Jan.

19

LIMITATIONS OF NATURAL-LANGUAGE FORMULAS

Natural-language formulas have several serious limitations, some of them obscure, others quite common. Even Excel experts can be tripped up by the following gotchas:

- Be extremely careful if you modify a worksheet that contains natural-language formulas, especially by adding or deleting rows or columns at the edge of a range. Excel does not redefine existing natural-language formulas when you revise your worksheet, nor does it give you a clue your formulas could be wrong. In the previous Figure 19.6, for example, if you enter =SUM(Jan) at the bottom of the first column and then add a new row just above the formula, Excel doesn't include the new row in your total. Even carefully examining every formula won't reveal this problem, because the natural-language formula appears to reference every cell under the heading Jan. After adding rows or columns or otherwise modifying a sheet, you must delete and re-enter the formula for it to work properly.

- If you use more than 32,764 natural-language formulas, Excel displays an out-of-memory message and might stop responding altogether. Although that sounds like an absurd number, it's not difficult to reach if you define a single natural-language formula and use AutoFill to extend it across a dozen columns and down a lengthy list.

- Natural-language formulas produce unexpected results if you merge cells in the headings above a column. In that case, the heading refers only to the column at the left of the selected range, because the contents of merged cells are actually stored in the top-left cell of the merged range.

- Finally, natural-language formulas choke when you use any of the following reserved terms as a row or column label: Complex, Imaginary, Workday, Convert, LCM, Yield, Delta, Multinomial, Disc, Networkdays, Duration, Quotient, Effect, or Received.

Have we convinced you yet that using natural-language formulas is a very bad idea? If you're sufficiently frightened by the potential for data loss or miscalculation caused by natural-language formulas, you should leave it disabled. If you're willing to take the risk, choose Tools, Options, click the Calculation tab, and click the Accept Labels in Formulas check box. If you turn off labels in formulas, Excel substitutes absolute cell or range references for any existing natural-language formulas; as a result, your formulas continue to work.

USING NAMED RANGES IN FORMULAS

For absolute control over cell and range references in formulas, use a range name instead of its row-and-column address. Unlike natural-language formulas, which rely on row and column headings, you explicitly define range names. When you refer to a named range in a formula, the effect is the same as if you had entered the absolute address of the named cell or range.

Using named ranges makes it easier for anyone looking at a worksheet to understand exactly how a formula works. That comes in handy when you share a workbook with a coworker, or when you look at a worksheet you designed long ago. On an invoice worksheet, for example, the following formula is instantly understandable:

```
=Quantity_Ordered*Unit_Price*(1+Sales_Tax_Rate)
```

The easiest way to name a cell or a range is to use the Name box, located just to the left of the Formula bar (see Figure 19.7). Select the cell or range you want to name, and then click in the Name box to highlight the entire cell address. Type a legal name for the cell or range, and press Enter to store the range name in the workbook.

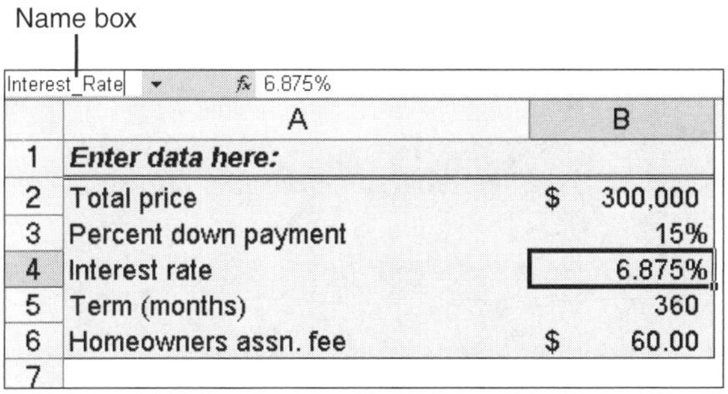

Figure 19.7
Select a range, and then click in the Name box and type the name you want to use for that range.

Name box

	A	B
1	**Enter data here:**	
2	Total price	$ 300,000
3	Percent down payment	15%
4	Interest rate	6.875%
5	Term (months)	360
6	Homeowners assn. fee	$ 60.00
7		

Interest_Rate ▾ *fx* 6.875%

The rules for assigning a *legal name* to a cell or a range are completely different from (and much more restrictive than) those that apply to the names of files and worksheet tabs:

- You can use a total of up to 255 characters in a range name.

TIP FROM
EQ & Woody

The point of range names is to make worksheets and formulas easier to understand. For clarity's sake, try to keep range names under 15 characters—the width of the Name drop-down list.

19

- The first character must be a letter or the underline character. You can't legally name a cell or range 4thQuarterBudget, but Q4Budget is acceptable.
- The remaining characters can be letters, numbers, periods, or the underline character. No other punctuation marks are allowed in range names. Spaces are forbidden; use the underscore character instead to form a legal name that's also easy to read.
- A cell or range name cannot be the same as a cell reference or a value, so you can't name a cell Q4, FY2001, or W2, nor can you use a single letter or enter a number without any punctuation or letters.

NOTE

When you name a cell or range, that name attaches itself to the absolute address you specify. If you move or copy a formula containing a reference to the named range, the reference continues to point to the original address rather than adjust to a new relative address. For this reason, you should use named ranges in formulas only when you want the formula to refer to an absolute address.

When constructing a formula, you can choose from a list of all defined names in the current workbook. After typing an equal sign or clicking in an existing formula, choose Insert, Name, Paste to display a dialog box that lists all defined names on all sheets in the current workbook. If the name you select is on a different worksheet, Excel automatically enters it by using the correct syntax, including the sheet name.

If you insert a cell or range reference in a formula by clicking a cell or range, Excel enters the defined name of the cell or range, if one exists. If you don't want this automatic substitution to take place, type the cell address directly, rather than clicking to enter it.

MANAGING RANGE NAMES

To manage names of cells or ranges stored in a workbook, choose Insert, Name. The Define Name dialog box (see Figure 19.8) lets you add a new name to an existing range, delete one or more range names, or change the reference for an existing name.

Figure 19.8
Use this list to manage named ranges in a workbook; to redefine an existing name, select a new cell or range in the Refers To box.

TIP FROM

EQ & Woody

You can assign more than one name to the same cell or range. Use different names if you intend to refer to the contents of a cell in several different formulas, and you want the names to match the purpose of each formula. For example, on a loan worksheet, you might refer to the same cell as AmountFinanced and AmountBorrowed, and then use the appropriate name in formulas on different parts of that worksheet.

→ You can also use the Go To Special dialog box to view and locate range names, a topic we cover in "Selecting Ranges of Data with the Go To Dialog Box," **p. 523**.

It's relatively easy to change the location that a cell or range name refers to: Choose Insert, Name, Define to open the Define Name dialog box, and then select the cell or range name from the Names in Workbook list. Select the contents of the Refers To box and click in the worksheet to select the new cell or range. When you use this technique, any worksheet formulas that refer to the range name automatically use the new location you defined.

Surprisingly, however, it's impossible to change a defined name in one step. Instead, you have to create a new name for an existing range, and then delete the old name. Open the Define Names dialog box, select the existing name, enter a new name in the Names in

Workbook box, and click the Add button. Then select the old name and click the Delete button.

 If some of the formulas in your workbook display error messages after you change or delete a range name, see "Checking Formulas Before Deleting Range Names" in the "Troubleshooting" section at the end of this chapter.

MANIPULATING DATA WITH WORKSHEET FUNCTIONS

Worksheet functions handle a broad array of tasks, from simple arithmetic to complex financial calculations and intricate statistical tests. Regardless of its complexity, every function consists of two parts: the function name and its *arguments*—the specific values the function uses to calculate a result. The *syntax* of a function defines what type of arguments it uses: text, numbers, dates, and logical values, for example. In most cases, you can substitute a cell or range address or another formula or function as an argument, as long as the data evaluates to the required data type. Some arguments are required, and others are optional. Arguments always appear to the right of the function name, inside parentheses; Excel uses commas to separate multiple arguments.

The following examples illustrate the syntax of some commonly used functions. Bold type means the argument is required. An ellipsis (…) means that the function accepts an unlimited number of arguments.

```
=TODAY()
=AVERAGE(number1,number2,...)
=IPMT(rate,per,nper,pv,fv,type)
```

TODAY() is one of the simplest of all worksheet functions. Whenever you open, save, or otherwise recalculate a worksheet that contains this function, Excel updates the value of the cell that contains this formula to display the current date, as stored in your computer's clock chip. This function is extremely common in formulas that calculate elapsed time, such as the number of days that have passed since you mailed an invoice or received a payment.

AVERAGE accepts up to 30 arguments (but requires only 1) and calculates the arithmetic mean of all values in the list, ignoring text and logical values. Although you can enter constant values in this formula, it's most commonly used to calculate the average of a range of numbers, such as monthly sales or budget results. If you calculate a year's worth of monthly expenditures in cells B20 through M20, for example, =AVERAGE(B20:M20) displays the average of the 12 monthly totals.

To calculate the amount of interest you pay each month on a mortgage, use the IPMT function. As the syntax description shows, you must supply a minimum of four values as arguments. This function requires (in order) the interest rate per period (rate), the specific payment period for which you want to calculate interest (per, a number between 1 and nper), the number of payment periods (nper), and the present value (pv, the amount of the loan). The final two arguments—future value (fv) and the type of loan (type)—are optional. Here, too, you're more likely to include a reference to a cell than the actual number in a formula that uses this function.

19

NOTE

> Although the Formula bar and Excel's help screens always display function names in capital letters, the names are not case sensitive. Use any combination of capital and lowercase characters; when you enter the formula, Excel converts the function's name to capitals.

ENTERING ERROR-FREE FORMULAS

For some functions, especially those with only a single argument, the easiest course of action is often to type them into a cell directly, using the mouse to select the cell or range address of any arguments.

When you begin to enter a new function or edit an existing one, Excel displays a ScreenTip just below the Formula bar. This yellow box displays all required arguments in bold type, with optional arguments in lighter type. After you enter an argument, the argument name serves as a link—click it to select the entire argument.

For functions with multiple arguments, however, especially those where you're not certain of the exact syntax, a fill-in-the-blanks form often ensures the proper results. The Insert Function dialog box allows you to enter any function and all its arguments quickly and accurately, by using a series of dialog boxes. The Insert Function dialog box is an expert Excel user's best friend: It makes errors nearly impossible, it provides constant feedback as you build a formula, and it includes hooks to surprisingly advanced help, including useful examples of some complex formulas.

You can use the Insert Function dialog box to build a function from scratch: You choose a function from a categorized list and then fill in the arguments using input boxes. Or you can enter part or all of the function and its arguments and use the Insert Function dialog box to edit specific arguments or debug a formula that isn't working as you expect.

To build a function from scratch, follow these steps:

1. Click to select the cell in which you want to add a formula, and then click the Insert Function button (the fx just to the left of the Formula bar). Excel inserts an equal sign in the Formula bar, positions the insertion point to its right, and opens the Insert Function dialog box.

NOTE

> When you type an equal sign in a cell or the Formula bar, Excel replaces the Name box (just to the left of the Formula bar) with the Function box. When you first use Excel, this list includes the 10 most popular functions; as you use the Insert Function dialog box, Excel replaces the entries on this list with the 10 functions you've used most recently. The last function you used is always the top selection in the Function box.

2. If the name of the function you want to use appears in the Select a Function box, click to select it. If the function you want to use is not on the Most Recently Used list,

choose a category. If you're not certain of the exact name of the function, enter a brief description or keyword in the Search for a Function box and click the Go button (see Figure 19.9).

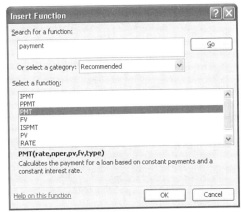

Figure 19.9

3. The text at the bottom of the Insert Function dialog box offers a brief explanation of the selected function and its syntax (click the Help on This Function link for a more detailed explanation). When you've selected the correct function, click OK. Excel adds the function to the Formula bar and opens a new dialog box with separate input boxes for each argument, as shown in Figure 19.10.

4. Click within the first argument box and fill in the required data. Note that the help text at the bottom of the dialog box is specific to the argument you're currently working with, and the data type required for each argument appears to the right of the input box.

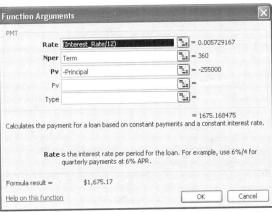

Figure 19.10

- Type text, numbers, and other constants directly in the input box.

- To add cell references by pointing and clicking, first click the Collapse Dialog button (at the right side of each argument input box) to roll most of the Insert Function dialog box up and out of the way. Next, select the cell or range to use for the selected argument, and then click the Collapse Dialog button again to continue.

- To use a function as an argument within another function, click to position the insertion point within the box for that argument and then select the function from the Function box to the left of the Formula bar. (See "Extra Credit: Nesting Functions Within Functions" at the end of this chapter for more details.)

- When entering constant values, you can include the percent operator (%) and minus signs (–) with numeric data. Look to the right of the input box to see the current value of each argument you enter. If the data is not of the type required by the argument, Excel displays the word Invalid to the right of the input box.

5. Repeat step 4 for other required and optional arguments. Look to the right of the equal sign for each argument to see its current value, using the data you've entered so far. To see the result of the formula itself, look at the text along the bottom of the dialog box.

6. After entering all required arguments, click OK to paste the complete function into the current cell, or click Cancel to start over.

TIP FROM

EQ & Woody

> *Debugging* a formula can be frustrating, especially when working with complex formulas containing several nested functions. Here's a backup strategy that allows you to freely experiment with formulas and functions without fear of losing your work or damaging a worksheet. Before editing a formula, remove the equal sign from the beginning of the formula and press Enter; then copy the formula to another cell. Without the equal sign, Excel treats the cell's contents as plain text and copies the formula exactly as it appears, with no adjustments. If your experiments are unsuccessful, copy the backed-up formula to the original cell and then restore the equal sign.

To use the Insert Function dialog box as a proofreading and reference tool, begin constructing your formula as usual, starting with an equal sign and the function name. After entering the first parenthesis, click the Insert Function button to open the Insert Function dialog box with the current function selected. Any arguments you've already entered will be in the dialog box as soon as it opens.

TOTALING ROWS AND COLUMNS AUTOMATICALLY

The most commonly used functions are also the easiest to enter. To insert a formula that adds a column or row of numbers automatically, click in a blank cell beneath any column of numbers (or at the end of a row of numbers), and then click the AutoSum button. Excel inserts the SUM function with the argument already filled in and selected. Adjust the selected range, if necessary, and then click the Enter box in the Formula bar or press Enter to store the formula in the active cell.

Use the drop-down arrow to the right of the AutoSum button to select the AVERAGE, COUNT, MAX, or MIN functions for the adjacent row or column. Select the More Functions option from the bottom of the list to open the Insert Function dialog box with the adjacent row or column selected as the default argument.

Two quirks in AutoSum are worth noting:

- First, if the range above or to the left of the cell containing the SUM formulas contains any blank cells, the range to be totaled stops there.

- Second, when the cell that holds the SUM function is at the end of a row and a column, AutoSum always selects the column.

In either case, the moral is the same: When using AutoSum, always check to be certain that the correct range is selected.

To automatically add totals for several adjacent rows or columns, select the cells directly beneath the columns or to the right of the rows and then choose an AutoSum function. Excel plugs in the selected formula for each row or column, just as if you had added each one individually. When you use the AutoSum button this way, you do not see a confirmation dialog box.

If you use AutoSum below an AutoFiltered list, the resulting formula uses the SUBTOTAL function instead. This syntax allows you to see a correct sum using only the filtered data; if you used the SUM function, the result would show all cells, including those hidden by the filter.

TIP FROM

EQ & Woody

> You don't need to enter a formula to make quick calculations. When you select two or more numbers in a worksheet, Excel displays a summary of the selected cells in the status bar along the bottom of the worksheet window. The default calculation is a simple total; look at the right side of the status bar and you'll see SUM=, followed by the total of the selected cells. Right-click anywhere on the status bar to display a shortcut menu that lets you choose a different calculation, including Average, Max, Min, Count (which counts the number of selected cells), and Count Nums (which counts only the number of selected cells that contain numbers). Use this feature in conjunction with selecting a column in a list, for example, to quickly spot the largest and smallest values in that field.

PUTTING WORKSHEET FUNCTIONS TO USE

Excel has over 300 functions, including those available in various add-ins. The following sections list some of the tasks you can accomplish by using functions in each category.

CALCULATING FINANCIAL FORMULAS

Excel includes a large number of financial functions—50 in all—covering everything from simple household budget problems, such as calculating a house payment, to complex tasks such as figuring the bond-equivalent yield for a U.S. Treasury bill (TBILLEQ) or the yield of a security that has an odd last period (ODDLYIELD).

Most of the more advanced financial functions, including those that calculate depreciation schedules (DB, DDB, SLN, SYD, and VDB) and internal rates of return (IRR, MIRR) are useful only if you have enough of an accounting or finance background to understand the underlying principles. However, a number of general-purpose functions are useful for a wide variety of calculations involving loans and investments. You can calculate the periodic payment for a loan or annuity using PMT, figure the net present value of an investment or loan with NPV, determine the interest and principal portion of a periodic payment with IPMT and PPMT, and calculate the future value of an investment (FV). These functions, and several more that cover the same ground, use some or all of the following common arguments:

- Future value (fv) is the amount that an investment or loan will be worth after all payments have been made. When dealing with investments, fv is usually positive; in the case of loans, fv is typically 0.

19

- Number of periods (nper) is the total number of payments or periods of an investment. Make sure the unit of measurement is consistent with the payment period; if you pay a 30-year mortgage monthly, nper is equal to 360 (30*12).

- Payment (pmt) is the amount paid periodically to an investment or loan. It cannot change over the life of the investment or loan. Typically, pmt includes principal and interest but no other fees or taxes. For a loan or investment, in which you are the one making payments, you typically enter pmt as a negative number; if you receive dividends or other payments (in other words, if you're the bank), pmt is generally a positive number.

- Present value (pv) is the value of an investment or loan at the beginning of the investment period. When you are the borrower, the present value of a loan is the principal amount that is borrowed, expressed as a negative number.

- Rate (rate) is the interest rate or discount rate for a loan or investment. Pay particular attention that nper and rate use the same scale as pmt. If you make monthly payments on a 30-year loan at 7.5% annual interest, use 7.5%/12 for rate (to convert the annual rate to a monthly rate, such as the payments) and 30*12 for nper (360, the number of monthly payments in a 30-year loan).

- Type (type) is the interval at which payments are made during the payment period, such as at the beginning of a month or the end of the month. In interest rate calculations over a long period of time, the difference can be substantial.

WORKING WITH DATE AND TIME FUNCTIONS

Use date and time functions for simple tasks, such as displaying today's date or the day of the week for a given date. If you run an organization whose members pay dues annually on their birthday, how do you create a list of birthdays sorted by month? If you sort by birthday, you'll end up with a list that's sorted by the members' ages. To sort properly, you'll have to create a column in which each row contains a formula that uses the MONTH function to convert a date to a month.

NOTE

> There is a profound difference between using a function to convert a value and using cell formats to change the display of a value. Functions return a different value from the value you use as an argument; when you change formats, on the other hand, the underlying value stored in the cell remains exactly the same.

→ For an overview of how Excel enters and manipulates dates as serial values, **see** "Setting Date and Time Formats" **p. 568**.

Date functions can help you perform even the most sophisticated calculations. For example, U.S. tax laws require that participants in some types of retirement accounts begin withdrawing funds and paying taxes as soon as they turn 70 1/2 years old. To calculate the first day of the month after a person reaches that age, enter the account holder's birthday in a cell named Birth_date, and then use the following formula to calculate the retirement date:

```
=DATE(YEAR(Birth_date)+70,MONTH(Birth_date)+7,1)
```

Table 19.1 lists the most useful date and time functions, along with examples of how to use each one.

TABLE 19.1   DATE AND TIME FUNCTIONS

Function Name	Description	How to Use It
TODAY(), NOW()	Return the current date or time as a serial value	No argument required; enter =NOW() to plug the current date and time into a cell; use TODAY() to enter only the current date.
YEAR(serial_number) MONTH(serial_number) DAY(serial_number)	Convert a serial date value to its year, month, or date	Useful when you need to separate the components of a date entered in a cell to create a list of all birthdays for all employees and sort it by month, for example.
WEEKDAY(serial_number)	Convert a serial date value to a weekday	Useful in formulas in which you want to calculate paydays or due dates. The result is a number from 1 (Sunday) to 7 (Saturday). Format the result using the "ddd" or "dddd" format to see the results as a day of the week.
HOUR(serial_number) MINUTE(serial_number) SECOND(serial_number)	Convert a serial date value to its hour, minute, or second	Useful when you need to separate the components of a time entered in a cell—to create a list of all starting times for a golf tournament, for example, grouped by hour.

19

You'll find an interesting collection of special-purpose date and time formats in the Analysis ToolPak, an Excel add-in. EOMONTH(TODAY(),0), for example, returns the last day of the current month—a useful calculation when working with payments that are due on the last day of the month. (Change the second argument to 1 to return the last day of next month, or -1 for the previous month.) Other date/time functions in the Analysis ToolPak include WORK-DAYS and NETWORKDAYS, which are useful when you're calculating project timelines. To install the Analysis ToolPak, choose Tools, Add-Ins, and select the Analysis ToolPak check box.

PERFORMING STATISTICAL ANALYSES

Excel includes a huge number of statistical functions, including such widely used measures as standard deviation (STDEV), normal distribution (NORMDIST), Chi test (CHITEST), and Student's t-test (TTEST). As with the financial functions, these are most useful to students and teachers in high-level mathematics classes (or people who have a firm grounding in the principles of statistical analysis after having completed such a class), but a handful are applicable to users with a general business background.

Excel includes not one but three functions for working with a set of values. AVERAGE returns the arithmetic mean (the total of all values, divided by the number of entries in the list); MEDIAN returns the value in the middle of the list; and MODE returns the value that occurs most frequently. Depending on the distribution of data in a sample, any one of these three functions might be more or less appropriate.

MIN, MAX, and COUNT are straightforward functions that calculate the minimum, maximum, and number of entries in a list. These functions (and several others) have variations that end in the letter A—MINA, MAXA, and COUNTA. Use COUNTA, for example, when you want to work with not just numeric values in a list, but all arguments, including text and those that evaluate to a logical result such as TRUE or FALSE.

USING DATABASE FUNCTIONS

Excel includes a dozen functions you can incorporate into formulas to analyze information in a list. These functions work with the same techniques as advanced *filters*—for each function, you define a criteria range, specify the location of a list, and select a column on which to perform calculations.

→ For details on how to use advanced filters in Excel lists, **see** "Finding and Filtering Data in a List," **p. 641**.

To work with any of these functions, choose Insert, Function, or click the Insert Function button on the Standard toolbar. In the Insert Function dialog box, select Database from the Function Category list. Choose any entry from the list on the right to see a brief description in the same dialog box, or click the Help button for step-by-step instructions on how to use the function and enter parameters.

Note that all 12 of these functions begin with the letter D (for *database*). All the D-functions take three arguments:

- **DATABASE**—The first argument is the range that contains your list; it must include the header row that contains column labels.

- **FIELD**—The second argument is the label over the column you want to summarize.

- **CRITERIA**—The final argument is the range that contains a condition you specify.

Use these functions to analyze whether values in a list meet specific criteria. For example, in a list that contains historical weather information organized by date, you can count all the rows in which the total rainfall for that period is greater than 0.1 inches.

PERFORMING MATHEMATICAL OPERATIONS

Given Excel's extensive mathematical capabilities, it's only natural that the list of worksheet functions includes 60 mathematical functions. Several handle advanced trigonometry calculations (COS, TAN, SIN, ACOS, ATAN, and ASIN, for example), and the PI function displays the value of Pi to 15 decimal places.

Use the ROUND and TRUNC functions to transform values for use in calculations. For example, if cell C16 contains the value 23.5674, use =ROUND(C16,2) to convert that value to 23.57; the second argument defines the number of decimal places. Use =TRUNC(C16,2) to lop off all digits beyond the number of decimal places you specify in the second argument. Because this function truncates the value rather than rounding it, the result is 23.56 rather than 23.57.

NOTE

> Although you can use cell formats to change the way information is displayed in a cell, these formats don't change the underlying information stored in the cell. Use the ROUND and TRUNC functions when you want to perform calculations based on a specific level of precision.

The MOD function divides one value by another and returns a remainder. One interesting use of this formula is to determine whether a given year is a leap year. If cell A1 contains the year to be tested, enter this formula:

```
=IF(OR(MOD(A1,400)=0,AND(MOD(A1,4)=0,MOD(A1,100)<>0)),"Leap Year", "Not a Leap
➥Year")
```

This tricky formula uses the logical operators IF, OR, and AND to test whether cell A1 is divisible by 400 or is both divisible by 4 and not divisible by 100. If either condition is true, it returns the text "Leap Year"; otherwise, it returns the text "Not a Leap Year."

To display the *absolute value* of a formula, so the result is always a positive number, use the ABS function. =ABS(A14-A16), for example, always returns the difference between the values in these two cells as a positive number, even if A16 is larger than A14.

One of the most interesting functions in this group is SUMIF(range,criteria,sum_range); use it to total a range of numbers based on whether they meet criteria you define. For example, if the range B2:B20 contains the names of club members and the range C2:C20 contains individual donations in an annual fund-raising drive, use the following formula to calculate the total for all donations that were solicited by Bianca Bott:

```
=SUMIF(B2:B20,"Bianca Bott",C2:C20)
```

COMBINING AND SEPARATING TEXT VALUES

It's easy to think of functions in mathematical terms, but some of the most useful functions work strictly with text. You can use text functions to pull specific information from a single *text value*, split a text value into multiple cells, combine text values into a single string, or convert one type of data (such as a number or date) into text, using a specific format.

When you want to combine (or *concatenate*) the text from two cells, use an ampersand. The following formula adds a space between the values in two adjacent cells:

```
=A1&" "&A2
```

19

For more sophisticated manipulation of strings of text, use any of Excel's 27 text and data functions. These functions are especially useful when you've imported text from another program or file. Simple text functions let you convert text from all capitals to lowercase letters (and vice versa) or convert a date value to text in a specific format. The following formula, for example, combines three functions to pull out just the last name from a complete name in cell A17:

```
=RIGHT(A17,LEN(A17)-FIND(" ",A17))
```

The task isn't as easy as it might first appear. Because the last name can be any length (Bott or Leonhard, for example), you first need to calculate the correct number of characters. For starters, use the FIND function to locate the space separating the first and last names. If the first name contains five letters, the formula FIND(" ",A17) returns the value 6. Next, use the LEN function to determine the total length of the name; by subtracting the value determined in the first step from this value, you can determine the exact length of the last name. Finally, use the RIGHT function to extract that number of characters from the input cell (A17), starting at the right side.

Table 19.2 lists the most useful text functions.

TABLE 19.2 COMMON TEXT FUNCTIONS

Function Name	Description	How to Use It
CONCATENATE(text1, text2,...)	Combine two or more text items	Generally, an ampersand (&) is easier.
UPPER(text), LOWER(text), PROPER (text)	Convert case of text, to all capitals, all lowercase letters, or initial capitals	=PROPER('pearson technology group') changes the first letter of each word to a capital letter— in this case, Pearson Technology Group.
FIND(find_text, within_text,start_num) SEARCH(find_text, within_text,start_num)	Find text in a cell	FIND is case-sensitive; SEARCH allows wildcard characters.
LEFT(text, num_chars) RIGHT(text, num_chars) MID(text,start_num, num_chars)	Extract text from a cell	Use with FIND and SEARCH to extract part of a text string for example, a part number from a lengthy product code.
TEXT(value,format _text) FIXED(number, decimals, no_commas) DOLLAR(number, decimals)	Convert number to text	For the TEXT function, specify any number format (except General) from the Category box on the Number tab in the Format Cells dialog box. Be sure to enclose the format in quotation marks: =TEXT(TODAY(), "mmmm d,yyyy".

19

Function Name	Description	How to Use It
CLEAN()	Remove unwanted	TRIM removes extra spaces from
TRIM()	characters from text	imported text, and CLEAN removes unprintable characters, such as might be found at the top or bottom of a file that contains formatting information that Excel can't interpret.

 If you have trouble concatenating two values, see "Converting Values to Text Before Concatenating" in the "Troubleshooting" section at the end of this chapter.

USING LOGICAL AND INFORMATION FUNCTIONS

Excel includes six *comparison functions*, which you can use to compare two values and define actions based on the comparison. Far and away the most popular and useful logical function is *IF*. The following is the syntax of the IF function:

=IF(**logical_test**,value_if_true,value_if_false)

Excel also includes 18 *information functions*, which give you information about cells, worksheets, and your system itself. For the most part, you'll use these functions to build error-handling and data-validation routines into a worksheet. Nine of these functions belong in a subgroup called the IS functions: ISTEXT, ISERROR, ISNUMBER, and so on.

By combining the IF function and the ISERROR function, you can avoid seeing error codes in a worksheet. The formula =IF(ISERROR(A5/A8)," ",A5/A8), for example, tests the value of the formula A5/A8 before displaying a result. If A8 is equal to 0, Excel displays nothing in the cell rather than the annoying #DIV/0! error message; if the value of A8 is other than 0 and the formula returns a valid result rather than an error message, Excel displays that result.

TIP FROM

> In many cases, *conditional formatting* is a better way to suppress error messages than using formulas. Select the cell in which you want to suppress error messages–A9, for instance–then choose Format, Conditional Formatting. In the Conditional Formatting dialog box, click the Condition 1 drop-down list and choose Formula Is. In the edit box to the right, enter the formula =ISERROR(A9). Next, click the Format button, and in the Format Cells dialog box, click the Color drop-down list and choose the white square. Click OK to close the Format Cells dialog box and click OK to close the Condition Formatting dialog box. Now, any error messages in that cell will appear as white text on a white background and will be invisible.

→ For a detailed discussion of conditional formatting, **see** "Using Conditional Formatting to Identify Key Values," **p. 584**.

TROUBLESHOOTING FORMULAS

The more complex the formula, the more likely you are to need time to get it working properly. Excel 2003 includes a variety of tools you can use to troubleshoot errors in formulas and in worksheets. This section discusses the most useful options.

HOW FORMULA AUTOCORRECT WORKS

Under most circumstances, Excel won't let you enter a formula using incorrect syntax. If you make one of many common mistakes in formula syntax or punctuation, Excel offers to correct the mistake for you, and generally the correction is appropriate. This feature, called Formula AutoCorrect, can detect and repair any of the following errors:

- Unmatched parentheses, curly braces, or single or double quotation marks.

- Reversed cell references (14C instead of C14, for example) or comparison operators (=< instead of <=).

- Extra operators, such as an equal sign or plus sign, at the beginning or end of a formula.

- Extra spaces in cell addresses (A 14 instead of A14), between operands, or between a function name and its arguments.

- Extra decimal points or operators—in general, Excel uses the decimal point or operator farthest to the left and removes all others, so 234.56.78 becomes 234.5678, and =23*/34 becomes =23*34.

- Incorrect range identifiers, such as a semicolon or an extra colon between the column and row identifiers.

- Implied multiplication—if you omit the multiplication sign and enter 2(A14+B14), for example, or use an x instead, Excel adds the correct sign.

RESOLVING COMMON ERROR MESSAGES

All Excel error messages begin with a number sign (#); in all, you might see any of seven possible error codes. To remove the error message and display the results you expect, you have to fix the problem either by editing the formula or changing the contents of a cell to which the formula refers.

Excel 2003 offers one innovative tool that helps identify possible errors and quickly resolve them. If the cell in question has triggered an error message, you see a small green triangle in the upper-left corner of the cell. Click to select that cell and a Smart Tag with a yellow exclamation point appears. Click that Smart Tag to display a menu like the one shown in Figure 19.11.

The top line in the Smart Tag menu displays the name of the error and is not clickable. Use additional menu choices to find possible causes and solutions for the error.

Table 19.3 lists the seven error codes you're likely to see when an Excel formula isn't working properly, along with suggested troubleshooting steps.

Figure 19.11
Click the Smart Tag to find clues to the cause of an error message and possible solutions.

TABLE 19.3   COMMON FORMULA ERROR CODES

Error Code Displayed	What It Means	Suggested Troubleshooting Steps
`#DIV/0!`	Formula is tr ying to divide by a zero value or a blank cell.	Check the divisor in your formula and make sure it does not refer to a balnk cell. You might want to add an error-handling `=IF()` routine or conditional format to the cell, as described earlier in this chapter.
`#N/A`	Formula does not have a valid value for argument passed.	`#N/A` means "No value is available." Check to see whether you have problems with `LOOKUP` functions. You can also manually enter the `#N/A` value in cells in which a value is temporarily unavailable, to prevent `#DIV/0!` errors.
`#NAME?`	Formula contains text that is neither a valid function nor a defined name on the active worksheet.	You've probably misspelled a function name or a range name. Check the formula carefully. In a natural-language formula, this error means Excel cannot identify one or both labels.
`#NULL!`	Refers to intersection of two areas that don't intersect.	You're trying to calculate a formula by using labels for a column and row that have no common cells. Choose new labels for the row or column or both.
`#NUM!`	Value is too large, too small, imaginary, or not found.	Excel can handle numbers as large as 10^{308} or as small as 10^{-308}. This error usually means you've used a function incorrectly—for example, calculating the square root of a negative number.
`#REF!`	Formula contains a reference that is not valid.	Did you delete a cell or range originally referred to in the formula? If so, you see this error code in the formula as well.

continues

19

TABLE 19.3 CONTINUED		
Error Code Displayed	**What It Means**	**Suggested Troubleshooting Steps**
#VALUE!	Formula contains an argument of the wrong type.	You've probably mixed two incompatible data types in one formula— trying to add text with a number, for example. Check the formula again.

CHECKING FOR ERRORS IN A WORKSHEET

As noted in the previous section, Excel tracks formula errors automatically as you work, displaying a green triangle in the upper-left corner of any cell that contains an error. You can also check for errors on a sheet manually, by choosing Tools, Error Checking. When you choose this option, Excel finds the first error (on the current sheet only) and displays a dialog box like the one shown in Figure 19.12. Use the Previous and Next buttons to highlight additional errors on the sheet.

Figure 19.12
Click the Show Calculation Steps button to step through each operation and debug a complex formula.

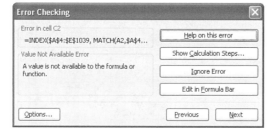

19

If the error is harmless and you don't want Excel to nag you about it any further, click the Ignore Error button. For simple errors where the fix is immediately obvious (a typographical error or a misplaced divisor, for instance), click the Edit in Formula Bar button to make the change directly, without closing the Error Checking dialog box.

For complex formulas, in which an error can be difficult to track down, click the Show Calculation Steps button. This button opens the Evaluate Formula dialog box (see Figure 19.13), which lets you drill down into a formula to find and fix the problem.

The initial view shows each element in the formula, evaluated to the result just before the error. Click the Evaluate button to step through the error. Keep clicking and you'll eventually return to the formula as entered, where you can walk through each element of the formula, moving from left to right. With each click, Excel evaluates another part of the formula.

For formulas that refer to other formulas in other cells, click the Step In button to follow the chain of references through as many steps as it takes to find the error.

Figure 19.13
Clicking the Step In button allows you to drill down into a formula in search of errors from another cell.

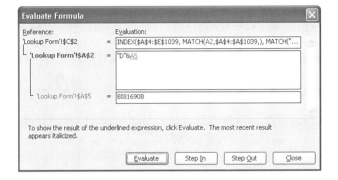

TIP FROM

EQ & Woody

If you inherit a worksheet that someone else has developed and you want to quickly check it for errors, take this precautionary step: Open the Error Checking dialog box, click the Options button, and click the Reset Ignored Errors button. This option ensures that you'll see all possible errors that Excel can detect, even if a previous user hid the error indicators.

Click the Options button on the Error Checking dialog box to specify which errors Excel should look for. For instance, Excel normally flags dates with two-digit years as errors (because of possible date arithmetic problems) and also calls out any formula that is inconsistent with other formulas in the same row or column. If you get tired of false alarms, clear any of the check boxes shown in Figure 19.14.

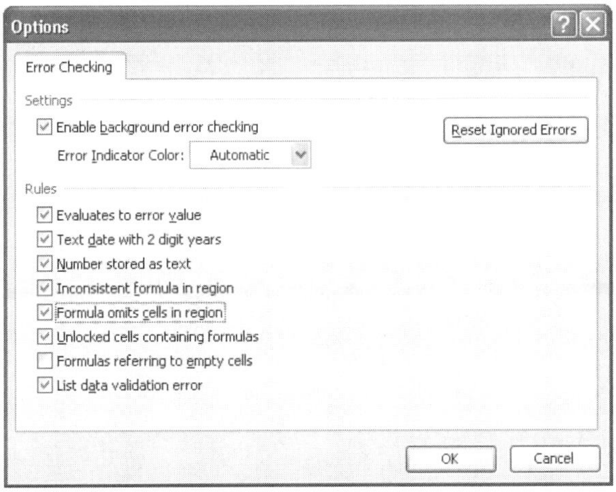

Figure 19.14
Use these options to prevent Excel from checking for certain types of errors.

Excel dutifully catches many common types of formula errors as soon as you press Enter. For instance, if you click in cell E8 and enter the formula =SUM(E1:E7)/E8, Excel will warn you that you're about to create a *circular reference*, in which one part of your formula refers to itself. Because the act of calculating the formula changes one of the values in the formula, you'll get a different result each time you calculate a formula that contains a circular reference. More subtle forms of circular references incorporate intermediate calculations that depend on the value in the current cell. For instance, if a formula in A8 refers to a value in E8, adding a reference to A8 into the formula in E8 will create a circular reference.

If you inadvertently create a circular reference, you can use the Circular Reference toolbar (View, Toolbars, Circular Reference) to identify the error and fix it. The drop-down list in this toolbar lists all such errors in the current sheet.

NOTE

> Some esoteric scientific calculations rely on circular references. In this case, you can specify the number of *iterations* you want to use when recalculating the formula. For a more detailed explanation, see the "Allow or correct a circular reference" Help topic.

USING THE RANGE FINDER TO LOCATE PARTS OF A FORMULA

When a cell that contains a summary formula doesn't display the correct result, the first place to look is at the cell and range references in that formula. If you've added new rows or columns, it's possible that the formula references the old range and doesn't include the new cells.

To match cell references in any formula with the actual worksheet cells, use Excel's Range Finder. When you select any cell that contains a formula and make it available for editing, Excel highlights each cell or range reference in that formula with a different color, and then adds an identically color-coded outline around the cells to which the range refers.

If you discover that a formula includes an incorrect cell or range reference, use the Range Finder to add or remove cells from the reference, or to select a completely different group of cells. Click the color-coded border on any cell edge to move the reference to a different cell; click and drag the square handle in any corner of the colored border to extend the selection. To record your changes, press Enter or click the green Enter Formula button next to the formula bar.

USING GOAL SEEK TO FIND VALUES

After you've constructed a worksheet and built several intricate formulas, you might discover that you can't easily get the answer you're looking for. A formula that uses the PMT function, for example, is designed to produce the total monthly payment when you enter the price and loan details. But what if you've determined your maximum monthly payment, you've shopped around for the best interest rate, and now you want to calculate the maximum loan amount you can afford based on those values? Rather than construct a new formula or use trial-and-error methods to find the right result, use Excel's Goal Seek tool to perform the calculations in one operation:

1. Start by opening the worksheet that contains the formula you want to work with, and then choose Tools, Goal Seek. Excel displays the Goal Seek dialog box shown in Figure 19.15.

Figure 19.15

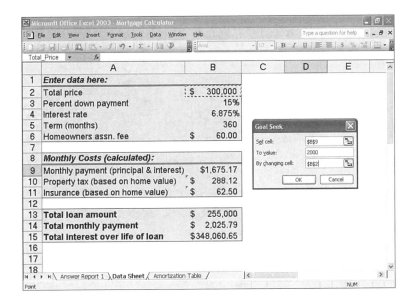

2. Fill in the three boxes to match the results you're trying to achieve. In the Set Cell box, enter the address of the formula whose results you want to control. In the To Value box, enter the amount the formula specified in the previous cell should equal. Finally, in the By Changing Cell box, enter the cell that contains the single value you want to change.

3. When you click OK, Excel runs through all possibilities and displays the Goal Seek Status dialog box, as shown in Figure 19.16. If you look at the worksheet itself, you'll see the values have changed to reflect the result shown here.

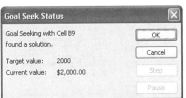

Figure 19.16

4. Click OK to incorporate the changed data into your worksheet; click Cancel to close the dialog box and restore the original data.

If your problem is more complex and can't be solved by changing a single cell, use the Solver add-in. Like other Excel add-ins, you must install this option before it's available on the Tools menu; choose Tools, Add-Ins, and click the Solver option to install it for the first time. Then choose Tools, Solver to display the Solver Parameters dialog box, as shown in Figure 19.17.

Figure 19.17
Use the Solver Parameters dialog box to specify more complex conditions for working backward to a formula's solution.

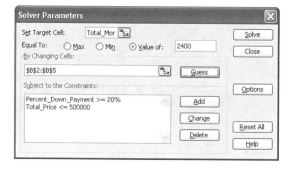

Select the cell that you want to adjust in the Set Target Cell box, click the Max, Min, or Value Of box, and enter a comparison amount. In the By Changing Cells box, select the cells you want to adjust. Note that unlike the Goal Seek feature, you can specify multiple cells here. Finally, enter any constraints you want to impose on the solution; for example, you can specify a maximum or minimum value for one or more of the changing cells. Click the Solve button to begin calculating.

When the Solver utility completes its calculation, it displays the Solver Results dialog box, shown in Figure 19.18. If Solver reports an error message, adjust the constraints and try again. If Solver successfully found a solution, you have three choices: Select the Keep Solver Solution option and click OK to change the values in your worksheet; choose the Restore Original Values option and click OK to cancel all changes; or click the Save Scenario button to create a worksheet scenario using the Solver results.

Figure 19.18
The Solver Results dialog box shows the results of a formula's calculations.

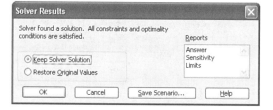

TROUBLESHOOTING

EDITING AN ARRAY FORMULA

I entered an array formula, but when I try to edit or copy it, the results change or I get an error message.

Editing an array formula is tricky. If the array formula was entered across multiple cells, you must select every cell that contains the array before you can edit it. If the array formula is contained in a single cell, you can edit it just as you would a conventional formula, but you must remember to press Ctrl+Shift+Enter to store your changes as an array formula. If you forget and press Enter, Excel stores it as a standard formula, with the wrong results. Finally, you'll notice some restrictions when you try to copy an array formula. If the destination range you select also contains the array formula, you'll get an error message; select a new destination range, or use AutoFill to copy the formula. Oh, and don't try to cheat by adding your own curly braces to create an array formula—the only way to enter an array formula is to press Ctrl+Shift+Enter and let Excel add the curly braces.

CHECKING FORMULAS BEFORE DELETING RANGE NAMES

After I deleted a range name in my worksheet, some of my formulas displayed error messages.

It's a frustrating fact of life: When you delete a range name from a worksheet, Excel does not automatically adjust any formulas that contain that range name. Even though it should, logically, be able to substitute the old cell address for the range name, it leaves the name there to torture you. After deleting a range name, you will see a #NAME? error in any cell that contains a formula with a reference to the deleted range name. Unfortunately, there's no easy way to determine which cell goes with the defunct name. If you spot these errors immediately after deleting the range name, press Ctrl+Z to undo your change. If you remember this possibility before deleting a range name, you can easily change any cells before deleting or changing the defined name. Press Ctrl+F to open the Find dialog box, enter the name of the cell or range, choose Formulas from the Look In box, and click Find Next to jump to and edit each cell that contains that name.

CONVERTING VALUES TO TEXT BEFORE CONCATENATING

When I try to combine a cell that contains text with one that contains a date, the result is nonsense. The cell that holds the date is correctly formatted, but the resulting text says something like "Today is 38059" instead of displaying a date.

As you've seen, Excel ignores the formatting of the original cell when concatenating the two values and instead displays the serial date value. Before concatenating a date with text, you must convert the date to text and choose a format. Use the TEXT function followed by a format in quotation marks. If the date is in cell A15, for example, use this formula to get the result you're looking for: `="Today is "&TEXT(A15,"mmmm d, yyyy")`.

EXTRA CREDIT: NESTING FUNCTIONS WITHIN FUNCTIONS

In some cases, it's necessary to use one function as the argument for another. *Nesting* functions within functions this way is common with logical functions such as IF, for example. You might use a set of nested functions to help you decide how much to pay on a handful of credit cards and installment loans, where your goal is to pay off the debts with the highest interest rate first and make minimum payments on those.

The sample worksheet shown in Figure 19.19 is built using the following principles:

Column B shows the current balance for each debt.

Column C lists the interest rate for each debt.

Column D calculates the minimum payment you want to make on each balance, at 5% of the current balance.

Cell E8 contains the total amount available for repaying your total debt load.

Figure 19.19

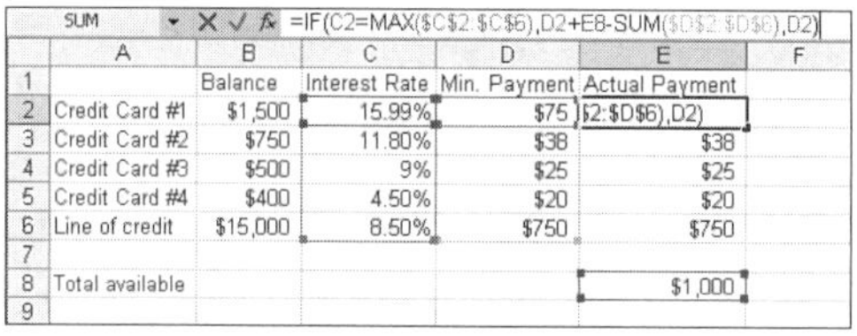

	A	B	C	D	E	F
	SUM	✗ ✓ fx	=IF(C2=MAX($C$2:$C$6),D2+E8-SUM($D$2:$D$6),D2)			
1		Balance	Interest Rate	Min. Payment	Actual Payment	
2	Credit Card #1	$1,500	15.99%	$75	$2:$D$6),D2)	
3	Credit Card #2	$750	11.80%	$38	$38	
4	Credit Card #3	$500	9%	$25	$25	
5	Credit Card #4	$400	4.50%	$20	$20	
6	Line of credit	$15,000	8.50%	$750	$750	
7						
8	Total available				$1,000	
9						

Each cell in column E contains a formula that enters the minimum payment for all rows except the one with the highest interest rate; for that value, the calculation adds whatever is left over from the Total Available amount after making all minimum payments.

The following formula performs the full calculation in a single step for the first row:

```
=IF(C2=MAX($C$2:$C$6),D2+E8-SUM($D$2:$D$6),D2)
```

Note that this example includes two levels of nesting, with the SUM and MAX functions nested within an IF function.

You can nest functions within functions within functions to create some clever effects. Say you want to add a date stamp to a worksheet, so whenever you print the worksheet, you'll see a large text label that includes your name and the current date. Enter this formula in a cell that is within the print range, substituting your name in the text string that begins the formula:

```
="Prepared by John Q. Smith, "&TEXT(TODAY(),"mmmm d, yyyy")
```

When nesting functions, note that the nested function must return the same value type (text, number, date, true/false) as the argument it's replacing. Unlike formulas containing constants or cell references, which can contain an unlimited number of nesting levels, Excel enables you to nest a maximum of seven levels of functions. If you need to perform more calculations than this, you'll have to break the formula into multiple steps and place each step in its own cell.

You can use the Insert Function dialog box to enter a nested function within another function. Begin entering the first function by using the Insert Function dialog box, as described earlier in this chapter. Click in the input box for any argument, and then choose another function from the Function box (this box is located to the left of the Formula bar, where the

Name box normally appears; it is visible only when the Function Arguments dialog box is open). As you enter the formula, you can switch between functions at any time by clicking the function's name in the Formula bar. If you choose a function that contains a nested function as an argument (as in the example shown here), the entire function appears in the input box, and the result of the function using current values appears to its right.

Figure 19.20

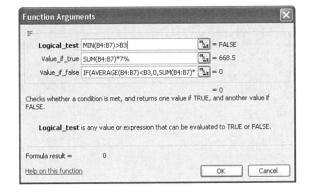

CHAPTER 20

WORKING WITH LISTS AND PIVOTTABLES

In this chapter

SLICING AND DICING DATA WITH LISTS

Excel is absolutely, positively not just for accountants and other number crunchers. For proof, take a look at the extensive set of features you can use to track information stored in list format. You've probably already figured out that Excel makes it easy to enter a column of names or dates and quickly sort them, but its list-handling features go much deeper. A list can include thousands of rows of data and dozens of columns, which you can use to filter, sort, and extract the details you're looking for. Want to do sophisticated cross-tabulations of data? That's no problem when you use the amazing PivotTable features.

You can enter data manually by creating a list, defining columns, and typing each row. Or you can import data from other programs or from Web-based repositories and then perform your own research and analysis. For example, you can do any or all of the following tasks:

- Keep a list of students or club members and track attendance for a series of classes or events

- Maintain an address list and use it to create mail-merge documents with Word

- Perform detailed analysis of statistical information, such as weather, population growth, and industrial or agricultural output

- Track your scores or times in a favorite hobby—golf or bowling scores, marathon times, and so on

In this chapter, we cover techniques for working with both standard lists and PivotTables.

CREATING A LIST ON A WORKSHEET

Excel's row-and-column structure makes it an ideal tool for organizing related information into a *list*. On an Excel worksheet, a list is a group of consecutive rows of related data. Conceptually, an Excel list is identical to a table in a flat-file database management program. Each *column* within a list is equivalent to a database *field*, and each *row* is the same as a *record* of data; headings in the top row represent the names of the fields. Within each column, you can enter text, numbers, dates, formulas, or hyperlinks. Excel does not impose any additional restrictions on the type of data that you can enter in a list.

Figure 20.1 shows a basic list, which can be distinguished from a simple range by the dark blue border around all four sides.

Excel 2003 includes several features designed to help you create and manage lists:

- You can designate a specific range as a list. When you do so, Excel adds a dark blue border around it, making it easy to see where your list begins and ends. You can convert a list back to a normal range at any time.

- The final row of the list range, marked by an asterisk in the first column, is called the *insert row*. When you enter information in this row, Excel automatically adds the row to your list and extends the list range accordingly.

- In any list range, you can show or hide a *total row*, which appears below the insert row. When this row is visible, you can click in any cell within the total row and choose from several functions to summarize the data in that column.

- The AutoFilter feature (which we discuss later in this chapter) is enabled automatically when you define a range as a list.

- Use options on the Data, List menu to create and resize lists, show or hide total rows, and hide the border on inactive (unselected) lists. Many of these same options are also available on the List toolbar.

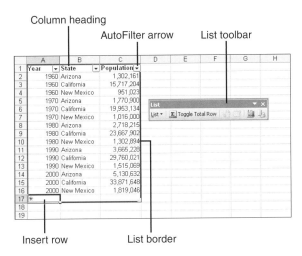

Figure 20.1
When you define a range as a list, Excel automatically enables AutoFilter for each column. To add a new row, click in the Insert row and enter the data.

NOTE

The Publish List option and four related commands on the List menu are useful only if you have access to a SharePoint server, which runs on Windows Server 2003. This option is irrelevant for most Office users in homes, schools, and small businesses.

You can sort list data in nearly any order, search for a specific bit of information, or use filters to find groups of data that match criteria that you specify. For complex lists, Excel can automatically create *outlines* that let you summarize and subtotal groups of records. Large, complex lists are a perfect starting point for PivotTable and PivotChart reports, which let you drag fields on a layout page to perform complex data-analysis tasks without having to construct a single formula.

→ For a full discussion of the wonders of PivotTables, **see** "How PivotTable and PivotChart Reports Work," **p. 652**.

Excel uses column labels in the first row of a list (also called the *header row*) to identify the names of fields used for sorting and filtering. Although you can create a list without a header row, we highly recommend that you include column labels for every list that you create or import. You must have a header row if you want to enter data using forms or use

20

the AutoFilter feature to find groups of records. If you use the Create List menu and specify that your list does not include headers, Excel automatically adds generic headers—Column1, Column2, and so on. In either case, when you use the Create List menu to define a range as a list, Excel applies bold formatting to make the column labels stand out from the data area.

TIP FROM

Ed & Woody

You don't need a header row to sort a range of data; to sort a data range that is not identified as a list and doesn't include column labels, be sure to select the No Header Row option when you sort.

To create a new list, select the range you want to use. The selection can be empty, or it can contain an existing list. Choose Data, List, Create List (or press Ctrl+L). Excel displays the dialog box shown in Figure 20.2.

Figure 20.2
If you leave the My List Has Headers box unchecked, Excel automatically adds generic headers to your list.

If your selection includes existing data with labels at the top of each column, select the My List Has Headers check box. Click OK to create the list. Excel automatically formats the header row (adding generic column headings if necessary), turns on AutoFormat, and adds the insert row at the end of the list. If your worksheet includes data in any row that is directly adjacent to the list range, Excel moves the list range and the existing rows to make room.

When creating a list, follow these basic guidelines:

- Whenever possible, define lists explicitly by choosing Data, List, Create List. Using Excel 2003, you can create as many lists as you want on a single worksheet.

→ For more details on how to manage multiple worksheets in a single workbook, **see** "Working with Multiple Worksheets," **p. 520**.

- Create a single header row with a unique label for each column. Descriptive headings are much more useful than the generic ones Excel creates. For lists you plan to print, you can add distinctive formatting to help make the column headings stand out even more, including larger font sizes and a border beneath the header row.

- Avoid leaving any blank rows or columns in your list. If you need to add data later, you can choose Data, List (or right-click the list area) to resize the list area or insert rows or columns within the list. Use the insert row at the end of the list to enter new data.

→ To prevent yourself or other users of a worksheet from entering invalid data, including blank cells, create data validation rules; **see** "Restricting and Validating Data Entry for a Cell or Range," **p. 534**.

■ To make it easier to enter data, freeze the worksheet panes just below the header row.

→ For instructions on how to freeze worksheet panes, **see** "Locking Row and Column Labels for Onscreen Viewing," **p. 532**.

To resize a list, click anywhere within the list and choose Data, List, Resize List. Drag the selection to add or remove rows or columns. Your selection must start with the existing header row and cannot overlap any other list. If you make the list smaller, Excel keeps any data that was in the rows or columns you excluded from the list.

Watch Out for Automatic Formatting

When you enter new data in an existing list, Excel automatically picks up formatting and formulas from the previous rows without requiring you to explicitly format cells in the new row. For example, if the first cell in the previous row is formatted in bold italic, Excel automatically applies that formatting as soon as you enter the data into the first cell in the new row. If the last cell in the previous row contains a formula that multiplies the values in the two previous cells, Excel adds that formula as soon as you enter data in the second of the two cells that make up that formula.

This feature isn't foolproof. For some inexplicable reason, Excel won't automatically pick up date formatting from the previous row, although it will consistently copy font formatting and attributes. Likewise, new rows pick up colors and shading consistently, but borders don't always extend as you expect. Although the documentation claims that Excel will pick up formatting and formulas that match three of the previous five rows, we found that this automatic feature works consistently only if the formatting appears in four of the previous five rows. Our advice? Don't rely on guesswork. Format the cells in your list range before you begin entering data, so that you can maintain control over the appearance of data you enter.

If you don't want Excel to automatically pick up formatting and formulas from previous rows, turn off this capability. Choose Tools, Options, and click the Edit tab. To automatically format new items that you add to the end of a list to match the format of the rest of the list, select the Extend Data Range Formats and Formulas check box.

SPEEDING UP REPETITIVE DATA ENTRY WITH AUTOCOMPLETE

Excel's default setup enables an option called *AutoComplete*, which is designed to speed up entering data in lists. As you type, Excel compares each character that you enter with other entries in cells directly above the active cell. If the opening characters match those of any other entry, Excel assumes that you want to repeat that entry and fills in the rest of the label. (This comparison applies only to cells that contain text; AutoComplete ignores numbers, dates, and times.)

If you want to repeat the previous entry, press Enter (or Tab or any arrow key) to insert the AutoComplete entry in the cell. Keep typing to enter a new value in the cell. Excel will not suggest an AutoComplete entry unless the string that you have entered identifies a unique entry in the list above the active cell.

TIP FROM

El & Woody

Instead of waiting for Excel's suggestion, you can select from a list of entries already in the column. To display the list, press Alt+down arrow, or right-click the cell and then choose Pick from List from the shortcut menu.

Some users find AutoComplete disconcerting, dangerous, or merely annoying because if you don't pay close attention, you risk accidentally entering the wrong data. You can easily disable AutoComplete: Choose Tools, Options, and click the Edit tab. Clear the check mark from the Enable AutoComplete for Cell Values box. Click OK to save the new setting and continue editing.

If you have a love-hate relationship with AutoComplete, create a macro that toggles this feature on and off. Assigning the macro to a toolbar button lets you turn on AutoComplete when you're entering data in a list where its capabilities are useful, and turn it off at all other times. Here's all the code you need:

```
Sub ToggleAutoComplete()
    Application.EnableAutoComplete = Not Application.EnableAutoComplete
End Sub
```

→ Don't confuse AutoComplete with AutoCorrect; for more details about this and other Office-wide Auto-features, **see** "Using AutoCorrect to Type Faster," **p. 98**.

AUTOMATICALLY FILLING IN A SERIES OF DATA

One common and tedious data-entry task is entering a sequence of numbers or dates in a column or row. Excel's *AutoFill* feature can handle this chore automatically by filling in information as you drag the mouse along a column or row. Use AutoFill to copy formulas or values; enter the days of the week, months of the year, or any series of numbers or dates; and even fill in custom lists of departments, category names, part numbers, and other information that you define.

Because of its tremendous number of options, even Excel experts sometimes have trouble coaxing the correct results out of AutoFill. Using Smart Tags makes this task somewhat easier. If using AutoFill has the wrong result, click the AutoFill Smart Tag to see a list of other options that enable you to select a different result, such as changing a simple copy to a series.

→ For more details about Smart Tags, see "Customizing Smart Tags," **p. 48**.

In general, using AutoFill will have one of the following results:

- **Copy data from one or more cells**—If the selection is not a sequence that Excel recognizes—for example, if you select a single cell that contains text—AutoFill copies the selection in the direction that you drag.

> Using AutoFill is an excellent way to copy a formula from one cell across a row or down a column. This technique is especially useful for copying formulas that total columns or rows. As you drag, AutoFill copies the formula, adjusting relative references as needed.

- **Copy formatting or values across a row or down a column**—Normally, AutoFill copies both formats and values from the cells that you start with. To choose one, make a selection and then hold down the right mouse button while dragging. When you release the mouse button, choose Fill Formatting Only or Fill Without Formatting. If you select a formula in the starting cell, either option copies the formula, with or without formatting.

- **Fill in a series of dates**—If you enter a date in any recognizable format, such as 4/10 or 5-23-04, AutoFill will extend the series in one-day increments. AutoFill also recognizes long and short versions of days of the week and months. If you enter Jan in the first cell, for example, AutoFill will continue the list with Feb, Mar, Apr, and so on; start with Wednesday, and AutoFill will extend the list with Thursday, Friday, Saturday, and so on. Excel also recognizes calendar quarters. If you enter Q1 in a cell and use AutoFill, you get Q2, Q3, and Q4, at which point the series starts over with Q1.

> When you reach the end of a finite AutoFill sequence, such as days of the week or months of the year, the sequence repeats. If you start with Monday, for example, the sequence starts over again after the seventh cell.

- **Fill in a series of numbers**—This is probably the trickiest AutoFill option. If you start with a single cell that contains the number 1 and use AutoFill to extend it, Excel will copy the number 1 to the rest of the cells that you select. To instruct Excel to AutoFill a series instead of copying the number, hold down the Ctrl key as you drag.

> When you insert a sequence of numbers, Excel assumes that you want to increment them by 1. Thus, if you start with 100, the sequence continues with 101, 102, and so on. To use a different sequence, enter values in at least two cells so that the sequence is apparent, and then select those cells and use AutoFill. For example, if you enter 100 and 200 in the first two cells and then select those cells and use AutoFill, Excel continues the series with 300, 400, and so on. You can also use this technique to enter a date series, such as every other day (Monday, Wednesday, Friday), every third month (Feb, May, Aug), or the 10th of each month (1/10, 2/10, 3/10). Enter the first two or three cells in the sequence, select the cells that you entered, and then extend the selection using AutoFill.

20

- **Fill in a series of numbered items**—If you enter any text plus a number (Chapter 1, Item 1, or Area 51, for example), AutoFill extends the selection by 1 (Chapter 2,

Chapter 3, and so on). Confusingly, this AutoFill option works exactly the opposite as it does on a series of numbers without text: In this case, hold down Ctrl to prevent Excel from extending the selection and copy the values instead.

- **Fill in a custom list**—If you've created a custom list (see the following section for step-by-step instructions), enter any item from that list in any cell, and then use AutoFill to add the remaining items in the list.

- **Fill in a trend series**—For this option, you must select a number of cells first and then drag with the right mouse button for more options. You can choose a *Linear Trend* series, in which Excel calculates the average difference between each value in the series that you selected and then adds it to (or subtracts it from) each succeeding value in the AutoFill range. Choose a *Growth Trend* series to have Excel calculate the percentage of difference between items in the series and apply that amount to each new value. These options are useful when you're trying to project future patterns, such as population growth, based on existing data.

To use AutoFill, follow these steps:

1. First, enter the initial value or values for the range. If the list begins a unique sequence—months of the year, for example, starting with Jan or January—you need to enter a value in only one cell. To AutoFill a sequence of numbers or dates with an increment value other than 1, enter the first two or three values in the series.

2. Point to Excel's *fill handle*—the small black square in the lower-right corner of the currently selected cell or range. When you point at the fill handle, the mouse pointer turns into a thin black cross.

3. Drag in any direction (up or down in a column, left or right in a row) to begin filling in values (see Figure 20.3). Hold down the Ctrl key as you extend the selection to switch the AutoFill action from copy to fill series, or vice versa.

Figure 20.3
As you drag, Excel automatically fills in values in your series—dates, in this example.

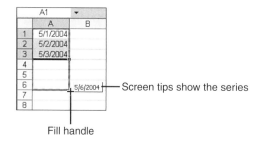

Screen tips show the series

Fill handle

NOTE

AutoFill works only in one row or column at a time. To extend a selection down and to the right, you must perform the AutoFill action in two steps.

4. ScreenTips display the value that will appear in each new cell as you extend the series. When you reach the final cell, release the mouse button to fill in the data.

5. If the AutoFill results are not what you expected, click the AutoFill Smart Tag to display a menu with additional options (see Figure 20.4).

Figure 20.4

TIP FROM

> You can also use AutoFill to remove items from a range without removing formatting. Select the entire range that contains the series. Aim the mouse pointer at the lower-right corner, but instead of dragging the fill handle down or to the right, as you normally would do to extend a series, drag it up (for a column) or to the left (for a row). This action makes the range smaller, removing those items that are no longer selected without affecting the formatting applied to those cells.

For maximum control over AutoFill options, hold down the right mouse button while dragging. When you release the mouse button, you can choose the appropriate option from the shortcut menu. Choose the Series option at the bottom of the shortcut menu to display a dialog box that lets you choose any option, including starting points and step values for a series, as in Figure 20.5.

Figure 20.5
If Excel can't recognize the progression in an AutoFill series, use this dialog box to specify series settings manually.

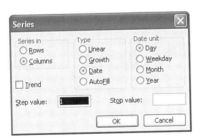

CREATING CUSTOM AUTOFILL LISTS TO FIT YOUR PROJECTS

You can also create a custom list, such as names of countries, budget categories, or department codes, and add the list to Excel. Excel adds custom lists to the Windows Registry, with each list appearing in the precise order in which you enter individual items. The result can be tremendous time savings for you if you regularly insert the same list into worksheets. AutoFill can insert any custom list in any row or column, anytime (and, as we'll demonstrate in the next section, you can also use a custom list as a sort key for the rest of your list).

TIP FROM

EQ & Woody

To copy a custom list from one computer to another, use the original custom list to fill in a range on a blank worksheet and then save the resulting workbook. On the computer where you want to import the list, open the saved workbook, select the list range, and use the Import button on the Custom Lists tab of the Options dialog box, as described in this section. It takes a few minutes at most, and it's foolproof.

To add a custom list to Excel, use either of the following procedures:

- If the list is short, you can type it directly into a dialog box. Choose Tools, Options, click the Custom Lists tab, select New List, and start entering items in the List Entries box, as shown in Figure 20.6. Be sure to enter each item in the correct order, and press Enter at the end of each line. When the list is complete, click the Add button.

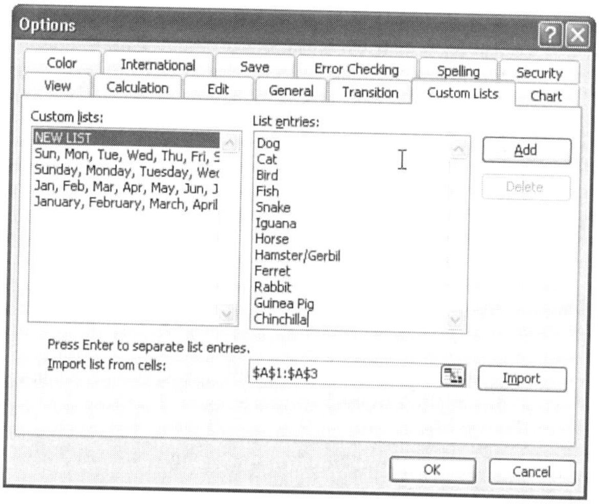

Figure 20.6

- If the list is already available in a worksheet, the process is even easier. Say that you've created a worksheet that contains all of your family budget categories in the exact order that you want to enter them every time. Open that sheet and select the worksheet range (column or row) that contains the list. Choose Tools, Options, click the Custom Lists tab, and click Import.

Your list is now available in any Excel worksheet that you open on this machine. To automatically add the custom list to a worksheet range, enter the first list item, use the fill handle to complete the list, and click OK.

SORTING LISTS

Excel's sorting capabilities let you view data in almost any order, regardless of the order in which you entered it. To quickly sort a list, first click a single cell in the column by which you want to sort, and then click the Sort Ascending button. Excel selects all the data in your list and sorts it alphabetically, using the column that contains the active cell. Click the Sort Descending button to sort in reverse order, using the same column. If you want to sort only a portion of the list, make a selection first, and then use the Tab key to move the active cell to the correct column. This option, used incorrectly, can make a mess of your database, so use it with caution.

TIP FROM

EQ & Woody

> If the order in which you enter data is important, add a column to your list and fill it with numeric values that you can use to identify each row, and then increment it by 1 for each new record. Re-sort using the values in this column to return the list to its original order. Don't use a formula for the data in this column, however—when you sort the list, the values will change and you won't be able to return to the original sort order.

When you choose ascending order, Excel always sorts numbers first, then most punctuation characters, and then letters, in ascending (A–Z) order, without regard to whether the letters are uppercase or lowercase. Excel generally ignores apostrophes and hyphens when sorting; if two entries are otherwise identical but one contains a hyphen, it will appear after the one that does not contain a hyphen. The precise order for punctuation follows the same order as the Unicode character set, as follows:

(space) ! " # $ % & ([dg]) * , . / : ; ? @ [\ ] [ct] _ [ag] { ¦ } [td] + < = >

SORTING BY MULTIPLE COLUMNS

By using the two sort buttons on the Standard toolbar, you can perform a multicolumn sort without ever using a dialog box. Perform each column sort in sequence, working your way up in reverse order to the sort order you want to see; Excel preserves the order of other columns in the list when you sort each succeeding column. In a budget worksheet for a large organization, for example, you might click in the Month column and click a sort button, and then do the same with the Category column and finally with the Department column. The result is to sort your list by department, then by category, and then by month.

The Sort dialog box lets you sort by up to three columns at one time; choose Data, Sort to open the Sort dialog box, as shown in Figure 20.7. Excel lets you specify up to three columns for your sort order, using ascending or descending order for each one.

Figure 20.7
This Sort dialog box shows three sort keys, each corresponding to a column label in the list.

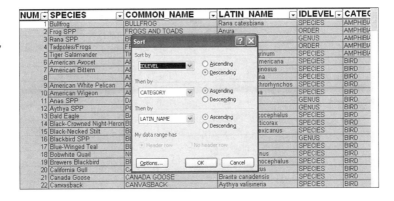

SORTING BY DATES OR CUSTOM SERIES

By default, Excel's sort options reorder data alphabetically or numerically. However, a basic A–Z or 1–10 sort isn't always appropriate. Dates and weekdays in text format represent a particular problem. For example, a list of modules for a school curriculum might include a column, formatted as text, that identifies the month in which a particular lesson should be taught. Or, a list of shift assignments for volunteers at the local community center might include a column of weekdays. Using the default sort order would put the month names and weekdays in alphabetical order—April, August, December, February, or Mon, Sat, Sun, Thu—when you actually want to sort the list in calendar order. You might also want to sort your list using a custom AutoFill list—by region, for example, or by budget category (see the previous section for details about how to create one of these lists).

Sorting by date or a custom series is available only when you use the Sort dialog box. To sort by text dates or using a custom series, follow these steps:

1. Click in the list that you want to sort, or select the region to be sorted.

2. Choose Data, Sort, and identify up to three columns for sorting. The column that contains the dates or custom list must be the first in the list.

3. Click the Options button in the lower-left corner of the Sort dialog box to open the Sort Options dialog box (see Figure 20.8).

4. Click the down arrow in the First Key Sort Order list box and select the appropriate series. The default selection includes four built-in lists—days of the week and months, in long and short versions. In addition, any custom lists that you've created will appear here. You can also choose a different orientation here—for most lists, the default setting, Sort Top to Bottom, is the correct choice.

5. Click OK to confirm the sort order that you selected; then click OK again to perform the sort.

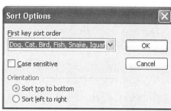

Figure 20.8

NOTE

By default, Excel does not distinguish between lowercase and capital letters when sorting. To change this setting, click the Options button in the Sort dialog box and check Case Sensitive. With this option enabled, Excel sorts lowercase letters ahead of capital letters.

As you can see, this option has one significant limitation—it is available only for the first sort key that you specify. If you're willing to sort in several steps, however, you can sort with a custom list or dates series in the second or third key. Perform each sort one column at a time. Remember to sort by choosing sort keys using the reverse of the order in which you want the final list to appear. To sort by month and then by budget category, for example, first use the Sort dialog box to sort by a single column, using the custom series that you've defined for budget categories. Then perform a sort using only the month column. The results will be in perfect order.

FINDING AND FILTERING DATA IN A LIST

When working with lists, you can use the Find shortcut (Ctrl+F) to search for any value in the list. That technique is useful if you want to jump quickly to a specific unique value in the list. More often, however, you'll want to extract details from a list instead of simply jumping to a single record. In that case, use *filters* to hide all records except those that match criteria that you specify. In a list that contains hundreds or thousands of rows, defining a filter helps you see a small number of related records together, making it easier to compare data and identify trends.

For example, in a list of daily high, low, and closing stock prices that includes data for many companies, you might want to see only those records in which the entry in the Symbol column is equal to KO (that's the Coca-Cola Company, for those who don't know ticker symbols by heart). Or, if you import product inventory information from a database into an Excel list, you can use filters to show only items that are currently out of stock, making it easy to build a reorder list.

AutoFilter options let you select information by choosing from drop-down lists of unique items in each column. You can also create custom filters using multiple criteria and combining criteria from multiple columns, or you can display only the top 10 (or bottom 10) entries in a list, by number or percentage, based on the contents of a single column.

NOTE

> Unlike sorts, which rearrange data in a list, filters do not change the underlying data. When you define a filter, you hide records that don't match the criteria that you define.

➔ For an overview of Office-standard Find and Replace tools, **see** "Finding and Replacing Text," **p. 93**.
➔ For details on database functions that let you analyze with data in lists, **see** "Using Database Functions," **p. 614**.

USING AUTOFILTER TO FIND SETS OF DATA

The easiest way to build a filter is with the help of Excel's AutoFilter capability. When this option is enabled, you can define criteria by choosing values from drop-down lists; as the name implies, an AutoFilter applies the filter to your list automatically, as soon as you select the criteria. When you understand how AutoFilters work, you can use them to narrow even massive lists.

When you define a list (using Data, List, Create List), the AutoFilter option is enabled by default. For lists that are not explicitly defined or where you have previously disabled the AutoFilter feature, you can create an AutoFilter manually by clicking anywhere in your list and choosing Data, Filter, AutoFilter.

When AutoFilter is on, a drop-down arrow appears to the right of each column heading in your list, as shown in Figure 20.9. Click the arrow to the right of the column label that you want to use as the first condition in the filter.

20

Figure 20.9
Drop-down AutoFilter lists let you narrow your selection by choosing from all unique values in that column.

	C	D	E	F
1	COMMON_NAME	LATIN_NAME	IDLEVEL	CATEGORY
2	DRAGONFLY/DAMSELFLY/WATE	Anisoptera/Zygoptera/Corixida	SUBORDER/SUE	Sort Ascending
3	DRAGONFLY/DAMSELFLY	Anisoptera/Zygoptera	SUBORDER/SUE	Sort Descending
4	DRAGONFLY/BEETLE	Anisoptera/Coleoptera	SUBORDER/ORE	(All)
5	DAMSELFLY/CADDISFLY	Zygoptera/Trichoptera	SUBORDER/ORE	(Top 10...)
6	DRAGONFLY	Anisoptera	SUBORDER	(Custom...)
7	DAMSELFLY	Zygoptera	SUBORDER	AMPHIBIAN
8	DUCK SPP	Anatinae	SUBFAMILY	BIRD
9	WINGED INSECTS	Pterygota	SUBCLASS	FISH
10	TIGER SALAMANDER	Ambystoma tigrinum	SPECIES	INVERTEBRATE
11	BULLFROG	Rana catesbiana	SPECIES	MAMMAL
12	WESTERN GREBE	Aechmophorus occidentalis	SPECIES	PLANKTON
				PLANT
13	RED-WINGED BLACKBIRD	Agelaius phoeniceus	SPECIES	REPTILE
14	WOOD DUCK	Aix sponsa	SPECIES	BIRD
15	NORTHERN PINTAIL	Anas acuta	SPECIES	BIRD
16	AMERICAN WIGEON	Anas americana	SPECIES	BIRD
17	NORTHERN SHOVELER	Anas clypeata	SPECIES	BIRD
18	GREEN-WINGED TEAL	Anas crecca	SPECIES	BIRD

Choose an item from the drop-down list to restrict the display to only rows that contain that item, or choose any of the options shown in the following bulleted list. Excel applies your criteria immediately, filtering out all rows except those that contain the value that you selected.

> **NOTE**
>
> Excel generates the drop-down list of AutoFilter values for each column automatically by pulling out all unique values from that column. As a result, every item on the drop-down list is guaranteed to be in that column, making it impossible to select an incorrect value. AutoFilter lists always display in ascending order.

Excel offers several AutoFilter choices:

- **Top 10**—Show the highest or lowest numeric values in a list by number or by percentage. Don't be misled by the name—when you choose this option, you see a dialog box that lets you select any number between 1 and 500; you can choose Bottom or Top, and you can specify percent as well. Use the settings in Figure 20.10, for example, to display the top 5% of all products in a list, based on the amount in the selected column. If the list contains 2,000 items, this setting will show only the top 100.

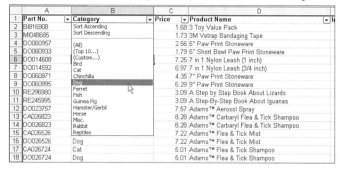

	A	B	C	D	
1	Part No.	Category	Price	Product Name	
2	BI816908	Sort Ascending	1.68	3 Toy Value Pack	
3	MI048685	Sort Descending	1.73	3M Vetrap Bandaging Tape	
4	DO060957	(All)	2.56	5" Paw Print Stoneware	
5	DO060933	(Top 10...)	1.79	5" Short Bowl Paw Print Stoneware	
6	DO014608	(Custom...)	7.25	7 in 1 Nylon Leash (1 inch)	
		Bird			
7	DO014592	Cat	6.97	7 in 1 Nylon Leash (3/4 inch)	
8	DO060971	Chinchilla	4.35	7" Paw Print Stoneware	
9	DO060995	Dog	6.29	9" Paw Print Stoneware	
10	RE296980	Ferret	3.09	A Step by Step Book About Lizards	
11	RE245995	Fish	3.09	A Step-By-Step Book About Iguanas	
12	DO023757	Guinea Pig	7.57	Adams™ Aerosol Spray	
13	CAD26823	Hamster/Gerbil	8.28	Adams™ Carbaryl Flea & Tick Shampoo	
		Horse			
14	DO026823	Misc.	8.28	Adams™ Carbaryl Flea & Tick Shampoo	
15	CAD26526	Rabbit	7.22	Adams™ Flea & Tick Mist	
		Reptiles			
16	DO026526	Dog	7.22	Adams™ Flea & Tick Mist	
17	CAD26724	Cat	5.01	Adams™ Flea & Tick Shampoo	
18	DO026724	Dog	5.01	Adams™ Flea & Tick Shampoo	

Figure 20.10

- **Custom**—Use comparison operators (covered in the next section) to define criteria. You can combine up to two criteria using this option.

- **Blanks**—Display only records that contain no data in the selected column. This option is available only if the selected column contains one or more blank cells.

- **NonBlanks**—Display all records that contain data in the selected column, hiding blank records. This option is available only if the selected column contains one or more blank cells.

- **All**—Show all records in the list. Use this option to remove AutoFilter criteria from a column.

AutoFilter criteria are cumulative; by combining criteria in different columns, you can successively filter a list to display an increasingly selective group of records. Although you can choose filter criteria in any order, it's best to start with columns that include the fewest options because the list of choices for succeeding columns will be narrower and easier to scroll through.

When you apply a filter to a list, Excel changes the color of the drop-down arrow for the column that you selected to blue. That is your only indication that a particular column is filtered. As the list in Figure 20.11 shows, Excel maintains the row numbers of the underlying list when you use an AutoFilter, hiding all rows that don't match the criteria that you specified.

Figure 20.11

Because an AutoFilter does not change the data in the underlying list, you'll see gaps in row numbering when you filter a list.

	SPECIES	COMMON NAME	LATIN NAME	IDLEVEL	CATEGORY
10	Tiger Salamander	TIGER SALAMANDER	Ambystoma tigrinum	SPECIES	AMPHIBIAN
11	Bullfrog	BULLFROG	Rana catesbiana	SPECIES	AMPHIBIAN
165	Frog SPP	FROGS AND TOADS	Anura	ORDER	AMPHIBIAN
166	Tadpoles/Frogs	FROGS AND TOADS	Anura	ORDER	AMPHIBIAN
187	Rana SPP	BULLFROG SPP	Rana spp.	GENUS	AMPHIBIAN
245					

To change AutoFilter criteria, click the blue arrow and select another value. To remove AutoFilter criteria for a single column, choose All from the AutoFilter list for that column. To remove all AutoFilter criteria from the list, choose Data, Filter, Show All. To restore a list to an unfiltered view with all rows visible, choose Data, Filter, AutoFilter. The check mark to the left of the AutoFilter menu entry vanishes, the drop-down arrows in the header row disappear, and your list returns to its full unfiltered state.

Excel does not automatically retain custom sets of AutoFilter criteria. When you save a worksheet that contains an AutoFiltered list, your list appears with AutoFilter settings intact when you reopen it. However, as soon as you choose a different AutoFilter option for a column (or disable the AutoFilter option completely), Excel discards any custom criteria that you've created for that column. To reapply those same AutoFilter criteria, you have to create a custom view or re-enter the criteria.

USING COMPARISON CRITERIA TO CREATE CUSTOM FILTERS

The AutoFilter drop-down list for each column allows you to select one and only one specific value. In some cases, that limitation gets in the way of finding the information that you need. For example, what if you want to search through your product list and find all items whose price is less than $10? Or, what if you want to find items whose name includes the text "puppy"? To create complex criteria in an AutoFiltered list, click the AutoFilter arrow for the column that you want to use, and then select the Custom option.

The Custom AutoFilter dialog box (see Figure 20.12) enables you to use any of the following *comparison operators*:

- Equals/does not equal
- Is greater than/is less than
- Is greater than or equal to/is less than or equal to
- Begins with/does not begin with
- Ends with/does not end with
- Contains/does not contain

Figure 20.12
Use the Custom AutoFilter dialog box to combine criteria; if you need more than two criteria, use an Advanced Filter instead.

You can also combine two criteria for a single column using the logical operator AND, or use the OR operator to tell Excel that you want to see records that match either of the criteria that you specify for that column.

Select a comparison operator for the first criterion, and then click in the box to the right of the comparison operator and enter the value that you want to use as a logical test. Or, use the drop-down list to select from all unique values in the column. If you add a second criterion for the same column, click And to select only rows in which both criteria are true; click Or to create a filter that shows rows in which either set of criteria is true.

TIP FROM

Although you're limited to only two criteria when you use AutoFilter's Custom option, you can easily work around this limitation by using Excel's capability to filter on criteria for two or more columns at once. Make a copy of the column that you want to use in your filter, and specify a separate set of criteria in the AutoFilter box for that column.

FILTERING WITH ADVANCED CRITERIA

Compared with the one-click ease of AutoFilters, Excel's advanced filters are downright cumbersome. Still, they're the only way to accomplish some tasks, such as defining more than three criteria for a single column or finding only unique values within a list that contains duplicate entries. Advanced filters also let you specify more complex criteria than you can use with AutoFilters, including criteria based on formulas.

To use advanced filters, start by creating a *criteria range* on the same worksheet that contains the list. Although you can add this range anywhere on the list, we strongly recommend that you place it directly above the list, where it's unlikely to be affected by any changes that you make to the sheet's design. Allow a minimum of three rows in the criteria range—one for the column labels, one for the criteria, and one to serve as a separator between the list and the criteria range.

TIP FROM

EQ & Woody

Add one extra row for each set of criteria that you expect to use when filtering the list. In almost all circumstances, you can get by with a criteria range of five rows, which allows you to add up to three sets of criteria for each column while still maintaining a one-row separation between the criteria range and the list.

Copy the column labels from the list to the first row of the criteria range. The resulting range should look something like the example shown in Figure 20.13, which also includes several criteria and shows the results of the filter on the list.

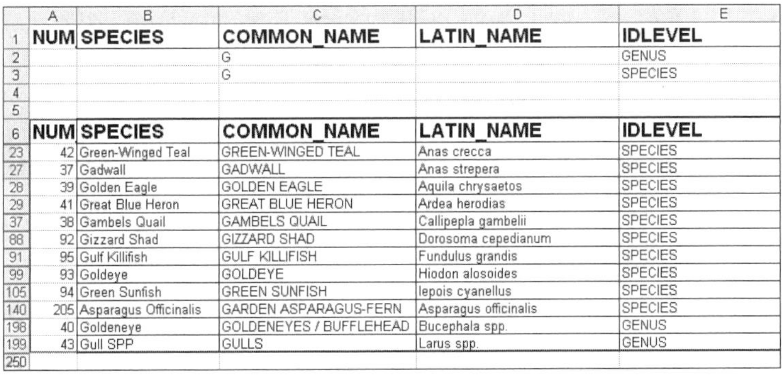

Figure 20.13
Always create the criteria range above the list, not below or alongside it; that placement keeps it from being scrambled when you extend or sort the list.

	A	B	C	D	E
1	NUM	SPECIES	COMMON_NAME	LATIN_NAME	IDLEVEL
2			G		GENUS
3			G		SPECIES
4					
5					
6	NUM	SPECIES	COMMON_NAME	LATIN_NAME	IDLEVEL
23	42	Green-Winged Teal	GREEN-WINGED TEAL	Anas crecca	SPECIES
27	37	Gadwall	GADWALL	Anas strepera	SPECIES
28	39	Golden Eagle	GOLDEN EAGLE	Aquila chrysaetos	SPECIES
29	41	Great Blue Heron	GREAT BLUE HERON	Ardea herodias	SPECIES
37	38	Gambels Quail	GAMBELS QUAIL	Callipepla gambelii	SPECIES
88	92	Gizzard Shad	GIZZARD SHAD	Dorosoma cepedianum	SPECIES
91	95	Gulf Killifish	GULF KILLIFISH	Fundulus grandis	SPECIES
99	93	Goldeye	GOLDEYE	Hiodon alosoides	SPECIES
105	94	Green Sunfish	GREEN SUNFISH	lepois cyanellus	SPECIES
140	205	Asparagus Officinalis	GARDEN ASPARAGUS-FERN	Asparagus officinalis	SPECIES
198	40	Goldeneye	GOLDENEYES / BUFFLEHEAD	Bucephala spp.	GENUS
199	43	Gull SPP	GULLS	Larus spp.	GENUS
250					

→ For more details on working with named ranges, **see** "Using Named Ranges in Formulas," **p. 604**.

Begin entering criteria in the row just below the column labels. You can enter text, numbers, dates, or logical values using comparison operators such as > and <. To find values that are greater than or equal to a specific value, use the >= operator. For example, >=1000 finds all values greater than or equal to 1000 in the specified column; in a text column, <C finds all entries that begin with A or B.

20

You can enter values in more than one column and in more than one row. When you do, Excel interprets your input as follows:

- For values in more than one column within a single row, Excel looks for records that match all values that you specify in the row, the equivalent of a logical AND.

- For values in the same column in separate rows, Excel displays records that match any of the values, the equivalent of a logical OR.

In essence, each row in the criteria range equals a single *condition*. By mixing and matching conditions, you can filter a list in many different ways, including the following:

- **Multiple conditions for one column**—Enter each condition in a separate cell under the column label in the criteria range. In the example shown in Figure 20.14, any row containing the value Dog, Cat, or Fish in the Category column will match.

	A	B
1	Part No.	Category
2		Dog
3		Cat
4		Fish

Figure 20.14

- **One condition in each of several columns**—Enter each condition under its respective column label in the same row. The example in Figure 20.15 will match rows in which the value in the Category column is Dog and the price is less than $10. Generally, this type of filter is much easier to apply using an AutoFilter.

	A	B	C
1	Part No.	Category	Price
2		Dog	<10

Figure 20.15

- **Multiple conditions in multiple columns**—Enter each set of conditions in its own row of the criteria range, and Excel will find rows in the list that match either set. Figure 20.16 finds any item in the Dog category whose price is less than $10, or any item in the Fish category whose price is greater than $20. This type of condition is nearly impossible to match with an AutoFilter.

	A	B	C
1	Part No.	Category	Price
2		Dog	<10
3		Cat	>20

Figure 20.16

To specify multiple criteria for the same column in the same row, add another column heading in the criteria range, using the same column label (extend the criteria range, if necessary, or replace the label for an existing column for which you're not defining conditions). For example, if you have a column called Amount, add a second column label, also called Amount, to your criteria range. Then, when you enter >3000 in one cell and <6000 in the other, both in the same row, Excel finds only records in which the Amount is between 3000 and 6000.

CAUTION

If you enter text in a criteria range, Excel finds all matching records that begin with that text. Thus, if you enter the letter F under the Category label, Excel finds all records whose category begins with F. To find only records that match the exact text that you specify, you must enter the value using the following format: `=""=text""` (where *text* is the value you want to use in your condition). Make sure to include both equals signs.

Finally, you can create conditions based on formulas. Although formulas can be a powerful way to filter a list, they are extremely challenging to enter, and the syntax is confusing. Unlike other conditions, which must appear under a label in the criteria range that matches the corresponding label in the list, you must not use a column label with a formula; enter the formulas in a cell beneath a blank label, or change the label above it so that it does not match a label in the list. Individual references in the formula should come from the column label or the first record of the list, and the formulas must evaluate to TRUE or FALSE.

In the example in Figure 20.17, we started with a simple list of orders, in which each row contains a transaction number, a price per box, and a number of boxes. We want to identify the orders that represent the highest cost, which we've arbitrarily defined as a total of $300.

Note that we've changed the label above the last column in the criteria range (cell C1) to read Big_Order. As you can see from the formula bar, the formula in cell C2 multiplies the value in the Amount column by the value in the Boxes column for the first row of the list (B6*C6) to see whether it's greater than 300. The result of this filter finds 9 matching rows.

Figure 20.17
The formula in cell C2 contains relative references to values in the first row of the database (row 6); note that the label above it does not match a label in the list itself.

	A	B	C
	C2	▾	*fx* =B6*C6>30
1	Trans_Num	Amount	Big Ord
2			FALSE
3			
4			
5	Trans_Num	Amount	Boxes
9	1004	$79.56	5
10	1005	$63.67	9
16	1011	$57.52	6
17	1012	$88.44	4
18	1013	$76.84	6
23	1018	$81.47	9
26	1021	$89.80	6
29	1024	$79.03	4
31	1026	$97.58	5

After you've created the criteria range and entered criteria, apply the filter to your list by following these steps:

1. Choose Data, Filter, Advanced Filter. The Advanced Filter dialog box appears (see Figure 20.18). Note that the values shown here correspond to values in Figure 20.17.

2. Click in the List Range box and then select the entire list, including the header row. (If you selected the list before opening the Advanced Filter dialog box, this range is already selected.)

Figure 20.18

3. Click in the Criteria Range box and select the portion of the criteria range that contains data. At a minimum, this must include one column label and one cell beneath that label. If your criteria include multiple rows, make sure that you select each row. The portion of the criteria range that you select must be a contiguous range.

4. Choose a destination for the Advanced Filter results, using the following options:

- To filter the list in place, as an AutoFilter does, accept the default option under Action.

- To extract records to another location, click the Copy to Another Location option; then click in the Copy To box and select the cell at the top-left corner of the range where you want the extracted records to appear (logically, this location is called the *extract range*). This location must be on the same worksheet as the list itself; if you want to extract specific fields, you must include column labels that correspond to the fields you want to extract. You do not need to extract every column from the list.

- To filter out duplicate records, select the Unique Records Only check box. If you filter the list in place, this option excludes those rows in which the values in every column are identical. If you extract the results to a new location and specify a subset of columns, Excel defines duplicates based only on the columns in the extract range.

TIP FROM

EQ & Woody

> By extracting unique records, you can quickly build a list of categories from a much larger list like the one in the examples shown here. Use no conditions in the criteria range. For the extract range, pick a cell below the list and enter the label of the column that you want to extract (Category, in this case). When you run the Advanced Filter, Excel displays a list of all the unique values in your Category column, with no duplicates.

5. Click OK to apply the filter.

TIP FROM

EQ & Woody

> Use range names to skip some steps in this process. If you create named ranges called Database and Extract, Excel automatically selects them in the Advanced Filter dialog box each time you use it. Excel automatically creates a named criteria range each time you use the Advanced Filter dialog box.

Advanced filters don't update automatically when you enter new values in the criteria range. To apply the new criteria, you need to reopen the Advanced Criteria dialog box and click OK. To remove an in-place filter from a list, choose Data, Filter, Show All.

USING FORMS TO ADD AND EDIT LIST DATA

Data forms provide a simple method for entering data into an Excel list. When you open a data form, Excel creates a dialog box on the fly, based on your list's column headings. When you enter data in the form, Excel fills in the correct columns, adding rows to the end of the list, if necessary.

TIP FROM

EQ & Woody

> Although you can also use data forms to view and search for information in lists, this technique is rarely worth it. Sorts, filters, and PivotTables are much easier ways to browse a list. The advantage of using a data form for data entry is that Excel automatically adds each row that you enter to the end of the list without requiring you to reposition the active cell.

To add records to an existing list with a data form, click to position the insertion point within your list, and then choose Data, Form. This displays a dialog box like the one in Figure 20.19. (The exact arrangement of columns, of course, depends on the header row in your list.) Click the New button to add a record to the list. When you press Enter, Excel stores the new row at the end of the list and displays a blank form for the next new record. Click Close or press Esc to return to the worksheet.

Figure 20.19
When you add a new record using a data form like this one, Excel automatically adds a new row at the end of the list.

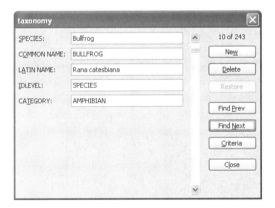

TIP FROM

EQ & Woody

> Is the data form too wide? Excel uses the width of the longest column in your list to determine the width of the form dialog box. Try narrowing any long columns to make the form easier to use.

In general, using data forms to search for information is inefficient. In one specific circumstance, however, this technique is useful. Say that you have a list that contains a large number of columns, some of which are extremely wide. Editing information in this type of list is a hassle because you have to continually scroll to the right to see all the columns in your list and then scroll back to see the beginning of the next row. If you need to edit a group of related records in a list like this, use the data form to locate specific records by entering criteria that identify data in your list:

1. Choose Data, Form to open a new data form. Click the Criteria button. Excel clears the data from the form and displays a blank box for each column in the list.

2. Enter your criteria for each column that you want to search. You can enter text or numbers. You can also use comparison operators, such as less than (<) and greater than (>) in the criteria that you enter in a form. To find records in which a particular column is blank, enter an equals sign (=) with no other text in that column. To narrow your search, enter criteria in multiple columns.

NOTE

If you search for a text string using a data form, Excel searches for columns that contain the entire string you entered. Use wildcards such as * and ? to search for columns that include a particular string. For example, type `*bullfrog*` in the Common_Name column, and Excel will find any record that contains that word anywhere within its name.

3. Click Find Next to move through the list looking for records that match the criteria you entered. If Excel can't find a matching record, you'll hear a beep. Click Find Prev to search in reverse order through the list.

After locating records with a form, you can change any data except calculated columns. Excel inserts your changes into the list as soon as you move to another row. When you use a data form to change a value that is used in a calculated column, you won't see the change in the calculated result immediately because Excel waits to recalculate columns until you move to another record. To update the calculation, press Enter to store your changes and then (if necessary) click Find Prev to return.

To delete the record currently visible in the form, click the Delete button. The effect is the same as if you had deleted all cells from that record in the list and then shifted the remainder of the list up.

NOTE

Using a data form, you can delete only one record at a time. Return to the list and select multiple rows to delete more than one record at once.

CAUTION

If you delete a row by mistake in Data Form view, you'll see a confirmation message warning you that you're about to delete the record permanently. Take this message seriously! When you delete a record using a data form, the Undo command is not available to restore the original data. The Restore button lets you discard changes that you've made to the current row, but only if you haven't moved to the next record and entered the changes on the worksheet.

IMPORTING AND EXPORTING DATA

Using Excel, you can create a list using data from a *text file*; you can also save a list to a text file. You import and export text files when you want to share lists between programs, such as mailing-list management software and database programs that cannot read Excel worksheet files.

To import a text file as a list, first position the insertion point in the cell where you want the data to appear. Make sure that no data appears below or to the right of the location that you select, or it could be overwritten. Then follow these steps:

1. Choose Data, Import External Data, Import Data.

2. In the Open dialog box, choose Text Files from the Files of Type list, select the file that you want to import, and click Open. The Text Import Wizard appears.

3. Specify how Excel should separate fields in your import file. Pick Delimited if the list uses characters such as commas or tabs to identify each field; choose Fixed Width if each field starts at the same position in each row.

NOTE

If the settings look correct here and you're confident that you don't need to adjust any other import options, click Finish to skip the remainder of the Import Text Wizard.

4. Click Next to display Step 2 of the wizard. If you're importing a *delimited* file, check that Excel has selected the correct options for your file. (In the example shown in Figure 20.20, we had to click the Comma check box before the wizard would correctly identify each field.) With a fixed-width file, click in the ruler to identify the beginning of each new column. Click Next again.

Figure 20.20
Be sure to specify the correct delimiters when importing a text file. Scroll through the Data Preview window, if necessary, to check a sufficient sample of records.

20

5. In the next step of the wizard, which is optional, choose formatting options for date/time and number fields, or specify any fields that you don't want to import. Click Finish to move to the last step of the process. Excel displays the Import Data dialog box.

6. Ensure that the cell you want to use as the top-left corner of the list is selected. Adjust this location if necessary, or click New Worksheet to create the list without disturbing existing sheets.

7. By default, Excel creates an external query to the original file, so that any changes you make to that text file can be reflected in your worksheet as well. If you want to permanently add the data to your worksheet and break the link to the external file, click the Properties button, clear the Save Query Definition box, and click OK to close the External Data Range Properties dialog box.

8. Click OK to add the new list to your worksheet.

To save an existing list in a text file that you can import into a database program, first make sure that the list you want to save is on its own worksheet, with no other data on that sheet. (If necessary, copy the list range to a new sheet before continuing.) Click to select the sheet that contains the list, choose File, Save As, and choose one of Excel's compatible delimited formats: CSV (comma-delimited) or Text (tab-delimited).

After importing data into a worksheet, you might end up with some blank cells. In some situations, you might want to replace those blanks with a value, such as "NA" or zero. To do so, follow these steps:

1. Select the range that contains the blank cells that you want to change. Don't select any other cells.

2. Press F5 to display the Go To dialog box.

3. Click the Special button and choose Blanks from the list of options in the Go To Special dialog box. Click OK to select all blank cells in the range.

4. Type the number or text that you want to enter in the blank cells, and then hold down the Ctrl key and press Enter. Excel enters that value in every formerly blank cell.

HOW PIVOTTABLE AND PIVOTCHART REPORTS WORK

PivotTables and PivotCharts are powerful tools for automatically summarizing and analyzing data without ever having to add a formula or function. As the name implies, you start with a list exactly like the ones we've discussed in the first half of this chapter; then you snap the rows and columns into position on a grid, and end up with a sorted, grouped, summarized, totaled, and subtotaled report. PivotTable reports are best for cross-tabulating lists— the more categories, the better. You can reduce a list of thousands of items to a single line, showing totals by category or department. Or you can create complex, multilevel groupings that show total expenses by department, grouped by budget category and by quarter. You can hide or show detail for each group with a quick double-click. You can change the view or grouping in literally seconds, just by dragging items on or off the sheet and moving them between row, column, and page fields.

Start with a list that contains multiple fields, and then use Excel's PivotTable Wizard to set up a blank PivotTable page with just a few clicks. Instead of sorting your list and entering formulas and functions, you drag fields around on the PivotTable page to create a new view of your list—Excel groups the data and adds summary formulas automatically. PivotCharts (which we discuss later in this chapter) are the visual equivalent of PivotTables, letting you create killer charts just as quickly, by dragging fields on a chart layout page.

Unlike subtotals and outlines, which modify the structure of your list to display summaries, PivotTables and PivotCharts create new, independent elements in your workbook. When you add or edit data in a list, the changes show up in your PivotTables and PivotCharts as well; because they're separate elements, you can easily change the structure of a PivotTable or PivotChart, too, and your changes won't mess up the data in the underlying list.

Figure 20.21 shows the four main *drop zones* on a blank PivotTable page. The PivotTable toolbar includes buttons for every field in your list. Use row fields and column fields to define how you want Excel to group your list. Data items define which fields contain the information you want to summarize. Page fields let you further refine your view by displaying a separate PivotTable for each item in a group, as though the table were on its own virtual page. You can use multiple row fields, column fields, or both, and you can specify which summary action you want Excel to perform on data items—the sum, average, or count of all related values, for instance.

Figure 20.21
Drag field buttons from the toolbar and drop them on the layout to build a PivotTable on-the-fly.

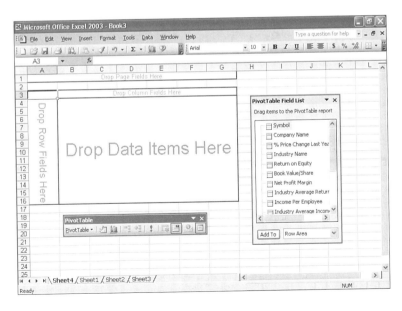

20

What can you do with a PivotTable? The number of uses is limited only by your imagination. Despite their dramatically different structures, for example, each of the following four PivotTables started with the same list of information about publicly traded stocks, which we downloaded from an Internet-based online service. In its raw form, with its grand total of 106,224 separate data points, the list is a prescription for information overload. Each of the 6,639 rows contains 16 data fields for an individual publicly traded company, including its name, ticker symbol, and industry category, the exchange on which it trades, its high and low stock price for the past year, and financial measurements such as net profit margin and return on equity.

A decade ago, you had to be a professional financial analyst with access to a mainframe computer to crunch numbers this thoroughly; today, you can manage your own money with nothing more than a web browser and some Excel know-how.

Figure 20.22 shows a simple PivotTable that lets you see at a glance how many companies are in each industry category, along with the average increase or decrease in stock price from companies in that category over the past year. This PivotTable consists of a single row field and two data items.

Figure 20.22
With no column fields and only one row field, this PivotTable quickly counts the number of companies in each category and calculates the average price change for the year.

	A	B	C
3	Industry Name	Number of Companies	% Price Chg Last Yr (Avg)
4	Closed-End Fund - Debt	360	-1.00
5	Savings & Loans	237	18.94
6	Business Software & Services	164	-38.23
7	Internet Software & Services	133	-22.66
8	Business Services	128	-21.35
9	Biotechnology	120	-45.73
10	Scientific & Technical Instruments	119	-24.45
11	Regional - Northeast Banks	116	14.96
12	Drug Manufacturers - Other	111	-33.29
13	Independent Oil & Gas	106	-7.48
14	Medical Appliances & Equipment	103	-18.11
15	Regional - Mid-Atlantic Banks	99	19.95
16	Communication Equipment	94	-31.54
17	Medical Instruments & Supplies	88	-24.90
18	Application Software	85	-27.05
19	Property & Casualty Insurance	75	-13.30
20	Restaurants	71	-19.31
21	Closed-End Fund - Foreign	71	-11.76

In Figure 20.23, more detail is added, displaying individual statistics for each company, and grouping the detail rows in alphabetical order by industry name. For this PivotTable, the data is arranged in report format, similar to the banded reports that high-end database management programs produce. Note that this PivotTable includes four data items instead of two, and a slew of Excel formatting options are used to make the report more readable—changing fonts and font sizes, aligning type and adding background shading, and standardizing the number of decimal points in each column.

To slice the data even more finely and add an extra analytical dimension, you can drag more buttons from the PivotTable toolbar to the row and column fields. Each row in the PivotTable is grouped using unique values in two categories, and there are two column headings as well, one for each unique value in the "Split in Last Year" column field.

(To make the PivotTable easier to read, the column headings were renamed from Yes and No to Split and No Split.) At the intersection of each row and column in the PivotTable, Excel counts the number of companies and calculates the average income per employee for all rows that match the row and column fields.

Figure 20.23
To hide gridlines and group-related items in bands such as these, choose a report format instead of the default table layout.

	A	B	C	D	E	F
1						
2						
			Avg of Net Profit Margin	Avg of % Price Change Last Year	52-Week Low	52-Week High
3	Industry Name	Company Name				
127		Petroleum Helicopters, Inc.	3.7	5.8	23.9	31.0
128						
129	Aluminum		2.3	(34.6)	71.4	155.4
130		Alcan Inc.	3.0	(25.1)	23.2	40.1
131		Alcoa Inc.	1.9	(41.0)	17.6	39.1
132		ALUMINUM CP CHN ADS	9.9	(17.5)	9.4	22.8
133		Century Aluminum Company	(2.6)	(50.9)	5.6	17.5
134		Commonwealth Industries, Inc.	0.9	(26.2)	4.2	8.1
135		Pechiney	0.8	(46.6)	11.4	27.8
136						
137	Apparel Stores		3.0	(22.8)	492.0	1,130.0
138		Abercrombie & Fitch Co.	12.2	0.7	15.0	33.9
139		American Eagle Outfitters, Inc.	6.1	(41.1)	9.8	27.2
140		AnnTaylor Stores Corporation	5.8	(28.1)	17.1	33.2
141		bebe stores, inc.	7.4	(48.3)	9.6	24.8
142		Big Dog Holdings, Inc.	3.4	(35.0)	1.8	5.6
143		Buckle, Inc.	8.0	(26.4)	15.5	25.5
144		Burlington Coat Factory Warehouse Corpora	2.7	(11.7)	15.4	23.5

The resulting PivotTable, shown in Figure 20.24, is a concise and crystal-clear cross-tabulation, giving you a side-by-side analysis of the number of stocks that split in the past year versus those that didn't, broken down by industry category and exchange.

Figure 20.24
Add a column field to quickly compare related data points. Notice that the worksheet pane is frozen to keep headings visible when scrolling, just as with an ordinary worksheet.

		A323	▼	*fx*	Regional - Mid-Atlantic Banks		
		A	B	C	D	E	F
3				Split in Last Year ▼ Data ▼			
4				Split		No Split	
5	Industry Name		Exchange ▼	Number of Companies	Avg Income Per Employee	Number of Companies	Avg Income Per Employee
140	Drugs Wholesale		AMEX	0	$ -	2	$ (174,500)
141			NASDAQ	1	$ 7,000	2	$ 54,000
142			NYSE	1	$ 22,000	2	$ 17,000
143	Education & Training Services		NASDAQ	1	$ 21,000	4	$ 16,500
144			NYSE	1	$ 12,000	2	$ 4,000
145	Electric Utilities		AMEX	0	$ -	3	$ 55,000
146			NASDAQ	0	$ -	2	$ 18,000
147			NYSE	3	$ 53,333	34	$ 31,618
148	Electronic Equipment		AMEX	0	$ -	3	$ 21,000
149			NASDAQ	1	$ 34,000	5	$ (400)
150			NYSE	0	$ -	1	$ 12,000
151	Electronics Stores		NASDAQ	0	$ -	3	$ -
152			NYSE	1	$ 6,000	3	$ 4,667
153	Electronics Wholesale		NASDAQ	0	$ -	5	$ 6,200
154			NYSE	0	$ -	2	$ (2,000)
155	Entertainment - Diversified		AMEX	0	$ -	2	$ 6,000
156			NYSE	2	$ 151,000	2	$ 24,500
157	Farm & Construction Machinery		AMEX	1	$ 13,000	0	$ -
158			NASDAQ	0	$ -	2	$ 12,500

There are literally hundreds of options in even a modestly complex PivotTable, but a PivotTable doesn't have to be large or complex to be effective. The PivotTable in Figure 20.25, for example, neatly summarizes more than 100,000 data points in just a few rows and columns.

20

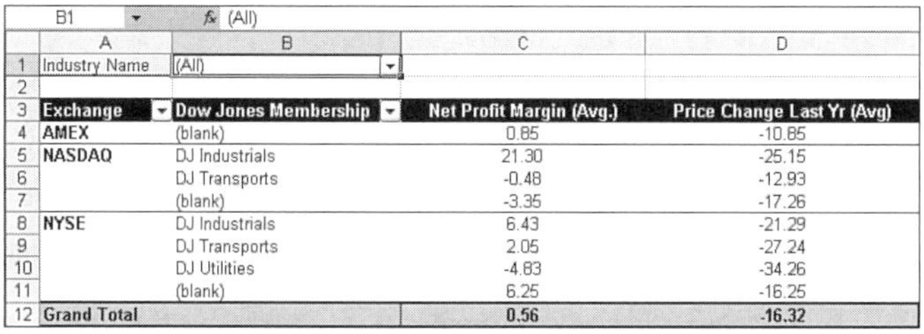

Figure 20.25
Notice the grand totals under the rows in this PivotTable. Use the page field in the top-left corner to filter the entire list.

	A	B	C	D
	B1	▼	ƒx (All)	
1	Industry Name	(All)	▼	
2				
3	Exchange ▼	Dow Jones Membership ▼	Net Profit Margin (Avg.)	Price Change Last Yr (Avg)
4	AMEX	(blank)	0.85	-10.85
5	NASDAQ	DJ Industrials	21.30	-25.15
6		DJ Transports	-0.48	-12.93
7		(blank)	-3.35	-17.26
8	NYSE	DJ Industrials	6.43	-21.29
9		DJ Transports	2.05	-27.24
10		DJ Utilities	-4.83	-34.26
11		(blank)	6.25	-16.25
12	Grand Total		0.56	-16.32

To produce this example, we used two column fields, two row fields, and one page field—a drop-down list that lets us filter the records in the entire table. Choosing (All) from the page field shows a summary of all data in the list; by selecting a different entry from the drop-down list, you can show the same breakdown for each industry name. Select one category at a time to flip through a series of otherwise identical PivotTables that focus on each category.

The layout Excel produced automatically included totals for each row and column; we kept only the grand total at the bottom of the PivotTable. We had to modify other default settings as well, including changing the default formula to calculate the average of our data items. To make the headings and totals easier to read, we did some rewording, and then changed fonts and alignment, added shading, and wrapped text.

WHEN SHOULD YOU USE A PIVOTTABLE?

PivotTables have several advantages over other worksheet models. Using the PivotTable Wizard, it's easy to create a PivotTable that summarizes all or part of a list in dozens of different ways. Trying to accomplish the same task by entering formulas manually would take days. Also, because PivotTables and PivotCharts do not change your existing data or its arrangement on the worksheet, you can freely experiment with different PivotTable layouts. Use the Undo button to roll back any changes you make in a PivotTable layout. If you want to start over, you can delete the PivotTable page and run the wizard again.

PivotTables are the correct choice when all your data is in a list or in an external database you can query from Excel. PivotTables are not appropriate for structured worksheet models that include data-entry cells, subtotals, and summary rows. A PivotTable won't do much good on an annual budget worksheet, for example, because it already includes rows, columns, and subtotals. On the other hand, if you enter the raw data in a list (or import it from an external database), with each row containing a month, department, budget category, and amount, you can easily re-create that same layout in PivotTable form—and you'll have many more analytical options available to you later.

CREATING A PIVOTTABLE

To create a PivotTable from an existing list, start with Excel's PivotTable Wizard. In this simple three-step process, Excel prompts you for basic details about the PivotTable you want to create, including the location of the data source and where you want the PivotTable to appear. After you finish with the wizard, you'll be able to lay out your data directly on the worksheet.

You can create and edit a PivotTable layout directly on the sheet, or you can edit PivotTable layouts the old-fashioned way, using the Layout dialog box. On a slow computer, or with extremely large lists, you might prefer to use this technique, because it doesn't actually begin rearranging data until you click OK. To open the Layout dialog box, click the Layout button in Step 3 of the PivotTable and PivotChart Wizard.

To build a new PivotTable, open the workbook that contains the list on which you plan to base the PivotTable. Then follow these steps:

1. Click anywhere in your list. To build a PivotTable from a subset of the data in your list, select the range that contains the data.

2. Choose Data, PivotTable and PivotChart Report. The PivotTable Wizard appears, as shown in Figure 20.26.

Figure 20.26
If you don't select a range first, the PivotTable Wizard assumes you want to base the new PivotTable on the entire list. Change the selection, if necessary, in the next step.

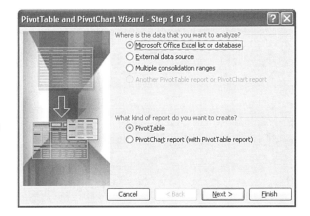

3. Specify the location of your data—typically an Excel list. If you choose the Multiple Consolidation Ranges option, Excel lets you select a group of data ranges from one or more worksheets. Click Next to move on.

4. The wizard asks you to specify the range in which your data is located. The default selection is your current list, or any range you selected before starting the wizard. Adjust the selection, if necessary, and click Next.

5. In its final step, the wizard asks you where you want to place the PivotTable. Choose the default option, New Worksheet.

20

CAUTION

> The PivotTable Wizard offers the option to place a PivotTable or PivotChart on an existing worksheet. In general, you should always choose to place a PivotTable on its own sheet. Adding a PivotTable to a sheet that contains data exposes you to the risk that changes you make to the list design will affect your PivotTable, or vice versa.

6. Click Finish to close the wizard and create a blank PivotTable page. Excel jumps to the new worksheet you just created and displays the PivotTable toolbar.

7. Drag field buttons from the PivotTable Field List and drop them into the appropriate regions in the layout. You must have at least one row or column field, and you must specify a data item.

TIP FROM

Ed & Woody

> If you're uncertain about exactly where to drop field buttons, watch the screen for two important clues. As the mouse pointer passes over each region of the PivotTable, Excel displays informative ScreenTips. When dragging fields around, watch the mouse pointer—it changes shape to match the PivotTable layout, and a blue highlight in the pointer shows which of the four regions (row, column, data, or page) is under the pointer at any given moment. If you can't figure out where to drop the selected field button, use the Add To list at the bottom of the PivotTable Field List window.

Don't be surprised if the PivotTable doesn't display properly at first. In particular, summary fields in the data area default to the SUM function. If you want to use COUNT, AVERAGE, or another summary function instead, see the next section.

EDITING AND UPDATING A PIVOTTABLE

After you create a PivotTable, it's easy to rearrange fields and data items. Drag fields from one place to another to change the display of data—from a row field to a column field, for example, if you want to see values side by side rather than one above the other. Right-click to display shortcut menus that let you adjust formatting and other options for each field. This section describes common procedures for editing PivotTables.

Use the PivotTable Field List to drag fields onto the layout. If you're uncomfortable with drag-and-drop operations, use the Add To drop-down list to choose where you want the field to appear. If the Field List isn't visible, right-click the PivotTable layout area and choose View Field List from the bottom of the shortcut menu. To make changes to the PivotTable report, use any or all of these techniques:

- To change the list or data source on which the PivotTable is based, click the PivotTable Wizard button on the PivotTable toolbar. Click Back twice to return to the beginning of the wizard and make the required changes, and then click Finish. If you add new rows or columns to a list, you might need to perform this step before the data or fields will be available.

- To add a new field to the layout, drag a field button from the PivotTable toolbar and drop it on the layout. If you're replacing an existing field, remove the old field first to reduce unnecessary calculations. When you drop a new field in the row or column area, Excel adds it as part of the hierarchy of fields that are already there and automatically groups items in the order in which they appear. Be careful to arrange these fields in the proper order. For example, if you have a list of product categories, each of which contains multiple products, place the category field to the left of the product name field, or the results will be nonsense.

TIP FROM

If your list includes two fields that have an absolute one-to-one correspondence, such as part numbers and part names, you can add them to the row area in either order and your list will appear correctly.

- To remove a field from any part of the PivotTable layout, drag the field button off the layout; when the pointer icon changes to include a red X, release the mouse button.
- To change the order of fields in rows, columns, or the data area, drag the field button and drop it in the correct location on the layout. Make sure you're pointing to the field button and not its label; you'll know you've aimed correctly when the mouse button turns to a four-headed pointer. Drag to another location and watch the mouse pointer and thick black lines for feedback on the correct "drop" location.

TIP FROM

Using the mouse to rearrange the order of data items on a PivotTable can be frustrating. It's usually easier to right-click the field button you want to move, and then choose any of the options on the Order menu. Typically, you can move the item left or right one position, or move it to the beginning or end of the list.

- To change the summary function used in the data area (from SUM to COUNT or AVERAGE, for example), right-click the field button in the PivotTable and choose Field Settings from the shortcut menu. That action opens the PivotTable Field dialog box, shown in Figure 20.27. Select a function from the Summarize By list; if you want to change the name from its default, do so in the Name box, and then click OK to save the change.

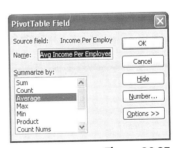

Figure 20.27

When you drag and drop buttons to arrange fields on a PivotTable page, Excel makes all sorts of decisions on your behalf. If these defaults aren't correct, the following sections will help you change them.

CHANGING SORT ORDER AND OTHER DISPLAY OPTIONS

The *default sort order* for rows and columns is usually alphanumeric. You can change the order of individual items by dragging them up or down (in the case of rows) or left or right (for columns). In other cases, you might want to adjust the default sort order. For example, if your PivotTable counts the number of items in each category, you might want to see categories with the highest number of items at the top of the list. To change the sort order, follow these steps:

Figure 20.28

1. Right-click the PivotTable button for the row or column field and choose Field Settings.

2. Click the Advanced button to display the dialog box shown in Figure 20.28.

3. Choose a sort order and the column by which to sort. The settings in Figure 20.28, for example, produce the list shown earlier in Figure 20.22, moving categories that contain the largest number of companies to the top of the list.

4. To show a specific number of records, choose Automatic from the AutoShow options section. This is a good way to create a "top 10" list, for example, showing only the categories that have the most items. Choose Top or Bottom from the Show drop-down list, and select a number between 1 and 255. Excel chooses records based on the sort order you defined in step 3.

→ AutoFilter can save a tremendous amount of time, if you know how to use it properly; **see** "Using AutoFilter to Find Sets of Data," **p. 641**.

5. Click OK to close the Advanced Options dialog box, and click OK again to close the PivotTable Field dialog box and return to the worksheet.

ADDING AND REMOVING COLUMN AND ROW SUBTOTALS

You can add subtotals to rows, columns, or both in a list. In some cases, Excel adds them automatically, even if they're not appropriate. Subtotals can add a useful way to see the impact of groupings in your PivotTable, or they can add clutter between rows and columns. Depending on the design of your PivotTable and what Excel did automatically, you might need to add or remove these subtotals. In some cases, you can remove subtotals with the right-click shortcut menu. Right-click any of the subtotals and choose Hide. To add subtotals, you need to use the dialog boxes. To work with subtotals, follow these steps:

1. Right-click the PivotTable button for the row or column heading that contains the subtotal, and choose Field Settings from the shortcut menu. Excel displays the PivotTable Field dialog box, as shown in Figure 20.29.

Figure 20.29
Use the Subtotals options to add, edit, or hide subtotals for a row or column.

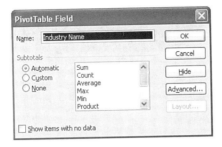

2. In the Subtotals section, choose Automatic to let Excel create subtotals for all items. Choose Custom and click a summary function to add one or more specific type of subtotals, such as Count and Average. Click None to remove all subtotals.
3. Click OK to exit the dialog box and make the changes you specified.

SWITCHING BETWEEN TABLE AND OUTLINE LAYOUTS

The default layout for a PivotTable, as the name implies, is a tabular format. But that grid-style arrangement is not always the most effective way to present data. When you're grouping a PivotTable by one row field and displaying data for a second row field, you probably want to use outline format instead; in that layout, the top-level row field appears in its own row, followed by each group of items. Which one should you choose? The question is partly dictated by the data in your table and partly by aesthetics; there is no right answer. Figure 20.30, for example, shows a table format. Figure 20.31 shows the same data arranged in outline format. In this case, the outline format is probably more appropriate, because each break in the grouping functions as a header for the list of details beneath it.

Figure 20.30
In tabular format view, the categories are arranged in a column to the left of the items to which they belong.

		Avg of Net Profit Margin	Avg of % Price Change Last Year	52-Week Low	52-Week High
Industry Name	Company Name				
	AFLAC Incorporated	8.0	15.8	24.2	33.5
	American Independence Corp.		34.9	5.2	8.7
	Aon Corporation	5.3	(40.1)	13.3	39.6
Accident &	Citizens Financial Corporation	(8.7)	(40.0)	3.4	8.9
Health	Everest Re Group Ltd.	9.0	(17.1)	42.6	72.2
Insurance	FPIC Insurance Group, Inc.	6.7	(40.8)	3.5	16.0
	MIIX Group, Incorporated	(68.8)	(75.4)	0.6	2.9
	Torchmark Corporation	15.1	(6.7)	30.0	41.8
	UNUMProvident	6.2	(67.8)	6.1	29.5
	Catalina Marketing Corporation	12.8	(45.6)	15.8	37.0
	Cordiant Communications Group plc	(51.9)	(70.2)	1.9	7.7
	Digital Generation Systems, Inc.	7.1	110.9	0.7	2.4
	Grey Global Group Inc.	(1.7)	(5.3)	508.0	832.0
	Havas	(2.9)	(66.9)	2.3	9.4
	Interpublic Group of Companies, Inc.	1.6	(70.2)	7.2	35.0
Advertising	Obie Media Corporation	(4.5)	(29.5)	2.0	4.2
Agencies	Omnicom Group Inc.	8.5	(38.1)	36.5	95.5

20

Figure 20.31
In Outline view, the categories appear more like headers, and you can use space on the page or screen more efficiently.

Industry Name ▾	Company Name	Avg of Net Profit Margin	Avg of % Price Change Last Year	52-Week Low	52-Week High
Accident & Health Insurance		(3.4)	(26.4)	128.8	253.1
	AFLAC Incorporated	8.0	15.8	24.2	33.5
	American Independence Corp.		34.9	5.2	8.7
	Aon Corporation	5.3	(40.1)	13.3	39.6
	Citizens Financial Corporation	(8.7)	(40.0)	3.4	8.9
	Everest Re Group Ltd.	9.0	(17.1)	42.6	72.2
	FPIC Insurance Group, Inc.	6.7	(40.8)	3.5	16.0
	MIIX Group, Incorporated	(68.8)	(75.4)	0.6	2.9
	Torchmark Corporation	15.1	(6.7)	30.0	41.8
	UNUMProvident	6.2	(67.8)	6.1	29.5
Advertising Agencies		(3.8)	(33.4)	625.5	1,156.9
	Catalina Marketing Corporation	12.8	(45.6)	15.8	37.0
	Cordiant Communications Group plc	(51.9)	(70.2)	1.9	7.7
	Digital Generation Systems, Inc.	7.1	110.9	0.7	2.4
	Grey Global Group Inc.	(1.7)	(5.3)	508.0	832.0
	Havas	(2.9)	(66.9)	2.3	9.4
	Interpublic Group of Companies, Inc.	1.6	(70.2)	7.2	35.0
	Obie Media Corporation	(4.5)	(29.5)	2.0	4.2
	Omnicom Group Inc.	8.5	(38.1)	36.5	95.5

To switch between tabular and outline formats, follow these steps:

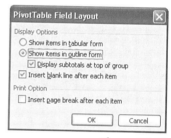

Figure 20.32

1. Right-click the PivotTable button for the row field that's farthest to the left, and choose Field Settings from the shortcut menu.

2. In the PivotTable Field dialog box, click the Layout button to display the dialog box shown in Figure 20.32.

3. To use a tabular layout, select the Show Items in Tabular Form option. To use an outline-style layout, select the Show Items in Outline Form option.

4. Adjust any other options—to add a blank line or a page break after each group, for example—and click OK.

To make the tabular view in Figure 20.30 easier to read, a hidden option was used. Right-click anywhere on the table, choose Table Options, and then check the Merge Layout option. The effect is to merge all cells for the outside row and column labels.

TIP FROM
EQ & Woody

Excel includes a broad selection of PivotTable AutoFormats, divided more or less equally between table and outline (report) layouts. Use AutoFormats to quickly switch between table and outline layouts while also adjusting formatting options.

REMOVING BLANK CELLS AND ERROR MESSAGES

Because PivotTables automatically summarize all data, it's common to see blank cells and error messages in the data area. #DIV/0 errors, for example, are especially common when calculating averages because in a long list, it's almost certain that some items will have no matches in a particular row-and-column intersection. For example, if you're calculating average sales with regions in the column area and product categories in the row area, some regions will have no sales for a particular category. These aren't really errors; instead, you want the table to display a label such as NA, for "Not Applicable."

Careful attention to blanks and error messages can make your PivotTable easier to read and make it look more professional. Here's how to adjust the appearance of blank cells and errors:

1. Right-click any part of the PivotTable and choose Table Options from the shortcut menu. Excel displays the PivotTable Options dialog box, as shown in Figure 20.33.

Figure 20.33
Use the options at the right of this dialog box to change the way a PivotTable displays blank cells and error messages.

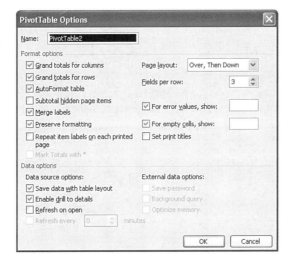

2. Select the For Error Values, Show check box. Click in the box to the right and fill in the information you want to display instead of the error message, such as NA.

3. Select the For Empty Cells, Show check box. If the field contains numeric data, enter 0 here; for a text field, enter the value you want Excel to display (NA, for instance) instead of leaving the cell blank.

4. Click OK to save your changes.

REFRESHING DATA IN A PIVOTTABLE

When you change the layout of a PivotTable, Excel automatically recalculates the resulting display of data. If you add or edit data in the underlying list, however, your changes do not appear immediately in the associated PivotTable. For PivotTable reports based on Excel lists, you must manually refresh the data in the PivotTable whenever you add, remove, or edit data. To be certain that the PivotTable reflects all recent changes, click the Refresh Data button on the PivotTable toolbar. If this toolbar isn't visible, choose Data, Refresh Data.

CREATING AND EDITING PIVOTCHARTS

A PivotChart is a chart based on data in a PivotTable. Like its row-and-column-based counterpart, you can rearrange a PivotChart by dragging field labels on a chart sheet. When you change the layout of a PivotChart, Excel automatically rearranges the corresponding data in your PivotTable, and vice versa.

In general, any time you can use a PivotChart instead of a conventional chart, you should jump at the opportunity, because they're so much easier to create and edit.

PivotCharts follow almost exactly the same rules as charts you create from a conventional worksheet. The default chart type for a PivotChart is a stacked column chart, but you can change this to any chart type except X-Y (scatter) charts, bubble charts, and stock chart types. Chart options are identical to those found in regular charts, although you'll discover that it's impossible to move certain items, including the plot area, chart title, and axis titles.

NOTE

Every PivotChart requires a PivotTable, which it uses as its data source. You cannot create a PivotChart without adding a PivotTable to your worksheet as well.

To instantly create a PivotChart from an existing PivotTable, first click in the PivotTable, and then click the Chart Wizard button. (You'll find this button on Excel's Standard toolbar and on the PivotTable toolbar.) The PivotChart appears on a new chart sheet. If you prefer to start from scratch, start the PivotTable and PivotChart Wizard and choose the PivotChart Report option. Excel docks the field list on the right side of the screen and displays the blank PivotTable chart, as shown in Figure 20.34.

Figure 20.34
To change the layout of a PivotChart, drag field buttons from the toolbar and drop them on the appropriate area.

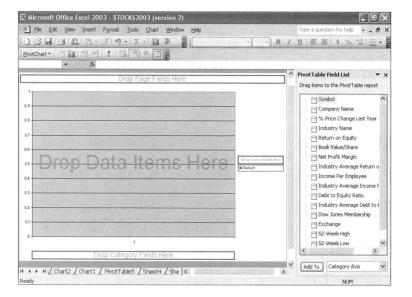

Of course, a chart doesn't include rows or columns, so the available drop zones on a blank PivotChart page are slightly different from their counterparts on a PivotTable. When you create a PivotChart from a PivotTable, row fields become category fields, and column fields become series fields. To change the arrangement of data in the PivotChart, drag field buttons from the PivotTable toolbar and drop them in one of four areas on the PivotChart. Category fields go below the chart, and series fields appear at the right of the chart. Drop data items directly into the body of the chart. If you want to add a page field, drag it to the region above the chart. Page fields are especially effective on a PivotChart, because they allow you to chart a subset of your data without having to remove or change data series. Click the drop-down arrow to the right of the page field to choose which item you want to display in the chart. The chart shown in Figure 20.35, for example, allows you to quickly compare data for each company within an industry category. If you used the All option for this chart, the display of more than 2,200 companies would be gibberish.

Figure 20.35
This PivotTable chart is a tremendous improvement over an ordinary chart, because you can use the page field (Industry Name) to quickly filter and redisplay the information.

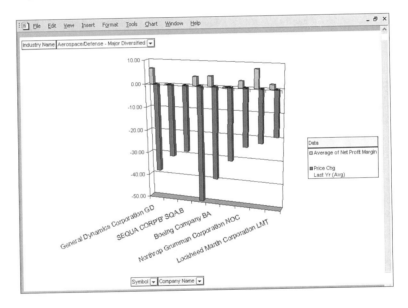

TIP FROM

EQ & Woody

There's no way to hide field buttons on a PivotTable, but you can remove clutter from a PivotChart. If you're happy with the chart layout, click the PivotChart button on the PivotTable toolbar and choose Hide PivotChart Field Buttons. Use the same menu choice to display the buttons again.

With PivotCharts, you can use the same formatting and editing options as with conventional charts. In particular, use right-click shortcut menus to choose a different chart type; format data series, axes, and the plot area; and add or edit colors and backgrounds to your chart.

→ For instructions on how to edit charts, **see** "Editing and Formatting Chart Elements," **p. 687**.

FORMATTING AND PRINTING PIVOTTABLES

When you first create a PivotTable, it picks up the generic look of a default worksheet, with plain 10-point Arial formatting for details and headings alike. To make your PivotTable more compelling, use Excel's formatting features to add emphasis to text and backgrounds or shading to cells, rows, and columns. You can also adjust the number format of data items.

→ For an overview of Excel's many formatting options, **see** Chapter 18, "Making Great-Looking Worksheets," **p. 559**.

You can format numbers and text in the data area of a PivotTable by selecting cells individually and choosing formatting options as you would in a normal worksheet. However, if you redefine your PivotTable later, you will lose this formatting. That can be exasperating if you're constantly losing, say, the number of decimal places you want to see in each data item. To apply number formatting that lasts, right-click any cell in the data items area and choose Field Settings from the shortcut menu. Click the Number button and choose a format from the dialog box.

TIP FROM

When you create a PivotTable or PivotChart on a new worksheet, Excel assigns a generic name to the new sheet. To make your worksheets easier to understand, right-click the tab, choose Rename, and give the sheet a new name that helps identify it. (You can also double-click the existing tab name to make it available for editing.) Right-click the PivotTable itself and choose Table Options to give the PivotTable itself a name, which you can use in dialog boxes and in the PivotTable Wizard.

Sometimes you need to adjust other formatting options as well. For example, you might want to change the alignment of a column of numbers, change to a new font, or add a background shade behind the column. Here, too, you have two options: If you right-click the cells in question and choose Format Cells, you'll have access to all common cell formatting options—Number, Alignment, Font, and so on. But as soon as you rearrange your PivotTable, those custom formats vanish.

To lock cell formatting in place regardless of what you do with your PivotTable, right-click the PivotTable button for the field you want to format and choose Format Cells from the shortcut menu. Adjust desired formatting options and click OK.

To make PivotTables look their best, take advantage of Excel's AutoFormat capability. After you've created a PivotTable, click the Format Report button on the PivotTable toolbar. You see a dialog box containing more than 20 ready-made formats. Select any format and click OK to apply the changes to your PivotTable.

If you don't like the AutoFormat you've applied to a PivotTable, it's easy to undo the changes. First, right-click any cell in the PivotTable, choose Table Options from the shortcut menu, and clear the check mark from the AutoFormat Table check box. Next, click the Format Report button to open the AutoFormat dialog box again. Scroll to the bottom of the list. Select the None option and click OK.

EXTRA CREDIT: GROUPING ITEMS IN A PIVOTTABLE

Excel PivotTables are capable of splitting data into groups, even when you haven't organized your data in advance. This is a powerful feature that's useful in a variety of circumstances. When you choose to group data in a PivotTable, Excel analyzes the field you've chosen and displays a dialog box with choices that are appropriate for that type of data. For example, if you have a year's worth of scientific data that records daily weather details for a particular location, you might want to group average temperature, rainfall totals, and other details by week or by month. If you have a list of textbooks and other course material in which each row contains a product name, its category, and a price, you might want to group the list of products by category, and then by price within groups: $1.00–$10.00, $10.01–$20.00, and so on.

In the example shown here, a worksheet-based list contains data from an automated weather-monitoring station that continuously records temperature, rainfall, relative humidity, barometric pressure, and other details. Each row contains a date and time stamp plus details for that sampling period. In total, the sheet contains two years' worth of data, with 24 hourly data points for each day. Here's how to create a report that shows monthly trends for all three years:

Figure 20.36

1. Create a PivotTable using the Date field in the Row area and the Temp and Rainfall fields in the Data area.

2. Right-click any entry in the Date column and choose Group and Show Detail, Group from the shortcut menu. As Figure 20.36 shows, Excel correctly determines these are dates and offers to group by month. Because the sample extends over several years, choose Months and Years, and then click OK.

3. Drag two more copies of the Temp field into the Data area and format each one to show a different summary: Average, Max, and Min. Adjust the names of each summary as well. This step allows you to see the average temperature as well as the high and low marks for each month during the two-year period. Format the Rainfall field using the Sum function.

4. Use the AutoFormat option to choose one of the Report formats. Adjust column formatting and number formats for each summary cell.

20

The results, shown in Figure 20.37, give a month-by-month snapshot of the weather, even though we started with a list that included only daily details.

Notice the final frill in this useful table: We hid the taskbar and chose View, Full Screen to make as much information as possible visible on the screen, hiding distracting toolbars and title bars.

Figure 20.37

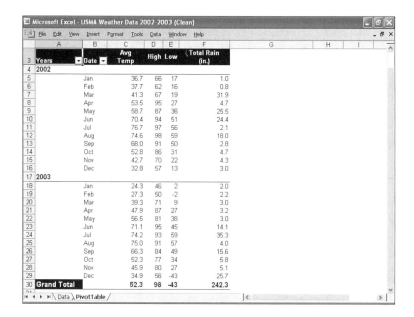

CHAPTER 21

TURNING DATA INTO CHARTS

In this chapter

EVERY PICTURE TELLS A STORY

For years, writers and illustrators have been trying to figure out the precise exchange rate between pictures and words. The standard made famous by the old aphorism, of course, is a thousand words per picture. But if you can replace even a hundred words of tangled, technical prose with a compelling visual image, you've made a great exchange.

Sometimes a chart doesn't need to replace any words at all. You can use a basic row-and-column worksheet grid to help you organize data and perform calculations, but it's difficult—and sometimes impossible—to analyze information and see patterns by staring at a sea of numbers. It's especially unfair to your readers to ask them to work with raw numbers.

Charts help you turn numeric data into visual displays in which you can identify trends and pick out patterns at a glance. By using lines, columns, bars, and pie slices to compare series of data over time and across categories, charts often provide clear answers to tough questions, such as these:

- **How fast have geographic regions grown in the recent past?**—A stacked column chart lets students of history and geography compare annual rates of population growth for two or more countries in a single display. The same type of chart can be used to compare growth in industrial or agricultural output as well.

- **Have school districts in your state seen improved test scores as a result of new educational initiatives?**—You might not be able to tell from a table packed with hundreds of individual data points, but a line chart can help you clearly see the highs and lows and identify any trends.

- **Just where does your family's money go?**—If you've broken out a year's worth of expenditures by category, a pie chart helps you see which categories are taking more than their fair share—and devise strategies for reining in those expenses.

ANATOMY OF AN EXCEL CHART

When you create a new chart, Excel allows you to place it on its own chart sheet or embed a chart object within the worksheet that contains the data you want to chart. Working with a chart on its own sheet gives you the maximum working room for editing and formatting; embedding a chart within a worksheet lets you easily see the data and chart side by side.

Excel automatically maintains links between worksheet data and its graphic representation on the chart; if you change the numbers or text in the data range, the columns, pie slices, and other graphic elements on the chart change, too.

To create a chart, use either of these two basic techniques:

- To create a chart and adjust all its options in four easy steps, click the Chart Wizard button on the Standard toolbar.

- To instantly create a chart on its own chart sheet using the default chart type, chart options, and formatting, open the worksheet that contains the data you want to chart. Select the range that contains the data you want to chart, and then press F11.

If the data you select is in a PivotTable, pressing F11 creates a new PivotChart on its own sheet using default formats.

You can choose from dozens of Excel chart types, ranging from basic bar charts appropriate in almost any simple analytical task to exotic data displays suited only for specialized scientific or engineering applications. Regardless of chart type, however, most charts include a set of standard elements and a palette of common options. Each row or column that contains numbers to be plotted, for example, makes up a data series. Each value within the series is called a *data point*. If the range you select for your chart includes worksheet headings, Excel uses them as labels along the category axis or value axis. The stacked-column chart in Figure 21.1 shows most of the common elements you'll encounter as you work with charts.

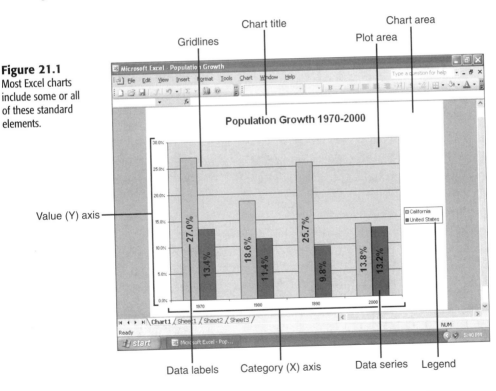

Figure 21.1
Most Excel charts include some or all of these standard elements.

continues

TIP FROM

Ed & Woody

To identify elements on an Excel chart, use the ScreenTips that pop up when the mouse pointer passes over objects. Even if you never use ScreenTips elsewhere, pay attention here because they are invaluable aids in identifying even the most obscure chart elements. Within the plot area, they identify the name of the data series and data points, as

continued

> well as the precise value of each data point. If you don't see these ScreenTips, this feature might have been disabled; to turn them back on, select Tools, Options, click the Chart tab, and select both check boxes in the Chart Tips area.

DATA SERIES

Each group of related data points in a chart is called a *data series*. In almost all cases, a series consists of a contiguous range in a row or column on a worksheet, and when plotted in the chart each data series has a unique color or pattern. You can plot one or more data series in a chart. Bar charts, area charts, and column charts, like the one shown in Figure 21.2, typically contain multiple series. Pie charts consist of only one data series, in which the total always adds up to 100%. A line chart might contain one or multiple series.

Figure 21.2
This ScreenTip identifies the name of the data series and the name and value of the data point under the mouse pointer.

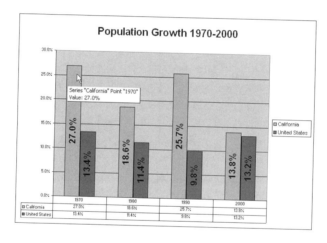

DATA MARKERS

Each point in a data series becomes a single *data marker* on a chart. In column, bar, and pie charts, each column, bar, or pie slice is a marker that represents one data point. In stacked column charts, each segment within each column or bar is a marker. In line, xy (scatter), and radar charts, you can use dots or symbols to identify all the data points on a series. For example, a line chart that compares the trends of two or more stock prices over time might use a triangle, a diamond, and a square to mark data points on different series. Marker characters appear in the legend, as shown in Figure 21.3.

21

TIP FROM

EQ & Woody

> Data markers are usually unnecessary when you're creating a chart that will be viewed online—instead of marker characters, use colors to differentiate between series. Markers are most useful when you intend to print a line chart in black and white and you want each line to be easily identifiable.

Figure 21.3
When you're printing in black and white, you can't tell that each line is a different color. Instead, use data markers to differentiate series; the marker characters appear in the legend.

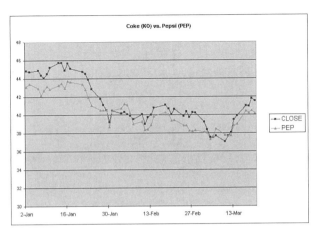

AXES AND GRIDLINES

Axes are the lines along each side of the plot area, which provide the scale for measurement or comparison of plotted data. The *category (X) axis* (usually horizontal) arranges your data by category—by time, for example, or by division or employee. The *value (Y) axis* (usually vertical) defines how you want to plot the worksheet data. In the default column chart, for example, taller columns represent bigger numbers. In combination charts (discussed later in this chapter), it's not unusual to see two value axes, both vertical. When you create a secondary value axis, the labels appear on the right of a column chart.

> **NOTE**
>
> In the default column chart type, the Y-axis is vertical and the X-axis is horizontal. Direction isn't important, however; what matters most is the type of data you plot along each axis. In any chart, the X-axis contains categories. On a 2D chart, the Y-axis is for values; in a 3D chart the values go on the Z-axis, with the Y-axis reserved for different series of data.

Gridlines are horizontal or vertical lines that extend through the plot area to help you visualize the connections between data points and values or categories. Gridlines start with the tick marks on an axis and extend through the plot area.

DATA LABELS, LEGENDS, AND TITLES

Data labels identify items on the category axis and define the scale of the value axis; you can also add labels to a single data marker, an entire data series, or all data markers in a chart. Depending on the chart type, data labels can show values, names of data series or categories, percentages, or a combination of these elements. Because of their tendency to clutter a chart, you should use data labels sparingly.

21

A *legend* is a color-coded key that identifies the colors or patterns that correspond to data series or categories. If you've defined data marker characters (as on a line chart), the legend includes the marker character as well.

Titles consist of descriptive text that identifies the chart or an axis. By default, titles are aligned to an axis or centered at the top of the chart.

TIP FROM

> Add a chart title when you want to provide a descriptive label for the entire graphic. If you plan to paste the chart in a highly formatted Word document or PowerPoint presentation, however, you might want to leave the title off the chart while working in Excel and add the text in Word or PowerPoint instead. That way, when you change your document or presentation design, the title will change as well.

PLOT AREA

In a 2D chart, the *plot area* is the region enclosed by the axes; it includes all data series. In a 3D chart, the plot area also includes category names, tick-mark labels, and axis titles. Right-click and select Format Plot Area to add borders or background colors, textures, and fill effects behind the plotted data.

CHART AREA

The *chart area* includes all chart elements. When you select the chart area, you'll see eight small black squares—one in each corner and one in the middle of each side. Right-click and select Format Chart Area to change all text elements to a specific font or to add a background color or texture behind the entire chart.

TIP FROM

> Many Excel experts don't even know this secret: After selecting any part of a chart, you can move in rapid succession to other parts of the same chart by pressing the arrow keys. Use the up- and down-arrow keys to select major chart elements. Use the left- and right-arrow keys to select every available chart element in succession, including individual points within each data series, as well as every color key and text entry in the legend. The Name box (just to the left of the Formula bar) identifies which element is selected.

WORKING WITH EMBEDDED CHARTS

If you chose to insert the chart as an object in an existing worksheet, it sits in its own layer on top of your data. Select the chart by clicking anywhere on it, and then point to one of its edges until the pointer turns into a four-headed arrow. Click and drag to slide the chart object into a new position. As you slide to any edge of the window, the worksheet scrolls in that direction.

When you move or resize cells underneath a chart object on a worksheet, Excel moves or resizes the chart as well. To change this link between chart and cells, right-click the chart area and select Format Chart Area from the shortcut menu. Click the Properties tab and select one of the three options in the Object Positioning section. Select Move but Don't Size with Cells, for example, if you want the proportions of a chart and all objects on it to remain exactly the same even if you move it.

To change an *embedded chart* to a *chart sheet*, and vice versa, right-click the plot area or chart area and select Location from the shortcut menu. The two choices on this dialog box let you enter a name for a new chart sheet or select the name of an existing sheet on which to place an embedded chart.

You can view an embedded chart in a window without moving it to its own chart sheet—a handy option when you want to edit or format an embedded chart without accidentally moving it or changing the zoom level of the worksheet. Right-click anywhere on the plot area or chart area of the embedded chart, and then select Chart Window from the shortcut menu. You can resize the window without affecting the position of the original embedded sheet. Right-click the title bar to print the chart, set page options, or run a spelling check. Click the Close (X) button to return to the worksheet window.

To resize an embedded chart, click once on the chart border to select the chart area. You'll see eight small sizing handles along the border—one on each side and one in each corner. Point to any of these black squares and drag the pointer—a two-headed arrow—in any direction to adjust the size and shape of the chart. As you drag, Excel adjusts the scale of all elements on your chart to match the new size and shape.

Excel doesn't add sizing handles to a chart on a chart sheet; instead, the default settings for the chart sheet use your default paper size and expand the chart area to fit the entire page. So, if you select a zoom level of 100%, you see the entire chart. To resize the chart area of a chart sheet for printing, select File, Page Setup, and then click the Chart tab. Select the Custom option to display sizing handles so you can change the dimensions of the chart, and then click OK to return to the chart sheet. You can now move or resize the chart.

USING THE CHART WIZARD FOR QUICK RESULTS

Expert users might be tempted to dismiss Excel's Chart Wizard as just another tool for beginners, to be avoided at all costs. Big mistake. Don't think of the Chart Wizard as a set of training wheels—instead, think of it as a highly structured, superbly organized interface that lets you efficiently deal with every chart option in four steps.

TIP FROM

Ed & Woody

Each of the four steps in the Chart Wizard corresponds to one of four choices on the shortcut menu that appears when you right-click the plot area or chart area of any chart. If you want to change only the data source of a chart, it takes fewer clicks to use the shortcut menus than to restart the Chart Wizard.

21

- In Step 1, use the Chart Type dialog box (see Figure 21.4) to select any of Excel's built-in chart types or select a custom chart type you've defined previously. Select a category from the Chart Type list, and then click the icon for the corresponding chart subtype that best represents the type of chart you want to create. If you selected a range of data before starting the Chart Wizard, click and hold the button below the chart types to see a preview of your data. Click Next.

- In Step 2, fill in or edit the Source Data dialog box to define the location of data series and values for use with labels and axes. If you selected data before starting the Chart Wizard, most of these decisions are already made for you.

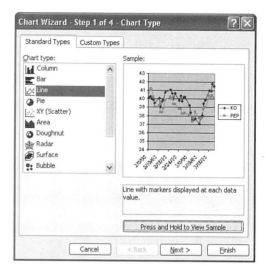

Figure 21.4

→ Choosing the best chart design for your data is a crucial step many Excel users overlook; **see** "Choosing a Standard Chart Type," **p. 679**.

- In Step 3, enter title text and configure the appearance of legends, gridlines, and other chart elements. Use any of the categories in the multitabbed Chart Options dialog box shown in Figure 21.5. (The exact options available depend on the chart type you selected in Step 1.) As you add title text and adjust other chart options, the preview window changes to show how your chart will look.

- In Step 4, use the Location dialog box to specify whether you want to create a new chart sheet or embed a chart object in an existing worksheet. If you want to review your choices or make any changes, click the Back button. Click Finish to close the wizard and add the chart to your worksheet.

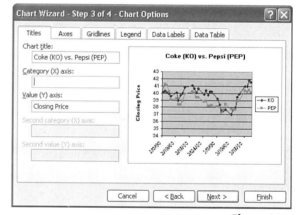

Figure 21.5

You can agonize over every detail of a chart, but sometimes it's more effective to breeze through the Chart Wizard first, using its default settings and ignoring most of the fine details. After you've created a solid foundation for your chart, you can tweak individual elements. You can also click the Chart Wizard button to restart the wizard any time after you've created your chart. Many of the choices will be much clearer when you see what the first draft of the chart looks like.

SELECTING DATA TO PLOT

Excel maintains links between worksheet data and the data series on a chart. When you create a chart, Excel automatically detects the data to be charted based on the current selection. If you select a single cell, Excel bases the chart data on the current region—an area that extends in each direction until you encounter the edge of the worksheet or a blank row or blank column. On the other hand, if you select a range of cells, Excel uses that range for the chart data.

NOTE

The number of points per series is limited to 32,000, and the total number of points per chart is limited to 256,000. The maximum number of series you can use in a chart is 255. If you have more series than this, you must filter your list before creating your chart. You should also seriously reconsider the point you're trying to make, because even Stephen Hawking would have trouble absorbing that much information at once.

Be sure the range you select includes all the data to be charted, as well as the labels you'll use for the categories. The range does not have to be contiguous. For example, to create a pie chart, you might want to select a row of column labels and a row of totals, ignoring the detail rows in between. Nor do you need to select all the data in a table, if all you want to chart is a subset of the data—for example, on a 12-month budget worksheet, you might want to show sales totals only for the months of October through December.

CAUTION

If the range you plan to chart ends with a row or column of totals, don't include those totals in your selection; otherwise, the totals will create one column or pie slice that overwhelms all the others in the chart.

When you select the data source, Excel attempts to identify category headings, value axis labels, and data series; it also chooses whether to plot data by rows or by columns. This choice is based on the number of items—if there are more columns than rows, Excel plots the data by column, placing the column headings along the category axis; if there are more rows than columns, or an equal number of rows and columns, Excel plots by row.

Changing the way data is plotted can help emphasize different trends and patterns. For example, Figure 21.6 shows a worksheet that contains a small range of data. When plotted by columns (left), the data emphasizes the trends for each decade, and you can see at a

21

glance that Arizona has grown at a faster rate than the other two Southwestern states and the United States as a whole. When plotted by rows, however (right), the chart encourages comparing how each state and the United States did on a decade-by-decade basis and to draw conclusions on the consistency of each state's growth.

Figure 21.6
Changing the way data is plotted–by columns or rows–can change the story a chart tells.

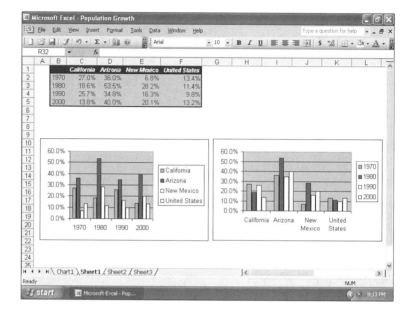

To reverse the order in which Excel plots the selected data, use one of two buttons on the Chart toolbar (if this toolbar is not visible, right-click the menu bar or any visible toolbar and choose its entry from the list). Click the By Row or By Column button to shift orientation. (This option is also available when you right-click the plot area and select Data Series, or in Step 2 of the Chart Wizard.) With some chart types and data, making this switch could render the chart incomprehensible; click the Undo button if that happens.

Normally, Excel plots data series from left to right and top to bottom. What do you do if your data source is arranged in alphabetical order, but you want to display the series in a different order—say, with the two most productive regions listed first, or with dates in reverse order? If you don't want to change the arrangement of data on the worksheet, you can change the plotting order of the data series:

1. Click any data series in the chart you want to change.
2. Select Format, Selected Data Series (or press Ctrl+1), and click the Series Order tab.
3. In the Series Order box (see Figure 21.7), select the series you want to move, and then click Move Up or Move Down. Repeat this step for each additional series you want to move. Watch the display in the Preview window to see the effect of your changes.
4. Click OK to apply your changes to the chart.

Figure 21.7

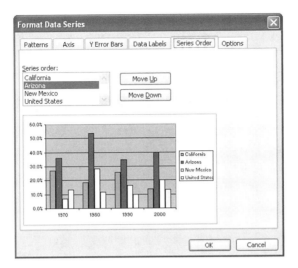

SELECTING AND CUSTOMIZING A CHART TYPE

When you create a new chart, Excel lets you select from 73 chart types in 14 categories (although a significant number of these choices are actually just minor variations of others in the same category). You can also choose from a gallery of 20 built-in custom chart types, and you can create and save your own chart types as well. The type of data you're planning to plot usually dictates which type of chart you should choose.

CHOOSING A STANDARD CHART TYPE

When you start the Chart Wizard, the first step is to specify what type of chart you want to create. After you create a chart, you can easily change it to a new type; right-click the chart area or plot area and select Chart Type, or click the Chart Type button on the Chart toolbar to display the Chart Type dialog box. The following sections discuss all the standard Excel chart types and describe how you can best use them.

COLUMN

This type of chart shows a comparison between values in one or more series, often over time. For example, as in the earlier examples in this chapter, you can show population growth in different states or countries over a number of years or decades. Stacked column charts further divide the total for each column; you might divide the United States into East, West, Midwest, and South and measure how each geographic region grew as a component of the entire country's population growth. Select a column chart when you want to show comparisons between different data points, especially those that change over time. Avoid this chart type if each series includes so many data points that you'll be unable to distinguish individual columns.

21

BAR

Think of a bar chart as a column chart turned on its side, with values along the horizontal axis and categories on the vertical axis. It de-emphasizes time comparisons and highlights winners and losers. Figure 21.8, for example, graphically illustrates how well each region has performed in a competition where the goal is to hit $1 million in donations.

Figure 21.8
Bar charts highlight winners and losers. In this example, it's easy to see which region is in the lead.

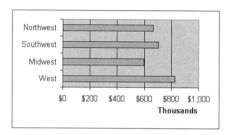

LINE

This chart type displays a trend, or the relationship between values over a time period. For example, Figure 21.9 plots a year's worth of monthly high temperatures for four U.S. cities. By placing temperatures on the value axis and using the category axis as the time scale, the dips and rises in the line show when the weather is getting cooler or warmer. Select a line chart when you have many data points to plot and want to show a trend over a period of time. Avoid this chart type when you're trying to show the relationship between numbers without respect to time, and when you have only a few data points to chart.

Figure 21.9
Line charts are most useful for showing trends over a period of time.

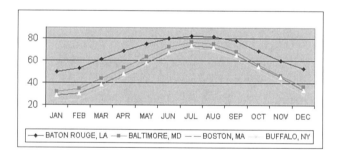

PIE

Pie charts show the relative size of all the parts in a whole—for example, the ethnic composition of a city. Pie charts have no x- or y-axis, and only one data series can be plotted. Use pie charts when you have only a few numbers to chart and want to show how each number contributes to the whole. Avoid this chart type when your data series includes many low numbers that contribute a very small percentage to the total. In this case, individual pie slices will be too small to compare.

XY (SCATTER)

Use a scatter chart to show correlations between different series of values when the element of time is unimportant—usually used for scientific analyses. For example, plotting daily high temperatures and ice cream sales over the course of a year will no doubt show clusters of high sales on hot days. Figure 21.10 shows a scatter chart that measures the correlation between risk and reward in stock investments (note the use of trendlines in both series). You can also create charts that plot two groups of numbers as one series of XY coordinates; this is the principle behind the price-performance charts you sometimes see in computer magazines. The correct arrangement of data on the worksheet, especially sorting, is crucial when creating this chart type.

Figure 21.10
Scatter charts help to illustrate correlations between two sets of data. We've used trendlines in this example to make the relationship even clearer.

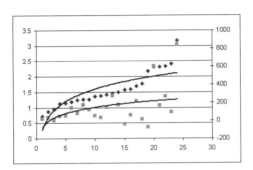

AREA

This chart type shows lines for parts of a series, adding all the values together to illustrate cumulative change. Unlike line charts, which emphasize the rate of change, area charts show the amount and magnitude of change. The area chart in Figure 21.11, for example, shows how much each region of a national nonprofit organization contributes to total revenues over the course of a year.

Figure 21.11
Area charts graphically illustrate cumulative changes—this example shows the year-long contribution of four regional divisions.

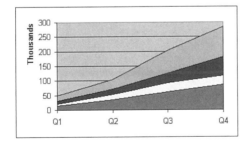

DOUGHNUT

The doughnut chart is similar to a pie chart, except that it can contain more than one data series. Each ring of the doughnut chart represents a data series.

21

RADAR

Each category in a radar chart has its own value axis that extends from the center of the chart. Lines connect all the values in the same series.

TIP FROM

> Are you baffled by some of these chart types? You're not alone. According to Microsoft, both doughnut and radar chart types are popular among Excel users in the Far East but are rarely used in the United States and Europe.

SURFACE

Select this chart type to add a topographic layer over a column or area chart. Instead of assigning a color to each series, this chart type assigns different colors to similar values. The result resembles a topographic map, which can be used to show relationships among large amounts of data that might otherwise be hard to see.

BUBBLE

Bubble charts are similar to scatter charts, except they contain three series of data rather than two. Instead of placing a uniform-sized dot at the point where each pair of x- and y-values intersect, the data markers are bubbles whose size is determined by the values in a third series. Bubble charts often are used to present financial or market research information.

STOCK

Four built-in chart types make tracking open/high/low/close prices over time possible, as in the example in Figure 21.12. Combination chart types in this category enable you to plot volume traded as well. You also can adapt these chart types for scientific use, to show high-low values in experimental data. When choosing one of these chart types, read the text under the Sample window carefully to ensure you've arranged your data correctly. The Office Assistant displays an error message if you have too many or too few columns, or if they are in the wrong order.

Figure 21.12
Each line in this stock chart shows the high, low, and closing prices for a selected ticker symbol on a specific day.

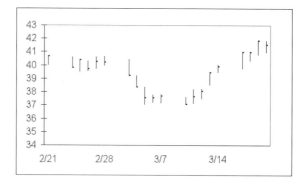

21

CONE/CYLINDER/PYRAMID

For the most part, these are simply glitzy versions of standard 3D column and bar charts. Options enable you to control whether each data marker tapers to a point or is tapered to the highest value in the series.

USING COMBINATION CHARTS

The list of standard Excel chart types includes several *combination charts*, which mix two chart types in a single graphic. The Line-Column chart type, for example, lets you format one series of data along a line and another in columns; you'll find this versatile chart type on the Custom Types tab of the Chart Types dialog box, along with other built-in custom designs.

In the Stock category on the Standard Types tab of the same dialog box, you'll find combination charts that let you plot high, low, and closing stock prices on a line, with trading volume in columns. In this case, you use two value axes, one to the left of the chart area and the other on the right.

The Pie-of-Pie and Pie-of-Bar combination charts, both available as subtypes in the Pie category, offer a clever solution when you have so many data points that your chart is difficult to read. As the example in Figure 21.13 shows, you can use a Pie-of-Bar chart to combine several smaller slices into a single large slice, and then show the detail in a separate chart connected to the original.

Figure 21.13
Use a Pie-of-Bar chart to keep small slices of the pie from getting lost.

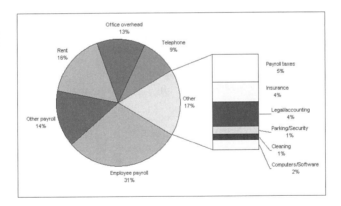

To create either of these combination chart types, open the Chart Type dialog box and select the Pie type; then select the appropriate chart subtype from the list on the right and click OK. To adjust which slices of the pie will go in the secondary (pie or bar) chart, right-click either pie and select Format Data Series. Then click the Options tab and adjust the settings as shown in Figure 21.14.

21

Figure 21.14
Use this dialog box to shift slices of a pie from the primary chart to the secondary chart.

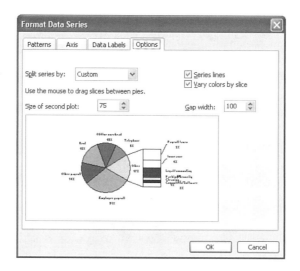

Using the Split Series By list, you can tell Excel to use a specific number of slices, or all slices below a certain value or percent. To move slices from the primary to the secondary chart, select the Custom option in this list; then close the Options dialog box and drag slices directly on the chart.

CREATING AND SAVING CUSTOM CHART TYPES

If you've extensively customized a chart, you can save its formatting settings and chart options in a named format. All the custom chart types you save appear on the Custom Types tab of the Chart Type dialog box. When you choose a custom chart from this list, Excel applies all the saved options and format settings from the selected chart type to the current chart. This is an especially effective technique for managing a collection of formatted charts you use regularly. It's also an effective way to maintain a consistent style across charts within an organization.

The Custom Types tab actually shows two groups of custom charts, drawn from a built-in gallery and a user-defined gallery:

- Click the Built-in option to see all the chart types in the Excel gallery, a collection of mostly combination charts. This file, Xl8galry.xls, is added to your system as part of the default Excel installation. On a typical installation for a U.S. English system, you'll find the built-in gallery in C:\Program Files\Microsoft Office\Office11\1033.

NOTE

The filename in the previous paragraph is not a typo. Even though Excel 2003 is version 11 (Excel 2000 was version 9 and Excel 2002 is version 10), the collection of built-in chart types uses the same format as those found in Excel 97 (version 8.0); to maintain compatibility, this file uses the Xl8 prefix. It's also worth noting that the date stamp on this file is from 1999, which suggests it hasn't been updated in a long, long time.

21

→ To learn how to use the Save My Settings Wizard to transfer this and other preferences from your old computer to a new one, **see** "Saving and Restoring Personal Settings," **p. 56**.

- Click the User-defined option to see a list of all user-defined charts. These details are stored in a file called `Xlusrgal.xls`, which Excel creates the first time you define a custom chart type. You'll find this file your personal profile; to open it in Windows Explorer, type `%appdata%\Microsoft\Excel` in the Run dialog box.

TIP FROM

Ed & Woody

> When you save a custom chart type, your entry in the user-defined gallery stores all formatting and chart options, including titles. If you want to enter a new title each time, replace the title text with a generic placeholder before saving the custom chart type.

To create a custom chart type, first select the chart sheet or embedded chart object whose format settings and options you want to save, and then follow these steps:

1. Click the Chart Type button on the Chart toolbar, or right-click the chart area or plot area and select Chart Type from the shortcut menu.

2. In the Chart Type dialog box, click the Custom Types tab; in the area labeled Select From, select User-defined. Excel filters the list to display only the Default chart type and other custom chart types you've previously created, as shown in Figure 21.15.

Figure 21.15
Click the User-defined option to see a list of all custom chart types you've previously created.

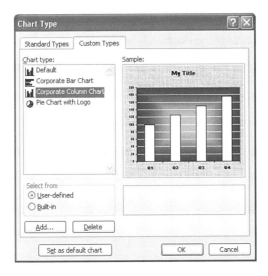

3. Click the Add button to display the Add Custom Chart Type dialog box shown in Figure 21.16.

21

4. Enter a name and description for your chart type. Then click OK to save your changes in the User-defined gallery.

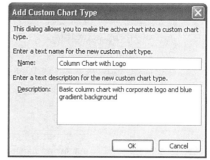

Figure 21.16

Excel's built-in gallery of chart types is a wildly inconsistent collection of several good-looking examples mixed with others that are staggeringly ugly. Although most users don't know it, you can edit this collection, and you can also add your own custom charts to the built-in gallery. Customizing the built-in gallery is a particularly good way to distribute standard chart types throughout an organization, while preventing users from modifying or deleting the chart types.

TIP FROM

EQ & Woody

To delete a custom chart type you've created, select its entry in the Custom Types tab, and then click the Delete button. You can't directly rename or modify a saved custom chart type; instead, apply the chart type to a new chart, modify it as necessary, save the resulting chart type under a new name, and then delete the existing chart type.

Custom chart types are stored as individual chart sheets in `Xl8galry.xls` (for built-in custom chart types) and `Xlusrgal.xls` (for user-defined chart types). Use the following techniques to manage the contents of the chart gallery:

- To rename or delete one or more chart types from the built-in gallery, open `Xl8galry.xls`, right-click the sheet you want to delete, and then click Rename or Delete.

- To add a new chart type to the built-in gallery, first save the new chart type in the user-defined gallery, being sure to give it a name and description. Then open `Xl8galry.xls` and `Xlusrgal.xls` and copy the chart tab from `Xlusrgal.xls` to `Xl8galry.xls`. Save both files.

Creating a Default Chart

The absolute quickest way to create an Excel chart is to select a data range and press F11. This creates a chart using all Excel's default chart options—on a clean installation of Office 2003, this is the Column chart type. If you prefer to use a different chart type as your default, open the Chart Type dialog box, select the chart type you want to use from either the Standard or Custom tab, and click the Set As Default Chart button. The next time you press F11, Excel will create a chart sheet using the current region or selected data with the chart options in your default chart type.

To reset the default chart type, open the Chart Types dialog box and click the Custom Type tab. Select the User-defined option in the Select From box; then click Default in the Chart Type list, and click the Delete button.

EDITING AND FORMATTING CHART ELEMENTS

Although the default chart settings are often good enough to get you started, Excel offers a broad range of chart options that give you complete control over the look of the chart and plot area. The easiest way to change many chart options is to rerun the Chart Wizard. The wizard's dialog boxes pick up your current chart settings and let you change chart types, edit the source data, apply new formatting, or change the location of your chart.

NOTE

All the techniques described in this section work equally well with embedded chart objects, chart sheets, and PivotCharts.

To adjust individual chart objects, first select the object (the chart title or the category axis, for example), and then change its properties.

TIP FROM

Ed & Woody

Selecting a specific chart object by pointing to it can be difficult, especially on a small chart with many elements crowding one another for space. Try this simple shortcut: Use the Chart Objects drop-down list at the left of the Chart toolbar. Selecting any item from this list selects that item in the current chart. Then click the Format button just to its right to display the Format dialog box for the selected object.

Excel also lets you add an enormous number of attention-getting elements in the drawing layer on top of a chart. For example, you can add text boxes to data markers to explain anomalies in your data or call attention to key numbers. If you select the chart or plot area and start typing, Excel begins creating a text box immediately. After you've added the desired text, you can then move it anywhere on the chart and reformat it to your liking.

→ To add, edit, and format text boxes, AutoShapes, callouts, and other drawn elements in charts, use the Office drawing tools; **see** "Using Office Drawing Tools," **p. 114**.

ADJUSTING CHART OPTIONS

Step 3 of the Chart Wizard displays a tabbed dialog box you can use to adjust various chart options. After you create a chart, you can display the same dialog box by right-clicking the chart area or plot area and selecting Chart Options from the shortcut menu. The following six categories of options might be available, depending on the chart type.

TITLES

Create titles that appear on the top of the chart or next to any axis. If the nature of data along each axis isn't immediately apparent, you can add explanatory text here, too. Click this tab and enter the text for the chart title and any available axes. In both locations, titles are nothing more than text boxes. The default font size for titles and other text objects on a

21

chart is 10 point. Typically, this setting results in chart titles that are too small and legends that are too large. Use the Font tab on the Format dialog box to adjust the size of each object.

AXES

Click Automatic to allow Excel to format and display the axes that are appropriate for the chart type you've chosen. Normally, Excel is capable of analyzing the data type and using the correct settings. If your category axis includes dates, the Format Axis dialog box allows you to set the options shown in Figure 21.17. Adjust the Minimum and Maximum settings if you want to restrict the charted portion of your data; for example, in a list of daily temperature readings that encompasses several years, you might want to see just a few months' results. Change the Base Unit option to chart time data using a different scale. For example, in a list that includes data for many days, select Month(s) or Year(s) to let Excel group the data before plotting.

Figure 21.17
Time-scale axes let you control the start and stop dates as well as the interval for the plotted data.

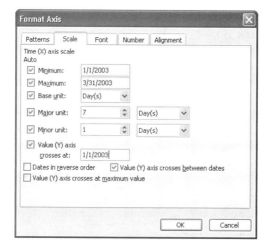

Use the Category and Time-scale options to solve a particularly annoying charting problem: If you select a time series that skips some dates, Excel might leave gaps in the category axis. If you construct a stock chart using daily high, low, and closing prices, for instance, your time series will be missing values for Saturdays, Sundays, and holidays, when the market is closed. Unfortunately, Excel insists on adding phantom markers for those days, messing up the smooth line you expect to see.

The solution is to convert the Time-scale axis to a Category axis. Right-click the chart axis and select Chart Options. Click the Axes tab and select the Category option under the primary Category (X) Axis. When you close the dialog box, Excel changes the display of data to a simple series, with no gaps. If you open the Format Axis dialog box, you'll see a different set of options, as shown in Figure 21.18.

Figure 21.18
If your time-scale axis includes some gaps in dates, convert it to a category axis. You might need to click the Categories in Reverse Order check box to display the dates correctly.

Format Axis

Patterns | Scale | Font | Number | Alignment

Category (X) axis scale

Value (Y) axis crosses
at category number: [1]

Number of categories
between tick-mark labels: [1]

Number of categories
between tick marks: [1]

☑ Value (Y) axis crosses between categories
☐ Categories in reverse order
☐ Value (Y) axis crosses at maximum category

[OK] [Cancel]

This dialog box also lets you control the placement of tick marks, which are the small lines that indicate where each item on the category axis is plotted.

TIP FROM

If you have more items on your category axis than will fit, use the Number of Categories Between Tick-mark Labels option to suppress some of them. Enter a value of 2 here to see every other label on this axis; enter 10 to see every 10th label. You can also use the settings on the Alignment tab to rotate the text on the category axis labels and make extra room.

GRIDLINES

Gridlines help readers see where data points cross category or value axes. You can set major and minor gridlines for each axis. Normally, Excel does a decent job of setting intelligent defaults, but you often can clean up a chart and make it easier to read by adjusting these settings. In general, you should try to use as few gridlines as you can get away with. Watch the Preview window to see the effect as you add or remove gridlines.

LEGEND

A chart legend identifies each data marker according to its color or pattern on a chart. Options on this tab let you move or reformat the legend. If you don't need to show a legend (perhaps because you want to label each column or pie slice individually), clear the Show Legend check box. The Placement options control where the legend first appears within the chart: Bottom, Corner, Top, Right, or Left. You can drag the legend box to position it more precisely later.

DATA LABELS

Use data labels when you want to display charted worksheet values, category labels, or percentages next to each point in a data series. Click the Legend Key Next to Label check box to add a color-coded key at the beginning of each label. The options in this dialog box control the placement and appearance of data labels for every data series. However, if you want to add labels for just one series, or even a single point, you can do so. Skip the Chart Options dialog box and instead open the Format dialog box for the series or point you want to label. Select the appropriate option on the Data Labels dialog box for that item.

DATA TABLE

Display a worksheet-style table directly in your chart to show the plotted worksheet data alongside the chart itself. Each row in the data table represents a data series. If your chart includes a relatively small amount of data, a data table can make an effective addition, as the example in Figure 21.19 shows.

Figure 21.19
Data tables give your audience both views of the data—the visual display as well as the underlying numbers.

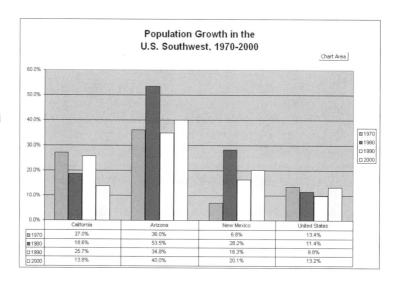

	California	Arizona	New Mexico	United States
1970	27.0%	36.0%	6.8%	13.4%
1980	18.6%	53.5%	28.2%	11.4%
1990	25.7%	34.8%	16.3%	9.8%
2000	13.8%	40.0%	20.1%	13.2%

NOTE

Data tables are available only in column, bar, line, area, and stock charts. You cannot add a data table to a pie, XY (scatter), doughnut, radar, surface, or bubble chart.

CHANGING NUMBER FORMATS

Use the right-click shortcut menus to change the number format of any item on a chart; to adjust the value axis, for example, right-click and select Format Axis. Click the Number tab in the Format Axis dialog box, and then select a format from the Category list. You can select a built-in number format or create a custom format, just as you can when formatting worksheet data. Click OK to apply the new format to your chart data.

→ To learn more about altering Excel's number formatting, **see** "Setting Number Formats," **p. 566**.

Normally, numbers that appear in Excel charts use the same format as the source data in the worksheet to which they're linked. If you change the format of the numbers in the chart, you break the link to the format in the worksheet. Under many circumstances you'll want to do exactly that—for example, if numbers in your worksheet use the Currency format with two decimal places, but you don't want to see a dollar sign or decimals in your chart. To reestablish the link so the data on the chart uses the same number format as the data on the worksheet, select the chart object (for instance, the Value axis), select its Format option, click the Number tab, and check the Linked to Source box.

CHANGING TEXT FORMATS

You can change the appearance of any text item on a chart. As with worksheet cells, Excel lets you change fonts as well as font sizes and character attributes. You can choose different colors for the text and its background. To keep labels from running into one another on any axis, rotate text to an angle.

TIP FROM

When you use the Chart Options dialog box to enter text for titles, Excel doesn't allow you to enter line breaks or change formatting within the title. After you place the title on the chart, however, you can select and format individual words or characters as well as the entire title. To add a line break to a title, click to position the insertion point within the title on the chart, and then press Enter.

To adjust font options for all text in your chart, right-click the chart area and select Format Chart Area. Click the Font tab of the resulting dialog box and adjust formatting as necessary. This dialog box is a great way to apply the same font to all text in your chart, but avoid the temptation to choose a standard size as well. In most cases, you'll want to specify different font sizes for different items, such as the chart title, axes, and legend.

To change text formatting for any text object on the chart, right-click the object and select its Format option. Click the Font tab and adjust options as desired.

TIP FROM

By default, text in an Excel chart is *scalable*—that is, as you resize the entire chart, the text gets larger or smaller so it remains in proportion with the rest of the chart elements. If you have carefully designed a text element and don't want its font size to change, turn off automatic scaling. Right-click the object and click the Format menu. On the Font tab, clear the check mark from the Auto Scale box.

21

Are the category axis labels crowding the axis itself? Use the Offset box to specify the distance between the axis labels and the axis itself; the higher the number, the more distance between the two points.

ADDING BACKGROUND COLORS, TEXTURES, AND PICTURES

The default background for charts is plain white, but you can add background colors, textures, pictures, and gradient fills to an entire chart, to just the plot area, or to individual items such as data markers. In 3D charts, you also can add images to the walls and the floor.

These features use the Drawing tools shared by all Office programs. If you've used Word to design a web page or created a presentation with PowerPoint, you can use the same backgrounds in Excel charts as in those files and then paste the charts into your web page or presentation with confidence that they'll match the existing design.

→ To learn how to change background colors in any Office document, **see** "Changing Background Colors and Line Formats," **p. 121**.

→ The Office Drawing tools enable you to easily add interesting visual effects; **see** "Adding Borders, Shadows, and 3D Effects," **p. 122**.

CHANGING THE SCALE AND SPACING OF AXES

To make a chart easier to read, you might also want to adjust the scale on the value axis. Normally, the values on this axis start with 0 and extend to a number past the highest number in your data series. You might want to change the scale to start at a higher number, so you can more easily see the difference between data points. You can also adjust the display of large numbers:

1. Right-click the value axis and select Format Axis.

2. Click the Scale tab to display the dialog box shown in Figure 21.20.

3. Enter the high and low values for the axis in the Minimum and Maximum boxes. Note that changing the default numbers automatically clears the check marks in the Auto column.

4. If you want to make large numbers— thousands or millions, for example— easier to read, select an option from the Display Units drop-down list. If you select Millions, for example, Excel will display $85,000,000 as $85.

5. Click OK to apply the changes to your chart.

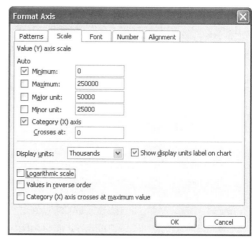

Figure 21.20

CHANGING THE DATA SOURCE FOR AN EXISTING CHART

How do you add, edit, or remove data series, category names, and axis labels when you've already created the chart? Use one of the following three techniques:

- If the *data source* is simple and straightforward, with easy-to-identify headings for categories and values, right-click the chart area or plot area and select Source Data. Click the Data Range tab of the Source Data dialog box and select the new data range. If necessary, specify whether the series is in rows or columns. Click OK to apply the changes to the current chart.

- To add, remove, or change an individual data series or the range that defines labels or names, click the Series tab on the Data Source dialog box and adjust the options there.

  For example, if your current chart includes five data series, one for each year from 2001 through 2005, you might want to remove the first two years and add the years 2006 and 2007 to bring the chart up to date. Select the 2001 entry from the Series list and click Remove, and then do the same for the 2002 series. Note that the category name and value labels adjust automatically when you use this option.

- To add or remove a single series from a chart embedded on a worksheet, select the data range that contains the headings and values you want to plot and drop it directly on the chart. Excel adds the data to the plot area, complete with new category labels and legend items, if necessary.

TIP FROM

EQ & Woody

> If you copy a worksheet range to the Clipboard, you can right-click the plot area or chart area and select Edit, Paste to add the series to an existing chart.

When you select a data series on an embedded chart, the Range Finder displays a colored line around the corresponding range within the data source; the Range Finder also adds a border around the value axis labels and category labels, using different colors for each. Drag the selection by using the rectangular handle in the lower-right corner of each selection to extend or move the data range for each series. On a chart where the data source consists of a single contiguous range, selecting the chart area causes the Range Finder to highlight all the data series in one color, the value axis labels in another color, and category names in still another color.

TIP FROM

EQ & Woody

> Excel uses the Range Finder only when the chart and its corresponding data range are on the same worksheet. Take advantage of this feature to debug problems in charts. If your chart is on a separate sheet, right-click the chart area and select Location; then click the As Object In option and select the worksheet that contains the charted data. Resize and reposition the chart object so it's near the corresponding range within the data source and use the color-coding to identify which data series is causing the problem. After you've fixed the chart, use the Location shortcut menu to move it back to its own chart sheet.

21

When using the Range Finder with charts, you should be aware of the following limitations:

- The Range Finder works only with a chart object that is embedded on the same worksheet as the data. It does not work with charts on chart sheets.

- You can drag to expand the data range or a given series to include new data in either direction; however, this technique works only for contiguous series. If any series consists of a noncontiguous range, you must use the wizard or the Data Source dialog box to select the data.

- When you click an individual data point, the Range Finder highlights the series that contains that point.

ADVANCED CHART OPTIONS

Excel's advanced chart options let you add details that help you spot trends more easily. For example, in a line chart that plots daily closing stock prices over time, you can add a trendline and a moving average that smooth out some of the peaks and valleys in the data. You can do the same with a column chart to show a smooth trend over time. Select the series, right-click, and select Add Trendline. For charts that project data, you can also add error bars that define the upper- and lower-error limits of your projections by using standard statistical measures. You'll find these options on the Error Bars tab of the Format Data Series dialog box.

NOTE

> For more information on how you can display detailed analyses in Excel charts, see *Special Edition Using Microsoft Excel 2003*, by Patrick Blattner (published by Que, ISBN: 0-7897-2953-9).

EXTRA CREDIT: CREATING A CUSTOM CHART LIBRARY

Why reinvent the wheel every time you create and format a chart? Build a library of good-looking custom charts, save them in your User-defined chart gallery, and call on them whenever you need them. The process is simple and straightforward:

1. Start with a blank worksheet. Enter a basic table of dummy data, like the range shown here. (Note we've hidden gridlines and added formatting to the range, just to make the sheet look good.)

2. Click anywhere in the worksheet outside the range you just created and click the Chart Wizard button. Breeze through the process of creating a basic column chart without any titles or additional formatting. Place this generic chart on the same sheet with your dummy data.

3. Use the Clipboard to make three, four, or more copies of this chart, and arrange them on the sheet. Now you're ready to begin customizing.

4. Right-click each chart in turn and set any or all of the following options:
   - Adjust the chart type if necessary.
   - Change the background colors for the chart area, plot area, fill area, gridlines, and data series. Choose a variety of complementary colors, including gradient

21

fills and textures available when you click the Fill Effects button on the Patterns tab of the Format dialog box for each item.

- Right-click the chart area, select Format Chart Area, and adjust the fonts for the entire chart. Then adjust the sizes of individual chart elements, such as axis labels and legends.

- Add chart titles and adjust the size and position of each. Because the title is just a text box, you can move it anywhere, including inside the plot area. Don't be afraid to make extra copies of the basic chart and experiment with them.

- If you're creating the charts to use on behalf of an organization, add elements such as logos or disclaimer text to each basic chart design.

5. Save the workbook that contains the charts so you can reuse them any time. If you're certain you'll want to use one or more chart designs, add them to the User-defined chart gallery.

Figure 21.21

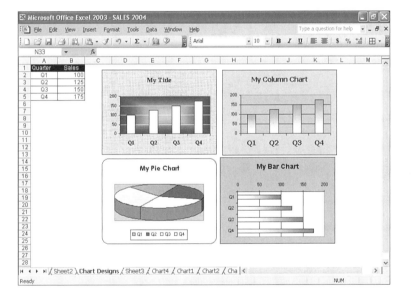

PART V

USING POWERPOINT

CHAPTER 22

GETTING STARTED WITH POWERPOINT

In this chapter

22

WHAT IS POWERPOINT GOOD FOR?

Most people think of PowerPoint as *the* tool for delivering sales pitches and boring speeches at business meetings. It's even been parodied for its capability to boil big ideas down to trite summaries, most famously by Peter Norvig in a version of Abraham Lincoln's Gettysburg Address done, brilliantly, as a stack of banal PowerPoint slides. (See it for yourself at `http://www.norvig.com/Gettysburg/`.)

Thankfully, PowerPoint isn't just for business. You can use it for class reports, for meeting agendas and wrap-ups, and as a tool to spark ideas in a brainstorming session. You can even use it for multimedia slideshows, if you keep the text to a minimum and use creative transitions to show off digital pictures and movie clips. In fact, PowerPoint is a useful tool anytime you need to communicate ideas to an audience in a sequential manner using a simple outline, with a few graphics mixed in to keep it from becoming too dull. You can even publish your presentation to a website where anyone can read it in a browser window.

Of all the programs in Office, PowerPoint is probably the easiest to use. In fact, it's so easy to get started that you might be tempted to skip these chapters and just start typing. If you do that, you'll miss some wonderful time-saving tips and tricks buried in the program, not to mention some techniques you can use to make your presentations more interesting.

But before we get to all that, let's start with the nuts and bolts of a PowerPoint presentation.

ANATOMY OF A POWERPOINT PRESENTATION

The basic building block of a PowerPoint presentation is the *slide*—a block of content the size of a computer screen that typically contains a title, some text, and perhaps a picture or chart. A PowerPoint presentation typically contains many slides.

Figure 22.1 illustrates a PowerPoint presentation made up of 30 slides. The default (Normal) view includes notes attached to the current slide, and a navigation panel on the left side that allows you to switch between a text outline and slide thumbnails.

A fully loaded slide (see Figure 22.2) includes at most six parts:

- The *title*, which usually sits at the top of the slide.
- *Body text*, the main part of the slide. More often than not, the text on a slide consists of a series of bulleted or numbered items. However, you can enter any kind of text in this part of a slide—bullets and numbers are not required.
- Some slides contain *content* in addition to text. You can add charts, tables, pictures, diagrams, and video clips to help illuminate your presentation.

Outline/Thumbnails   Slide

Figure 22.1
PowerPoint's Normal
view includes most of
the information you
need to assemble a
presentation.

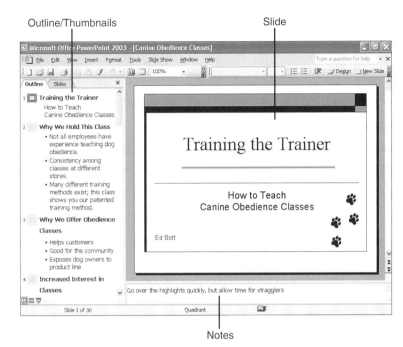

Notes

Graphic   Slide Title   Text

Figure 22.2
All the components of
a PowerPoint slide are
shown here, with
slide thumbnails in
place of a text outline.

Outline/Thumbnails

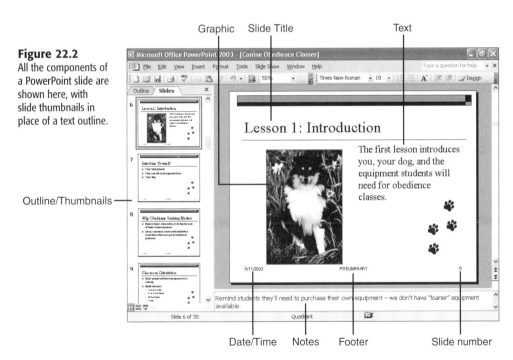

Date/Time   Notes   Footer   Slide number

22

NOTE

Text and content sit inside resizable and movable containers called *placeholders*, which you can see if you click the text or graphic in the slide pane. PowerPoint help screens sometimes refer to the placeholder and the text or content it contains as a "text object" or a "graphic object."

- If you choose to display the *date and time*, these items appear at the lower-left corner by default.

- The *footer*, another optional element, appears by default at the bottom of the slide, in the middle.

- Finally, you can choose to display a *slide number*; its default position is in the lower-right corner.

Most presentations begin with a *title slide*, which typically includes the title of the presentation, the speaker's name, and other introductory details. If you're planning a presentation as a class project, you might include the class name and number—Sociology 101, for instance; for a presentation to a business or civic group, you might include your name and the name of the organization you represent. Other slides in a presentation can also be title slides—you might use a title slide to introduce different portions of a long presentation, for example—but in most cases, you'll have just one title slide in a presentation, and it will serve as the first slide.

NOTE

Don't be confused by the terminology. A *title slide* is, in most cases, a slide that introduces a presentation. A *slide title*, on the other hand, is usually the first line on a slide.

POWERPOINT FILE TYPES

PowerPoint uses three main file types: Presentation, Template, and Slide Show. For the most part, you can construct and deliver simple presentations without ever having to deal with the differences among these types of files. But before you can effectively use PowerPoint's advanced formatting options, you have to understand its file formats.

The Office 2003 Setup program registers a collection of PowerPoint file types. When you view the list of registered file types in Windows Explorer, you'll see the three major types listed in Table 22.1 (there are also some variant HTML file types that work much the same as these).

TABLE 22.1   POWERPOINT FILE TYPES

File Type	File Extension	Default Action
PowerPoint Presentation	*.ppt	Open
PowerPoint Template	*.pot	New
PowerPoint Slide Show	*.pps	Show

Thus, from an Explorer window, if you double-click an icon whose file type is Presentation (.ppt), PowerPoint opens the file for editing. When you double-click an icon whose file type is Template (.pot), however, PowerPoint creates a new presentation, based on the template, and takes you to the first slide so you can begin editing. Finally, if you double-click an icon whose type is Slide Show (.pps), PowerPoint runs the show without ever showing you any of its slide-editing tools.

Here's the punch line: The internal structure of all three file formats is exactly the same. You can save any presentation as a Template or Slide Show file, and the contents of the file remain the same.

N O T E

> You might find inconsistent references to these three file types scattered throughout PowerPoint's Help files and dialog boxes. In this book, we use the three terms defined in this section—Presentation, Template, and Slide Show—to differentiate among the three file types.

When should you use each file type? Follow these general guidelines:

- Use the Presentation file type (.ppt) when you plan to edit the presentation and/or work with its design. To save a file as file type Presentation, choose Presentation from the Save As Type list in the Save As dialog box.

- Use the Template file type (.pot) when you create a presentation that you want to use as the basis for creating new presentations, or if you expect to "borrow" the presentation's design for use in other presentations. To save a file as a Template, choose Design Template from the Save As Type list in the Save As dialog box. When you select this file type, PowerPoint immediately changes the Save In location to the default Templates folder.

- Use the Slide Show file type (.pps) for presentations that you no longer need to edit or design. (Although it's possible to open this type of file from within PowerPoint, this is not the default action when you double-click its icon on the desktop or in an Explorer window.) Choose this file type if you want to start a slide show directly from the desktop, or if you want someone else to be able to double-click a file icon and see the show. To save a file as a Slide Show, choose PowerPoint Show from the Save As Type list in the Save As dialog box.

22

TIP FROM

EQ & Woody

> Because all three file types are internally identical, it's easy to change file types. Just open the file in PowerPoint, choose File, Save As, and then choose a different format from the Save As dialog box. If you're comfortable working with file extensions in an Explorer window or at a command prompt, you can change a file type by changing the three-letter extension at the end of the filename; for example, changing the file extension from .ppt to .pps converts a Presentation into a Slide Show.

FILE COMPATIBILITY ISSUES

Using PowerPoint 2003, you can open and edit files created in any version of PowerPoint. In fact, you can freely share presentations you create in PowerPoint 2003 with anyone using PowerPoint 2003, PowerPoint 2000, or PowerPoint 97, because all of these versions use the same file format. Older versions may not be able to take advantage of every feature in PowerPoint 2003 (animated GIFs, for instance, will display as static illustrations in PowerPoint 97), but the file will be unaffected by any changes.

In the unlikely event that you need to share files with someone using PowerPoint 95, you must save them in an alternate format. To do so, choose File, Save As and select PowerPoint 97-2003 & 95 Presentation (*.ppt) in the Save as Type box. When you choose this option, PowerPoint saves two copies of your presentation in the same file—one in PowerPoint 95 format, the other in the standard PowerPoint presentation format—and anyone can open, view, and edit the presentation by using any version of PowerPoint.

NOTE

> When you save a PowerPoint 2002/2003 presentation in PowerPoint 95 format, you lose many components of your presentation. Animated chart elements, hyperlinks, and macros, among other elements, all disappear. In addition, file size usually swells: PowerPoint 95 has comparatively crude picture-compression capabilities.

CREATING A PRESENTATION

When you choose File, New, PowerPoint presents you with a familiar task pane that includes a variety of options for creating or opening presentations (see Figure 22.3).

CREATING A BLANK PRESENTATION

When you create a new, blank presentation—by choosing Blank Presentation in the New Presentation pane or by clicking the New icon on the Standard toolbar—PowerPoint generates a new presentation and displays the Slide Layout task pane (see Figure 22.4).

When you begin with a blank presentation, PowerPoint starts with a single title slide. Although it's a tedious way to work, you can build your presentation from this view, one slide at a time. Aim your mouse pointer at the layout that matches the kind of slide you want to add, click the arrow to the right of the slide layout icon, and choose Insert New Slide from the menu.

Figure 22.3
PowerPoint lets you choose whether you want to open an existing presentation, create a new presentation with or without content, or pull in a template.

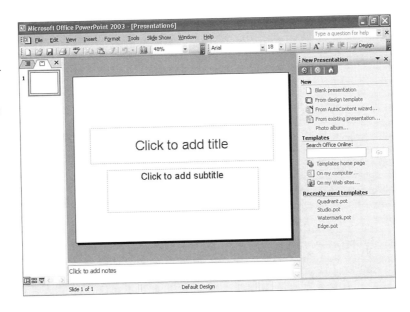

Figure 22.4
Use the Slide Layout pane to specify which placeholders will go on a slide and where they will sit.

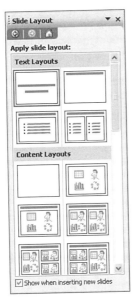

→ For tips on negotiating the layout maze, **see** "Picking the Best Slide Layout," **p. 726**.

In a blank PowerPoint presentation, each new slide you create is completely free of any design elements whatsoever. You get a white background, with text formatted in the Arial font (44-point for slide titles and 32-point for body text) and generic round bullets.

It is hard to imagine a layout more dull than this default design. To replace it with one that contains coordinated colors, fonts, and graphics, click the Design icon on the Formatting

22

toolbar (or choose Slide Design from the drop-down list at the top of the task pane). The Slide Design pane (see Figure 22.5) appears.

TIP FROM

Initially, PowerPoint installs only a limited selection of its design templates. To make the entire collection of templates available, scroll all the way to the bottom of the Slide Design pane and click Additional Design Templates. (If you kept the installation files on your hard drive, you won't need the Office CD.) If that's not enough, a quick search of the Internet will turn up literally thousands of downloadable templates of varying sophistication. You can also create your own templates, either from scratch or by modifying a template you found elsewhere. Don't be afraid to experiment!

When you click the icon for a design template, PowerPoint immediately applies the design to all slides in your presentation. The icons offer a thumbnail-sized preview of the design, but there's no substitute for experimentation. Feel free to apply different designs to the current presentation and then flip through the slides to see what each design looks like; if your presentation includes important content, create a copy first so that you don't have to worry about inadvertently messing up the existing design.

If you regularly prepare presentations for an organization or company that has certain standards for all presentations—logo in a specific location, identification of title slides, and so on—you might want to customize PowerPoint's "blank" presentation so that it reflects those standards. That way, whenever you begin a new presentation you'll have the basic requirements out of the way before you type your first bullet point.

To replace the PowerPoint default blank presentation with one of your own design, follow these steps:

1. Create the presentation you want to use as the "blank" presentation. Add slides, customize slide masters, and change designs until you're satisfied that the basic arrangement is a good starting point for any new presentations you create.

2. Choose File, Save As. In the Save as Type box, choose Design Template.

3. Type **Blank** in the File Name box and click Save.

TIP FROM

By default, PowerPoint saves your new blank presentation in your personal Templates folder (to view the contents of this folder, click Start, Run, enter %appdata%\ Microsoft\Templates in the Open box, and press Enter). To make this change for all the users in your organization, you must copy the Blank Presentation design template file into the personal Templates folder for each user.

→ For more details on how and where Office programs organize files, **see** "Creating New Files," **p. 66**.

22

With a Blank Presentation file in the correct location, all "blank" presentations—whether created via the New Presentation task pane or using the New icon on the Standard toolbar—will be based on that file.

STARTING POWERPOINT WITH A DESIGN TEMPLATE

Don't like the idea of starting with a completely blank slate? If you click From Design Template in the PowerPoint New Presentation pane, PowerPoint transports you to the Slide Design pane, and lets you pick a design for the presentation before you roll up your sleeves and begin adding new slides.

> **NOTE**
>
> A *design*, in this case, includes a background, font specifications for the title slide and other slides in the presentation, default bullets, and a handful of lesser settings—title locations, footers, slide numbering, and the like.

Click the arrow at the right side of the design template icon and click Show Large Previews to see more detail for each design (see Figure 22.5). The default menu option, Apply to All Slides, adjusts your presentation so that the new layout applies to the single slide in your new presentation as well as any new slides you might add.

Figure 22.5
Switch to this larger preview to get a better picture of what each design template looks like.

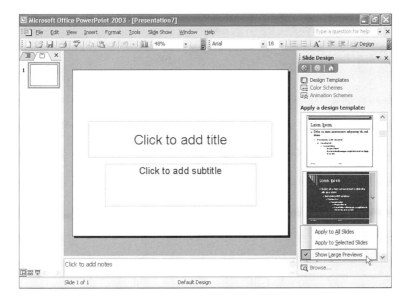

> **TIP FROM**
>
> *Ed & Woody*
>
> Want more designs? Scroll to the very bottom of the list of thumbnails in the Slide Design task pane and click the Design Templates on Microsoft.com link. This opens Internet Explorer and takes you to the Microsoft Office Templates website, where you can browse through a searchable collection of extra designs.

22

BUILDING A PRESENTATION FROM "CANNED" CONTENT

PowerPoint ships with dozens of prefabricated presentations with a business focus, many of which combine decent visual effects with reasonable suggestions for presenting your own content. On the New Presentation task pane, click From AutoContent Wizard to select from a list of built-in templates covering a wide variety of situations—Recommending a Strategy, Communicating Bad News, Selling a Product or Service, and Company Meeting, for instance.

These generic templates can be a helpful way to get started (providing they cover the topic you want), but they also run the risk of limiting your creativity. In our experience, most advanced PowerPoint users will find that their own custom presentations provide a better starting point. For instance, if you're preparing for the annual meeting of a statewide charity organization, you probably want to start with a presentation that includes the history of the organization, its goals, its current status, and its plans for the coming year. Using this content as a jumping-off point, local chapter leaders can customize the presentation for their city or town and get results in a fraction of the time they would spend by starting from scratch.

To add your own presentation to the AutoContent Wizard, follow these steps:

1. Create and save a presentation that you want to put in the AutoContent Wizard. You might want to start with one of PowerPoint's built-in presentations, adding your own content and design elements. Or you can begin by stripping an existing presentation down to its most generic form.

2. Save the resulting file in either Presentation format (*.ppt) or Design Template format (*.pot) in your personal Templates folder (`%appdata%\Microsoft\Templates`).

3. Start the AutoContent Wizard by clicking From AutoContent Wizard on the New Presentation task pane, and click Next to jump to the second step, Presentation Type.

4. Choose the category most appropriate to your presentation: General, Corporate, Projects, or Sales/Marketing. (If you select "All," PowerPoint adds the new presentation type to the General category.) Click Add (see Figure 22.6).

5. Select the presentation or design template file you saved in Step 2 and click OK. When you return to the wizard, click Cancel.

Presentations added in this manner work just like the built-in templates, except the full filename, including the .ppt or .pot filename extension, appears in the wizard's second pane. If you no longer want a custom presentation to appear in this list, select it and click Remove. (The original file remains intact.)

COPYING THE DESIGN OF AN EXISTING PRESENTATION

So, you've found a presentation with just the right design elements, even if the content is completely different from what you need.

Figure 22.6
Add your own presentations to the AutoContent Wizard using the Add button here.

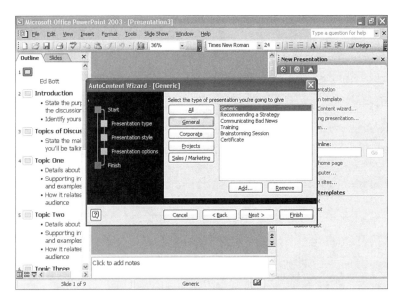

PowerPoint makes it easy to recycle the design of an existing presentation. If you have the original presentation file, you can "borrow" its design without changing the content of your current presentation in any way.

Just choose Format, Slide Design. Scroll through the Apply a Design Template List and click the one you want to use. If you've downloaded a template or saved an existing presentation that isn't on the list, click the Browse link at the bottom of the Slide Design task pane, locate the presentation you want to use, and click Apply.

The design of the chosen presentation is applied automatically to your current presentation.

IMPORTING FROM A WORD OUTLINE

Have you been asked to give a presentation based on an existing report or other document? If you can import the document into Word and convert its headings to Word's default "Heading 1" style, the rest is a snap.

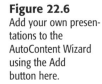

TIP FROM

To convert a Word document into an outline that can be used in PowerPoint, you need to learn just a few simple Word shortcuts. In Word, click to select the paragraph you want to turn into a slide title and press Ctrl+Alt+1, which applies the Heading 1 style. For the text that will go into bullet points, press Ctrl+Alt+2 (Heading 2). Want bullet points beneath the bullet points? Press Ctrl+Alt+3 (Heading 3). Save the document and import it into PowerPoint for quick results.

Outlines in Word can be imported directly into PowerPoint in either of two ways. From inside Word, choose File, Send To, Microsoft PowerPoint. From inside PowerPoint, choose

22

File, Open; in the Files of Type box choose All Outlines, select the Word document, and then click Open.

When you import a Word document, Level 1 headings (formatted "Heading 1" in Word) turn into the titles of new slides. Level 2 headings turn into top-level bullet points. Level 3 headings become second-level bullet points, and so on. In essence, the outline that you see in Word's Outline view is translated into a PowerPoint outline. Any body text beneath existing headings is discarded.

Each time PowerPoint encounters a Level 1 heading in Word, it starts a new slide and uses the Level 1 heading text for the slide's title. In other words, your presentation will include exactly one slide for each Level 1 heading in the Word document.

NOTE

You can also import files saved in HTML formats and turn them into a PowerPoint outline. (From the drop-down Files of Type list in the Open dialog box, choose All Web Pages.) During the import, PowerPoint turns each top-level heading into a new slide; all text underneath each heading is placed in a text box on the corresponding slide.

You can also insert an outline into the middle of an existing presentation. Select the slide you want the outline to follow, and then choose Insert, Slides from Outline. PowerPoint converts the outline to new slides and inserts them after the selected slide.

VIEWING A PRESENTATION

PowerPoint starts in Normal view. You can return to this view at any time by choosing View, Normal, or by selecting the Normal View icon on the View bar in the lower left corner of the screen. In Normal view, you can see either a text outline of your presentation or thumbnails of all the slides in the left-most pane. The current slide appears in the main pane, with the slide's notes just below it.

Normal view is highly customizable. To dismiss the left navigation pane and the notes pane temporarily, leaving only the current slide, click the X at the top left of the navigation pane. To restore both panes, choose View, Normal (Restore Panes). You can also click and drag the edge of any pane to resize that portion of the view. Compare the configuration of Figure 22.7, for instance, with the default view shown earlier in Figure 22.1. We dragged the border of the outline pane nearly all the way to the right and set the Zoom menu to 30%. Using this arrangement allows you to concentrate on content, leaving just a small preview of the current slide and any accompanying notes.

TIP FROM

EQ & Woody

The outline and notes that appear in Normal view's two respective panes are unformatted by default. For example, if you've italicized a word in a particular slide's title, that formatting does not appear in Normal view's outline pane. To force the outline and notes panes to display actual formatting, click the Show Formatting button on the Standard toolbar. Click this button again to restore the basic unformatted view.

Figure 22.7
Customize
PowerPoint's Normal
view to customize on
the outline.

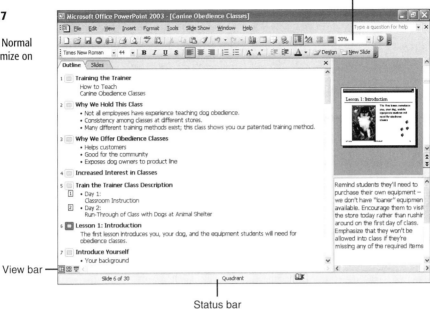

Zoom menu

View bar

Status bar

Although Normal view gives quick and easy access to most of the options you'll typically want to use, each of the individual views available via the View bar comes in handy for specific tasks.

ORGANIZING IDEAS IN THE OUTLINE PANE

You can do most of the important work on a presentation—that is, content, content, content—without ever leaving the outline pane.

TIP FROM

EQ & Woody

The outline pane becomes much more useful when it's accompanied by the Outlining toolbar. To make these handy buttons visible, right-click the main menu bar or any visible toolbar and select Outlining from the list of available toolbars.

Any text you type in the outline pane immediately to the right of a slide number becomes the title of the slide; subsequent outline points turn into bulleted items in the slide's text placeholder. Highlight, click, and drag to move outline text or entire slides. To select an entire slide, move the mouse pointer under the slide number until it turns into a "northwest arrow"—meaning that the arrow points upward and to the left. Click and the slide is selected.

→ Details on setting outline levels are in the next chapter; **see** "Editing Slides," **p. 729**.

USING SLIDE SORTER VIEW TO REARRANGE A PRESENTATION

Slide Sorter view (see Figure 22.8) gives you an opportunity to see the entire presentation all at once, move slides around, control the transition effects that bind the slides and animation together on an individual slide, and perform easy, one-click previews of animations and transitions.

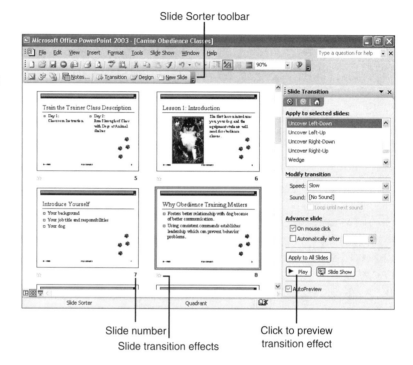

Figure 22.8
Slide Sorter view makes it easy to check transitions and animations.

Move to Slide Sorter view by selecting the Slide Sorter view icon in the View bar, or by choosing View, Slide Sorter. Use the Zoom menu to configure the size of the thumbnails (and, by extension, the number of thumbnails visible on the screen).

PowerPoint transitions control how a slide makes its initial appearance onscreen. Animations, on the other hand, control how components of the slide appear, after the slide is onscreen. For instance, you might use an animation to cause bullet points to "zoom" onto the slide, one after the other, with a brief delay between each bullet.

Bring up the Slide Transition task pane by clicking the Transition button on the Slide Sorter toolbar. To work with animations, choose Animation Schemes from the Slide Design task pane.

Slide Sorter view is the easiest place to perform the following common tasks:

- **Rearrange slides**—Click and drag any slide to a different position.
- **Add slides**—Right-click the space between two slides and choose New Slide from the shortcut menu.

22

- **Delete slides**— Select one or more slides and then press the Delete key. (To select multiple slides, hold down Control while clicking.)

- **Set transition effects**—Select one or more slides and then use the Slide Transition pane to pick and fine-tune the transition you like.

- **Preview transition effects**—Click the Preview button to the left of the slide number, or click Play at the bottom of the Slide Transition task pane.

- **Apply an animation to the contents of a slide**—Use the Animation Schemes list on the Slide Design task pane to pick one of PowerPoint's ready-made animations, or use the Custom Animation task pane to build your own animation from scratch.

PREVIEWING YOUR PRESENTATION IN SLIDE SHOW VIEW

At any point in the process of developing a presentation, you can preview the show itself.

To see the presentation starting with the currently selected slide, just pick a slide (in any view) and click the Slide Show View icon on the View bar. This starts the show and allows you to use the same navigation techniques you would use if you were actually giving the presentation to an audience (for example, click to advance the slide, press Esc to exit). When the show is over, you return to the view you were using before starting the slide show. If you want to see the entire presentation, starting with the first slide, click Slide Show, View Show. Alternatively, press F5.

TIP FROM

EQ & Woody

> If you hold down the Control key as you click View Slide Show, the show appears in a small window that occupies the upper-left quadrant of the screen. Click elsewhere in the PowerPoint window to hide the show while you edit or create a slide; click the Resume Slide Show button to return and see your changes.

ADDING NOTES

The simplest way to add or modify notes is in Normal view, where you can expand the notes pane as needed to accommodate lengthy notes.

If the small notes pane isn't big enough to work with comfortably, choose View, Notes Page to switch to Notes Page view. This view, which doesn't have its own button on the View bar, hides the outline and shows you a full-page as it will appear when you print out your notes for reference (see Figure 22.9).

If the notes for any particular slide extend beyond one page, Notes view expands the text area downward to accept what you type. If you print the notes for that particular slide, however, they'll be truncated at one page. Multi-page notes appear in Normal view.

Figure 22.9
Notes Page view hides the outline and shows only the notes for one slide at a time.

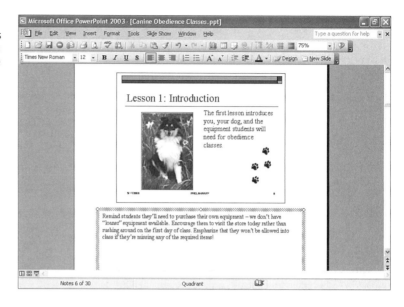

VIEWING PRESENTATIONS IN A WEB BROWSER

If you save your presentation as a web page, the entire presentation can be viewed with a web browser (see Figure 22.10). The person looking at your presentation need not have PowerPoint installed to see all the details and navigate the presentation fully. (Note the navigation buttons along the bottom of the presentation, which allow the viewer to show or hide the outline and notes pane, to jump from slide to slide, and to display the presentation as a slide show.)

Figure 22.10
This PowerPoint presentation is being viewed through Internet Explorer.

→ To learn how to save your presentation as a web page, **see** "Creating Presentations for the Web," **p. 788**.

To get full effect of the browser-viewing option, the person viewing the presentation should be running Internet Explorer version 5 or later, Firefox 1.0 or later, or Netscape/Mozilla version 5 or later. Although you can create presentations that show up on earlier versions of these browsers, there are extensive limitations on what they can do.

CAUTION

This browser-viewing capability might not perform precisely the way you expect. In particular, you might be disappointed with the way diagonal lines (for example, in AutoShape callouts), WordArt, and Organization Charts appear when viewed in a browser window.

Before you expend a lot of effort developing a presentation for the Web, flesh out a few of the most complex graphics, stick them in a slide, and choose File, Web Page Preview. That will give you a good indication of how the final presentation will appear, at least when using the browser installed on your PC. If you discover a display problem, consider saving the org chart or AutoShape as a standard graphic and inserting it into a slide instead. Save the original as a hidden slide so that you can edit it later.

MANAGING SLIDE SHOWS

PowerPoint has several useful tools and techniques you can use to manage presentations. If you work in Slide Sorter view, it's easy to copy, move, insert, or delete slides. But there are some tricks. To paste a slide at the beginning of a presentation, go into Slide Sorter view, click to the left of the first slide, and then paste.

If you want to copy slides from one presentation and put them in another, select the slide you want the imported slides to appear after (in Slide Sorter view, click between the slides), and then choose Insert, Slides from Files. The Slide Finder dialog box appears, as shown in Figure 22.11.

Figure 22.11
Slide Finder lets you pick and choose which slides to copy into the current presentation.

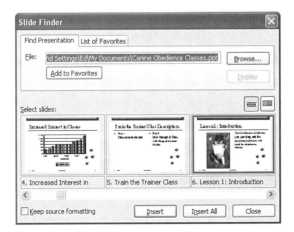

22

Find the file containing the slides you want to copy, and then click the Display button. Click each slide in turn and click Insert. Click the Add to Favorite button to add the current presentation to the list of presentations on the Favorites tab. Choosing this option saves a few clicks if you regularly build new presentations using slides in a select few existing presentations.

NOTE

The Slide Finder's List of Favorites tab is maintained independently of the Windows (and Office) Favorites folder.

PowerPoint lets you mark specific slides as *hidden*. Hidden slides appear in all views except Slide Show view, and they don't show up when the presentation is run. You can use hidden slides to prepare material that doesn't have to be in your presentation but might come up in a Q&A period, for example.

To hide a slide, switch to Slide Sorter view, select the slide to be hidden, and click the Hide Slide icon. You'll know that the slide won't be shown in the presentation because a "not" sign appears over the slide number.

CAUTION

You can hide slides while working in other views—select the slide, and then choose Slide Show, Hide Slide. When you use this technique, Normal View will show the slide number with a slash through it. That tells you the slide is hidden.

When you add a new slide to a presentation, you must specify what kind of slide you want (unless you paste one in). To specify the type of new slide, choose a *thumbnail* sketch from the Slide Layout pane (refer to Figure 22.6).

→ For tips on getting the slide layout right, **see** "Picking the Best Slide Layout," **p. 726**.

If you deliver PowerPoint presentations regularly, you might have a main presentation that needs only a bit of tweaking for use with a variety of audiences. For example, you might have one version for teachers and a slightly different version for administrators. Or you might have short and long versions of a presentation, choosing one or the other depending on the time allotted for your talk. PowerPoint makes it easy to keep all your slides together in one file, but build separate, custom slide shows for specific situations.

To create a custom show, choose Slide Show, Custom Shows, New. The Define Custom Show dialog box appears, as shown in Figure 22.12.

Select the slides you want to appear in the custom show and click Add. Note that you can move a slide—so it appears in a different sequence in the custom show—by clicking the up arrow or down arrow. Type in a name for the custom show, and click OK. Repeat this process for other variations on the main show. You can now run any custom show any time you want; open the Custom Shows dialog box again, select the name of the show, and click Show.

Figure 22.12
Pick and arrange existing slides to be incorporated in a custom show.

You can also use custom slide shows as a way to create alternate paths within a longer presentation. Move to the slide in your presentation where you want to branch out to one of these custom shows. Select a location for the link (perhaps in the body text, or in a drawing), and click the Hyperlink icon. In the Link To pane on the left side of the dialog box, pick Place In This Document. Scroll to the bottom of the list, as shown in Figure 22.13.

Figure 22.13
Hyperlink to one of the custom shows—for example, Executive Briefing.

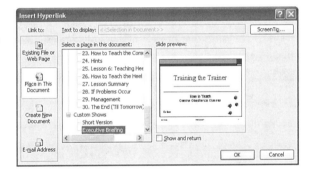

Choose the custom show you want to link to, and click OK. From that point on, whenever you encounter the slide with the hyperlink, click it to display the custom show.

To return to the main presentation after the custom show runs, select the Show And Return check box.

TIP FROM

EQ & Woody

> Alternatively, you can create a hyperlink on the last slide in the custom show to jump to whatever point in the main presentation you like.

→ For details about hyperlinking inside your presentation, **see** "Using Hyperlinks," **p. 719**.

You can tell PowerPoint that you want it to run a custom show, instead of the "normal" show, whenever you start a slide show. To do so, choose Slide Show, Set Up Show. In the Set Up Show dialog box (see Figure 22.14), select a custom show from the Custom Show list in the Show Slides area.

Figure 22.14
Have PowerPoint run a custom show automatically by using the Custom Show setting.

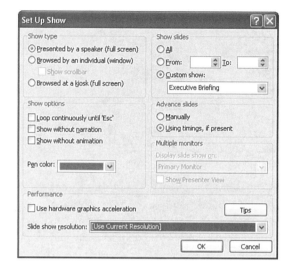

Custom shows can be a powerful feature. For example, you can put all your slides relating to a given topic inside one PowerPoint file, and then pick and choose the slides you want to give for your main presentation. Set up a custom show called Main, and then choose Main as the default show. That way, all your slides stay in one presentation file, the Main presentation runs whenever you start a slide show, and you can easily and quickly add and remove slides from the Main presentation.

NAVIGATING THROUGH A PRESENTATION

PowerPoint presents myriad ways to navigate in a presentation.

MOUSE AND KEYBOARD SHORTCUTS

In addition to the navigation methods you've probably used (left mouse button to advance to the next slide, Backspace key to back up to the previous slide, Esc to end the current slide show), PowerPoint also supports a wide variety of mouse and keyboard shortcuts:

■ To advance from one slide to another, or perform the next animation on the current slide, you can click the left mouse button—but you can also press Enter, N (for Next), page down, right arrow, down arrow, or the spacebar. You can also right-click the screen during a presentation and choose Next.

■ To move to the previous slide, or activate the preceding animation on the current slide, you can press Backspace—but you can also try P (for Previous), page up, left arrow, or the up arrow. Or you can right-click the screen and choose Previous.

■ To end a presentation, in addition to the Esc key, you can right-click and choose End Show.

22

An almost-complete list of navigation controls is available by right-clicking the screen during a presentation and choosing Help, by pressing F1, or by referring to the Help topic "Slide Show Controls." Most of the controls are obscure, but a few might be worth memorizing:

- B (for Black) or pressing the period key toggles between displaying a black screen and showing the current slide
- Similarly, W (for white) or pressing the comma key toggles a white screen
- Tab cycles among all the hyperlinks on a slide

The black- and white-screen options are useful when you're giving a slide show and you come to a point where you want to talk without the help of slides. Clearing the contents of the screen allows your audience to focus on you without being distracted by the contents of the last slide.

TIP FROM

Ed & Woody

> This doesn't appear to be documented anywhere, but pressing the Home key during a presentation returns you to the first slide. Similarly, pressing the End key sends you to the final slide.

USING HYPERLINKS

Hyperlinks allow you to turn text, graphics, pictures, or almost anything else on a slide, into a "hot" link. Those hot links can point just about anywhere—a specific slide, the first or last slide in a presentation, the next or previous slides, files (whether on the local hard drive, or accessible through the network), specific locations inside Word documents or Excel workbooks, and much more. As shown previously in Figure 22.13, you can even link to a custom show within the current presentation by using the Bookmark button in the Insert Hyperlink dialog box.

If the computer you're using for the presentation is connected to the Web (or if the presentation itself is on the Web), hyperlinks can also connect to web pages.

The easiest way to establish a hyperlink is to start by selecting whatever you want to hyperlink from (that is, the text, drawing, picture, and so on, that will be "hot" during the presentation), and then click the Insert Hyperlink icon on the Standard toolbar. (If you prefer, you can choose Insert, Hyperlink, or use the Office-wide shortcut Ctrl+K.)

The problem with hyperlinking to an object that requires another application, of course, is that there's no way to hyperlink to the next slide in your presentation. If you hyperlink out to an object that requires a program other than PowerPoint—to a web page, say, or a Word document—when you close that program, PowerPoint is still there, and you've gone back to the "linked from" slide; you'll have to click to move on to your next point.

TIP FROM

Ed & Woody

> If you hyperlink to an entire PowerPoint presentation, you can run through that presentation and, when it's done, you are back where you started, at the "link from" slide.

ADVANCED NAVIGATION WITH ACTION SETTINGS

Action Settings are an older variation on hyperlinks that let you link to a few unusual locations in a presentation—in particular, the "last slide viewed." Action Settings also let you start a program, run a macro, and/or combine sounds with all the preceding.

If you want to be able to "jump back" to the previously viewed slide, your best bet is to set up an Action Button (see next section) with an Action Setting that moves to the previously viewed slide. This option allows you to link to a single slide from several different locations and set up a "Return" button that always goes back to the right place. Action Settings allow you to navigate in powerful ways that aren't possible with hyperlinks.

To open the Action Settings dialog box (see Figure 22.15), select the text or graphic you want to make "hot," and then click Slide Show, Action Settings.

Figure 22.15
Action Settings provide the only (easy) way to return to the previously viewed slide.

Note that you can specify separate actions for a mouse over—where you move the mouse pointer over the "hot" area—and for a mouse click.

NAVIGATION SHORTHAND WITH ACTION BUTTONS

PowerPoint makes some kinds of hyperlinking easy by attaching predefined hyperlinking information to a group of AutoShapes called Action Buttons.

If you want to add a button that allows you to immediately move to the end of the presentation, use an Action Button. If you're creating a presentation for the Web and want to create your own Next Slide and Previous Slide buttons, instead of relying on PowerPoint's built-in navigation bar, Action Buttons make it easy.

To place an Action Button on a slide, select the slide and, on the Drawing toolbar, choose AutoShapes, Action Buttons. (Equivalently, you can choose Slide Show, Action Buttons.) The buttons look just like AutoShapes (see Figure 22.16).

Figure 22.16
Predefined Action Buttons cover many of the common hyperlinking bases.

Several of the Action Buttons (for example, the question mark, information sign, video camera) don't hyperlink to anything in particular; they just put the picture on the slide and bring up the Action Settings dialog box.

Most of the Action Buttons, however, have predefined actions associated with them. You can insert buttons on your slides to move to the first or last slide in the presentation, to go to the next or previous slide, or to return to the last viewed slide.

EXTRA CREDIT: SUPERCHARGING POWERPOINT WITH A FREE ADD-IN

Using nothing more than PowerPoint, you can create impressive presentations that mimic an old-fashioned slide show. If you're willing to work within PowerPoint's limits, you can add sound and video to individual slides. But if you want to blend video clips, HTML, audio, and a set of PowerPoint slides into a single show that will play back over the Internet, you need something a little extra.

You need a free add-on called Microsoft Producer 2003. At 46MB, you'd better have a high-speed Internet connection to download it. But the wait is worth it. Producer lets you do any or all of the following:

- Capture narration and synchronize it with your slides using a simple wizard
- Capture high-quality audio and video and add it directly to your presentation
- Create presentations that play back properly on Macintosh computers and in non-Microsoft browsers
- Embed presentations into HTML frames within a website and allow viewers to save stopping points, speed up playback, and easily fast-forward or rewind through the show
- Create multiple versions of your show in different bit rates or using different versions of the Windows Media format

Producer has a steep learning curve, and it isn't for the casual PowerPoint user. But if you're ready to turn pro (or at least semi-pro) this is an excellent addition. You'll find it at
http://www.microsoft.com/office/powerpoint/producer/prodinfo/default.mspx.

Figure 22.17

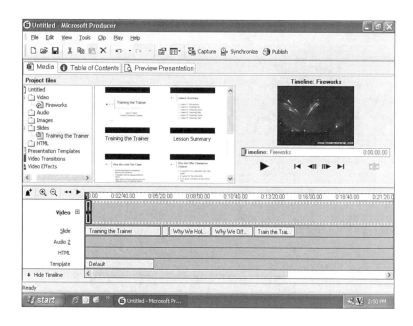

BUILDING YOUR PRESENTATION

23

EDITING THE PRESENTATION OUTLINE

The fastest, easiest, and safest way to edit the text of your presentation is by working with the outline. Flip into Normal view, choose the Outline tab from the navigation pane on the left side of the screen, and enter or edit text here to quickly build content.

EDITING SLIDES IN OUTLINE VIEW

If you have a good idea of what you want to say—or if you're willing to use one of Microsoft's ready-made presentations to suggest content—the simplest way to get a presentation on its feet in no time is to work directly on the outline. Enter text for the slide's title and body, and then you can select, click and drag, copy, move, and delete, just as you would in any other Office program.

TIP FROM

Ed & Woody

> To maximize the editing area when working with an outline in Normal view, click the divider between the Outline pane and the slide and drag it to the right as far as you can while still being able to see the current slide. If you want to see formatted text in your outline, click the Show Formatting button on the Outlining toolbar.

You can use the Tab key while in Outline view to demote one outline level. When you press the Tab key, PowerPoint demotes the current line of text—that is, it moves the current line one level lower in the hierarchy. (You can accomplish the same result by clicking the Demote button on the Outlining toolbar.)

Similarly, you can promote a line one level by pressing Shift+Tab (essentially the "back tab" key). Clicking the Promote button on the Outlining toolbar does the same thing.

NOTE

> The Tab key behaves differently in the outline pane, where it promotes and demotes lines in the presentation's hierarchy. When you're working in the slide pane, a tab is just a tab.

When you promote a line in the outline to the highest level, it becomes the title of a new slide. Thus, a quick and easy way to insert a new slide in a presentation is to press Enter and press Shift+Tab (or click the Promote button) as many times as necessary to reach the top level. (The new slide uses the generic Title and Text layout.)

You can type your entire presentation this way, promoting and demoting as you go: When you type a line at the highest level of the hierarchy, it automatically becomes the title of a new slide; any line below the top level turns into a bullet point (nested however deep you might want) in the slide's text placeholder.

If your slides start getting too wordy and you want to turn high-level bullet points into slides of their own, select the points (one at a time, holding down the Shift key as you click each one from top to bottom) and promote them to the highest level. PowerPoint automatically turns all of them into slides, with the old high-level bullet points now serving as titles.

REORDERING SLIDES

Use the Move Up and Move Down arrows to rearrange text in the outline, and thus in the slides. To do so, click inside the line you want to move, or select a group of lines. Then click the Move Up or Move Down arrows until the lines are positioned correctly.

NOTE

When working with the outline, you can select any group of lines, even if they appear in different slides, as long as they are contiguous.

TIP FROM

You might find it easier to use Slide Sorter view to perform extensive reordering, or to reorder a large presentation. Slide Sorter view gives you a lot more flexibility for drag and drop; it also shows you more of the presentation at one time.

→ For a detailed discussion of Slide Sorter view, **see** "Using Slide Sorter View to Arrange a Presentation," **p. 712**.

EXPANDING AND COLLAPSING

PowerPoint also makes it easy to hide all the bullets under a slide's title (commonly called *collapsing* the outline) or display every line (*expanding*). Collapsing an outline to just the titles lets you see the overall organization and flow of your presentation, without being distracted by details. Expanding allows you to work on all the bullet points, and compare them across slides. Click inside the slide you want to change (or select a number of contiguous slides) and click the Collapse button to hide all the detail, or click Expand to show all the detail.

NOTE

PowerPoint does not have the capability to expand or collapse to a particular level in the hierarchy: It's an all-or-nothing setting. Either you see all the lines in a slide, or you see just the title.

If you want to collapse or expand all the slides in the presentation in one fell swoop, click the Collapse All or Expand All buttons on the Outlining toolbar.

PICKING THE BEST SLIDE LAYOUT

Although it's easy to add a new slide to a presentation, choosing the right slide layout isn't always so simple.

PowerPoint supports two broad categories of slides: *title slides* (typically the first slide in a presentation), and "regular" slides (which, confusingly, are usually just called "slides"). PowerPoint has one predefined layout for title slides, and almost two dozen predefined layouts for regular slides.

Slide layouts aren't static: You can change a slide's layout by selecting the slide, choosing Format, Slide Layout, and clicking a layout in the Slide Layout task pane.

CHOOSING A SLIDE LAYOUT

Whether you're applying a layout to a brand-new slide, or changing the layout of an existing slide, PowerPoint presents you with the Slide Layout choices shown in Figure 23.1.

Figure 23.1
The Slide Layout pane gives you more than two dozen different ways to organize a slide.

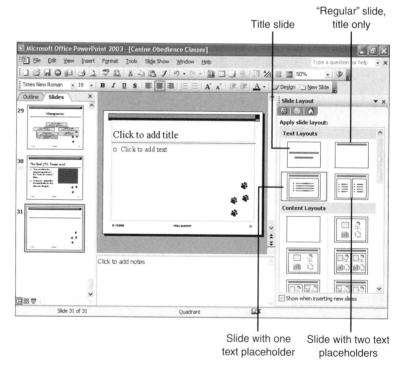

If you choose the first thumbnail in the Slide Layout pane, PowerPoint turns the new slide (or selected slide) into a title slide. Title slides are treated differently from other slides in a presentation—they're formatted independently of the rest of the slides, using the *Title Master*. They generally don't have bullet points and they generally do have a subtitle, so make sure you really want a title slide before making this choice.

→ For more information on editing title slides, **see** "Using the Title Master," **p. 736**.

→ For more information on editing title slides, **see** "Using the Title Master," **p. 736**.

NOTE

The distinction between a title slide and a "regular" slide comes into play because of the way master formatting changes ripple through a presentation. The only way you can manually turn a "regular" slide into a title slide is by applying this first layout, the one called "Title Slide" in the Slide Layout pane.

Other slide thumbnails in the Slide Layout dialog box (refer to Figure 23.1) contain one or more of the following:

- **Text placeholders**—Typically for bulleted and numbered lists.
- **A general "content" placeholder**—Ties into PowerPoint's Insert Object function. The standard content on offer here includes a simple grid (that is, a table), a Microsoft Chart chart, clip art, a picture (from a file), a diagram/org chart, or a media clip.

→ For instructions on using the chart drawing tool, **see** "Simple Charts," **p. 142**.
→ To use Office's Org Chart drawing system, **see** "Organization Charts," **p. 142**.

- **Combinations of "content" and text**—The placeholders are arranged in various configurations.

TIP FROM

EQ & Woody

Placeholders can be resized or dragged to fit your requirements. You need not settle for the size or placement established in the Slide Layout dialog pane.

The general "content" placeholder is a superset of the individual clip art, chart, media clip, and org chart placeholders. In general, you do not limit your choices by using the Slide Layout pane's Content Layouts, as opposed to the Other Layouts.

USING PLACEHOLDERS

With few exceptions, every slide layout has a title placeholder, which reserves space for the title of the slide; this text also appears at the highest hierarchical level in the presentation's outline.

Most slides also have at least one text placeholder. The contents of the text placeholder appear in the outline as points underneath the highest hierarchical level.

Slides that have two text placeholders generate separate outline sections for each placeholder. As you can see in Figure 23.2, PowerPoint gives each placeholder a number, which is used in the outline to keep track of what text belongs in which placeholder.

All the other kinds of slide layout placeholders are special kinds of graphic placeholders: table, chart, org (organizational) chart, clip art, media clip, and general "content" placeholders all contain graphics that don't appear in the outline. The only real difference among all these graphic placeholders, in fact, is the kind of link they provide to retrieve the graphic.

Figure 23.2
Multiple text place-holders receive separate numbers, as indicated in the outline pane.

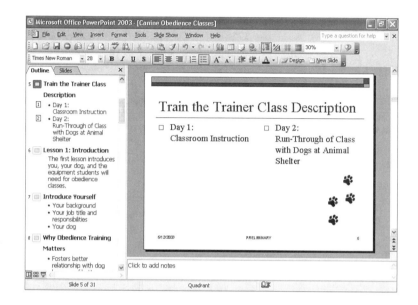

NOTE

You cannot manually insert a placeholder on a slide. Instead, you have to use the Slide Layout task pane. If you copy or paste a text placeholder, it appears as a text box on the slide, and any text you type is not available in the outline. As a result, you cannot add a third text placeholder to a slide.

GOING OUTSIDE THE PLACEHOLDERS

Not all slide activity takes place within placeholders. In fact, any of the items that can go in one of the many content placeholders can also be placed directly on the slide—no place-holder required.

There are two benefits to using the content placeholders to position graphics and other non-text items: First, as the name implies, this technique holds a place open on the slide so PowerPoint can scale the inserted graphic or other object properly and move other place-holders out of the way as needed. Second, placeholders provide easy links to specific kinds of objects. If neither of these characteristics matters on a given slide, consider bypassing content placeholders entirely.

Graphics and drawings (for example, items generated by the Drawing toolbar, or any graphic from the Insert menu) that are placed directly on a slide go in the drawing layer.

→ To learn more about how the drawing layer stores graphics and drawings for your presentation, **see** "Working with the Drawing Layer," **p. 114**.

Note, in particular, that text entered in the drawing layer (say, inside a callout or a text box that you create using the Drawing toolbar or by choosing Insert, Text Box) does not appear in the outline.

EDITING SLIDES

Slides can contain text, bulleted and numbered lists, tables, and other content such as clip art and charts. In most cases, you can make changes to each of these elements directly on the slide itself, in Normal view.

23

ADDING AND EDITING TEXT

The highest-level points in a presentation's outline appear as slide titles. Everything else in the outline appears in the slides' text placeholders. The outline links to the slide strictly and exclusively via the title placeholder and the text placeholder.

If you try to enter more text than a placeholder can accommodate, PowerPoint automatically tries to shrink the text to fit within the confines of the placeholder. First, it tries to reduce the spacing between lines. If that doesn't work, it shrinks the size of the font. If you start to see your text shrinking, maybe it's time to take another look and see whether you need to trim some verbiage or split the slide into two.

→ To work from the outline, **see** "Editing the Presentation Outline," **p. 724**.

Whenever PowerPoint shrinks text to fit in a placeholder, an AutoFit Options action menu appears (it resembles the AutoCorrect action menu). If you don't want PowerPoint to squeeze the text into the placeholder, click the button and choose Stop Fitting Text to This Placeholder from the menu. When you choose this option, your text will spill over onto the face of the slide. This action menu also gives you the options to split the text on the current slide into two slides, to continue on a new slide, or to change to a two-column layout (which will only help if your bulleted list consists of very short items).

TIP FROM

EQ & Woody

> On presentations that adhere to strict design guidelines, auto-fitting text damages the integrity of the design; it might also make the slide too hard to read. To turn off AutoFitting, choose Tools, AutoCorrect Options, click the AutoFormat As You Type tab, and clear the AutoFit Body Text To Placeholder and AutoFit Title Text To Placeholder options.

If you choose to continue on a second slide, the final bullet point on the overextended slide becomes the first bullet point on the new slide. If you opt to split the text between two slides, PowerPoint tries to balance the quantity of text on each slide. In either case, you will probably need to modify titles and tweak text on the original slide or the new slide (or both).

TIP FROM

> In a bulleted list, use Ctrl+Tab to insert a tab character into the text. Pressing the Tab key by itself changes the bullet level.

You might also place text anywhere in the drawing layer—which is to say, on "top" of the slide—by inserting a text box or using one of the many different kinds of AutoShapes.

→ To get text into the drawing layer, **see** "Adding Text to a Drawing," **p. 123**.

In the case of AutoShapes, PowerPoint lets you type in text that extends beyond the ends of the shape. In text boxes, PowerPoint expands the text box downward to accommodate all the text you care to add. In both cases, any text that extends beyond the edge of a slide when viewed in the slide pane does not show up on the slide when you view the slide show or print that slide.

You can apply formatting to any text on a slide by selecting the text and then choosing the formatting. If you want to change the formatting on all slides, however—say, change all the titles on all the slides to a new font, or make all the first-level bullet points on all the slides green—you should use the Slide Master.

TIP FROM

> You can change all instances of a font (typeface) with another font by choosing Format, Replace Fonts.

→ For an explanation of how Slide Masters work, **see** "Using Slide Masters," **p. 738**.

PowerPoint applies AutoFormatting while you type, changing fractions (1/4 to ¼), ordinals (1st to 1ˢᵗ), "smart" curly quotes, dashes, and the like. It will also change a single quote in front of a number into a curly quote ('04 to '04), with the curl pointing in the correct direction, change (c) into a copyright symbol, and change several different combinations of : and) into a ☺ smiley face.

 If you're frustrated because some of your Word AutoCorrect entries don't work in PowerPoint, see "Not All AutoCorrect Entries Work in PowerPoint" in the "Troubleshooting" section at the end of this chapter.

→ For advice on making AutoCorrect work the way you want—and to turn the vexing changes off—**see** "Using AutoCorrect to Type Faster," **p. 98**.

WORKING WITH BULLETED AND NUMBERED LISTS

Most of the text you enter on slides appears as bulleted—or possibly numbered—items.

You can pick bullets or a numbering scheme when the insertion point is in any text, whether in the title placeholder, text placeholder, or even on the drawing layer.

If you've applied a Slide Design to your presentation, PowerPoint has probably already selected a bullet character and formatted it with a color from the default palette for that design. To change a bullet—say, to use a picture as a bullet—go through the Bullets and Numbering dialog box.

Click within the line you want to change, or select all the lines to change, and then choose Format, Bullets and Numbering. (Equivalently, right-click and select Bullets and Numbering.) The Bullets and Numbering dialog box appears (see Figure 23.3).

TIP FROM

Although you can change the bullet character for a single line, you will usually want to change all the bullets on a slide. To customize an entire presentation, perform these steps using the Slide Master rather than an individual slide.

23

Figure 23.3
PowerPoint lets you choose any character or picture as a bullet.

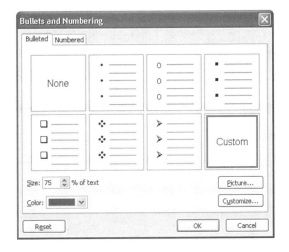

Choose a bullet character from the list of preset options, or click Customize to select a different character from any available font. You can also use a picture in any Office-compatible graphics format—GIF or JPEG, for example—as a bullet. To do so, click Picture (see Figure 23.4), and use one of the built-in bullets, or click Import to bring in a picture of your own.

TIP FROM

PowerPoint stores the bullets just once, so you needn't be overly concerned about swelling file sizes if you stick to just one or two picture bullets. Your primary concern should be how legible the bullet will be in your presentation. Simple line art drawings—say, a pointing finger or a starburst—can help make your point. Washed-out photographs rendered in tiny sizes will only leave your audience squinting.

The Size *nn*% of Text box in the Bullets and Numbering dialog box (refer to Figure 23.3) adjusts the size of the bullet (whether picture or character), scaling it to the point size of the text. You can select any size between 25% and 400%.

Figure 23.4
Choose a picture from among the ones offered, or import your own.

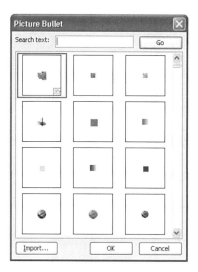

NOTE

The Color drop-down list box in the Bullets and Numbering dialog box applies only to characters; it does not affect the color of a picture used as a bullet.

Numbered paragraphs renumber themselves as you add new items and delete or move existing ones. Follow these steps to number the lines in a slide:

1. Click within the line you want to number, or select a range of lines to be numbered. Auto numbering is supported only for the highest-level paragraphs; if you select lower-level paragraphs, they are ignored.

2. Choose Format, Bullets and Numbering. (Or right-click and select Bullets and Numbering from the shortcut menu.)

3. In the Bullets and Numbering dialog box, click the Numbered tab.

4. Pick the type of numbering you want—fairly simple Roman and Arabic numbers as well as alphabet sequences (a,b,c) are supported on the Numbered tab.

5. If you have a long numbered list that extends over multiple slides, specify a starting value other than 1.

The size and color formatting options mentioned for bullets earlier in this section apply to numbers, too.

If you want to construct multiple-level numbering schemes (for example, 1.1, 1.2, 1.3, 2.1, 2.2), you have to type and maintain the numbers manually.

WORKING WITH TABLES

PowerPoint supports two different methods for constructing tables. Using the older Insert Table approach, you specify the number of rows and columns, and then place the table in the slide. The freeform Draw Table feature lets you draw custom tables by using the mouse.

NOTE

> Although tables created in PowerPoint look a lot like Word tables, there are fundamental differences, both in options and in implementation—the version in PowerPoint isn't nearly as powerful. If you need advanced cell formatting (for example, rotating text within cells), use the Draw Table feature in Word and then paste the resulting table into your presentation.

23

TIP FROM

> Don't forget to use the Clipboard when it makes sense! Pasting a Word table into a slide brings the table in as a graphic. That gives you the opportunity to scale the table by simply clicking and dragging the sizing handles. You don't want to do this with every table, but it's a handy trick to use when necessary.

To place a simple table on your slide, choose Insert, Table, or click the Insert Table button on the Standard toolbar. Specify how many rows and columns you want in the table and click OK; the table appears in a content placeholder that automatically positions itself in the most logical place. For instance, if the insertion point is currently in an empty text placeholder, the placeholder for the new table replaces the text placeholder. If the insertion point is in a text placeholder that already contains text, PowerPoint shrinks the text placeholder and adds the new table in a placeholder that appears to the right.

You can click and drag the resizing handles on the outer edge of the table to resize it. You can also adjust each line in the table by letting the mouse pointer hover until it turns into a parallel line pointer, and then click and drag.

TIP FROM

> If you specify a slide layout that includes a content placeholder and then click the Insert Table icon, PowerPoint inserts this more rigidly formatted kind of table.

To draw your own table freehand, do the following:

1. Click the Tables and Borders icon on the Standard toolbar.
2. On the Tables and Borders toolbar, click the Draw Table button. Your mouse pointer changes into the shape of a pencil.

3. Immediately draw a rectangle that defines the outer boundaries of your new table. The new table appears in a text box in the drawing layer. To customize the table, do any of the following tasks:

- Use the pencil to draw horizontal or vertical lines within the table wherever you want.
- Enter text in a table cell by clicking inside the cell and typing.
- To erase an unwanted line, click the Eraser button, point to an existing cell border, and click.
- Align text, split and merge cells, set border and fill colors, insert cells, and more by using the other options on the Tables and Borders toolbar.

4. When you're done drawing, press the Esc key to turn the pencil back into a normal mouse pointer.

TIP FROM

Clicking the Insert Table button, the simpler approach for most table creation tasks, changes the mouse pointer into the Draw Table tool. Press Esc to restore the normal mouse pointer.

Of course, you can import tables from Word, Excel, or other sources by using simple copy and paste, or PowerPoint's Insert, Object, or Edit, Paste Special options. Word's table functions are somewhat more powerful than those in PowerPoint: They include the capability to rotate text to any angle, sort, and sum, for example.

To maintain control over the look of the pasted results, always use Paste Special when inserting tables. As explained later, Office uses HTML as its default format when you choose a simple Paste, and the results will generally be unsatisfactory.

If you can't see all the cells in your Excel table after pasting it into a PowerPoint slide, see "Excel Tables Don't Display Properly" in the "Troubleshooting" section at the end of this chapter.

ADDING PICTURES, DIAGRAMS, AND CLIP ART

Use the full array of Office drawing tools (available on the Drawing toolbar) to insert pictures, clip art, and text boxes, add WordArt and AutoShapes, set colors, connect AutoShapes with lines, draw shadows, and so on.

→ For details on how to find and insert ready-made graphics from the Office clip art collection, **see** "Using Clip Art," **p. 138**.

→ To work in the drawing layer, **see** "Using Office Drawing Tools," **p. 114**.

Grids and guidelines help you line up drawing items; you can be a little imprecise as you add items and then, when you're finished, allow PowerPoint to line things up precisely. When working with pictures and other drawing tools, it's helpful to show gridlines on the screen. To do so, choose View, Grid and Guides (see Figure 23.5) and select the Display Grid On Screen check box.

Figure 23.5
PowerPoint lets you control the granularity of its grid, and whether drawings should be snapped to the grid.

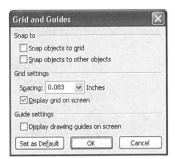

Sometimes you want to know how far a picture lies from dead center. That's where drawing guides come in handy. If you choose to Display drawing guides onscreen, you'll get horizontal and vertical lines that you can use to gauge how far any particular item on the slide sits, compared to dead center (see Figure 23.6). Click the guide, and its distance from center appears as a ScreenTip. You can drag the guides into any position you like, making even fine layout tasks easier.

Figure 23.6
PowerPoint's drawing guides—one horizontal, one vertical—are shown here. Note that we've "parked" pictures in the unused region around the slide.

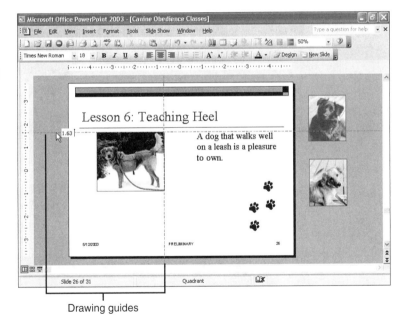

Drawing guides

In the Grid and Guides dialog box, you can take your pick of two Snap To check boxes. You can choose to line up shapes so they snap to the grid, or use the Snap Objects to Other Objects setting to make them automatically abut each other or share a common axis.

PowerPoint also allows you to park pictures in the gray area outside a slide, but still in the slide pane. This option can come in handy if you have a few different pictures you're considering for the slide, but can't make up your mind which one would be best: Parking them in the margin lets you swap them in and out quickly. To get a picture into the margin, click and drag on the picture, moving it to the edge of the pane. It takes a little practice to get a picture positioned this way, but the picture remains handy without appearing on the slide itself. (This option is most useful in Normal view when you close the Outline/Slides pane on the left.)

Organizing Formats with Master Slides

23

Behind every great PowerPoint presentation lurk masters that control the presentation's appearance: the Title Master, Slide Master, Notes Master, and Handouts Master. Each master stores detailed formatting information for title slides, "regular" slides, speaker's notes, and hardcopy handouts, respectively.

These masters control many facets of the slides themselves—backgrounds, fonts (typeface, point sizes, colors, and the like), bullets, locations for all the main components, tabs, and indents. You can also use masters to specify pictures—a logo, for example—and "boilerplate" text that appears on all slides.

TIP FROM

EQ & Woody

If you want to put a graphic, a piece of text, or any other type of object on a bunch of slides, add it to the Slide Master. Repeat the process with the Title Master, too, if you want the same object to appear on title slide(s).

Masters ensure a uniform appearance for your entire presentation. If you're preparing a presentation on behalf of an organization that already has a standard slide show template, use it.

When you create a blank presentation, PowerPoint creates three generic masters—Slide, Notes, and Handouts. When you apply a Design Template to your presentation, PowerPoint adds a Title Master. For presentations that use a consistent design for every slide, one set of masters—that is, one Title Master, one Slide Master, one Notes Master, and one Handouts Master—will normally suffice. In special circumstances, however, you might want to create multiple sets of masters. Throughout most of this section, we assume that your presentation has only one set of masters.

→ For details on how to work with more than one set of master slides, see "Creating Multiple Master Slides," **p. 746**.

To work with master slides, choose View, Master, and then select Slide Master (which, confusingly, displays the Title Master and Slide Master), Handout Master, or Notes Master.

Using the Title Master

The *Title Master* controls "title" slides—typically just the first slide of your presentation. If you create a presentation using the AutoContent Wizard or any of the presentation templates that are installed along with PowerPoint, your presentation includes one title slide, at the beginning.

Many presentations can benefit from multiple title slides, each based on the same master slide: Title slides can help you organize long presentations, emphasize when you're making a transition from one topic to another, or provide cues for custom presentations. You can insert a title slide anywhere in a presentation at any time. To convert any specific slide to a title slide, open the Slide Layout task pane, select the slide you want to convert to a title slide, and click the Title Slide layout (the first one in the task pane). This is the only method PowerPoint supports to convert a "regular" slide into a title slide.

→ For help on setting slide layouts, **see** "Choosing a Slide Layout," **p. 726**.

Making changes to the Title Master automatically changes all the title slides in your presentation. For example, if you change the Title Master's subtitle to 36-point Arial bold, all the title slides in your presentation will have their subtitles changed to 36-point Arial bold.

TIP FROM

If your presentation has only one title slide, and you don't intend to use the presentation to create new presentations—or use its design to modify the design of other presentations—there is absolutely no reason to change the Title Master.

To bring up the Title Master, choose View, Master, Slide Master. This switches the display into Slide Master view, adds a New Slide Master button to the Formatting toolbar, and displays the Slide Master View toolbar. Then click the Title Master in the thumbnail pane on the left. Can't tell the Title Master from the Slide Master? Hover the mouse pointer over each slide to see the ScreenTip that identifies each one (refer to Figure 23.7).

Figure 23.7
Use Slide Master View to manage the design of all slides in a presentation. The ScreenTip shows the name of the current design and the slides to which the master applies.

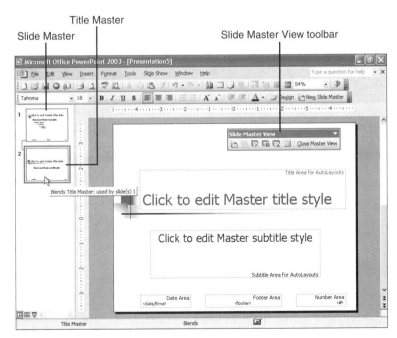

A typical Title Master includes placeholders for the title and subtitle, as well as a background design (usually assigned by the design you apply from the Slide Design task pane). Some Title Masters also have placeholders for a date, footer, and/or slide number.

To change the formatting of the title or subtitle, click inside the placeholder and apply font or paragraph formatting. Similarly, you can click inside the date, footer, or slide number placeholders—if they exist—and adjust their formatting.

For example, if you want the title on all title slides to be left-aligned (instead of centered), click once inside the title placeholder and click the Align Left button on the Formatting toolbar.

Similarly, you can resize or move any of the placeholders on the Title Master. If you move the subtitle placeholder down a half inch on the Title Master, the subtitles on all title slides will move down half an inch.

PowerPoint ignores any text you type into the title or subtitle placeholders on the Title Master. But if you type text into the date, footer, or slide number placeholders, PowerPoint repeats the text on all title slides. So, if you want the slide number on each title slide to say Slide *n*, click the Number Area placeholder and type the text Slide (being sure to add a space after it) in front of the <#>.

TIP FROM

EQ & Woody

> If you accidentally delete one of the five placeholders, you can restore it. Choose Format, Master Layout, select the check box for the deleted placeholder, and click OK. The new placeholder appears in its default location.

You can override Title Master settings on individual title slides. For example, to move the subtitle on a slide or to add a picture to just one title slide, jump to the slide and make the change.

When you override a Title Master setting on an individual slide, you break the link between that setting and the master; subsequent changes won't affect that setting. For example, if you change formatting for the subtitle on the first slide in your presentation, and later change formatting for the subtitle on the Title Master, the subtitle on the first slide won't change. Even changing the Title Master entirely by applying a new design template won't restore the link.

To restore the link between a slide and its master, you have to open the Slide Layout task pane, click the arrow to the right of the Title Slide layout, and choose Reapply Layout from the menu.

USING THE SLIDE MASTER

Whenever you want to change all the slides in your presentation (except the title slides) in exactly the same way, you should change the *Slide Master*. If you want to put a logo on all your slides, for example, add the graphic to the Slide Master instead of editing each individual slide. The same is true if you want to put identical text on all the slides—or change a color, modify a font, or use a different kind of bullet.

The Slide Master includes two default placeholders—one for the title of the slide and a text placeholder designed primarily to hold bulleted lists.

The terminology PowerPoint uses for these two default placeholders takes some explanation. The "Title Area for AutoLayouts" applies to any slide layout that contains a title. The "Object Area for AutoLayouts" appears to be an ordinary text placeholder, but it's not. Any changes you make to this placeholder apply to all slide layouts that contain any kind of object, not just text. Thus, if you make the placeholder smaller by dragging its right border toward the center of the slide, as we've done in Figure 23.8, the change affects all slide layouts. After making this change, if you create a new slide using the Title, Text And Content layout, PowerPoint will squeeze the text placeholder and the content placeholder into the smaller area defined by the Object Area on the Slide Master.

Figure 23.8

Changing the size or shape of the Object Area for AutoLayouts changes the layout of slides containing any type of text or content.

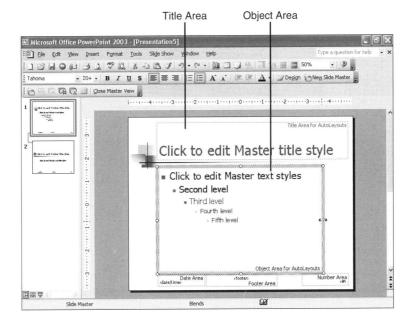

General instructions for the Slide Master mirror those for the Title Master, described in the previous section:

- Any text that appears in the Title Area and Object Area is strictly explanatory. Although you can edit the default text, any text you add in either location does not appear in your presentation.
- Click inside a placeholder to change formatting.
- Resize or move placeholders at will.

- Type text into the date, footer, or slide number placeholders to have it appear on all slides.

- When you work on an individual slide and override settings on the Master—creating different settings for that slide—you break the link to the Master.

 Are you confused by PowerPoint's seeming reluctance to update some of the slides in your presentation when you update the slide master? See "Slide Master Link Damage" in the "Troubleshooting" section at the end of this chapter.

In a Slide Master, you can set formatting and bullets for each level of bulleted text in the body of your presentation. The easiest way to accomplish this task is by applying a design template. To change the formatting of the bullet points in your presentation manually, Choose View, Master, Slide Master to switch into Slide Master view. Then click the Slide Master thumbnail for editing. To change the formatting of text in the highest-level bullet points, click the line that reads "Click to enter Master text styles" and apply the formatting.

- You can change the font, font size, font color, and indent level.

- To change the bullet character used on all slides based on this Master Slide, choose Format, Bullet, and choose the bullet you like.

Repeat this process for the second-, third-, fourth-, and fifth-level bullet items by clicking the appropriate line and applying the formatting.

TIP FROM

E Q & Woody

To "tighten up" the distance between the bullet and text, choose View, Ruler, and adjust the tab stops (see Figure 23.9). PowerPoint aligns each level's bullet and text with the stops shown on the ruler.

Figure 23.9
To change the location of bullets and text in the body of a presentation, adjust tab stops in the Slide Master.

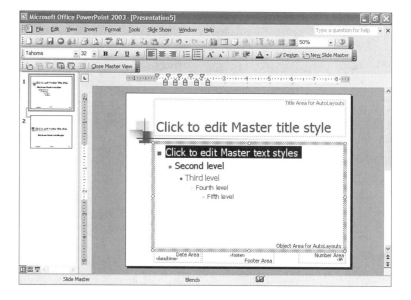

CAUTION

> Changing font formatting of the title placeholder on the Slide Master also changes the title placeholder on the Title Master. So, for example, if you change the Slide Master to make the title on all "regular" slides 36-point Arial, PowerPoint changes your Title Master, too, so *its* title is 36-point Arial.
>
> The Slide and Title masters do not share paragraph formatting, however; if you right-align the Slide Master's title, for example, the Title Master's title remains unchanged. In addition, formatting changes you make to one type of master (Date, Footer, and Number Area, for instance) do not apply to the other.

CHANGING THE BACKGROUND OF EVERY SLIDE

If you want a logo, a graphic, or a drawing item to appear on all "regular" slides, place it on the Slide Master. Any object in the Slide Master's drawing layer appears in the drawing layer of all nontitle slides in the same location it occupies on the Slide Master.

Text you place on the Slide Master behaves the same way. For example, in a presentation that contains sensitive data, you might want to add the word CONFIDENTIAL to every slide; for a presentation that's under construction, you might want to stamp DRAFT on every slide. To put identical pieces of text on every "regular" slide, follow these steps:

1. Switch into Slide Master view (choose View, Master, Slide Master) and select the Slide Master.

2. Click the Text Box icon in the Drawing toolbar. Draw a text box on the Slide Master and adjust its size and position as necessary.

3. Click in the text box and enter the text you want to repeat on all slides. This text will appear in the drawing layer on all the "regular" slides in your presentation, and thus will not show up in the outline.

4. To apply formatting to the box itself, right-click the edge of the box and choose Format Text Box. You might want to draw a thick line around the box, for example, or change its background color.

Similarly, if you want a logo, fixed text, or other drawing item to appear on all title slides, put it on the Title Master.

You'll find by far the richest vein of background customizing options when you learn how to develop, modify, and apply designs. Use these techniques to customize the Master Slides included with PowerPoint's ready-made designs, or devise your own masters and store them for future use.

→ To work with designs, **see** "Applying and Modifying Designs," **p. 747**.

WORKING WITH HEADERS AND FOOTERS

If you're used to working with headers and footers in Word or Excel, PowerPoint's Header And Footer dialog box might be confusing initially. On a slide, you'll search in vain for a header. Paradoxically, though, you can move the Footer Area placeholder, which normally appears centered at the bottom of the slide, to any location—including the top. The Notes Master and Handout Master contain both a Header Area and a Footer Area, positioned by default at the top left and bottom left of printed pages; you can move these placeholders anywhere on the page as well.

In addition, all masters include placeholders for the date and slide number, which normally appear at the bottom of the slide but can be moved anywhere on the slide. When working with any of these elements on the Title Master or Slide Master, follow these guidelines:

- The Date Area placeholder can show the current date—that is, the date the slide show is being presented. To add a date field of this sort, choose View, Header And Footer, click to select the Date And Time box, and select the Update Automatically check box. If you want to track different versions of a presentation as you change it, use the Fixed option instead and enter a descriptive text label (it doesn't have to include the date); remember to enter a new description when you save an updated version of the presentation.

- The Footer Area placeholder can carry any text you want, and you can drag it to any location on the slide. You can use this element to label each slide with the name of a school or civic organization, the class you're preparing it for, or even with the title of the presentation itself.

- The Number Area placeholder can be confusing if it appears near other numbers on a slide. Slide numbers are rarely useful (you might rely on them as a visual reminder of how many slides are left), and they're frequently distracting. If you decide to use slide numbers, keep them subtle, and remember that you can always make the font smaller than the default provided by PowerPoint.

If you look closely at a Slide Master, you'll see that these three placeholders all have dummy values enclosed in angle brackets (< >):

- The Date Area placeholder includes a dummy value called `<date/time>`.
- The Footer placeholder includes a dummy value called `<footer>`.
- The Number Area placeholder includes a dummy value called `<#>`.

To show (or hide) the date/time, footer, or slide number placeholders and their contents, do the following:

1. Choose View, Header and Footer to open the PowerPoint Header and Footer dialog box; if necessary, click the Slide tab (shown in Figure 23.10).

2. Select the appropriate check boxes to display any or all of the three placeholders on all slides; clear the check mark to hide the selected placeholder.

3. Use the entries under the check boxes to define what, if anything, replaces the dummy entries—the current date or a footnote, for example.

4. Click Apply To All to make the change to all "regular" slides in your presentation. To apply the same change to title slides, too, clear the check mark from the Don't Show on Title Slide box.

Figure 23.10
Use this dialog box to specify which place-holders appear, and replacements for the three Slide Master dummy values.

NOTE

When working in Master Slide view, the Apply option is grayed out and unavailable. If you open the Header And Footer dialog box from Normal view, you can change the display of dates, slide numbers, and footers on an individual slide (click Apply) or on the Slide Master (click Apply To All). If you're certain you don't want to use one of these placeholders, you can safely delete it.

TIP FROM

EQ & Woody

If you are likely to use the same headers or footers or other master elements in additional presentations, save a copy of the presentation as a template.

REMOVING SLIDE MASTER ELEMENTS FROM A SINGLE SLIDE

You can have the slide number appear on every slide except one. You might need to do this if one slide includes a big chart, for example, and you need every square inch of slide space to hold it. You might think that you could select the slide number placeholder on a single slide and press the Delete key to remove it. If you try it, however, you'll see that this approach doesn't work.

In fact, removing elements of the Slide Master from an individual slide is an all-or-nothing proposition: You get all of them, or you get none of them. This can be particularly vexing when the design you've chosen includes a graphic object—and most of the designs included with PowerPoint include graphics—or when you have a graphic element, such as a logo, that's supposed to appear on all slides.

To remove *all* the Slide Master elements (except the Title Area placeholder and Object Area placeholder) from a single slide:

1. Select the slide.
2. Choose Format, Background.

3. Select the Omit Background Graphics from Master check box.

4. Click Apply.

CAUTION

> Do *not* click Apply to All. Doing so will remove all the elements from all the regular slides in your presentation.

If this method is too drastic—you want to remove only one element, for example, on just one slide—you can cover the element up, instead of removing it:

1. Create a small rectangle by clicking the Rectangle icon on the Drawing toolbar.

2. Make the rectangle just slightly larger than the Master Slide element you want to eliminate. If you need to adjust the size in finer increments than the tool normally allows, press the Alt key while making the adjustments.

3. Drag the rectangle over the Master Slide element.

4. Click the down arrow next to the Fill Color icon. There should be a color very close to the background color available at the beginning of the first or second line of color swatches. Choose the color closest to the background color.

5. Click the down arrow next to the Line Color icon. Choose the same color you just chose for the fill color, or choose No Line.

If you match the colors carefully, your audience will never know.

To accomplish the same trick on multiple slides, even those with fancy multi-colored backgrounds, make a copy of the master slide, remove the element from the copy, and then use this master for the slides where you want the one element removed.

CREATING SPEAKER NOTES AND AUDIENCE HANDOUTS

The *Notes Master* and *Handout Master* behave differently from the Title and Slide masters; their only function is to provide extremely rudimentary instructions for printing speaker notes and audience handouts.

Speaker notes and *handouts*, in PowerPoint, are designed to be printed on letter-size paper. Each page typically holds one slide. On speaker notes, the slide appears at the top of the page, with the notes for that slide at the bottom. Handouts, by contrast, consist solely of printed copies of the slides.

To set PowerPoint printing options for speaker notes:

1. Go into Notes Master view by choosing View, Master, Notes Master. You will almost always want to adjust the Zoom factor, using the Zoom icon on the Standard toolbar.

2. Apply formatting to the Notes Body Area just as you would to the Slide Master's text placeholder: Click the desired bullet level, and apply text formatting.

3. Resize and/or move the slide placeholder and the Notes Body Area.

4. Move the header placeholder, footer placeholder, date/time placeholder, and page number placeholder (marked "Number Area"). Note that you can type text into any of these placeholders and the text will appear on the notes.

5. Control the appearance and contents of those four placeholders by choosing View, Header and Footer, Notes and Handouts, and setting the check boxes accordingly.

When you're satisfied with the formatting, print the speaker notes—choose File, Print, choose Notes Pages in the Print What box, and click OK.

TIP FROM

Ed & Woody

Color slides—particularly those with dark backgrounds—invariably print better on a black-and-white printer if you select the Grayscale check box in the Print dialog box. Choose the View Color/Grayscale icon on the standard toolbar to preview the presentation in Black and White.

Choose View, Master, Handout Master to see the layout for your handouts. As Figure 23.11 illustrates, you can use buttons on the Handout Master View toolbar to change the page layout so that each page includes two, three, four, six, or nine slides. If you choose the three-slides-per-page layout, PowerPoint adds blank lines next to the slides so the audience can take notes. You can also move or format the Header Area, Footer Area, Date Area, and Number Area (which contains a page number rather than slide numbers, as in the presentation itself). Here, too, you can type text into any of these placeholders and the text will appear on the handouts.

Figure 23.11
The three-slides-per-page handout layout saves paper and gives your audience room to add their own notes on the right.

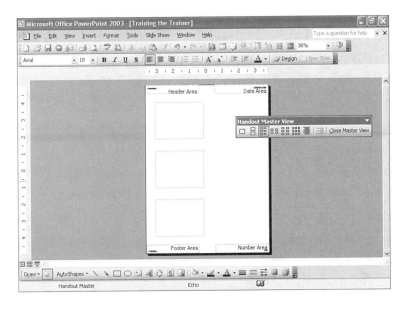

23

TIP FROM

Ed & Woody

> The only reason to use the Handout Master view is if you want to add text or graphics to your handouts. You can adjust headers and footers using the Header And Footer dialog box, and you can choose a layout for printing handout sheets from the Print dialog box. (Choose File, Print, select Handouts from the Print What box, and choose a number from the Slides Per Page list.)

CREATING MULTIPLE MASTER SLIDES

By default, every slide in a presentation has an associated set of up to four master slides. For most presentations, as we noted earlier, this configuration is perfectly adequate.

In some cases, however, you might want to associate certain slides in your presentation with a different set of masters than the standard Slide Master. For example, if you and a classmate or colleague are collaborating on a presentation, you might want to set up a "point/counterpoint" presentation, where your "point" slides all have one look, but your colleague's "counterpoint" slides are different. The main part of the presentation would flip-flop between point and counterpoint slides, with each set of slides showing a different graphics design—on the point slides, a woman facing to the right; on the counterpoint slides, a man facing left. To create this design, you would establish one set of masters for the point slides, and another set of masters for the counterpoint slides.

To create a second Slide Master, use either of these options:

- Right-click any empty space below the current crop of masters and choose New Slide Master from the shortcut menu (or, alternatively, choose Insert, New Slide Master). This option produces a completely blank master that doesn't incorporate any elements from the design you've used.

- Right-click an existing Slide Master and choose Copy; then point to any empty space below the existing masters, right-click, and choose Paste. The new master slide is a perfect copy of the original, including design elements. For the new slide, PowerPoint adds a number and an underscore to the beginning of the name; if your presentation uses the Blends design, the new Slide Master is called 1_Blends Slide Master.

TIP FROM

Ed & Woody

> If you go to the trouble of creating and customizing master slides, take the final step and give each one a descriptive name. Right-click the master slide and choose Rename Master from the shortcut menu.

When you create a new presentation from scratch, all the slides are associated with one set of masters. If you want to use a second (or third, or fourth...) set of masters, you have to manually associate the slides in your presentation with the additional masters. The following steps assume you've already created a second Slide Master to use in your presentation:

1. In Normal view, click the Design button on the Formatting toolbar. This brings up the Slide Design pane. All existing master slides appear at the top of the Apply a Design Template box, under the heading Used In This Presentation.

2. Select the slides that you want to associate with the second set of masters.

3. Click the down-arrow to the right of the newly created Slide Master and choose Apply to Selected Slides.

CAUTION

> Working with multiple masters can be a daunting and potentially confusing adventure, and we recommend it for experts only. For new slides, PowerPoint continues to use the original masters. If you change designs, slides created using the additional masters do not reflect the background, fonts, and colors of the new design.

23

APPLYING AND MODIFYING DESIGNS

PowerPoint designs control the appearance of a presentation. By allowing you to save, modify, and reuse designs—including dozens of Microsoft-supplied samples—PowerPoint makes it easy to create presentations that are visually appealing and consistent. Consistency is especially important when you want a group of presenters from the same organization to share a common look.

Don't be intimidated by the presentation designs included with PowerPoint. These designs are only a starting point. Feel free to adapt, combine, customize, and tweak to your heart's content. If you come up with a presentation that really gets your point across, save the presentation as a template and use it to design new presentations.

A design is a set of four masters—a Title Master, Slide Master, Notes Master, and Handout Master—along with a group of color settings called Standard color schemes. Between them, the four masters completely control the look and feel of a presentation: background design, color, and pictures; fonts, sizes, and attributes; bullet points; and location and contents of placeholders. In other words, it includes practically everything except the content itself. The color schemes make it easy to change groups of color settings.

→ To change every slide in a presentation, **see** "Organizing Formats with Master Slides," **p. 736**.

→ To modify the colors of all the slides, **see** "Using Color Schemes," **p. 752**.

NOTE

> PowerPoint's dialog boxes and Help files use a variety of design-related terms to describe variations on templates. A *design template* (sometimes referred to as a *presentation design*) typically includes only design elements (that is, four masters and the color scheme), with no other slides. A *content template* (also known as a *presentation template*) contains a group of slides with title text and bullets.

CHOOSING THE BEST DESIGN FOR YOUR PRESENTATION

Nothing detracts more from a good presentation than a poor design. To choose the best possible design for a presentation, weigh the following—consider your audience, your image, and your message. For a serious, low-key presentation to a conservative group, stick with a no-nonsense design. If you're trying to impress your audience with your energy and ability to project bold ideas, go with bold graphics and vivid colors.

After you have a clear vision of the image you want to project, you're ready to choose a design. To pick a design for your presentation, follow these steps:

1. Start with an existing presentation or create a new blank presentation. Bring up the Slide Design pane by clicking Design on the Formatting toolbar.

2. In the Apply a Design Template list, choose a design you like.

TIP FROM

If you can't quite make out the designs, click the down-arrow to the right of one of the offered designs, and choose Show Large Preview. PowerPoint enlarges the thumbnails so they take up the entire width of the pane.

3. If you haven't installed all the designs that came with Office (which is the case if you performed a standard install), scroll to the bottom of the list and click Additional Design Templates. Insert your Office CD, if necessary, and PowerPoint will bring in the rest of the templates that ship with Office.

TIP FROM

Serious PowerPoint users should install all the templates. Few designs are over 50KB in size, and most presentations are under 150KB. Adding all the available templates takes up only a few megabytes of disk space.

4. If you still haven't found a design you like, scroll to the bottom of the list and click Design Templates on Microsoft Office Online to look for updated designs on the Web. Or click the Browse button at the bottom of the Slide Design pane. From that point you can look for designs on your hard drive or your network.

5. When you've found a suitable design, double-click it. PowerPoint throws away the masters it's currently using, replacing them with those in the design or presentation that you've chosen, rippling those changes through your presentation.

MODIFYING AN EXISTING DESIGN FOR YOUR PRESENTATION

Many PowerPoint designs include groups of drawing objects that you can move, resize, and otherwise modify to suit the needs of a particular presentation.

For example, the Fireworks design (see Figure 23.12) consists of a picture of a firework burst on a black background. The rectangle in the upper right holds the fireworks.

Figure 23.12
You can move or delete components of a design.

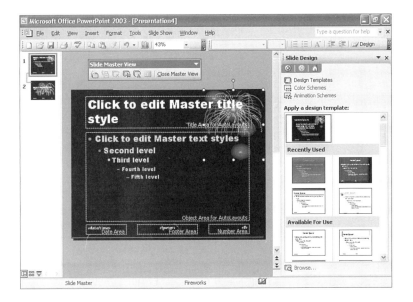

At first glance, this might not appear to have much bearing on the quality of your presentations. Think of it this way: Every single graphic element in every single PowerPoint presentation—whether it's from Microsoft or any other source—can be lifted and moved to your presentations. So, for example, if you see a color-layering technique in a presentation, but you don't like the colors, you can lift the design (see the preceding section), and then work element-by-element on the Slide Master to retouch each piece. Or you can selectively add, remove, copy, or move any element to any location you like. That comes in handy if you need more room on an existing design.

For example, if you wanted to emphasize the fireworks in Figure 23.12, and trim back a bit on the title placeholder, this is how you would do it:

1. To apply the Fireworks design, click the Design button on the Formatting toolbar. In the Slide Design task pane, click Fireworks.

2. Choose View, Master, Slide Master to go into Slide Master view.

3. To select the rectangle with the picture of the fireworks on it, click the fireworks. You might have to jockey around a bit to get outside of the title placeholder.

TIP FROM

Ed & Woody

Some of the more complex designs have many different elements. If you think that might be the case with the design you're using, click the design, click Draw on the Drawing toolbar, and choose Ungroup. If you do that with the fireworks graphic you just selected, you'll find that there are many components to the fireworks—it isn't a simple, single drawing.

4. Drag the sizing handle on the lower left to expand the fireworks. Then click and drag to resize the title placeholder and text placeholder.

5. When you're done, click Close Master View on the Slide Master View toolbar, and the changes will take effect.

Use this same technique to resize, move, or delete any of the drawings that appear on the background in this (or any other) design.

TIP FROM

Ed & Woody

> To maintain design uniformity in the presentation, you might want to make the same changes to the Title Master. Unfortunately, PowerPoint has no automated tools to help; you must make the changes manually. One shortcut that will make things easier: If you cut a graphic or other object from one master and paste it to another, the pasted object appears in the exact same position on the second slide.

CHOOSING THE BEST BACKGROUND

The background of your presentation—the "canvas" that sits behind all elements on a slide—offers a wide range of possibilities. The background might include solid colors, gradient fills of one or two colors, textures, or patterns; you can also import a graphic file (in GIF, JPEG, Windows Metafile, or any compatible graphics format) to use as the background.

In addition to the fundamental design principles that we discussed earlier in this chapter, your selection of a background should be influenced by the medium you'll use for the presentation.

If you're going to make the presentation in a darkened room on a large, high-contrast screen, you can get away with just about any combination of colors. But if you're making your presentation in a low-contrast situation (in a room where ambient light will fall on the screen, for example, or on a portable in which some members of your audience might not be able to view the screen directly), make sure you use light letters on a dark background, or vice versa. Those who have trouble discerning colors in low-contrast situations (not to mention the color-blind, who most frequently have trouble distinguishing green and red) will thank you.

Finally, if you intend to print the presentation—or show it on an overhead projector—stick to very light backgrounds. Although there are tricks for improving the printed appearance of almost any presentation, if your most important destination is hardcopy, you should design the presentation from the ground up to comply.

→ For tips on getting the most out of hardcopy, **see** "Printing Your Presentation," **p. 795**.

To change the background, do the following:

1. Apply the design you want and go into Slide Master view (View, Master, Slide Master).

2. Choose Format, Background. You see the Background dialog box (see Figure 23.13).

Figure 23.13
Apply quick background changes, or select Fill Effects in the drop-down list to use PowerPoint's extensive set of tools for changing backgrounds.

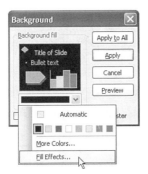

3. Build your background using any of the following techniques:

   • To select a solid background color, choose a new color from the drop-down list. (For a more extensive selection, click More Colors.)

   • To create a one- or two-color gradient, click Fill Effects and select options from the Fill Effects dialog box (see Figure 23.14).

   • Use the other tabs of the dialog box to add patterns or textures (you can use the samples included with PowerPoint or import your own). You can also import a picture to use as the background; the picture will be stretched to fit the slide.

Figure 23.14
The Fill Effects dialog box offers comprehensive tools for creating the "canvas" behind your slides.

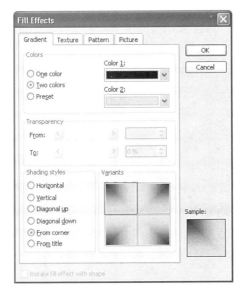

→ For advice on working with graphics, **see** Chapter 5, "Using Pictures and Drawings," **p. 113**.

4. When you've constructed the background you want, click Apply to update the Slide Master, and have the changes take effect throughout your presentation.

For consistency's sake, you might want to make the same changes to the Title Master.

CHANGING THE BACKGROUND ON SELECTED SLIDES

Sometimes your presentation will include one or two slides that absolutely demand a different background. Maybe the colors in a photo clash with the background color. Perhaps the bars of a chart don't stand out well enough against a color that's otherwise perfect for the rest of the presentations.

If you don't want to change the background for every slide in your presentation, use the same techniques described in the preceding section on individual slides. Select the slide you want to change, and follow the instructions. In the last step, make sure you click Apply. (If you click Apply to All, you'll change the Slide Master, and every slide in the presentation will take on the new background.)

USING COLOR SCHEMES

A *color scheme* (see Figure 23.15) consists of eight colors, one for each major type of element in a presentation. Each of PowerPoint's ready-made color schemes consists of foreground and background colors that work well together.

Figure 23.15
A color scheme has eight defining colors.

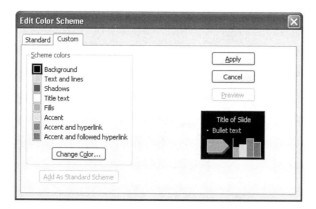

You can create your own color schemes by using any colors that your video settings will support (refer to Figure 23.15 and see Table 23.1).

TABLE 23.1 COLOR SCHEME COMPONENTS

Component	Description
Background	The color behind all text and objects on the slide; on slides with gradient-filled backgrounds, it's the primary color.
Text and Lines	The color of the font in the text placeholder, and the outline color for items in the drawing layer.
Shadows	The second color in a gradient-filled background; it doesn't appear to have anything to do with the "shadow" color of shadowed text.

Component	Description
Title Text	The color of the font of text in the title placeholder. It's also the color of the highest-level bullet in the text placeholder.
Fills	The background color of items in the drawing layer, and the color of the bars for the first set of data in a chart. It has nothing to do with gradient fills.
Accent	The only use we've found for the *Accent* color is for the bars representing the second set of data in a chart.
Accent and Hyperlink	The color of the text of hyperlinks that haven't been "followed" (that is, clicked and activated). It's also the color of the third bars in charts.
Accent and Followed Hyperlink	The color of hyperlinked text that has been "followed," and it's the color of the fourth bar in charts.

Just as you can change any detail on a master slide, you can change the colors in the current presentation by changing the color scheme of any master. PowerPoint saves color schemes along with the design; if you apply a new design, PowerPoint discards any previous color changes and applies the color scheme from the new design to your presentation.

PowerPoint uses colors from the color scheme in many different places. For example, the Background dialog box (refer to Figure 23.13) offers colors from the current color scheme as its first choice, and the colors used to create graphics in many standard designs change when you change color schemes.

CHOOSING A NEW COLOR SCHEME

To apply a color scheme to your presentation, first apply the design you want to use. Make sure only one slide is selected and follow these steps:

1. Click the Design button on the Formatting toolbar. This opens the Slide Design task pane.

2. From the options at the top of the task pane, choose Color Schemes. The task pane changes to show a selection of standard color schemes, as shown in Figure 23.16.

3. Click any color scheme offered here to apply it to all slides based on the master used by the current slide. (You must perform this step twice to change colors for title slides and regular slides.) Or click Edit Color Schemes at the bottom of the task pane and use the Custom tab (shown earlier in Figure 23.15) to create your own scheme. Click Apply to save your changes on the current presentation.

NOTE

To save a color scheme, click the Add As Standard Scheme button on the Custom tab. From that point on, the new scheme shows up on the Standard tab.

Figure 23.16
Standard color schemes vary depending on the design.

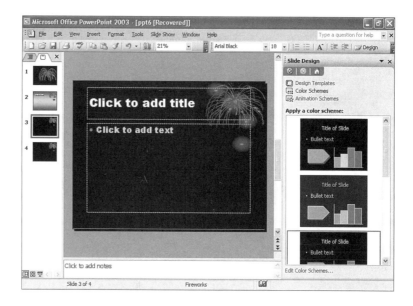

The Standard color schemes for a presentation are saved with the masters. Thus, if you create a new Standard color scheme, and save it as a Design Template or Presentation, that Standard color scheme will be available whenever you apply the design to a different presentation.

CHANGING COLORS ON SELECTED SLIDES

If you decide you need to change one color on a slide—perhaps it clashes with a picture or doesn't contrast enough with a chart—you might want to consider changing the entire color scheme for that slide.

The procedure for changing the color scheme for a single slide (or a selection of slides) is nearly identical to the procedure outlined in the preceding section. First, select the slides you want to individually colorize; then, in step 3, click the down arrow to the right of the color scheme preview and choose Apply to Selected Slides instead of Apply to All Slides.

COPYING A COLOR SCHEME

It's easy to create, store, and modify color schemes; use the Standard color scheme technique described in the preceding two sections. Unfortunately, it's difficult to copy a color scheme from one presentation to another, or from one design to another. That can pose a problem if you want to use the same color scheme (or a group of color schemes) across many different designs—for example, if you want to replace the colors in a set of designs with your school colors. You can re-create the color schemes manually in each design or presentation, but the process is time-consuming and error-prone.

Fortunately, there is an undocumented method for transferring a color scheme from one presentation (or design) to another:

1. Open or create a presentation in which at least one slide contains the color scheme you want to copy. Call this slide the "color source slide." Click the Slide Sorter button to switch to Slide Sorter view.

2. Open the presentation to which you want to transfer the color scheme. Call this the "destination presentation." Switch to Slide Sorter view in this presentation, too.

3. Click the color source slide, and then click the Format Painter button on the Standard toolbar.

4. Switch to the destination presentation and click once on any slide. Your preferred colors are transferred to this slide in the destination presentation.

5. Click the Design button on the Formatting toolbar to open the Slide Design task pane, click Color Schemes, and then click Edit Color Schemes. In the Edit Color Scheme dialog box (refer to Figure 23.15), the custom settings you see will match the color scheme you copied from the original presentation.

6. Click the Add As Standard Scheme button on the Custom tab. Click the Standard tab and verify that the color scheme you copied is now a standard color scheme for this slide.

7. Click the Apply to All button so that this new Standard color scheme will be applied to the Slide Master. The destination presentation now includes the color scheme you copied.

8. Save the presentation (or its design).

If you want to restore the original formatting to the destination presentation, switch into Slide Master view, bring up the Edit Color Scheme dialog box, and click the first standard color scheme.

CHANGING PARAGRAPH AND TEXT FORMATTING

Not all presentation text is created equal, and not all text falls into PowerPoint's relentless and presumed point-by-point-by-point format. Sometimes you might want to center a line of text, to make it stand out. In other presentations, you might want to ensure that each top-level bullet point has an extra bit of space after it, to make the presentation more readable from the back of the room. Then there's the inevitable bold text, and italic, and even the fontographer's nightmare, bold italic. All these treatments have a place in your repertoire of presentation tricks.

In general, PowerPoint paragraph and text formatting options mirror those available in Word. Select whatever you want to change—paragraphs, words, characters—and then apply the change. To change paragraph or text formatting for all the "regular" slides in your presentation (that is, all slides except title slides), change the Slide Master. To change paragraph or text formatting for a title slide, it's generally easier to change the slide directly—providing your presentation has just one title slide.

USING PARAGRAPH FORMATTING

All the standard paragraph formatting settings found in Word are at your disposal, including alignment (right, center, and left), spacing (double and triple), and so on. These options are accessible directly from the Format menu.

NOTE

> To remove bullets from a paragraph, click inside the paragraph, choose Format, Bullets and Numbering, and click None, or click the Bullets button on the Formatting toolbar.

To change tab stops and adjust the behavior of tab characters, you must use the ruler (choose View, Ruler to make it visible).

Some tab formatting options you might use in other Office applications do not exist in PowerPoint. For example, there is no easy way to put a tab stop in every cell of a table; you have to enter them all manually.

USING FONTS

Professional designers recommend you stick with one font for titles and another for text—better yet, use the same font for both. Using too many fonts detracts from a presentation.

To adjust any font effects, select some text, right-click, and choose Font from the shortcut menu. All standard effects are available in the Font dialog box: color, bold, italic, bold italic, underline, shadow, emboss, and superscript/subscript. You can also adjust the elevation of superscripts and subscripts in the Offset box.

If you're planning to deliver your presentation on a large screen, avoid italicized fonts, which often end up looking like wavy blobs. You can use underline instead, to emphasize a word or phrase, but underlining is traditionally reserved as a substitute for italic. If you absolutely must emphasize a word, bold is probably your best choice.

REPLACING FONTS THROUGHOUT A PRESENTATION

If you're trying to change all the Times New Roman in a presentation to Garamond, you might be tempted to change the Title Master and Slide Master, and call it a day.

Unfortunately, if you've applied any manual formatting to individual slides, the "link" between the slide and its master might be broken. In that case, even if the master is updated, the slide might not make the switch.

→ To change every slide in your presentation, **see** "Using the Title Master," **p. 736**.

To truly change all occurrences of Times New Roman to Garamond, choose Format, Replace Fonts. Choose Times New Roman from the Replace drop-down list; choose Garamond from the With list. Click OK to apply the change throughout the presentation—even in the masters. This solution is especially useful when you inherit a presentation created by someone who used a font you don't have.

> **NOTE**
>
> This technique changes only the font; you can't use the dialog box to change point size.

TROUBLESHOOTING

NOT ALL AUTOCORRECT ENTRIES WORK IN POWERPOINT

An AutoCorrect entry works fine in Word, but the exact same entry doesn't work in PowerPoint.

Any AutoCorrect entry in Word that produces a formatted result will not be available in PowerPoint. If you need the AutoCorrect entry, open Word, delete the entry, and replace it with one that doesn't produce a formatted result.

EXCEL TABLES DON'T DISPLAY PROPERLY

After using Paste Special to put an Excel table in a slide, the placeholder is big enough, but the table doesn't line up correctly. As a result, I can't see all the cells on the slide.

Double-click the table to open it in Excel 2000. Use the arrow keys to make the top-left cell in the range active. Click anywhere outside the table to return to the PowerPoint editing window. In most cases, this technique will line up your table properly.

SLIDE MASTER LINK DAMAGE

I changed the Slide Master, but some of the slides in my presentation haven't been updated with the changes.

If you do something odd (for example, delete one of the placeholders in a slide), it's possible to break the link between a slide and the Slide Master. After the link has been broken, changes to the Slide Master are no longer propagated to the slide. To reset the link, select the slide, bring up the Slide Layout pane by choosing Format, Slide Layout, click the arrow to the right of the layout that's most appropriate for the slide, and choose Reapply Layout.

EXTRA CREDIT: CREATING TOP-NOTCH NOTES AND HANDOUTS

PowerPoint's canned layouts for speaker notes and handouts have the singular advantage of being easy to use. If you just want your audience to have a place to scribble notes about your talk, these basic templates will do the trick.

But for truly professional-looking leave-behinds, consider sending the presentation to Word, which offers much better formatting and printing options than the basic notes and handout layouts in PowerPoint. After polishing your presentation to perfection, choose File, Send To, Microsoft Word. Using the choices in the Send To Microsoft Word dialog box, Word creates a new document with blank lines next to the thumbnails, in a format suitable for handouts (see Figure 23.17).

You can use all of Word's editing tools to add content and sizzle to the resulting document, or insert the presentation into an existing document, such as a corporate backgrounder or product datasheets.

After you've finished creating your handouts, consider how your audience will use them before you begin your presentation! When audience members can look at your handout and jump ahead to a topic that specifically concerns them, you may find it difficult to keep their attention focused on what you're saying. The solution? Hand out a one- or two-page summary of your presentation before the talk begins, with room for your audience to jot down comments and questions, but pass out the unabridged handouts *after* your presentation is complete.

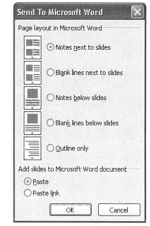

Figure 23.17

CHAPTER 24

ADDING SIZZLE TO A PRESENTATION

In this chapter

BANISHING BORING SLIDE SHOWS

If you're in a hurry, you can whip out a PowerPoint slide show in minutes. Type in an outline, pick a preset design, save your file, and—voila—instant presentation. Alas, that quick and dirty technique also results in a boring presentation, and if your audience has any experience with PowerPoint they'll know instantly that you didn't put much effort into your slide show.

It takes only a little time and energy to liven up a presentation. In this chapter, we focus on the tricks that add instant visual interest without requiring a design degree or hours of careful tweaking. By adding animations, you can turn a static, 2D slide show into one that sizzles. Add sound and multimedia and you move into a completely new dimension.

At the end of this chapter, we also explain how you can use PowerPoint's bag of tricks to create slide shows from digital photos. In fact, if you leave titles and text to a minimum, your audience doesn't need to know that you created the show with PowerPoint.

USING TRANSITIONS TO CONTROL PACING

PowerPoint makes it easy to control what your audience sees on the screen when you move from one slide to another. You can arrange things so that one slide replaces another onscreen, just as it would if you clicked through a carousel of 35mm slides. Or you can add wipes, dissolves, and other varieties of eye-catching (and frequently distracting) transitions. Properly done, transitions (sometimes also called *transition effects* or *slide transitions*) provide a breathing space between slides. Improperly done, your presentation will look amateurish and detract from making your point—which, after all, is the purpose of PowerPoint.

The nature of that breathing space lies totally at your control—a subtle, quick fade to black; a pixelated dissolve that leaves the old slide in view for quite some time; shutters and checkerboards; and dozens more. Transitions can help add an ambience to your presentation. You might want a more abrupt transition if you're trying to project a snappy, rapid-fire image, and a more relaxed transition when the situation calls for a less formal approach.

Mixing and matching transitions jars the audience every bit as badly as ransom-note mixed fonts. For that reason, we recommend that you select one transition and use it exclusively throughout your presentation, with perhaps a few slides here and there getting "special treatment"—just to keep the audience awake.

When dealing with transitions, it's always easiest to work in Slide Sorter view.

→ For tips on using Slide Sorter view, **see** "Using Slide Sorter View to Rearrange a Presentation," **p. 712**.

NOTE

Although you might think that a transition is defined between slides—showing how to *fade out* on the first slide and *fade in* on the next—PowerPoint doesn't work that way. Instead, you assign a transition to a slide, and that particular transition takes place when the slide is shown—it's a fade-in effect.

TIP FROM

Ed & Woody

By creatively using transitions, you can simulate some slide animation effects that simply aren't possible with PowerPoint's built-in animation tools. For example, in a presentation that shows the geographic changes in Eastern Europe over time you might want to put together a map with each country fading into position, but you want some countries to disappear after two or more mouse clicks, so that you can emphasize the changes in the map. PowerPoint doesn't offer a "hide after *N* mouse clicks" animation option, so you can't animate that slide directly. In these cases, use a transition to fake animation: Build two slides—one to show the "before" image and the other for the "after" image—and then run a quick transition between the two. Your audience will be impressed.

24

APPLYING A TRANSITION TO ONE SLIDE

To set a transition for a single slide, select that slide (by displaying it in Normal view or clicking the slide in Slide Sorter view), and then choose Slide Show, Slide Transition. This brings up the Slide Transition task pane (see Figure 24.1).

Available transitions

Figure 24.1
The Slide Transition pane makes it easy to apply and modify transitions.

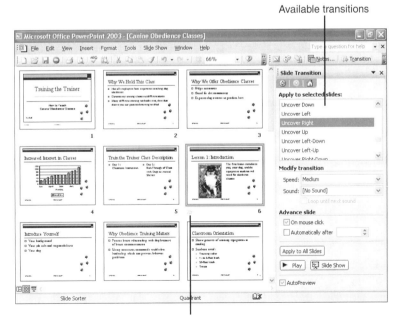

Preview transition and animation

Select the slide with which you want to use a particular transition, and then select the transition effect you want from the Apply to Selected Slides list. PowerPoint shows you a preview of the transition you selected; in Slide Sorter view, it also adds a small icon just below the bottom-left corner of the slide, as shown in Figure 24.1. To see the transition again, click this icon, or click Play at the bottom of the Slide Transition task pane.

TIP FROM

Ed & Woody

If you want your transitions and animations to appear when your presentation is viewed from a web browser, you must choose Tools, Options, General, Web Options, and select the Show Slide Animation While Browsing check box.

APPLYING A TRANSITION TO A GROUP OF SLIDES

To assign the same transition to a group of slides, switch to Slide Sorter view and select the slides with which you want to use the same transition. Hold down the Ctrl key as you click to select single slides, or hold down the Shift key and click to select a contiguously numbered group.

TIP FROM

Ed & Woody

To select all the slides in the presentation, click one slide, and then press Ctrl+A.

Select the transition you want from the list on the Slide Transition pane.

PowerPoint goes through a preview of the transitions and animations on all the selected slides. (To stop this mass preview, press Escape.) To see the transition and animation on an individual slide, click the Preview Transition icon below the slide. To repeat the transitions and animations for all the slides, click Play on the Slide Transition task pane.

CAUTION

When you apply a transition to a slide, PowerPoint replaces any transitions you previously applied to that slide.

CONTROLLING SLIDE TRANSITION SPEED

The Slide Transition pane gives you additional control over the transition between slides. You can

- Set the speed to slow, medium, or fast.
- Tell PowerPoint how you want to advance to the next slide during a presentation—manually, by clicking the mouse, or automatically, after a preset interval. Note that this

setting controls how the slide exits and is thus unrelated to the transition effect you set for the current slide.

■ Make PowerPoint play a sound during the transition.

> In general, resist the temptation to select the Loop Until Next Sound check box, which is certain to distract almost any audience, unless you have a specific impression in mind: a suspenseful tick-tick-tick leading up to the next slide, for example, might be appropriate. But consider the reaction if a question from the audience takes you 10 minutes to answer—with the tick-tick-tick going all the time.

The two Advance settings—On Mouse Click and Automatically After—operate independently. If you activate both options, PowerPoint shows the next slide when the timer expires, or when you click the slide, whichever comes first. If you leave both boxes unchecked, the slide advances only when you press the spacebar, the Enter key, or one of PowerPoint's other keyboard presentation *control keys*.

→ For a definitive list of presentation control keys, **see** "Mouse and Keyboard Shortcuts," **p. 718**.

24

ANIMATING TEXT AND OBJECTS ON A SLIDE

Just as you use transition effects to control how a slide fades in, you use *animations* to control how the individual elements of a slide make their appearance. By showing one bullet point at a time, for example, you can make sure your audience concentrates on what you're saying now rather than reading the rest of the bullets on your slide and mentally calculating how much longer you're going to speak.

The most rudimentary form of slide animation displays each bullet point on a slide one at a time: You click the mouse (or tap the spacebar) and the slide's title appears. Click again, and the first bullet point appears onscreen. Keep clicking to display each bullet point on the list. Other animations let you specify that bullet points fly in or zoom from any direction. You can also choose fades, dissolves, wipes, and other visual effects.

TIP FROM

> PowerPoint's selection of ready-made animation schemes is conveniently divided into three groups: Subtle, Moderate, and Exciting, with each group of effects appearing under a bold heading. We recommend you stick with Subtle for the most part. Reserve the Moderate and Exciting effects for the special slide that really deserves to stand out from the pack.

You can apply animations to almost any part of a slide, and then activate the animations by clicking the mouse or using PowerPoint's built-in timers. Used sparingly, these animations can add punch to your presentation, augmenting your spoken words with powerful visuals. Say you have a graph that illustrates the growth in the number of websites created each year since the birth of the World Wide Web in 1993. You could show the whole graph, all at one time, and emphasize the spike in the final number verbally. Much more effectively, however, you could have the bars fly onto the graph one at a time—building up, in your narration, to the spike in the most recent year.

You can use animations to coordinate sounds, so they play as predetermined parts of the slide appear. You can also place text on a slide, one character, word, or paragraph at a time. For example, use animations to start movies and other types of video clips at predetermined intervals after the slide first appears. Or use them to dim or change the color of items on the slide, in conjunction with the appearance of a new item.

TIP FROM

EQ & Woody

For sophisticated animation effects, break the clip-art objects apart, and then animate each element separately. Duplicating elements and using flying effects can also create the illusion of motion.

ANIMATING BULLET POINTS

Animating the arrival of bullet points on a slide gives you control over how much information your audience sees, and when. Moving one bullet point at a time onto the slide lets you keep your audience running at your pace, particularly if you know that people in the audience have a tendency to read ahead. Also consider using bullet animation if you want to save some surprising or emphatic points for the end of the slide.

CAUTION

If you remove the capability to advance a slide based on mouse clicks (by clearing the On Mouse Click check box in the Slide Transition task pane), you also remove the capability to animate bullet points with a mouse click. Instead, if you've provided an automatic advance time (in the Automatically After *nn:nn* box), PowerPoint divides that time equally among the bullet points, and presents each in turn, automatically.

If you select the Automatically After *nn:nn* check box on the Slide Transition task pane, PowerPoint shows each of the bullet points automatically if you don't click soon enough. Here, too, each bullet point is given an equal amount of time.

TIP FROM

EQ & Woody

If you have animated bullet points, don't forget to show them as you're making the presentation! You would be amazed how many presenters talk "to" multiple animated bullet points on a slide, show the first point, and then forget to click to put the other bullet points on the screen so their audience can follow along.

To animate "flying" bullet points the easiest way, choose from the Animation Schemes on the Slide Design task pane:

1. Bring up the Animation Schemes portion of the Slide Design task pane by choosing Slide Show, Animation Schemes (see Figure 24.2).

Figure 24.2
Animation schemes
are on the Slide
Design pane.

2. Select the slide or slides you want to take on the specified animation. (Selecting multiple slides is easiest in Slide Sorter view. To select multiple slides in Normal view, first click in the Slides pane on the left side of the screen.)

3. Select an animation from the Apply to Selected Slides list. Look at the first slide you selected to see a preview of the slide's transition, followed by the animation. If you want to see the transition and animation again, click the Play button on the Slide Design task pane; in Slide Sorter view, you can also click the slide's Preview Transition and Animation button, which is just below the slide on the left.

PowerPoint's collection of built-in animation effects is impressive, but if you don't see the animation effect you want, you can create your own. For example, you can bring in second- and lower-level bullet points one at a time, or specify that bullet-point text should appear onscreen one word or character at a time. To build your animation from scratch, use the Custom Animation task pane; we explain how to use this feature in "Advanced Animation," later in this chapter.

TIP FROM

If you want your transitions and animations to appear when your presentation is viewed from a web browser, you must choose Tools, Options, General, Web Options, and then select the Show Slide Animation While Browsing check box.

ANIMATING TITLES

The trickiest part of animating the title of any slide lies in understanding precisely when the animation will take place. Some preset animations include animated bullets, and others don't. When you click to advance to a slide with an animated title using preset animations, your presentation proceeds in one of two ways (assuming the Slide Master itself isn't animated):

- **If the bullet points are not animated**—The background appears, along with all the slide's bullet points. Shortly thereafter, the title appears, using the chosen animation. You don't have to click.

- **If the bullet points are animated**—The slide background appears. Shortly thereafter, the title appears, using the animation you specified. Click to display the first bullet on the slide. Click again to show each succeeding bullet.

It's easy to animate titles by using most of the preset animations available on the Slide Design pane's Animation Schemes list. To see for yourself how animated bullets work, start with a preset animation that includes this feature, such as Flash Bulb.

The easiest way to apply one of these preset animations to a slide's title is via the Animation Schemes section of the Slide Design task pane, as described in the previous section. As soon as you choose the animation, watch the selected slide to see what the animation entails. The Big Title effect, for instance, super-sizes the slide title, brings it to the foreground for a moment, and then fades the title back to its normal size and position.

ADVANCED ANIMATION

In the preceding two sections, you saw how to apply PowerPoint's prebuilt animations with titles and bullet points. By creating a custom animation, you can go far beyond the preset choices for animating items on a slide. For instance, every one of PowerPoint's preset animations displays an entire high-level bullet point and all the lower-level points below it at the same time. Using a custom animation, you can arrange for top-level bullet points to appear onscreen first, followed one at a time by second-level bullets. You can have the title appear after the bullet points, or have the characters or words in the title appear in a specific sequence. This section shows you how to build custom animations, again concentrating on bullets and titles.

TIP FROM

EQ & Woody

> For help in learning how to create custom animations, try applying a preset effect from the Animation Schemes task pane first, before switching to the Custom Animation task pane. When you do so, PowerPoint shows the individual steps of the preset animation so that you can see how it works and customize it in whole or in part.

In the following example, we'll create a custom animation effect that allows us to display secondary bullet points individually:

1. In Normal view, bring up the slide that contains the elements you want to animate. For this example, we're using a slide that has bullet points at both the first and second levels. If you've already applied any preset animations, remove them by choosing No Animation from the Animation Schemes section of the Slide Design task pane.

2. Choose Slide Show, Custom Animation. The Custom Animation task pane appears (see Figure 24.3).

Figure 24.3
To build a custom animation from the ground up, remove any preset animations and start with a blank Custom Animation task pane.

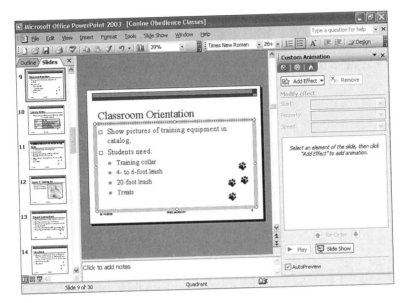

3. Select the items on the slide you want to animate. To animate the slide's bullet points but not its title, select only the text placeholder (which contains all the bullet points), as in Figure 24.3.

4. Click the Add Effect button and choose the effect you want. In Figure 24.4, we're about to apply an Entrance effect called Fly In to all elements in the text placeholder.

Figure 24.4
PowerPoint has hundreds of animation effects. For each element of a slide, you can control the entrance and exit motion and font effects (from the Emphasis menu), or you can apply any motion that you can draw.

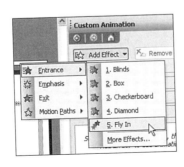

5. PowerPoint shows the first animation—in this case, the bullet point that starts with "Show pictures of…"—in the timing review list. Click the downward-pointing chevron (double arrow) below the first animation, and PowerPoint shows you all the bullet points and their sequence (see Figure 24.5). The timing review list indicates that on the first mouse click, the first bullet ("Show pictures of training …") appears. On the second mouse click, the second bullet point and its four secondary bullet points appear.

Figure 24.5
The timing review list shows what each mouse click will do. Sequence numbers to the left of the bullet points repeat that information.

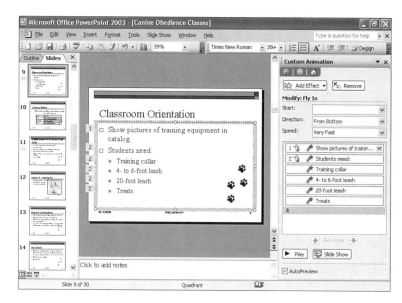

6. Each bullet point should appear in turn—in this example, two mouse clicks (each indicated by a mouse icon) and four unnumbered items that are associated with the second click. Click the first unnumbered bullet point ("Training collar"), select the down-arrow to the right, and choose Start on Click (see Figure 24.6).

7. Continue in this manner until all the bullet points have their own sequence numbers, 1 through 6 (see Figure 24.7).

8. Finally, to verify your choices, click the Slide Show button at the bottom of the Custom Animation pane. The heading should come up as soon as the slide appears. Click once, and the first bullet point comes up. Click again and you get the second bullet point, and so on. This level of control is not available in any of the standard Animation Schemes.

NOTE

You can apply completely separate animations to individual bullet points on a slide. For example, you can have the first bullet point wipe from the left, and have the second spiral from the top. Just because you *can* do this, however, doesn't mean you *should*. The results are usually a mess. Stick with one effect.

Figure 24.6
You can adjust the appearance of each bullet item individually.

Figure 24.7
Each bullet point appears in turn, as indicated by the numbers 1 through 6.

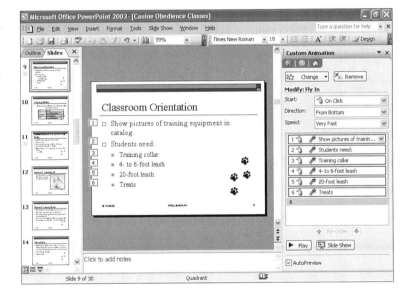

When you make a presentation, any item on the slide that isn't animated shows up as soon as the slide hits the screen. Animated items appear next, normally in top-to-bottom order. Sometimes you don't want the slide's elements to appear from top to bottom, however; you might have a picture that you want to appear before the bullets, or a video clip that should show before the title comes up. Using the Custom Animation pane, you can control the order in which animated items appear.

To arrange the order in which animations appear:

1. In Normal view, select the slide with the animations that need to be reordered.

2. Open the Custom Animation task pane by choosing Slide Show, Custom Animation.

3. Click the number to the left of any one animated item whose order you want to adjust.

4. Use the Re-Order arrows at the bottom of the timing review list to move the selected item up or down in the list.

5. Repeat steps 3 and 4 for any additional items you want to reorder.

As we noted earlier, you can select one of PowerPoint's preset Animation Schemes as a starting point for customization and then open the Customize Animation pane to modify it slightly.

For example, if you like the Boomerang and Exit effect (found near the bottom of the Exciting category in the Animation Schemes list), but want it to apply to both first- and second-level bullets, try this:

1. In Normal view, select the slide you want to animate.

2. Choose Slide Show, Animation Schemes. On the Slide Design task pane, choose the Boomerang and Exit scheme from the Animations Schemes list.

3. Open the Custom Animation task pane to see all the components of the Boomerang and Exit scheme, detailed in the timing review list.

4. Click to the right of the first bullet point you want to change, and choose Start on Click.

5. Adjust the remaining bullet points. When you're ready, click Slide Show and make sure the animation does what you want.

 If you're frustrated because you can't copy custom animation effects from slide to slide, see "Custom Animation Tricks" in the "Troubleshooting" section at the end of this book.

TIP FROM

To add a custom animation to every slide, animate the Slide Master. You can apply any animation effect to any item on the Slide Master—title, text, background pictures, date/time, footer, and slide number. You can also animate the Title Master. If you use the AutoContent wizard to create a presentation, you'll discover that many of PowerPoint's "canned" presentations use this trick.

To coordinate the arrival of each character in a title with a sound (say, a typewriter clacking), here's how you coordinate sounds with characters:

1. In Normal view, select the slide whose bullet points you want to animate. Bring up the Custom Animation task pane (choose Slide Show, Custom Animation).

2. Choose the item you want to animate—for example, the title. Click Add Effect (or, if the item already has an effect, click Change), and choose Entrance, More Effects, Color Typewriter.

NOTE

The list of menu choices on the menus attached to the Add Effects and Change buttons are dynamic. As you use individual choices from the More Effects menu, PowerPoint adds your choices to these menus, saving you a click or two when you reuse those same effects. If you've used the Color Typewriter option recently, for instance, you'll find it on the Entrance menu, without having to detour to the More Effects list.

3. In the timing review list, click the down arrow to the right of the title, choose Effect Options, and choose Typewriter in the Sound box (see Figure 24.8).

Figure 24.8
You can match any sound with any effect. Here a typewriter sound announces the arrival of each character.

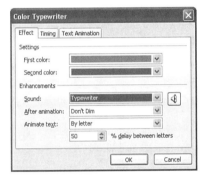

When the title appears on the slide, each character flies in, accompanied by the sound you selected—in this example, a typewriter. (Don't let the effect name limit your creativity. By using modern fonts and other sounds, you can create an interesting effect that has no association at all with an old Underwood or Selectric.)

ANIMATING THE DRAWING LAYER

PowerPoint allows you to animate any items in the drawing layer—text boxes, drawings, AutoShapes, clip art, charts, embedded Excel or Word objects, org charts, and more. Before you try, however, it's important that you understand how the drawing layer works, and how to use it in conjunction with the Custom Animation dialog box.

→ For an explanation of how Office programs use the drawing layer, **see** "Working with the Drawing Layer," **p. 114**.

Say you've created a dramatic slide that features your organization's new president. You've added a scanned photo to the slide, and you want the photo to "dissolve" onto the screen with applause—and you hope the audience will join in. Here's how:

1. Display the slide in Normal view and click to select the picture.

2. Choose Slide Show, Custom Animation.

3. In the Custom Animation task pane, click Add Effect, Entrance, More Effects, and then choose Fade (see Figure 24.9).

Figure 24.9
If you select an item on a slide and then choose an animation, PowerPoint applies the animation only to the selected item.

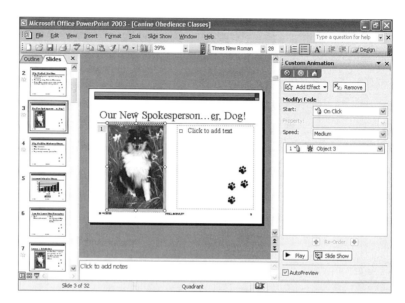

4. Click the down arrow in the timing review list next to the picture. Choose Effect Options. In the Sound box, pick Applause, and click OK.

Now when the slide appears on the screen, the picture will "fade in," accompanied by the sounds of applause.

Use similar techniques to animate any object on the drawing layer. For example, you might want to have a text box that says "We Hit Our Target!" on top of a slide showing the success of a fund-raising effort, animated to appear after you've had a chance to talk about the numbers. Custom animations also let you introduce text in AutoShape callouts or text boxes one word or letter at a time.

HIDING AND UNCOVERING SLIDE CONTENTS

There's a trick to using items in the drawing layer that all too frequently escapes PowerPoint users. If you carefully match the color of a shape in the drawing layer to the color of the background, you can use animation on these shapes to *hide* parts of your presentation.

Say you have a slide that includes an organizational chart, and you want to unveil each member of the organization, one at a time. PowerPoint offers only basic options when it comes to organizational charts, in noteworthy comparison to the long list of fancy effects you can accomplish with charts you create with Excel or Microsoft Graph. Here's how to use animations to show one piece of the org chart at a time:

1. Create the slide and organizational chart. For best results, make sure the slide's background is a solid color.

2. Click the Rectangle tool on the Drawing toolbar. Draw a rectangle around the top box in the org chart, extending down so that it covers the vertical line at the bottom of the box. If you have trouble covering the rectangle precisely and need more control, hold down the Alt key as you drag.

3. Click the Fill Color button on the Drawing toolbar. Select the color that most nearly matches the background color. (If you're using defined color schemes, you should be able to select an exact match.)

4. Click the Line Color button on the Drawing toolbar. Select the same color you selected in the preceding step.

5. Repeat steps 2, 3, and 4 to draw rectangles around each box, including appropriate sections of the connecting lines.

6. Choose Slide Show, Custom Animation, select the Rectangles AutoShapes you added to the slide, and choose whatever Animation Effect suits your fancy. In the timing review sequence list, arrange the order so the first Rectangle is the last in order. Use the Effect Options choices to add any additional effects (applause, for example).

The presentation will now reveal each piece of the org chart when you click the mouse.

ANIMATING CHART COMPONENTS

You can animate every piece of a chart separately. For example, to dramatically demonstrate five years of steady growth, try sliding each bar in the chart up from the bottom of the slide, one after the other. To focus on the differences between economic growth in the economies of Europe and Asia over the past 30 years, show the bars for Europe first, and then reveal the corresponding bars for the Asian economy.

Before you undertake this advanced animation, make sure you understand how to create a chart in Excel or Microsoft Graph, how to insert a chart into a slide, and how to use the Custom Animation dialog box.

→ To learn how to create a chart in Excel, **see** "Selecting and Customizing a Chart Type," **p. 679**.

To animate an Excel chart, you must put the chart in a slide's object placeholder. To put an existing Excel chart into a chart placeholder, first create the chart in Excel and copy it to the Clipboard. Then display the slide in PowerPoint and use the Slide Layout pane to apply a layout of the suitable size and shape. The ideal choice, of course, is a Content or Text and Content layout, but you can actually use any layout. PowerPoint is smart enough to paste the chart into the correct location and replace a text placeholder with an object placeholder if necessary.

After creating the new slide, choose Edit, Paste. PowerPoint places your chart in the slide as an embedded Excel object. You can double-click the chart to edit it using Excel. At this point, you can animate the chart.

To make each bar of a bar chart appear independently on the screen, follow these steps:

1. Open the slide that contains the chart. Select the chart and choose Slide Show, Custom Animation.

 If you can't see the Slide Show menu and you can't make the Task Pane appear, see "Where's the Task Pane?" in the "Troubleshooting" section at the end of this chapter.

2. In the Custom Animation task pane, choose Add Effect and pick an Entrance effect such as Diamond.

3. Click the down arrow next to the chart object in the timing review list and choose Effect Options. On the Chart Animation tab, choose the method you want to use to introduce chart elements: The chart can come in all at once; by Series (that is, all similarly colored bars appear, followed by all bars with the next color, and so on); by Category (each group of bars that falls into one group on the y-axis appears, and then the next group); or by individual bars within each Series or Category (see Figure 24.10).

Figure 24.10
Individual bars in a chart appear in the sequence defined on the Chart Animation tab.

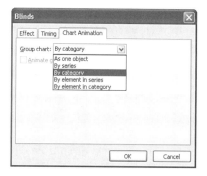

4. Test your animation by clicking the Play button.

Because PowerPoint gives you the capability to present data by Series or Category, the animation sequence for chart effects can be complex. Use the Play button as you work to make sure the order is correct.

ADDING MULTIMEDIA TO YOUR PRESENTATION

PowerPoint puts you in the director's chair when it comes to adding sounds, clip art (including pictures with movement such as animated GIFs), extended musical accompaniment, and even movie clips. But just because it *can* be done doesn't necessarily mean it *should* be done. Multimedia components in a presentation tend to overwhelm the audience. Be sure you really want to draw your audience's attention away from what you're saying before you insert a multimedia clip.

ADDING MUSIC, SOUNDS, AND VIDEO CLIPS

The easiest way to add multimedia to a presentation is to apply one of the content place-holders from the Slide Layout task pane:

1. In Normal view, select the slide on which you want to include a media clip (sound or movie).

2. Bring up the Slide Layout pane by choosing Format, Slide Layout.

3. In the Slide Layout pane, select one of the Content Layouts, Text and Content Layouts, or one of the Other Layouts that includes the "321" clapboard.

→ To change the layout of the slide, **see** "Choosing a Slide Layout," **p. 726**.

4. Back in the slide, rearrange the placeholders as necessary to fit both the clip and text (if any) on the slide. (If you don't want text on the slide, remove the text placeholder.)

5. If you used a content layout, click the video camera in the lower-right corner. If you used a selection from the Other Layouts category, double-click the icon to choose the appropriate media type. The Media Clip dialog box appears, with choices representing the type of content you selected.

→ For details on taking advantage of Office's extensive Clip Organizer, **see** "Using Clip Art," **p. 138**.

6. Choose the sound or motion clip you want, and then click OK. The Media Gallery inserts the clip you selected into the media clip placeholder on your slide, and then asks: "How do you want the movie (or sound) to start in the slide show?" Choose Automatically if you want the movie/sound to begin as soon as the slide appears. If you choose When Clicked, you'll have to click the picture (or the speaker that symbolizes a sound) to play the sound or show the video during the presentation.

> **NOTE**
>
> You'll find animated GIFs in the Clip Organizer. Office 2003 does not include any tools that allow you to edit an animated GIF; to change one of these images, you must use a program specifically designed to handle this graphic format, such as Magic Viewer from Crayonsoft (*http://www.crayonsoft.com/*).

Other methods for adding multimedia to a slide include the following:

- To place a clip in the drawing layer, choose Insert, Picture, Clip Art (or equivalently, click the Clip Art icon on the Drawing toolbar). This brings up the Clip Art task pane—thus giving you the widest latitude in choosing what kind of clip you want to use.

- To bypass the Media Gallery and choose a picture from files stored on your computer or network, choose Insert, Picture, From File.

- Use Insert, Movies and Sounds if you know what kind of multimedia clip you want to insert: Movie from Clip Organizer brings up the Clip Organizer with Motion Clips alone available; Sound from Clip Organizer does the same, with Sounds. The Movie from File and Sound from File options allow you to select media stored in external files.

- Also use Insert, Movies and Sounds if you want to play a CD track, or if you want to record a custom sound to go with the slide.

→ For more information on sounds, **see** "Using CD Audio and Recorded Audio," **p. 778**.

All the preceding methods insert a multimedia clip into your presentation for playback by PowerPoint itself. For maximum control over media objects, embed a Windows Media Player object on a slide. The following guidelines can help you decide when you should use this option:

- Do you want anyone viewing the presentation to be able to start, stop, and jump through the media clip? PowerPoint includes only basic controls for starting, ending, and looping. Media Player includes extensive capabilities for fast forward, marking and jumping to segments, editing, and the like. A Media Player Object can even display a working "Play/Stop" slider on the slide.

- You cannot adjust the PowerPoint animation multimedia effects of a Media Player object (see the next section).

- If you test a presentation with one version of Media Player and then run it on a computer that is significantly less powerful or uses a different version of Media Player, you might notice significant differences.

To embed a Windows Media Player object in a slide, choose Insert, Object, and then choose Media Clip, MIDI Sequence, Video Clip, or Wave Sound. Any of those choices will embed an object that plays back with Windows Media Player.

CONTROLLING A VIDEO OR SOUND CLIP

To change the behavior of a video or sound clip after you place it on a slide—whether it's in a placeholder or in the drawing layer—right-click the clip (or the speaker icon representing a sound object) and choose Custom Animation. On the Add Effects menu (or the Change menu, if an effect is already applied), you'll notice a new Sound Actions or Movie Actions menu that allows you to define Play, Pause, or Stop effects. After applying an effect, choose Effect Options and use the Movie Settings or Sound Settings tab to see options that apply only to the type of media clip you've inserted.

Use these options to create a video introduction to a slide with bullet points. The slide should appear first, with the title and background. Then, as quickly as PowerPoint can manage, the video clip should play. Finally, after the clip is over, the video should disappear and your bullet points should slide onto the screen.

Here's how to do it:

1. Select the slide you plan to use, and enter its title and bullet points.

2. To place the video clip in the drawing layer, choose Insert, Movies and Sounds, Movie From File. Select the file and click OK.

3. When PowerPoint asks, "How do you want the movie (or sound) to start in the slide show?" click Automatically.

4. Resize the movie clip window and position it where you want the movie to appear. Ignore the bullet points for the time being—they won't be there when the video runs—and concentrate on getting the movie clip positioned properly.

5. Right-click the movie clip window and select Custom Animation. You'll see the movie file appear at the top of the timing review list, with a 0 next to it (indicating that the movie will run as soon as the slide appears).

6. Select the Text placeholder and the title, click Add Effect in the Custom Animation task pane, and select an effect to assign to all the text on the slide. In Figure 24.11, we've used the Fly in effect. The bullet points appear in the timing review list directly below the animation.

Figure 24.11
The timing review list indicates that the Fireworks.wmv animation will run before the bullet points appear.

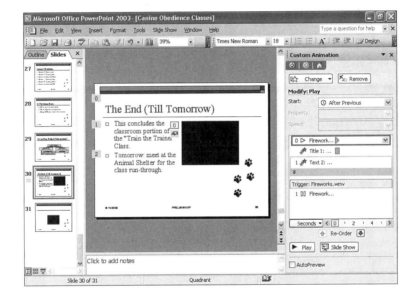

7. Click the down arrow next to the media clip at the top of the timing review list. Choose Effect Options. In the Play Movie dialog box (see Figure 24.12), click the Movie Settings tab and select the Hide While Not Playing check box. Then click the Effect tab and choose Hide After Animation from the After Animation drop-down list. This combination of settings ensures that the movie clip will play and then disappear, before the bullet points arrive. Click OK to close the Play Movie dialog box.

8. Click the down arrow next to the entry for the bullet points in the timing review list (in this example, it's labeled as Text 2), and select Start After Previous. This setting ensures that the first bullet point will appear immediately after the movie clip finishes.

Click Play on the Custom Animation pane and you'll see how all this ties together.

Figure 24.12
Specify that you want the movie clip to disappear when it's done playing.

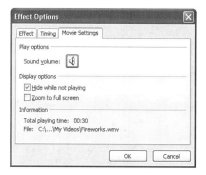

TIP FROM

Loop and rewind options vary depending on the type of multimedia clip you select. To work with these settings, click the Effect and Timing tabs in the Play Movie dialog box.

USING CD AUDIO AND RECORDED AUDIO

You can use recorded audio (such as a narration) or a track from a music CD as a dramatic way to introduce a slide or a presentation. You could even use this technique in combination with a series of timed animations to run a dramatic series of slides, complete with audio, before you take the stage.

The simplest way to synchronize audio with recorded music is to use Windows Media Player (or another music player) to "rip" the track into Windows Media or MP3 format, and then synchronize that sound with the slide. If you are unable to rip a track from CD (or unwilling to do so because of copyright concerns), you can play a track from an audio CD as soon as a specific slide appears during a presentation. In either case, follow these steps:

1. In Normal view, select the slide. If you plan to play a track from CD, insert the CD you want to use in the PC's CD-ROM drive.

TIP FROM

If you have enabled CD AutoPlay on your system, Windows will begin playing an audio CD as soon as you insert it into the drive. When this happens, PowerPoint won't be able to take control of the CD to let you select a track. To give control back to PowerPoint, open Windows Media Player (or whatever program is configured as the default for playing CDs) and stop the CD. Close the player to let PowerPoint use the CD.

2. Choose Insert, Movies and Sounds. To play a "ripped" track, choose Sounds from File. To play a track from a CD, choose Play CD Audio Track. If you select a CD, PowerPoint responds with the Movie and Sound Options dialog box (see Figure 24.13). Choose the recorded file(s) or track(s) you want to play and click OK.

Figure 24.13
As long as you have the CD in your PC's drive, PowerPoint automatically calculates how much time it will take to play the tracks you select.

3. PowerPoint asks how you want the sound to start in the slide show. If you want the music to start the moment this slide hits the screen, choose Automatically. If you select When Clicked, you'll have to click the slide's speaker or CD icon before the track(s) will play.

4. If you want to make any more changes to the animation, right-click the speaker or CD icon and select Custom Animation. Use any of the options described earlier in this chapter.

Whether they're launched from a file or a CD, audio tracks have all the flexibility of any other kind of animation. PowerPoint can launch an audio track automatically, and individual tracks can appear in any order, before or after other animated elements on a slide.

NOTE

PowerPoint doesn't identify the actual CD in the CD-ROM drive; it knows only to play the tracks you've specified, no matter which CD might be in there. If you forget to put a CD in the drive when running a presentation, PowerPoint continues as if there were no track(s) to be played. Whenever possible, you should use audio files instead of CDs.

If your PC has a functioning microphone, you can record a sound to be played with slides—you can even prerecord narration for every slide and, using timed advancing on the slides, deliver an entire presentation without being physically present. Choose Insert, Movies and Sounds, Record Sound, and follow the instructions.

CAUTION

Audio clips in presentations viewed over the Web can slow down the process horribly, unless the viewer has a high-speed connection.

Using Action Links to Combine Effects

You can tie each animated element on a slide to a hyperlink or action setting. When you click a hyperlinked element or an item that includes an action setting, the animation takes place before the hyperlink or action setting kicks in.

→ For information about hyperlinks in general, **see** "Working with Hyperlinks," **page 847**.

→ For hyperlink information specific to PowerPoint, **see** "Using Hyperlinks," **page 719**.

Combining custom animation and action settings needn't be overly confusing because they typically operate on different slide components. For example, you can apply a sound "animation" to the appearance of bullet points on a slide, but you can apply the sound "action setting" only to the words (and characters) in the bullet point.

Surprisingly, however, there's one action that you can implement only through hyperlinks and action settings: the mouse over. All the fancy animation techniques discussed in this chapter are tied to mouse clicks, or internal timers.

For example, if you want to make a video clip start by passing the mouse over the clip, you *must* use action settings. Select the clip, choose Slide Show, Action Settings, and then adjust options on the Mouse Over tab.

→ For details, **see** "Advanced Navigation with Action Settings," **p. 720**.

Troubleshooting

Custom Animation Tricks

I created a slick custom animation for one slide, but I can't figure out how to copy the animation effects to other slides in my presentation.

Although PowerPoint has no built-in way to copy a custom animation from one slide to another, here's an undocumented trick that lets you reuse custom animations: Make a copy of a slide, and then change the title and bullets on the copy. The copy includes all the custom animation settings of the original.

For example, if you've created a nifty custom animation on slide 20, how do you move it to slides 17, 18, and 19? You could edit the animation settings for each of the other three slides, but that's a cumbersome process. Instead, make three copies of slide 20, and then move the existing text from the old slides to the copies. Delete the old slides when you've finished.

Where's the Task Pane?

I added a chart to my slide and am trying to animate its elements, but the Slide Show menu is unavailable and I can't figure out how to make the task pane appear.

You double-clicked the chart, causing it to open for editing. As a result, the PowerPoint menus changed to those that allow you to work with charts. Press the Escape key or click anywhere else in the chart to return to the slide. Then click the chart object once to select it without activating it for editing.

EXTRA CREDIT: USING POWERPOINT TO SHOW OFF DIGITAL PHOTOS

Most people think of PowerPoint as a tool for creating presentations that consist of bullet points and titles in an outline format. But if you focus only on the graphics, you can use PowerPoint to create a dazzling slide show out of a collection of digital photos. You can use this technique to build a slide show for a family event, such as Grandma's 75th birthday or a family reunion. You can also use it to help members of a club or organization relive a recent event, such as a picnic or competition. The best part is that the show can run unattended, looping back to the beginning when it hits the last slide. That way anyone who walks past the monitor or TV on which you're displaying the slide show can see the whole thing even if they arrive late.

You'll have best results if you start with a photo editing program. Select the photos you want to use, crop as needed, and convert them to the correct format. Rename the collection, if necessary, and then save all your photo files to a single folder (or subfolders within a single folder, if you have a large collection).

You can now begin creating your PowerPoint slide show. Create a new presentation and create the background you want to use. Keep it simple—you don't want the background to fight with photos that may be complex.

When creating each slide, use any of the layouts in the Content Layout category. For slides with title placeholders, use the Title and Content layouts, and then click the photo icon to insert a file from a Browse dialog box. If you choose the Blank layout, you can add photos individually by choosing Insert, Picture, From File. Repeat the process to add a second or third or fourth photo to a slide, and then move the photos around as needed.

What about the New Photo Album option on the Insert, File menu? It produces quick results by allowing you to choose a group of photos and then quickly turn each one into a slide. Unfortunately, it centers each photo and resizes it to fill the full height or width of the slide, which usually results in a boring presentation.

After you've finished placing your photos on slides, use the tools described in this chapter to add background music or narration, create smooth transitions between slides, and save the whole thing in Slide Show format.

CHAPTER 25

DELIVERING A PRESENTATION WITH STYLE

In this chapter

PLANNING YOUR PRESENTATION

You've finished preparing all your slides. You've created a visually interesting presentation with transitions that help move the narrative along. Now all you have to do is stand and deliver.

Far too many presentations fail because the presenter doesn't anticipate what could reasonably go wrong, or doesn't prepare for questions that can be answered with a few facts, figures, or slides.

On the other hand, some less-than-flashy presenters with solid but uninspired slides regularly draw raves from appreciative audiences. Why? Because they step through points logically and in sequence, and when questions arise, they have solid answers, ready and waiting—and right at hand in their speaker notes.

THE IMPORTANCE OF PREPARATION

It's no secret, and no coincidence, that the best presenters rehearse their presentations over and over, in front of different groups that closely parallel the target audience. Before they stand up on stage, they take apart their presentation, slide by slide, and then edit, reorganize, put it back together, and test it again.

You might be tempted to practice in front of a mirror, and if your primary concern is the mechanics of the presentation, that's a reasonable approach. But if you want to get a point across, nothing beats jumping into the lion's den. Practice delivering the presentation to people who are willing to stop you when they don't understand, and make suggestions when your points miss their mark. If you're working on a pitch to a nonprofit, invite some members of the organization to listen to a preview. If you're preparing a classroom presentation, see if your study group will act as a trial audience.

PowerPoint includes a number of tools that will help you prepare, refine, and ultimately deliver the presentation. But in the final analysis, they won't help a bit unless you have the content down pat. The best presentations practically deliver themselves.

ORGANIZING YOUR REMARKS WITH SPEAKER NOTES

Some people are capable of delivering a perfect presentation without notes. But what if you don't have a photographic memory or weeks to rehearse? For those of us who are chronically short on spare time and brain cells, there's no substitute for PowerPoint's *speaker notes*.

→ For an overview of notes, **see** "Adding Notes," **p. 713**.

The easiest way to construct and maintain notes is in PowerPoint's Normal view, where the Notes pane appears below the slide. Normally, this window displays only a few lines; to look at all the notes for a given slide, go to Notes view by choosing View, Notes Page.

You can do little to change the appearance of the Notes page, except for adjusting tab stops. Because default tab stops start at one inch, you might find yourself running out of room if you indent text on a note page that contains lots of text; follow these steps to adjust the tabs and give the indented text a little extra room:

1. In Normal or Slide Sorter view, select the slide with the notes that you want to change.

2. Choose View, Notes Page. Then bring up the ruler by choosing View, Ruler.

3. Click once to position the insertion point in the notes placeholder below the slide. Then click and drag on the bottom of the ruler to adjust the tab stops.

To change the tab spacing on all your Notes pages, bring up the Notes Master (choose View, Master, Notes Master), adjust the tab stops on the ruler, and save your changes to the master.

TIP FROM

Ed & Woody

If you can anticipate any questions your audience might ask when a particular slide is on the screen, consider typing the question (and a possible answer, of course) at the bottom of the Notes page for that slide. To make it easier to identify the questions while you're flipping through your notes, set them off in bold or italic.

USING POWERPOINT'S TIMER TO REHEARSE A PRESENTATION

When you practice a presentation, PowerPoint can start a timer to keep track of the amount of time you spend on each slide and on the presentation as a whole. These timings can be useful in several situations:

- Timing your presentation helps you identify slides that are too complex or contain too much detail. If you find yourself spending five minutes explaining a single slide, consider simplifying the slide or splitting it into two or more. Likewise, if you discover you're racing through one part of your presentation, taking only a few seconds on each slide, that might be a clue that those slides are too elementary.

- PowerPoint timers help you set up the presentation so that slides advance automatically. This capability might be useful if, for example, you need to have both hands free to work with a physical prop. In this case, you can use the timings from your rehearsals to specify how long PowerPoint should display each slide before advancing.

- With the help of a special timer on the Rehearsal dialog box, you can plan your presentation so you don't overrun a tight time slot. The Rehearsal timer appears onscreen to tell you how long you've spent on each slide. Although few people use the Rehearsal timer during a final presentation, it can help you keep on top of timing during the preparation phase.

To rehearse a presentation using the timer, follow these steps:

1. Gather all the notes you'll need, and then open the presentation in PowerPoint, preferably using the same computer you'll use when you actually deliver the presentation.

2. Choose Slide Show, Rehearse Timings. As your presentation begins, the Rehearsal dialog box appears onscreen (see Figure 25.1).

Figure 25.1
Keep track of the time spent on each slide by using the Slide Meter.

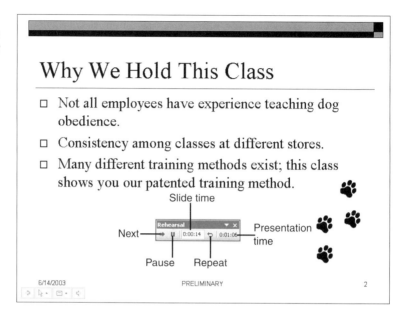

3. Run through your presentation normally. Try to speak at a natural pace, using your notes if necessary, and click your way through slides and animations.
   - Watch the Slide Time box to see how much time you've spent on the current slide. If you bump into an unexpected snag—you lose your place in your notes, for example—click the Pause button to stop the clock. Click Next to proceed.
   - If you get flustered, click Repeat to "turn back the clock"—that is, reset the time on the current slide to zero, and subtract the appropriate amount of time from the Presentation Time counter. Resume your presentation at that slide.

NOTE

Clicking the Repeat button causes animations to repeat, starting with the first animation on the slide, but you must click once on the screen before the first repeat animation appears.

4. When you finish the presentation, PowerPoint tells you how long the entire presentation took, and asks whether you want to update the times associated with each slide to reflect the latest numbers. If you click Yes, the timing numbers appear in Slide Sorter view, to the lower left of each slide (see Figure 25.2).

Figure 25.2
The results of the last (accepted) timing run appear to the lower left of each slide.

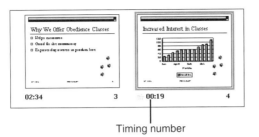

Timing number

Unfortunately, there is no way to keep a history of timing runs, or to selectively re-record timings on a slide-by-slide basis. You must either accept all the new times, or reject them all. You can manually adjust the timing of a single slide by choosing Slide Show, Slide Transition, and entering a time in the Advance Slide box.

NOTE

> If you show the same slide more than once (such as if you back up or use it in a custom show), the timer keeps statistics only for the final time it appears.

To set an individual slide so that it advances automatically after a specific amount of time, you must use the Slide Transition dialog box.

→ For details on timing, **see** "Using Transitions to Control Pacing," **p. 760**.

DELIVERING A PERFECT PRESENTATION

The perfect presentation makes your point. It's that simple. Ultimately, of course, you control the quality of your presentation, but a few tricks can help you master the mechanics of presenting.

RUNNING A SLIDE SHOW

PowerPoint contains an enormous—even overwhelming—variety of options to help you run a slide show. One piece of advice rises above all others: If you're not sure what to do next during a presentation, right-click the screen. Don't press Escape. Right-click.

The right-click context menu available from the presentation screen gives you instant access to nearly every option you'll ever need to run a slide show. For example, you can jump to any slide if you know the title; you can move backward, or blank the screen, or perform a dozen other important gyrations—even if you don't remember the shortcut key for a particular obscure option. Unless you need to create a new slide in the middle of your presentation (it happens), right-click to steer your way out of trouble.

25

CREATING PRESENTATIONS FOR THE WEB

The fact that web browsers are practically ubiquitous might tempt you to save your PowerPoint presentation as a web page and hit the road with only a browser to make the presentation (for an idea of what the result looks like, see Figure 22.10 on page 714).

In many situations, saving your presentation as a web page is a good idea:

- Internet Explorer is available just about anywhere you go, so you needn't worry whether PowerPoint is installed on the PC you'll use for your presentation.

➔ Some presentation details might not make the transition to a browser, however; **see** "Browser Compatibility Issues," **p. 845**.

- Running in a browser in full screen mode—with toolbars and menus hidden—your presentation will look almost exactly the same as if you were using PowerPoint for the show.

- It's a great "Road Warrior" fallback. If your notebook dies a few minutes before you have to give the presentation, you can easily connect to the Net from another PC and be right back in business.

- The outline shown in the browser (on the left side of Figure 22.10) can actually make presenting easier—although viewers might find it distracting. For example, if you forget which slide contains a specific bullet point, you can expand and collapse the outline dynamically to find the point, and then jump to the slide in question with one click.

But there are also potential problems when you rely on a web server and a browser for your presentation:

- Unless there's a wide communications pipeline straight from your presentation PC to the web server, a browser-based presentation always runs slower than a presentation run in PowerPoint—in some cases, much, much slower. You can reduce this performance penalty by saving the web page to portable media (CD, DVD, or USB flash drive) and running it from a local drive.

- When you're running in a browser, some of the PowerPoint presentation navigation techniques don't work. Pressing the Enter key and the spacebar doesn't advance slides. Pressing B doesn't blank the screen. And, if you right-click a slide, you get the browser's context menu, not PowerPoint's.

If you decide to use a browser to make your presentation, always practice with the browser you're going to use.

 If you're having problems getting your transition and/or animation effects to display in a web browser, see "Viewing Transition and Animation Effects in a Browser" in the "Troubleshooting" section at the end of this chapter.

Another excellent reason to save a presentation as a web page is to allow your audience to view the presentation at their leisure, without the benefit of your commentary. By posting the results on your website, you can provide ready access to your slide show without having to worry about whether your audience has PowerPoint installed. If you regularly save presentations as web pages, consider adjusting some of the settings available for this format by choosing Tools, Options, and then clicking the Web Options button on the General tab.

In the Web Options dialog box, the options available on the General tab, shown in Figure 25.3, are unique to PowerPoint. (Settings on the other five tabs affect all Office programs.) To eliminate the annoyance of forcing your audience to click several times to see all parts of a slide, for instance, you might want to turn off slide animations by clearing the Show Slide Animation While Browsing box.

Figure 25.3
These options are unique to PowerPoint presentations saved as web pages.

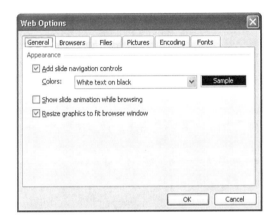

To save a presentation for use on the Web, choose File, Save as Web Page. This option saves your presentation in the Single File Web Page format using the .mhtml extension. The resulting file can be opened in Internet Explorer 5.0 or later.

If you plan to post the presentation on a website where people might want to view it using another browser, such as Firefox, click the Publish button and choose the All Browsers Listed Above option. This saves the file as a standard HTML page instead.

SETTING UP A SLIDE SHOW

When creating a presentation, you can add a variety of features, including narration, animations, and preset timings. When you deliver the presentation, however, you may be using a different computer than the one you created. In addition, you may want to tweak the settings of the slide show to match its intended use, especially if someone other than you will be the presenter.

TUNING YOUR PRESENTATION FOR YOUR HARDWARE

When you take your slide show on the road, you may be asked to use a different computer than you're used to. This can cause two problems:

- Performance may suffer if you use demanding transitions and animations. Effects that work well on your top-of-the-line desktop computer may poke along on a computer with a less robust video card, a slower CPU, and insufficient RAM.

- Your carefully drafted design may turn into a crowded, unreadable mess if the video resolution of the presentation machine is significantly less than the computer you used to create the show.

To deal with either of these problems, you need to make some adjustments. Choose Slide Show, Set Up Show. The resulting dialog box (see Figure 25.4) includes several useful options.

Figure 25.4
To avoid problems when showing a presentation at a lower resolution, use the options in the Performance box.

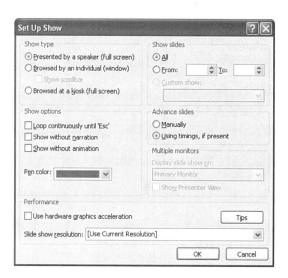

Two areas in particular are worth noting here. Consider selecting the Show Without Narration and Show Without Animation check boxes if you notice that the presentation is dragging unacceptably on the presenting machine. If you know that your target machine is going to use a specific resolution—say, 800×600—adjust the Slide Show Resolution setting in the Performance box and preview your show *before* you hit the road. If any slides look odd or distorted, you can edit them in advance.

USING TWO MONITORS

If you have dual monitors set up and recognized by the operating system (including a setup in which you connect your notebook or desktop PC to a TV in addition to a standard monitor or LCD screen), you can tell PowerPoint to show the presentation on one monitor, while you control the presentation in a normal-like view on the other monitor.

NOTE

> Windows XP builds the support for multiple monitors into the operating system and pro-
> vides an additional feature called DualView, often used in portable computers. For more
> details, see the Knowledge Base article at
> http://support.microsoft.com/default.aspx?scid=283674.

The primary monitor, which you use to control the presentation, displays the presentation
in Normal view. Alternatively, you can have PowerPoint display "presenter tools," which
give you slide thumbnails, buttons for showing the next and previous slide, a timer, speaker
notes, and a black screen button. The secondary monitor shows the usual presentation full-
screen.

To set up a presentation for dual monitors, choose Slide Show, Set Up Show, and in the
Multiple Monitors box, point PowerPoint to the secondary monitor. If you want "presenter
tools" to appear on the primary screen, click the Show Presenter Tools check box.

USING HIDDEN SLIDES TO ANTICIPATE QUESTIONS

If you anticipate a question and have the answers handy in your presentation notes, your
audience will be impressed. If you can cut immediately to a new slide that answers that
question, your audience will sit up and take notice.

Hidden slides offer a clever way to prepare for topics that you want to bring up only if someone asks. If you anticipate that someone in your audience might ask a question about slide 4,
for example, here's how to be ready with a slide that answers the question:

1. Switch to Slide Sorter view and click after the final slide in the presentation. Click New
   Slide on the Slide Sorter toolbar, and create the slide that will answer the expected
   question.

2. Double-click to open your new slide in Normal view and add whatever content you
   need. Then, in an inconspicuous location, add a text box (saying, perhaps, "Back to presentation") or a picture to use as a button to return to the originating slide.

TIP FROM

EQ & Woody

> On the Drawing toolbar, if you choose AutoShapes, Action Buttons, and select the
> "return" action button in the lower-left corner, it will achieve exactly the same results as
> steps 2 and 3 here. The only difference is that you'll end up with the default "return"
> icon image.

3. Right-click the picture or text box and select Action Settings. On the Mouse Click tab
   of the Action Settings dialog box, click Hyperlink To, and choose Last Slide Viewed
   from the offered drop-down list. Click OK to save this setting. During the presentation, you'll be able to click this hyperlink, and return to the originating slide.

→ For details on action settings, **see** "Advanced Navigation with Action Settings," **p. 720**.

4. Choose Slide Show, Hide Slide. (In Slide Sorter view, you can select the slide and click the Hide Slide button.) Because the slide is hidden, it never appears in the normal course of a presentation.

5. Return to slide 4 and create a hyperlink to this new, hidden slide. Attach the hyperlink to a small picture or piece of text—anything that will jog your memory without alerting your audience that you've prepared a "hidden" answer to a specific question.

→ For more about hyperlinks inside PowerPoint, **see** "Using Hyperlinks," **p. 719**.

When you deliver the presentation, if a member of the audience asks the question, click the hyperlink, discuss the issues on the hidden slide, and then click the "Back to presentation" button at the bottom of the hidden slide to return to the main presentation. To see this hidden slide technique in action, see "Extra Credit: Anticipating Questions with Hidden Slides" at the end of this chapter.

TIP FROM

Ed & Woody

> You can use the same technique if the answer to a question requires more than one slide. Instead of creating a hyperlink that jumps to a specific slide, however, create one that jumps to a custom presentation. You can branch back from the end of the custom presentation with yet another hyperlink that's specifically tied to the originating slide— just remember to use it during the presentation!

25

Hidden slides are marked in Slide Sorter view and in the Slides navigation pane with a slash through the slide number. In the Hyperlink dialog box, you can spot hidden slides by looking for those that have the slide number in parentheses.

→ For more on custom shows, **see** "Creating a Blank Presentation," **p. 704**.

WRITING OR DRAWING ON SLIDES

Sometimes in the course of delivering a presentation, you might want to "draw" on a slide: Like a commentator on a TV football broadcast, you can use circles and arrows to drive home a point. You can use a fine-line ballpoint option, a thicker felt tip instrument, or a broad highlighter, and in all these pen options you choose the color.

To begin marking up a slide while your slide show is running, right-click the screen and choose Pointer Options, Pen. Choose one of the three pen types and then click the pen-shaped pointer to draw on the slide.

If you use the pen regularly, you'll appreciate the following shortcuts:

■ The default color for the Ballpoint and Felt tip options is red; the Highlighter option uses yellow. To change pen colors, right-click the screen, choose Pointer Options, Ink Color, and choose among the colors offered.

■ When you finish marking up the slide, you can restore the pointer to an arrow by pressing Escape. (Don't press Escape a second time, however, or you'll suddenly exit your presentation!)

- To quickly switch between the currently selected pen type and the arrow pointer, press Ctrl+P (pen) and Ctrl+A (arrow).
- To erase all that you have drawn on a slide, press E on the keyboard.
- When using the mouse pointer to draw, press Enter or the spacebar to advance to the next animation or slide.

In previous versions of PowerPoint, all annotations disappeared as soon as you left the slide, and the drawings could not be retrieved under any circumstances. In PowerPoint 2003, the "ink" used for annotations is persistent. Any mark-ups you make on a specific slide are visible when you return to the slide. When you exit the slide show, PowerPoint gives you the opportunity to save your annotations. This option comes in handy if you scribble notes to yourself during the course of the presentation and want to act on those notes after you return to the office.

TAKING NOTES DURING A SLIDE SHOW

Besides the free-form annotation capability described earlier in this chapter, PowerPoint also allows you to make formal notes during a presentation by modifying the speaker notes for an individual slide. To do so, right-click the slide in question during a presentation and choose Screen, Speaker Notes. This option opens a pop-up window into which you can type your notes.

TIP FROM

EQ & Woody

> If you're using PowerPoint on a portable computer running Windows XP that supports the DualView feature, you can see your presentation in Normal view on your computer screen while the audience watches the slide show on the second monitor. Using this configuration, you can add slides, change text, revise speaker notes, and otherwise adjust your presentation on the fly, with your audience unaware that you're making things up as you go.

PACKAGING A PRESENTATION FOR USE ON OTHER COMPUTERS

A presentation doesn't always require a stand-up presentation. Sometimes, in fact, a carefully crafted presentation can literally deliver itself. If you've created a PowerPoint presentation that you want to allow other people to view even when you're not around, you can tie the pieces of the presentation into a tidy package and copy it to a CD. The secret? Use the Package for CD feature in PowerPoint 2003.

Packaging a presentation involves three steps:

1. Select the files you want to include on the CD. You can include multiple presentations and add supporting files, such as embedded TrueType fonts and music or video clips.

2. Adjust any or all of the following options:

- Specify whether you want the presentation to play automatically (Autorun) when inserted into a Windows computer.

- Decide whether you want to include the PowerPoint Viewer.

- Password-protect confidential presentation files so that only authorized users can open or edit the files. The PowerPoint Viewer will prompt for an Open or Modify password based on the options you select.

3. Save the package. Using Windows XP, you can save directly to a compatible CD burner or save the results to a folder and then use a third-party program to burn the saved folder to a CD.

TIP FROM

Using the Package for CD feature is an effective way to archive presentations for safe-keeping. A single CD can easily contain more than 100 typical presentations. If you use CDs as an archive medium, you needn't include the PowerPoint Viewer, and you can turn off AutoRun as well.

A saved presentation delivered through the PowerPoint Viewer looks exactly as it would if you were to present the slide show from PowerPoint. Transitions, animations, navigation techniques, and other features are unchanged. You can't add annotations, of course, and making any changes requires that you open the presentation in PowerPoint and save the changed file to a new CD.

SAVING A PRESENTATION ON A CD

After you've polished your presentation to a high gloss and you're satisfied with its content and design, you can copy it to a CD using the following steps:

1. With the presentation open in PowerPoint, choose File, Package for CD. The Package for CD dialog box appears, as shown in Figure 25.5.

2. Change the default name in the Name the CD box. Although this step is optional, we recommend that you do so to make it easier to identify the CD when you open it using the My Computer window. The name you enter must be 16 characters or fewer.

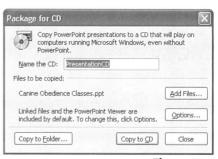

Figure 25.5

3. The current presentation is included by default and cannot be removed. To include other files on the CD (such as additional presentations or supporting media clips), click the Add Files button and use the Browse dialog box to select the files.

4. Click the Options button and adjust any of the options shown in Figure 25.6. By default, the PowerPoint Viewer is included, all presentations are played automatically, and passwords are left blank. This is your opportunity to add, open, or modify passwords. Click OK.

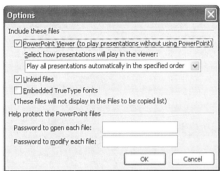

5. After inserting a blank CD into your CD-R or CD-RW drive, click Copy to CD to begin recording. If your computer does not include a compatible CD burner, click Copy to Folder instead, choose a name and location for the saved folder, and click OK. You can burn the saved folder to a CD later.

Figure 25.6

USING THE POWERPOINT VIEWER

When you use the AutoRun option on a CD-based presentation, it should require no effort from the intended audience beyond inserting the CD into the appropriate drive. If the person who created a CD chose not to use the AutoRun option, or if AutoRun is disabled on the target computer, open the CD in Windows Explorer, double-click the pptview icon, and choose the saved presentation from the Open dialog box, which appears automatically when the Viewer opens.

25

PRINTING YOUR PRESENTATION

Eventually, you'll want to print out a presentation. Print options let you generate speaker notes for you, handouts for your audience, and copies of the slides for you to study and revise while you're sitting on a plane or stuck in traffic.

CHOOSING WHICH ELEMENTS TO PRINT

When you choose File, Print, PowerPoint opens the Print dialog box, shown in Figure 25.7. Several of the options shown here are unique to PowerPoint and allow you to exercise excellent control over printed pages.

CAUTION

> Avoid the Print button on the Standard toolbar unless you're absolutely certain you want to send your entire presentation to the default printer using current settings. If you have any doubts, press Ctrl+P instead, or use the File, Print menu. To be on the safe side, consider customizing the Standard toolbar by eliminating the Print button and replacing it with the Print… button (note the ellipsis following the button name), which always displays the Print dialog box first.

The Print What box offers four different choices, as shown in Table 25.1.

Figure 25.7
Although many Print options are common to all Office programs, those at the bottom of this dialog box are unique to PowerPoint.

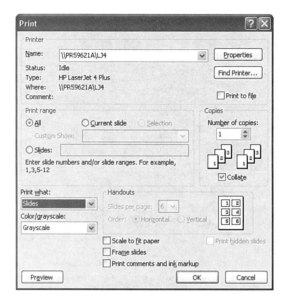

TABLE 25.1   PRINTING OPTIONS

Print What	Means
Slides	One slide per page, portrait, the slide fills up the whole page
Handouts	Multiple slides per page, based on the number in the Slides Per Page box, formatted according to the Handout Master that has the same number of slides per page
Notes Pages	One slide per page, formatted according to the Notes Master
Outline View	No slides, only outline text, formatted according to the Outline setting on the Handout Master

→ For details on notes and handouts formatting, **see** "Creating Speaker Notes and Audience Handouts," **p. 744**.

TIP FROM

Ed & Woody

Before sending a long presentation to a color printer, click the Preview button on the Print dialog box. This gives you one last opportunity to look over the proposed printed output and make sure that your color copies will turn out as you expect.

PREPARING A COLOR PRESENTATION FOR A BLACK-AND-WHITE PRINTER

When you print PowerPoint slides on a black-and-white printer, you might be disappointed at the way Windows translates color to black-and-white pages. Shadowing in graphs loses much of its definition. All but the lightest backgrounds completely obliterate any nuances in the foreground—to the point of obscuring text, in many cases.

For the best-quality printed output, use PowerPoint's built-in grayscale converter, which is optimized for the colors in presentation designs. By taking liberties with your slides—converting dark backgrounds to light when needed, for example—it produces extremely readable black-and-white output.

To preview what your slides look like when viewed through this special grayscale converter, click the Color/Grayscale button on the Standard toolbar. You'll be sent into Color/Grayscale View, with a toolbar that lets you tweak the grayscale settings.

You can also see how your slides will look by using PowerPoint's Print Preview: Just choose File, Print Preview.

To print using the Grayscale converter, click the Print button while in Print Preview, or choose File, Print, and select the Grayscale option at the bottom of the Print dialog box.

TROUBLESHOOTING

VIEWING TRANSITION AND ANIMATION EFFECTS IN A BROWSER

I've added transitions and animation effects to my slides, but they don't appear when I view my presentation in a web browser.

If none of your transition or animation effects appear in the browser, open the presentation and choose Tools, Options. On the General tab of the Options dialog box, click the Web Options button. On the General tab of the Web Options dialog box, select the Show Slide Animation While Browsing check box. Click OK to close each dialog box, and save your presentation.

EXTRA CREDIT: ANTICIPATING QUESTIONS WITH HIDDEN SLIDES

If you can anticipate a question from your audience, you'll be miles ahead if you have a slide ready to answer it. For example, this first slide might elicit the question, "How did customers find out about these classes?"

In anticipation of the question, you could construct a slide like the one shown next, and place it in the presentation immediately after the first slide. Hide the second slide (Slide Show, Hide Slide), add an action button to the first slide that jumps to the hidden slide, and add an action button to the hidden slide that returns to the last slide viewed.

→ For details on linking to a hidden slide and returning to the main presentation, **see** "Using Hidden Slides to Anticipate Questions," **p. 791**.

By constructing the presentation in this way, if someone asks the question, "How did our students find out about these classes?" you can click the question mark icon, give the answer, and continue with your presentation. If nobody asks the question, you don't click the question mark icon, and the presentation proceeds normally—the second slide will never appear.

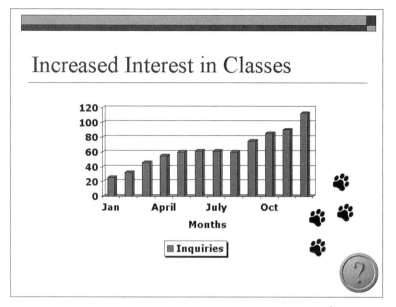

Figure 25.8

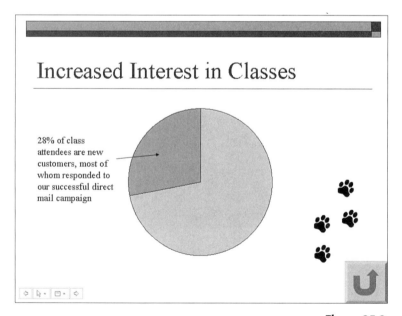

Figure 25.9

ADVANCED TASKS AND FEATURES

CHAPTER **26**

USING MACROS TO AUTOMATE OFFICE TASKS

In this chapter

GETTING STARTED WITH MACROS

Office *macros* are small computer programs that perform tasks on your behalf. And when we say small, we mean very small. A skilled programmer can create a macro that does something meaningful with just a few lines of program code, written in the underlying programming language of Office, Visual Basic for Applications (VBA).

You don't have to be a programmer to create powerful macros using Office. Using Word, Excel, or PowerPoint, you can turn on a macro recorder. As you perform a series of tasks, the recorder captures the effect of your clicks and keystrokes in a macro that you can play back later to perform the same task.

The more you know about macros and VBA, the more you're able to use them effectively. In this chapter, we explain how macros work, how to troubleshoot recorded macros, how to use the VBA editor, and how to manage a collection of macros.

WHAT CAN YOU DO WITH A MACRO?

Most of the time, you use the individual programs that make up Microsoft Office interactively—typing text, inserting graphics, formatting, saving, and printing. That's fine when you're creating new content, but it's no fun at all when you have to perform the same task regularly. Even a procedure that requires only three or four mouse clicks can become unbearable if you have to repeat it several times a day. The problem is even more acute if you perform any weekly tasks using Word or Excel where the step-by-step instructions are so complicated you have to print out a "cheat sheet." If you have any such complicated task on your daily or weekly to-do list, you're a prime candidate to create a macro that automates that task using a single command.

Macros can be surprisingly short—even a one-line macro can perform helpful tasks—or they can run for hundreds of lines, with loops and variables and input boxes, and other elements you normally associate with a full-fledged programming language. You don't need to be a programmer to automate much of your work with macros. All you need is a basic understanding of the underlying application and a willingness to step through a few lines of code.

With rare exceptions, you can create a macro to automate any task you can do manually in Word, Excel, or PowerPoint. (Automating Outlook is far more difficult, partially because it lacks a macro recorder and partially because the rules for writing macros collide head-on with the security restrictions that are an essential part of the program. For that reason, we don't discuss Outlook macros in this book and don't recommend that anyone but certified VBA experts even attempt to create them.)

Macros are ideal for automating routine drudge work—those everyday tasks that normally require multiple menu selections and mouse clicks. For example, you can use macros to do any of the following tasks:

- Print letters and companion envelopes for a mailing—selecting the correct paper trays for letterhead, additional pages, and envelopes.

- Apply complex formatting rules—everything from scanning reports to ensuring that all "Level 1" headings start with a number, to validating the searchable keywords in a memo, to correcting common typographical mistakes such as two spaces following a period.

- Collate and aggregate worksheets, complete with charts and custom pivot tables, based on Excel spreadsheets submitted by individuals working on separate parts of the project. When changes come, roll the new numbers into the master report in minutes.

- Retrieve data from an Excel membership list and generate letters in Word for all members who haven't signed up for an upcoming event or who haven't paid their annual dues.

You can use macros for simple tasks, such as toggling a group of Word or Excel settings for a specific task, or for complex document assembly processes. You can assign a macro to a toolbar button, a keyboard shortcut, or a menu command.

After you create a macro, you can share it with others by distributing the template in which the macro is stored. Those using the macro only need to know that clicking the button, or choosing the menu item, creates the report. They needn't know a thing about macros or VBA, or even how to modify their toolbars or menus. You can do it all for them, easily, with a macro.

→ For more information about Word templates, **see** "Managing Styles and Templates," **p. 465**.

WHAT SHOULDN'T YOU DO WITH MACROS?

Each individual Office program includes features that help you automate tasks without having to use macros. When there's a good alternative to writing a custom macro, the alternative is almost always preferable:

- For inserting boilerplate text into documents, workbooks, or slides, it's usually more efficient to use AutoCorrect or AutoText entries.

- Before you write a custom macro to find and replace characters, try Word's extremely capable Find feature.

- Excel's automatic data-entry and list-management features can help you accomplish many complex tasks without having to work with VBA code.

→ For hints on how to bring in boilerplate text, **see** "Using AutoCorrect to Type Faster," **p. 98**.
→ To tailor a Find in Word, **see** "Finding and Replacing Text and Other Parts of a Document," **p. 345**.

VBA BASICS

Visual Basic for Applications version 6.3 is a key component of Office 2003. It's a *development environment*—the place where programmers write and test programs. VBA is included with Office, at no additional cost. Even if you have no programming experience, you can leverage your knowledge of Office applications to learn VBA programming techniques on the side.

26

VBA contains an internal hierarchy that enables you to organize and manage your programs. At the lowest level, the individual *macros* (more accurately, *procedures*: snippets of programming code in subroutines and functions) do the work. Groups of procedures get organized into modules. Modules can then combine with custom dialog boxes that a macro programmer creates (VBA calls them *UserForms*) to make up a *project*. When things happen to a dialog box (say, the user types something, or clicks a button), procedures respond to the actions. In addition, procedures can change the contents of the dialog boxes, and make them appear and disappear (see Figure 26.1).

Figure 26.1
VBA's basic internal hierarchy enables you to organize and manage your programs.

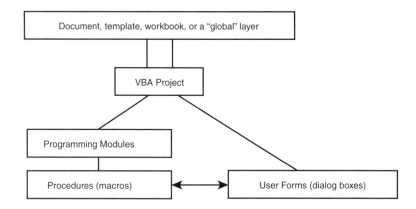

The project is then attached to a document, template, workbook, or presentation—depending on which Office application you're using. In Word, Excel, and PowerPoint, VBA projects don't have an independent existence; they're always attached to a document, template, workbook, or presentation.

If you don't plan to become a VBA programmer, you can forget about all projects, modules, and forms and just create individual macros that are tied to individual documents, templates, or workbooks.

USING THE VISUAL BASIC EDITOR

The *Visual Basic Editor* (see Figure 26.2) is the tool you use to view and edit Office macros.

To open the Visual Basic Editor in any Office program, choose Tools, Macro, Visual Basic Editor. The Visual Basic Editor sits in its own window, separate from the Office application that opened it. For the simple tasks that we describe in this chapter, you'll use only the code window, where you can see the code created by the macro recorder and directly edit it. If you're interested in exploring the editor in more detail, use its excellent Help files.

Project Explorer   Code window

Figure 26.2
The Visual Basic
Editor usually con-
tains two "dockable,"
resizable panes, plus
a large open area for
writing programs and
creating custom
dialog boxes.

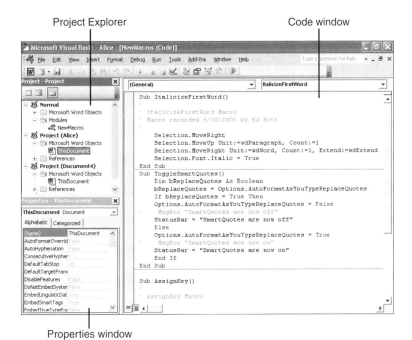

Properties window

HOW OFFICE APPLICATIONS STORE MACROS

No two Office applications handle macros the same way. Although the precise details are
complex, here's a quick summary of how each Office application stores macros:

- **Word**—Word can store macros in documents, templates, or the global template known
  as Normal.dot. When you open a document, macros in its associated template become
  available. If you store templates in the Office11\Startup folder, Word gives you access
  to macros stored in those templates whenever you start Word.

→ For details on template locations, **see** "Where Does Word Store Templates?," **p. 465**.

- **Excel**—Excel stores macros in workbooks or templates. Unlike Word, Excel does *not*
  maintain a link between a workbook and the template you use to create it; if you add or
  edit a macro in a template, that macro is available only in new workbooks you create
  with that template. Excel automatically opens all workbooks in the Office11\Xlstart
  folder when it starts, including the hidden workbook Personal.xls. Thus, all macros in
  Personal.xls are available all the time.

→ For details on templates, **see** "Customizing Excel," **p. 552**.

- **PowerPoint**—PowerPoint stores macros in presentations and templates. Like Excel,
  PowerPoint uses templates only to create new files, so adding or editing macros in a
  template will not affect existing presentations based on that template. PowerPoint does
  not have a Startup folder or anything resembling a global template. Macros written or
  recorded in earlier versions of PowerPoint should work in PowerPoint 2003.

→ To understand the role of templates in PowerPoint, **see** "PowerPoint File Types," **p. 702**.

26

CAUTION

> Unless you're a skilled programmer, avoid trying to automate anything but the most routine PowerPoint tasks with VBA. Compared with Word and Excel, its ability to help you with everyday tasks is incomplete. There's no easy way to copy macros from one presentation to another short of copying and pasting code in the Visual Basic Editor. The lack of a global template makes it difficult to manage macros, and there is precious little documentation unless you dive into the Visual Basic Editor.

- **Outlook**—Outlook stores all of its macros in one place, and all macros are available all the time. Outlook does not support recorded macros, and security restrictions make many of its features difficult for all but experienced programmers to work with. We don't recommend trying to create or edit Outlook macros unless you're a skilled programmer.

USING OBJECT MODELS

The fundamental building blocks of VBA remain the same, no matter which application you're using. An IF statement in VBA/Word, for example, works like an IF statement in VBA/Excel. That's one of VBA's great strengths, for as soon as you learn VBA with one Office application, you can apply much of what you know to other Office applications—or even to non-Microsoft applications, such as AutoCAD, which use VBA as their macro language.

Still, VBA has to accommodate the differences in each application. You work with words, sentences, and bookmarks in Word, you use formulas, cells, and ranges in Excel, and you work with tables and reports in Access. Those parts of VBA that differ between applications are embodied in the *object model* for that application. The object model provides the means for working with an application.

Word's object model, for example, includes objects that let you create and change documents, paragraphs, and footnotes. Excel's object model works with workbooks, charts, and pivot fields. PowerPoint's object model has presentations, slides, and sound effects. Outlook's object model includes contacts and e-mail messages. FrontPage actually has two object models, one for web pages themselves (with tags, themes, Webs, and the like) and the other for the FrontPage editor (with styles, text, and tables). The Access object model has reports, forms, and images.

The object model is important because it defines precisely how VBA can interact with an application. That, in turn, imposes limitations on how the macro recorder can work, because the recorder must generate a valid VBA program.

RECORDING SIMPLE MACROS

Word, Excel, and PowerPoint all allow you to record macros. (Although Outlook lacks a macro recorder, you can record macros while creating a message if you've configured the program to use Word as its e-mail editor.)

In theory, when you turn on the macro recorder, VBA "watches" as you perform some action or series of actions. When you turn off the recorder, you can replay the resulting recorded macro to replicate that series of actions.

In practice, you'll more often use the macro recorder to eliminate the tedious steps of creating a macro. Unfortunately, a recorded macro rarely solves a real-world problem by itself. After recording a macro, you'll typically need to make some modifications.

You can also use the recorder to capture the steps of a particular task, and then copy all or part of the recorded macro into a larger macro.

HOW THE MACRO RECORDER CAPTURES ACTIONS

As anyone who's used the Office *macro recorder* for more than a few minutes can tell you, the macro recorder can't record every single action you take. There are two fundamental reasons why the recorder can fail:

- The action you take might not have an exact translation in the application's object model. For example, if you record a macro in PowerPoint to change first-level bullet points in a presentation to 18-point bold, the macro won't work because PowerPoint's object model doesn't include commands for working with first-level bullet points.

CAUTION

> This type of failure, generally completely undocumented, happens without any warning to you. The recorder doesn't stop; there's no other feedback. You know the failure occurred only because the macro fails to work when you play it back.

- The action you take might be ambiguous; in other words, the recorder might not be able to tell exactly what you want to do. For example, if you type this paragraph into a new, blank Word document and use the mouse to select it, the VBA/Word macro recorder has no way of knowing what you're trying to do. Are you selecting the current paragraph? Or are you selecting the first paragraph that starts with the word "The"? Maybe you really want to select the tenth paragraph in the document. Or the first one with more than a hundred words. That's why the recorder usually won't record mouse actions—there's just too much ambiguity, most of the time, when you use the mouse.

26

After you turn on the macro recorder, it records the effect of your actions, not the actions themselves. The full effect of your actions goes into the recorded macro, not the means you used to apply them. For example:

- If you choose File, Open, type mydoc, and click OK, the recorder notes that you opened Mydoc.doc—not that you went through all the clicking.
- If you choose Format, Font, and change the font to Wingdings, the recorder records the fact that you changed the font to Wingdings—but it also picks up all the other formatting settings that happened to be set by default in the Font dialog box, including font size, bold, italic, underline, and so on.

- If you open a dialog box, navigate to a specific tab, and then stop recording the macro, the recorder ignores your actions because you didn't actually *do* anything. You can't use this technique to automate the process of opening a specific dialog box to make a selection.

- If your insertion point is inside a paragraph in a Word document, and you want to tell the recorder to select the first word in that paragraph, double-clicking the first word in the paragraph will not work. If you try to double-click the first word in the paragraph, the recorder won't let you do it. The recorder can't record your double-click action because it's ambiguous: You know that you want to select the first word in the current paragraph, but there's no way to specify that precisely by clicking with the mouse. For all the recorder knows, you might want to select the 50th word on the page, or the 1st word on the 10th line, or the last capitalized word in the paragraph.

When recording, instead of using the mouse, you'll frequently have to resort to obscure keyboard navigation keys. To move to the beginning of the current paragraph in Word, press Ctrl+↑. To select the word to the right of the insertion point (the first word in the paragraph, if you previously moved to the beginning of the paragraph), press Ctrl+Shift+→. To italicize the word, press Ctrl+I.

TIP FROM

ER & Woody

Nobody, but nobody, memorizes all of Word's obscure key combinations. To create a lengthy document listing them all, click Tools, Macro, Macros, type `listcommands`, and press Enter. Click Current Menu and Keyboard Settings, and then OK. Unfortunately, there's no easy equivalent for PowerPoint or Excel.

RECORDING A MACRO

Word, Excel, and PowerPoint include simple macro recorders that all work in essentially the same way. To record a macro in Word, for example, follow these steps:

1. Create a new document or open an existing document.

2. Choose Tools, Macro, Record New Macro. In the Record Macro dialog box (see Figure 26.3), click in the Macro Name box and type a name (`ItalicizeFirstWord`, in this example).

Figure 26.3
Replace the generic Macro1 name with a descriptive macro name, but don't use spaces or punctuation marks.

NOTE
> Macro names can contain up to 255 letters and numbers, but no spaces or other punctuation marks. Names must start with a letter, and cannot duplicate certain reserved names (for example, cell addresses in Excel).

3. Choose a location for the macro (the current document or a template, for example). If you want to assign the macro to a keyboard shortcut or toolbar button, click the respective button. (You can change either shortcut assignment after the macro has been recorded. See the "Troubleshooting" section at the end of this chapter.) The Description box includes the name of the currently logged-on user, along with the current date; if you wish, you can enter additional explanatory text about the macro. Click OK to begin recording.

4. You'll see the Recording pointer, which includes a picture of a cassette tape beneath the familiar arrow. In addition, the Stop Recording toolbar appears on the screen (the Excel and PowerPoint versions of this toolbar are slightly different, but both include a Stop Recording button). Perform any actions you want to record in your macro.

5. Click the Stop Recording button on the Stop Recording toolbar.

To record macros in Excel and PowerPoint, follow the same steps.

TESTING THE MACRO

After recording a macro, it's essential that you test it to see whether it works the way you expect. To quickly run a Word macro, follow these steps:

1. Open a document or create a new document. If necessary, click to position the insertion point at an appropriate location in the document.

CAUTION
> Don't use a "live" document when testing. Always work with a backup copy or a dummy document you create just for testing.

2. To run the macro, choose Tools, Macro, Macros. You'll see the Macros dialog box shown in Figure 26.4.

3. Click the name of the macro you want to run and press Enter or click Run. If all goes well, the macro performs the task you intended.

4. For more complete troubleshooting, click in another location within the document, and repeat steps 1–3.

Using the Macro dialog box lets you run all currently available macros, regardless of which program you're using. If you're going to use the macro regularly, it's easier to assign the macro to a menu or a keyboard shortcut, as we explain later in this chapter.

Figure 26.4

All available macros appear in the Macros dialog box.

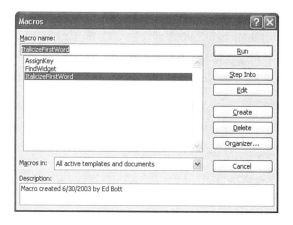

TROUBLESHOOTING RECORDED MACROS

Macros rarely work right the first time. Recorded macros, in particular, frequently require some tweaking before they work as intended. If the macro you recorded doesn't work, re-record it and see whether you can use a different method for accomplishing the same result. Edit a recorded macro only when it works most of the time, but occasionally fails to work the way you expect, or triggers an error message.

STEPPING THROUGH AND EDITING RECORDED MACROS

Fortunately, Office makes it relatively easy to edit a recorded macro. It even supports you in your bug-extermination efforts by allowing you to run the macro program one line at a time, and see what the effect of each command might be. Here's how to use the Visual Basic Editor to step through a macro recorded in Word (the steps in Excel and PowerPoint are virtually identical):

1. Create a new document or open an existing document and position the insertion point as necessary. For example, to test a macro that italicizes the first word in a paragraph, be sure to click inside a paragraph in the current document.

2. Choose Tools, Macro, Macros. Select the name of the macro you want to troubleshoot, and click Step Into. The Visual Basic Editor opens, with your macro visible in the right pane (see Figure 26.5). You'll see a large yellow arrow appear to the left of the Sub line, and the Sub line will be highlighted.

3. Arrange the windows on your desktop so you can see both the program (in this case, Word) and the Visual Basic Editor at the same time (see Figure 26.6). Click the window holding the Visual Basic Editor.

4. To begin executing the VBA code one step at a time, press F8, or choose Debug, Step Into. The first line of the macro—the Sub line—executes.

5. Press F8 again, and watch carefully as the macro performs the next actions; repeat this process, one command at a time.

6. When you reach the End Sub line, the Visual Basic Editor stops. You can start all over again, if you like, beginning with step 4.

Figure 26.5
When you step into a macro for trouble-shooting, the line that's about to be run appears highlighted.

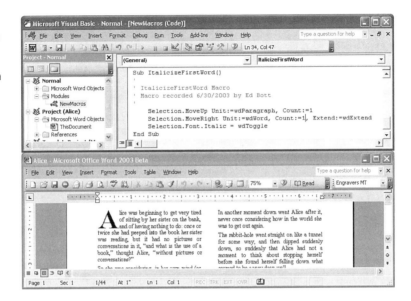

Figure 26.6
By default, recorded VBA/Word macros show up as sub-routines (beginning with the word Sub) in the Normal project's NewMacros module.

26

Frequently, you'll be able to identify the location of the problem (or problems) in a macro by stepping through it in this way. Although the solution might not be at all clear—there are lots of VBA commands, and each one behaves in a different way—being able to narrow the problem down to a line or two can make a huge difference.

After you isolate the line that you suspect is causing the problem, position the insertion point within that line and press F1. That action brings up context-sensitive VBA Help, which might present a possible solution.

Follow the same procedures to step through VBA/Excel and VBA/PowerPoint macros; you'll find recorded macros in the current workbook or presentation, in a module called Module1. Press F8 to step through the macro.

COMMON RECORDED MACRO MISTAKES

When a recorded macro doesn't work as you expect, chances are the problem is one of several common errors. Table 26.1 lists common mistakes and suggested troubleshooting steps.

TABLE 26.1 COMMON MACRO PROBLEMS

Macro Error	Troubleshooting Suggestion
A key combination doesn't work the way you thought it would.	Many navigation keys have easy-to-understand descriptions (select next word, or move down one paragraph), but they behave oddly in unusual circumstances—inside a Word table, cell, or at the end of a document, for example. Find a different key combination that accomplishes the same task in a slightly different way.
Formatting commands overwrite existing formatting.	When you apply formatting using the Format menu, the application might replace all formatting with the new format. If you want to add the new formatting—for example, bold-facing a word while leaving intact other attributes, such as italic—use shortcut keys to apply formatting (Ctrl+B to apply bold).
A repeating macro doesn't do the entire job.	Recorded macros rarely incorporate the kind of repetition you anticipate. To create a macro that loops properly, you almost always have to edit it manually. (One exception—Replace All will loop through an entire document, worksheet or presentation.)

In addition, any number of unusual circumstances can trigger errors in recorded macros. For example, if you search for the word "widget" in a document where that word is in a footer and not in the body of the document, the search will succeed. When you record that action in a VBA/Word macro, everything appears to work just fine. But when you play back the recorded macro in the same document, Word won't find the word you're looking for no matter how many times you run it—in fact, it will trigger a Run Time Error. The recorded version of the Find operation works differently from the interactive version when it comes to footers.

TESTING AND BULLET-PROOFING MACROS

Just because a macro appears to work in a handful of simple tests doesn't mean that the macro will work correctly all the time. Word macros are notorious for working properly inside simple documents, but failing—without any warning whatsoever—when run on a table, or in text boxes, or on pictures, or in a document with Track Changes enabled, in headers and footers, comments, footnotes, and on and on. It can be devilishly difficult to find the problems and, once found, to figure out how to fix them.

Will your recorded macro work properly every time you run it? Frankly, there's no way to know for sure—VBA macros hardly fall into the category of "provably correct" computer programs—but you can improve the odds of a macro working correctly by employing two time-honored testing techniques:

- Trace through the logic. In most cases, that means stepping through the macro, as explained earlier in this section. Watch for behavior or settings that you don't understand.

- Test it in a wide variety of circumstances. Try to think of odd situations that might make the macro fail, and then see whether it does. Ask a friend to test a macro, if possible, because testers will think of situations that just don't occur to you.

For example, the ItalicizeFirstWord macro example (in the "Recording a Macro" section earlier in this chapter) should italicize the first word in the current paragraph, but in one particular case it won't. When the insertion point is at the beginning of a paragraph, this macro italicizes the first word of the *preceding* paragraph. Running through the macro a step at a time reveals that the culprit is the MoveUp command; when you point to that command and press F1, the context-sensitive help suggests several examples. The solution? You have to MoveRight once before performing a MoveUp, to stay in the original paragraph.

The recorded ItalicizeFirstWord macro contains a second problem as well. When you run the macro, and then leave the insertion point in the same paragraph and run the macro again, it *removes* the italic formatting from the first word. Stepping through the macro again lets us see the problem: The Selection.Font.Italic line toggles the italic attribute on and off. According to the Help file, the Italic property "can be set to `True`, `False`, or `wdToggle`." Changing the value from `wdToggle` to `True` causes it to work properly.

When you modify the ItalicizeFirstWord macro so that it looks like the one in Figure 26.7, you'll find that both problems have disappeared.

Figure 26.7
Compare this code to the contents of Figure 26.6. Two small changes ensure that the recorded macro works properly.

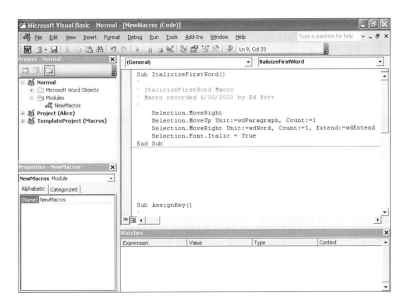

26

RUNNING MACROS

Although each of the Office programs offers myriad ways to run macros, three simple methods in Word, Excel, or PowerPoint will get you going:

- Choose Tools, Macro, Macros to open the Macros dialog box, which contains a list of all currently available macros. Use this technique for macros you run only infrequently.

- Before you start recording a macro, you can choose to assign the macro to a menu (Word only) or a specific key combination (Word or Excel).

- After recording a macro, you can assign it to a menu, a toolbar button, or a key combination.

→ For details on setting up macros as menu items, **see** "Customizing Built-In Menus," **p. 43**.

In addition, you can set macros to run each time you start a program. For example, you can record a macro that maximizes the Excel window whenever you start Excel. Or you can set up a macro to run every time you open or close a specific document. You can assign a macro to a picture or a piece of text, or set up a macro to run at a specific time. Your macros can even take over built-in Office functions such as printing.

MANAGING MACROS

All of the main Office programs include built-in tools for creating and deleting macros:

1. Choose Tools, Macro, Macros, and you'll see the Macros dialog box (see Figure 26.8).

Figure 26.8
If more than one document, template, workbook, or presentation is open, you can narrow down the list of macros by making a choice in the Macros In box.

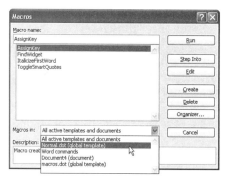

2. To create a new, empty macro, type a name for the new macro, choose a location for it in the Macros In box, and click Create. VBA creates a new subroutine with the given name, and puts you in the Visual Basic Editor, ready to start typing your macro.

Word places newly created macros in a module called NewMacros. Excel and PowerPoint put them in modules called Module1, Module2, and so on. If you want to place your new macro in a specific module, use the Visual Basic Editor.

TIP FROM

EQ & Woody

> If you want to easily copy and move individual macros in Word, you'll want to move them out of the NewMacros module and give them their own module.

3. To delete a macro, click the macro's name and click Delete.

Of all the Office applications, only Word provides any tools for copying and moving macros—and even then, you have to move or copy an entire module full of macros at a time. To copy a VBA/Word module or UserForm (custom dialog box) from one document or *template* to another, or to delete or rename a module or UserForm:

1. Choose Tools, Macro, Macros, and click the Organizer button. The Word Organizer opens (see Figure 26.9).

Figure 26.9
The Word Organizer can copy or move modules or UserForms—so-called "macro project items"—but not individual macros.

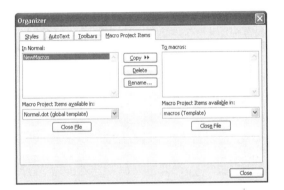

2. Click the Macro Project Items tab. You'll see a list of all modules and UserForms in the current document (on the left side of the dialog box) and in the Normal "global" template (on the right side of the dialog box).

→ For detailed information on how to work with Normal.dot, **see** "Customizing the Normal Document Template," **p. 459**.

3. If necessary, select different "from" and "to" documents or templates from the Macro Project Items Available In boxes. (Note that you can copy in either direction, left-to-right, or right-to-left.) If the document or template isn't available in these lists, click Close File, and then click Open File and select the correct document or template.

4. Click once to select the module or UserForm you want to copy, delete, or rename, and then click the appropriate button to complete the action (the arrows on the Copy button show you which file you'll copy from and to). Note that you cannot move a module in a single action: You must copy it, and then delete it.

Modules often contain more than one macro, and the Word Organizer won't tell you the names of the macros in a module. Be careful that you don't copy or delete the wrong macros, or rename the wrong module.

26

CAUTION

If you use macros that are confidential or proprietary, be sure you know what macros are in a module before you copy and distribute it. Because the individual macro names never appear in the Organizer, it's easier to make a mistake than you might think.

 If you're stumbling over roadblocks when trying to distribute a Word macro (or module) to other people, see the "Troubleshooting" section at the end of this chapter.

To copy, move, delete, or rename an individual macro in Word, Excel, PowerPoint, Outlook, Publisher, or FrontPage, you have to use the Visual Basic Editor, as described in the next section.

MACRO SECURITY

Macros can save time and energy, but an ill-conceived macro can (intentionally or unintentionally) destroy data and otherwise wreak havoc. For example, a macro that automates file management tasks by deleting old files could inadvertently wipe out a whole folder full of files if you don't define its parameters carefully.

You can have a high degree of confidence in macros you write yourself, but you should never trust a macro you receive from someone you've never met. Word macro viruses, especially the notorious Melissa virus, were all the range in the late 1990s. Today, they're no longer a critical security concern, but new varieties still appear on occasion. You run the risk of encountering this type of malware every time you open a document, workbook, or presentation that comes from an outside source.

What is a *macro virus*, and how likely are you to encounter one? Here are some simple facts every Office user should know:

- A computer "virus" is just a program that propagates. A macro virus uses a macro language (such as VBA or VBScript) as the means of propagating. A large percentage of macro viruses aren't harmful in any way.

- Some viruses corrupt data in subtle ways by rearranging words and phrases in documents, or adding the word "not" in random locations. The payload of the relatively obscure W97M.Thus.AJ virus actually encrypted the first 32KB of any open Word file, rendering it unreadable and unrecoverable. These are the most insidious viruses because, without full and detailed backups, it's nearly impossible to restore documents to their original state.

- Other serious macro viruses erase selected data files or groups of files from your hard drive. They may also attempt to delete key program files or alter the Windows registry.

- You're far more likely to receive an infected file from a coworker, a friend, or a network server than by downloading documents from the Internet. Similarly, you are far more likely to lose data due to a dumb mistake or a hardware problem than to a macro virus.

26

- Most macro viruses were originally written for Office 97. Security changes in Office versions since that time have made it impossible for a macro virus to run without significant actions on the user's part.

- Almost all virus scares are precisely that—scares—with little or no foundation in reality.

The vast majority of macro viruses rank as amateurish and poorly written, and can hardly survive in the wild. Some, however, have proven themselves robust—and destructive. For the most part, as we'll see in the next section, Office 2003 protects you from virtually all macro viruses—even those you author yourself—unless you go to extraordinary lengths to remove this protection.

USING DIGITAL SIGNATURES TO VERIFY A MACRO'S SOURCE

Office 2003 includes a number of innovative methods to help protect you from macro viruses. *Digital signatures* lie at the heart of the approach most frequently encountered by Office users.

A digital signature identifies the source of a macro. Developers must apply for digital signatures from *certifying authorities*, which verify the identity of developers before issuing them a signature. Certifying authorities can revoke a certificate after issuing it, if they discover evidence that a developer is distributing viruses or unsafe software.

When you use Word, Excel, PowerPoint, or Outlook to open a data file that contains digitally signed macros, you'll see a Security Warning dialog box that contains information about the signature and asks whether you want to enable the macros. Figure 26.10 shows the options available when you try to load a Word template that contains a digitally signed macro project on a computer where macro security is at its default setting, High (see the following section for a discussion of Office macro security levels).

26

Figure 26.10
When your security settings are on High, you can't enable macros until you confirm that you always want to trust the author of those macros—the "publisher," in Office terms.

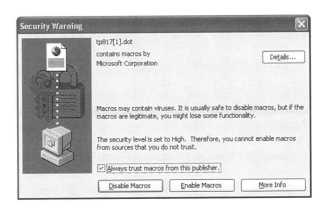

If you select the Always Trust Macros from This Publisher check box, Office adds that digital signature to its Trusted Publishers list. From that point on, you will be able to open signed macros from that source without having to click through a dialog box.

By contrast, when your macro security is set to High and you try to load an unsigned macro, all Office programs refuse to allow you to open the macros at all. In the case of Word, the Enable Macros button is disabled. In Excel, you see the dialog box shown in Figure 26.11, which explains your options.

Figure 26.11

With macro security set to High, Excel refuses to open any macros that aren't digitally signed.

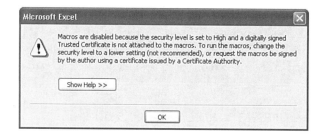

How do you decide whether to trust a publisher? Use your judgment, and err on the side of suspicion. A digital signature identifies the company (or person) that claims to have written a macro. It does *not* tell you anything about the author. A macro signed "A-Z Developers Inc." could have originated with a terrorist in Timbuktu. Similarly, certificates can be generated with any name, so if you find a macro signed "Bill Gates" on the website http://www.virusheaven.com, you should doubt its veracity. It's up to you to decide whether you trust the company (or person) that signed the macro.

You can inspect the contents of the certificate by clicking the Details button on the Security Warning dialog box. The signature contains a wealth of information. Click the View Certificate button to follow the chain of trust back to the original certifying authority and decide whether you can safely trust this source.

After installing a certificate, you can revisit the Security dialog box, click the Trusted Publishers tab, and view the details about that certificate. If you decide that it wasn't such a good idea to trust that source after all, click the Remove button to remove the installed certificate.

CONFIGURING OFFICE SECURITY LEVELS

Digital signatures work in conjunction with each application's *security level* to determine which macros will or will not run. In Word, Excel, PowerPoint, and Outlook, you have a choice of four different security levels (see Table 26.2). For example, you might decide it's OK to run any macro in a template you download from Microsoft's Office Online site (http://www.microsoft.com/office), because you know it was tested carefully before being made available for download. On the other hand, you probably never want to run a macro you receive from a completely unknown source on the Internet. To open the Security dialog box (see Figure 26.12), choose Tools, Macro, Security.

Figure 26.12
If you understand the implications of digital code signing and the possible threat from macro viruses, the Medium setting will generally suffice.

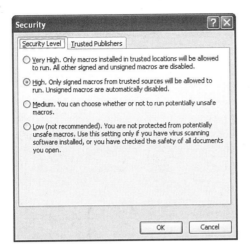

TABLE 26.2 OFFICE 2003 SECURITY LEVELS

Security Level	Macro Restrictions
Very High	Signed and unsigned macros are allowed to run only if the Trust All Installed Add-ins and Templates option (on the Trusted Publishers tab) is selected and the macros are stored in a specific trusted folder on your local hard disk. This option is primarily for use on corporate networks or by programmers.
High	Only valid digitally signed macros from a previously identified "trusted source" will run automatically. If the macro is signed, but the source isn't listed as a "trusted source," you will be given the opportunity to accept or reject the certificate (refer to Figure 26.12) and add the source to the trusted list. In all other cases, macros are disabled.
Medium	Much like the High setting, except that users have the option to enable or disable macros if there's a problem with the signature (for example, it was incorrectly applied), or if there's no signature at all.
Low	All macros are enabled, without regard to the presence of a digital signature.

The default security setting in Word, Excel, PowerPoint, and Outlook is High.

TIP FROM

EQ & Woody

Consider setting Word and Excel security to Medium. If you leave this option set on High, Word and Excel discard unsigned macros, and you'll never know they existed.

BLOCKING ACCESS TO THE VISUAL BASIC PROJECT

Most macro viruses propagate by creating copies of themselves: They build macros attached to documents, which, in turn, infect other Office users. To create a copy, the virus has to be

26

able to get at the part of VBA that's used to write new programs. The virus then proceeds in a manner that's similar to what you would use to write or record a macro, except the virus does it all by using programs.

The part of VBA that's used to build new macros (and modify old ones) is called the Visual Basic Project.

Office 2003 automatically prevents programs from getting into the Visual Basic Project unless you specifically, deliberately allow macros to get in. You can only allow macros access to the Visual Basic Project if you choose Tools, Macro, Security, click the Trusted Publishers tab, and select the Trust Access to Visual Basic Project check box (see Figure 26.13).

Figure 26.13
Unless you have a specific reason to allow macros to create and modify other macros, leave the Trust Access to Visual Basic Project check box unselected.

26

It's rare that anyone—even professional macro programmers—will grant programmatic access to the Visual Basic Project. Leaving this box unselected effectively neutralizes all macro viruses created before December 2000.

PROTECTING YOUR PC AND NETWORK FROM VIRUSES

Office 2003 incorporates virus-detection technology that allows antivirus programs to "hook into" Office; an up-to-date antivirus program that includes this hook can examine a file for viruses before allowing an Office program to open the file. (That's why you'll frequently see the message "Requesting a virus scan" at the bottom of an application's window whenever you open a file.) This antivirus scan operates independently of digital signatures, and it has been proven effective in reducing the impact of macro viruses as well as conventional viruses that arrive as file attachments in Outlook.

It's impossible to stop every macro virus, but you can dramatically reduce the risks to your computer (and any other computers that are connected on the same network) by following these procedures:

- For Word, Excel, PowerPoint, and Outlook, keep the digital security setting on Medium for users who understand the implications of macro viruses and need to run macros from external sources. Leave this setting on High for all others.

- Purchase, install, and regularly update one of the major antivirus software packages. Make sure the program you select is compatible with Office 2003.

- Stay informed of the latest virus (and antivirus) developments. All the major antivirus software vendors maintain websites with up-to-the-minute news: The Symantec Security Response site for Norton AntiVirus is at `http://www.symantec.com/avcenter`; the McAfee Virus Information Library is at `http://vil.nai.com/vil`.

TIP FROM

Ed & Woody

> How many times this week have you received a breathless e-mail warning you about a deadly new virus? Is the latest warning real, or the figment of someone's grossly overactive imagination? For the definitive answer, head directly to Rob Rosenberger's Virus Myths Home Page at `http://www.vmyths.com`. Rob's voice of reason stands in stark contrast to much of the mindless virus-clamoring you'll hear on the Net. And, he knows his stuff.

BUILDING INTERACTIVE VBA PROGRAMS

Some macros work by themselves, with no user intervention required. The ItalicizeFirstWord macro, which you recorded earlier in this chapter, falls into the "no hands required" category. It runs from start to finish and, except for starting it, the user doesn't have to do a thing. In fact, all recorded macros run without any user intervention, because the recorder doesn't have the intelligence necessary to know when to pause for user input when it's required.

More powerful macros interact with the outside world—for example, a macro might stop and let you select a file from a browse box, or display a message and wait for you to click OK. You can also set up timers to let a macro pause for a predetermined amount of time—to display a message without requiring the user to click OK, for example.

Here's how to create a simple macro that requires user intervention. It just counts to five:

1. In Word, Excel, or PowerPoint, choose Tools, Macro, Macros. In the Macro Name box, type **Counter** and click Create. VBA creates a subroutine called Counter, as shown in Figure 26.14.

2. Type the code you see in Figure 26.15. Take advantage of the Auto features of the Visual Basic Editor when it offers to complete a line for you.

3. Now run the program by clicking the Run Sub/User Form button.

The Office application should respond by displaying a series of five message boxes, with the numbers between 1 and 5, as in Figure 26.16.

Figure 26.14
VBA (in this case, VBA/PowerPoint) puts together all the details you need to get started with the macro called Counter.

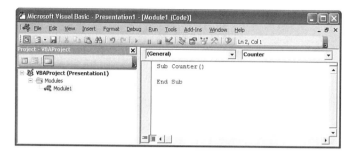

Figure 26.15
The program loops five times, each time showing the current value of i in a message box.

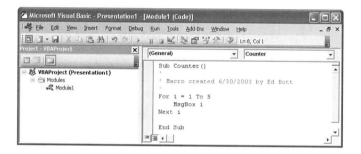

Figure 26.16
When run in PowerPoint, Counter's message boxes all display the title "Microsoft PowerPoint."

Each time the box appears, the macro stops and waits for the user to click OK. After the message box has been cleared, the macro picks back up where it left off.

In VBA parlance, clicking OK is an *event*—something that happens outside the macro program itself. In this case, the Counter macro responds to the event of an OK click by continuing in its loop.

Windows lives and dies by events. In fact, events lie at the heart of interactive Windows programs in general, and VBA programs in particular: If the user clicks *this* (say, a Cancel button), the program should do *that* (perhaps clear out the dialog box); if the user types something over here (such as a filename), the program should do something over there (maybe open the file). Events, and responses to events, are of paramount importance when designing and programming VBA systems that interact with a user.

You'll most often work with events when you design your own custom dialog boxes to enable the user to interact with a macro. VBA contains an extensive toolkit for constructing custom dialog boxes. You can choose from a wide variety of items—VBA calls them *controls*—and place them wherever you want on a custom dialog box.

The controls used by VBA are the same controls you use when working with Windows dialog boxes.

The more useful VBA controls are listed in Table 26.3.

TABLE 26.3   CUSTOM DIALOG BOX CONTROLS

Name	Description
Label	Static piece of text on a custom dialog box that the user can't change.
Text Box	Location set aside on a custom dialog box where the user is permitted to type in text.
Command Button	A button the user can click. OK and Cancel are the two most common kinds of command buttons, but you can create command buttons of any size, containing any descriptive text.
Check Box	A box the user can check or clear to make a yes-or-no choice.
Option Button	Also known as a radio button, designed to enable the user to pick one and only one option from several alternatives. You set up option buttons in a group on your custom dialog box: As soon as the user clicks one of the option buttons in the group, all the others get cleared out automatically by VBA.
List Box	Drop-down list of several options. The user clicks the down arrow to the right of the list, and can pick, at the most, one.
Image	A picture. VBA lets you put pictures anywhere on a custom dialog box.

In short, any control you've ever seen in a Windows dialog box (including scrollbars, spin buttons, drop-down combo boxes, and more) are available for your use in building custom dialog boxes.

26

Table 26.4 lists some of the more common events that VBA tracks inside custom dialog boxes, and makes available to your programs. You can write pieces of VBA code to respond to the events as they occur.

TABLE 26.4   VBA EVENTS

Name of Event	What It Means
Click	If you ask it to, VBA notifies your program when the user clicks a command button, picture, or some other part of the custom dialog box.
Double-click	VBA determines when a double-click (as opposed to two single clicks) has occurred, and notifies your program accordingly.
Mouse Move	You can set up the dialog box so that VBA tells your program when the mouse has moved over a command button, picture, or anywhere else on a custom dialog box.

continues

TABLE 26.4 CONTINUED	
Name of Event	**What It Means**
Key Press	When the user presses a key—generally while the insertion point sits in a text box—you can have VBA notify your program of the fact, and tell the program which key has been pressed.

That's just the tip of the event iceberg. VBA can track and log almost any event you can conceive—anything the user might do on or to a custom dialog box that you've constructed—and send a notification to your program.

CODE SNIPPETS YOU CAN USE

Although it would take a book this size to explore the VBA object model for just one of the Office applications, most of the programming chores you'll encounter boil down to a handful of common techniques. This section gives you working code you can plug into your macros to overcome the most common problems.

USING VBA TO NAVIGATE OFFICE DOCUMENTS

One of the first tasks most beginning VBA programmers undertake is to figure out how to move around a document using VBA commands. Navigation is a fundamental capability of all the versions of VBA in Office 2003.

NAVIGATING WORD DOCUMENTS WITH VBA

In Word, you will frequently want to move the insertion point (VBA calls it the "Selection") within a document. It's easiest to understand how VBA/Word accomplishes this navigation by trying a few different VBA/Word commands, and watching what happens on the screen:

1. Open (or create) a Word document that has several paragraphs of text as a test document, so you can see what is going on with each of the different commands.

2. Bring up the VBA Editor by pressing Alt+F11. Arrange the screen so that you can see both the VBA Editor and the Word document at the same time.

3. Find a convenient project in the Project Explorer (say, MyMacros.dot or Normal) and double-click it. Navigate down to a Module. Use Insert, Procedure and create a new subroutine called Navigate.

4. In between the Sub/End Sub pair, type each of these commands, one at a time. Press F8 to step through the subroutine. Watch where the selection point ends up in the Word document:

```
Selection.HomeKey unit:=wdStory, Extend:=wdMove    'Moves to the beginning
➥of the doc
Selection.EndKey unit:=wdStory, Extend:=wdMove     'Moves to the end of the doc
Selection.MoveLeft unit:=wdCharacter, Count:=1, Extend:=wdMove 'Move left
➥one char
```

```
Selection.MoveRight unit:=wdWord, Count:=1, Extend:=wdMove 'Move right one
➥word
Selection.MoveUp unit:=wdParagraph, Count:=1, Extend:=wdMove ' Move up one
➥para
ActiveDocument.Bookmarks("test").Select  'Selects the bookmark "test"
```

NAVIGATING EXCEL WORKBOOKS WITH VBA

In Excel, you're less likely to use the insertion point, and will most frequently refer to cells by name or location. Use the method in the preceding section (working with a project such as Personal.xls or Macros.xls) to write and test each of these commands:

```
Range("A1") = "First Cell" 'Put the text "First Cell" in cell A1
Cells.SpecialCells(xlLastCell) = "Last Cell" 'Put the text "Last cell" in the last
➥used cell
Range("test").Rows(1) = "First Row" 'Put "First Row" in top cells of the range
➥"test"
Range("test").Rows(1).Columns(1) = "First Cell in test" Upper left cell of "test"
```

NAVIGATING POWERPOINT PRESENTATIONS WITH VBA

With the possible exception of Publisher, PowerPoint presents the greatest challenge in navigating the object model. For example, to change the title of the third slide to Hello, you have to resort to this kludgy technique:

```
ActivePresentation.Slides(3).Shapes.Title.TextFrame.TextRange = "Hello"
```

USING VBA TO AUGMENT FIND AND REPLACE

Another common activity, finding and replacing text from a VBA program, can be challenging. The primary difficulty lies in figuring out precisely when VBA performs the Find (or Replace) command. Much of the work in implementing a Find is in setting up all the parameters properly.

USING FIND AND REPLACE VBA CODE IN WORD

In Word, if you want to find and replace all occurrences of one string with another, you needn't resort to looping through the document. Instead, the simple VBA snippet in Listing 26.1 will suffice.

LISTING 26.1   REPLACEOLDWITHNEWSTRING

```
With ActiveDocument.Content.Find
    .ClearFormatting
    .Replacement.ClearFormatting
    .Text = "old string"
    .Replacement.Text = "new string"
    .Execute Replace:=wdReplaceAll
End With
```

26

NOTE

> Be sure to use the `.ClearFormatting` property to modify both the `Find` and `Replacement` objects. Otherwise, you might inadvertently search for formatted text using leftover settings from a previous search.

Because this succinct piece of code doesn't refer to the Selection, the user won't see the document scroll and the mouse pointer move while the macro runs. That has its advantages and disadvantages. On the plus side, the macro will run faster because the screen isn't updated each time you find the string. On the minus side, the user might think the macro has frozen her PC, because there's no visible sign of life until the macro finishes (unless the macro writes updates to, for example, the status bar).

If you want to loop through a document and count the number of occurrences of, say, "string," moving the selection as you go, use a program like that in Listing 26.2.

LISTING 26.2   COUNTOCCURRENCESOFSTRING

```
intCount = 0
'Move to the beginning of the document
Selection.HomeKey unit:=wdStory
With Selection.Find
    .ClearFormatting
    .Text = "string"
'   Find the first occurrence of "string"
    .Execute
'   Loop while "string" is found
    While .Found
'       Increment the counter
        intCount = intCount + 1
'       And look for another occurrence
        .Execute
    Wend
End With
MsgBox "Found " & Str$(intCount) & " occurrences"
```

USING FIND AND REPLACE VBA CODE IN EXCEL

In Excel, the general approach is similar. For example, to replace `"old string"` with `"new string"` in all the cells of the active worksheet, use this:

```
Cells.Replace What:="old string", Replacement:="new string", LookAt:= xlPart,
SearchOrder:=xlByRows, MatchCase:=False
```

Always explicitly include values for `LookAt` (whether Excel must match the contents of the entire cell, or if only a partial match suffices), `SearchOrder`, and `MatchCase`, to avoid picking up leftover settings from a previous Find/Replace operation.

If you want to restrict the replacing to a specific named range (such as Database), try this technique:

```
Range("Database").Replace What:="old string", Replacement:="new string",
➥LookAt:=xlPart, SearchOrder:=xlByRows, MatchCase:=False
```

USING VBA TO APPLY FORMATTING

VBA gives you full control over formatting, although the mechanics of applying formatting can be obscure. For example, if you want to change a selection of text to italic in Word or Excel, this command does the trick:

```
Selection.Font.Italic = True
```

But to turn selected text italic in PowerPoint, you have to jump through this hoop:

```
ActiveWindow.Selection.TextRange.Font.Italic = True
```

Similarly in Publisher:

```
Selection.TextRange.Font.Italic = True
```

Formatting text as you place it in a document, spreadsheet, or presentation is a more complex process. Say you want to insert this sentence into a Word document:

> Please join us at the *Heartstrings* gala.

It's easiest to "type" text into the document, interrupting the macro's typing to switch to italic and back. Listing 26.3 has the code that will do it.

LISTING 26.3   TYPEWORDFORMATTEDSTRING

```
With Selection
    .TypeText "Please join us at the "
    .Font.Italic = True
    .TypeText "Heartstrings"
    .Font.Italic = False
    .TypeText " gala."
End With
```

Excel's in-cell formatting works in a completely different way. Instead of interrupting the typing to switch to italic and back, Excel requires you to dump all the text into the cell, and then go back and make selected characters italic. To put that same sentence in the selected Excel cell, use the code in Listing 26.4.

LISTING 26.4   INSERTEXCELFORMATTEDSTRING

```
With Selection
    .Value = "Please join us at the Heartstrings gala."
    .Characters(23, 17).Font.Italic = True
End With
```

The same concepts apply in PowerPoint as in Excel, although the actual commands vary a bit, as in Listing 26.5.

26

LISTING 26.5   INSERTPOWERPOINTFORMATTEDSTRING

```
With ActiveWindow.Selection.TextRange
    .Text = "Please join us at the Heartstrings gala."
    .TextRange.Characters(23, 17).Font.Italic = True
End With
```

Publisher works similarly:

```
.TextRange.Characters(23, 17).Font.Italic = True
```

Sometimes you want to use formatting as a *selection criterion*. Say you want to loop through a Word document and make sure that all the `"Heading 4"`–style paragraphs start with the text `"(d)"`. The program in Listing 26.6 will do it.

LISTING 26.6   ADDDTOHEADING4

```
'Move to the beginning of the document
Selection.HomeKey unit:=wdStory
With Selection.Find
    .ClearFormatting
    .Style = "Heading 4"
    .Format = True
    .Text = ""
'   Find the first occurrence of "Heading 4"
    .Execute
'   Loop while "Heading 4" is found
    While .Found
'       Move to the beginning of the paragraph
        Selection.Collapse
'       Select the first three characters
        Selection.MoveRight unit:=wdCharacter, Count:=3, Extend:=wdExtend
        If Selection.Text <> "(d)" Then
            Selection.Collapse
            Selection.TypeText "(d)"
        End If
'       Move on to the next paragraph
        Selection.MoveDown unit:=wdParagraph, Count:=1
'       And look for another occurrence
        .Execute
    Wend
End With
```

The `.Format` = `True` setting in the `Find` loop in Listing 26.6 ensures that Word looks for paragraphs with the specified formatting.

USING VBA TO LOOP THROUGH COLLECTIONS

VBA abounds with *collections*. All the files currently open in an application, for example, define one common collection. Other collections include all the bookmarks in a document, or all the named ranges in a workbook.

Sometimes you know exactly which member of a collection you're trying to find. For example, the VBA/Excel command

```
Workbooks("Book1.xls").Activate
```

scans the Workbooks collection, and brings up the workbook called Book1.xls.

At other times, however, you want your program to look at all the members of a collection, one at a time, to see which one meets certain criteria. For example, you might want to loop through all the slides in a presentation to select the one with the most verbiage in a text placeholder.

The VBA command For Each enables you to step through all the members of a collection. In Word, the FontNames collection contains a list of all the fonts available in Word. Listing 26.7 shows you how to loop through the collection, displaying the name of each font in its own message box.

LISTING 26.7 DISPLAYFONTNAMES

```
'Variables in "For Each" statements must be Variants or Objects
Dim varFont As Variant
For Each varFont In FontNames
    MsgBox varFont
Next
```

After you see how For Each works, it's only a small step to write a VBA/Word program that prints a list of all the fonts available on your machine. Taking input from the user for point size and a test sentence, Listing 26.8 shows you how that might be done.

LISTING 26.8 PRINTFONTNAMES

```
Dim varFont As Variant
Dim intPoints As Integer
Dim strTestString As String
intPoints = 11
intPoints = InputBox("Print list at what point size?", "PrintFontNames",
➥intPoints)
If intPoints <= 0 Then GoTo Cancel
strTestString = "The quick brown fox jumped over to greet the lazy
➥poodle."
strTestString = InputBox("Test print text:", "PrintFontNames",
➥strTestString)
Documents.Add
Selection.TypeText "Samples at " & Str$(intPoints) & " points."
Selection.TypeParagraph
Selection.TypeParagraph
For Each varFont In FontNames
    Selection.Font.Size = 11
    Selection.Font.Name = "Arial"
    Selection.TypeText varFont & ": "
    Selection.TypeParagraph
    Selection.Font.Name = varFont
    Selection.Font.Size = intPoints
```

26

continues

LISTING 26.8   CONTINUED

```
        Selection.TypeText strTestString
        Selection.TypeParagraph
        Selection.TypeParagraph
    Next
Cancel:
```

TROUBLESHOOTING

CHANGING THE KEY COMBINATION FOR A MACRO

I recorded a macro and told Word to run it whenever I press Shift+F5. I changed my mind after discovering that Word has a built-in command already assigned to Shift+F5. How do I change the macro so it runs when I push Shift+F6, and restore Word's built-in command to Shift+F5?

Click Tools, Customize; then press the Keyboard button at the bottom of the dialog box. In the Categories list on the left, click Macros; then, in the Macros list on the right, select the name of the macro that you recorded. In the Current Keys box at the lower left, click the unwanted keyboard shortcut (in this case, Shift+F5), and then click Remove. That removes the Shift+F5 key assignment for your recorded macro and restores the assignment to Word's default command. Click in the Press New Shortcut Key box, and press Shift+F6. Click Assign; then click Close twice. Shift+F5 will revert to the old Goback function. Shift+F6 will run your recorded macro.

MISSING PERSONAL.XLS

I've looked in the Project Explorer, but I can't find my Personal Macro Workbook.

If you don't have a Personal Macro Workbook (stored as Personal.xls), the simplest way to create one is to flip back to Excel and record a do-nothing macro: click Tools, Macro, Record New Macro, and make sure you choose Personal Macro Workbook in the Store Macro In box. Click OK, and then click the Stop button. Excel automatically creates Personal.xls to store the recorded macro.

DISTRIBUTING MACROS INFORMALLY

I've created a few Word macros that I would like to share with a few friends, but every time I try, they say they're unable to open the macros. What am I doing wrong?

The biggest problem when trying to share macros is security; any time Word opens a template or a document that contains macros, it applies the current security settings. If you and your co-workers are using sensible security settings (Medium or High), Word refuses to run those macros. You can digitally sign the template (or document) to silence Word's squawks of protest, but that's overkill if all you want to do is share a few simple snippets of code. A much easier alternative is to simply copy the body of the macro into an e-mail message—

without the Sub line at the beginning and the End Sub line at the end. In the rest of the message, include these simple instructions on how to create a simple macro:

> Select the macro code and press Ctrl+C to copy it to the Clipboard. Click Tools, Macro, Macros, type in a name for the macro, and click Create. Click to position the insertion point in the blank space between Sub and End Sub and then press Ctrl+V to paste the macro code. Click File, Close and Return to Microsoft Word.

If your co-workers follow these instructions, the macro will be ready for them to use in any document, with no security warnings to bypass and no futzing around with odd files or folders.

EXTRA CREDIT: GETTING READY TO TACKLE VBA

Ready to start working with VBA? Good. Take a few moments to organize your screen and customize the Visual Basic Editor. That way, you won't have to hunt and click so much to get going. (To start the Visual Basic Editor, just start your favorite Office program and press Alt+F11.)

The behavior of the Visual Basic Editor is controlled by choosing Tools, Options and clicking the Editor tab. In particular, consider selecting the Require Variable Declaration check box. That will protect you from the single most common source of programming errors—misspellings.

If you do a lot of VBA programming, do yourself a favor and take advantage of the Windows support for multiple monitors. That way, you can keep the Visual Basic Editor window open on one monitor and view the current Office application on the other monitor. If you have only a single screen to work with, arrange your windows so that the application is in the top half of the screen and the Visual Basic Editor is in the bottom half. In either of these configurations, you can step through your program,

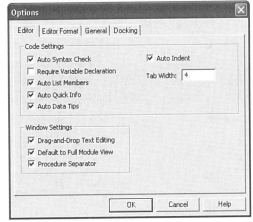

Figure 26.17

keeping track of the active command in the Visual Basic Editor window, while watching the effects of your program in the top window.

As you become more proficient, you might want to add the Immediate Window (choose View, Immediate Window) so that you can change variable values as the program runs and test unfamiliar VBA commands. You might also want to get rid of the Properties window (in the lower-left corner; View, Properties Window) if you won't be working with custom-built dialog boxes.

Even if you're new to programming and have only just begun writing your first VBA programs, you should always keep several tips in mind:

- Use lots of comments. Yes, you can remember precisely what each line of code in your program does, and what each variable's duty in life might be. But when you look at your program a year from now, it will all be gibberish unless you add a lot of comments now, while it's still fresh in your mind.

- Don't be afraid to experiment. You aren't going to break anything. The real beauty of VBA is that you can try something, see how (or whether) it works, and then try something else. Amazing things have been discovered by trial and error.

- Remember that nothing is perfect, and VBA certainly follows that rule. Although VBA itself is reasonably stable and predictable, the underlying object models in all the Office applications have lots and lots (and lots and lots) of rough edges. Go slowly, step through all your programs, and be observant.

- Test. Then test some more. Then give your program to 10 friends, and have them all test it even more. Everyone has a slightly different configuration, and odd settings can throw off even the most well-conceived program.

- Keep your sense of humor. Programming is fun. But it's also hard work. The machine isn't out to get you—even though there will certainly be days when you think it is.

- Ask questions. Nobody knows it all. And even if they did, by the time they figured out the last nuance of the last feature, they would've forgotten what they knew in the first place.

- No matter what happens, there's always another revision. VBA is a dynamic language and every new version brings some exciting new capabilities. Stay on top of the wave, and you'll be able to solve problems that would curl the hair of mere mortals.

CHAPTER **27**

USING OFFICE TO CREATE WEB PAGES

In this chapter

OFFICE AND THE WEB

You may think of Office as a way to produce letters and spreadsheets, but it's also a first-rate Web-authoring tool. Or, more precisely, it's a *collection* of great Web-authoring tools. As in previous versions, you can save just about any Office document in Web format.

With a few exceptions, you can choose to save most types of Office documents in HTML, the language of the Web. When you use HTML format, your Word documents, Excel workbooks, or PowerPoint presentations take on an extra dimension: Anyone with a compatible web browser can open the saved file and see your document just as you created it (subject to some formatting limitations, which we discuss later in this chapter); anyone who has installed the Office program that was used to create the original document can open the file for editing as well.

When you save an Office document as a web page, virtually every bit of data and formatting is preserved during the "round trip" from Office program to web page and back again. You can create and modify documents using Office programs, publish them as web pages, and know that you'll still be able to make changes to the underlying document.

Word 2003 also incorporates the capability to save "filtered" web pages, which strip away Office-specific tags and leave behind only basic HTML. This feature, which is not available in any other Office program, produces a smaller, less complex HTML file that displays approximately the same formatting as the original page; however, you lose the capability to read the file back into Word and retrieve all formatting.

TIP FROM

EQ & Woody

> Although it sounds good in theory, the filtered HTML generated by Word uses style tags that instantly identify the resulting page as having been created by Word; if you're an HTML purist and you want only bare-bones HTML tags for your website, use a different editor.

NOTE

> This chapter is designed to show how Office programs work with HTML-formatted pages. It won't make you an expert on Web-page design or managing websites. If you want to build a first-class website using Office-compatible tools, you should look at Microsoft FrontPage, a member of the Office family that includes first-rate tools for creating web pages and publishing those pages to web servers. We've used FrontPage 2003 extensively, and we can say with confidence that FrontPage 2003 is an excellent program that directly tackles many of the objections Web designers had to previous versions of FrontPage. If you're serious about Web design and you use Office, we strongly suggest you take a close look at FrontPage 2003.

USING HTML, XML, AND XHTML

HTML (Hypertext Markup Language) is the fundamental language of the Web. It defines a set of embedded instructions, called *tags*, that control how information is displayed in a browser, and how the browser is to react to certain events. For instance, the <h1> and </h1> tags mark the beginning and end of a first-level heading, which even the most rudimentary browser can render in a large, bold headline font. Because HTML files are composed of plain text, they are ideal for sharing across otherwise incompatible computer platforms.

HTML is the basic (some would say "old") technology that drives the Web: Any browser will support early versions of HTML, and most HTML pages based on the classic (read: "old") tags will display perfectly well in any browser. But like so many other components of the Web, HTML has evolved on Web time, mutating so quickly that it's difficult to keep track of the various standards from day to day.

Office applications take advantage of many *Extensible Markup Language (XML)* tags, which go well beyond the capability of standard HTML to describe and present data. Using XML, a developer can create custom tags that define any sort of data or formatting, for use on the Web and elsewhere. Whereas HTML is based on standard tags defined by the World Wide Web Consortium (W3C), XML tags can be highly customized so that they precisely fit the needs of the developer; collections of XML tags can in turn be shared as *schemas*.

Today, the integration of XML and HTML has resulted in a successor to plain-vanilla HTML called Extensible HyperText Markup Language (XHTML). Most sophisticated Web developers use XHTML to create the complex, interactive pages you see on the Web. Similarly, most advanced Office features rely on XHTML to help documents survive the round-trip between the application that created them and the browser.

NOTE

For more details on the XML standard, point your browser to the home page of the W3C XML Activity group at `http://www.w3.org/xml`. For details on the XHTML specification, see `http://www.w3.org/MarkUp`.

The following XHTML features in particular are key to the ability of Office programs to save documents in Web formats:

- *XML namespaces* specify the location of schemas that define the custom tags used in a document. In the case of Office 2003, the XLM namespace declaration looks something like this:
  ```
  <html xmlns:o="urn:schemas-microsoft-com:office:office"
  xmlns:w="urn:schemas-microsoft-com:office:word"
  xmlns="http://www.w3.org/TR/REC-html40">
  ```

- *Style sheets* allow a Web designer to specify exactly how the browser should interpret a tag. Style sheets can be embedded directly in a page, or they can be saved in a separate file and *attached* to a page or an entire site. If you visit a site whose style sheet declares that all <h1> headers appear in blue, then they'll always appear in blue when viewed using a browser that supports style sheets.

- *Cascading style sheets (CSS)* make style sheets more flexible by allowing inheritance (similar to Word's "Based On" styles), and automatically generated text and graphics.

27

They extend basic HTML with style properties that define fonts, colors, margins, and other formatting properties. If you view a web page that contains a CSS in a browser that can't interpret it, the browser displays the page using its default fonts and layout properties.

■ *Dynamic HTML (DHTML)* allows a web page designer to add effects to text and images, such as hiding or displaying a block of text when the user clicks it.

The structural differences between HTML, XML, and XHTML are extensive and are beyond the scope of this book. At any rate, you don't need to know the details of HTML or XML tags to create formatted documents in an Office program; when you save a document as a web page, Office handles all those details. In addition, most modern browsers (including Internet Explorer 5.0 or later, Opera 5.0 or later, and all Mozilla-based browsers including Firefox 0.9 or later and Netscape 6.0 or later) follow the XHTML specifications and should thus be able to render a page written using XHTML tags.

HOW OFFICE PROGRAMS HANDLE WEB PAGES

Word, Excel, and PowerPoint include a Save As Web Page option on the File menu that lets you translate the file you're currently working with into Web format; you can save it locally or publish it to a web server. (Because Outlook isn't a document-based program, it doesn't include a Save As capability. As we'll see later in this chapter, there are only a few Web-based tricks you can use with Outlook.) When you create a new document or edit an existing one in Word, Excel, or PowerPoint and save it as a web page, the resulting file uses XHTML in place of the application's native format. You can view the source code using a text editor such as Notepad or WordPad.

The requirement for HTML compatibility extends throughout Office—so much so, in fact, that Microsoft has adopted HTML as its primary format for use on the Clipboard. If you copy data from Excel to PowerPoint, for example, the data is translated into HTML as an intermediary format. If you copy anything from a web browser into one of those Office applications, it should come across completely intact, although the formatting may bend and twist to conform to the styles present in the target program.

CAUTION

> The ability of Office programs to generate complex HTML can be a double-edged sword for experienced Web designers who are accustomed to tweaking source code in a simple text editor. If you create a web page in Word, for example, and then edit the page manually, there is *no* guarantee that Word will maintain your manual edits or display the page as you intended (although it leaves tags intact that it doesn't understand). The possibility of Word modifying a handwritten tag can be confusing and frustrating to experienced Web-page designers.

When you save a document in Web format, the result may consist of more than one file. The source code, of course, is saved as a text file with the extension .htm. If your document includes any graphics or linked files, those are saved by default in their own folder, which has the same name as the document file. When you use Windows Explorer to move or copy the document file, the linked files automatically go along for the ride. If you publish the file to a web server, remember to include the folders in this file as well.

TIP FROM

For complex documents with many linked graphics, you may have better results choosing File, Save As, and then choosing Single File Web Page from the Files of Type list. This format embeds all linked files into a single file with the .mht extension. You can view the saved file in Internet Explorer (but not in a non-Microsoft browser such as Firefox), and you can open it for editing in the Office program you used to create it. The only thing you can't do is inspect the source code of the underlying document file.

If you encounter broken links after renaming an Office document that you've saved as a web page, see "The Right Way to Rename an HTML Document" in the "Troubleshooting" section at the end of this chapter.

Any Office document you save in Web format contains an HTML tag that identifies the program that originally created the file. As a result, when you look at the file in Windows Explorer, you see that its file type is HTML Document, and its icon is a modified version of the icon used for documents saved in the program's native format. If you examine the source code for the saved file, you'll see two blocks of tags near the top of the document. As long as these blocks remain intact, Office will have no problem recognizing which program is the correct one to use for editing purposes.

REMOVING OFFICE-GENERATED HTML TAGS

In addition to the Save As Web Page option, Word allows you to save a document in Web Page, Filtered format. This option, which is not found in any other Office program, generates comparatively clean HTML. A document that has been saved in Web Page, Filtered format contains embedded styles and section breaks, thus preserving much formatting; however, all Office-specific XML tags, such as those that contain document properties and Word fields, are stripped away. The cost of this option, naturally, is that you are then unable to open the resulting document in Word with all of its original formatting information intact.

There is no easy way to remove Office-specific tags from documents created by other Office programs.

27

VIEWING OFFICE DOCUMENTS IN A BROWSER WINDOW

Word, Excel, and PowerPoint allow you to easily see how a web page will appear in your default browser window: Choose File, Web Page Preview. Office saves a copy of the document in a temporary directory in Web format, and then opens the saved HTML document in a browser window.

In Word, Excel, and PowerPoint, you can modify your document so it looks better in a specific browser. Choose Tools, Options; then click the Web Options button on the General tab. On the Browsers tab, select your preferred browser from the Target Browsers list, as shown in Figure 27.1. For maximum compatibility with practically any browser, choose Microsoft Internet Explorer 3.0, Netscape Navigator 3.0 Or Later as the target. For the best-looking pages with full access to advanced Office features, choose Microsoft Internet Explorer 6.0.

Figure 27.1
Choosing a target browser lets you control the complexity of HTML code when you save an Office document as a web page.

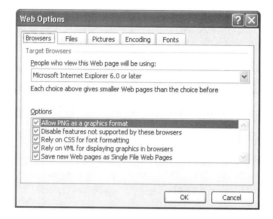

TIP FROM

Are you concerned about leaving traces of sensitive documents behind when you pre-view them in a web browser? You needn't worry, as long as you remember to com-pletely close the program you used to create the original document. When you do so, Office cleans out the temporary folder used to store these preview copies. To verify that the folders and the files they contain are truly gone, open Windows Explorer, enter the address `%userprofile%\Local Settings\Temporary Internet Files\Content.mso` (be sure to include the percent signs), and verify that folders with names such as WordWebPagePreview and ExcelWebPagePreview are not present.

What You Can (and Can't) Do with Office

27

Should you use an Office program to create web pages? If so, which one? There are no uni-versal answers to those questions. Instead, the correct answer varies, depending on the task you're trying to accomplish and your level of Web sophistication.

Each program has its own strengths, weaknesses, nuances, and gotchas. If you're trying to maintain a complex website, with a constantly changing lineup of links, or if your pages contain scripts and custom HTML tags, FrontPage is your only reasonable choice.

FrontPage uses all the Office import filters, so it's easy to open almost any kind of file and turn it into a web page. Because Word, Excel, and PowerPoint support HTML as a native file format and common copy format (and FrontPage's native file format has always been HTML), copying and moving data among these Office applications is a breeze.

In general, if you're serious about page design and, especially, Web-site management, you should always use FrontPage, unless

- You already know one of the other Office applications well, and you want to put together a handful of simple web pages with minimal fuss.

- You know that an existing Web template designed in Word contains all the elements you need for a simple website.

- You've created a PowerPoint presentation and you want to make it easily available to friends, customers, or associates.

- You want the specific controls provided by Excel (spreadsheet, chart, and PivotTable). Even then, it's a good idea to run the data through Excel, and do everything else with FrontPage.

- You want a special feature in one of the Office programs (Outlook's calendar publisher, for example, or one of the Word Web Wizards) that precisely meets your needs.

In this section, we examine the strengths and weaknesses of each Office program when it comes to authoring and editing web pages.

WORD

With a few small exceptions (such as diagonal cell borders, weird text formatting, and shaded paragraph backgrounds), anything you can put in a Word document will appear on a web page. Even the items that don't appear on the page will survive a round-trip: Write a VBA/Word macro for a document, save it as a web page, then open the web page in Word, and the macro works just fine.

Word is an excellent choice for creating and maintaining relatively simple web pages. Although it has no features for tracing or maintaining hyperlinks across a site, experienced Word users will find it easy to use and understand. The extensive frames capabilities (available when you choose Format, Frames) make it easy to create framed web pages, as in the example in Figure 27.2.

Previous versions of Word included a handful of templates and a wizard devoted exclusively to creating web pages. These choices are no longer available in Word 2003 (nor are they greatly missed). If you want to create a web page from scratch, switch to Word's Web Layout View, create your page using Word's normal layout and formatting tools, and save it in web page format.

EXCEL

As with Word, a few Excel features won't appear when you save a workbook as a web page: Custom views, nested functions, scenarios, and some advanced formatting don't appear on the web page. Nonetheless, those features all survive a round-trip, and Excel does a good job of not clobbering tags it doesn't understand.

27

Figure 27.2
Use the Frames tool-bar to add frames to any Word document whose ultimate destination is the Web.

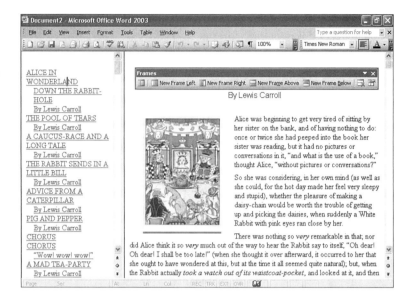

You can use Excel to publish almost anything to the Web, including entire workbooks. Excel is a particularly good choice for quickly turning static tables or lists into neat web pages, and charts pose no problem except with ancient browsers. The most interesting Excel web pages, however, are those that provide interactivity. To create an interactive web page, click the Publish button on Excel's Save As dialog box and then select the Add Interactivity check box, as shown in Figure 27.3.

Figure 27.3
Interactive spread-sheets, charts, and PivotTables start with the Add Interactivity check box.

The degree of interactivity depends on the remote user's browser and whether he has the correct components installed:

- You can allow anyone using Internet Explorer 5.01 with Service Pack 2 or later to view the data, just as it would appear in an Excel workbook. The first time a remote user loads a web page containing an interactive Web component, he may see an error message containing a link to a page at Microsoft's website where the Office 2003 Web Components are available for download. After this package is installed, the page should display properly.

- If the computer accessing the interactive web page has Excel 2003 installed, the remote viewer can use the Web-based worksheet in fully interactive mode to change data, move or copy cells, change formulas, and the like, and see the impact of those changes in spreadsheets, charts, or PivotTables. These capabilities are blocked on a computer that has only the Office 2003 Web Components installed.

CAUTION

> If you expect that some persons will use older Internet Explorer versions or any non-Microsoft browser to open a web page you create in Excel, do not use Web components to add interactivity. Only Internet Explorer 5.01 SP2 or later is able to display content using the Office Web Component package.

POWERPOINT

PowerPoint is suitable for generating web pages if you are willing to abide by its strict structure: PowerPoint creates a slide show on the Web, and not much else.

Although the format of the slide show offers a great deal of flexibility—you can put slide titles in a pane, for instance, and you can set up your own navigation buttons if the ones at the bottom don't ring your chimes—the end result is a PowerPoint slide show, pure and simple.

→ If you want to publish your PowerPoint presentations to the Web, **see** "Creating Presentations for the Web," **p. 788**.

OUTLOOK

Outlook uses the Internet for all sorts of features, but with one exception, it isn't designed to create web pages. That one exception is a humdinger, however. With a few mouse clicks, you can turn your Outlook calendar into a professional-looking web page. The resulting page, which looks great in just about any browser (see Figure 27.4), encompasses all your meetings and appointments for any range of dates you specify.

→ To learn more about using Outlook to publish your calendar, **see** "Extra Credit: Publishing a Calendar as a Web Page," **p. 321**.

27

Figure 27.4
Outlook will publish your appointment calendar (or that of your business or other organization) to the Web.

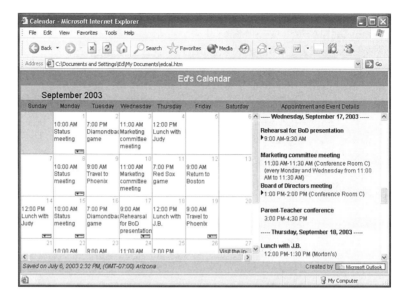

MOVING BETWEEN HTML AND OFFICE FORMATS

When Office applications create HTML files, they store the identity of the creating program in an XML tag at the beginning of the document. For example, a web page created in Word 2003 will contain these tags after the opening <head> tag:

```
<meta name=ProgId content=Word.Document>
<meta name=Generator content="Microsoft Word 11">
<meta name=Originator content="Microsoft Word 11">
```

When you open an HTML file in Internet Explorer, the File/Open routine looks for these tags; if it finds one, it adds the originating program's icon to the Internet Explorer toolbar. To begin editing the page, just click that icon, which automatically launches the associated program and loads the document.

If you look closely at the icon associated with any Office document, you can easily see the difference between documents saved in the native format and those saved in various HTML and XML formats. A small icon in the upper-left corner identifies the originating application; Figure 27.5, for instance, shows four documents created by Word and saved with the same name, each in a different format.

 If you need to open an HTML file in an Office application other than the one that originated it, see "Opening Office-Generated HTML Files" in the "Troubleshooting" section at the end of this chapter.

Traditional HTML files are plain-text files; they cannot contain graphics. If you construct a web page in Word, Excel, or PowerPoint, and the page contains a picture, the application has to store the picture outside the HTML file, and create a link to the picture within the text of the HTML file.

Figure 27.5
The icon attached to a file tells you which Office program created it. The differences can be hard to distinguish in a tiny dialog box.

TIP FROM

EQ & Woody

> You can save files in Single File Web Page format (also known as Web Archive or MHTML format). Most non-Microsoft browsers (including Firefox) are unable to cope with this file format, which stores HTML source code and associated graphics in a single file with the .mht file extension. To save a file in this format, choose File, Save As (or File, Save As Web Page). Then choose Single File Web Page in the Save As Type box.

All the Office applications will translate the graphic, if need be, into a GIF or JPEG file, which can be readily viewed on the Web. The rest of the story, however, isn't so simple.

Word, Excel, and PowerPoint solve the problem using the same elegant (if potentially dangerous) way that Windows does when you save a web page from Internet Explorer: During the Save operation, the program creates a folder with the same name as the file and then copies graphics (and other linked items) to that folder. If you use Word to create a web page that contains several graphics and then save it using the filename Annual Report.htm, Word creates a folder Annual Report Files, which contains all the graphics from the original page, translated (if necessary) into GIF or JPEG format. You'll find this folder in the same location as the page that contains the file you saved.

CAUTION

> The links between the HTML file and the graphics are hard-coded to refer to an appropriately named subfolder. (For those of you who might have encountered this problem in other guises, Office stores relative addresses, not absolute addresses.) If you move an Office-generated HTML file within Windows Explorer, you must move the supporting folder and all the contents along with it or the links will be broken. If you move an HTML file in Windows Explorer, it automatically moves the supporting folder as well. However, if you rename the underlying file or folder in Windows Explorer, you immediately break the link and the page no longer displays properly.

27

You can change this behavior, if you like, so all the files—main page and supporting files alike—go into a single folder. (It's fairly easy to identify the supporting files, which are based on the same filename as the main file.) To do so in Word, Excel, or PowerPoint, choose Tools, Options, click the Web Options button on the General tab, and then click the Files tab.

Outlook's calendar pages behave differently. The main calendar page and all its supporting data are dumped into the same folder. If you save a calendar in Outlook, we strongly recommend that you create a new folder to store it.

NOTE

> Office saves VBA projects in a binary file called Editdata.mso and stores it along with associated files for that page. Similarly, Word, Excel, and PowerPoint store XML-formatted lists of support files in Filelist.xml, and PowerPoint and Outlook store cascading style sheets in various *.css files.

WEB-PAGE DESIGN ESSENTIALS

Web-page design is an art unto itself, with a broad array of graphic considerations that don't apply when you're working with printed media. Most computer magazines run design articles from time to time, and no two seem to agree on what constitutes an outstanding design. A topic as simple as frames versus no frames can trigger the journalistic equivalent of a barroom brawl.

That said, all would-be Web-page designers should keep a few simple tips in mind:

- Obey the Web design corollary to the KISS principle—Keep It Small, Stupid. Nobody likes to wait for downloads.

TIP FROM

> You have to dig into a properties dialog box to find out how big your Word document or Excel worksheet is. By contrast, FrontPage offers a handy indicator on its status bar that tells you approximately how long the page you're constructing will take to download at various speeds. If you build lots of complex, graphics-rich pages, this is yet another reason to consider switching to FrontPage as your primary authoring tool.

- Avoid ransom note typography. Using two different fonts on a page serve to distinguish headings from body text. Using three or more fonts just annoys people and may convince them to click another link and go read something else.

- Make colors work together. Magenta text on a red background might be (barely) legible on some monitors. It won't be legible at all on many. Whenever possible, use the preselected PowerPoint color schemes or Word themes to ensure that everything blends together smartly.

- Don't break the law. Copyright protection applies in cyberspace, too. It might be easy to reproduce copyrighted work on your page, but that doesn't make it legal.

BROWSER-COMPATIBILITY ISSUES

When you publish a Word document, a PowerPoint presentation, or an Office-generated page to a server that's widely accessible on the Web, you don't know exactly what software your visitors will be using when they view it. The more traffic you have, the more important it is that you anticipate problems. Many of these problems can be traced back to fundamental differences in the way various web browsers work.

Specific, known limitations include these:

- If you use Excel to create interactive web pages, they can be viewed only with Internet Explorer 5.01 or later, and only on computers that have installed the Office 2003 Web Components. Anyone who tries to view the page using a non-Microsoft browser such as Firefox will be rewarded with an error message.

- Documents created with Office programs and saved in Web format use HTML, XHTML, and XML tags. Thus, at least in theory, the content of any Office-generated page should be visible in almost any modern browser. In practice, some formatting might be lost, especially in older browsers. For complex pages, your best bet is to view the pages in a variety of target browsers to see if you can identify compatibility problems before your users do.

- Some Office document elements—most notably drawing layer objects, including organization charts—don't look very good in any browser, including Internet Explorer. Be cautious of how the various browsers render carefully crafted graphics in the drawing layer.

VIEWING HTML SOURCE CODE

Office 2003 includes a little-known component called the Microsoft Script Editor. Don't let the name fool you: Yes, you can use this development environment to insert VBScript and JScript into Office documents intended for use on the Web. But it's equally handy at simply viewing the source code of Word documents saved in HTML format. (The command is unavailable when you use Word to view or edit a document saved in Word's native format.)

In Word, choose View, HTML Source to open Microsoft Script Editor and display the raw source code of the current document. As you can see in Figure 27.6, this display shows a Text Editor window and a Project Explorer pane. The HTML source is color-coded to help distinguish tags, parameters, text, and other elements.

Microsoft Script Editor is strictly an expert-level tool. Click the Help button to read its excellent explanations and tutorials (from the Contents tab, be sure to explore the sections that explain the structure of Office documents, found under the heading "HTML in Microsoft Office Applications"), and it's most useful as a way to see how Office files are built.

27

Figure 27.6
Use Microsoft Script
Editor to inspect the
HTML source code of
a document.

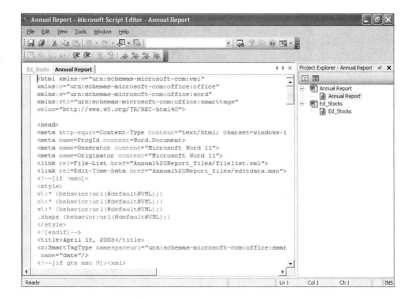

TIP FROM

Excel and PowerPoint don't offer options to view the HTML source of workbooks or presentations saved in Web format, but you can do it, if you're willing to take an extra step. Open the workbook or presentation in Internet Explorer. On the taskbar, you'll see an icon representing the program originally used to create the file—Excel or PowerPoint. Click the down arrow to the right of this button to see additional choices, one of which should be "Edit in Microsoft Word." Click this choice to open the file in Word. From there, you can choose View, HTML Source.

PREVIEWING AND TESTING WEB PAGES

As the most important—and most frequently overlooked—step in creating web pages, testing is a necessity after you go beyond a single HTML page with no attached graphics.

Depending on your computer and your network, you might be able to use any or all of the following options for testing:

■ If you have a good web page design tool, such as FrontPage, the Web preview available in the tool will probably suffice for layout and general debugging. FrontPage also has a Preview in Browser feature (File, Preview in Browser), which pulls up the browser of your choice. Failing that, the Web Page Preview command on the File menu in Word or Excel will do in a pinch.

■ At the next level, you can double-click an *.htm or *.html file, and your browser will attempt to load it. (Equivalently, you can start the browser and type the filename, or drag and drop the file onto the browser.) This is a good quick-and-dirty approach for verifying layout problems in different browsers, and can also identify some (but not all) problems with graphics and hyperlinks.

TIP FROM

E&Woody

> If you flip between an Office program and your browser to check on the status of your page, make sure you save your changes in the originating program before opening or refreshing the page in the browser.

- If you have installed a web server on your own computer, you can use it as a "staging area" for testing purposes. Likewise, if you have access to a client/server network running Windows 2000 Server or Windows Server 2003, you might be able to test your pages on the web server included with those operating systems. Contact your network administrator for details about how to connect to the web server.

- After you're on the Web, you might find it advantageous to "hide" the main page for a few days, to shake out any final bugs. You can do that by calling the main page in the default folder Index0.htm, for example, and instructing your testers to use that page instead of the default Index.htm or Index.html.

WORKING WITH HYPERLINKS

All Office programs allow you to add hyperlinks in your documents. Every hyperlink has two parts: The *display text* is the clickable part of your document, and the *address* is the URL, bookmark, filename, e-mail address, or other destination that opens when the link is clicked.

If you don't select any text before opening the Insert Hyperlink dialog box, the display text shows the name of the destination you select. You can and should change the display text to something more descriptive. To keep the link short, click the ScreenTip button and enter a longer bit of explanatory text.

CAUTION

> As soon as you change even a single letter of the Text to Display box, that text is frozen in place. That can produce bizarre consequences if the display text is a URL and you then click a different URL in the Address box. That's why it's always better to use a word or phrase for the display text.

27

To add a link in any Office document, follow these steps:

1. Select the text you want to use for your display text and then choose Insert, Hyperlink. This opens the common Insert Hyperlink dialog box, shown in Figure 27.7.

2. In the Link To pane along the left side of the dialog box, choose the type of destination you want to use for your hyperlink. The contents beneath the display text change according to your selection:
   - Choose Existing File or Web Page to browse for a file or folder that already exists. You can choose from files in the current folder, pages in your browser's history, or files you've opened recently.

Figure 27.7
The Insert Hyperlink dialog box allows you to create "hot" links to web pages, files, or locations within files, with a few simple clicks.

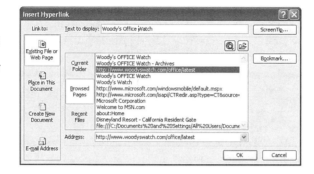

- Choose Place In This Document if you want to select a Word document bookmark, a cell or range name in an Excel workbook, or a slide in a PowerPoint presentation, as in Figure 27.8.

Figure 27.8

- Choose Create New Document to create a new file using the same program as the one in which you're inserting the hyperlink. You can change the folder in which the new document is stored, and you can also specify that you want to edit the document now or later.
- Choose E-mail Address to create a mailto: link. Options allow you to enter an e-mail address and a subject.

3. If you chose a file or web page, you can optionally click the Bookmark button to specify a named bookmark in that file or page.

4. Click OK to save your changes.

Hyperlinks can be copied, moved, or deleted, much as you would copy, move, or delete text. To remove a hyperlink but leave the display text intact, right-click the display text and choose Remove Hyperlink.

You can find advanced discussions about hyperlinking as it pertains to each individual Office application throughout this book.

TROUBLESHOOTING

THE RIGHT WAY TO RENAME AN HTML DOCUMENT

I needed to rename a web page that I created using Word. Using Windows Explorer, I renamed the page and the folder containing linked graphics; now, I see only red Xs where the pictures should be. What did I do wrong?

When you saved your document, links to the graphics were embedded in the document using the folder name as it existed at that time. When you open the file, it's looking for the folder with its original name. The best way to rename a file saved as a web page is to reopen it in the Office program that created it. Save it under the new name, and then open Windows Explorer and delete the old file. When you delete the old file, Windows should also delete its matching folder.

OPENING OFFICE-GENERATED HTML FILES

I created a Word document and saved it as a web page, and now I want to edit it in FrontPage. Every time I try to open the HTML file in FrontPage, however, Word opens instead.

Office is outsmarting you. Because it sees the XML tag at the top of the document indicating that the page was created with Word, it assumes that you always want to open this page in Word. To use FrontPage as your editor instead, you have several options; the following two are the easiest:

- Open the web page in Internet Explorer, click the arrow to the right of the Edit button on the browser's Standard toolbar, and then choose Edit with Microsoft FrontPage.

- From FrontPage, choose File, Open; in the Open dialog box, right-click the icon for the file you're trying to open, and choose Open in Microsoft FrontPage.

EXTRA CREDIT: VIEWING AND EDITING OFFICE DOCUMENTS IN A WEB BROWSER

You don't have to convert Office documents into Web format to post them on a web server. A web page designer can create a hyperlink that points directly to a Word document, Excel workbook, or PowerPoint presentation saved in its native format. When you open that page and click the link, Internet Explorer displays a security warning like the one shown here.

What happens next? As with so many things involving Windows and Office, that depends.

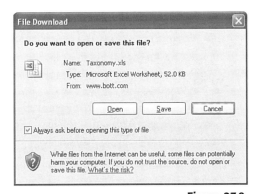

Figure 27.9

If the person who clicked that link is using Internet Explorer and doesn't have Office installed, Windows looks for a program that can handle that file type. Clicking the Open button displays the file in a separate window using that program—in the case of most Word documents, for example, Windows will use Wordpad. If Windows can't find a compatible program, the Open button is missing and the user has only the option to save the file or cancel.

If the person who clicked that link is using Internet Explorer and does have Office installed, the experience is much more interesting. In that configuration, you can click Open and the file will appear within the browser window. (In technical terms, Internet Explorer is acting as a "container" for the Office program.) The contents of the document look just as if they were appearing in the program window. You can scroll through the pages of a Word document, click tabs to switch between worksheets in an Excel workbook, and view a PowerPoint presentation complete with slick transition effects. But there are some noteworthy differences, as you can see here:

Figure 27.10

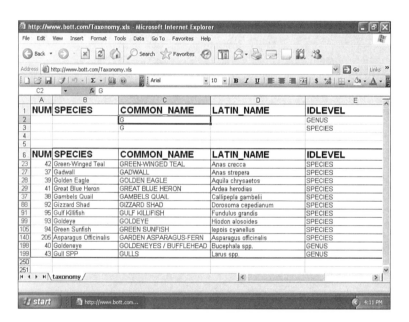

Look carefully at the toolbars and menus in the browser window. The toolbar buttons control browser functions, but the pull-down menus are from the program that actually opened the document—in this case, Excel. Internet Explorer's Favorites menu is shoehorned between the Edit and View menus, Excel's Window menu is missing (because you can't open multiple documents in a browser container), and you can choose from *two* Help menus—one for Internet Explorer, the other for Excel.

Normally, the toolbars for the program that created the document are hidden. To make the Standard and Formatting toolbars visible, as they are in this example, click the Tools button on Internet Explorer's toolbar. To display additional toolbars, choose View, Toolbars and select from the list of available toolbars.

If you edit a document within a browser window, be careful. When you exit the page, your changes are discarded without being saved. If you use the Save button on the creating program's toolbar, it has no effect, nor will you be able to save the changed document to the web server where it's stored. The only way to preserve your changes is to choose File, Save As and save a copy of the document in a location where you have read-write permissions.

CHAPTER 28

Using Office on a Tablet PC

In this chapter

OFFICE 2003 AND THE TABLET PC

If you use a portable PC running Windows XP, Office 2003 works exactly the same as it does on a desktop PC. There's one significant exception to this rule, however: Using Windows XP Tablet PC Edition, you have access to a set of unique features that are ideally suited to educational environments.

In design, a Tablet PC is a notebook computer with a few hardware twists. The most obvious is the input device—a pen-shaped stylus that takes the place of a mouse and allows the user to select and manipulate text and objects, make menu selections, and click buttons. The pen also serves as a way to draw lines, sketch diagrams, and tap out text using an onscreen keyboard. Most importantly, you can use the pen to scribble your own notes right on the screen, just as if you were jotting them down on a piece of paper.

NOTE

> If you have a Tablet PC, make sure you have the latest updates. In particular, be sure to install Service Pack 2 for Windows XP, which includes a slew of Tablet PC–specific updates that change the operating system version to Windows XP Tablet PC Edition 2005. After you install Office 2003, get the Office 2003 Ink Recognition Update, which greatly improves the ability of Office programs to decipher your handwriting. It's available from `http://office.microsoft.com`; click the Downloads link and search for the December 10, 2004 Improved Ink Recognition Update.

Office 2003 recognizes when it's been installed on a computer running Windows XP Tablet PC Edition and automatically installs code that takes advantage of the hardware. The most noteworthy change is that the screen appears in portrait orientation, with the taskbar appearing along the bottom of the screen rather than on the right. This configuration allows you to interact with your document just as you would with a piece of paper. Figure 28.1 shows Word running on a Tablet PC.

Everything you add to a document using the Tablet PC's pen is called *ink*. In Office, ink is a full-fledged object type with its own properties and behaviors, just like AutoShapes and pictures. Ink sits in the drawing layer, and you can use the Format Ink dialog box and options on the Drawing toolbar to change the color and width of the ink. You can select an ink annotation, copy it to the Clipboard, and then paste it into another Office program—or into any application that supports ink. Office 2003 supports ink in the following ways:

- **Annotations**—Mark up a Word document, Excel workbook, or PowerPoint slide using your own handwriting. While delivering a PowerPoint presentation, you can take notes directly on the slides and then save the results.
- **Writing**—Create and send handwritten e-mail messages, add text or drawings to a Word document or PowerPoint slide, or copy handwritten notes from another program. As we explain later in this chapter, ink appears in the drawing layer; to convert handwritten comments into text and add them in the text layer, you must go through a conversion step.

28

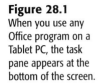

Figure 28.1
When you use any Office program on a Tablet PC, the task pane appears at the bottom of the screen.

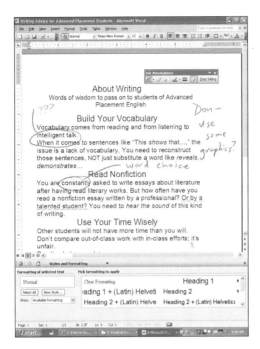

- **Comments**—In Word, but not in PowerPoint or Excel, you can add handwritten comments to a document. These notes appear in comment balloons and can be tracked on a per-user basis.

Although ink sits in the drawing layer, it actually contains some attributes normally associated with text. You can use the surprisingly accurate handwriting recognition capabilities of Windows XP Tablet PC Edition to convert your scribbled notes into text, which can then be pasted into a document. More often, though, you'll want to save ink as ink.

TIP FROM

You need a Tablet PC to create ink in an Office document. (The one exception is in Slide Show view in PowerPoint, where you can create ink annotations using any computer.) However, you don't need any special hardware to work with ink that has been saved in a document. The ink is treated as an object, the same as a drawing object. If Windows XP Tablet PC Edition is running, you can work with the ink as ink; on all other Windows versions, the ink behaves as if it were a drawing.

The pen is an excellent tool for creating short notes and marking up existing documents. It's much less appropriate for creating new documents or entering large amounts of text; in either of those cases, a keyboard is a far better input device. For basic note taking, your best choice is a new member of the Office family called OneNote. Although it's not included with Office 2003 Student and Teacher Edition, it's a worthwhile edition; in fact, because it's

28

so well suited to the hardware, many Tablet PC makers include a free copy of OneNote with their computers. This versatile program (shown in Figure 28.2) acts like an endlessly expandable file folder, on which you can jot notes, draw pictures, and insert scraps from web pages and from other documents. Although OneNote is also useful on a desktop computer, it realizes its full potential on a Tablet PC.

Figure 28.2
OneNote is a member of the Office family that is particularly effective on Tablet PCs.

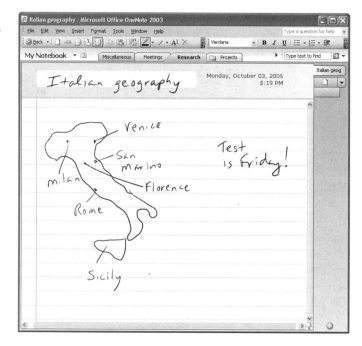

→ For more details about using OneNote, see "Using OneNote with Office," **p. 862**.

ENTERING AND EDITING TEXT ON A TABLET PC

On a Tablet PC, the standard way to enter text into dialog boxes and programs that don't recognize ink (such as Notepad) is to use the Tablet PC Input Panel. The easiest way to summon this box is to hold the pen directly over the screen (without touching the screen), until you see the Input Panel icon appear. Tap this icon with the pen tip and the Input Panel appears.

The Input Panel floats over the current window. The three icons on the left allow you to select one of its three text entry options: Writing Pad, Character Pad, and On-Screen Keyboard. When you use the Writing Pad (shown in Figure 28.3), you write just as if you were using a piece of paper. The ink recognizer interprets your letters at the bottom of the panel, and if you reach the end of the input box it helpfully adds another line. You can click the recognized word to correct a single character or to choose a different word from the recognizer's dictionary. If the results are acceptable, click Insert to add the text at the current insertion point, just as if you had typed it.

Figure 28.3
When you use the Writing Pad, the Tablet PC Input Panel turns handwriting into text and sends it to the current insertion point.

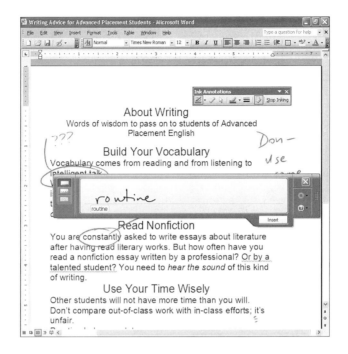

For some tasks, the handwriting recognition offered by the Input Pad actually gets in the way. This might be the case if you're entering scientific terms that aren't in the dictionary. In that case, you can click the Keyboard icon in the Input Panel and use the onscreen keyboard to fill in precise values. (See Figure 28.4.)

Figure 28.4
Using the On-Screen Keyboard is a more accurate way to enter text that isn't included in a standard dictionary.

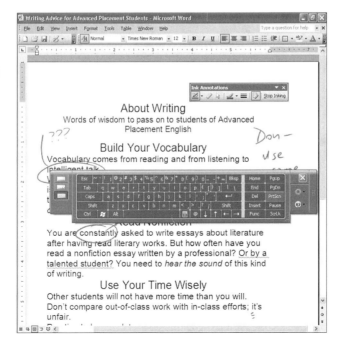

28

The third variation of the Input Panel is the Character Pad, shown in Figure 28.5. In this mode, you enter characters one at a time, and each character is recognized independently; the ink recognizer doesn't try to match your input with its dictionary. This tool is most useful when filling in dialog boxes and password prompts.

Figure 28.5
Use the Character Pad to enter passwords and filenames in dialog boxes, one character at a time.

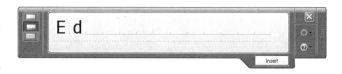

In Office 2003, the only reason to use the Input Panel is to make minor edits to a document or to fill in a dialog box. For all other text input tasks, use the Ink Drawing and Writing toolbar. This toolbar is only available on a computer running Windows XP Tablet PC Edition, and only in Word, Excel, or PowerPoint (and in Outlook when using Word as the e-mail editor).

To begin adding ink to a document, choose View, Toolbars, Ink Drawing and Writing (or right-click any menu or toolbar and choose Ink Drawing and Writing from the list). Click the pen button at the left of the toolbar to begin inking with the default black felt-tip style; click the arrow to the right of the button to choose a different pen style or color from the drop-down list. In Word, a drawing canvas appears in your document, and you can begin writing anywhere within that canvas, as shown in Figure 28.6.

Figure 28.6
To stop writing, click the Stop Inking button on the toolbar.

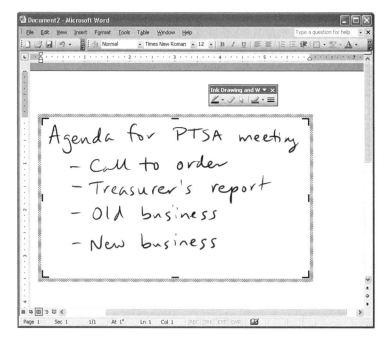

→ For an explanation of how the drawing canvas in Word works, see "Working with a Drawing Canvas," **p. 116**.

When you add ink writing to an Excel worksheet or PowerPoint slide, the ink appears in the drawing layer, directly on top of the current work surface. As with any drawing object, you can select, move, copy, delete, resize, or format the ink.

If you change your mind about something you wrote using ink, click the Eraser button. This changes the mouse pointer to an eraser icon. Tap the eraser icon on any existing ink to remove it from the page.

You can convert any ink to text and then paste the converted text into any Office document (or anywhere that the Clipboard's Paste command is available). Select the ink, right-click, and choose Copy Ink As Text from the shortcut menu.

One of the most effective uses of text input on a Tablet PC is for short e-mail messages. Using Word as your e-mail editor, click the pen button on the Ink Drawing and Writing toolbar and write your message in the drawing canvas. Click the To button to choose a recipient from the Outlook Address Book, and click Send. Your handwritten content appears as an embedded graphic within an HTML-formatted e-mail message, which can be read by anyone with an HTML-capable e-mail client. Figure 28.7 shows what your recipient will see if he or she uses Outlook 2003.

Figure 28.7
Use a Tablet PC to create short handwritten e-mail messages. The message body appears as a graphic object.

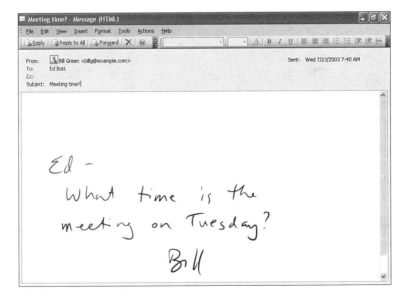

28

TIP FROM

Entering text as ink in the body of a message is easy. Filling in the address and subject fields is slightly more difficult. Clicking the To button gives you point-and-click access to your entire Outlook Address Book. You can also use the Tablet PC Input Panel to enter the first few characters of the recipient's address, and then allow AutoComplete to finish the job. For the subject, you can use the Input Panel, or try the Tablet PC's text recognition feature. Enter the subject at the top of your e-mail message. When you've finished writing the message body, click the Select Objects button on the Ink Drawing and Writing toolbar. Select the ink you entered for the subject text, right-click, and choose Copy Ink As Text. Now right-click in the Subject box and paste the text.

USING INK TO ADD ANNOTATIONS AND COMMENTS

You can freely ink anywhere on a Word document, PowerPoint slide, or Excel worksheet. The most common reason to do so is to mark up an electronic document, just as you would add handwritten comments to a printed copy of that document. These freehand comments, which sit in the drawing layer on top of any text in the text layer, are called *annotations*. In addition, Word allows you to add handwritten comments that appear in balloons when viewed in Print Layout view.

→ For details on how to work with Word's comments and other revision-tracking features, see "Sharing Documents," **p. 355**.

In Word, it's easy to distinguish between ink writing and ink annotations. Ink writing is allowed only within a drawing canvas, whereas ink annotations appear on the document itself. In PowerPoint and Excel, the difference is less obvious, because both writing and annotations appear on the document.

Here's the crucial distinction that separates annotations from writing: Ink annotations are integrated with the Reviewing toolbar. With the click of a button, you can show or hide all annotations on the current document. A common Ink Annotations toolbar allows you to enable or disable annotations. Each program has a slightly different way of letting you show or hide annotations:

- In Excel, click the Show Ink Annotations/Hide Ink Annotations button on the Reviewing toolbar or the Ink Annotations toolbar.

- In Word, choose View, Markup; or click the Show/Hide Markup button on the Ink Annotations toolbar; or click the Show menu on the Reviewing toolbar and select or clear the Ink Annotations item.

- In PowerPoint, choose View, Markup; or click the Show/Hide Markup button on the Reviewing toolbar or the Ink Annotations toolbar.

You can use annotations to make editing marks (drawing a line through text you want deleted, for instance), scribble short questions, highlight words and phrases, or add drawings. By default, annotations appear in a red felt-tip pen. As with ink writing, you can change the pen style to a ball point or a highlighter, and you can change the color as well.

28

To begin marking up a document, choose View, Toolbars, Ink Annotations (or right-click any menu or toolbar and choose Ink Annotations from the list). Click the pen button at the left of the toolbar to begin inking with the default red felt-tip style; click the arrow to the right of the button to choose a different pen style or color from the drop-down list. Figure 28.8 shows a marked-up PowerPoint slide.

Figure 28.8
Use ink annotations to suggest changes in an Office document without affecting the document's content.

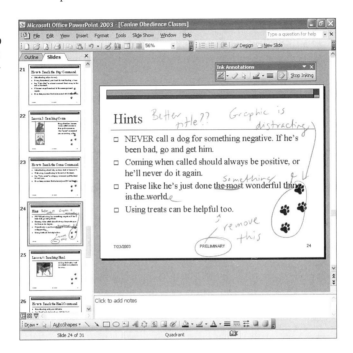

One big advantage of ink annotations is that anyone—with or without a Tablet PC—can remove them with just a few mouse clicks. If users embed comments directly with a document, you risk inadvertently leaving a comment behind, with potentially embarrassing effects. But after dealing with all ink annotations, you can remove them using the following techniques:

- In Word, display the Reviewing toolbar, click the drop-down arrow to the right of the Reject/Change/Delete Comment button, and click Delete All Ink Annotations in Document. All annotations in the current document are deleted instantly, with no confirmation. You can undo this action.

- In Excel, display the Reviewing toolbar and click Delete All Ink Annotations. You are prompted to confirm that you want to delete all ink annotations on all worksheets in the current workbook. You can undo this action; however, you lose the undo capability as soon as you save the current workbook.

- In PowerPoint, you can remove markup from a single slide or the entire presentation. Click the drop-down arrow to the right of the Delete Comment button on the

28

Reviewing toolbar and choose Delete All Markup on the Current Slide or Delete All Markup In This Presentation.

If you want to show or hide ink annotations on a printed copy of a document, worksheet, or presentation, choose File, Print. In Word, choose Document Showing Markup from the Print What box to show annotations; choose Document (the default) to hide annotations. In PowerPoint, select or clear the Print Comments and Ink Markup option on the Print dialog box. In Excel, ink annotations appear on printed pages if the annotations are visible on the screen; you can't control print options separately.

If ink annotations won't stay put within a Word document, see "Locking Documents When Using Annotations" in the "Troubleshooting" section at the end of this chapter.

USING ONENOTE WITH OFFICE

In its basic form, a Tablet PC resembles a pad of paper. Most of us are used to jotting down notes of phone conversations, class lectures, shopping lists, and other sorts of random, freeform text; so it's tempting to think of doing the same with a Tablet PC. Although you can press Word into service for an occasional handwritten document of this sort, it's ill-suited to this task on a day-to-day basis. Word's drawing canvas greatly limits your ability to enter and edit text, and you're still faced with the dilemma of how to save, organize, and search multiple documents containing ink-based text.

That's where OneNote comes in. The newest member of the Office family was designed with freeform note taking as its central task. OneNote is not available in any of the Office editions; you have to purchase it separately.

OneNote uses a page-and-folder metaphor to keep your freeform notes organized. The main data file for OneNote is a notebook. Tabs along the top of the OneNote window function as folders within the open notebook; when you click a tab, you can create new pages within that folder. For the current folder, each page gets its own tab along the right side of the window. Although you can use OneNote on a desktop PC and type notes onto pages, it's especially effective on a Tablet PC, thanks to its ability to store ink. You don't need to convert your notes into text; OneNote automatically includes ink-based content in its searchable index, making it possible for you to quickly locate words and phrases anywhere within a notebook.

If you have OneNote installed on your computer, you can use it in combination with other Office programs in the following ways:

- Choose File, E-mail (or press Ctrl+Shift+E) to insert and attach the current OneNote page to an e-mail message using Outlook. The message contents appear as a picture; if the recipient has OneNote installed, she can open the attachment and add it to her own notebook.

- You can create Outlook task items directly from within OneNote. Select any text, typed or handwritten, and click the Create Outlook Task button on the Standard toolbar.

28

OneNote converts your handwritten selection to text, if necessary, and fills in the task form for you.

- Reuse any OneNote selection in any Office program. Use the Paste Options button to control the format of the pasted content.

TROUBLESHOOTING

LOCKING DOCUMENTS WHEN USING ANNOTATIONS

I added some annotations to a Word document and then made some edits. Now all the annotations are in the wrong place. How can I keep this from happening?

When you insert annotations, they appear in the drawing layer and "float" on the page. If you underline a sentence and then add a new sentence before the underlined sentence, the text shifts down the page, but the ink stays where you originally added it. To ensure that your annotations stay in sync with your document's content, you need to lock the document's layout. Choose Tools, Protect Document, select the check box under Editing Restrictions, and select either Comments or No Changes (Read-Only). Click Yes, Start Enforcing Protection to make your changes effective.

INDEX

bullet points, converting to slides, 725

bulleted/numbered lists
tightening up to text, 740
working with, 730-732

character attributes, changing, 108

color schemas
choosing, 753-754
copying, 754-755
overview, 752-753

design templates
accessing/finding more, 706-707
applying, 706
copying between presentations, 708-709
versus designs, 747
starting with, 707

designs
backgrounds, choosing, 750-751
choosing effectively, 748
modifying existing designs, 748-750
overview, 747
Title Master changes, 750
ungrouping, 749

Excel charts, importing, 674

Excel tables, troubleshooting, 757

file types, 702-704

fonts, 756

hardware considerations, 789-790

headings, positioning, 580

hidden slides, 791-792, 797

hyperlinks, utilizing in slides, 719-720

importing HTML files, 710

importing Word outlines, 709-710

keyboard shortcuts, 718-719

legacy compatibility issues, 704

macros. *See* macros

master slides
backgrounds, global changes, 741
font formatting, 741
Handout Master, 744-746, 757-758
headers and footers, 741-743
multiple master slides, creating, 746-747
Notes Master, 744-745, 757-758
overview, 736
paragraph formatting, 741
removing elements from single documents, 743-744
Slide Master, 738-740
Title Master, 736-738
troubleshooting, 757

Microsoft Producer 2003, 721

multiple monitors, utilizing, 790-791

notes, adding, 713

overview, 13

outline panes, organizing with, 711

Package for CD feature, 793-795

paragraph formatting, 755-756

pictures/diagrams/clip art, adding, 734-736

placeholders
going outside of, 728-729

manually inserting, 728
restoring, 738
types of, 727
utilizing, 727-728

presentations. *See* presentations (PowerPoint)

printing, 795-797

Repeat button, 786

slide layouts, 726-727

Slide Show view, 713

slide shows. *See* slide shows

Slide Sorter view
managing slide shows, 715-718
rearranging presentations, 712-713

slides. *See* slides (PowerPoint)

speaker notes
modifying during slide shows, 793
organizing remarks with, 784-785

spell-check, setting up, 50-51

tables, 733-734

text formats, changing, 755

timers, rehearsing with, 785-787

VBA
limitations of, 806
navigating presentations with, 825

Viewer, 795

views (presentations), 710-711

web browsers, viewing presentations in, 714-715

Web presentations, 797, 841

PowerPoint Viewer, 795

.pps files. *See* **slide shows**

Q - R

How can we make this index more useful? Email us at indexes@quepublishing.com

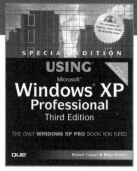